ECSCW 2005

ECSCW 2005

Proceedings of the
Ninth European Conference on
Computer-Supported Cooperative Work,
18–22 September 2005, Paris, France

Edited by

Hans Gellersen
Lancaster University, U.K.

Kjeld Schmidt
IT University of Copenhagen, Denmark

Michel Beaudouin-Lafon
Université Paris-Sud, France

and

Wendy Mackay
INRIA, France

 Springer

A C.I.P. Catalogue record for this book is available from the Library of Congress.

ISBN 13 978-90-481-7015-9 (PB)
ISBN 10 1-4020-4023-7 (e-book)
ISBN 13 978-1-4020-4023-8 (e-book)

Published by Springer,
P.O. Box 17, 3300 AA Dordrecht, The Netherlands.

www.springeronline.com

Printed on acid-free paper

Table of Contents

viii

From the editors

Welcome to the proceedings of ECSCW 2005, the 9th European Conference on Computer Supported Cooperative Work.

Founded in 1989, ECSCW was always a forum for researchers from a variety of disciplines and perspectives, and it has long since become one of the most respected venues for publishing research on the technical, empirical, and conceptual aspects of supporting collaboration by means of computer systems. Furthermore, as an international conference, ECSCW attracts high quality submissions from all over the world — this year from authors representing a record 30 countries.

ECSCW'05 received 125 submissions, a notable increase over previous years, which posed a significant challenge to the members of the Program Committee who had to spend countless hours assessing manuscripts and offering guidance in order to put together the final program. Each paper was initially reviewed by three members of the Program Committee, and in a second phase discussed among its reviewers so as to reach consensus as to its merit. By the end of the review process, we had 413 reviews on file, as well as extensive email discussion threads for each submission. At the end of this process, the top–rated papers, as well as those that were deemed controversial, were selected for discussion at the PC meeting and read by an additional PC member to ensure an informed discussion. Finally, in the two-day PC meeting, 24 papers were selected for our single–track paper program, a highly competitive 19% acceptance rate.

We hope that, as a result of the review process we adopted, all authors received detailed and constructive comments to their submission, whether or not it was accepted for publication, and believe that the process enabled us to assemble an outstanding program. We thank the members of the Program Committee for their insightful and constructive contributions to the process.

In addition to the paper program, ECSCW'05 also provided a number of other participation categories, including a doctoral colloquium, workshops on topics of special interest, as well posters, videos and demonstrations. Together these provided rich opportunities for discussion, learning, and exploration of the wide range of issues and challenges in the field.

Several organisations provided financial and logistical assistance, and we are grateful for their support. In particular, we thank AFIHM, the French association for Human-Computer Interaction, for supporting ECSCW'05 in cooperation with INRIA, the French National Research Institute in Computer Science..

Finally thanks must go to all the authors who entrusted their work to us, and to everyone who attended ECSCW'05 and enjoyed the program we helped to assemble. None of this would be possible, or worthwhile, if it were not for your research in this field. Your continued support of this conference is most gratifying.

Hans Gellersen and Kjeld Schmidt

ECSCW 2005 Conference Committee

Conference Co-chairs:

Michel Beaudouin-Lafon, Université
Paris-Sud, France
Wendy Mackay, INRIA, France

Program Co-chairs:

Hans Gellersen, *Lancaster University,
UK*
Kjeld Schmidt, *IT University of
Copenhagen, Denmark*

Conference Committee:

Tutorials:
Liam Bannon, *University of Limerick,
Ireland*
Workshops:
Susanne Bødker, *University of Aarhus,
Denmark*
Demos & Videos: Nicolas Roussel,
Université Paris-Sud, France
Posters:
Catherine Letondal, *Institut Pasteur,
France*
Volkmar Pipek, *IISI, Germany*
Doctoral Consortium:
Lucy Suchman, *Lancaster University,
UK*
Toni Robertson, *University of
Technology Sydney, Australia*

Organizing Committee:

Student Volunteers:
Jean-Baptiste Labrune, *INRIA, France*
Local Arrangements:
Catherine Girard, *INRIA, France*

ECSCW 2005 Program Committee

Mark Ackermann, University of Michigan, USA

Liam Bannon, University of Limerick, Ireland

Jakob Bardram, University of Aarhus, Denmark

Geof Bowker, Santa Clara University, USA

Peter Carstensen, IT University of Copenhagen, Denmark

Matthew Chalmers, University of Glasgow, UK

Joëlle Coutaz, University of Grenoble, France

Giorgio De Michelis, University of Milano-Bicocca, Italy

Alain Derycke, University of Lille, France

Paul Dourish, University of California, Irvine, USA

Prasun Dewan, University of North Carolina, USA

Anind Dey, Carnegie Mellon University, USA

Monica Divitini, Norwegian University of Science and Technology, Norway

Keith Edwards, Georgia Institute of Technology, USA

Geraldine Fitzpatrick, University of Sussex, UK

Rebecca Grinter, Georgia Institute of Technology, USA

Tom Gross, Bauhaus-University of Weimar, Germany

Carl Gutwin, University of Saskatchewan, Canada

Christine Halverson, IBM T.J. Watson Research Center, USA

Jon Hindmarsh, King's College London, UK

Lars Erik Holmquist, Viktoria Institute, Sweden

Gerd Kortuem, Lancaster University, UK

Kari Kuutti, University of Oulu, Finland

Paul Luff, King's College London, UK

Gloria Mark, University of California, Irvine, USA

Keiichi Nakata, International University Bruchsal, Germany

Philippe Palanque, University of Toulouse, France

Wolfgang Prinz, Fraunhofer FIT, Germany

Dave Randall, Manchester Metropolitan University, UK

Toni Robertson, University of Technology Sydney, Australia

Tom Rodden, University of Nottingham, UK

Yvonne Rogers, Indiana University. USA

Mark Rouncefield, Lancaster University, UK

Albrecht Schmidt, University of Munich, Germany

Carla Simone, University of Milano-Bicocca, Italy

Lucy Suchman, Lancaster University, UK

Yasuyuki Sumi, University of Kyoto, Japan

Ina Wagner, Technical University of Vienna, Austria

Volker Wulf, University of Siegen, Germany

H. Gellersen et al. (eds.), ECSCW 2005: Proceedings of the Ninth European
Conference on Computer-Supported Cooperative Work, 18-22 September 2005, Paris,
France, 1–22.

Ways of the Hands

David Kirk, Andy Crabtree and Tom Rodden

School of Computer Science & IT, University of Nottingham, Nottingham, UK.

Abstract. This paper presents an ethnographic analysis of the nature and role of gestural
action in the performance of a remote collaborative physical task. The analysis focuses
on the use of a low-tech prototype gesturing system, which projects unmediated gestures
to create a mixed reality ecology that promotes awareness in cooperative activity. CSCW
researchers have drawn attention to the core problem of the distortion effect along with
the subsequent fracturing of interaction between remote ecologies and have emphasized
the need to support the 'projectability' of action to resolve this. The mixed ecology
resolves the distortion effect by enabling a remote helper to project complex object-
focused gestures into the workspace of a local worker. These gestures promote
awareness and thus enable helper and worker to coordinate their object-focused actions
and interactions. Analysis of the socially organized use of the system derives key
questions concerning the construction of mixed ecologies more generally, questions
which may in turn be exploited to drive the design of future systems.

Introduction

The theme of 'awareness' has come to play a central role in CSCW research and a
range of technical solutions have been developed to explore ways in which
computer-based systems and applications might enable people engaged in
cooperative activity to 'take heed' of one another and *align* and *integrate* their
individual actions. Understanding and promoting awareness through design is of
fundamental concern to CSCW then, as awareness is a primary means by which
coordination 'gets done' (Hughes et al. 1994). Early research in the field was
devoted to exploring the potential benefits of audio-video 'media space'
technologies to promote awareness amongst remote parties. However, as Schmidt
(2002) points out, the expected benefits from these technologies never

materialized. The root of the problem was that media spaces 'distorted' participants' natural awareness practices (Heath and Luff 1991), subsequently 'fracturing' interaction. Of particular concern was the effect of media space technologies on the range of human gestures that are central to the face-to-face coordination of collaborative tasks.

> The emergence of a gesture, its progressive movement and graduated appearance within the local environment, its complex operation on the periphery of the visual field, is distorted by the technology. It renders the recipient insensitive to the interactional tasks of the movement ... It is interesting to note that in video mediated communication, individuals assume and attempt to preserve the presupposition of a common frame of reference and the interchangeability of standpoints. Indeed their visual conduct is systematically designed with respect to a common mutual environment. Speakers for example, shape their gestures as if the potential recipient will view it in the way in which it is designed. Yet by providing limited access to the other and 'transforming' the appearance of a gesture, the technology introduces an incongruous mutual environment and a curious subsidence into the foundations of socially organized interaction. (Heath and Luff 1991)

Research subsequently diversified from the communication paradigm that underpinned the development of media spaces, and interest in the socially organized properties of space burgeoned in particular. The spatial paradigm sought to promote the continuity of awareness through the development of 'shared spaces' or digital ecologies, situating audio and video alongside other media in collaborative virtual environments (CVEs) where participants were 'immersed'. The spatial paradigm has been explored by a great many researchers and in many different ways, though it has notably being extended through the development of *mixed reality boundaries* (e.g., Koleva et al. 1999). Mixed reality boundaries situate the shared ecology in the physical environment beyond the desktop and make it possible for remote participants to engage in 'collaborative physical tasks' – i.e., object-oriented tasks that take place in the real world but which are, at the same time, mediated through a digital environment. Actually accomplishing collaborative physical tasks via CVEs and in mixed reality settings inevitably brings the communication paradigm back into consideration however (Hindmarsh et al. 2000), which in turn leads us back to the distortion effect and the fracturing of interaction between ecologies that emerges from it (Luff et al. 2003).

Despite well-founded criticism (Dourish et al. 1996), researchers did not abandon the communication paradigm (or the face-to-face organizational aspects of at least) and recent attempts to address the problem of distortion have led to the emergence of *dual ecologies* (Kuzuoka et al. 2004). Dual ecologies are at the present time remote audio-video environments that seek to support collaboration between distributed parties through the further development of communication devices that resonate with participants' natural interactional practices (and therefore, it is hoped, prevent the fracturing of interaction between ecologies). Of key concern is the development of support for the 'projectability of action' between remote ecologies.

"By 'projectability' we mean the capacity of participants to predict, anticipate, or prefigure the unfolding of action ... The discussion of projectability is inseparable from the issue of ecology. A participant's actions are afforded by the properties of the environment. One participant can project the forthcoming actions of another participant by making sense of his/her actions in relation to the surrounding objects and environment ... " (Kuzouka et al. 2004)

In this paper we seek to address the distortion effect and extend the field of research by marrying the communication and spatial paradigms together through the development of a *mixed reality ecology* to support the effective projectability of gesture and thereby resolve the distortion effect. Whereas the nature of dual ecologies is to have two separate ecologies (one for each participant, remote and local), with communication between them mediated by some interaction device, a mixed reality ecology consists of a mixed reality surface that is overlaid onto the real world ecology. This allows a remote participant to talk to, monitor and intervene in the task actions of another participant (Kirk and Stanton Fraser 2005). Bodily actions are projected into the physical task space, thereby conjoining both the communicative and spatial elements of two workspaces into one hybrid workspace. Specifically, the mixed reality ecology enables one participant to project her hands into the physical space of the other participant and to coordinate his physical task actions. The mixed reality ecology provides the 'common frame of reference' that is presupposed in and essential to naturally occurring interaction and retains the relational orientation and unmediated nature of naturally occurring gesture. The technology employed to create the mixed reality ecology (derived from low-tech prototyping methods) is well established (consisting of video cameras, a projector, and a TV in this case). What is novel and of importance here is the mixed reality ecology created by the technology, its ability to redress the distortion effect, and its consequences for 3D object-focused interactions. In order to understand the potential of mixed reality ecologies to promote awareness in cooperative physical activities, we conducted a series of lab-based experiments, which were subject to qualitative analysis. Below we describe the technological arrangement of the mixed reality ecology, the nature of the experiments, how they were studied, what we found, and the implications that these findings have for CSCW systems design.

Supporting the Projectability of Gesture

There are currently two main classes of systems support for projectability: *linked* gesture systems and *mediated* gesture systems. Linked systems support collaboration around the construction of shared (often digital) 2D artefacts. Linked systems largely emerged from the efforts of designers to support remote collaboration amongst themselves using video connections. Research into the potential of linked systems has led to the development of a range of video-based technologies. These include VideoDraw, which provides a 'virtual sketchbook' that allows participants to see each other's drawings and projects video of their accompanying hand gestures directly onto one another's drawing space (Tang and Minneman 1990); VideoWhiteboard, which extends VideoDraw by projecting digital shadows of hand and upper body gestures (Tang and Minneman 1991); and ClearBoard, another shared drawing tool that projects video feed of head and gaze movements through the shared surface (Ishii and Kobayashi 1992). More recent developments have extended linked systems to support distributed multi-party interactions with a wider variety of applications. These include the Agora system (Kuzuoka et al. 1999), which projects video of the documents on a local desk and the gestures, gaze, and bodily orientations implicated in using them onto a remote desk and vice versa; and VideoArms (Tang et al. 2004), which captures the arm movements of participants in particular locations and digitally recreates them as 'virtual embodiments' that are available across the shared workspace.

Mediated systems are more diverse in character and seek to exploit computational devices to articulate gesture. Early systems such as Commune (Bly and Minneman 1990) explored the use of digital tablets and styli as a means to articulate gesture around shared drawings. More recent research has exploited 'telepointer traces' – i.e., interaction histories for virtual embodiments - that visualize a participant's recent movements in a shared workspace (Gutwin and Penner 2002). Current research seeks to move beyond articulating gestures in 2D environments to understand how they might be manifest in the real world to support the physical manipulation of 3D objects. This class of mediated system is largely concerned to support remote help giving or instruction. The DOVE system (Ou et al. 2003, Fussell et al. 2004) supports remote interaction between local workers and remote helpers by allowing helpers to overlay pen-based gestures onto a video stream of the worker's task space, the results of which are displayed to the worker on a linked video window adjacent to their task space. Whilst local workers are made implicitly aware of the remote helper's view in the DOVE system, the worker still needs to extrapolate from the illustrated gestures presented on a video feed to their own local ecology. In other words, the local worker needs to 'decode' and realign the gesture in relation to her perspective on the task space; needs to *embed* the gesture in her local ecology in order to articulate its meaning and align and integrate her actions accordingly. Efforts to embed gesture in the worker's local environment are currently being pursued through robotics. The development of GestureMan (Kuzuoka et al. 2004) seeks to move gesture beyond the interface and *situate it in the remote worker's local workspace*, though distortion and fracturing of the two ecologies has proved to be a continuing problem (Luff et al. 2003).

Our own research seeks to explore the use of gesture in collaborative physical tasks. We exploit the direct and unmediated representation of gestures within a linked system to promote mutual awareness between participants located in asymmetric ecologies. We support the accomplishment of collaborative physical tasks through a mixed reality surface that aligns and integrates the ecologies of the local worker and the remote helper. To effectively embed remote gestures in the local ecology we exploit direct video projection (Figure 1a). Specifically, a video camera is used to capture images of the remote helper's hands and the gestures she makes are then projected onto the desk of the worker. The projection overlays the helper's hands on top of the worker's hands (rather than being face-to-face or side-by-side). This provides her with the same orientation to the worker's local ecology and creates a mixed reality surface at the level of the task space. The actions carried out at the mixed reality surface are captured by a second video camera and passed back to a TV monitor situated on the remote helper's desk. This arrangement establishes a common frame of reference. It allows the worker to see the helper's hands and hand movements in his local ecology. It allows the helper to see objects in the worker's local ecology, to see the worker's actions on the objects in the task space, and to see her own gestures towards objects in the task space. In turn, this 'reciprocity of perspectives', where the helper can see what the worker is doing and the worker can see what the helper is doing, provides for mutual awareness and enables the helper and worker to align and integrate their actions through the effective combination of gesture and talk (Figure 1b).

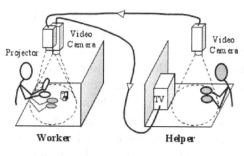

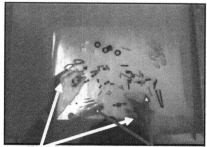

Figure 1a. Projecting gesture into the worker's local ecology.

Worker's hands   **Helper's hands**

Figure 1b. The mixed reality surface: a reciprocity of perspectives.

Experiments in the Mixed Reality Ecology

In order to establish the *prima facie* efficacy of the mixed reality ecology we carried out a series of lab-based experiments involving 24 pairs of participants (student volunteers from various backgrounds) in the performance of a collaborative physical task, namely, assembling a Lego® kit. Participants were randomly assigned roles, one becoming a remote helper and the other a local worker. The remote helper had the kit's instructions and a video-gesture link to the local worker's task space. The local worker had physical contact with the items to be assembled, but no specific knowledge of how to assemble the pieces in front of him, and relied on the assistance of the remote helper to assemble the Lego model correctly. Both parties were located in the same room but were not able to see each other. The participants could talk to each other however, so no technical configuration was required to transmit audio. Pre-experiment demonstration introduced the participants to the system and they engaged in a simple assembly task to familiarize themselves with the technology. Once participants understood how the system operated they were instructed that they had 10 minutes to construct as much of the model as they could.

Assembling a Lego kit encompasses a variety of *generic task elements*, such as item selection, pattern matching, physical manipulations (rotate, insert, attach) and error checking. In this respect the assembly task offers the opportunity to explore some of the demands that may be placed on real world applications of the system: on the remote guidance of machine and equipment repair or remote artefact and specimen examination, for example. The use of Lego meant that we could model a complex array of interactions and thus inform the development of future applications of the underlying technology. A central feature of interaction is the clear asymmetry between the roles of the participants. Essentially one of the participants is an expert guiding the task or providing expert assistance and support, and the other is a worker who has less knowledge about the artefact or the operations to be performed on the artefact to bring about some desired result (such as assembling a particular model with the Lego pieces or diagnosing a particular machine fault). As the design of Lego is such that the connection of pieces is rather intuitive, little effort is required to learn how to put the pieces together and the worker's attention is instead directed towards artefact manipulation (assembling the model), which requires quite a high level of skill and dexterity. The task expertise of the helper was rapidly generated by giving them a set of clearly designed instructions, which accompany all Lego kits. Of course, all instructions no matter well designed are 'essentially incomplete' (Suchman 1987) and the work of *articulating* just what they mean 'here and now' for just these parties in just this situation is, in many respects, the focus of the experiments. We restrict our account of this articulation work (Schmidt and Bannon 1992) to the nature and role of gesture. It should be said, however, that the use of gesture is thoroughly intertwined with standard conversational mechanisms (Sacks et al. 1974), though space necessarily restricts our treatment of this intertwining.

The standard approach to studying lab-based experiments is essentially quantitative in character and largely concerned with establishing performance parameters and other salient metrics (see Kirk 2004 for these results). As we are concerned to understand the potential of unmediated gesture in mixed reality ecologies to promote awareness in cooperative activity, we elected to complement the standard approach with qualitative study as well. Our approach is motivated by the observation that "an experiment is, after all, just another socially organized context for cognitive performance" (Hollan et al. 2000). Lab-based experiments might be studied ethnographically then (ibid.) to complement standard user modeling approaches with detailed observation and careful analysis of the cooperative work of the experiment. Ethnographic study in turn allows us to explicate the socially organized properties of the experiments, bearing in mind Schmidt's caveat that the social organization of cognition is not be found in some "internal realm" but in the intersubjective practices whereby "actors effortlessly make sense of the actions of coworkers" (Schmidt 2002). The social organization of awareness is to be found, then, in the "practices through which actors align and integrate their distributed but interdependent activities" (ibid.). Those practices are done in bodily ways and through bodily movements. Accordingly, and following Suchman (2000), when examining video recordings of the experiments we pay particular attention to the bodily practices that participants engage in to "mediate interaction" and "highlight objects for perception", thus promoting awareness in cooperative activity.

The Mediating Body in Cooperative Activity

Below we present a series of vignettes that illustrate the cooperative work of the experiments and the bodily practices organizing that work. In bodily detail the vignettes display the range of gestures implicated in the collaborative assembly of the Lego kit. A standard treatment of gesture in a design context is to borrow classification schemes (taxonomies or typologies) from the social sciences to organize findings and inform design (see Bekker et al. 1995 for a classic example). We make no effort to reconcile our findings with existing taxonomies, however, for reasons best articulated by Adam Kendon, a leading figure in the study of gesture:

> "The various typologies of gesture that have been put forward are in part attempts to classify gestures in terms of the information they encode, albeit at very general levels. These typologies are often logically inconsistent, in many cases formed on the basis of rather hasty observation with a good admixture of 'folk' categories thrown in ... gestures that consistently occupy extreme ends of these dimensions (with little weighting on the others) get distinguished as "types" - but I don't think a typological way of thinking is very helpful. Rather, it tends to obscure the complexity and subtlety [of gesture]." (Kendon 1996)

In order to develop a broader understanding of the potential of gesture to promote awareness in cooperative activity we replace a concern to cast our findings in terms of existing taxonomies, with a concern to understand the 'stroke of gestural phrases'. That is, to understand what gestures 'say' and 'do', what the gesture is 'meant for', or, more definitively, what the situational 'business' of the movement is. In addition to this, we wish to understand the 'content' of the stroke. As Kendon puts it,

"It is often said that gesticulation is idiosyncratic, each speaker improvising his own forms. So far as I know, no one has ever really tested this claim. My own experience in gesture-watching suggests to me that people are far more consistent in what they do gesturally than this 'idiosyncrasy' claim would lead one to imagine ... [There are] similarities in the patterning of gestural action and such patterns are socially shared - hence there is conventionalization to a degree affecting all kinds of gesturing." (ibid.)

The content of the stroke refers to the compositional character of gestural phrases - to the emergence of distinct patterns of gestural action. It is with an eye towards carefully describing *particular patterns of gestural phrase* and *the business or work that they do* that we approach analysis of the ways in which the body (and the hands in particular) mediates interaction and highlights objects for perception (Sudnow 1978). In turn, this approach might enable us to identify how gestures promote awareness as an integrated aspect of collaborative practice. Below we present a series of vignettes that articulate the patterns of gestural phrase 'at work' in our experiments and the ways in which they functioned (the helper's hands are highlighted to aid the visibility of her gestures).

'The Flashing Hand'

Before assembly begins the participants must first *align themselves* in the mixed reality ecology such that their movements and gestures might be understood in relation to the arrangement of (the Lego kit in this case) and each other's gestural activities. In other words, the participants must establish to their satisfaction that they share a common frame of reference that permits the reciprocity of perspectives. This is achieved through variants of the 'flashing hand' gesture:

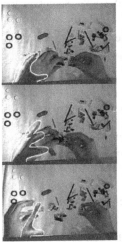

The worker is picking up pieces of the kit and looking to see how they fit together. The helper moves her hand towards the worker's left hand.

As the helper's hand approaches the worker's left hand she says, "Is this your left hand?" The helper then starts to wiggle her fingers.

The worker then moves his hand into closer proximity with the helper's, copies the wiggling motion and says "Yeah."

Figure 2. The Flashing Hand Gestural Phrase

The 'flashing hand' gets its name from the wiggling movement of the helper's hand, which brings the helper's hand in and out of alignment with the workers and gives the impression that the worker's hand is flashing. Whilst simply done, it is used to establish the reciprocity of perspectives that is essential to mutual awareness and the coordination of task actions. Although indication of which hand is being referred to could be done by a simple pointing gesture, this form of gesture makes implicit reference between worker and helper to their comparative alignment to the artefacts. The mixed reality ecology enables the helper and the worker to effectively inhabit the same place and it is by this overlaying of hands in similar ways to the vignette above, and in the ways that follow, that the participants maintained reciprocity throughout the experiment.

'The Wavering Hand'

Having established reciprocity of perspectives, the participants begin the assembly task. The most obvious way in which gesture might promote awareness and coordination in cooperative object-focused activity is through an unfolding order of what is taxonomically referred to as deixis - 'pointing' in vernacular terms - at the particular items to be selected for assembly. Our experiments show that coordinating the selection of items for assembly is more subtle and complex than simply pointing, however. Whilst deixis does make up a large part of gesturing behaviour it usually occurs as a component feature of a larger gestural phrase. The 'wavering hand' illustrates the point. In the following vignette the helper is trying to get the worker to pick up a black L-shaped piece of Lego. Having been asked if he has "got an L-shaped piece" the worker scans the items in front of him and picks one up, but it is yellow (and therefore the wrong item). The helper responds as follows:

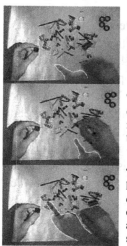

The helper reaches forward with his hand as he starts to look himself for the black L-shaped piece.

The helper's hand then wavers over the work surface, mirroring his visual scan over the pool of possible items.

This lateral movement of the hand is followed by a final and decisive pointing movement over the required item, which is accompanied by the helper saying, "One of those I think."

Figure 3. The 'Wavering Hand' Gestural Phrase

Combined with talk, the 'wavering hand' makes the worker aware of the helper's search and location of the required piece, and in turn enables the worker to select the correct item. The ability to support cooperative activity through unmediated gesture reduces the amount of time required to secure a common orientation to material tasks of work. Systems that do not support deictic gesturing require that a great deal more verbal instruction be issued to achieve mutual awareness and the integration of tasks. Even though current systems have been built to support deictic gestures, mechanisms of projection still require a great deal of articulation work either to embed the gesture or to understand the specific meaning of a gesture. However, with unmediated gesture there is, at the same time, both an interactional *richness* and an *economy* that facilitates awareness and coordination on a moment-by-moment basis. Thus, and for example, as the 'wavering hand' moves from side-to-side it mirrors the visual scanning of the helper suggesting that the he is 'looking for the piece too' and promotes awareness of the search for the item. The local worker is made aware that the piece has been located when the 'pointing finger of the wavering hand' and the helper's utterance "One of those I think" together highlight its presence at a specific place in the worker's ecology. Without the economy and richness of movement that the unmediated representation of gesture affords, such use of demonstrative pronouns and deictic expressions would not be possible. Those affordances are provided by the mixed reality ecology, which aligns both the location and the representation of the remote helpers' gestures. In turn, this means that the local worker does not need to reconcile gestures dislocated from the actual task space (such as those presented on a separate screen, for example) or interpret the meaning of artificial representations of gesture embedded in the task space.

'The Mimicking Hand' (with One or Two Hands)

As the experiments unfolded it became apparent that different gestural patterns were implicated in the accomplishment of the different activities that make up the overall assembly task. As demonstrated by Fussell et al. (2004) those gestures that go beyond mere deictic reference are often the most important in terms of facilitating task performance. Whilst the 'wavering hands' make the worker aware of *just what pieces are to be selected* and coordinate selection, the 'mimicking hands' gesture is one of a range of gestures that are concerned with *ordering the assembly* of selected pieces. The following vignettes illustrate the role of the 'mimicking hands' gesture, with one and two hands respectively, in the ordering of assembly. In the first vignette, the worker has picked up what the helper has called the "main construction type bit":

The helper then prompts the worker to rotate the piece prior to attachment. Her flat hand indicates the piece's current orientation.

The gesture unfolds as the flat hand is rotated to its side and the helper says, "If you flip it a hundred and eighty degrees like that."

The gesture is completed as the helper rotates her hand 180°, and is then repeated for effect.

Figure 4a. The 'Mimicking Hands' Gestural Phrase (with one hand)

Here the 'mimicking hand' enables the helper to make the worker aware of the relative orientation of the Lego kit (what way up it should be, what way pieces should face, etc.) In the second vignette, the worker exploits hand gestures to show how the pieces should be manipulated and fitted together.

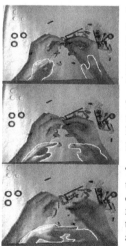

The helper places her hands at the edge of the table watching the worker assemble two pieces. The worker moves the pieces around as if unsure of how they connect together.

The helper says, "So they lie next to each other", extending her fingers to mimic the primary axis of the pieces.

The gesture comes to a close as the helper indicates the direction of the movement required to fit the pieces together by docking her hands and saying, "Like that".

Figure 4b. The 'Mimicking Hand' Gestural Phrase (with two hands)

The 'mimicking hands' make the worker aware of the ways in which pieces fit together. This requires the arrangement of subtle and complex movements of the hands and fingers to articulate the particular way in which particular pieces should be oriented in 3D space, the spatial relationships that hold between pieces, and the ways in which they should be manipulated and moved so that they fit together. In the above vignette, for example, we can see that positioning of the helper's hands enables the worker to see the proper relation of the two pieces. This in turn enables the worker to orient the two pieces correctly and the 'docking hands' shows how they should fit together given that orientation. While unsophisticated, the technological arrangement at work here nevertheless allowed helpers to use their hands in intuitive ways to articulate the complexities of assembly.

'The Inhabited Hand'

Of course, ordering the assembly of a complex 3D object did not always run smoothly. Practical difficulties of orientation frequently occurred and workers could not always understand just how pieces were meant to fit together. To remedy this the helper would perform the 'inhabited hand' gesture. In this vignette the helper seeks to clarify instructions and to help the worker move a piece he has been struggling with into the right orientation and in the right direction:

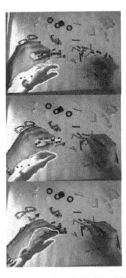

The helper places her hand on top of the worker's, forms it into the same shape and says, "If you rotate."

The helper then rolls her hand forwards. Saying "Rotate your hand like that, yeah."

The helper then brings her hand back to its original position before repeating the gesture .

Figure 5. The 'Inhabited Hand' Gestural Phrase

The 'inhabited hand' makes the worker aware of the fine-grained movements that need to be done to align pieces and make them fit together. This is achieved by placing the hand in the same position as the worker's and making the same shape of the hand, a specific movement that indexes the verbal instruction to it. Through this movement the helper models how the worker is to hold the piece and shows the desired angle of rotation of the hand, making the worker aware of just how he needs to manipulate the piece to assemble it. It is not simply a case of showing the worker how the piece should be rotated however, which can be achieved by showing a representation of the piece in initial and final states, but is a literal instruction on the actions required to achieve the final state (which in this instance is to hold the piece in the left hand just "like that" so that it can be easily inserted into the piece held in right hand). The helper thus demonstrates just what is to be done with the hand to obtain the correct orientation of the piece and make it fit with its partner. Here we can see that the mixed reality ecology enables a level of interaction not easily achieved via other means, effectively allowing the helper to embody the hands of the worker to synchronize the task to hand.

'The Negating Hand'

Other practical difficulties populated the assembly of the Lego kit, particularly the selection of wrong pieces. Such mistakes were highlighted and corrected through the 'negating hand' gesture. In the following vignette the remote helper has instructed the worker to put two particular pieces together. The worker goes to pick up the wrong piece, however:

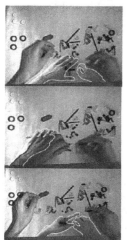

The helper lays her hand flat on the desk over the wrong piece and says, "Forget about this."

The helper moves her hand in a sweeping movement, emphasizing which piece is to be ignored.

The helper then points at the correct piece, which is now in the worker's right hand and says "Just this piece."

Figure 6. The 'Negating Hand Cover' Gestural Phrase

The 'negating hand' gesture makes the worker aware of his mistake and highlights the correct piece for assembly by combining covering, sweeping, and pointing movements of the hands and fingers. Effectively, the gesture says 'not that, but this'. Although rapidly accomplished such gestures are complex and while laser dots, drawn lines, or virtual embodiments may be used to refer to and highlight particular objects in a shared ecology, fluid interaction and the ability of the recipient to make sense the situational relevance of the gesture are dependent upon the alignment of both the gestural representation *and* its spatial position within the ecology. The advantage of using gestures projected into the task space is that it allows the 'spatial reference' of a gesture to be held intact, as gestures are presented relative to their objects of work, readily enabling workers to see and repair their mistakes. The use of unmediated representation also allows gestures to retain their natural temporal characteristics, being both rapid and fluid and reconstituted on an *ad hoc* basis and avoiding excessive temporal residue such as the cluttered screen that results from a series of sketch-based gestures (though this may be a double-edged sword to some extent, as there may be some benefit to be gained from a degree of permanence on certain occasions).

'Parked Hands'

It will come as no surprise to say that assembly activities were oriented around turn-taking, especially as one party had the assembly instructions and the other was obliged to follow them. In addition to employing standard conversational mechanisms (Sacks et al. 1974) the participants developed a particular gestural pattern to signal and accomplish the taking of turns. We refer to this pattern as the 'parked hands' gesture and it is illustrated in the following vignette. Through employing the gestures described above the helper has managed to guide the worker through the assembly of a particular section of the Lego kit and the task now is to assemble its partner:

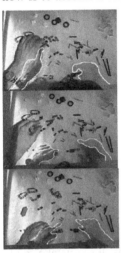

The helper points out a piece and says," Assemble that exactly the same as the other one."

The helper then withdraws his hands and parks them at the edge of the ecology.

The worker assembles the section and the helper says, "Yeah, okay, and then put that on here." The helper points to a specific location and then parks her hands again.

Figure 7. The Parked Hands Gestural Phrase

The 'parked hands' gesture indicates that a turn has been completed and that it is now the turn of the worker to undertake the instructions delivered. Moving the hands out of the parked position indicates that helper is about to take another turn, issuing new instructions accompanied by appropriate gestures. This simple but elegant gesture makes the worker aware when a turn is about to be taken and when it has been completed and enables the worker to coordinate his actions with the helper's instructions.

Promoting Awareness through Gesture

The gestural phrases that we have identified in our study elaborate a corpus of patterns of gestural action that integrate awareness in practice in the mixed reality ecology (Table 1). They do not represent general taxonomic elements and their coincidence with, divergence from or elaboration of existing types is irrelevant. Emphasis is instead placed on the ability of gesture to promote awareness and (thus) on the situated 'business' or function of particular gestural patterns in action. As Schmidt (2002) points out,

> Awareness is an attribute of action. Doing one thing while taking heed of other relevant occurrences are not two parallel lines of action but a specific way of pursuing a line of action, namely to do it heedfully, competently, mindfully, accountably. In a CSCW context 'awareness' does not refer to some special category of mental state existing independently of action but to a person's being or becoming aware of something.

The patterns of gestural phrase we have identified make it visible how participants promote awareness of the tasks they need to accomplish and come to integrate and align their activities using non-verbal behaviours as well as speech. Each gestural phrase provides a way for the mediating body to highlight objects for perception and to make what Crabtree et al. (2004) describe as "a host of fine-grained grammatical distinctions". These marry utterances (such as verbal instructions) to specific actions (such as the selection and orientation of pieces and the manipulations required to fit them together, etc.), which in turn provides for the coordination of tasks.

Gestural Phrase	Business of Phrase
Flashing Hand	Establish reciprocity of perspectives
Wavering Hands	Indicates search for and location of items and coordinates selection of correct pieces.
Mimicking Hands	Orders assembly of pieces by indicating how pieces should be oriented for assembly and how pieces should be joined together
Inhabited Hand	Shows fine-grained movements that need to done to align pieces and make them fit together.
Negating Hand	Repairs mistakes and clarifies instructions
Parked Hands	Orders turn-taking

Table 1. Corpus of gestures that promote awareness in the mixed reality ecology

The corpus indicates that a rich grammar of gestural action is implicated in the organization of interaction around shared artefacts. This grammar enables participants to 'project' awareness of the tasks to hand and to integrate their actions accordingly. Its effective expression is afforded by the mixed reality ecology, which aligns the participants' distinct ecologies and their gestural phrases. The alignment of ecologies and expression of a rich grammar of gestural action that it affords *resolves* the distortion effect and fracturing of interaction between ecologies.

16

While existing systems support the expression of gesture, they still effect a separation between the ecologies of the participants. The GestureMan system (Luff et al. 2003), for example, fractures interaction as it fails to comprehensively reflect the remote helper's actions. Whilst extensions to the system have sought to address the problem of projectability of action, the mediated expression of gesture still does "not operate ideally" (Kuzouka et al. 2004). This is, in part, attributed to the temporal character of expression – to the timing of gestures and their placing within collaborative interaction. However, it is also recognized that representing the "movement, shape and motion" of gesture is also critical to the enterprise (ibid.). The DOVE system (Ou et al. 2003, Fussell et al. 2004) seeks to overcome these problems by overlaying sketches onto the worker's ecology. However, these gestures are removed from the working surface and their relation to task artefacts must be extrapolated by the worker if they are to gain practical purchase, again fracturing interaction.

The effort to align separate ecologies in ways that resolve distortion and the fracturing of interaction, revolves around the reconciliation of space, time and motion in direct relation to a shared object of work. The spatial, temporal and motional coherence of projected action is maintained in the mixed ecology as the ecology 'forces' worker and helper to adopt the same orientation. From this position they see things from the same perspective and see what the other sees *from same point of view that the other sees it*. By 'forcing' orientation, the spatial, temporal and motional coherence of projected actions is preserved then. Furthermore, the richness and economy of projected action – of unmediated gesture - means that participants do not have to 'decode' abstract representations of gesture, but can effortlessly make sense of the actions of coworkers. Embedding the remote helper's gestures into the local worker's task space in direct relation to his local orientation unifies separate ecologies and promotes awareness between the two by enabling a rich texture of grammatical phrases to be coherently articulated and expressed. It is this 'phenomenal coherence' of gesture – i.e., the *situational relevance and intersubjective intelligibility* of gesture that the mixed ecology promotes. Phenomenal coherence prevents distortion and the fracturing of interaction between separate ecologies and it is the ability of technology to support phenomenal coherence that represents a long-tern challenge for design.

Designing Mixed Ecological Arrangements

In this paper we have introduced the core notion of a mixed reality ecology and explored the ways in which it might be exploited *by users* to support interaction between a remote helper providing advice and guidance to a local worker. The low-tech prototype we have constructed to explore the potential of mixed reality ecologies exploits the direct unmediated projection of gestures to support phenomenal coherence. It provides a common frame of reference that promotes awareness between remote ecologies and enables participants to align and integrate their collaborative activities. Our analysis has shown that the mixed reality ecology provides an expressive medium allowing participants to exploit a subtle and complex range of naturally occurring awareness practices, which we have articulated in terms of a corpus of 'gestural phrases'. But what relevance do our experiences have for design more generally and to the development of technological arrangements supporting *remote users engaged in cooperative work on physical objects* in particular?

First and foremost our experiences suggest that there is a need for a shift in design orientation, particularly in the ways in which we consider the use of technology to support remote collaboration on physical tasks. The primary orientation to design at the current time places technology in the role of linking two distinct ecologies and essentially focuses on repairing the discontinuity or 'fracture' between them. In contrast, we think it is necessary to design for phenomenal coherence from the outset and see the role of the technology as one that is concerned to develop a shared environment that blends and mixes interaction between ecologies, thereby enabling participants to construct a 'world known in common' - a 'world' that is intersubjectively intelligible to participants and which provides for the situational relevance of gesture. Essentially it can be argued that current approaches to design support only one of the two key features of phenomenal coherence. The class of systems represented by DOVE, for example, support intersubjective intelligibility but not situational relevance (gestures must be made relevant by the local worker to the task). And on the other hand, the class of systems represented by GestureMan support situational relevance but not intersubjective intelligibility (that the robot is pointing at 'this' or 'that' is clear but what the pointing means in the absence of other subtle gestural cues is not so clear).

The design of mixed ecologies requires us to think carefully about key features of interaction that require support. Reflecting on our analysis of the mixed reality ecology, we would suggest a number of key questions become critical to the design of mixed ecological arrangements more generally:

- *How are participants' gestures placed within a mixed ecology?* Our arrangement directly projects gestures, overlaying them onto the shared task space to create a common frame of reference. Three key elements are central to this achievement.

    - *Aligning the orientation of participants* so that their gestural actions are interpretable in terms of a common orientation to the object of collaboration. This entails projecting the remote helper's gestures so that they share the same bodily relation to a physical object as that of the local worker's Thus, the remote helper's view of the shared ecology is identical to the local worker's.

    - *Aligning the effects of remote gestures and local actions* so that they are understood within the particular context of the activity taking place. Projecting remote gestures into the local helper's task space and in direct relation to the physical object being manipulated situates interaction at a hybrid surface that not only aligns the participants orientation but marries remote and local actions together to create a shared, mutually intelligible context for collaborative action.

– *Projecting gestures to coherently reflect arrangements of collaborative activity* so that the display of gestures supports the arrangements of cooperation underpinning the task. In the current case our display strongly reflects the asymmetric nature of the task at hand in that a remote helper is giving instruction to a local worker. The local worker sees the remote gesture directly projected on the surface in front of him while the remote helper sees the remote surface through a monitor, thus providing for the mutual intelligibility of gesture between participants.

- More broadly we think it important for design to consider *how participant's actions and gestures are captured as part of a mixed ecology*. We would stress that the capturing of gesturing should be as lightweight and distract as little as possible from the activities to be supported by the mixed ecology. In our case we have used simple video capture and transmission rather than having the remote helper explicitly manipulate a secondary gesture interface. This arrangement meant that participants did not have to manage gestures separately and that their gestures are situated within the cooperative activities to hand. This blending of gesture and action helps promote a mutual sense of a shared ecology of action.

- We also think it important to consider *how gestures are represented and commonly understood in a mixed ecology.* In particular are the representations of participant's gestures readily intelligible within a mixed ecology or do they require a significant reinterpretation? A number of technologies have been used to represent remote gestures, the most notable of these being video sketching and remote pointing technologies. Our use of projected hands reduces the cost of interpreting remote gestures and provides for the situational relevance and intersubjective intelligibility of gestural actions in our mixed ecology.

Approaching the design of remote gesture systems by first tackling these key questions will allow designers to construct more effective mixed ecologies. By designing with the view to making disparate ecologies as mixed and overlapped as possible the purpose of the technology will no longer be to repair fractured interactions. It will instead be to support strong intersubjective understanding and awareness of remote collaborator's joint activities in a shared environment.

Conclusion

The mediation of awareness in remote interactions is of central concern to CSCW and is particularly germane when considering object-focused interactions (which have been plagued by the inability to adequately support intersubjective awareness in collaborative activities on 3D artefacts). Early efforts explored the communicative potential of 'media spaces', exploiting audio and video technologies to promote awareness amongst geographically dispersed parties located in remote locations or ecologies of work. Use of these technologies highlighted the distortion effect, where the salience of users' natural awareness practices - and of their gestures in particular - was obscured by the technology, thus undermining the foundations of socially organized interaction and resulting in the fracturing of interaction between ecologies.

Recent efforts have suggested that the distortion effect may be remedied by developing support for the 'projectability' of action and of gesture in particular. Technologies that have sought to do this have been designed with aim of reducing the fracture brought about by linking two distinct ecologies together. For different reasons fractured interaction is still a major issue to be contended with in both the DOVE system and the GestureMan systems, however. Our approach has been to utilise low-tech prototyping to explore how a system can be designed from the perspective of creating a mixed ecology rather than attempting to repair a fracture. Using video projection we have created a mixed reality surface at the level of the task space, allowing a remote helper to project their gestures directly into a local worker's environment. The 'forced' orientation and unmediated projection of gesture in the mixed ecology enables users to exploit natural awareness practices and align and integrate their object-focused actions and interactions.

The ability of a mixed reality ecology to effectively promote awareness was explored through lab-based experimentation that involved participants in a relatively complex collaborative physical task where there was an asymmetry of worker roles and functions. Our ethnographic approach to the analysis sought to explicate the ways in which the body mediated interaction and highlighted objects for perception. The pattern and function of gestural action was discerned, revealing a corpus of 'gestural phrases' that were integral to interaction and which promoted collaborative awareness and the coordination of tasks. Each gestural phrase performed a different function, enabling the participants to establish and maintain the reciprocity of perspectives that is essential to interaction, to select pieces for assembly, to orient pieces for assembly, to manipulate pieces and fit them together, to repair mistakes, and to signal turn taking and turn completion. In this the mixed reality ecology successfully conveys and preserves gesture's spatial, temporal and motional or 'phenomenal' coherence with reference to shared objects of work. Its ability to do this is dependent on the technological arrangement used to facilitate interaction. We have mooted several key questions which address the technological character of mixed ecology systems and which might drive the development of future systems supporting remote collaboration. Such systems might unify fractured ecologies, providing support for seamless object-focused interaction between remote parties and for the natural awareness practices that secure real world, real time collaboration.

Acknowledgement

The research on which this article is based was funded by UK Engineering and Physical Sciences Research Council 'Equator Interdisciplinary Research Collaboration' (EPSRC GR/N15986/01), www.equator.ac.uk

References

Bekker, M., Olson, J. and Olson, G. (1995) "Analysis of gestures in face-to-face design teams", *Proceedings of DIS '95*, p. 157-166, Michigan: ACM Press.

Bly, S.A. and Minneman, S.L. (1990) "Commune: a shared drawing surface", *Proceedings of Office Information Systems1990*, p. 184-192, Cambridge, Massachusetts: ACM Press.

Crabtree, A., Rodden, T. and Mariani, J. (2004) "Collaborating around collections", *Proceedings of the CSCW '04*, pp. 396-405, Chicago: ACM Press.

Dourish, P. Adler, A., Bellotti, V. and Henderson, A. (1996) "Your place or mine?", *Computer Supported Cooperative work: The Journal of Collaborative Computing*, vol. 5 (1), p. 33-62.

Fussell, S. et al. (2004) "Gestures over video streams to support remote collaboration on physical tasks, *Human-Computer Interaction*, vol. 19 (4), pp. 273-309.

Gutwin, C. and Penner, R. (2002) "Visual information and collaboration", *Proceedings of CSCW '02*, p. 49-57, New Orleans: ACM Press.

Heath, C. and Luff, P. (1991) "Disembodied conduct: communication through video in multi-media office environment", *Proceedings of CHI '91*, p. 99-103, New Orleans: ACM Press.

Heath, C. and Luff, P. (1992) "Media space and communicative asymmetries", *Human-Computer Interaction*, vol. 7, p. 315-346.

Hindmarsh, J., Fraser, M., Heath, C., Benford, S. and Greenhalgh, C. (2000) "Object-focused interaction in collaborative virtual environments", *ACM ToCHI*, vol. 7 (4), p. 477-509.

Hollan, J., Hutchins, E. and Kirsh, D. (2000) "Distributed cognition: toward a new foundation for human-computer interaction research", *ACM ToCHI*, vol. 7 (2), p. 174-196.

Hughes, J. et al. (1994) "Perspectives on the social organization of work", *Field Studies and CSCW* (COMIC Deliverable 2.2), p. 129-160, Lancaster University.

Ishii, H. and Kobayashi, M. (1992) "Clearboard", *Proceedings of CHI '92*, p. 525-535, Monterey: ACM Press.

Kendon, A. (1996) "An agenda for gesture studies", *Semiotic Review of Books*, vol. 7 (3), p. 8-12.

Kirk, D.S. (2004) "Performance effects of using a mixed reality surface for collaborative physical tasks", *Equator Technical Report*, University of Nottingham.

Kirk, D.S. and Stanton-Fraser, D. (2005) "The effects of remote gesturing on distance instruction", to appear in *Proceedings of CSCL 2005*, May 30-June 4, Taipei: ISLS.

Koleva, B., Benford, S. and Greenhalgh, C. (1999) "The properties of mixed reality boundaries", *Proceedings of ECSCW '99*, p. 119-137, Copenhagen: Kluwer Academic Publishers.

Kuzuoka, H. et al. (1999) "Agora: a remote collaboration system that enables mutual monitoring", *Proceedings of CHI '99*, p. 190-191, Pittsburg: ACM Press.

Kuzouka, H., Kosaka, J., Yamazaki, K., Suga, S., Yamazaki, A., Luff, P. and Heath, C. (2004) "Mediating dual ecologies", *Proceedings of CSCW '04*, p. 477-486, Chicago: ACM Press.

Luff, P. et al. (2003) "Fractured ecologies", *Human-Computer Interaction*, vol. 18 (1), p. 51–84.

Ou, J. et al. (2003) "Gestural communication over video stream: supporting multimodal interaction", *Proceedings of ICMI '03*, p. 242-249, Vancouver: ACM Press.

Sacks, H., Schegloff, E., and Jefferson, G. (1974) "A simplest systematics for the organization of turn-taking in conversation", *Language*, vol. 50, p. 696-735.

Schmidt, K. and Bannon, L. (1992) "Taking CSCW seriously: supporting articulation work", *Computer Supported Cooperative Work: An International Journal*, vol. 1 (1), pp. 7-40.

Schmidt, K. (2002) "The problem with 'awareness'", Computer Supported Cooperative work: The Journal of Collaborative Computing, vol. 11 (3), p. 285-298.

Suchman, L. (1987) *Plans and Situated Actions: The Problem of Human-Machine Communication*, Cambridge: Cambridge University Press.

Suchman, L. (2000) "Embodied practices of engineering work", *Mind, Culture & Activity*, vol. 7 (1), p. 4-18.

Sudnow, D. (1978) *Ways of the Hand: The Organization of Improvised Conduct*, London: Routledge.

Tang, J.C. and Minneman, S.L. (1990) "VideoDraw:", *Proceedings of CHI '90*, p. 313-320, Seattle: ACM Press.

Tang, J.C. and Minneman, S.L. (1991) "VideoWhiteboard: video shadows to support remote collaboration", *Proceedings of CHI '91*, p. 315-322, New Orleans: ACM Press.

Tang, A. et al. (2004) "Embodiments and VideoArms in mixed presence groupware", *Technical Report 2004-741-06*, Department of Computer Science, University of Calgary.

H. Gellersen et al. (eds.), ECSCW 2005: Proceedings of the Ninth European
Conference on Computer-Supported Cooperative Work, 18-22 September 2005, Paris,
France, 23–43.

A Design Theme for Tangible Interaction: Embodied Facilitation

Eva Hornecker

Interact Lab, Dept. of Informatics, University of Sussex, GB

eva@ehornecker.de

Abstract. This paper presents parts of a design framework for collaboratively used tangible interaction systems, focusing on the theme of *Embodied Facilitation*. Systems can be interpreted as spaces/structures to act and move in, facilitating some movements and hindering others. Thus they shape the ways we collaborate, induce collaboration or make us refrain from it. Tangible interaction systems provide virtual and physical structure - they truly embody facilitation. Three concepts further refine the theme: Embodied Constraints, Multiple Access Points and Tailored Representations. These are broken down into design guidelines and each illustrated with examples.

Introduction

Tangible User Interfaces (TUIs) have become a hot topic in HCI. Until recently, research was mostly technology-driven, focusing on developing new systems. A special issue of 'Personal & Ubiquitous Computing' on 'tangible interfaces in perspective' (Holmquist, Schmidt and Ullmer, 2004) marks a change in focus towards conceptual analysis. Yet, there is still a lack of theory on *why* tangible interaction works so well (Dourish, 2001). Cooperation support might be the most important, domain-independent feature of TUIs, but this issue has attracted even less explicit attention. Many researchers agree that TUIs are especially suited for collocated collaboration and build systems aimed at group scenarios (e.g. Stanton et al, 2001; Ullmer and Ishii 2001). Nevertheless, conceptual papers (as in the mentioned special issue) tend to brush over this issue by briefly mentioning visibility of actions and distributed loci of control as collaborative affordances. User studies focusing on group interaction are still scarce, even though we know from CSCW research that collaborative use often poses different (and possibly contradictory) requirements to single-user usability. We therefore lack concepts for analyzing and understanding the collaborative aspects of tangible interaction and design knowledge on how to design *for* collaboration.

This paper focuses on part of a framework that offers four themes and a set of concepts for understanding and designing collaboratively used tangible interaction systems (for an overview: Hornecker, 2004b). The framework builds on results from a PhD project on the collaborative use of tangible interfaces (Hornecker, 2004) and on recent studies in related areas (Hornecker and Stifter, 2004, Hornecker and Bruns, 2004). Just as interaction design aims to create opportunities *for* experience, one can design *for* cooperation and create a 'force field' encouraging and inducing collaboration. The framework aims to help in creating such 'force fields' by offering "design sensitivities" (Ciolfi, 2004, Fitzpatrick, 2003) and soft guidelines. The framework theme focused on here is *Embodied Facilitation*. Tangible interfaces/interaction systems embody facilitation methods and means by providing structure and rules, both physically and procedurally. Any application can be understood as offering structure that implicitly directs user behavior by facilitating some actions, and prohibiting or hindering others. It thus influences behavior patterns and emerging social configurations. With Tangible interaction systems, structure is not only in software, but also physical. They can truly embody facilitation.

I now describe what 'tangible interaction' means, summarize the overarching framework and present the *Embodied Interaction* theme. The following sections deal with the concepts relevant to embodied interaction and design guidelines derived, illustrated by examples. I conclude on open questions and related work.

A Framework for the Design of Tangible Interaction for Collaborative Use

From the characterizations of tangible interfaces/interaction found in literature, we can distinguish a data-centered view, pursued in Computer Science and HCI; a perceptual-motor-centered view, pursued by Industrial and Product Design; and a space-centered view influenced from Arts and Architecture:

- *Data-centered view:* Physical representation and manipulation of digital data (Ullmer and Ishii, 2000; Dourish, 2001) or the interactive coupling of physical artifacts with "computationally mediated digital information" (Holmquist, Schmidt and Ullmer, 2004). Research often explores types of coupling. These systems are usually referred to as *"tangible interfaces"*.
- *Perceptual-motor-centered view:* Bodily interaction with objects, exploiting the "sensory richness and action potential of physical objects", so "meaning is created in the interaction" (Djajadiningrat, Overbeeke and Wensveen,

2004). Design takes account of skills and focuses on expressiveness of movement, e.g. rhythm, force and style (Buur, Jensen and Djajadiningrat, 2004). The design community prefers the term *'tangible interaction'*.

- *Space-centered view:* A combination of real space and real objects with virtual displays (Bongers, 2002). "Interactive systems, physically embedded within real spaces, which offer opportunities for interacting with tangible devices, and so trigger display of digital content or reactive behaviors" (Ciolfi, 2004). This is termed *'interactive/interactivating spaces'*.

The concept of *tangible interaction* has a much broader scope than Ullmer and Ishii's (2000) description of tangible interfaces: "giving physical form to digital information" and its subsequent physical control, which is often referred to or used as a definition (data-centered view). *Tangible interaction* is not restricted to controlling digital data and includes tangible appliances or the remote control of *real* devices. Because it focuses on designing the interaction (instead of the interface), resulting systems tend less to imitate interaction with screen-based GUIs (as does placing and moving tokens) and exploit the richness of embodied action (Buur, Jensen and Djajadiningrat, 2004). Interaction with 'interactive spaces' by walking on sensorized floors or by simply moving in space further extends our perspective on 'tangible' interaction. Instead of using a restrictive definition that excludes some of these interesting system variants, it seems more productive to address this larger design space. Thereby we leave the somewhat artificial confines of any definition behind, and can interpret these attempts at conceptualization as emphasizing different facets of a related set of systems.

The Design Framework Themes

The framework (Hornecker, 2004b) is structured around four themes, which are not mutually exclusive, but interrelated, offering different perspectives. Each theme consists of three or four concepts, which are broken down into concrete guidelines. In this section will present the four overarching themes and later focus on one. For each theme a short argument is given as to why it is relevant for tangible interaction (referring to the definitions given above).

Tangible Interaction Systems for collaborative use should carefully exploit:

- *Tangible Manipulation:* Tangible Manipulation is bodily interaction with physical objects. It is interacting with hands and the body. Tangible interaction is observable and legible, allowing for implicit communication and peripheral awareness. The objects react in a physical, material way. Design can deliberately exploit tangibility, emphasizing the direct interaction with physical objects, which have distinctive material qualities.
- *Spatial Interaction:* Tangible interaction is embedded in real space. We are spatial beings; we live and meet each other in space. Our body is a reference point for perception. Spatial qualities have psychological meaning. Real

space is inhabited and situated. Real places have an atmosphere. Spatial interaction is observable and often acquires performative aspects. Design can exploit the qualities of space and the resources it offers.

- *Embodied Facilitation:* With tangible interaction we act/move in physical space and in system space (software). Software defines virtual structure, determining the interaction flow. Physical space prescribes physical structure. Both types of structure allow, direct, and limit behavior. Tangible interaction systems embody structure. Design can enforce social structure and we can learn from facilitation and pedagogical methods how to do this.
- *Expressive Representation:* Tangible Interaction is about physical representation of data. Hybrid representations combine tangible and virtual elements. These communicate to us and have expression. In interaction we 'read' and interpret representations, act on, modify and create them. We share externalizations of our thinking, which provide shared reference, remember our traces and document common ground. Design can create legible, expressive representation.

The framework is organized on three levels of abstraction. The themes offer perspectives (or viewpoints) and argumentation of an abstract, theoretical level. They define broad research issues such as the role of space for tangible interaction. Themes are each concretized with a set of concepts. Concepts provide analytical tools for describing empirically found phenomena and help to summarize generic issues, to pinpoint design mistakes and successes. However, concepts are quite abstract and employing them to support design necessitates understanding the argumentation behind them. For a design framework, a level of more directly applicable design guidelines is needed. These should be easily communicable and comprehensible for people working on practical design projects, but not interested (or not having time) for the underlying theory.

Furthermore, different researchers and research communities might focus on different levels. To explain general phenomena or analyze empirical studies, themes and concepts might be most useful. When designing systems, one might experimentally follow some guidelines, testing their usefulness and exploring the design space. To quickly enable people to roughly understand what the more abstract concepts mean, 'colloquial versions' have also been developed. It should be emphasized that these are not strict rules, but rather soft guidelines, close to Ciolfi's (2004) "design sensibilities" or Fitzgerald's (2003) sensitizing concepts.

Embodied Facilitation

We can interpret systems as spaces or structures to act and move in, thereby determining usage options and behavior patterns. They enforce social configurations and direct user behavior by facilitating some movements and hindering others. Thus, they shape the ways we can collaborate; they can induce us to collaborate or make us refrain from it. From pedagogy and facilitation we can learn about how structure, both physical and procedural, can be shaped to support and direct group processes. With tangible interaction systems, which are embedded in real space and physically embodied, this space is both a literal one (physical space and objects) and metaphorical one (software determining action spaces). Tangible interaction systems can thus truly embody facilitation.

The background that underpins this approach is an exploration of analogies between interaction design and group pedagogy or facilitation (for details see: Hornecker 2004c). Both interaction design and facilitation/pedagogy can be interpreted as the design of 'spaces for human communication, interaction and experience'. Similar to architectural spaces, these are appropriated and inhabited by users. They furthermore offer and prescribe structure, predetermining feasible adaptation and movement paths. Interaction design cannot 'design experiences' just as the structure provided by facilitation can only foster certain experiences or processes, but not automatically produce them. I became aware of what can be learned from facilitation and pedagogy for interaction design when evaluating a system in a group setting (Eden, Hornecker and Scharff, 2002). Seemingly trivial design decisions (such as system size, placement and number of tools) had a huge impact on group behavior, session dynamic and atmosphere. My knowledge of facilitation methods helped to explain these phenomena and informed the systems redesign. With the theme of Embodied Facilitation, I propose to utilize this analogy by intent and to apply 'facilitation knowledge' to interaction design.

As stated previously, this paper focuses on the *Embodied Facilitation* theme. Each theme (offering a specific perspective on tangible interaction) is elaborated by a set of concepts. The three concepts related to embodied facilitation are now summarized as a question in colloquial language to give a quick, but rough idea of what they are about. Then the concepts are explained in detail and the corresponding design guidelines are presented and illustrated with examples.

Embodied Constraints: Does the physical set-up lead users to collaborate by subtly constraining their behavior?

Multiple Access Points: Can all users see what's going on and get their hands on the central objects of interest?

Tailored Representation: Does the representation build on users' experience? Does it connect with their experience and skills and invite them into interaction?

Concept: Embodied Constraints

Constraints restrict what people can do and thereby make some behaviors more probable than others. Embodied constraints refer to the *physical system set-up* or *configuration of space and objects*. They can ease some types of activity and limit what people can (easily) do. Thereby they determine probable trajectories of action. Some embodied constraints provide implicit suggestions to act in a certain way. Others require people to collectively work around them, leading to the adoption of interaction patterns that indirectly foster collaboration. Using such subtle mechanisms, we can encourage and induce people to collaborate. Shape and size of interaction spaces e.g. act as embodied constraints, which bring groups together, focusing on a shared object, or which hinder communication.

The design guidelines are:
- Exploit constraints that require groups to:
  - distribute the task   - help each other out   - coordinate action
- Provide a shared 'transaction space'

Guideline: Exploit Constraints that Induce Helping and Coordination

Sometimes constraints that at first sight seem restrictive and hinder usability have positive effects on social interaction. In evaluating and redesigning the Envisionment and Discovery Collaboratory (EDC) (Eden, Hornecker and Scharff, 2002, Hornecker, 2004) we started to use the term 'embodied constraints' to understand and pinpoint some of these phenomena.

The EDC was developed at the Center for Lifelong Learning and Design to support co-located participatory urban planning (Arias, Eden and Fischer 1997). It provides an augmented game board and allows tangible interaction with computational simulations projected upon an aerial photo. We assessed two system versions by having two groups use them in a role-play of a neighborhood meeting on re-design of a local bus route. The sessions and subsequent discussions were videotaped and an interaction analysis was carried out. One system version uses a horizontal SMARTBOARD™ that allows drawing with fingers to create, move or delete objects and pen sketching, but cannot handle simultaneous interactions or detect physical objects. The second system version, the PITA-BOARD, is based upon a chessboard grid (http://www.dgtprojects.com) that registers RFID tags embedded in objects. Thus it comes closer to the vision of a tangible interface with tangible manipulation.

Figure 1. Embodied constraints by structure and size of EDC SMARTBOARD version: (a) helping each other to change interaction mode (menu in front) and (b) handing over of tools (a pen).

During analysis we found that constraints forced participants to coordinate actions, and as a result fostered group awareness and cooperation. Such constraints can consist of shared or restricted resources that must be coordinated, or of structures encouraging reciprocal helping. Examples are a menu for selecting interaction modes on the SMARTBOARD (create, move, delete...) or a limited supply of tangible tools. The sheer size of the SMARTBOARD necessitated mutual helping and handing over of tools (figure 1), indirectly fostering collaboration and awareness. It also made it physically impossible for one person to take over control of the entire interaction space. Participants found these to be valuable effects; they advised us to keep the system that large. With the much smaller PITA-BOARD we observed markedly less of these behaviors. From group dynamics it is known that situations requiring coordination and help do improve reciprocal liking and group cohesion. Such situations occurred at the very beginning of the session and initiated content-neutral cooperation, possibly making people more willing to cooperate on more salient issues later-on. Working with interaction modes (one global menu with create, move, delete... tools) had negative effects from a task-oriented view and led to frequent breakdowns, but required participants to be highly aware of each other and to coordinate activity. Here the annoyance was higher than the benefits. Nevertheless, participants could imagine employing similar (less disruptive) constraints to foster collaboration.

Physical or system constraints requiring coordination and sharing of resources thus embody facilitation methods that foster cooperation and structure group processes. From a viewpoint of task analysis, constraints seem counterproductive. However, easing the task is not the most important goal for all situations; less straightforward social or cognitive effects may be more critical. Nevertheless, as the modal interaction example demonstrates, constraints need to be carefully chosen so as not to disturb and irritate participants. Lessons learned for re-design included enlargement of the PITA-BOARD, so people would be forced to help each other and could not control the entire board. We also consciously provided enough tools for several participants to be active at once, but only a restricted number of each, so they would need to help each other and coordinate use.

Figure 2. The size of the CLAVIER necessitates several people for a more complex soundscape.

A further example for embodied constraints originates from a very different system. Seven installations created by students were shown on three nights in summer 2002 at a public festival in a park in Bremen. A description and analysis of the SENSORIC GARDEN, using concepts on interactivity to explain *why* some installations successfully attracted visitors' engagement and what made others fail, is given in Hornecker and Bruns (2004). Here I focus on the CLAVIER: a walkway with light sensors triggered by walking across it (figure 2). Colored spotlights reacted where one put one's feet. Triggered midi drums and beats produced an ambient sound environment. Visitors danced to the music, jumped from light to light and created music. This installation attracted many interactors and a constant gathering of observers. Some people even danced with umbrellas in the rain. Others used umbrellas and other objects to trigger multiple sensors.

In several ways the system encouraged people to implicitly and explicitly cooperate. Visitors, by inadvertently passing, interacted musically with intentional interactors. Furthermore, its size necessitated the activity of several people to produce a complex soundscape, as a single person could only trigger a few adjacent sounds. The installation in this way encouraged group creativity. While the CLAVIER exemplarily illustrates the spatial interaction theme, these effects also make it a good example for the embodied constraints given by the sheer size of an interaction area. Additionally, by necessitating large-scale bodily interaction, it transforms interaction into a public performance (a concept from the tangible manipulation theme), makes actions visible, and supports full body interaction (concepts from spatial interaction theme). This shows how the themes are interconnected, offering different perspectives on related phenomena.

There is considerable evidence that the physical set-up affects social interaction patterns, an issue getting relevant in research on distributed displays. E.g. Rogers and Rodden (2003) found that groups tend to nominate one participant for writing on a white board and line up before it. When sitting around a table, roles are more flexible. The physical constraints of a white board mean that standing in front blocks view and physical access for others. Only one or two persons can simultaneously have physical access. A point on a table can be accessed by more people. Buur and Soendergaard (2000) observed different behaviors and discussion styles for various room set-ups. Needing to stand up and go to a wall to show a video made people refrain from it. Discussions tended to be abstract and general. Being able to show clips while staying seated, people would quickly do so and referred more to concrete video clips and specific observations.

Guideline: Provide a Shared Transaction Space

Kendon (1990) introduced the term *transaction space* in his explanation of the F-formation. A persons' transaction space is formed by the half-circle before the upper body, that (s)he can see and act within. It is framed by body orientation and posture. "An F-formation arises whenever two or more people sustain a spatial and orientational relationship in which the space between them is one to which they have equal, direct and exclusive access" (Kendon, 1990, p. 203). If people stand in a circle or surround a table, their transaction spaces overlap and create a shared one. Kendon found that establishing, changing and leaving an F-formation correlates with beginning, participating in, and ending social interaction and that changes of the configuration give subtle social signals (see also: Suzuki and Kato 1995). As people seem to interpret its establishment as indication that social interaction is appropriate, implicit creation of an F-formation might stimulate group interaction. This can explain why surrounding an image on a table produces a different atmosphere and interaction style than the same image on a wall.

A shared transaction space provides shared focus (if a representational object attracts attention), while allowing for peripheral awareness. Systems that render sides of a table unavailable to users affect the shape of transaction spaces (Scott, Grant and Mandryk, 2003) and thereby the interaction. A transaction space, by providing exclusive access, also limits communication to those sharing it. There is a natural limit to its size determined by visibility and audibility.

The focus-providing effect of the EDC's shared transaction space can be seen well on evaluation videos. Even from only a bird's eye view of the table, one can discern from the rapid activity and gesturing on the SMARTBOARD that people mostly look at the aerial photo. Nevertheless, the fluidity of interaction and conversation demonstrates high awareness. Figure 3 a shows a group surrounding the enlarged PITA-BOARD highly focused on the map and on group activity.

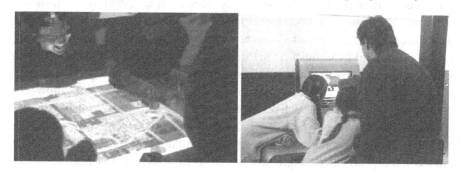

Figure 3. (a) The enlarged PITA-BOARD provides a shared transaction space. (b) Size and form of the Electrical Telegraphy hands-on exhibit support small group interaction.

An evaluation of a museum exhibition in Vienna on media evolution provided further examples of the effects of specifically formed transaction spaces (Hornecker and Stifter, 2004). The exhibition combines traditional object exhibits, computer-augmented hands-on exhibits, touch screens, interactive installations and computer terminals. Evaluation combined logfile analysis with qualitative observation and visitor interviews. Observation revealed interesting differences in interaction patterns with installations types, in particular in terms of group sizes. While most touch screens or computer terminals tended to be used by one visitor and only rarely by two, interactive installations were often surrounded by groups of up to five persons. Figure 3 b shows a family exploring a hands-on exhibit on electrical telegraphy. The image illustrates how its size and form limit the number of people able to focus on it. By providing a hands-on device in the foreground (not visible: Morse ticker and letter wheel) the screen is moved to the rear; focus shifts between device and screen. Size and form of an interaction space (or system) act as a specific type of embodied constraint delimiting access.

Concept: Multiple Access Points

Access points refer to the options to access and actively manipulate relevant objects. Access is an issue of power, highly influencing group dynamics. We can analyze systems in terms of the resources they offer for accessing and interacting with the objects of interest and in terms of privileges and limitations of access. Restricted resources affect the power play and may even entice people into conflict and competition for control. Sufficient resources and non-privileged access create a more egalitarian situation, allowing everyone to participate and to have a say (abstracting from factors such as hierarchies), making it difficult for individuals or subgroups to take over control. *Access points* determine the opportunities to observe and to become involved hands-on with relevant objects.

Researchers comparing single and multiple mouse conditions for children's games found different interaction structures (Stewart et al, 1998). In multi-mouse conditions significantly more cooperation and communication took place, conflict was reduced, children interacted more, were more on equal terms and did not drop out of the activity as much as in the single mouse set-up. Stanton et al (2001) conclude on a study with tangible props for children's storytelling: "If everyone has a prop, then everyone has a vote". Multiple input devices allow for simultaneous action, easing active participation, reducing time constraints and supporting fluent switches between individual and group work (Stewart et al, 1998). By allowing parallel and non-verbal contributions they shift power away from the verbally articulate, aggressive or self-assured members of groups.

Observational studies of design sessions often find fine-grained synchronization of simultaneous multimodal activities. Simultaneous activity not only speeds up interaction, it also displays shared understanding and distributes ownership (Hornecker, 2004). Visible representations provide focus and shared reference; they anchor discussions (Arias, Eden and Fischer, 1997, Henderson 1999). Public interaction triggers communication and negotiation. Access points are influenced by size and form of artifacts and shared space (Scott, Grant and Mandryk, 2003), determining the physical configuration or arrangement of a group and affect audibility, visibility and manual accessibility.

The design guidelines are:

• Give multiple points of interaction

- Allow for simultaneous action
- Give equal access - no privileges

Guideline: Give Multiple Points of Interaction

Multiple interaction objects distribute control in a group, make it difficult for individuals to take over control, and lower thresholds for shy or timid persons to become active. Whereas in the original PITA-BOARD version, bus stops were 'stamped' with a tool onto the map, the new version provided as many stop tokens as could be used (figure 4 a). This made it easier to relocate stops and to keep track of 'unused' stops. At the same time, it became difficult for a single participant to remain in control and set all stops.

There is reason to believe that touching objects creates a sense of ownership and aids cognitive and emotional appropriation (cp. Buur and Soendergaard, 2000). When distributing creation and manipulation of representations over a group, these can thus become truly shared objects. This belief was strengthened by observing the SMARTBOARD-group taking turns in drawing the final bus route at the end of the session, *explicitly* involving everyone. Members of a workshop using a redesigned PITA-BOARD version did the same. While access to the modal menu on the SMARTBOARD was limited to those next to it (an embodied constraint enforcing coordination and help), access to the board for other actions was not restrained. Not being forced to aggressively acquire control over interaction devices lowers thresholds. Even though there was no equal distribution (achieving this is probably illusionary), the more quiet or shy group members gestured lively and made important contributions in manipulating items.

The CLAVIER installation from the SENSORIC GARDEN provides another example for multiple points of interaction (figure 4 b + c). While here the visitors' bodies constitute interaction devices, input points are distributed, allowing several persons to be active without being in each other's way. This allowed for incidental simultaneous activity and for cooperative dancing and composing.

The setup as an embodied constraint often also limits access points. In the exhibition evaluation (Hornecker and Stifter, 2004) it was observed how different types of installations attracted different visitor constellations. Computer terminals were almost always used by single persons (figure 5 a), as screens and seating suit this best. Although of same screen size, the ORF-ARCHIVE (radio and TV clips) was quite often occupied by pairs. The seat and the small screen allow up to two people to see and be active. Having only two of these stations gave an incentive, and the seat seemed to provide a sense of intimacy while being comfortable enough for two because of sideward space. In contrast, hands-on installations were frequently surrounded by groups with several people interacting. Several visitors can move the physical beads of the ABACUS (figure 6 a) at once and the set-up provides space for observers. The large screens of the GLOBAL STORAGE (figure 6 b) installation are interacted with via laser beam pens. The large projection affords many observers and a number of laser pens are attached to long strings, allowing multiple visitors to move about and be active.

Figure 4: (a) Many interaction objects (PITA-BOARD) and (b, c) input at various loci (CLAVIER)

Figure 5: (a) Terminals suit single users. (b) The ORF-ARCHIVE is used by up to two visitors.

The idea of analyzing size and form of systems in terms of providing access points originated from observing students work with LEGO MINDSTORMS™. In several groups of five, two people only observed and soon got distracted. It was salient that more than three people can simply not touch the robots simultaneously (limiting participation in building and testing) and block view for others. The option to touch something can thus be a scarce resource to start with. Small objects or surfaces make it difficult to reference via gestures for large groups. Large objects on the other hand may provide many access points. Yet, their size means that one can only access a certain subset at a time. The CLAVIER provides an example where this effect is positive in fostering cooperation.

Guideline: Allow for Simultaneous Action

Multiple points of interaction ease simultaneous interaction, but do not necessarily permit it. Often systems provide several input devices, but require sequential input, ignoring parallel events or reacting delayed. The PITA-BOARD allows for simultaneous interaction, while the SMARTBOARD does not. Having to alternate and sequentialize actions caused multiple breakdowns, even though participants were highly aware of each other. Alternating actions was felt to be demanding. Simultaneous interaction speeds up work that can be done in parallel and thereby helps the group to concentrate on issues requiring negotiation and on developing shared understanding. It also allows less vocal group members to have a say, as they do not need to wait for a free time slot or need to interrupt.

Figure 6: Hands-on exhibits (a) ABACUS and (b) GLOBAL STORAGE afford small groups

Figure 7: Simultaneous action on new PITA-BOARD (a) introductory phase (b) mapping land use

Most examples given in the previous section for multiple points of interaction apply here as well. Simultaneous interaction thus supports multiple points of interaction. Yet, it is not a design guideline that should be followed slavishly. Physical constraints that sequentialize actions can serve to give necessary order to an interaction process or to ensure equal rights (e.g. a waiting queue).

Guideline: Give Equal Access – No Privileges

Privileged access to system features naturally gives more power to those privileged. Besides affecting the interaction process it changes the atmosphere by evoking certain assumptions and expectations, in particular by delivering implicit social signals on hierarchies and expertise. Equal access refers to giving everybody equal options; it does not mean everybody should have one of every tool or that all interaction devices should provide the same functionality.

In assessing the EDC (Eden, Hornecker and Scharff 2002) we found that privileged access of facilitators to system functions affected the power play of sessions. Facilitator access to PITA-BOARD features via mouse and keyboard, invisible and unpredictable to participants, made them feel as guests, not allowed to 'own' the system space. In comparison, the SMARTBOARD group quickly learned how to close error messages (appearing on the table) and took over this task. Making the means of controlling the system invisible and non-observable does not enable users to learn and become 'experts'. Providing privileged access to some group members gives implicit *signs of ownership*. When re-designing the PITA-BOARD, we eliminated privileged access by providing means to control the simulation by manipulating objects on the game board (Figure 8 b). Combined with other improvements, the new version provided a much better experience, allowed for equal access, and enabled everybody to take over system control.

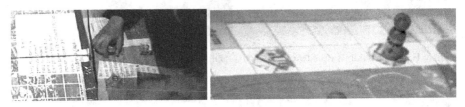

Figure 8. (a) A menu pops up unexpectedly within participants' manual space, who cannot see facilitator actions. (b) The new PITA-BOARD version has an extra 'admin-space'.

Another kind of privilege relates to optimal viewpoints, due to e.g. a vertical screen next to a table (cp. Scott, Grant, Mandryk, 2003). With the EDC, there was no optimal, and therefore privileged place, as most icons were easily identifiable, even if upside down, and the aerial photo has no implicit orientation. Orientation and positioning are much more critical for text. Privileged viewpoints are a result of the type of representation used as well as size and form of interaction spaces.

Concept: Tailored Representations

The concept of *tailored representations* refers to a different type of access, which is cognitive and emotional instead of manual or visual. Discussions of tangible interfaces often highlight the intuitiveness of interaction. Focusing only on intuitiveness neglects the skills and knowledge of people (cp. Buur, Jensen and Djajadiningrat, 2004) and may result in systems that don't scale up to experienced users and complex domains. While intuitive usability is important in giving new users access, we also must consider expert users and specialists. Representations that connect with users' experiences and skills invite them into interaction and empower them. Representations that do not connect do exclude and silence users, who cannot relate, understand, and contribute. Representations need to be adequate for the task, the domain and the user group. Intuitiveness is thus relative.

Nevertheless, it is important to ease initial access on the basic level of manipulating relevant objects. If we cannot figure out how to interact with a system, it is of no help if the representation is legible. Users should be able to quickly explore the basic syntax of interaction. Over time they might acquire the more complex syntax of advanced interaction (learnability). Experience-orientation thus refers more to the semantics of interacting with a representation.

Representations that build upon users' experiences can become tools for thought as thinking prop or external memory, and can complement verbal communication by allowing people to gesture, refer to visible objects and manually demonstrate something (Norman, 1994; Hutchins and Klausen, 1998). Adequately chosen representations thereby ease participation in discussions. Henderson (1999) describes the gatekeeper function of design representations that control access, invite or discourage participation and define the range of allowed actions. Representations can privilege perspectives (different notations being easier to read and manipulate for specific professions) and become symbolically owned territory. Good representations offer several layers of legibility, are accessible for people with differing knowledge areas, and provide a shared reference. Then they can serve as boundary objects (Star and Griesemer, 1989).

Another aspect of representations and materials is that these trigger people's imagination and creativity (Rettig, 1994). The selection of materials provides a trajectory for thought, for the positive or the negative. What is not available or not visible will be thought of less. Similar to facilitators, system designers should be aware of the responsibility they carry in deciding upon available materials and representations, as these might affect the decisions of people using them.

The design guidelines are:
• Build on the experience of the group and its members
• Make the interaction intuitive enough for easy access
• Allow the semantics to rely on specific knowledge

Guidelines on Intuitiveness and Experience-Orientation

Interaction with the PITA-BOARD tokens was perceived by all participants as intuitive. In analyzing the videos, no interaction problems could be detected after an initial phase of finding out how to place tokens on the board. A new introductory phase for exploring the system in a playful way (figure 7 a) gave participants the opportunity to get accustomed to its reactions. Many common methods for citizen participation in urban design use aerials as maps distort and abstract geographical relations. Furthermore, map reading must be learned, it is an acquired skill. Aerials might relate more to inhabitants' experience, with landmarks being easy to identify and street shapes visible. Ernesto Arias (personal communication) emphasizes the importance of selecting an appropriate level of abstraction in participatory urban design, such as very literal, figurative building blocks: "Some laypeople need a tree-tree, not a green general block". After a while categories become well known and more abstract blocks can be introduced.

The systems introduced so far have all been of the 'walk up and use' kind, meant for public places or participatory meetings. A recent study provides a better example of the difference between intuitiveness and experience-orientation.

Together with students I carried out a user study on the TANGIBLE IMAGE QUERY (Matkovich et al 2004). This system offers architects inspiration through serendipitous searching in collections of images. Users define a search by laying colored objects onto the input area. The underlying algorithm searches for color distributions. The study participants were architecture and computing students. While manipulation of input and querying was intuitive, the search results required habituation and were initially irritating. One major finding was that the attitude of participants towards the system depended largely on their relation with images (as architects, art lovers or avid photographers) and their ability to find value in being inspired and surprised (instead of finding "what I searched for").

Figure 9. (a + b) Study participant at the TANGIBLE IMAGE QUERY with query results

Examples for this concept are not yet sufficient, as the systems studied so far did not address specialized and experienced professional users and the TANGIBLE IMAGE QUERY has no collaborative use context. Nevertheless the concept is important to Embodied Facilitation, and therefore needs to be presented here.

Conclusions and Outlook

In this paper I presented a theme for design and analysis of collaboratively used tangible interaction. Tangible interaction encompasses a broad scope of system and interfaces sharing aspects of tangibility, physical embodiment of data, bodily or embodied interaction and embedding in real space. It encompasses approaches from HCI, computer science, product design and interactive arts. Following a short summary of the overall framework, I focused on the *Embodied Facilitation* theme. Its basic idea is that tangible interaction systems provide procedural as well as physical and spatial structure, which shapes the ways we act. It can induce collaboration, foster it or make us refrain from it. Thus, tangible interaction systems embody styles, methods and means of facilitation.

The theme of Embodied Facilitation was broken down into three concepts. These were concretized with design guidelines and illustrated with examples. *Embodied Constraints* are aspects of the physical set-up that subtly constrain peoples' behavior or provide implicit suggestions for action, encouraging collaboration. The guidelines suggest (a) employing constraints that require groups to distribute the task, to help each other out and to coordinate action, and (b) providing shared 'transaction spaces'. The concept of *Multiple Access Points* makes us consider systems in terms of how many people can see what is going on and lay hands on the objects of interest. The guidelines suggest (c) giving multiple points of interaction, (d) allowing simultaneous action and (e) giving equal access, not privileging some users. *Tailored Representations* take account of users' experiences and skills, inviting and empowering them. The guidelines suggest (f) building on experience and (g) making interaction intuitive enough for easy access, but (h) allowing the semantics to rely on specific knowledge.

In its current state, the overall design framework should be read as a proposal, backed by examples and arguments. There are several directions for future research. To demonstrate its utility as a *design framework*, practical design studies employing concepts and guidelines are required. These could involve design of new and redesign of existing systems, or adjusting a previously single-user system to collaborative use. Other studies could systematically explore the design space given by specific (sets of) guidelines. A further direction for research relates to the frameworks' general applicability to CSCW. Illustrative examples so far stem predominantly from entertainment, design and negotiation support. To demonstrate its general utility, examples from other application areas are required. It is furthermore open whether the framework covers collaboration distributed over time and space. Further research questions concern the relations between some of the concepts and guidelines. Transaction spaces and access points are clearly positively related. Seen as absolutes, multiple access points and constraints are in tension. Different configurations may prompt different interaction patterns, such as providing a tool for every second or third group member. Similar questions could be studied in detail empirically. The concrete influence of size and form of interaction spaces or the number of access points is still unclear. Is there a systematic relation between task, access points, number of actors and evolving interaction patterns? Considering the number of guidelines in the overall framework there will be many more detailed research questions.

It is important to remember that the guidelines are meant to sensitize designers, not to be slavishly followed. While it is tempting to make concepts operational, we need to be wary of transforming analytic terms, meant to sharpen perception, into rules and measurements. Design needs sensitivity and judgment. Sometimes it might even be best to temporarily discourage collaboration, prevent observation and restrict access, turning the guidelines from *do's* into *don't's*. Which guidelines should be applied and which take precedence over others, will depend on the task and the larger context of an activity, requiring further investigation on indicators for the applicability of guidelines and priorities in-between guidelines.

The contributions of this paper towards understanding the relation of embodied interaction and collaboration consist of: framework themes and concepts which support high-level analysis; complemented with guidelines to support design; and a research agenda. The framework is illustrated with several examples. It furthermore contributes to research on interactive exhibits, where space is an intrinsic issue (e.g. Ciolfi, 2004), as these served as major illustrative domain.

To round up, I will put my own framework into the context of related work. There are several frameworks aimed at the design for social interaction and a number of frameworks on tangible interfaces/interaction. With its soft guidelines and 'design sensitivities' my framework shares characteristics with others that offer concepts as 'sensitizing devices' and support designing for social interaction (Ciolfi, 2004, Dourish, 2001, Fitzpatrick, 2003). These frameworks are not prescriptive, do not offer recipes, and thus need to be interpreted and appropriated in response to concrete situations. Although operationalized to a greater extent, the framework presented here is meant to be continually evolving and open.

Previous frameworks on tangible interfaces/interaction have focused mainly on defining terms, categorizing, and characterizing systems (e.g. Ullmer and Ishii, 2000, some articles in 'Pervasive & Ubiquitous Computing' special issue 2004). While supporting the structural analysis of systems and detection of uncharted territory, these approaches offer little advice when designing for specific real world situations. Furthermore, these frameworks seldom address the human interaction experience or are restricted to solitary users. Suzuki and Kato (1995) and Arias et al (1997) did pioneering work on acquiring a better understanding of how tangible interaction affords social interaction and collaboration, but found few followers. Even though many TUIs supporting collaborations have been developed and some field-tested, analysis often remains domain-specific and yields few generalizable concepts (for a literature overview see Hornecker 2004).

This framework contributes to the larger research agenda of Embodied Interaction. While sharing the goal of understanding tangible interaction with Dourish (2001), my view on embodiment is more in line with Robertson (1997, 2002). Dourish's perspective on embodiment focuses on the social construction of meaning, whereas Robertsons starting point (in the tradition of French phenomenologist Merleau-Ponty) is the living, feeling, responsive body as our primary means of experiencing the world, the world being its milieu. In embodied interaction the living body encounters and enters into dialogue with the world. Dourish (2001) states that social action is embedded in settings, which are not only material, but also social, cultural and historical, focusing his analysis on the latter. While the social has been elaborated, materiality has been less discussed. Understanding system embodiment in the sense of being *physically manifested* takes materiality seriously. I aim to unfold these aspects, inquiring into the interweaving of the material/physical and the social. Similar to Robertson (1997) and Fitzpatrick (2003) I am interested in how we accomplish communication and collaboration and how designed environments can support this.

Several framework themes and concepts not focused upon within this paper relate to topics discussed by other authors. E.g. social and atmospheric qualities of places (Ciolfi, 2004, Dourish, 2001) are part of the spatial interaction theme. The concepts of *non-fragmented visibility* and *performative action* are related to Dourish's (2001) discussion of accountability and observable action and build heavily on work from Robertson (1997). The concept of *embodied constraints* is at the same time related to and in intrinsic tension with *configurability*, focused on by other authors as an important system quality, but often with little reference to collaboration (Dourish, 2001, Jaccucci, 2004). This is a productive tension, as understanding the effects of embodied constraints makes the needs for configurability apparent. Moreover, it may give us insight on where exactly configurability is desirable and where (and how) system designers should provide structure – at least initially – in order for social processes to start evolving (cp. Hornecker 2004c). That "by configuring space in different ways, different kinds of behaviours can be supported" has often been stated (e.g. Dourish 2001). However discussion usually stops here. There have been only few attempts (e.g. Rogers and Rodden, 2003) to dig deeper and understand these relations. Affordances as 'exploitation of physical constraints' are often merely seen in terms of usability and provision of legible cues. With my framework and in particular with the theme of Embodied Facilitation presented here I extend the analysis to less straightforward, indirect (or second-order) social effects.

Acknowledgments

Jacob Buur pushed and helped me to go on, identify core ideas, fuse them into structure, focus on the essentials, and keep it simple. Thanks for the challenge and encouragement. Years ago Michael Heger gave me and my HDA-TG teammates a hands-on education in facilitation that imbues this work. Mark Stringer, Paul Marshall and Geraldine Fitzpatrick commented on different versions of this paper and helped polishing it. Special thanks to Geraldine for getting me to Sussex.

References

Arias, E., Eden, H. and Fischer, G. (1997). 'Enhancing Communication, Facilitating Shared Understanding, and Creating Better Artifacts by Integrating Physical and Computational Media for Design'. In *Proc. of DIS '97*, ACM. pp.1-12.

Bongers, B. (2002): 'Interactivating Spaces'. In *Proc. of Symposium on Systems Research in the Arts. Informatics and Cybernetics.*

42

Buur, J., Jensen, M.V. Djajadiningrat, T. (2004). 'Hands-only scenarios and video action walls: novel methods for tangible user interaction design'. In *Proc. of DIS'04*. ACM, pp. 185-192.

Buur, J. and Soendergaard, A. (2000): 'Video Card Game: An augmented environment for User Centred Design discussions'. In *Proc. of DARE'00*, ACM. pp. 63-69.

Ciolfi, L. (2004): *"Situating 'Place' in Interaction Design: Enhancing the User Experience in Interactive Environments"*. Ph.D. Thesis, University of Limerick.

Djajadiningrat, T., Overbeeke, K. and Wensveen, S. (2002): 'But how, Donald, tell us how?' In *Proc. of DIS'02*, ACM. pp. 285-291.

Dourish P. (2001): *Where the Action Is. The Foundations of Embodied Interaction*. MIT Press.

Eden H., Hornecker E. and Scharff E. (2002): 'Multilevel Design and Role Play: Experiences in Assessing Support for Neighborhood Participation'. In *Proc. of DIS'02*, ACM. pp. 387-392.

Fitzpatrick, G. (2003) *The Locales Framework: Understanding and designing for Wicked Problems*. Kluwer Publishers

Henderson, K. (1999): *On Line and On Paper*. Cambridge, MIT Press.

Holmquist, L., Schmidt, A. and Ullmer, B. (2004): 'Tangible interfaces in perspective: Guest editors' introduction'. *Personal and Ubiquitous Computing* 8(5). pp. 291-293.

Hornecker, E. (2004): *Tangible User Interfaces als kooperationsunterstützendes Medium*. PhD-thesis. University of Bremen. Dept. of Computing, July 2004.

Hornecker, E. (2004b): 'A Framework for the Design of Tangible Interaction for Collaborative Use'. In *Proc. of Danish HCI Research Symposion*. University of Aalborg. pp.57-61.

Hornecker, E. (2004c): 'Analogies from Didactics and Moderation/Facilitation Methods: Designing Spaces for Interaction and Experience'. *Digital Creativity* Vol. 15 No. 4. pp. 239-244

Hornecker, E. and Bruns F.W. (2004): 'Interactive Installations Analysis - Interaction Design of a Sensory Garden Event.' In *Proc. of IFAC/IFIP/IFORS/IEA Symposium on the Analysis, Design and Evaluation of Human-Machine Systems*.

Hornecker, E. and Stifter, M. (2004). *Evaluationsstudie Ausstellung medien.welten Technisches Museum Wien*. Unpublished project report. TU Vienna & TMW

Hutchins, E. and Klausen, T. (1998): 'Distributed Cognition in an Airline Cockpit'. In Engeström, Middleton (eds.) *Cognition and Communication at Work*. Cambridge Univ. Press. pp. 15-34.

Jacucci, G. (2004): *Interaction as Performance. Cases of configuring physical interfaces in mixed media*. PhD thesis, University of Oulu

Kendon, A. (1990): 'Spatial organization in social encounters: The F-formation system'. In Kendon (1990). *Conducting interaction*. Cambridge Unviversity Press. pp. 209-237.

Matkovic, K., et al (2004): 'Tangible Image Query'. In *Proc. of Smart Graphics*. pp. 31-42.

Norman, D. (1994*): Things that Make Us Smart*. Addison Wesley, Reading. Mass.

Rettig, M. (1994): 'Prototyping for Tiny Fingers'. *Communications of the ACM* 37 (4), pp.21-27.

Robertson T. (2002). 'The Public Availability of Actions and Artefacts'. *CSCW* 11 (3-4), 299-316.

Robertson T. (1997). 'Cooperative Work and Lived Cognition. A Taxonomy of Embodied Actions'. In *Proc. of E-CSCW'97*, pp. 205-220.

Rogers, Y. and Rodden, T. (2003): 'Configuring spaces and surfaces to support collaborative interactions' In: O' Hara, et al (eds.) *Public and Situated Displays*. Kluwer. pp.45-79

Scott, S. D., Grant K. D and Mandryk R. L. (2003): 'System Guidelines for Co-located Collaborative Work on a Tabletop display'. In *Proc. of E-CSCW'03*. pp. 159-178

Stanton, D. et al. (2001): 'Classroom Collaboration in the Design of Tangible Interfaces for Storytelling'. In *Proc. of CHI'01*, ACM. pp. 482-489.

Star, S. L. and Griesemer, J. (1989): 'Institutional Ecology, "Translations" and Boundary Objects'. *Social Studies of Science* 19. pp. 387-42.

Stewart, J., Rayborn, E., Bederson, B. and Druin, A. (1998): 'When Two Hands are Better Than One'. In *Proc. of CHI'98,* Extended Abstracts, ACM. pp. 287-288.

Suzuki H. and Kato H. (1995): 'Interaction-level support for collaborative learning: Algoblocks - an open programming language'. In *Proc. of CSCL 1995*, pp. 349-355.

Ullmer B. and Ishii H. (2000): 'Emerging frameworks for tangible user interfaces'. *IBM Systems Journal* 39(3-4), pp. 915-931.

H. Gellersen et al. (eds.), ECSCW 2005: Proceedings of the Ninth European
Conference on Computer-Supported Cooperative Work, 18-22 September 2005, Paris,
France, 45–64.

Supporting High Coupling and User-Interface Flexibility

Vassil Roussev
Department of Computer Science
University of New Orleans
vassil@cs.uno.edu

Prasun Dewan
Department of Computer Science
University of North Carolina
dewan@cs.unc.edu

Abstract. Collaborative systems that automate the sharing of programmer-defined user
interfaces offer limited coupling flexibility, typically forcing all users of an application to
share all aspects of the user interfaces. Those that automatically support high coupling
flexibility are tied to a narrow set of predefined user-interfaces. We have developed a
framework that provides high-level and flexible coupling support for arbitrary,
programmer-defined user interfaces. The framework refines an abstract layered model of
collaboration with structured application layers and automatic acquisition, transformation,
and processing of updates. It has been used to easily provide flexible coupling in
complex, existing single-user software and shown to support all known ways to share
user-interfaces. Coupling flexibility comes at the cost of a small amount of additional
programming. We have carefully crafted the framework to ensure that this overhead is
proportional to the degree of coupling flexibility desired.

Introduction

Collaborative environments today (such as *NetMeeting,Webex,* and *LiveMeeting*)
typically have two components: a shared-window application-sharing system that
allows sharing of collaboration-unaware applications and a set of applications,
such as a whiteboard and a distributed presentation tool, that are collaboration
aware. The reason for providing the shared-window system is that the cost of
implementing collaboration-aware applications is high. The reason for providing a
special set of collaboration-aware applications is that a shared window system
provides a very tightly coupled and inflexible model of collaboration in which
What You See Is What I See (WYSIWIS). Collaboration-aware applications
relax/extend this model in several ways. This is illustrated by the *NetMeeting*,
LiveMeeting, and *Webex* whiteboards. They support sharing of a subset of the
user-interface objects: for example, Figure 1(b) shows that the line drawn by user
1 is shared but the line-selection mode used to draw the line is not. Moreover,
they support both synchronous and asynchronous communication of changes to

shared objects. For example, text insertions are sent as they are made. On the other hand, as a user draws a new line, the other users get no feedback (Figure 1 (a)). It is only when the line is completed that others user see it (Figure 1 (b)).

From a software-engineering point of view, it is important for the application-sharing system and collaboration-aware applications to share a single set of high-level abstractions for coupling user interfaces. However, in current systems, high-level coupling abstractions limit either the coupling flexibility or the user-interface flexibility. Those that provide high user-interface flexibility, like *NetMeeting*, restrict the coupling to near-WYSIWIS sharing. Those that provide high coupling flexibility restrict the user-interface to a textual display. Thus, none of these systems can support the variety of coupling modes implemented in collaboration-aware graphical applications supporting loose coupling. These include whiteboards, *MS PowerPoint* presentation systems (e.g., *Webex* , *LiveMeeting*), structured idea-finding systems (Prante 2002), and even table-top and large-display applications (Tse 2004). As a result, all of these applications must be implemented manually. While this has been an open problem for more than a decade, it remains an active issue because of the overhead of implementing collaborative applications. In fact, in the CSCW 2004 conference, the developers' workshop, "Making application-sharing easy," was devoted to the issue of how to relax the coupling of current near-WYSIWIS application-sharing systems.

We have addressed this question by developing a high-level framework that supports both high coupling and user-interface flexibility. Section 2 describes the research work related to our own, Section 3 and 4 discuss the components of our framework, Section 5 details our experiences with coupling complex, existing, single-user code, and Section 6 presents conclusions and future directions.

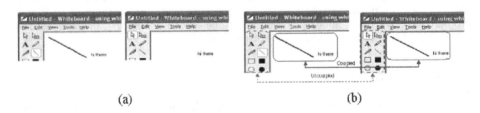

(a)   (b)

Figure 1 Non-WYSIWIS coupling in NetMeeting Whiteboard

Related Work

The coupling between two user-interfaces defines which parts of them are shared and when a change to a shared part in one user-interface is reflected in the other. Multiple coupling policies have been developed for two main reasons. First, users should be allowed to use a coupling policy that reflects their level of collaboration. For example, two users may wish to see the same or different visualization of some data depending on whether their discussion is about the visualization or the data. Second, the system should be allowed to choose a level of coupling that gives the desired quality of service. For example, *NetMeeting* and other commercial collaboration-aware applications do not support immediate or synchronous remote updates to a graphical object being dragged (Figure 1) probably because of jitter problems in a wide-area network, while some systems that address these problem do support incremental graphical updates (Dyck 2004).

The relationship between user-interface and coupling technology is demonstrated by shared window/screen systems, which share the user interface (UI) by intercepting the I/O stream of a collaboration-unaware application. They collect the input from different users into the single I/O stream expected by the application, and replicate the single application output stream for each user. The result is that each user sees the same sequence of outputs. The degree of coupling, then, depends on the abstraction level of the output. In a screen-sharing system, the entire screen is replicated, while in a shared window system, only the shared windows are replicated. Stream-based sharing of this form is formalized in Chung and Dewan (2001), which provides sharing of an abstract I/O stream, to which the specific I/O stream of a system/application must be translated.

Stream-based sharing does not support sharing at multiple degrees of abstraction such as the ability to share either the same or different visualization of some data. The PAC (Coutaz 1987) and MVC (Krasner 1988) architectural frameworks provide a way to formally describe these two levels of sharing. MVC, in particular, divides an interactive application into a Model, a View, and a Controller, which address semantics, output, and input, respectively, of the application. The controller invokes methods in the model to inform it of input; model sends notifications to all of its views of any changes to its state. Different views can respond to these notifications in independent ways, thereby creating different visualizations of the model. The MVC framework is often simplified in later systems to the Model/View framework, in which the view and controller are combined into one object because of the many dependencies among them in editor-based applications, where input consists of editing output.

Some collaborative systems based on the Model/View framework provide sharing of either component. Model sharing is provided by allowing the views to be created on the displays of different workstations. View sharing is provided by creating each view as a physical replica of a single logically shared object. Different systems provide different mechanisms to keep a model consistent with its views and the different view replicas consistent with each other. *Rendezvous* and *Weasel* (Graham 1996) use declarative constraints, *GroupKit* (Greenberg 1994) uses table updates, *DISCIPLE* (Wang 1999) uses *JavaBean* events, *JViews* (Grundy 1998) uses a more general `ChangeDescription` object, and *Colab* (Stefik 1987) supports broadcast methods that are invoked on all replicas. Some of these systems, such as *Rendezvous*, centralize the model while others, such as

GroupKit and *JAMM* (Begole 1999), replicate it, while addressing display synchronization, externalities, and other replication issues.

These systems allow arbitrary user-interfaces to be created by the programmer-defined view objects. However, their support for coupling is limited in several ways. They cannot support fine-grained sharing of model or view objects. For example, they cannot support the *RTCAL* collaborative calendar application (Sarin 1985), which allows sharing of public, but not private, appointments of a user. Moreover, they do not provide automatic support for asynchronous sharing of shared objects. Most of the above systems support only synchronous sharing. The exception is *JViews*, which also supports asynchronous sharing by logging events, but requires users to manually flush the logs and resolve any inconsistencies. Furthermore, they do not allow users to dynamically change between model and view sharing. The level of sharing is fixed at compile time based on whether a shared or normal view object is used. Finally, they do not support sharing at a lower-level of abstraction than views, in particular screen or window sharing.

The design of *Suite* (Dewan 1992) shows that coupling inflexibility of other (concrete) collaborative systems can be addressed if the system coupling the UIs is also the one that automatically generates them. This knowledge is used to support fine-grained, synchronous, asynchronous, and multi-layer sharing policies, and dynamic changes to them. The problem is that these policies apply only to the limited set of user interfaces generated by the system, which does not include graphical interfaces such as a whiteboard.

One way to achieve the coupling flexibility of *Suite* and UI flexibility of systems supporting programmer-defined views is to provide an architecture for easily adding new coupling implementations. This approach has been taken in several systems such as *DISCIPLE*, *AMF-C* (Tarpin-Bernard 1998), and *JViews*. While it is important to offer extendibility/composability, it is also crucial to recognize the commonality in the coupling policies supported by existing software and provide high-level support for these policies. The experience with *Suite* has shown the benefit of providing high-level support for a comprehensive set of coupling policies. Fifteen years after it was developed, as far as we know, no new coupling policy has been identified for the (textual) UI it supports.

The layered architecture model of Dewan (1998) provides a way to reason about multiple levels of sharing for arbitrary user-interfaces. It assumes that input and output are processed by a series of layers, where each layer abstracts the I/O received by the lower layer. An example of such a series of layers is the screen, window, view and model layers. The layers communicate interaction events to implement the user-interface of the application. A collaborative architecture can be modeled by a (possibly empty) series of shared layers followed by a series of "replicated" layers that communicate coupling events to share their state.

The "replicas" can diverge by sharing a subset of the objects managed by them and queuing changes to shared objects before transmitting them to peer replicas. This model is abstract in that it does not describe the exact form of communication across layers. Thus, it does not provide a system that automates multiple levels of sharing, serving only to define them informally.

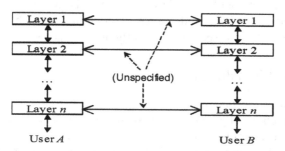

Figure 2 Layered model

Our framework combines and extends the various approaches/concepts described above. It defines an open, composable architecture for implementing coupling that can be considered as a concrete, automatable version of the abstract layer architecture above. Based on user-defined descriptions of application layering, it supports sharing of any subset of layers. More generally, it provides high-level support for a set of coupling policies that is comprehensive in that it covers all known coupling policies. Like *Suite*, it is able to support dynamic changes to the coupling policy.

Overview

To make our discussion concrete, we first consider the implementation of a multi-user Outline application in *Java* from the point of view of the application programmer. Our starting point is a single-user model/view implementation where the model has the recursive structure (of subsections) shown on Figure 3 and the view is the tree interface on Figure 4.

```java
public class Outline {
  String getTitle();
  void setTitle(String title);
  void insertSection(int i,Section);
  void removeSection(int);
  Section getSection(int);
  void getSection(int,Section);
  int getSectionCount();
}
```

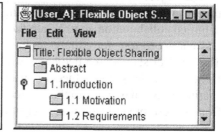

Figure 3 Example *Outline* object definition   Figure 4 Example *Outline* user interface

To add collaboration support using our infrastructure, the developer must: **a)** register the roots of the shared object structure (`Outline/OutlineView`); **b)** provide specifications so that the rest of the shared object structure (title, sections, and subsections) can be extracted automatically; **c)** provide update notifications of user updates to the outline; and **d)** provide layer descriptions to enable dynamic transition between model and view coupling. Depending on the coding conventions used and the desired degree of coupling, steps b), c), and d) are optional. For the rest of this section, we briefly present each step of the process.

Registration and Initialization

Figure 5 illustrates the necessary additions to the startup code of the original application. The un-highlighted code is single-user code that would have to be written even if no coupling was desired. It creates an outline model and view, informs the view about the model, and displays the application window.

```
public static void main( String[] argv) {
    SystemBoot.initAll( argv);
    // --- Single-user initialization
    Outline outline = initOutline();
    JFrame outlineView = initOutlineView( outline);
    outlineView.setVisible( true);
    // ---
    ColabJMenu.addColabMenu(outlineView);
    PropertyRegistrar.register(outline, "Outline");
    PropertyRegistrar.register(outlineView, "OutlineView");
    ObjectBrowser.addRootObject(outline);
    ObjectBrowser.setVisible(true);
}
```

Figure 5 Initialization code for example application

The highlighted code is the added collaboration-aware code, which is external to the model and view. It adds a special collaboration menu (Figure 6) to the window that allows users to execute collaboration-aware commands to transmit pending updates. It registers the outline model and view with the infrastructure, which uses pattern specifications to decompose these objects, and assigns unique global ids to the tree of objects rooted by them. Finally, it instantiates an object browser (Figure 7) to enable flexible coupling specification by the user.

The object browser is an application-independent user interface component through which users control the sharing of application objects. The idea is to have a unified collaboration control interface in order to save development effort and to allow users to transfer collaboration experience from one application to another. The browser shows, in a dedicated window, a tree representation of the structural hierarchy of the shared objects registered with the infrastructure. To change the sharing, a user navigates to the desired object and selects a specific sharing policy from a list of predefined ones, or customize one on the fly (Section 3.5).

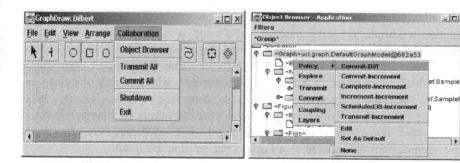

Figure 6 Collaboration menu attached to an application

Figure 7 Object browser with policy selection pop-up menu

Object Structure Specification

To present the GUI on Figure 7, and to enable fine-grained coupling in which different layer components are coupled differently, we must derive the logical structure of the shared objects. Ideally, this should be accomplished automatically, as it is the case in *Suite*. However, *Suite* assumes that the entities are defined by concrete data types such as records and arrays, which expose their structure. Our framework assumes entities are encapsulated objects and cannot automatically decompose an object without making any assumptions about it.

Our approach to address this problem is to build on the fact that code naming conventions used to convey information to other developers can also be used by our framework to decompose an object. We support a language for describing object components or *properties* based on the relationships among the signatures of methods used to access them. This approach is more fully motivated and described in Roussev (2000); Roussev (2003)—here describe it "by example" to give a concrete idea of how it is used, based on Outline object of Figure 3.

The properties of instances of this type are defined by two definitions. The first definition states that a simple property *<PropName>* of type *<Type>* is defined whenever two property methods, "getter" and "setter" can be found such that the constraints on their signatures described above are met:

```
type = simple
methods
  getter = <Type> get<PropName>()
  setter = void set<PropName>(<Type>)
name = <PropName>
```

Similarly, the following definition describes a variable-sized sequence property, *<PropName>*, whose elements are of type *<ElemType>*:

```
type = sequence
methods
  insert = void insert<PropName>(int,<ElemType>)
  remove = void remove<PropName>(int)
  lookup = <ElemType> get<PropName>(int)
  set   = void set<PropName>(int, <ElemType>)
  count = int get<PropName>Count()
name = <PropName>
```

Together, these two definitions describe the two properties in the outline example—a simple property named "Title" and a sequence property named "Section". In a property definition, free variables such as *<PropName>*, *<ElemType>*, and *<Type>* must be unified to the same values in all uses. These free variables allow property definitions to describe a whole family of interfaces. In fact, an interface is a property definition with no free variables. The overhead of creating property definitions is amortized over the family of classes/interfaces that use the conventions encoded by them. For example, the *JavaBeans* convention definition is shared by all object classes that use them.

The property-description language comes with a *Java*-based introspection mechanism to dynamically determine the properties of an object and invoke the methods to read/write them. For example, it provides the following method to determine the properties found:

```
Property[] mp = Introspector.getProperties(className, specs);
```

It also provides a way to access the methods for handling a property:

```
Method getter = property.getMethod("getter");
```

The *Java* Method class allows runtime invocation of its instance:

```
getter.invoke(target, null);
```

In our specific example, the developer would not have to give any specifications as our implementation by default supports *JavaBeans* properties, as well as *sequence* and *table* properties. Depending on the coding style, additional specs may be necessary for other applications. We should point out that the definitions are given in separate *XML* files and are reusable across applications.

Update Notification

In order to provide automatic coupling, the infrastructure must learn of user updates to the shared structures. Ideally, the application should notify the infrastructure of each incremental update. However, this may require more effort than the developer is willing to invest and/or more than the user actually needs. Therefore, we give a range of sharing options and specify the implementation effort required for each one of them.

Asynchronous fine-grained diff-based sharing can be achieved without any notification support from the Outline application. We have developed a general property-based diffing algorithm (Roussev 2003) that can derive the fine-grained updates from successive snapshots of the object's state. The properties used in the Outline are supported by default so no additional effort is required. Thus, upon a user command (or timer expiration) the infrastructure performs diffing and communicates any discovered updates. For applications using other property types, specific diff operations may need to be defined as separate methods that can be shared across applications using the corresponding property type.

Incremental, synchronous sharing can be achieved by announcing update events. This can be accomplished in one of two ways—by directly using the infrastructure-defined event model, or by translating existing application events into the model. The first option requires an extra line of code at the end of each method of the shared object that modifies the state (such as `setTitle`, `insertSection`, `removeSection`, and `setSection`). For example,

```
public void setTitle(String title) {
...
Coupler.dispatch(new PropertyOperation(this.getGID(),"title", "setter",newObject[] {title}));
}
```

The second option may be more attractive for component-based applications that already have their own events. Our implementation provides two general-purpose reusable event adapters for translating *AWT* and *JavaBeans* events.

Delayed semi-synchronous sharing that communicates changes when they reach a certain completion or correctness level requires *synchronization* events to be transmitted (Sections 4.2-4.3). A synchronization event is a meta-event that labels a preceding update as having certain level of completion and/or correctness. For example, typing a character in the title would trigger an update notification, while pressing <Tab> might indicate that the change is complete.

In practice, model-level objects (i.e., `Outline`) must be aware of the level of correctness of each change, as it is their job to ensure it. Hence, they only need to pass along this information by tagging the updates as `Parsed`, or `Validated`. In terms of implementation, this corresponds to one more line of code for each modifier method. Indicating a `Complete` editing operation for the Outline is slightly more complicated—in our prototype it took an additional 15 lines of code.

Application Layering Specification

Recall that, to increase coupling flexibility, *Suite* provides sharing at two levels (model and view) that can be dynamically switched at run-time. This is possible because the system builds the UI and knows the precise application layering. However, in our model, we support arbitrary layers and thus need an alternative mechanism—developer-provided layer descriptions. To illustrate, consider the layer decomposition for the Outline application shown on Figure 8 and its corresponding (partial) *XML* description given on Figure 9.

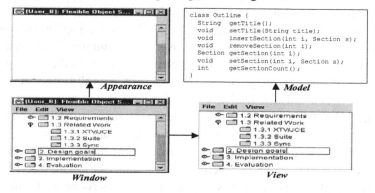

Figure 8 Layer decomposition for Outline application

At the lowest level is the *window* layer, which consists of the single application window through which all objects are edited. The *view* layer consists of the window's menu-bar and a JTree object through which the outline object is edited. The *appearance* layer consists of the elements of the application window that do not affect the state of the outline, such as the scrollbar. In this example, a user action may trigger one of two sequences of events. If the user performs an action that modifies the outline, the process triggers three causally related notifications at the *window*, *view*, and *model* layers, respectively. If a user action concerns only the *appearance* layer (e.g., scrolling), it triggers a sequence of two causally related notifications—at the *window* and *appearance* layers.

```
<object class = "outline.Outline">          <layer_dependencies>
   <layer name="model"><ALL/></layer>         <window>
</object>                                        <view>
<object class = "outline.Section">                <model/>
   <layer name="model"><ALL/></layer>            </view>
</object>                                         <appearance/>
<object class = "java.swing.JTree">           </window>
   <layer name="view"><ALL/></layer>         </layer_dependencies>
</object>
   ...
```

Figure 9 Layer definitions for Outline application

Thus, if *window* sharing is specified, all notifications from other layers will be suppressed. If *view* sharing is specified, then *model* and *window* notifications will be suppressed. Similarly, if *model* sharing is specified, *window/view* events are suppressed. Since the *appearance* layer is independent of both the *model* and *view* layers, its sharing can be turned on/off independently of the *model* and the *view*.

Coupling Specification

To complete the overview, we present the coupling control interface seen by the user. Using the object browser (Figure 7), the user selects a layer, an object, or an object property and then selects the desired policy from a pop-up menu. This is either a named (predefined) policy or a custom one built on the fly. The drop-down list in the browser allows different policies for the interaction with different users to be selected. The *Group* value shown is a default for all participants.

Policy customization is invoked by selecting 'Edit' from the pop-up menu, which brings up the policy editor (**Error! Not a valid bookmark self-reference.**). A detailed explanation of the different policy parameters is given Section 4.2 but the essential idea is to define the conditions under which updates are transmitted/received. The policy shown on the figure is asynchronous fine-grained diff-based sharing: updates are obtained using diffing, sent whenever the user chooses to commit them and are installed as soon as they are received. After editing is complete, the user has the choice of *Apply*-ing it to the target object/property, or *Save*-ing it as a named policy.

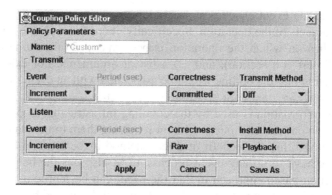

Figure 10 Coupling policy editor

In summary, depending on the desired level of support, a developer needs 20-45 lines of application code and several *XML* specifications to incorporate all features of the synchronous, event-based sharing for the Outline application. Programmers can incrementally add the code and learn the concepts behind it as more coupling flexibility is required. Users will be able to immediately take advantage of the new features using the same control interface.

Framework

Update Events

The layered model leaves unspecified the communication of (1) interaction events that go up and down layers and (2) coupling events that go across layers. The interaction events should be left unspecified in a collaboration framework to accommodate arbitrary programmer-defined UI. However, automating replica coupling implies making some assumptions about the coupling events.

The interaction events supported by the Model/View framework provide a basis for designing and understanding coupling events. The framework supports an asymmetric communication model, where the communications up and down are different in nature. A view informs the higher-level model layer about an input event by directly invoking a model-specific method in it. On the other hand, a model informs its lower-level view layers about state changes by sending view-independent notifications to them. A view processes the notification by retrieving the state of the model in which it is interested, and calling a view-specific method to update its own state. In our framework, we combine these approaches when defining (replica) update events, recognizing the fact that an object generating such an event is also capable of processing it. As in the notification-based approach, a replica does not directly call methods in its peers, and as in the direct-method invocation approach, it does not have to map notifications to the methods that process them. The events are symmetric in nature and are defined in terms of properties to support fine-grained coupling.

An update event encodes an operation invoked on a property of a replica and the arguments of the operation. Specifically, it contains: (1) the global identifier of the replica on which the operation is performed; (2) the name of the operation (e.g., "insert" on section); and (3) a list of arguments. For example, inserting a new section into the outline would be associated with an event of the form:

```
<"Outline","section","insert",{2, section}>.
```

This information is used by the coupling infrastructure to perform a reflective invocation on remote replicas without requiring them to translate the event. Thus, this approach has the benefit of direct method invocations in that a target object does not have to do any event processing. It also has the benefit of the indirect notification-based approach in that the event can be sent to a variable number of targets, and more important, can be "intelligently" handled by the system.

Parameterized Update-Event Handling

On the surface, there does not seem to be any need for special handling of update events, beyond translating these events to corresponding replica methods. In fact, this is all we need if (1) each replica responds to property updates by generating corresponding update events, (2) all of these updates must be made synchronously to all of the other replicas, and (3) replicas are not concurrently updated in inconsistent ways. If these three assumptions do not hold, then special acquisition, processing, and installation phases, respectively, are needed (Figure 11).

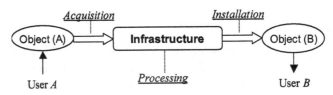

Figure 11 Phases of update handling

In the acquisition phase, a description of the update to a shared property is either received from the changed replica or generated by the infrastructure. In the processing phase, the infrastructure filters, buffers, transforms, and communicates the update to the remote parties. Finally, in the installation phase, the update is merged with the current state of the remote object to which it is delivered. Each of these phases is controlled by user-specified, interrelated parameters.

These parameters are associated with (properties of) each replica of a shared object to allow users to autonomously control event handling. As the acquisition and installation are local operations performed on the source and target objects, respectively, these are controlled by the corresponding parameters of these two objects. The processing operation, on the other hand, involves both objects as it determines what is shared by the two objects and when it is shared. As the users owning these objects should be allowed to independently specify the nature of sharing, our framework uses processing parameters of both the sending and receiving objects which place restrictions on *outgoing* and *incoming* events, respectively. We use a *Suite*-like reconciliation mechanism based on conservative matching. By conservative we mean that of the two versions of each processing parameter (outgoing and incoming), we pick the one that supports less sharing and, thus, come up with an *effective* coupling policy. For example, if one replica wishes a property to be shared while the other does not, the effective sharing policy does not share it. Realizing that an outgoing policy that is more liberal (sends out more events) than its incoming counterpart would lead to the communication of events that will be held at the receiver site for delivery, we perform the matching at the sending site to avoid sending such events in the first place. Hence, the receiving site does not perform filtering of incoming events but proceeds directly to install them. Performing the policy matching at the sender, as Suite does, implies that policy changes must be sent to the corresponding user(s) every time a user modifies the incoming policy. This, however, is a good trade off because policy updates are infrequent relative to object updates.

With each shared property, we associate four different parameters: *Acquisition, Transmission, Correctness,* and *Installation.* The second and third parameters generalize the semantics of corresponding *Suite* parameters to arbitrary user-interfaces, while the first and last form our extension to the model to handle existing objects and concurrent updates, respectively. Below, we describe the meanings and values of each parameter in our model, and the pros and cons of choosing different values.

Acquisition. This parameter controls the method used to obtain a replica property update. Currently, we distinguish among four different acquisition methods: *Read, Log, Effective Log,* and *Diff,* as well as the special value of *None* which indicates that property updates should not be acquired (or shared).

To illustrate the differences among the acquisition methods, consider the simple scenario of a user inserting a new section in the list of sections in the outline. The object may respond to the update in three ways:

1. It may conform to our event model and announce an update event exactly encoding the operation and its parameters. In this case, the acquisition parameter must be set to *Log* or *Effective-Log*. In the former case, each update event is logged until the processing parameters require it to be transmitted. Over time, the log of operations can become rather long if, for example, one of the users is off-line for a prolonged period of time. Therefore, log-based systems provide mechanisms for compressing the log by removing operations whose effects will be undone by subsequent operations. If such compression is desired, then the acquisition parameter must be set to *Effective Log*. We have developed a generic scheme that performs log compression for static and dynamic properties based on the operations defined on them. The disadvantage of this acquisition method is that the remote user does not see each operation invoked by the local user and may not see the rationale behind the changes.

2. It may conform, not to our event model, but instead to the more general model-view model, which only requires that a notification be sent that the object has been changed. In this case the acquisition parameter must be set to *Read* to tell the infrastructure to record the end result of the user action by obtaining the complete state of the object – in this example, the section list. While this

approach is attractively simple, it does not work well when different parts of an object are concurrently edited by multiple users and we would like to merge their work by combining the edited components (e.g. different sections).

3. It may not announce any update event. In this case, the acquisition parameter is set to *Diff* to ask the infrastructure to derive the fine-grained operations from successive snapshots of the object's state. We have developed a general property-based diffing algorithm to support this acquisition method (Roussev 2003), however, it cannot support incremental coupling.

Transmission. This parameter controls the transmission of updates based on the communication operation performed on the shared entity and has four possible values: *Increment, Complete, Scheduled,* and *Transmit*. Each individual update such as insertion of a character and the dragging of a line is an *Increment* operation. A *Complete* operation is executed whenever the user has indicated that he is "finished" editing the value, e.g., hitting <tab>, releasing the mouse. The semantics of this application-dependent operation is defined by synchronization events (Section 4.3). A *Scheduled* operation is triggered by timer expiration and has two parameters: execution time and a period. The operation is first triggered at the specified wall-clock time, and it is then triggered periodically. The *Transmit* operation is executed whenever the user explicitly requests it by pressing a <Transmit> command provided by the infrastructure. This generalizes the *send* command provided by a mail client by requiring the sender to explicitly indicate when updates must be sent. The transmission parameters correspond to the notification parameters identified in Shen (2002) for text editors and interaction parameters supported for document editing in *PREP* (Neuwirth 1994).

Correctness. One of the problems of incremental coupling is that a user's mistakes are seen by others. That, however, may be desirable in some cases. For example, a tutor may help a student with fixing semantic errors in a program. This parameter lets collaborators choose the degree of correctness of shared changes. Its possible values (in increasing order) are *Raw, Parsed, Validated,* and *Committed*. By default, any updated value is *Raw*, unless it has undergone a successful syntactic check after which it is elevated to *Parsed*. If the value has also passed a check for semantic correctness, it becomes *Validated*. The exact semantics of syntactic and semantic checks are defined by synchronization events discussed below. *Committed* values are explicitly designated by the user by executing an infrastructure-provided <commit> command.

Installation. Once an update is acquired and processed, it needs to be installed on the remote object. We distinguish among three different ways in which this can be achieved: *Replay, Real-time Replay, Merge,* and *None*. The *Replay* option is the simplest choice—the operations are replayed one after the other, with the user likely to have a "fast forward" experience in which minutes of collaboration are compressed into seconds. *Real-Time Replay*, replays the events at the rate at which they were executed at the transmitting site. The *Merge* installation option refers to the use of a merge procedure (Munson 1997) that integrates the update with the current version of the object. This is necessary when the simple replay of the updates is not sufficient. *None* ignores remote updates entirely.

Synchronization Events

The user command that completes a series of incremental changes (e.g. mouse button release), as well operations to parse/validate a value, are application-specific. We define standard synchronization events that allow such information to be passed along to the infrastructure in an application-independent fashion.

A synchronization event redefines the values of the transmission and correctness attributes of the property operations that are still in the buffer. Such an event is a four-tuple consisting of: **(a)** a global identifier of the object on which the operation(s) are performed; **(b)** the name of the property affected where null implies all properties of the object; **(c)** a new value for the transmission parameter (*Increment, Complete, Scheduled,* or *Transmit*); and **(d)** a new value for the correctness parameter (*Raw, Parsed, Validated,* or *Committed*). Thus, the tuple <"Outline","section","Complete","Raw"> specifies that all property operations on the *section* property of the object named "Outline" should be relabeled as *Complete* and *Raw* unless they have higher values already. Once relabeled, all affected events must be reevaluated with respect to the current sharing policy and sent out if necessary.

Application Layer Model

Update and synchronization events provide a basis for flexible coupling but their naïve use raises some correctness issues. Suppose that the outline title is edited through a text field and both the text field and the outline object provide notifications about changes to their state to the infrastructure. An infrastructure that does not take into account the dependency between the states of the text field and the outline would produce incorrect results by replicating the notifications at both the text field and the Outline object. Thus, a character insertion by one user would be lead to a duplicate insertion on other replicas. The causally related notifications occur as a result of user actions being translated from a less abstract to a more abstract layer, with each step triggering a separate notification.

The most common solution among existing infrastructures is to provide sharing at one fixed layer (e.g., shared-window systems provide sharing at the window layer). The shared layer processes events received from remote replicas the same way it processes local events and propagates the results to upper (more abstract) layers, thereby achieving the sharing of those layers as well. This approach automatically eliminates the correctness problem but limits coupling flexibility.

To overcome this, we introduce an *XML* layer description language. An application layering definition consists of two parts: layer mapping and layer dependencies. The layer mapping is a set of tuples of the form <class, property, layer> specifying that the named *property* of all object instances of the given class belongs to the given *layer*. If the *property* is NULL, then all properties in the class are implied. If no explicit definition is given for a particular class, we recursively lookup the definitions for the superclasses until an appropriate one is found. Once layers have been defined, the dependencies between them are specified as shown on Figure 9.

In addition to correctness, this generic layer model also gives us a high-level mechanism for sharing specification by dynamically changing the shared layer. Sharing a higher layer is a trivial task because we move from tighter sharing modes to more relaxed ones. However, the reverse process is non-trivial in the general case. Consider the following scenario: Initially, users are using asynchronous sharing of the model (i.e., they may have different versions of the shared object). If they want to switch to *view* sharing, the infrastructure must first bring the outline model versions into a consistent state using a merge procedure. To switch to *window* sharing, both the *view* and the *appearance* must be consistent beforehand. In general, to switch the sharing from a higher (more abstract) layer L_k to a lower one L_m, the infrastructure ensures that all layers that depend on L_m must be brought into consistency first.

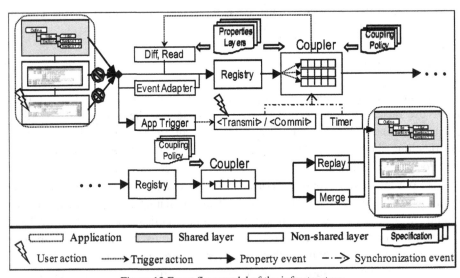

Figure 12 Event flow model of the infrastructure

Putting It All Together

Our infrastructure is not involved in communicating interaction events that go between layers but handles communication of events that are passed across layers (Figure 12). These events may be created explicitly by the programmer as update events or implicitly by a *diff* or *read* operation in response to a synchronization event. In both cases, they are delivered through a static, 'well-known' replicated object called the Coupler. An event passes through the registry first to register dynamic additions/deletions to the shared object structure. Next, the event is filed with each of the outgoing queues associated with individual users, and it is then evaluated with respect to each of the corresponding policies based on user and the target object. Events that meet the minimum requirements set by the policy are immediately sent to their respective recipients using an event multicast service.

After the remote site receives the incoming event, it is processed along the same lines as outgoing events. First, the local registry and dependency tables are updated, then the local `Coupler` looks up the installation policy, selects the installation method, and applies the updates to the application object. The difference between Figure 2 and Figure 12 graphically illustrates how we have refined the abstract layer model by defining the communication between peer replicas and a generic mechanism for dynamically selecting the shared layer.

The programmers are not concerned with the details of the low-level event flow described above, which is driven by high-level code and the overhead of specifying this code is proportional to the degree of flexibility desired.

Case Study Evaluation

To understand how well we can add flexible coupling to existing complex single-user applications. One of these is *GraphDraw*, which is a *Visio*-like application provided as part of the *GEF* (Graph Editing Framework) developed at the University of California by *Jason. Robbins*. The basic goal of *GEF* is to provide a UI toolkit for the development of various applications requiring graph editing, such as circuit design, or a *Petri* net editor. *GraphDraw* is fairly simple; it consists of 9 *Java* classes that define two types of graph nodes and two types of graph edges and registers them with the framework, which handles everything else. *GEF*, consist of 171 *Java* classes totaling over 26,000 lines of code.

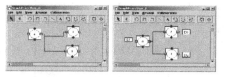

Figure 13 *Graph* layer sharing

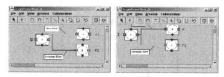

Figure 15 *Graph view* and *figure* sharing

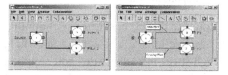

Figure 14 *Graph view* layer sharing

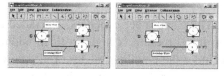

Figure 16 *Window* layer sharing

A *GEF* graph diagram consists of three basic layers—a *graph* layer, a *graph view* layer, and a *figures* layer. The graph layer represents the abstract graph (nodes and edge) being edited. The *graph view* provides the specific graphic representation through which users can manipulate the nodes and edges of graphs.

The *figures* layer consists of a number of standard shapes, such as ovals, rectangles, and text boxes that can be used to annotate the graph. We also define a *window* and an *appearance* layer much like we did for the *Outline* application.

This layer decomposition can be used to support multiple combinations of the layers. It is possible to share only the *graph* layer, that is, the graph but not its visual appearance and annotations (Figure 13). Sharing the *graph view* layer (Figure 14) leads to the sharing of the topology *and* its graphic presentation but not the annotations. To also share the annotations, we must as the infrastructure to couple both the *graph view* and *figures* layers (Figure 15). In all of the above cases, users retain the freedom to navigate autonomously and edit the graph concurrently. Sharing the window layer *window* layer (Figure 16). This is the WYSIWIS sharing supported by shared-window systems. As Table I below suggests, it was fairly easy to interface *GraphDraw* and *GEF* with our infrastructure. They employ only three basic patterns in the object structures we want to share—standard simple (*JavaBeans*) properties, as well as two versions of *set* properties very similar to the *sequence* property given earlier. The bulk of the interfacing effort was concentrated on three event adapters that translate *GEF*-defined events into property and synchronization events. All changes were linear code with a total of only four `if` and six `for` statements; almost 20% of the code changes were `import` statements.

We similarly interfaced our infrastructure with a graphical editor and the *Java Swing* toolkit. The latter experiment resulted in an application sharing system that allows the sharing of collaboration-unaware *Swing* applications. The interfacing effort in both cases was very similar to the presented *GraphDraw/GEF* case.

Action	GraphDraw Modified	GEF Modified	GEF Added	Total
Total Lines of Code	26	76	102	204
Affected Classes	5	13	4	22
Code Complexity				
`import` statements	11	15	12	38
`if` statements	0	3	1	4
`for` statements	0	5	1	6

Table I Code statistics for *GraphDraw* application adaptation

These and other experiences detailed in Roussev (2003) confirm our claim that the infrastructure is high-level. In addition, as Sections 2 and 4 have shown, it includes the coupling modes of all known high-level infrastructures and supports programmer-defined user interfaces. Thus, it satisfies the requirements of providing higher coupling and user-interface flexibility.

Figure 17 shows the practical benefits of satisfying these requirements. In current systems, application sharing systems and collaboration-aware applications do not share any high-level abstractions, making the cost of implementing them high. This is probably the reason why more collaboration-aware applications such as a spreadsheet have not been developed. Moreover, changing the coupling is a heavyweight operation requiring manually switching between two different systems. To illustrate, suppose we wish to share the *NetMeeting* (*LiveMeeting*, or *WebEx*) whiteboard in a WYSIWIS manner so that we can browse the drawing together. This requires its addition to the set of applications shared by the application-sharing system. Now suppose we wish to switch to a collaboration mode in which we can scroll independently. This requires us to (1) remove the whiteboard from the set of shared applications and (2) use its native collaboration support to re-establish the conference. If we do not take the first step, then two different systems would try to simultaneously support sharing without coordination. As Figure 17 shows, we allow application-sharing systems and collaboration-aware applications to share a common-set of high-level abstractions. Moreover, we can dynamically switch the coupling in a collaboration-aware application, with the system ensuring causally dependent events are not duplicated. Given the low cost of developing collaboration-aware applications, we expect application-sharing to be used only for closed systems that we cannot introspect or whose events we cannot intercept.

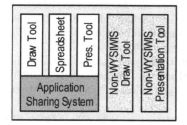 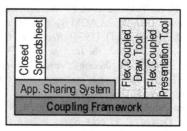

Figure 17 Coupling framework impact

Conclusions and Future Work

While there has been much effort in developing and automating general software architectures (such as MVC) for single-user interactive applications, there has been relatively less attention paid to multi-user applications. We have taken an important step to address this problem by refining/formalizing the abstract/informal layered architecture with several novel concepts for supporting all known coupling modes without making assumptions about the user-interface. These include (1) property-based decomposition to support fine-grained coupling, (2) update events, unifying method- and notification-based communication, (3) flexible acquisition, processing, and installation of these events, (4) synchronization events to support multiple degrees of update synchronization, and (5) layer definitions allowing users to dynamically choose shared layers.

Our preliminary experience has shown that changing complex, existing code to interface with our infrastructure requires a few mundane changes to it consisting mainly of writing event adapters. Further research is needed to verify that this holds for a larger set of existing single-user applications/toolkits and adapt the framework in response to problems uncovered by this research. It would also be useful to automate other abstract collaboration architectures.

Acknowledgements

This research was funded in part by *Microsoft* and NSF grants ANI 0229998, EIA 03-03590, and IIS 0312328.

References

Begole, J. e. a. (1999). 'Flexible Collaboration Transparency: Supporting Worker Independence in Replicated Application-Sharing Systems'. *ACM TOCHI* **6**(2): 95-132.

Chung, G. Dewan, P. (2001). *Flexible Support for Application-Sharing Architecture.* Proceedings of the European Conference on Computer-Supported Cooperative Work (ECSCW), Bonn.

Coutaz, J. (1987). *PAC, an Object Oriented Model for Dialog Design.* Proceedings of Interact.

Dewan, P. (1998). 'Architectures for Collaborative Applications'. *Trends in Software, special issue on CSCW* **7**: 169-194.

Dewan, P., Choudhary, R. (1992). 'A High-Level and Flexible Framework for Implementing Multiuser User Interfaces'. *ACM Transactions on Information Systems* **10**(4): 345-380.

Dyck, J., Gutwin, C., Subramanian, S., Fedak, C. (2004). *High-Performance Telepointers.* Proc of the ACM Conference on Computer-Supported Cooperative Work (CSCW), Chicago, IL.

Graham, T. C. N., T. Urnes, et al. (1996). *Efficient Distributed Implementation of Semi-Replicated Synchronous Groupware.* ACM Symposium on User Interface Software and Technology.

Greenberg, S., Marwood, D. (1994). *Real-Time Groupware as a Distributed System: Concurrency Control and its Effect on the Interface.* CSCW, Chapel Hill, NC

Grundy, J. (1998). *Engineering component-based, user-configurable collaborative editing systems.* Proc of Conference on Engineering for Human-Computer Interaction (EHCI).

Krasner, G., Pope, S. (1988). 'A Cookbook for Using the Model-View-Controller User Interface Paradigm in Smalltalk-80'. *JOOP* **1**(3): 26-49.

Munson, J., Dewan, P. (1997). Sync: a Java framework for mobile collaborative applications. *IEEE Computer.* **30**: 231-242.

Neuwirth, C. e. a. (1994). *Computer support for distributed collaborative writing: Defining parameters of interaction.* CSCW, Chapel Hill, NC.

Prante, T. e. a. (2002). *Developing CSCW Tools for Idea Finding - Emperical Results and Implications for Design.* CSCW, New Orleans, LA.

Roussev, V. (2003). *Flexible Sharing of Distributed Objects Based on Programming-Patterns.* Ph.D. Thesis, Department of Computer Science, Chapel Hill, Univeristy of North Carolina.

Roussev, V., Dewan, P., Jain, V. (2000). *Composable Collaboration Infrastructures based on Programming Patterns.* CSCW, Philadelphia, PA

Sarin, S., Greif, I. (1985). 'Computer-Based Real-Time Conferencing Systems'. *IEEE Computer* **18**(10): 33-49.

Shen, H., Sun, C. (2002). *Flexible Notification for Collaborative Systems.* CSCW,New Orleans,LA.

Stefik, M. e. a. (1987). 'Beyond the Chalkboard: Computer Support for Collaboration and Problem Solving in Meetings'. *Communications of ACM* **30**(1): 32-47.

Tarpin-Bernard, F., David, B.T., Primet, P. (1998). *Frameworks and Patterns for Synchronous Groupware : AMF-C Approach.* (EHCI), Heraklion, Greece.

Tse, E., Histon, J., Scott, S., Greenberg, S. (2004). *Avoiding interference: how people use spatial separation and partitioning in SDG workspaces.* CSCW, Chicago, IL.

Wang, W., Dorohonceanu, B. and Marsic, I. (1999). *Design of the DISCIPLE Synchronous Collaboration Frameworks.* IMSA, Nassau, Grand Bahamas.

H. Gellersen et al. (eds.), ECSCW 2005: Proceedings of the Ninth European
Conference on Computer-Supported Cooperative Work, 18-22 September 2005, Paris,
France, 65–82.

A Groupware Design Framework for Loosely Coupled Workgroups

David Pinelle and Carl Gutwin

Department of Computer Science, University of Saskatchewan, Canada
david.pinelle@usask.ca, carl.gutwin@usask.ca

Abstract. Loosely coupled workgroups – where workers are autonomous and weakly
interdependent – are common in the real world. They have patterns of work and
collaboration that distinguish them from other types of groups, and groupware systems
that are designed to support loose coupling must address these differences. However,
loosely coupled groups have not been studied in detail in CSCW, and the design process
for these groups is currently underspecified. This forces designers to start from scratch
each time they develop a system for loosely coupled groups, and they must approach
new work settings with little information about how work practices are organized. In this
paper, we present a design framework to improve the groupware design process for
loosely coupled workgroups. The framework was developed to provide designers with a
better understanding of how groupware systems can be designed to support loosely
coupled work practices. It is based on information from CSCW and organizational
research, and on real-world design experiences with one type of loosely coupled group—
home care treatment teams. The framework was used to develop Mohoc, a groupware
system for home care, and the system and underlying framework were evaluated during
two field trials.

Introduction

Loosely coupled workgroups are common in the real world, and they have been
identified in a number of domains including education, healthcare, knowledge
work, and mobile service work (Hasenfeld 1983; Pinelle 2004). Workers in these
groups are weakly dependent on one another and can function autonomously,
often without the need for immediate clarification or negotiation with others
(Olson and Teasley 1996). They have patterns of work and collaboration that

distinguish them from other types of groups, and groupware systems that are designed to support loose coupling must address these differences. However, they have not been studied in detail in CSCW, and it is not clear what their design requirements are, or how groupware should be developed to address their needs.

Groupware design for loosely coupled workgroups is underspecified, and groupware designers must start from scratch when they develop a system for one of these groups. Designers cannot make use of others' design experiences in similar groups, and must approach the work setting with little information about how work practices are organized. This makes it easy to overlook important work characteristics that are relevant to design, often leading to systems that are not well-suited for supporting work in context.

In this paper, we present a design framework to improve the groupware design process for loosely coupled groups. The framework has two main parts: a contextual model that describes loose coupling in the workplace, and a set of design approaches for developing groupware applications that support loosely coupled work practices. The design framework is based on information from CSCW and organizational research, and on real-world design experiences with one type of loosely coupled workgroup—home care treatment teams in Saskatoon Health Region (SHR).

The framework was used to develop Mohoc, a groupware system that supports loosely coupled work practices in home care. The Mohoc system supports current home care workflows, including managing clinical documentation, planning treatments, and scheduling appointments with patients. It emphasizes autonomous work activities, but also provides opportunities for workers to collaborate and share information using low-cost communication and coordination features.

The framework was evaluated during two field trials where home care treatment teams in SHR used the system to support the services they provided to shared patients. Results were analyzed to determine how well the design framework performed in the design process. The results suggest that the framework was able to fill its role in specializing the general CSCW design process for loosely coupled groups by adding consideration for work and collaboration patterns that are seen in loosely coupled settings. However, further research is needed to determine whether these findings generalize to other loosely coupled workgroups.

In the next section, we provide a brief discussion of literature on loose coupling and groupware design. We provide a brief overview of the home care work context, and then we present the framework. We then describe how the framework was used to develop the Mohoc groupware system, and present the results of two field trials in SHR.

Loose coupling and groupware design

Organizational research from management, organization science, healthcare, education, and sociology has the potential to help inform the design of CSCW applications. Studies from these areas can help improve the analysis of target work settings and can help to identify important organizational patterns that are relevant to system design, but that are otherwise easily overlooked.

In this research, we used organizational research literature to help build a framework for groupware design for loosely coupled workgroups.

In organizational research, the term "loose coupling" is used to describe relationships between elements in social systems. These elements can be people or organizational units, such as groups, departments, or divisions. Weick (1976) describes loose coupling in education:

> By loose coupling, the author intends to convey the image that coupled events are responsive, but that each event also preserves its own identity and some evidence of its physical or logical separateness. Thus, in the case of an educational organization, it may be the case that the counselor's office is loosely coupled to the principal's office. The image is that the principal and the counselor are somehow attached, but that each retains some identity and separateness and that their attachment may be circumscribed, infrequent, weak in its mutual affects, unimportant, and/or slow to respond. Each of those connotations would be conveyed if the qualifier loosely were attached to the word coupled. Loose coupling also carries connotations of impermanence, dissolvability, and tacitness all of which are potentially crucial properties of the 'glue' that holds organizations together. (p. 3)

In a later paper, Orton and Weick (1990) formulate a more precise definition of loose coupling. They argue against using what they describe as a unidimensional interpretation of loose coupling that views loose and tight coupling as opposite extremes along a scale. In this view, "tightly coupled systems are portrayed as having responsive components that do not act independently, whereas loosely coupled systems are portrayed as having independent components that do not act responsively" (p. 205). Orton and Weick advocate using a dialectical interpretation of loose coupling that describes system elements according to their distinctiveness and responsiveness. Elements are distinctive if they are well-defined and semi-autonomous, and elements are responsive if they react to the actions of other elements in the system:

> If there is neither responsiveness nor distinctiveness, the system is not really a system, and it can be defined as a noncoupled system. If there is responsiveness without distinctiveness, the system is tightly coupled. If there is distinctiveness without responsiveness, the system is decoupled. If there is both distinctiveness and responsiveness, the system is loosely coupled. (p. 205)

In CSCW literature, loose coupling in the workplace has been discussed as a potential design dimension, but not in detail. In a discussion of organizational structure in research and development (R&D) work, Grinter et al. (1999) show that organizations adopt different coupling patterns depending on work interdependencies and on the physical relationships of workers and workgroups. They equate co-location with tight coupling and high communication requirements, and physical distribution with loose coupling and reduced communication requirements.

Olson and Teasley (1996) describe loose and tight coupling in design teams at an automotive manufacturer using two work dimensions: the required response time, and the required level of interaction between collaborators. They state that in tightly coupled work, workers are directly dependent on each other, and immediate interaction is needed to coordinate work. In loosely coupled work, "people need to be aware of others' activity and decisions, but without the need for immediate clarification or negotiation. The work can proceed in parallel." (p. 422)

Churchill and Wakeford (2001) suggest that the level of coupling in mobile groups can be used as a design dimension for technologies to support mobile collaborators. They describe two coupling styles for mobile workers: tight mobility and loose mobility. In tight mobility, mobile collaborators need real-time synchrony with others in order to communicate and coordinate work. In loose mobility, mobile workers asynchronously access documents or information – while they still co-operate with others, the collaborative requirements are reduced. Loose mobility, then, represents a form of loosely coupled interaction specific to mobile groups. It implies that workers are not regularly synchronized with others, and that asynchrony serves an important role in information sharing between workers.

In previous work, we discussed loosely coupled work patterns in home care treatment teams, and presented a preliminary set of design principles for developing groupware applications for loosely coupled collaborators (Pinelle and Gutwin 2003). We discussed the discretionary nature of collaboration in loosely coupled work, and the preference workers had for low-cost collaboration such as low-level awareness and asynchronous communication instead of synchronous communication, which required significant effort to initiate. From an analysis of home care work, we proposed several groupware design strategies, including: preserving workers' flexibility in managing their workdays, consolidating fragmented information repositories that are maintained by the workers, and supporting low cost communication and coordination.

In this paper, we build on our past work on loose coupling (Pinelle and Gutwin 2003). We present a formal design framework that is partially based on our work in home care, but that also incorporates findings from related studies of loosely coupled work from organizational research. The framework describes common work and collaboration patterns seen in loosely coupled settings, and it also provides a set of groupware design approaches that significantly expands on those that we previously presented.

Setting

This research was carried out as part of a project to develop a groupware system to support collaboration in home care treatment teams in Saskatoon Health Region (SHR) in Saskatchewan, Canada. The design framework grew out of design work in home care and was developed for three reasons:

- Current CSCW studies provided limited guidance on designing groupware for the setting.
- Current groupware systems did not adequately address the needs of the workers. For example, groupware systems such as instant messaging, shared calendars, newsgroups, and existing workflow systems did not provide adequate support for teamwork, taskwork, autonomy, and flexibility.
- There were extensive studies on loose coupling in organizational research fields that characterized home care work practice and that had the potential to provide guidance in analysis and design for loose coupling in general (e.g. Orton and Weick 1990; Scott 1985; Hasenfield 1983).

Initial observations and interviews with workers in the home care setting contributed to the development of the framework. The framework was later used in the design of Mohoc, a clinical information system for home care, and it was evaluated during two field trials where Mohoc was deployed for a combined total of 6 months. The SHR home care setting is described in more detail elsewhere (Pinelle and Gutwin 2003; Pinelle 2004). We provide a brief overview here.

Patients who receive home care services in SHR are treated in their homes by clinicians from several disciplines. The set of community-based workers who share a common patient are called a home care treatment team, and teams can include members from as many as seven different disciplines, including occupational therapists, physical therapists, nurses, dieticians, social workers, case managers, and home health aides. Since each worker treats multiple patients during a workday (usually 6-15 depending on the discipline), and since teams are formed around patients, each worker is a member of multiple teams.

Regardless of the discipline, home care workers spend most of their time carrying out a limited number of tasks. Most of their time is spend planning their workday, visiting patients, driving between patients' homes, and filling out paperwork. With the exception of home health aides, workers have significant discretion in carrying out their daily activities, and managers act primarily in advisory roles.

Treatment teams members work together in a loosely coupled fashion. Since team members share a common patient, their work is interdependent. However, work practice is not organized to facilitate interaction within teams, so collaboration is infrequent. Workers are mobile, maintain different schedules, and work out of different locations. This often makes it difficult for them to determine others' locations and availabilities, and it can require significant effort for them to initiate contact with others. Workers may occasionally see each other in their offices, but these meetings are often sporadic since there are no fixed office hours, and since some disciplines begin visiting patients earlier than others. Each discipline maintains a separate set of paperwork for each patient, and this paperwork is carried with workers in the field so that they can access it at the point of care. This makes paperwork unavailable to team members from other disciplines, even though the content is potentially valuable.

In multidisciplinary teams, each worker is recognized as the expert in their discipline's practice domain, and it is acknowledged by others that they are the best suited to make decisions that fall within that area. This professionalism and knowledge specialization effectively partitions the work that takes place in home care since each worker is usually able to focus on their separate concerns and leave other areas to workers from other disciplines.

Even though collaboration and information sharing can be difficult, the reduced interdependence seen in home care has some benefits. For example, the mobile work environment seen in home care is unpredictable—workers may be delayed while driving between patients' homes or while delivering treatments. Loose coupling gives workers the flexibility that they need to handle this uncertainty since they do not need to consult others when plans and schedules need to be revised.

Design Framework

The design framework was developed by synthesizing existing information on loose coupling in CSCW and organizational research. It was also based on observations and interviews with home care workers. These included four rounds of semi-structured interviews, and each round consisted of 7 one-hour interviews. Each round included an interview with a member of each home care discipline in SHR. In addition, approximately 60 hours of field observations were carried out with workers from each of the disciplines. The data collection and analysis processes are described in further detail in Pinelle and Gutwin (2003).

The framework was developed to help designers consider important characteristics of loosely coupled work practice while designing groupware systems. The framework attempts to improve the design process by:

- clearly defining loose coupling and loosely coupled groups for groupware designers;
- providing a set of concepts that designers can look for when approaching a new work setting;
- providing a description of collaboration patterns, work patterns, reasons, and outcomes seen in loosely coupled workplaces;
- providing a set of approaches for designing groupware systems that are appropriate for work practice in loosely coupled groups.

The framework has two main parts, each of which supports a different step in the design process: a contextual model, and a set of design approaches. The contextual model describes loose coupling in the workplace, and it acts as a theoretical foundation for the rest of the framework. The design approaches provide guidance on developing groupware applications that are tailored to work practices in loosely coupled settings.

Operational Definitions for Loose Coupling

We propose operational definitions for "loose coupling" and "loosely coupled groups." Our goal was to develop definitions with few ambiguities so that designers can identify loose coupling in the workplace.

Defining loose coupling

In this section, we provide definitions for loose and tight coupling in social systems. The definitions are general and can be used to describe relationships between a range of system "elements", which can include organizations, groups, or individuals. The definitions are partially based on definitions by Orton and Weick (1990).

We define loose and tight coupling using three dimensions: interdependence, distinctiveness, and integration. Interdependence describes the strength of linkages between system elements. Interdependence refers to "the extent to which the items or elements upon which work is performed or the work processes themselves are interrelated so that changes in the state of one element affect the state of others" (Scott 1987, p.214). Integration indicates the level of coordination seen in interaction patterns between system elements (Bertrand 1972, pp. 26). Distinctiveness indicates the degree to which elements are well defined and semi-autonomous (Orton and Weick 1990). The definitions follow:

Loose coupling. Loose coupling exists between two or more elements when:

1) *Low interdependence.* Each element's actions affect the other elements weakly and/or infrequently.

2) *High differentiation*. Elements are distinct, logically separate, and self-contained.

3) *Low integration*. Interaction to manage interdependence does not take place regularly between elements.

Tight coupling. Tight coupling exists between two or more elements when:

1) *High interdependence*. Each element's actions affect the other elements significantly and regularly.

2) *Low differentiation*. Elements are not self-contained or distinct.

3) *High integration*. Interaction to manage interdependence takes place regularly between elements.

The differentiation described in these definitions can operate at different levels. For example, when the elements are two people, differentiation can indicate well-defined roles that give a logical separation to the work of each individual. When the elements are groups, high differentiation can indicate separation of function or purpose between the groups.

The low interdependence described in the loose coupling definition indicates that elements' actions will not strongly impact other elements. This is described in detail by Weick (1982):

Loose coupling exists if A affects B (1) suddenly (rather than continuously), (2) occasionally (rather than constantly), (3) negligibly (rather than significantly), (4) indirectly (rather than directly), and (5) eventually (rather than immediately). Connections may appear suddenly, as in the case of a threshold function; may occur occasionally, as in the case of partial reinforcement; may be negligible, as when there is a damping down of response between A and B due to a constant variable; may be indirect, as when a superintendent can affect a teacher only by first affecting a principal; and may occur eventually, as when there is a lag between legislator voting behavior and response by his or her electorate. (p. 380)

Defining loosely coupled groups

In this section, we propose a definition for "loosely coupled groups." The three criteria for loose coupling (interdependence, differentiation, and integration) provide a basis for developing the definition. However, given differences in work patterns over time and differences in relationships between group members, it can be difficult to classify a group as a "loosely coupled group" in an absolute sense. This type of classification seems most appropriate when loose coupling represents the primary relationship pattern between members of the group, and when the coupling patterns are relatively stable over time. Given this qualifier, occasional and brief shifts to tight coupling do not prevent a group from being "loosely coupled", since work will settle back into a loose pattern. The definitions follow:

Loosely coupled groups. Loosely coupled groups meet the following criteria:

1) *Low interdependence*. Each group member's actions affect the other members weakly and/or infrequently.

2) *High differentiation*. Each group member has a distinct and mutually understood role. Roles may be defined by professional disciplines, job descriptions, skills, knowledge specialization, or through periodic planning.

3) *Low integration*. Members do not interact regularly to manage interdependence.

4) *Stability*. In spite of brief and intermittent shifts in coupling style, the high differentiation—low integration patterns remain stable over time.

Tightly coupled groups. Tightly coupled groups meet the following criteria:

1) *High interdependence*. Each member's actions affect the other members significantly and regularly.

2) *Low differentiation*. Each member may or may not have a distinct role.

3) *High integration*. Members interact regularly to manage interdependence.

4) *Stability*. In spite of brief and intermittent shifts in coupling style, the low differentiation—high integration patterns remain stable over time.

Contextual Model: Understanding Loose Coupling in the Workplace

In order to build groupware that supports loosely coupled work situations, it is first necessary to understand loose coupling in the workplace. In the next sections, we present a "contextual model" for loose coupling that describes common work practices in loosely coupled workgroups. It is based on previous work in organizational research, small group research, and CSCW research, and it has three main parts: a set of reasons for the adoption of loose coupling, a set of outcomes of the adoption of loose coupling, and a description of interaction patterns between loosely coupled collaborators.

Reasons for loose coupling

Several factors can contribute to the adoption of loose coupling in the workplace, and they can occur at different levels—at the organizational level, at the group level, at the interpersonal level, or in the external environment. Common contributing factors include: uncertainty in the work environment that requires rapid adaptation by work units, unpredictable tasks that are difficult for managers to monitor and evaluate, employees that are professionals or that have a high level of knowledge specialization, and barriers that interfere with routine collaboration (e.g. physical distribution, mobility, and schedule variability).

Table I. Summary of reasons for loose coupling

Reasons	
Environmental uncertainty and complexity	The system operates in an uncertain and/or complex environment (Orton and Weick 1990; Scott 1985; Aldrich 1979; Lei et al. 1996; Hasenfield 1983)
Non-routine and unpredictable tasks; ambiguous evaluation criteria	Tasks are not routine and are difficult to plan and predict, and evaluation criteria are unclear and poorly defined (Hasenfeld 1983)
Professionalism; specialized knowledge and expertise	The organization has professional employees; employees have specialized knowledge (Kouzes and Mico 1979; DiTomaso 2001; Scheid-Cook 1990)
Limited opportunities for interaction	Workplace factors interfere with interaction and can include: physical distribution, schedule variability, worker mobility, physical environment constraints, organization / group size and complexity (Olson and Teasley 1996; Bellotti and Bly 1996; Fagrell et al. 2000; Smith 1973; Monane 1967)

Table I summarizes the underlying reasons that can lead to the adoption of loose coupling. While each of the reasons can contribute to loose coupling, causality is not always clear, and in some cases, some conditions may be the result of the adoption of loose coupling (Foster 1983, p. 13).

Outcomes of loose coupling

The adoption of loose coupling impacts the patterns of work and collaboration that are seen in groups and organizations. A common outcome of loose coupling is worker autonomy, which is usually associated with a corresponding weakness in managerial oversight. Loose coupling also allows significant adaptability since each worker and work unit is able to sense and rapidly adjust to their local work environment because their autonomy frees them of the need to consult other individuals or work units when making routine decisions.

Table II summarizes the outcomes associated with the adoption of loose coupling. They are not necessarily good or bad (Firestone 1985, p.5; Weick 1976). Instead, the utility of each outcome depends on the specific circumstances confronted in the work situation (Scott 1987, p. 254).

Table II. Summary of outcomes of loose coupling

Outcomes	
Information buffers	Workers maintain local information repositories (Kmetz 1984)
Autonomy and behavioral discretion	Workers are free to use their own discretion in determining their behavior (Aldrich 1979; Tyler 1987; Perrow 1999)
Sensitivity to environmental stimuli	The system has several distinct "sensors", so it is sensitive to environmental stimuli (Weick 1976; Staber and Sydow 2002; Brusoni and Prencipe 2001)
Adaptability	Workers are able to adapt to the environments that they encounter locally (Rubin 1979; Horne 1992; Lutz 1982; Scott 1987)
Weak authority structure	Authority structures are limited in their ability to sanction subordinates (Staber and Sydow 2002; Lorsch 1973)

Patterns of interaction in loose coupling

Since interdependence is weak in loose coupling, well-established communication channels may not exist, and when more intense collaboration is needed, it can require significant effort. Since workers are autonomous, they can often exercise their discretion in initiating interactions with others, and weak interdependence can enable them to utilize channels that are slow and sparse (e.g. memos or email rather than face-to-face meetings). Low-cost collaboration mechanisms are generally preferred since work is not usually organized to facilitate regular interactions. We summarize coordination and communication in loosely coupled workplaces in Table III.

Table III. Summary of patterns of interaction in loose coupling

Patterns of interaction	
Coordination	Voluntary rather than directed coordination (Litterer 1965) Low-cost coordination strategies • Unexamined assumptions (Gamoran et al. 2000) • Common socialization (Weick 1980; Hasenfeld 1983) • Mutually understood roles, task partitioning (Hasenfeld 1983; Litterer 1965)

	▪ Adjustment without negotiation (Pinelle and Gutwin 2003)
Communication	Tolerance for low efficiency (Staber and Sydow 2002) Tolerance for "non-rich" media (Daft and Lengel 1986) ▪ Email, text messaging ▪ Memos Can be uneven and indirect (Staber and Sydow 2002; Weick 1982)

Design Approaches

The work patterns seen in loosely coupled workgroups have implications for the way that groupware systems should be designed to support them. Unlike more tightly coupled groups, work is primarily autonomous, and communication and coordination occur less often. These patterns suggest that designs should place more of an emphasis on features that support autonomous work, and should support direct collaboration, but only at the workers' discretion.

Table IV presents a set of design approaches that suggest how groupware systems should be designed to support loosely coupled workgroups. They were developed for settings where loose coupling is seen in the workplace, and where it is not the intent of the designer to change the current coupling style. The design approaches are based on the contextual model and on observations from home care in Saskatoon Health Region.

Each approach is based on loose coupling characteristics in the contextual model and presents a design recommendation that suggests how groupware systems should be designed to support loosely coupled work practice. The approaches emphasize the importance of support for autonomous work, and of support for low-cost communication and coordination mechanisms. For example, some of the approaches highlight the value of using low-cost coordination support such as low-level awareness of others' actions so that workers can coordinate their activities without the need for costly explicit negotiation.

Table IV. Summary of design approaches

Design approach	Description
Support autonomy and flexibility	Support current work practices without tightening interdependence between workers since this can reduce autonomy, professional discretion, and flexibility
buffers	Shift select pieces of information from locally maintained information buffers to a merged repository to help improve coordination and awareness of real-world activities.
Support individual workspaces and discretionary sharing	When information maintained by a worker is shared with the rest of the team, the sharing should be at the worker's discretion so that they can selectively protect information.
Integrate collaboration with features for individual work	Support for collaboration should be integrated with features that support individual work. Collaborative features should be unobtrusive and should not interfere with workers' abilities to utilize other more frequently used features.
Facilitate asynchronous awareness	Support awareness of the activities that others carry out in the groupware system. Awareness representations should persist over time to accommodate varied schedules and autonomous work patterns.
Support loose coordination	Support loose coordination, where minimal effort and minimal direct negotiation is needed by the users.
Support loose communication	Provide support that lowers the amount of effort that is required to initiate communication.

Support shifts to tighter coupling	Support periods of direct interaction and periods of no interaction. Support for tighter coupling can be handled in two ways: support for direct communication within the application and/or support for arranging direct communication in the real world.
Preserve flexible group organization	Allow workers to determine their level of involvement in collaborative situations. They should have the flexibility to determine how involved they want to be in a given group, and involvement levels should be conveyed to others.

Mohoc

We used the contextual model during the analysis of the home care work setting, and then we used the design approaches to develop Mohoc, a groupware application to support loosely coupled work in home care treatment teams. Each design approach is instantiated in user interface and interaction features in the system (see Table V), and Mohoc provided a means of investigating the value of the underlying design framework in the home care context.

The main reason for developing groupware support for home care was to improve information access by workers and to lower the amount of effort needed to communicate and to coordinate tasks within treatment teams. The system was developed to support current autonomous work activities, including: managing clinical documentation, planning treatments, and scheduling visits with patients. It makes information generated through those activities available to other team members so that they can coordinate activities more closely and without the need for direct negotiation.

The Mohoc system is an asynchronous groupware system that uses a client-server architecture. The system was developed to operate using wireless networks (CDPD and 1X) that are unreliable and at times unavailable. To address this, the system supports disconnected work, and stores data locally. When network connections become available, the client application forwards transactions to the server, and the server sends cached transactions to the client. All transactions are stored in FIFO queues, so transactions are always sent in the order that they occurred. The Mohoc client was initially developed to operate on laptop computers with wireless modems. Later, Pocket Mohoc, a Pocket PC version of the client, was developed to support home health aide workflows since they require only a subset of the functionality that is needed by professional workers.

Mohoc has three main user-interface screens, and each screen supports a distinct step in the daily activities of home care workers. The *schedule view* allows the worker to view their weekly schedule and allows them to plan and set their weekly appointments. The *daily agenda view* allows the worker to access an interactive daily agenda that can be revised as the workday unfolds. The *chart view* allows workers to access an interactive chart for each of their patients, and it provides electronic versions of their forms so that they can fill out their daily paperwork for the selected patient. Collaboration support is provided as an adjunct to these autonomous work activities. This is done using tools for explicit communication which include a group discussion tool and sticky notes that can be placed on the shared workspace or in documents. The system also provides several types of awareness information to help workers to coordinate their work activities without expending significant effort including: viewing histories and modification histories for shared artifacts (e.g. clinical documents or communications), awareness flags that indicate when new artifacts are added or when existing artifacts are modified, and awareness representations that are displayed in tools that support individual work.

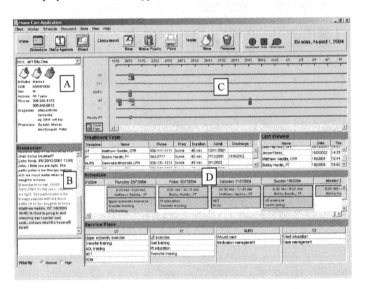

Figure 1. Chart view with cover page selected. A: Client summary region. B: Discussion tool. C: Document overview region. D: Document viewing region.

Figure 1 shows a screenshot of the chart view and illustrates several of the design approaches. The screen is primarily used for maintaining clinical documents such as assessments, progress notes, and discharge summaries. The documents are merged into a shared document repository so that they are accessible by all team members. A timeline-based overview of this space is shown in C, and area D displays the content of the selected document. The overview area (C) also shows the private document space that is available to the physiotherapist worker who is logged into the system. A line at the bottom of the overview region is labeled "Private PT", and it contains documents that were created by the user and that are not viewable by others. In Figure 1, area D shows the chart view "cover page", a summary page that displays information about other workers that treat the selected patient. For example, an area labeled "Last viewed" shows the times and dates when other workers accessed the selected patient's chart. The area labeled "Schedule" shows the patient's schedule, the times the patient will be visited by other workers, and the treatments the workers will provide. Communication tools are also shown. Sticky notes are attached to the patient's chart and are shown in A, and a group discussion tool is shown in B. These are both attached to the workspaces used to carry out autonomous work activities, but can be selectively ignored by workers.

Field Trials

We carried out two field trials where the Mohoc system was used by home care teams to support team members' daily activities. The field trials allowed the groupware system and the underlying design framework to be evaluated. During the trials, participants used the client application to support the care of patients who consented to participate in the trials.

Prior to each trial, each worker participated in two training sessions. Each session lasted between 45 minutes and 1 ½ hours, and duration varied with the technical expertise of the trainee. First, each participant was trained on the care and maintenance of the client device (laptop or handheld) and modem, and on the operating system installed on the device. Each worker also received preliminary training on the client application. Workers were given the client device and were encouraged to use them so that they could become more familiar with the technology. A second training session was scheduled with each worker 2 weeks after the first session. During the second training session, workers were given in-depth training on the client application, and on field trial logistics.

The first trial lasted 2 ½ months. During that time, Mohoc was used by a treatment team of six home care workers from five different disciplines, and the team used the application to support the treatments that they provided to a single shared patient. The second field trial was larger in scope—it lasted 3 months and included 3 patients and 10 participants, and it included the Mohoc and Pocket Mohoc applications. The underlying intent of the second trial was to expand on the investigation started in the first, but with patients with conditions varying in acuity. This variation, it was hoped, would provide an opportunity to examine different levels of interdependence within treatment teams so that a range of work patterns could be considered.

During each field trial, two types of data collection procedures were used. First, two rounds of interviews were conducted with each participant. The first round was conducted midway through the trial, and the second was conducted at the end of the trial. All interviews were audio recorded for later analysis. The interviews were semi-structured and focused on gathering information about how features were utilized by participants and about participants' opinions of features. They also provided an initial look at how the system impacted work practice. Second, participants' interactions with the system were recorded using system logs. System logs contained timestamps and information about the specific interactions that workers carried out with the application.

During the trials, participation varied with each participant's level of involvement in patient care. Over the course of 162 days, there were a total of 240 unique sessions where a participant logged into the system and generated at least one network transaction. There were a total of 5153 transactions during the trials. A transaction was an action taken by a user that generated a network message that was sent to the server. On average, participants carried out 21.47 transactions per session. At times, some participants accessed the system sporadically, but the field trial duration enabled enough data to be collected from each user so that a reasonable evaluation could be carried out. Additionally, a range of system features were used by the participants over the course of the trial, and this generated enough data to allow most of the major features (and the underlying design approaches) to be evaluated.

Results

Each design approach was instantiated in features found in the Mohoc system, and this mapping was used to evaluate the design approaches (see Table V). Each approach was evaluated by analyzing field trial data to determine how successful the corresponding system features were at supporting work and collaboration in home care teams. Interview data and system logs were analyzed to determine:

- patterns of system use,
- participants' opinions of the features,
- the impact that the system had on work practice (based on participant report).

Most of the features that implement the design approaches were well received during the field trials. Table V summarizes the field trial results. Each design approach is listed along with the Mohoc features that instantiate the approach. The result summary column provides a brief description of the evaluation result for each approach. The evaluation results are positive in most instances and indicate that most of the features were successfully integrated into existing work practices in home care, and that support for low cost collaboration features was beneficial to workers during the trials. Overall, this suggests that most of the design approaches are useful at adding consideration for loosely coupled work practice to groupware design in a way that allows the system to be successfully incorporated into existing work practices.

Table V. Summary of field trial results

Design approach	Mohoc features	Result summary
Support autonomy and flexibility	Supports current autonomous workflow, does not force explicit collaboration	System used primarily to support autonomous activities: documentation, scheduling
Consolidate information buffers	Stores clinical documents in a shared document repository	Participants regularly viewed others' clinical documents and had a positive view of this feature
Support individual workspaces and discretionary sharing	Allows documents to be maintained in unshared personal workspaces	Individual space used to leave notes to self, for experimentation, and to temporarily store documents until completion
Integrate collaboration with features for individual work	Provides collaboration tools that are associated with individual workspaces; Embeds collaborative information in tools for individual work	Collaboration features used less frequently than individual work features; used to augment workers' current work activities
Facilitate asynchronous awareness	Tracks viewing and modification histories for artifacts; flags new / newly modified content	Participants reported using flags to track relevant content; modification histories to manage shared editing of documents
Support loose coordination	Embeds information about others' treatment times and treatment activities in scheduling tools to facilitate adjustment without negotiation	Several participants reported using information in the system to tailor treatment activities and times
Support loose communication	Provides asynchronous communication tools: sticky notes, group discussion tool	Used to communicate primarily urgent information (falls, hospitalizations). Participants report more communication than in unsupported work.
Support shifts to tighter coupling	Provides limited information about others' availabilities to facilitate face-to-face and phone conversation	Participants found information useful; would have liked more detail to facilitate phone conversations while in office
Preserve flexible group organization	Provides information about others' treatment frequencies	Participants did not report making use of this feature

The features that support autonomous work activities were used most frequently. Workers primarily used the system to maintain clinical documents, to manage their schedules, and to update patients' treatment plans. Many participants also utilized their personal, unshared workspace regularly. They often left incomplete documents in their personal space, and once they were completed, they moved them to the shared workspace so that they were viewable by others. Others maintained personal notes and reminders using sticky notes even though the feature was initially intended for use as an interpersonal communication tool. This is illustrated by the following example:

Interviewer: "You left sticky notes for yourself? How did you use them?"

Nurse: "I put things in there to remind myself to pass on messages to other people. Like, for example, an LPN. Or I left a message to myself to pick up a particular type of supply. Something that I may would have written in my own calendar book or something, or put a nurse to nurse memo on the front of our file, so instead of...put it on there as a reminder to me to do something in particular, so I used it that way."

During interviews, several participants reported modifying their treatments and schedules based on information that was provided through Mohoc's coordination features. In a discussion about the schedule tools and the shared document repository, a participant offered an example of how she tracked another worker's treatment activities since they had direct relevance to her own treatments:

Participant: Last week <patient name>'s chest was bad so <worker's name> was in there every day, and I mean, I could pick up on that, that I wouldn't normally pick up on. So that is probably the biggest advantage, that you can see what the other people are doing and that they've...noticed any changes in <him/her> or whatever.

Features that support explicit communication were used more intermittently than autonomous work features. However, the frequency of communication that did take place was greater than what was seen during observations of unsupported work. Most of the communication that took place was not routine in nature, but instead was used to inform the team of unusual occurrences or observations such as patient hospitalizations or health emergencies. For example, during the second field trial, a patient was hospitalized and a participant posted a brief public message using the discussion tool: "daughter came called EMS went to hospital." During an interview, a participant describes the value of the communication support in allowing more direct communication, but suggests that the true value is to pass on "a little message" rather than to sustain regular communication:

Interviewer: How did the communication support, like the discussion and the sticky notes, impact your work?

Participant: Yeah, that's not something we had the sort of ability to do anyway before. You know, a message or something. And we really need it. Because there's no connection. Even with the home health aides, they're never in the office at the same time that we are, so there is never an opportunity to pass on a little message. It's always got to be second hand through the supervisor to them kind of thing, so it's always a three way system. So this let me talk to them without going through the supervisor first.

Some of the design approaches could not be fully evaluated due to oversights in the implementation or due to limited utilization of features by participants. In the next paragraphs, we discuss two approaches that were difficult to evaluate: supporting shifts to tighter coupling and supporting flexible group organization.

Support shifts to tighter coupling. The field trial results suggest that supporting shifts to tighter coupling may be valuable, but the Mohoc system missed opportunities for supporting this approach fully, and as a result, it was not evaluated as extensively as it could have been. The Mohoc system did not record information about workers' office hours, which would have helped facilitate meetings and phone conversations in the office. Participants recommended the addition of this information in exit interviews during the trials. While this approach does not need to be revised given the evidence available from the trial, it would benefit from further evaluation in other settings.

Support flexible group organization. The Mohoc system did not provide different participation modes, making it difficult to fully evaluate this approach. For example, the system did not allow workers to indicate to others that they are less involved with a patient so that more involved members can notify them when increased involvement is needed. Since support for this approach was only minimally provided, it was not possible to fully evaluate its usefulness.

Discussion

Loose coupling is common in many work domains including education, health care, and knowledge work, but it has not previously been studied in detail in CSCW. In this research, we attempted to address the need for a more informed approach to designing groupware systems for loosely coupled workgroups by developing a design framework based on literature in organizational research fields, and on findings from home care treatment teams. The framework provides a contextual model that characterizes loose coupling in the workplace, and a set of design approaches for tailoring systems to the work practices in loosely coupled settings.

Our evaluation findings from home care are generally positive and suggest that the framework was useful in specializing the groupware design process for loose coupling. However, since the framework was only evaluated in a single setting, further research is needed to determine how well it will generalize to other loosely coupled groups. Furthermore, the framework was developed concurrently with home care data collection activities, so it is a possible that the framework may be tailored to the home care setting rather than to loosely coupled groups in general, and that evaluation results may also reflect this bias.

One of the difficulties we encountered in evaluating the design framework is that the theoretical components are difficult to test in a rigorous fashion since there are limited controls in a field study. Furthermore, since the ultimate test of a design framework is in how well it contributes to the development of systems that are well suited to the needs of the users, the theoretical propositions cannot be tested directly. Instead, the system itself must act as a surrogate for the framework during an evaluation. This makes it difficult to evaluate a framework with a high level of rigor, since, for example, it is difficult to measure how well features instantiate a framework and to what degree. It is also difficult to attribute success of failure of an implementation to the framework in entirety, since design is an imprecise activity, and since success or failure may be due to factors that fall outside of the framework's focus. We acknowledge that this is a preliminary step in understanding design for loosely coupled workgroups and that significant further work needs to be carried out. In part, we hoped to overcome some of these limitations by basing many of our theoretical assumptions on literature on loose coupling in organizational research fields. However, the design approaches extend beyond organizational research, and it is here that further validation is needed the most.

References

Aldrich, H. (1979): *Organizations and Environments*, Prentice Hall, Englewood Cliffs, NJ.

Bellotti, V., Bly, S. (1996): 'Walking away from the desktop computer: distributed collaboration and mobility in a product design team', *Proc. CSCW'96*, ACM Press, pp. 209-218.

Bertrand, A.L. (1972): *Social Organization: A General Systems and Role Theory Perspective*, F.A. Davis, Philadelphia.

Brusoni, S., Prencipe, A. (2001): 'Managing knowledge in loosely coupled networks: exploring the links between product and knowledge dynamics', *Journal of Management Studies*, 38(7), pp. 1019-1035.

Churchill, E.F. and Wakeford, N. (2001): 'Framing mobile collaboration and mobile technologies', in Brown, B., Green, N., Harper, R. (eds.): *Wireless World: Social and Interactional Implications of Wireless Technology*, New York, Springer-Verlag.

Daft, R.L., Lengel, R.H. (1986): 'Organizational information requirements, media richness and structural design', *Management Science*, 32(5), pp. 554-571.

DiTomaso, N. (2001): 'The loose coupling of jobs: the subcontracting of everyone?', in Berg, I. and Kalleberg, A.L. (eds.): *Sourcebook of labor markets: evolving structures and processes.*, Kluwer Academic/Plenum, New York, pp 247-270.

Fagrell, H., Forsberg, K., Sanneblad, J. (2000): 'FieldWise: a mobile knowledge management architecture', *Proceedings CSCW 2000*, ACM Press, pp. 211-220.

Firestone, W. (1985): 'The study of loose coupling: problems, progress and prospects', in Kerckhoff, A. (ed.): *Research in Sociology of Education and Socialization*, Greenwich, CT, JAI Press, 5:3-20.

Foster, W. (1983): *Loose-coupling Revisited: A Critical View of Weick's Contribution to Educational Administration*, Victoria University Press, Victoria, Australia.

Grinter, R.E., Herbsleb, J.D., Perry, D.E. (1999): 'The geography of coordination: dealing with distance in R&D work', *Proc. GROUP 1999*, ACM Press, pp. 306-315.

Hasenfeld, Y. (1983): *Human Service Organizations*, Prentice Hall, Englewood Cliffs, NJ.

Horne, S. (1992): 'Organization and change within educational systems: some implications of a loose-coupled model', *Educational Management and Administration*, 20(2), pp 88-98.

Kmetz, J.L. (1984): 'An information-processing study of a complex workflow in aircraft electronics repair', *Administrative Science Quarterly*, 29(2), pp. 255-280.

Kouzes, J.M. and Mico, P.R. (1979): 'Domain theory: an introduction to organizational behaviour in human service organisations', *Journal of Applied Behavioural Sciences*, 15(4), pp. 449-469.

Lei, D., Hitt, M.A., Goldhar, J.D. (1996): 'Advanced manufacturing technology: organizational design and strategic flexibility', *Organization Studies*, 17(3), pp.501-523.

Litterer, J.A. (1965): *The Analysis of Organizations*, John Wiley & Sons, New York.

Lorsch, J.W. (1973): 'An open-system theory model for organizational research', in Negandhi, A.R. (ed.): *Modern Organizational Theory: Contextual, Environmental, and Socio-cultural Variables*, Kent State University Press, Kent, Ohio, pp. 132-144.

Lutz, F.W. (1982): 'Tightening up loose coupling in organizations of higher education', *Administrative Science Quarterly*, 27, pp. 653-669.

Monane, J.H. (1967): *A Sociology of Human Systems*, Meredith Publishing, New York.

Olson, J.S. and Teasley, S. (1996): 'Groupware in the wild: lessons learned from a year of virtual collocation', *Proc. CSCW 1996*, ACM Press, pp. 419-427.

Orton, J.D. and Weick, K.E. (1990): 'Loosely coupled systems: a reconceptualization', *Academy of Management Review*, 15(2), pp. 203-223.

Perrow, C. (1999): *Normal Accidents: Living with High-risk Technologies*, Princeton University Press, Princeton, NJ.

Pinelle, D. (2004): *Improving Groupware Design for Loosely Coupled Groups*, Ph.D. thesis, Department of Computer Science, University of Saskatchewan, Canada.

Pinelle, D. and Gutwin, C. (2003): 'Designing for loose coupling in mobile groups', *Proceedings of GROUP 2003*, ACM Press, pp. 75-84.

Rubin, I.S. (1979): 'Retrenchment, loose structure and adaptability in the university', *Sociology of Education*, 52(4), pp. 211-222.

Scheid-Cook, T.L. (1990): 'Ritual conformity and organizational control: loose coupling or professionalization?', *The Journal of Applied Behavioral Science*, 26(2), pp. 183-99.

Scott, W.R. (1987): *Organizations: Rational, Natural, and Open Systems*, 2nd ed., Prentice-Hall, Englewood Cliffs, NJ.

Scott, W.R. (1985): 'Systems within systems: the mental health sector', *American Behavioral Scientist*, 28(5), pp. 601-618.

Smith, P.B. (1973): *Groups Within Organizations: Applications of Social Psychology to Organizational Behaviour*, Harper & Rowe, London.

Staber, U., Sydow, J. (2002): 'Organizational adaptive capacity - a structuration perspective', *Journal of Management Inquiry*, 11(4), pp. 408-424.

Tyler, W. (1987): 'Loosely coupled schools: a structuralist critique', *British Journal of Sociology of Education*, 8(3).

Weick, K.E. (1982): 'Management of organizational change among loosely coupled elements', in Goodman, P.S. (ed.): *Change in Organizations: New Perspectives on Theory, Research, and Practice*, Jossey-Bass, San Francisco.

Weick, K.E. (1980): 'Loosely coupled systems: relaxed meanings and thick interpretations', Paper presented at the Annual Meeting of the American Educational Research Association, Boston, 1980.

Weick, K.E. (1976): 'Educational organizations as loosely-coupled systems', *Administrative Science Quarterly*, 21, pp. 1-21.

H. Gellersen et al. (eds.), *ECSCW 2005: Proceedings of the Ninth European Conference on Computer-Supported Cooperative Work, 18-22 September 2005, Paris, France*, 83–102.

Formally Analyzing Two-User Centralized and Replicated Architectures

Sasa Junuzovic, Goopeel Chung* & Prasun Dewan

Department of Computer Science
University of North Carolina at Chapel Hill, NC, USA
Department of Computer and Information Science
Westfield State College, MA, USA*

sasa@cs.unc.edu, gchung@cs.wsc.ma.edu, dewan@cs.unc.edu

Abstract. We have developed a formal performance model for centralized and replicated architectures involving two users, giving equations for response, feedthrough, and task completion times. The model explains previous empirical results by showing that (a) low network latency favors the centralized architecture and (b) asymmetric processing powers favor the centralized architecture. In addition, it makes several new predictions, showing that under certain practical conditions, (a) centralizing the application on the slower machine may be the optimal solution, (b) centralizing the application on the faster machine is sometimes better than replicating, and (c) as the duration of the collaboration increases, the difference in performances of centralized and replicated architectures gets magnified. We have verified these predictions through new experiments for which we created synthesized logs based on parameters gathered from actual collaboration logs. Our results increase the understanding of centralized and replicated architectures and can be used by (a) users of adaptive systems to decide when to perform architecture changes, (b) users who have a choice of systems with different architectures to choose the system most suited for a particular collaboration mode (defined by the values of the collaboration parameters), and (c) users locked into a specific architecture to decide how to change the hardware and other collaboration parameters to improve performance.

Introduction

Two main architectures have been used to support the sharing of a program among multiple users: centralized and replicated. In the centralized architecture, the shared program executes on a computer belonging to one of the collaborators, receiving input from and broadcasting output to all users. In the replicated architecture, a separate replica of the program executes on the computer of each user, receiving input from all users and producing output for only the local user.

Both architectures have been popular in commercial and research systems. In fact, often a single collaborative system supports both architectures. For example, NetMeeting and Webex provide the centralized architecture for application sharing and the replicated architecture for whiteboard sharing. Chung and Dewan (2001) allow the choice of architecture to be made at application start time while their later results (2004) allow it to change at runtime.

The choice of the architecture affects the semantics, correctness, and performance of the shared program. In this paper, we focus on performance. Previous studies on the performance of collaborative architectures have been restricted to gathering empirical data. To the best of our knowledge, no previous work has developed an analytical performance model.

An analytical model is an attractive idea for two main reasons. First, like analytical models in other computer science fields, it increases our understanding of the subject analyzed. In the case of collaboration architectures, it helps us better understand and compare the event flow and performance of the centralized and replicated architectures. Second, empirical data can inform us about the performance of a collaborative application only under the collaboration conditions used in the measurements. In general, there exists an infinite design space of collaboration modes defined by a variety of collaboration parameters such as network latency and processing power. An analytical model can predict the performance for the entire design space modeled.

As a first step towards meeting these two goals, we have developed a formal performance model for centralized and replicated architectures involving two users, giving equations for response, feedthrough, and task completion times. Our model takes into account collaboration parameters such as network latency, processing powers of the computers used, command-processing time, think time, and degree of participation of each user in the collaboration. The model provides a better understanding of the event flow in the centralized and replicated architectures. It also explains previous empirical results and makes several new predictions. We have verified these predictions through new experiments for which we synthesized logs based on parameters gathered from actual collaboration logs.

The rest of this paper is organized as follows. We first present related work on the performance of collaborative architectures. Next, we develop the mathematical equations comprising the analytical model. We then validate our model against empirical data shown in previous work and through new experiments. Finally, we end with conclusions and directions for future work.

Related Work

Unlike in traditional computer science fields such as databases and operating systems, there has been relatively little work in the collaboration domain on studying the performance of system architectures, even though, arguably, performance is more important in this field because of the human in the event-processing loop. As mentioned earlier, existing studies have been confined to gathering empirical data. Moreover, there have been very few studies that have directly targeted collaboration. One can, however, make some collaboration implications indirectly from studies of distributed window systems.

Nieh, Yang, Novik et al. (2000) conducted experiments that measured the relative performances of two distributed window systems, the Linux implementation of VNC (Hopper, 1998) and Microsoft's Windows 2000 RDP implementation. The architecture used was essentially a two-user centralized architecture with the user at the hosting site inactive. Such a setup gives an idea of the performance experienced by a remote user interacting with a centralized program, assuming the host site does not become a bottleneck. These studies compared two different implementations of the centralized architecture and do not addresses the relative performances of different architecture configurations.

Wong and Seltzer (2000) measured the network load for various remote user operations. Danskin and Hanrahan (1994) measured the frequencies of these operations. Together, these two results give an idea of the actual bandwidth requirements for a variety of remote desktop tasks. Two other studies, one involving Microsoft's Terminal Services (NEC, 2000) and the other by Droms and Dyksen (1990) showed that average and maximum network bandwidth requirements of remote desktop operations can vary greatly. Again, these studies do not address the relative performances of different architecture configurations. This limitation was addressed by the following two works.

Ahuja, Ensor, Lucco et al. (1990) performed experiments to compare the network load imposed by the centralized and replicated implementations of a shared drawing program. They found the following three results. (1) When output was not buffered, there were 6 times as many output events as input events. (2) When output was buffered, there were 3.6 times as many output events as input events. (3) An output event was about the same size as an input event – about 25 bytes (presumably not including network headers).

Like Ahuja, Ensor, Lucco et al. (1990), Chung and Dewan (2004) compared the centralized and replicated architectures, addressing response and task completion times instead of network load. They showed that (a) low network latency favors the centralized architecture and (b) asymmetric processing powers favor the centralized architecture. As these conditions can change dynamically, they developed a system that supports architecture changes at runtime. They also performed experiments showing that when a user with a powerful computer joins the collaboration, it is useful to dynamically centralize the shared program to the new user's computer.

We use previous work to identify collaboration parameters relevant to performance, and we extend it by (a) defining an analytical model that explains existing results about response, feedthrough, and task completion times, and (b) performing new kinds of experiments that validate results predicted by the analytical model not shown previously.

Formal Analysis

As mentioned above, we use response, feedthrough, and task completion times as performance metrics. We define the response (feedthrough) time of a command to be the time that elapses from the moment the command is input to the moment the inputting (non-inputting) user views the corresponding output. We define the task completion time for a particular user as the time that elapses from the moment the collaboration session begins to the moment the user sees the final output. We have not yet considered other important metrics such as jitter (Dyck and Gutwin, 2004).

Developing an analytical model is a complex task, especially when deriving the task completion time for the replicated architecture. Therefore, we make certain assumptions in this first cut at a performance model of collaboration architectures. The major assumption we make is that the collaboration involves only two users, who we denote as $user_1$ and $user_2$. We will describe other assumptions as we introduce our collaboration parameters:

Processing powers of collaborators' computers: As shown by earlier work, a centralized architecture may offer better performance than a replicated architecture when the difference between the processing powers of the users' computers is high as the faster computer can act as a high-performance server for compute-intensive tasks. Thus, it is important to consider processing powers in our equations. We assume that $user_1$'s and $user_2$'s machines have processing powers of p_1 and p_2 MHz, respectively. We assume that the work required, measured in CPU cycles, is the same for all input commands and refer to it as w. Without loss of generality, we assume that $p_1 > p_2$, that is, $user_1$ has a faster computer than $user_2$. Thus, $w/p_1 < w/p_2$, or in other words, an input command is processed faster on $user_1$'s computer than on $user_2$'s computer.

Network latency: Previous work has also shown the influence of network latency on response and task completion times. In a centralized architecture, network latency affects the feedback time of the remote user. In both architectures, it influences both users' feedthrough times, and hence the task completion time when there is coupling between the two users, that is, when a user cannot input the next command before he sees the output for the previous command entered by the other user. For simplicity, we assume that the network latency between the two machines is constant and denote it as d.

Number of input commands by each user. This can have a large impact on the performance of an architecture. To illustrate, assume a centralized architecture in which one of the users provides all the input. If the active user's computer is hosting the program, then the task completion time is independent of network delays. This is not the case if the active user is on the other computer. We will see later that not only is the degree of participation of each user important but also the total of input commands by each user, as differences in the performances of architectures can get magnified the longer the collaboration lasts. We let c_1 and c_2 denote the total number of input commands by $user_1$ and $user_2$, respectively.

Think time before each input command. We assume that the think time for each input command is constant and denote it as t.

Number of answered $user_1$'s input commands. An input command by $user_1$ is answered if $user_2$ inputs a command after it. Thus, the number of $user_1$'s answered commands equals the number of input commands by $user_1$ unless $user_1$ inputs last. In this case, the last burst of input commands by $user_1$ is not answered. We let a denote the number of $user_1$'s answered commands. Note that $a \le c_1$.

Number of input subsequences. An input subsequence ends and a new one begins every time $user_2$'s input command is followed by $user_1$'s command. Also, an implicit start and end of the first and last subsequences occur at the start and end of the collaboration session. As we will see, during each subsequence in the replicated architecture case, there are periods of time during which $user_1$'s faster computer is waiting for $user_2$'s slower computer to catch up. These idling periods are important because they affect the replicated architecture's task completion time. We denote the number of subsequences by s.

Number of user input commands in a subsequence. We assume that $user_1$ is the first user to enter a command. Recall that $user_1$ has c_1 and $user_2$ has c_2 total input commands, and that both users input in each subsequence, except when $a < c_1$, that is, when only $user_1$ inputs in the last subsequence. We let $c_{1,i}$ and $c_{2,i}$ denote the number of input commands in subsequence i by $user_1$ and $user_2$, respectively.

While we know of no data identifying the number of users in a computer-supported collaborative session, we believe a significant number of such sessions involve two users based on the fact that most telephone conversations are two-way calls, many research papers have two authors, many games involve two users, and pair programming requires exactly two users. Thus, our two-user assumption does not make our work impractical. Assuming constant command-processing times is reasonable in whiteboards, instant message clients, games, and several other widely used programs that offer a small number of commands of similar complexity. For example, a command to draw a rectangle is processed very similarly to one that draws an oval. Assuming constant low think times is reasonable in closely-coupled interactions in which it is considered impolite to keep collaborators waiting. When think times are large, assuming they are constant is less reasonable, but large think times dominate the task completion time, and as a result, their specific values do not matter as much. Even if some of these assumptions are considered somewhat simplistic, as mentioned above, the main goal of this paper is to motivate research in analytical performance models of collaboration architectures rather than be the last word on them.

In two-user collaborations there are three architectures to consider: (1) the shared program is centralized on the faster computer, (2) the program is centralized on the slower computer, and (3) the program is replicated. The reason for considering (2) is that in a centralized system, the user initiating the collaboration is the one whose computer hosts the program. By comparing (1) and (2) we can estimate the benefit of (a) adding a constraint on users that requires the one with the faster computer to initiate the session in a static system and (b) changing the architecture at runtime in a dynamic system. Below, we derive the response, feedthrough, and task completion times for these three architectures.

Response Times in Centralized Architectures

In cases where a user's input commands are processed by processed by the local program, the local program replica processes each input command immediately after the local user provides it, keeps processing it without interruption, and finally generates an output message. Hence, if $user_1$ is hosting the centralized architecture, his response time is w/p_1, and if $user_2$ is hosting the centralized architecture, his response time is w/p_2. Now, consider the case where a user's input commands are processed by processed by a remote program instance. Each of his input commands must first travel to the remote program instance, which then immediately starts processing the command upon receipt. The remote program instance processes the input command without interruption, and finally generates an output message, which, then, must travel back to the input provider's computer. Therefore, $user_2$'s local response time is $2d+w/p_1$ in centralized architectures with $user_1$ hosting, and $user_1$'s local response time is $2d+w/p_2$ in centralized architectures with $user_2$ hosting. Hence, we have

$$\text{Resp}_{Cent}U_1 = w/p_1 \qquad \text{if } user_1 \text{ is hosting} \qquad [\text{Eq. 1.1}]$$
$$\text{Resp}_{Cent}U_1 = 2d+w/p_2 \qquad \text{if } user_2 \text{ is hosting} \qquad [\text{Eq. 1.2}]$$
$$\text{Resp}_{Cent}U_2 = w/p_2 \qquad \text{if } user_2 \text{ is hosting} \qquad [\text{Eq. 1.3}]$$
$$\text{Resp}_{Cent}U_2 = 2d+w/p_1 \qquad \text{if } user_1 \text{ is hosting} \qquad [\text{Eq. 1.4}]$$

Response Times in Replicated Architectures

In the replicated architecture, each user's input command is processed by the local replica without synchronizing with the other replica. Thus, $user_1$'s and $user_2$'s response times in the replicated case are w/p_1, and w/p_2, respectively. Hence,

$$\text{Resp}_{Rep}U_1 = w/p_1 \qquad [\text{Eq. 2.1}]$$
$$\text{Resp}_{Rep}U_2 = w/p_2 \qquad [\text{Eq. 2.2}]$$

Task Completion Times in Centralized Architectures

We calculate here the centralized architecture task completion time for $user_1$ and assume $user_1$ inputs first. Figure 1(a) below illustrates the elements of an example task completion time in a centralized architecture scenario where the shared program is centralized on $user_1$'s faster computer. In this interaction sequence, $user_1$ enters inputs 1, 2, 5, and 6, while $user_2$ enters inputs 3, 4, and 7. Let L_i denote the ith contiguous period of time during which the centralized program is busy *locally* processing or waiting for input commands from the *local* user, $user_1$. Let R_i denote the ith contiguous period of time during which the program is waiting for input commands from the *remote* user, $user_2$. Since a collaboration session starts when the centralized program starts processing the first input command of the session and ends when it finishes processing the last input command of the session, L_i must immediately be followed by R_i, which then must be immediately followed by L_{i+1}. Therefore, the total task completion time equals $\Sigma L_i + \Sigma R_i$.

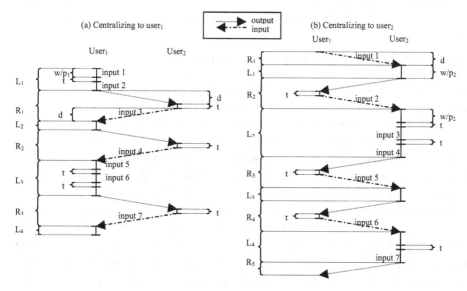

Figure 1. Centralized Architecture Time Diagram

ΣL_i: This term includes two components: the time used to *locally* process the input commands of both users and the think times of the *local* user, $user_1$. The first component is $(c_1+c_2)w/p_1$ and the second one is $(c_1-1)t$ as $user_1$ spends t think time before inputting a command for all commands but the first. Thus, we have

$$\Sigma L_i = (c_1+c_2)w/p_1+(c_1-1)t \qquad \text{[Eq. 3]}$$

ΣR_i: As shown in Figure 1(a), waiting for an input command from $user_2$ consists of three parts: the network delay in transmitting the output for the previous command from $user_1$'s computer to $user_2$'s computer, the think time t of *user₂* before inputting the next command, and finally the network delay in transmitting *user₂*'s input command to *user₁*'s machine. Thus, we have

$$\sum R_i = c_2(2d+t) \qquad \text{[Eq. 4]}$$

From equations 3 and 4, we can derive the total task completion time for a centralized architecture in which the faster user, *user₁*, is the host.

$$\text{task}_{cent}U_1 = \sum L_i + \sum R_i = (c_1+c_2)w/p_1+(c_1+c_2-1)t+2c_2d \qquad \text{[Eq. 5.1]}$$

As the three terms above show, it consists of the time required to process all input commands, the time it takes to think before all commands but the first one, and the network delays incurred in receiving the input commands from and in sending the outputs of the previous commands to the remote user.

If we consider Figure 1(b), then we can similarly reason about the task completion time of a centralized architecture in which the slower user, *user₂*, is the host. In this case, all the processing is done by *user₂*'s computer, and the delays are incurred for *user₁*'s commands. As this the dual of the previous case, the task completion time mirrors equation 5.1.

$$\text{task}_{cent}U_2 = \sum L_i + \sum R_i = (c_1+c_2)w/p_2+(c_1+c_2-1)t+2c_1d \qquad \text{[Eq. 5.2]}$$

Task Completion Time in Replicated Architecture

Deriving the replicated architecture task completion time is significantly different and more complicated than deriving it for the centralized case for several reasons. First, the faster computer may have to wait for the slower one to catch up because of processing time differences. Second, this wait occurs, not after each input command, but instead, when control switches from the user with the fast computer to the user with the slow computer. Finally, the wait time depends not only on the processing power difference but also on the network delays and think times.

Figure 2 below illustrates the elements of an example task completion time in the replicated architecture scenario during which *user₁* enters inputs 1, 2, 5, and 6, and *user₂* enters inputs 3, 4, and 7. This example illustrates our derivation of the task completion time. We will calculate the task completion time for *user₁* only. As before, let L_i denote the ith contiguous period of time during which the program on *user₁*'s computer is busy *locally* processing input commands or waiting for input from the *local* user, *user₁*. Let R_i denote the ith contiguous period of time during which the program on *user₁*'s computer is waiting for input commands from the *remote* user, *user₂*.

$\sum L_i$: As in the centralized case, the shared program on *user₁*'s computer must process all of the input commands and wait for the think time, t, before each command entered by *user₁* except the first one. Thus, we have

$$\sum L_i = (c_1+c_2)w/p_1+(c_1-1)t \qquad \text{[Eq. 6]}$$

$\sum R_i$: In order to calculate the time the faster computer waits for the slower one, we divide the task completion time into subsequences and then add up the time all the subsequences contribute. A subsequence i consists of $c_{1,i}$ $user_1$'s consecutive input commands followed by $c_{2,i}$ $user_2$'s consecutive input commands. In case $user_1$ provides the last input command in a subsequence, the last subsequence is composed only of $user_1$'s input commands. We refer to such a subsequence as a half subsequence as opposed to a full subsequence. Therefore, a task sequence is composed of full subsequences and possibly another one half subsequence. The first subsequence is different from the others in that both computers are ready to process the first input command in the subsequence. Therefore, we treat it differently from the others. We now calculate $\sum R_i$ in terms of its components.

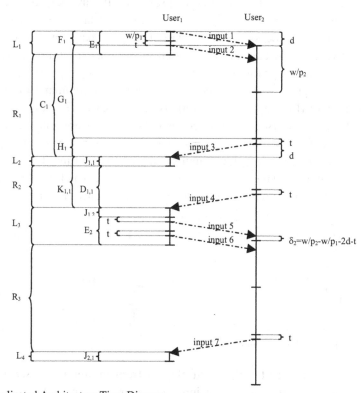

Figure 2. Replicated Architecture Time Diagram

$\sum R_i$ in First Subsequence

C_1: C_1 is defined as the time that elapses from the moment $user_1$'s program replica finishes processing the last input command by $user_1$ in the subsequence to the moment it begins processing the first input command by $user_2$ in the subsequence. Figure 2 graphically shows that $C_1+E_1=F_1+G_1+H_1$. Therefore, $C_1=(F_1+G_1+H_1)-E_1$. We next calculate the values on which C_1 depends.

E_1: E_1 is defined as the time that elapses from the moment $user_1$'s program replica begins processing $user_1$'s first input command in the subsequence to the moment it finishes processing *user₁*'s last input command in the subsequence. This includes processing $c_{1,1}$ input commands by *user₁* and a think time of *t* for each of these commands except the first. Thus, we have

$$E_1 = c_{1,1}w/p_1+(c_{1,1}-1)t \qquad\qquad \text{[Eq. 7]}$$

F_1: F_1 is defined as the time that elapses from the moment *user₁*'s first input command in the subsequence leaves *user₁*'s computer to the moment *user₂*'s program replica begins to process it. Therefore, F_1 is the network delay between the users' computers, *d*. Thus, we have

$$F_1 = d \qquad\qquad \text{[Eq. 8]}$$

G_1: G_1 is defined as the time that elapses from the moment *user₂*'s program replica begins processing *user₁*'s first input command in the subsequence to the moment it finishes processing *user₁*'s last input command in the subsequence. There are two cases to consider here based on whether the think time, *t*, is less than the difference in processing times of an input, $w/p_2-w/p_1$. If $t \le w/p_2-w/p_1$, then *user₂*'s computer will never be idle waiting for a command to arrive from *user₁*'s computer (Figure 2), except initially. In this case, $G_1 = c_{1,1}w/p_2$, the time required to process *user₁*'s input commands in the subsequence on *user₂*'s computer. But if $t > w/p_2-w/p_1$, $\delta_1 = t-(w/p_2-w/p_1)$, *user₂*'s program replica will finish processing *user₁*'s previous input command by the time it receives *user₁*'s next input command. Thus, G_1 increases by $\delta_1(c_{1,1}-1)$, which is the time *user₂*'s computer is idle while *user₁*' inputs in the first subsequence (Figure 3). Hence,

$$G_1 = c_{1,1}w/p_2 \qquad\qquad \text{if } \delta_1 = t-(w/p_2-w/p_1) \le 0 \qquad \text{[Eq. 9.1]}$$
$$G_1 = c_{1,1}w/p_2+\delta_1(c_{1,1}-1) \qquad \text{if } \delta_1 = t-(w/p_2-w/p_1) > 0 \qquad \text{[Eq. 9.2]}$$

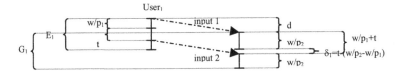

Figure 3. Illustrating G_1 if $t > w/p_2-w/p_1$

H_1: H_1 is defined as the time that elapses from the moment *user₂*'s program replica finishes processing *user₁*'s input commands in the subsequence to the moment *user₁*'s program replica begins to process *user₂*'s first input command in the subsequence. Once *user₂*'s program replica finishes processing *user₁*'s commands in the subsequence, *user₂* spends *t* time thinking about the output of *user₁*'s last input command and then enters his first input command in the subsequence. Therefore, H_1 consists of *user₂*'s think time, *t*, and the network delay between the users' computers, *d*. Thus, we have

$$H_1 = t+d \qquad\qquad \text{[Eq. 10]}$$

user₁'s replica begins processing *user₂*'s first input command in the subsequence immediately. Therefore, by the definitions of C_1, E_1, F_1, G_1, and H_1, it must be the case that $C_1 = (F_1+G_1+H_1)-E_1$. Based on equations 7, 8, 9.1, 9.2, and 10, the wait time that elapses from the moment $user_1$'s replica finishes processing $user_1$'s last input command in the subsequence to the moment it begins processing $user_2$'s first input command in the subsequence, is

$$C_1 = 2d+c_{1,1}(w/p_2-w/p_1)-(c_{1,1}-2)t \qquad \text{if } t-(w/p_2-w/p_1) \leq 0 \quad \text{[Eq. 11.1]}$$
$$C_1 = 2d+(w/p_2-w/p_1)+t \qquad \text{if } t-(w/p_2-w/p_1) > 0 \quad \text{[Eq. 11.2]}$$

The C_1 component of $\sum R_i$ in the first subsequence tells us how long $user_1$'s faster computer must wait for $user_2$'s first input command in the subsequence after processing all of $user_1$'s input commands in the first subsequence. However, $\sum R_i$ in the first subsequence also includes the time $user_1$'s computer must wait for $user_2$'s computer while processing $user_2$'s input commands in the first subsequence. $user_1$'s program replica will wait from the moment it processes $user_2$'s j^{th} command in the subsequence until $user_2$'s $j+1^{st}$ command of the subsequence arrives. This time is equal to $D_{1,j}$ and for $user_2$'s j^{th} input command. Figure 2 shows $D_{1,1}$.

$\sum D_{1,j}$: $\sum D_{1,j}$ is the summation of the wait times during the time period in which $user_1$'s program replica is processing $user_2$'s input commands in the first subsequence. We now show that $\sum D_{1,j}$ equals $\sum (K_{1,j}-J_{1,j})$.

$K_{1,j}$: $K_{1,j}$ is defined as the time that elapses from the moment $user_1$'s program replica begins processing $user_2$'s j^{th} command in the subsequence until $user_1$'s program replica begins processing $user_2$'s $j+1^{st}$ command in the same subsequence. Since $p_1 > p_2$ and $t \geq 0$, we have $w/p_1 < t+w/p_2$, that is, the time $user_1$'s program replica takes to process $user_2$'s input command, w/p_1, is less than the time it takes $user_2$'s program replica to process the same input command, w/p_2, and the time, t, during which $user_2$ thinks before inputting his next command. As a result,

$$K_{1,j} = w/p_2+t \qquad \text{[Eq. 12]}$$

$J_{1,j}$: $J_{1,j}$ is the time that $user_1$'s replica requires to process $user_2$'s input command. Hence,

$$J_{1,j} = w/p_1 \qquad \text{[Eq. 13]}$$

By the definition of $D_{1,j}$, $K_{1,j}$ and $J_{1,j}$, $D_{1,j} = K_{1,j}-J_{1,j}$. As a result, from equations 12 and 13, we have

$$\sum D_{1,j} = \sum (K_{1,j}-J_{1,j}) = (c_{2,1}-1)(t+w/p_2-w/p_1) \qquad \text{[Eq. 14]}$$

In other words, when $user_2$ is inputting a command, $user_1$'s computer must wait for the think time and extra time it takes $user_2$'s computer to process the command for all $user_2$'s input commands in the subsequence except the last.

$V_1 = C_1+\sum D_{1,j}$: C_1 and $\sum D_{1,j}$ account for all components of $\sum R_i$ in the first subsequence. Based on equations 11.1, 11.2, and 14, we have:

$$V_1 = 2d+(c_{1,1}+c_{2,1}-1)(w/p_2-w/p_1)+(c_{2,1}-c_{1,1}+1)t \qquad \text{if } t-(w/p_2-w/p_1) \leq 0 \text{ [Eq. 15.1]}$$
$$V_1 = 2d+c_{2,1}t+c_{2,1}(w/p_2-w/p_1) \qquad \text{if } t-(w/p_2-w/p_1) > 0 \text{ [Eq. 15.2]}$$

$\sum R_i$ in Non-First Subsequences

$V_i = C_i + \sum D_{i,j}$ accounts for all components of $\sum R_i$ in subsequence i, where $i > 1$. The other subsequences are different from the first subsequence for the following reason. In the first subsequence, $user_2$'s computer is ready to process the first input command of $user_1$ in the subsequence as soon as it arrives. However, in other subsequences, $user_2$'s program replica may still be processing the last input command of the previous subsequence by the time the first input command of the current subsequence reaches it. As in Figure 2, this occurs if $w/p_2 - w/p_1 > 2d + t$, that is, if the difference in command processing times is greater than the time it takes for the last input of the previous subsequence to reach $user_1$'s computer, for $user_1$'s computer to process it, the think time before $user_1$ enters his first input command of the current subsequence, and the time it takes for this input to reach $user_2$'s computer. This additional delay increases the processing time for all non-first subsequences by $\delta_2 = w/p_2 - w/p_1 - 2d - t$.

Hence, the processing time equations 15.1 and 15.2 for the first subsequence can be generalized for non-first subsequences as follows:

$V_i = 2d + (c_{1,i} + c_{2,i} - 1)(w/p_2 - w/p_1) + (c_{2,i} - c_{1,i} + 1)t$ if $t - (w/p_2 - w/p_1) \leq 0$ [Eq. 16.1]

$V_i = 2d + c_{2,i}t + c_{2,i}(w/p_2 - w/p_1)$ if $t - (w/p_2 - w/p_1) > 0$ [Eq. 16.2]

$V_i = (c_{1,i} + c_{2,i})(w/p_2 - w/p_1) + (c_{2,i} - c_{1,i})t$ if $t - (w/p_2 - w/p_1) + 2d \leq 0$ [Eq. 16.3]

We can now calculate $\sum L_i + \sum R_i$ which is the same as $\sum L_i + \sum V_i$.

$\sum L_i + \sum R_i$: Recall that c_1 and c_2 are the total number of commands by $user_1$ and $user_2$, respectively, s is the number of full subsequences, and a is the number of $user_1$'s answered commands. Then the task completion time for a replicated architecture, based on equations 6, 16.1, 16.2, and 16.3 is

$task_{rep} = (c_1 + c_2)w/p_1 + 2sd + (a + c_2 - s)(w/p_2 - w/p_1) + (c_1 + c_2 - a + s - 1)t$

            if $t - (w/p_2 - w/p_1) \leq 0$ [Eq. 17.1]

$task_{rep} = (c_1 + c_2)w/p_1 + 2sd + c_2(w/p_2 - w/p_1) + (c_1 + c_2 - 1)t$

            if $t - (w/p_2 - w/p_1) > 0$ [Eq. 17.2]

$task_{rep} = (c_1 + c_2)w/p_1 + 2d + (a + c_2 - 1)(w/p_2 - w/p_1) + (c_1 + c_2 - a)t$

            if $t - (w/p_2 - w/p_1) + 2d \leq 0$ [Eq. 17.3]

In equation 17.3, δ_2 is subtracted as it does not occur in the first subsequence.

Feedthrough in Centralized Architectures

Recall that the feedthrough time for a command is defined as the time that elapses from the moment the command is input to the moment the non-inputting user sees its output. In centralized architectures, feedthrough depends on whether the inputting user is local or remote to the computer hosting the centralized program. If the *local* user provides the input, the *remote* user will see the output once the input command is processed and the output traverses the network. If the *remote* user provides the input, the *local* user will see the output once the input command reaches the local computer and the local computer processes it. Thus:

$$\text{Feed}_{\text{CentTo}}U_1 = w/p_1+d \qquad \text{if } user_1 \text{ hosts the program} \qquad [\text{Eq. 18.1}]$$
$$\text{Feed}_{\text{CentTo}}U_2 = w/p_2+d \qquad \text{if } user_2 \text{ hosts the program} \qquad [\text{Eq. 18.2}]$$

Feedthrough in Replicated Architectures

Consider first feedthrough to commands input by the slower user, $user_2$. Such a command must traverse the network and be processed by the faster user's computer before the latter sees its output. Thus,

$$\text{Feed}_{\text{RepFor}}U_2 = w/p_1+d \qquad\qquad [\text{Eq 19.1}]$$

The feedthrough time of commands input by the faster user, $user_1$, is more complicated because if $t < (w/p_2-w/p_1)$, the slower computer falls further behind the faster computer with each consecutive input entered by the faster user, as illustrated in Figure 2. In this case, consider, command, j, entered in the first subsequence. As this is the first subsequence, $user_2$'s computer processes the first command as soon as it arrives. Hence:

$$\text{Feed}_{\text{RepFor}}U_1^{1,j} = d+w/p_2 \text{ for } j = 1 \qquad\qquad [\text{Eq 19.2}]$$

As $t < (w/p_2-w/p_1)$, the feedthrough will increase by $(w/p_2-w/p_1-t)$ for each subsequent command by $user_1$ in the subsequence. Hence:

$$\text{Feed}_{\text{RepFor}}U_1^{1,j} = d+w/p_2+(j-1)(w/p_2-w/p_1-t) \text{ for } j \geq 1 \qquad [\text{Eq 19.3}]$$

If $t \geq (w/p_2-w/p_1)$, the slow computer is ready to process each command by $user_1$ as soon as it arrives. Thus:

$$\text{Feed}_{\text{RepFor}}U_1^{1,j} = d+w/p_2 \quad j \geq 1 \qquad\qquad [\text{Eq 19.4}]$$

Recall that there are two cases to consider for the non-first subsequences. If $w/p_2-w/p_1 \leq 2d+t$, the slow computer is ready to process the first command in the subsequence as soon as it arrives. In this case, the feedthrough equations given above for the first subsequence apply to all subsequences. Otherwise, the term $w/p_2-w/p_1-2d-t$ is added to the equations given above for the first subsequence.

Formal Analysis Validation

We have given above both mathematical proofs and intuition for justifying the performance model. In addition, it is important to back these with experimental results that validate it for a large number of values of collaboration parameters. Ideally, these experiments should also show its practicality. Several approaches could be used to gather the experimental data.

- Live interaction: Under this approach, pairs of users would perform a collaborative task multiple times as the architecture and system parameters are varied in a controlled manner each time.

- Actual logs: Another approach is to use logs of actual collaborations and assume that these are independent of the system parameters such as architecture, machines used, and network delays. These logs can then be replayed under different values of system parameters.
- Synthetic logs: With this approach, the user logs can be created by varying the user parameters using some mathematical distribution such as Poisson's.

Since users cannot be relied upon to perform the same sequence of actions and have the same think times in different collaborative sessions, the live interaction approach is impractical. The other two approaches require a large number of logs to ensure that a wide range of values for user parameters are covered. This is not a problem for synthetic logs, but such logs do not address the practicality concern as it is not clear parameter values based on mathematical distributions represent reality. Logs of actual interaction are not provided in any public database and we were unsuccessful in obtaining them from researchers who we knew had logged their collaboration tasks. Thus to use the actual-log approach, we would have to gather a large number of actual logs ourselves, which is beyond the scope of our work: the analytical model is our primary contribution and the experiments are addressed mainly to validate the model. In other fields such as real-time systems where benchmarks are not widely available, it is customary to resort to the synthetic-log approach to validate new theoretical results. We did a little better by using a hybrid of the synthetic and actual log approaches. We recorded a small number (8) of actual logs to obtain realistic values of some user parameters and then used these values to create a large number (30) of synthetic logs that we then replayed in the actual experiments using different architectures and system parameters.

We used the same program for recording the actual logs and replaying the synthetic logs. The program is the distributed checkers program used by Chung and Dewan (2001, 2004) which allows a group of users to play against the computer. We chose this program for two reasons. First, it is a computer-intensive task, allowing us to validate the effect of processing time differences. Second, the user study participants knew the game rules, so no user training was needed.

Recall that we assume that an input command takes exactly w CPU cycles to be processed. In Checkers, a user's move consists of two actions: picking up and putting down a piece. To make our response and feedthrough measurements valid, we group the multiple input commands for a single move into a single input command. Also, the computer calculation of the next move depends on the piece positions and is hence not constant. Thus, we report the average response and feedthrough times over all the moves in a single game.

We focus on actor-observer interaction mode in which one user, the actor, makes all the inputs, which are at the end acknowledged by the other user, the observer. The acknowledgement is needed to tell the actor that the observer has seen all the moves and they can proceed to their next task (e.g. post mortem of the game.) Focusing on the actor-observer allows us to show practical results in the limited space available while addressing many common collaborative tasks, such as an expert demonstrating to others or a pupil being tested by a tutor.

To approximate the think times and logs for the actor-observer mode, we gathered actual user logs in which a single user played against the computer. Table I shows the values of user parameters obtained from these studies, which were used in the synthetic logs.

Number of moves			Think Time (s)		
Min	Med	Max	Min	Med	Max
21	44	72	0.11	4.5	41.2

Table I. Measured User Parameter Values Used In Synthetic Logs

The system parameters, processing powers and network delays, also have to be realistic. We used two computers, a Pentium 1.5M laptop and a P2 400Mhz desktop, which have a processing power difference that can be expected when two users collaborate. Both computers are connected on a local LAN. Based on Chung's and Dewan's experiments, we added 72, 162 and 370 ms to the LAN delays to estimate half the round-trip time from a U.S. East Coast LAN-connected computer to a German LAN-connected computer, German modem-connected computer, and Indian LAN-connected computer, respectively. As LAN delays vary during an experiment, we performed it ten times and report the average performances for these ten trials. Our measured numbers are consistent with our model. We do not have space to give all of our measurements. We report a sample of them next when we discuss and validate the new predictions made by our model.

Applications of our Model

The application of our work consists of (1) explaining previous experimental results, and (2) making new predictions.

Explaining Architecture Performance Results

Chung and Dewan showed that (a) low network latencies favor a centralized architecture and (b) asymmetric processing powers favor a centralized architecture. These results were interesting because they went against the common assumption that a replicated architecture always outperforms a centralized one. In their experiments they used a think time of zero and a centralized case in which the faster computer executed the program. Under these conditions, equation 5.1 applies for the centralized architecture task completion time, and equations 17.1 and 17.3 apply to the replicated architecture. For brevity, we consider only 17.3

here. To compare the task completion times of the two architectures, we can subtract equation 17.3 from equation 5.1. A negative result means that the centralized architecture has a better task completion time, and vice versa.

$$\text{task}_{cent}U_1 - \text{task}_{rep} = 2d(c_2-1) - (a+c_2-1)(w/p_2 - w/p_1)$$

Assume that c_2, the number of input commands entered by $user_2$, is always greater than 1. Also assume that the number of $user_1$'s answered input commands, a, is greater than or equal to 0. Thus, the term $2d(c_2-1)$ will increase as d, the network delay, increases, which favors the replicated architecture. On the other hand, the term $-(a+c_2-1)(w/p_2-w/p_1)$ in the same equation will become more negative as the processing power difference, $w/p_2-w/p_1$, increases, which favors centralizing the program to $user_1$'s machine. This is consistent with the results by Chung and Dewan. Next we consider new predictions made by our analytical model. In all of the cases we consider below, we assume the actor-observer mode defined earlier.

Choosing the Placement of the Centralized Program

Sometimes replication is not an option – a user may be bound to a centralized system or the shared program cannot be executed correctly in the replicated architecture. Our model, somewhat counter-intuitively, predicts that centralizing the program on the slower computer may give better task completion and response times but worse feedthrough times than centralizing to the faster computer.

This occurs when the actor is the user on the slow computer. The relevant task completion time equations are 5.1 and 5.2 and the relevant response time equations are 1.3 and 1.4. Consider the task completion and response time difference equations for the two centralized architectures:

$$\text{task}_{cent}U_1 - \text{task}_{cent}U_2 \qquad\qquad \text{Resp}_{Cent}U_2[1.4] - \text{Resp}_{Cent}U_2[1.3]$$
$$= 2d(c_2-c_1) - (c_1+c_2)(w/p_2-w/p_1) \qquad = 2d - (w/p_2-w/p_1)$$

We can set $c_1 = 1$ because the observer, $user_1$ in this case, provides one input at the end to acknowledge end of collaboration. We assume that c_2, the number of input commands entered by $user_2$, is always greater than 1. Thus in the task completion time difference equation, the term, $2(c_2-1)d$, will increase as d, the network delay, increases, which favors centralizing the program to $user_2$'s slower machine. However, since $c_2 > 1$, the $(1+c_2)(w/p_2-w/p_1)$ term in the equation will increase with the processing time difference, $w/p_2-w/p_1$, which favors centralizing the program to $user_1$'s machine. The same conditions apply to the response time difference. For feedthrough, however, centralizing on the fast computer gives a lower value, as shown below. In both centralized architectures, either $user_1$'s input command or its output will traverse the network before $user_2$ sees the output. Therefore, the feedthrough will be lower when centralizing to $user_1$'s faster computer as it processes input commands faster than $user_2$'s slower computer.

$$\text{Feed}_{cent}U_1 - \text{Feed}_{cent}U_2 = w/p_1 + d - w/p_2 - d = -(w/p_2 - w/p_1)$$

To experimentally validate this scenario, we used the median observed think time of 4.5s. The results in Figure 4 confirm our analyses. As we see, centralizing on the slow computer offers relative gains of as much as 69% for response time and 10% for the task completion time. As expected, when think times dominate the task completion time, the relative task completion time difference is not large.

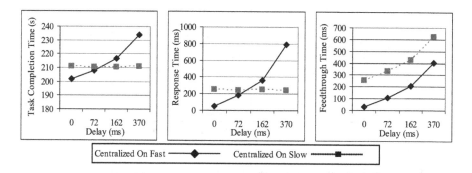

Figure 4. Task Completion, Response, and Feedthrough Times of the Slow Actor

Centralized and Replicated Task Completion Times

Our model also predicts that in certain collaboration modes, the task completion time advantage one architecture has over another can be significant. In particular, a centralized architecture with the faster user's computer hosting may enjoy such an advantage over a replicated architecture when think times are low and the user with the faster computer, $user_1$, is the actor. The relevant equations are 5.1, 17.1, 17.2, and 17.3. We consider 5.1 and 17.1 only which give the task completion time difference as

$$task_{cent}U_1\text{-}task_{rep} = 2d(c_2\text{-}s)\text{-}(a+c_2\text{-}s)(w/p_2\text{-}w/p_1)+(a\text{-}s)t$$

As before, we can set $c_2 = 1$ because the observer, $user_2$ in this case, provides one input at the end of the collaboration. We assume that c_1, the number of input commands entered by the actor, $user_1$, is always greater than 1, all of which are answered. Hence, $c_1 = a > 1$. Because the collaboration consists of one full subsequence, $s = 1$. Thus, $2(c_2\text{-}s)d = 0$ and $(a+c_2\text{-}s) = a$. We assume that t, the think time, is less than $(w/p_2\text{-}w/p_1)$, the processing time difference. Thus, the task completion time difference, which equals $-a(w/p_2\text{-}w/p_1)+(a\text{-}1)t$, is negative. Since the faster user inputs all the commands but one, the network delays are not a factor. Hence, processing the input commands only on the faster computer is better than replicating because the slower computer falls further behind the faster one with each input command which increases the task completion time as predicted by the model.

To experimentally validate this scenario, we used the minimum observed think time of 110ms as it needed to be less than the time difference for processing an input command to make the above equations hold. We show the experiment results with LAN delays (0ms). The results for other delays are consistent but are omitted for brevity reasons. Figure 5 confirms our analysis. It shows that the centralized architecture can be as much as 6.3s faster or as much as 58% quicker in completing the task than the replicated architecture.

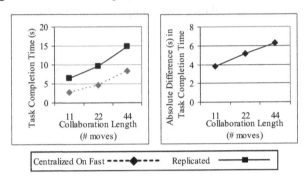

Figure 5. Task Completion, Response, and Feedthrough Times of the Slow Actor

Collaboration Length Effect on Task Completion and Feedthrough Times

Our model also predicts that for certain collaboration conditions, the advantage in task completion and feedthrough times one architecture has over another gets magnified as the length of the collaboration increases.

As above, this occurs when think times are low, that is, $t < w/p_2 - w/p_1$, and the user with the faster computer, $user_1$, is the actor. In the above analysis, we show that in this collaboration mode, the centralized architecture with $user_1$'s computer hosting completes the task in $a(w/p_2-w/p_1)-(a-1)t$ time faster than the replicated architecture. Since a, the number of answered $user_1$'s input commands, increases with collaboration length, this difference gets magnified according to the above task completion time difference equation. Intuitively, the time that elapses from the moment the faster computer processes an input command and to the moment the slower computer processes the same command increases between consecutive inputs by the actor because the slower computer falls further behind the faster one with each input command. Figure 5 verifies our analysis.

Consider now the feedthrough times. Since the entire collaboration consists of consecutive actor's input commands followed by a single input command from the observer, there is only one subsequence in the collaboration. Thus, the relevant feedthrough time equations are equations 18.1 and 19.3. According to these equations, the feedthrough time difference is:

$$\text{Feed}_{\text{CentTo}}U_1 - \text{Feed}_{\text{RepFor}}U_1^{1,j} = -(w/p_2-w/p_1)-(j-1)(w/p_2-w/p_1-t) \text{ for } j \geq 1$$

The maximum value of j is a, the number of $user_1$'s answered input commands. Consider the feedthrough of $user_1$'s last input command. With the same reasoning as above, we can argue that the feedthrough of $user_1$'s last input command will, in the replicated case, increase with collaboration length as predicted by the model.

We validate this indirectly using task completion time results in Figure 5. The time $user_2$ views the output to $user_1$'s last input command is exactly the task completion time minus the time it takes to process $user_2$'s only input. Since the previous result showed that the absolute task completion time difference increases with collaboration length in favor of the centralized architecture, we can conclude that the feedthrough time of $user_1$'s last input message will behave the same.

Other Predictions

Our model makes the following additional predictions. In some cases, the replicated architecture optimizes the feedback time but not the task completion time. In other cases, centralizing to the slower computer may offer equivalent task completion and feedback times as replicating. Moreover, as the think time increases, the architecture choice makes no significant difference to the task completion time (though it does influence the response and feedthrough times). This happens for two reasons. The obvious one is that think times dominate the task completion time. The more interesting one we found is that the users who had high think times also had smaller number of moves. As we saw above, relative difference in task completion times of replicated and centralized architectures decreases as input sequence length decreases. We do not deduce or validate these predictions through experiments because of lack of space.

Conclusions and Future Work

This paper makes several contributions.

First, the analysis offers a better understanding of the event flow in centralized and replicated architectures and explains previous experimental results.

Second, the analysis provides several new conclusions regarding the performances of two-user architectures such as (a) centralizing the application on the slower machine is sometimes the optimal solution, (b) centralizing the application on the faster machine can be better than replicating, and (c) as the duration of the collaboration increases, the difference in performances of centralized and replicated architectures gets magnified.

Third, the analysis provides guidance for users with varying degrees of choice regarding the collaborative systems they use. For users who are bound to a particular collaboration system, we offer an analysis of how changes to the collaboration parameters can help improve performance. Given a choice of systems that support a single collaborative architecture or that bind a session to an architecture at session start time, we provide a way to make a better decision about which system or architecture to select to obtain optimal performance. When a system supports runtime architecture changes, we help decide which architecture to use as the user and system parameters change.

Lastly, as secondary contributions we report results of our user studies. The logs we collected from actual usage give values of user parameters such as think times and number of user actions that are relevant to performance. The performances we report from the replays of synthetic logs generated from the user parameters constitute new empirical results in this area.

Further work is needed to make and verify additional predictions based on our analyses, use actual user logs for making measurements, relax assumptions made in our analysis, and build a system module that automatically changes the architecture based on the analysis and current values user and system parameters. We hope this first-cut at a formal model will be a catalyst for such work.

Acknowledgements

This research was funded in part by *Microsoft* and NSF grants ANI 0229998, EIA 03-03590, and IIS 0312328. We also thank Tynia Yang, Ankur Agiwal, John Calandrino, Enes Junuzovic, Jason Sewall, Stephen Titus, and Ben Wilde, our user study participants, who volunteered their time on a very short notice.

References

Ahuja, S., Ensor, J.R., Lucco, S.E. (1990): 'A Comparison of Application Sharing Mechanisms in Real-time Desktop Conferencing Systems', *Proceedings of the conference on Office Information Systems*, 1990, pp: 238-248.

Chung, G. and Dewan P. (2001): 'Flexible Support for Application-Sharing Architecture', *Proceedings of the European Conference on Computer Supported Cooperative Work*, 2001.

Chung, G and Dewan P. (2004): 'Towards Dynamic Collaboration Architectures', *Proceedings of the 2004 ACM conference on Computer Supported Cooperative Work*, 2004.

Danskin, J., Hanrahan, P. (1994): 'Profiling the X Protocol', *Proceedings of the 1994 ACM Conference on Measurement and Modeling of Computer Systems*, 1994, pp: 272-273.

Droms, R., Dyksen, W. (1990): 'Performance Measures of the X Window System Communication Protocol', *Software – Practice and Experience (SPE)*, vol. 20, no. S2, 1990, pp: 119-136.

Dyck, J., Gutwin, C. Subramanian, S., Fedak, C. (2004): 'High-performance Telepointers', *Proceedings of the 2004 ACM conference on Computer Supported Cooperative Work*, 2004.

NEC 2000: 'Windows 2000 Terminal Services Capacity and Scaling', *NEC*, 2000 .

Nieh, J., Yang, S. and Novik, N. (2000): 'A Comparison of Thin Client Computing Architectures', *Technical Report CUCS-022-00 Columbia University*, November 2000.

Richardson, T., Stafford-Fraser, Q., Wood, K., Hopper, A. (1998): 'Virtual Network Computing', *IEEE Internet Computing*, vol. 2, no. 1, January/February 1998, pp. 33-38.

Wong, A., Seltzer, M. (2000): 'Evaluating Windows NT Terminal Server Performance', *Proceedings of the 3rd USENIX Windows NT Symposium*, July 1999, pg: 145-154.

H. Gellersen et al. (eds.), ECSCW 2005: Proceedings of the Ninth European
Conference on Computer-Supported Cooperative Work, 18-22 September 2005, Paris,
France, 103–122.

Working Together Inside an Emailbox[1]

Michael J. Muller and Daniel M. Gruen

Collaborative User Experience / IBM Research, Cambridge MA, USA

{michael_muller, daniel_gruen} @us.ibm.com

Abstract. In this paper we look at a situation in which email is not simply a channel for collaboration and communication but a site of collaboration itself, involving email inboxes that are jointly accessed by more than one person. We conducted two studies of shared email usage. We learned about a diversity of shared email practices in 14 schools, museums, and support centers through semi-structured interviews and (where feasible) site visits. We also explored in depth one type of shared email usage: executives and assistants sharing an emailbox. We describe the strategies that people use today to meet their collaborative needs by exploiting mailbox structures they currently have. We close with a discussion of email as a site of reinvention – i.e., where users' work practices have given existing technology new meanings.

Introduction

Many studies in the past have examined the role email plays in people's work and personal lives, the methods they use to manage and organize mail, and the problems people face from ever increasing volume and overload (Bälter, 1998; Ducheneaut and Bellotti, 2000; Sproull and Kiesler, 1991; Whittaker and Sidner, 1996). In these studies, email is viewed as a tool for communication and collaboration, generally in support of some other task or activity (see also Bellotti et al., 2003; Boardman, 2002; Muller at al., 2004).

---

[1] A brief report of this work appeared as a poster at CSCW 2002 (Muller & Gruen, 2002).

By contrast, this paper focuses on the interesting situation in which email itself is the object or site of the collaboration. Such situations exist in several contexts. One context is the collaboration that occurs between managers and assistants who share access and responsibility for the same mail file. A broader class of contexts occurs when organizations or individuals establish an email alias to a function or service, so that clients and/or customers have a simple way of finding that function or service. We will consider each of these cases, beginning with diverse examples of this broader class.

Email Aliases to Functions, Services, or Roles

Many organizations have provided an email alias to a function or service. Using generic wording, examples include the following:
- Information@museum.org
- Admissions@school.edu
- Recruiters-hotline@company.intranet.com
- orders@catalog-merchant.com

A common configuration involves a group or team in-box, to which information and queries are sent. In some cases, complete workflow systems are built to support these settings; in others, teams have devised procedures and tools to manage their work. In addition, individuals and organizations have made less formal arrangements to enable and coordinate activities in shared mailboxes.

This study helped us to understand the diversity of shared email usages, in which individuals and organizations have improvised working practices to make a technology designed for individual use into a technology suited for shared use – a process called "reinvention" in the sociotechnical systems literature (e.g., Tornatsky and Fleischer, 1992; see below). This first study also provides a general context for our second, in-depth examination of how assistants and their executives have adapted email for their joint use.

Executives and Assistants

During visits to our company's Executive Briefing Center, chief information officers and other high-level executives of our customers mentioned a need for mechanisms to support the way executives and assistants work together. It became clear that they were interested both in technological solutions, and in understanding the practices others in similar situations have developed. We also began to believe that executives and/or their assistants had begun redefining (or reinventing) email features – i.e., that they had taken existing features, but used them in novel and inventive ways.

The insights learned through this study also suggest features and capabilities that would be useful to individual email users in their own email work. And they point to the fact that, to some extent, most users do have some need to collaborate around email; for example, the email writer who forwards a copy of a message to a colleague to check over it before sending it out, or the recipient who forwards a message to a colleague for handling.

An Earlier Study of Assistants

In an earlier study, we observed meetings in which assistants and managers reviewed received mail together ("Mail Sessions", discussed below) with the goal of informing the design of a computerized collaborative assistant by understanding human assistants work practices (Gruen et al., 1999). We reported five categories of work by the human assistants:

- **Pre-Processing:** Assistants frequently gathered additional information and prepared items in other ways before passing them to the manager.
- **Filtering/Prioritizing:** Assistants selected the messages that needed the manager's attention, and often ordered them by priority. They also determined if any required that they interrupt the manager immediately.
- **Adding Relevant Information:** Assistants provided additional information, such as a reminder of a sender's affiliation, both when first presenting a message and while the manager read it.
- **Delegating Complex Tasks:** Assistants frequently performed a number of complex steps in response to a single, often brief, request.
- **Peripheral Awareness/Drawing Attention to Items of Interest:** Assistants frequently pointed out information they thought their manager's would find important, such as the mention of a colleague in a message.

In the current study we look in detail at how assistants and executives communicate and collaborate around email, in service of the above goals.

Shared Mailboxes in Diverse Organizations

Our broad examination of shared mailboxes in organizations presented operational difficulties. The concept of shared mailboxes is so counter-intuitive that many people who work in this manner do not think about it in these terms. Further, some people who work in this way consider it to be a strange kind of work-around, and were therefore somewhat embarrassed to talk about it. Some companies arrange their shared mailboxes in ways that they prefer to keep private. In one example, a company did not wish to reveal that an executive's published email address was *never* read by that executive. In a second example, a company was reluctant to acknowledge that its customer care operations were conducted by a separate "out-sourced" company. As a result, our ability to collect sample artifacts and verbatim recordings of our interviews and observations was severely restricted.

Our interviews began with an explanation of what we meant by "shared email" or "shared mailbox." Discussions then proceeded in an opportunistic manner, pursuing the most interesting aspects of each informant's experience. We attempted to collect relatively simple data (e.g., "how many people share this mailbox or alias?"), but some of our informants considered even that kind of data to be too revealing. We also asked for stories or broad-based accounts (e.g., "how do multiple users of this mailbox coordinate their work?"), and we were somewhat more successful at collecting this kind of informal account.

In this broad-based approach, we conducted telephone interviews at three online catalogue companies, a corporate internal human resources hotline for recruiters, a corporate executive's public email addresses, two corporate webmasters, a college/graduate institution, and a student organization.

In addition, we conducted preliminary telephone interviews followed by field visits and observations a museum customer-relations site, two corporate customer-support sites, and one school.

Findings

Our report on the shared mailboxes begins with an introduction to the sites, and then a thematic summary of findings that showed interesting similarities and differences across sites, from the largest to the smallest team sizes. The Minority Student Organization's novel use of the shared mailbox is presented last.

Sites: Online Catalogue Companies

We conducted telephone interviews with three online catalogue companies, and conducted follow-up site visits at two of them. Each company published an email address on the company's website, and often communicated that address to customers in emails and in printed materials. When each customer's email arrived at the alias, it was put into a general mailbox or, for more specialized mail-handling technology, into a queue for analysis and processing. In some cases, a human agent gave each email a cursory examination, and routed it into an appropriate queue for a specialized team. In other cases, the company's website required users to self-categorize their emails through pull-down menus. The self-categorizations were recorded as part of the emails' headers, and were used for automatic queuing to specific teams with specific competencies.

These sites were the most operationally complex. They had the largest numbers of people *directly* involved in dealing with the emails (but see "Museum" and "Executives' public email addresses," below, for larger groups of people who might be involved in a more diffuse way). Teams of workers acted in an email version of a traditional customer-care call-in center. In all cases, the respective company offered more products than any one worker could know about, and workers made routine reference to both online and paper product descriptions and help information. These sites typically applied well-defined work-quality norms to their work, including criteria for responsiveness, accuracy, and identity/branding requirements. These themes are pursued in the "Identity" theme section, below.

A second aspect of complexity at these sites was coordination. In the simplest terms, coordination was needed to make sure that each customer's email was answered by only one employee – however, this coordination issue became more complex in practice (see the "Coordination" theme section, below).

A third aspect of complexity – knowledge management – was a result of the size of the teams handling various customer requests or inquiries. While team size varied according to a number of factors (customer demand, particular sales campaigns, seasonal issues), the overall staffing of customer response centers was between 20 and 40 people. Sites varied in how they supported employees' responses to high-frequency customer questions. These observations will be pursued further in the "Knowledge Management" theme section, below.

Site: Museum

The Museum's shared email usage was similar in some ways to the online catalogue companies. The Museum' website maintained an active online presence, which was used by schools, other museums, and individual members/customers. The site provided information about exhibits, schedules, programs, and travel directions. The website provided an email alias through which people could ask questions and make arrangements for visits. A small team (fewer than 20 people, with much seasonal variation and only modest training) answered those emails.

In practice, the most frequent users of the Museum's customer response center were schools that wanted to arrange for class visits to the Museum. Arrangements for the visits usually involved steps that included initial inquiries, initial commitments, and then (in the majority of cases) major changes to those commitments. The customer response center was well-versed in dealing with all of those easily-recognized phases of visits.

A second high-frequency work item was the correction of unintentional double-billing of customers' credit cards. Again, the customer-response center had well-defined and well-documented ways to deal with these issues.

A third type of inquiry was less standardized. This inquiry was a request for information about the contents of a Museum exhibit, or about one of the topics that fell within the Museum's mission. In these cases, the task of the customer response center was to route the request to the appropriate staff expert. This set of work practices will be pursued in the "Coordination" theme section, below.

Site: Corporate Webmasters

We interviewed two members of an informal team of corporate Webmasters.[2] Members of this team worked in a diversity of roles within the company's Information Technology (IT) departments. They had a rotation of serving as "webmaster of the day," and one of the responsibilities of the webmaster of the day was to read the email addressed to "webmaster@[company-name].com", with an informal commitment to "leave the mailbox empty" at the end of their shift or day of webmaster duty. It was thus the responsibility of each webmaster of the day to resolve any issues that came through the mailbox – at least to the extent of assigning the task or problem to an appropriate staff member.

Site: Human Resources Recruiter Hotline

The Human Resources (HR) Recruiter Hotline was an internal support activity within its company, for technical members of the company's staff who spent a small amount of their time at university campuses, recruiting new employees. These recruiters were not professional HR workers. They therefore often fielded students' questions for which they did not know the answer; they also needed to hand off any resumés that they received to an HR professional. The HR department provided an intranet website to support these recruiters, but of course the HR department could not anticipate every question. Moreover, the recruiters were often at university campuses during the day, and could relay their questions to the HR staff only during the evenings (when no one was available to answer questions). The HR department provided a single email alias for recruiters' questions, as well as for electronic resumés; a small team (n=2-4) of trained, full-time HR professionals read the emails, returned answers (or obtained answers and then relayed them), and received and processed the resumés.

Site: Corporate Executives' Public Email Addresses

We found one corporate internet website that offered direct email access to certain executives – e.g., "send an email to Sean" (we have changed the name). We were surprised to learn that the named executive read exactly *none* of the emails. We were also surprised to learn that the company in question published email addresses for several key executives, and that all of the emails to those addresses were read by the same clerical worker. The clerical worker had no formal background or training for this task; it appeared that the worker and her supervision had defined the responsibilities in an ad hoc manner, over time. If the

---

[2]   The title of "webmaster" is used for an astonishing variety of corporate roles, ranging from very senior members of Information Technology organizations, to temporary workers who maintain the text contents of a few web pages. We restricted our investigation to people who had broad and senior responsibilities for corporate internet or intranet infrastructures.

executives read none of the emails, we asked, then what was the purpose of the published addresses? The manager of the clerical worker explained that many inquiries to the company were addressed to top executives, but were more properly handled by other people in the company. Some of the inquiries were about company finances, and some were about employment (often including an electronic resumé that could be relayed directly to the HR department's email alias, as described in the preceding section). Some of the inquiries were technical, including proposals for products; these were often referred to the relevant expert in the company.

We encountered a number of coordination and knowledge management issues with this role, as described in the appropriate thematic sections, below.

Sites: Grade School and Graduate Institute

We conducted telephone interviews with the people who read emails send to aliases of the form "information@school.edu" – one at a Grade School, and one at a Graduate Institute. We were permitted to make a site visit (but not an observation) at the Grade School. At both of these organizations, the person who read the email had primarily clerical and/or receptionist responsibilities, and acted largely as an initial screener and router of inquiries. Thus, the emails were part of a diversity of routine communication-routing tasks for this worker.

Initially, this responsibility appears to be similar to that of the Corporate Executives' Public Email Addresses (above), but there were important differences. The corporate situations involved large and (often) geographically distributed work forces; the clerical worker found experts either by consulting a corporate directory, or by asking for advice from local management. By contrast, at the Grade School and the Graduate Institute, the clerical worker relayed inquiries to people in the same building – often people with whom s/he was on a first-name basis. These differences in remoteness and impersonality will be discussed further in the "Coordination" theme section, below.

Site: Minority Student Organization

We interviewed a past leader of a minority student engineering association (we will refer to this group as the Minority Student Organization in this paper). The Student Organization's use of a shared email address was in subtle contrast with the use of the organizations profiled above. The Student Organization was largely unconcerned with *incoming* email, which was usually sent directly to named members of the organization in their own personal email inboxes. Rather, the Student Organization used its shared email address for *outgoing* emails, in order to present a consistent "face" to other organizations. This usage will be detailed in the "Identity" theme section, below.

Comparing and Contrasting Sites: Emergent Themes

Four major themes emerged from reflection and analysis of the broad investigation into shared mailboxes:[3] Generalized architectures; Coordination; Identity; and Knowledge management. We will consider each theme, in turn, integrating experiences at various sites to describe and explore each theme.

Theme: Architectures

Looking across the sites, we found several general architectural approaches to the problem of adapting the single-user technology of email into a multiple-user point of collaboration.

Relatively small-scale sites, including Human Resources Hotline, Webmasters, Corporate Executives, Grade School, and Graduate Institute, appeared to use a simple architecture, in which one or more email aliases fed directly into a conventional emailbox. In general, a single person would access that mailbox at a time, although there were significant exceptions. The small-scale architectures left emailboxes largely unchanged, except for the addition of an email alias. Most of the adaptations for sharing the mailbox were carried through work practices, such as the "webmaster of the day" role. This use of work practices to implement sharing of a single-user interface was also the case for the Student Organization.

In contrast, the larger-scale applications had a very different, customized architecture. The customer response centers divided their incoming emails into distinct groups of messages on different topics (e.g., different product groups or different industry segments). Different teams of employees handled messages from these different groups of emails. In some cases, employees were assigned to teams because of their knowledge or because of specific training that qualified them to resolve customer inquiries on particular products or for particular industry segments. In other cases, it appeared that employees were assigned to different teams as a matter of load-balancing among the message queues.

Although we did not interview systems architects, we discerned two distinct configurations to manage these groups of email messages. One configuration used formal queues into which email messages were placed, and the other configuration used separate but conventional emailboxes in place of queues. The queue-based configuration was a specialized application that took messages from email and put them into a different and non-email-mediated work-management system. The multiple-emailbox configuration was a sophisticated use of the kinds of resources that are supposed by some email systems.

---

3   In addition to these four content- and work- related themes, we also heard a lot about the problem of spam ("junk" email), which was described as having measurable impacts on productivity at some of the corporate sites. Strategies for dealing with spam are beyond the scope of this paper.

Theme: Coordination

The differences between these two architectures are important. In the cases of the queues, any number of people could work on the same queue, because the act of accessing a message also removed that message from the queue. In the case of the emailboxes, accessing a message did not remove it from the inbox, and therefore "we can have a maximum team size of two people" [informant, customer response center 2] for each inbox, with one person reading the newest messages, and the other person reading the oldest messages in the inbox.

Other differences were also important. Queue-based systems generally provided the means of tracking each message, if necessary, as well as means of tracking each person who worked on the queue. By contrast, mailbox-based systems were less governable. A common way to avoid having more than one person working on a message at the same time was for the first person to move the message from the shared inbox and into her/his own inbox. Unfortunately, "after that, no one can find the message" [informant, Museum]. If the person who had moved the message left work before the messages was answered or resolved, then no one else knew where the message was. An illness or a holiday could cause a message to remain "lost" (from the perspective of everyone else on the team) until the absent person returned

In general, managers of shared mailboxes believed "no, we don't have any coordination problems" [e.g., manager, customer response center 1]. However, our interviews and our observations showed that there were low-frequency and seemingly inevitable coordination problems, even in the queue-based customer response center. One manager admitted, "We are struggling as to how to organize our messages – by person [employee] or date or client or what" [manager, customer response center 1]. As the managers said, coordination around *single* email messages was easy in a queue-based system – but only (as the workers informed us) if a customer did not send in multiple messages. During an evening shift, our principal informant told us that he checked for multiple messages by calling out to the only other employee who was working that queue – "he's like my wing man" [informant, customer response center 1]. This strategy for coordination would, of course, break down with more people on each queue, or with a larger work force during a daytime shift.

A second set of coordination issues occurred around the forwarding of emails. As noted in the site descriptions, above, part of the work of many of the sites was to forward inquiries to a subject matter expert if they could not be resolved by the employee who first read the message. This was a common event at the Museum site, and a moderately frequent event at both customer response centers. It was the dominant activity on the executives' public email address site, where the clerical worker who read the email acted primarily as a router to other people in other parts of the company.

We asked how these forwarded emails were tracked, and we received very different answers. As noted above, queue-based customer-response operations often provided for tracking within the email-queue technology. By contrast, situations that made use of simpler mailboxes required more active human management of tracking. Some members of the customer response centers kept records of messages that they had sent to other departments, and followed-up to make sure that the recipient of the forwarded message answered it; this assurance of an answer had become part of the quality-of-service metrics for that center. By contrast, for the executives' public email addresses site, neither the clerical worker nor her/his management tracked any message, so there was no way to determine if a particular inquiry had received a response. The two educational sites both had informal, face-to-face-based ways of tracking responses.

Identity

The Museum site made an effort to send most outbound replies out through the same mailbox as the inbound inquiries, even if employees had to go through extra steps to make this happen. The manager of the Museum team spoke of maintaining a "single point of contact" – a concept which was echoed by the managers of both customer response sites (e.g., "a single identity to the customer"). This use of the same email identity for both outbound and inbound messages was considered helpful for several reasons:

- First, the practice made the emailbox (or its alias) a known and reliable way for customers to reach the company. In an informal way, the emailbox began to function as a brand.
- Second, the practice reduced the salience of any particular employee in the customer response center, because customers were encouraged to write back to the center as a whole, and not to a particular person in the center. This, of course, had both positive and negative implications – less personal treatment, but greater likelihood of a quick response.

Another customer care center added its own distinctive signature phrase at the end of each email, and required that all response emails have the same subject line, "[company-name] Replies...". Thus, the customer care center had turned the email subject line into a kind of brand.

The strongest case of identity-management for outbound messages occurred for the Minority Student Organization. This group was concerned to maintain its organizational relationships over a number of years with funders and recruiters, despite the fact that is officers changed every year or at times every semester. They believed that busy people at funding agencies or in human resource departments would be more likely to respond if the email's "from" line were the name of the Minority Student Organization, rather than the name of a particular student. In this case, the "from" line was used exactly as a brand is used. The company that required each response to a customer to have a subject line containing the phrase "[company-name] Replies..." was accomplishing much the same objective – to re-purpose common features of email so as to emphasize an identity or brand to its email correspondents.

Knowledge Management

While many of the sites were concerned to manage their own identities *out* to their customers, none of the sites had any means of managing issues related to the *incoming* identities of their customers. The manager of customer response center 1 lamented that what was really needed was a customer relationship management (CRM) solution – i.e., a database that would track communications with a particular customer, in such a way that all workers in the center would be able to get background on the characteristics of that customer, and would be able to reconstruct the history of past interactions with that customer.

This inability to track emails by originating customer is one of a number of examples of knowledge management (KM) issues in shared mailbox systems and work practices. As noted above in the "Coordination" theme section, tracking of messages by any indexical term was a problem, and companies were "struggling" about the best attributes to use to organize emails into groups. These problems extended to the resources that employees used to find information and to resolve problems, including both printed materials (from one-page memos to technical manuals whose combined pages were almost a meter in thickness), and social knowledge of whom to ask for help (including both co-workers within each customer response center and subject matter experts outside of the customer response centers). Although there were databases of such information, we saw many instances of hand-annotated printed material, and place-marked technical manuals – i.e., inscriptions of private knowledge onto personal materials, with no way to share them to the larger team.

Another major area of KM difficulties occurred in the re-use of standardized or "boilerplate" text in multiple email messages. As mentioned in the site descriptions of customer response centers in Online Catalogue Companies and the Museum, workers often had to respond to similar or identical customer inquiries over and over again. In two of the sites, the company provided a set of standard paragraphs that could be copied into these responses; in a few cases, there appeared to be legal requirements that certain phrases or sentences be used. However, most employees also maintained their own collections of private texts that they would copy into their responses to customers. One company encouraged employees to share these resources, but other companies considered these employee-originated resources as being of questionable quality, requiring a formal approval process before they could be shared with other employees (for a more detailed examination of the production of knowledge, and of the authority to create knowledge for others, see (Muller and Millen, 2000).

Summary

Our study of work practices in shared email showed us
- A variety of architectural configurations supporting shared email usage
- A diversity of work practices, ranging from opportunistic use of standard email features (one worker at a time in small-scale sites) to re-purposing of common email features into new significance (e.g., branding in "subject" and "from" lines) to new application-like configurations for better tracking and load management (large-scale sites)
- Dense and varied patterns of coordination and collaboration, ranging from simple routing to collaborative problem-solving to situations requiring awareness of the work of others within a common online work environment.
- Many partially-realized opportunities to share knowledge, experience, and competence

These observations form a backdrop for our second, in-depth investigation into the issues faced by assistants and their executives in management of shared email.

Assistants and their Executives

For the in-depth study of executives' assistants, we conducted semi-structured interviews with sixteen assistants to high-level managers and executives in a large technology corporation. All assistants shared access to their manager's main email account, and were responsible in various ways for dealing with the mail.

This investigation aimed at analytic depth, in contrast to the breadth-oriented study of shared mailboxes in diverse organizations. We obtained access to the assistants through the corporation's Senior Assistant's Council, an organization established to support the corporation's higher-level assistants. The Senior Assistant's Council participated with us in the content and wording of the questionnaire we used to guide our interviews, to be sure it covered issues they knew were important in the language assistants commonly used. This process itself was an educational one for us, as we got a clearer understanding of the range of responsibilities assistants held. The council also gave us access to the online discussion space in which questions and tips, including several suggestions for dealing with email, appeared.

All assistant in this study used Lotus Notes as their main email application, and for calendaring and scheduling.

Interviews

Each of the sixteen semi-structured interviews lasted 45-60. All but two of the interviews were conducted by phone. All but one of the sessions was audiotaped (one of the subjects preferring not to be recorded.). Throughout the interviews we asked for specific anecdotes, stories, and examples that illustrated the points the assistants were making.

The semi-structured interviews began with our asking about the setting in general and the role the assistant played, including the general business functions of the group, the people involved, and their collaborative tools. We asked the assistant to describe a typical day, or, if it was easier, to start by describing what they were working on that day. We then asked more directed questions about the email that arrived, its volume, how it was organized, how often they checked it, who had access to it, and to describe what they did with it. We asked how they communicated with their manager about mail, if they sent mail on behalf of the manager, how they knew to do so, and how the manager knew that they had sent the mail. We asked about deleting and filing of email. Finally, we asked generally about how the practices and systems the assistants and managers used together had evolved, what problems they had encountered, and what they had done to solve them.

Findings

Assistants described the overall goals of their work in terms of the performance of the manager they supported. One said simply the goal was to "make the boss look good." In practice, this involved keeping the office running smoothly, making sure managers were where they were supposed to be on time, and making sure they were prepared with the information and materials they needed to be effective.

Other descriptions of goals included:

"keep everything running smoothly and in order" (s1)

"make his day run as smoothly as it can, make sure he gets to where he needs to be"(s8)

"to make [the manager's] job as easy as possible, make the day run as smoothly as possible"(s9)

"insure the office is run smoothly, that there are no conflicts," and making sure the manager *"is confident whether he is going to meet with internal or external people." (s14)*

"trying to keep everything in order, to minimize escalations" (s7)

"to make sure he could make it through the day without missing something," and *"to make sure he didn't have to worry about preparing for things."(s16)*

"make sure [the manager] is where he needs to be and has all pertinent information for meetings." (s5)

Specific responsibilities included managing email, managing the calendar, answering phones, and making travel arrangements. As mentioned above, an overarching responsibility involved keeping the manager informed of the day's schedule, and making sure the manager had documents and information as needed throughout the day.

Eight of the assistants reported the manager receiving over 100 messages on a typical day, with half of those reporting 150 messages a day or more. Six estimated between 30 and 50 messages. One reported "at least 20", and one said the volume varied substantially from day to day. All but two of the subjects reported checking the mail "constantly" or "all day", with the others checking "about every half hour," or "several times a day, perhaps once an hour." The Lotus Notes program allows users to keep several mailboxes open at a given time, and assistants reported shifting frequently throughout the day between their own and their manager's mailboxes.

Most assistants reported preparing packets for their managers to use containing information they needed for each of their meetings throughout the day, or for each of the days during which they were traveling. These packets often included printed copies of crucial emails, the executive's calendar, and the (increasingly rare) physical mail that pertained to the meetings or travel periods.

Assistants' Shared Email Challenges

Several key challenges recurred in the assistants' discussion of how they worked with their managers' email.

Awareness of Past Activity

All assistants reported the need to be aware of actions the other person had taken on a given message. While in general, this referred to needing to know if a message had been forwarded, filed, or responded to, three assistant mentioned the importance of knowing if a manager had in fact read a message. As there was no direct way to have this awareness, assistants resorted to two main strategies:

- Assistants frequently checked the "sent mail" folder to see if the manager had replied to messages or generated new ones (5 assistants), and
- Managers and assistants copied each other when sending mail (9 assistants).

Assistants reported dissatisfaction with both of these mechanisms. Checking a separate folder (or even searching in a list) for messages required extra actions, and managers occasionally forgot to cc or bcc their assistant on mail they sent.

As mentioned above, three assistants reported the need to know if their manager had read a message. This is because they saw a part of their role being to keep the manager up to date on important new information. Absent any technological way to know if the manager had read a message, they resorted to calling, instant-messaging, or in some cases sending additional email messages asking "did you see the message about X."

These difficulties of the assistants are similar to some of the problems that we observed in the first study. In that study, we encountered difficulties in knowing who was doing what (or who had *done* what) in large-scale teams or queues in the customer response centers. And we observed that the clerical employees who routed emails for the Grade School, Graduate Institute, and Corporate Executives' Public Email Addresses sites had no formal or online way of determining whether people had acted on the messages that they had forwarded. Similarly, only one of the customer response centers had any mechanism for closure on a forwarded message, and the informal work practices (also involving cc messages) were often not followed.

Awareness of Current Activity

Three assistants reported a desire to know what actions their manager was taking at that moment. They described situations in which this would have been useful both in seeing that the manager was already dealing with a message, and in being able to communicate additional information related to the message.

Communicating About Messages

All assistants described the need to communicate about messages and the actions to be taken with them. Mechanisms they used included:

- Using folders to indicate actions to be taken (such as "[*Assistant-name*]-To-Do", or "Print");
- Using folders to delegate items to others who shared the emailbox;
- Leaving notes by editing the messages themselves and inserting new text, in a way clearly recognizable as being added by the assistant;
- Sending separate emails about the message to the manager, or from the manager to the assistant's personal account;
- Using another medium, such as telephone, chat, or face-to-face discussion.

Some manager-assistant pairs used folders not only as a way to categorize messages for filtering or storage, but also to indicate actions in a way similar to ad-hoc workflow. For example, the manager would place an item they wanted printed into a folder marked "Print". The assistant would print the message, and then remove it from the folder or place in it a folder marked "Done."

In some cases, a team of assistants would share access to the manager's mailbox. For example, one manager had one assistant for email, telephone and calendaring, a second assistant who acted as an executive assistant and accompanied him to meetings, and a third "technical assistant" who served as the key liaison to the other managers who reported to the manager. Folders were used as a way of delegating a message to a specific assistant, or to indicate that an assistant had taken responsibility for a specific message. These practices are of course similar to patterns observed in the first study, in which messages in large-scale centers could be routed to specific inboxes or queues, to be worked by specific functional teams.

Four assistants reported editing an incoming email message to add comments for the manager to see. In many cases, these were summaries of a longer message, distilling the essential points for the manager, and sometimes including other relevant information. In others, they would include a description of how the assistant had handled an item, or a question on what to do with it. For example, a long, wordy message inviting the manager to give a presentation might be summarized by a few words added at the top: "They're inviting you to give a talk. It's the week you're in Denver. I've told them no."

Assistants would occasionally send messages from their personal accounts to their manager's account to draw their attention to an important message, ask a question, or describe how they handled a situation. Managers sent messages to their assistant's accounts to ask questions or request actions, sometimes forwarding a relevant message they had received.

Keeping Up With Incoming Mail

Assistants expressed the importance of keeping up with the incoming mail. Two common methods for dealing with incoming mail were:
- Scheduling regular meetings with the managers to review the day's email
- Using folders to separate mail by priority.

Five assistants reported daily, scheduled meetings with the manager to discuss new correspondence needing the manager's attention. Although these meetings often covered a range of issues, they were commonly known as "Mail Sessions." All five reported conducting some form of these meetings by phone when the manager was traveling. A nice feature of these meetings was that they bundled together small discussions that would otherwise require separate interruptions, while insuring that the issues would be addressed in a timely fashion.

Four assistants reported creating electronic folders specifically aimed at separating new mail by priority. For example, one subject described a folder marked "Today", with items requiring immediate action or needed for that day's activities; a folder marked "For-Action", with items requiring some activity or decision by the manager; a folder marked "FYI", with items of the manager "would want to know about" but which required no specific action; and a folder marked "Personal", containing the managers personal Human Resources items and correspondence from family and friends.

Five assistants reported trying to keep the quantity of mail in the generic inbox down to a minimum, in one case to "about half a screen-full", in another "down to about ten or twenty messages". These messages represented items that required additional actions to file, delegate, reply, or act upon them in some other way. The set of messages in this view thus served as an indication of some of the work the assistant and/or manager still needed to perform.

Dealing With Volume of Saved Mail

Email messages were frequently saved, both for the specific information they contained and because they served as a record of past activities and contacts. Four assistants reported that they hardly ever deleted anything except for obvious junk mail. One reported that she would often delete earlier entries in an email thread if the later messages contained the text of the prior ones quoted as history. Another reported going through saved mail older than 30 days every month and removing items that were no longer needed.

The assistants employed several strategies to organize the mail they saved:

- Filing items in folders by subject or project;
- Filing items by sender or category of sender;
- Filing items by date (typically current month and year).

These different filing strategies are almost identical to the problematic approaches that the manager of Customer Care Center 1 reported he was "struggling" with. However, perhaps because of the lower overall volume of emails, these strategies appeared to be more effective for the assistants. Despite the fact that the quantity of saved mail continued to increase over time, assistants reported little trouble in finding older items when needed. A common strategy for locating past messages was to go to an "All Documents" view which showed all messages regardless of the folders in which they had been placed. Assistants sorted the view by name and/or date, or ran a text search by keyword. Six assistants reported using this strategy as their main method for finding old messages, and each of the others mentioned it as a backup strategy in case they couldn't easily find a message by looking in specific folders.

Date-Related Messages

Three assistants used dated "tickler" folders to store printed messages that were relevant to events occurring on future days. Numbered from 1-31, these folders referred to the date in the current or next month, with a separate future folder for items more than 31 days in the future.) Each evening, the assistant would extract the documents the manager would need to be informed for meetings and other events the following day. These would either be given to the manager at night to take home, or left in a "today" folder to be looked at first thing in the morning.

Printing Messages

Assistants frequently printed messages, either to store in physical folders associated with a project or date, to have active items they needed to work on easily available ("hot items", in the terms of one assistant), for placement in the packets given to the manager (such as with material for a meeting or trip), or to bring in to the Mail Sessions that five of the assistants reported having. These printed items were often annotated with pen or sticky-notes indicating the actions taken or which needed to be taken.

Interestingly, one of the common requests by managers was for the assistant to print a message or attachment. At first this struck us as odd; why didn't the manager simply print the message? Upon further discussion, it became clear that the request meant more than simply instructing the software to send it to the printer. The assistant would print the message, staple or bind it as needed, and then leave it in a place (such as on the manager's desk) where it would be seen.

Discussion

Bellotti and Ducheneaut (2000) described "Email as Habitat," arguing that email is more than just a frequently used application, but rather the place in which many workers spend most of their time and which guides and shapes their work. Our study suggests that it can be important to ask *who else is in that place with you*, and argues for email not only as personal habitat but as a shared, collaborative workplace. As such, it deserves the same support known to be important for teams in other shared environments. This includes situational awareness of current and past activity, joint understanding and construction of goals, communication, coordination of actions, and resources that can be shared, discussed, referred to, and jointly constructed (Schmidt & Bannon, 1992; Olson & Olson, 1999). In a related development, emailboxes and other messaging environments may also become sites of task management on an individual or group basis (Bellotti et al, 2003; Boardman, 2002; Muller et al., 2004).

In these studies, features of email that had been developed primarily with the single user in mind were re-purposed to support collaboration among two or more people. For example, folders were used as work-routing or load-balancing mechanisms, to signal priority or to communicate actions to be taken or which were taken. A feature allowing received mail to be edited was used to add additional information about a message, or to report on how an issue had been handled. Standard portions of the email header ("subject" and "from" lines) were re-purposed into statements of corporate identity or branding opportunities. Messages were forwarded between managers and assistants as a way of drawing attention to them, and to discuss how they should be handled. The size of the current inbox served as a representation of currently outstanding activities.

This use of available structures to support collaboration parallels a key aspect of the distributed cognition approach (Hutchins, 1995), in which cognition is seen to occur not just within the head of an individual but through the manipulation of representational state by actors in interaction with external artifacts. Here, various configurations of workers used traditional email features in novel ways to support and coordinate their collaborative email work. Activity Theory might characterize the shared email repository as a form of mediation, a social tool containing emails as social objects owned by a community of workers (e.g., Nardi, 1996).

These accounts are examples of reinvention by the users of existing features of email. Reinvention occurs when users discover new, unanticipated uses for existing technologies (Tornatsky and Fleischer, 1992). In our study, users treated message lists as performance reports, comment fields as instructions, mailboxes as identity statements, and folders as action-requests or status indicators. By turning the technology to new purposes, they "reinvented" it in usage, even if they did not change its internal functionality. This concept has been important in HCI and CSCW studies of group decision support systems (Bikson and Eveland, 1996), telephony services (Antón and Potts, 2001), and IT adoption (Muller and Millen, 2001), informed in part by earlier research from social studies of technology (e.g., Rogers, 1995; Sproull and Kiesler, 1991; Tornatsky and Fleischer, 1992). Reinvention has also been a theme in users' re-purposing of technology in the participatory design tradition (Floyd, 1987).

When we consider our findings through the lens of reinvention, we see typical evolutionary cycles. As Bikson and Eveland note, "Successful technologies are usually those that can achieve reciprocal adaptation with the social organization" (1996, p.436). Our informants were in various stages of adapting the technology to their work practices (subfolders, workflows, special forms of forwarding, report-generation), and of adapting their work practices to the technology (assignment of incoming traffic, work-arounds to achieve a common "from" address, social protocols to track assignment to subject matter experts). As we consider improvements to email, we should be mindful of this dialogue between technology and use. As Bikson and Eveland conclude, "Without invention, there are no tools. Without reinvention, there are no uses" (1996, p. 437).

Conclusions

Collaboration through shared emailboxes is an example of how tools developed primarily with individual users in mind are re-purposed to support shared work. We have described a variety of situations in which formal or informal teams share responsibility for an emailbox, and as the use of email increases, we would expect the number of such situations to increase as well. A growing body of evidence supports the notion of email as the place in which many workers "live". The studies described here suggest expanding our view of email — not just as individual habitat, but as a collaborative space in which people work together.

Acknowledgments

Thanks to Regina Tassone for assistance in conducting the interviews and in collating data. Thanks also to members of the Senior Assistants Council who assisted with the study.

References

Antón, A.I., and Potts, C. (2001). Functional paleontology: System evolution as the user sees it. *IEEE Conf. on Software Engineering.* Toronto ON Canada: IEEE.

Bälter, O. (1998). *Electronic Mail in a Working Context.* Doctoral Dissertation, Royal Institute of Technology, Stockholm.

Bellotti, V., Ducheneaut, N., Howard, M., Smith, I., "Taking Email to Task: The Design and Evaluation of a Task Management Centered Email Tool," *Proc. CHI 2003,* Ft. Lauderdale FL USA: ACM.

Bikson, T.K., and Eveland, J.D. (1996). Groupware implementation: Reinvention in the sociotechnical frame. *Proc CSCW'96.* Cambridge MA USA: ACM.

Boardman, R., "Workspaces that Work: Towards Unified Personal Information Management," *Proc. HCI2002.*

Ducheneaut, N. and Bellotti, V. (2001). "Email as a Habitat: an Exploration of Embedded Personal Information Management." In *ACM Interactions,* September-October, 2001.

Floyd, C. (1987). Outline of a paradigm change in software engineering. In G. Bjerknes, P. Ehn, and M. Kyng (eds.). *Computers and democracy: A Scandinavian challenge.* Brookfield VT USA: Gower Press.

Gruen, D., Sidner, C., Boettner, C. and Rich, C. (1999). "A Collaborative Assistant for Email." In *Proc. CHI'99,* Extended Abstracts. Pittsburgh PA USA: ACM.

Hutchins, E. (1995). *Cognition in the Wild.* Cambridge, MA: MIT Press.

Muller, M.J., and Gruen, D.M. (2002). Collaborating *within* – not *through* – email: Users reinvent a familiar technology. Poster at CSCW 2002.

Muller, M.J., Geyer, W., Brownholtz, B., Wilcox, E., and Millen, D.R. (2004). One hundred days in an activity-centric collaboration environment based on shared objects. *Proc. CHI 2004.*

Muller, M.J., and Millen, D.R. (2000) Social construction of knowledge and authority in business communities and organizations. Presented at Human Computer Interaction Consortium meeting, February 2000. Available as TR 01-03 under "Papers" at http://www.research.ibm.com/cambridge (verified 4/25/05).

Nardi, B. (1996). *Context and Consciousness: Activity Theory and Human-Computer Interaction.* Cambridge MA USA: MIT Press.

Olson, J and Olson, G. (1999). "Computer Supported Cooperative Work." In *Handbook of Applied Cognition,* Durso and Dumais, Eds. Sussex: John Wiley and Sons.

Rogers, E. (1995). *Diffusion of innovations* (4th ed.). New York: Free Press.

Schmidt, K. and Bannon, L. (1992). "Taking CSCW Seriously: Supporting Articulation Work." *Computer-Supported Cooperative Work,* 1(7), 7-40.

Sproull, L. and Kiesler, S. (1991). *Connections: New Ways of Working in the Networked Organization.* Cambridge: MIT Press

Tornatsky, L., and Fleischer, M. (1992). *The processes of technological innovation.* Lexington MA USA: Lexington Books.

Whittaker, S. and Sidner, C. (1996). "Email Overload: Exploring Personal Information Management of Email." *Proc. CHI'96.*

H. Gellersen et al. (eds.), ECSCW 2005: Proceedings of the Ninth European Conference on Computer-Supported Cooperative Work, 18-22 September 2005, Paris, France, 123–142.

Emergent Temporal Behaviour and Collaborative Work

Lesley Seebeck[*#], Richard M Kim[*] and Simon Kaplan[#]

[*]The University of Queensland; [#]Queensland University of Technology, Australia

lesley@itee.uq.edu.au; r.kim@uq.edu.au; s.kaplan@qut.edu.au

Abstract. Although collaboration manifestly takes place in time, the role of time in shaping the behaviour of collaborations, and collaborative systems, is not well understood. Time is more than clock-time or the subjective experience of time; its effects on systems include differential rates of change of system elements, temporally non-linear behaviour and phenomena such as entrainment and synchronization. As a system driver, it generates emergent effects shaping systems and their behaviour. In the paper we present a systems view of time, and consider the implications of such a view through the case of collaborative development of a new university timetabling system. Teasing out the key temporal phenomena using the notion of temporal trajectories helps us understand the emergent temporal behaviour and suggests a means for improving outcomes.

Introduction

Socio-technical systems are complex and change with time. Brittle systems handle such changes poorly, while plastic systems are more able to adapt to changing circumstances and requirements. While most readers would consider this assertion to be self-evident, we nonetheless have at best a poor understanding of the drivers underpinning the dynamic of socio-technical systems, and in particular the temporal factors at work in this dynamic. We believe that understanding these drivers will help us to better comprehend system-level behaviours, thus informing good (i.e., more plastic) system design.

Time contributes to the wicked behavior of design problems (Seebeck and Kaplan, 2004), and constitutes a fundamental driver of social systems. Irreversible, time forces change on systems; systems in turn must find some means to handle its effects, or risk a loss of integrity, even dissolution (Luhmann, 1995:41-52). We contend that temporal behavior within socio-technical systems is not the simple enumeration of processual steps, but an *emergent characteristic of the systems and their compositional elements*. While time and its effects are not contributors to all the characteristics of system wickedness, a deeper understanding of temporal effects should improve our ability to cope with that wickedness.

We begin by briefly introducing a case study of the development of a university timetabling system. We will then investigate time and its characteristics and construct a means of analyzing time in systems using the case to illustrate our ideas and argument. Lastly, we draw some conclusions regarding accounting for temporal effects in the design of collaborative systems.

The Case

One of the authors conducted a 12-month longitudinal case study concerning the introduction of a novel academic scheduling system at an Australian university referred to as ASU. He conducted interviews with key players and had access to project and steering committee meetings and teleconferences with the vendor, all of which were taped and transcribed, and had access to project documentation including tenders, notes and policy documents. Kim and Kaplan (2005) describe the co-evolutionary aspects of this case from an actor-network perspective without considering the temporal aspects that we shall consider here.

ASU's Central Timetabling section coordinated class timetabling using a software application called OLDSIS. Schools would enter their scheduling requirements into OLDSIS specifying day, time, class size and room requirements. Once all the requests from the schools had been collated, Central Timetabling would initiate the space optimization function in OLDSIS to automatically allocate centrally controlled rooms against the Schools' predefined timetable. Over recent years however OLDSIS became increasingly unstable and was unsupported by its vendor. Fearing that they would 'break it' if they attempted to re-optimize room allocations, Central Timetabling decided to commence the process by rolling the prior year's timetable forward each year and then adjust the allocations manually.

There was a perception amongst senior management that the university timetable contained significant inefficiencies due to the inability of OLDSIS to produce a 'fully optimized timetable' (i.e., a timetable which optimizes day and time allocations for a class as well as finding an available room), for which it was never designed, to say nothing of its inability to reliably optimize room allocation against a fixed timetable, for which it *was* supposedly designed. Therefore, in August 2002 the university tendered for a replacement for its class and examination timetabling systems. The final decision came to a choice between two systems: COMMONSIS, developed by an English company; and an offering from Stellar, a US company.

Within the national context, two-thirds of Australian universities and six of the seven institutions that ASU regards as its peers use COMMONSIS. Stellar on the other hand offered the mature STRIPES, which like OLDSIS optimized room allocation against a fixed day/time/staff timetable, and its planned flagship product STARS, based on STRIPES and nearing the end of development, which claimed to fully optimize day/time/room/staff assignments. Although Stellar had no sales outside of North America, they tendered and demonstrated STARS saying that it would meet all of the tender requirements without customization. In August 2003 ASU awarded the contract to Stellar. The reasons for that decision will not be examined here except to say that ASU felt that "COMMONSIS [had] had its hour in the sun" and considered it advantageous to be involved in the design and development of a new scheduling system, not least because ASU thought it could influence the design of STARS to best suit itself.

At the time of writing, STARS has yet to be implemented at ASU, 21 months after its first due date, and after four subsequent missed delivery dates. To help us understand why this outcome eventuated, we consider how temporal behaviour influences socio-technical systems and system development and how the lack of understanding of temporal issues and drivers on the part of both Stellar and ASU significantly contributed to these outcomes.

Why Time is Important

When we design complex socio-technical systems, such as computer supported collaborative work (CSCW) systems, we are designing both for, and within the context of, wider socio-technical systems. Such systems are *complex adaptive systems* (Kaplan and Seebeck, 2001): irreducible, heterogeneous, many-bodied systems which exhibit non-linear, emergent behaviour, and all the characteristics of 'wickedness'. The temptation — and often the expectation — in the face of wickedness is to design for the known, defined by the user, the developer or the client organization, and for the static. But without a better understanding of the drivers of wickedness, which can render even careful design brittle or irrelevant, system design remains hostage to complexity and contingency. A similar attention to deep system drivers may be found in Murphy's (2001) consideration of nature's temporalities; in Dourish's (1995) effort to identify a generic set of behaviours underpinning socio-technical systems; and in

Alexander's efforts to understand patterns inherent to good design (1979; 2002). We are concerned with that which makes systems change, shift, evolve and so elude easy diagnosis: time.

In system analysis and design, time and its socio-technical effects are infrequently considered explicitly (Bluedorn and Denhardt, 1988; Butler, 1995; Lee and Liebenau, 2000). There are, of course, a number of worthy exceptions. Time has a not inconsiderable literature within sociology, including Sorokin and Merton (1937), Zerubavel (1981), Adam (1990), and Gell (1992). Within the CSCW field, Reddy and Dourish (2002) investigate the temporal rhythms apparent in an intensive care unit. Huy and Mitzberg (2003) similarly suggest that there's a time and place — a rhythm of change — particular to different organizations, and change should not be forced outside of those rhythms. Orlikowski and Yates (2002) differentiate between objective and subjective time, arguing that in practice people and organizations 'temporally structure' their environments and work. Temporal pacing, like entrainment in organizations (Ancona and Chong, 1996), has been identified as a means of shaping group work (Gersick, 1988; 1994) as well as of dominating industries (Brown and Eisenhardt, 1997). But generally these authors focus on temporal phenomena without addressing their underlying causes.

Time's exclusion leads to problems such as that identified by Dix et al (1998) — the neglect of long pauses, delay and gaps in favor of the interaction in the here and now. Time typically is assumed to be linear; proceeding in unitary step-wise intervals; and homogenous, its effects experienced uniformly across the system — if not simply a constant (Seebeck and Kaplan, 2004). Change in at least part of the system, and often the wider environment, is often held constant. Even within the CSCW discipline, the focus has been more on what people actually do in terms of their work and workplace (eg Bannon, 1995; McCarthy, 2000; Suchman, 1995), and less on how that work might change over time, as a result of economic, technological, social or demographic change.

In part, the exclusion of explicit consideration of temporal effects can be explained through humanity's habit of discounting over time; lower, short-term gains are preferred over higher, but longer-term gains (Fehr, 2002). But when human endeavor *does* plan for longer-term systems and outcomes, then time must be factored in. Time is a major consideration in systems, system development and projects. Artifacts such as calendars, synchronisation, and planning and budgeting cycles enable the coordination of highly complex systems; such is the purpose of the university timetabling system described in our case.

There also are less obvious uses of and challenges presented by time. Teams and management use 'pacing' to achieve outcomes and to resist centrifugal tendencies in organizations (Ancona and Chong, 1996; Gersick, 1988; 1994). Beer (1974) observed that bureaucracies use time as a coping mechanism: delay can be used to eliminate problems, or to aggregate data to a level more easily handled. In our planning efforts we seek to see *through* time, a uniquely human characteristic (Luhmann, 1995). In doing so, we make our best estimate of the system state at some future point and then behave accordingly; the longer the leap through time, the greater the risk of divergence between expectation and reality; too timid a projection, the more likely events will overtake us.

Unpacking Time in Systems

Unpacking our understanding of time, and how time affects systems, is key to accounting for time and improving system design and management. Time is neither uniformly distributed nor homogenous nor linear. This is beyond merely people's perceptions, and the notion of constructed time (Butler, 1995; Nowotny, 1994), but resides deep within the system and its dynamics — it extends beyond the social (Gell, 1992:89). Time in systems has three key behavioural characteristics: different elements have differing rates of change; time affects the system non-linearly; and interacting elements with similar temporal characteristics will tend to synchronize.

Differing rates of change: All socio-technical systems, such as CSCW systems, workplaces, even information systems, are comprised of many interacting parts, whether modularised and interdependent, as within an IT system, or free-flowing and non-hierarchical, as in society more generally. Each part or agent within the system has its own integral temporal behaviour. For example, our bodies respond to circadian rhythms, entrained by the natural environment (Strogatz, 2003). Artifacts decay unless attended to and maintained on a regular basis. Rest and replenishment and a resumption of normal temporal patterns must balance periods of abnormal, usually increased, tempo. But change does not occur in lockstep across the system: eg, we do not alter the database structure or hardware each time we enter new data.

This insight allows us to conceptually partition a system temporally. While there are various means of partitioning systems, Brand's model (1994) offers a user-friendly means of differentiating 'layers' via their relative rates of change. In our university example, the academic year evolves slowly, set by tradition and constrained by adjacent systems such as the high school year. The set of degrees offered by the university evolve more quickly, and the individual subjects within degrees more quickly still. The content of individual lectures evolves yet faster. Each of these represents a layer; to the extent that these layers can evolve relatively independently the system comprising the university's academic offerings achieves a degree of plasticity. Similarly, the information and communications technologies used for pedagogical purposes within ASU are evolving more rapidly than those used to support the university's 'back-office' business processes.

In our case, there is a natural rhythm to university timetabling generated by the flow of semesters, commencement and graduation. The ASU timetable achieved a degree of stability over time, as subjects and staff changed relatively slowly, allowing a consensus to be reached based on mutual expectations. But several years ago, ASU adopted a new academic information system that in turn forced changes to degree structures and subject offerings throughout the university. ASU management seemed to recognize the deep nature of those changes and worked hard to identify and plan for their consequences. However, with the timetable, ASU imagined Stellar could deliver solutions within the temporal cycles of its own planning processes; Stellar, however, would discover that its deeply-embedded assumptions about how timetabling should work would make this impossible.

Non-linearity: The modern conception of time assumes a mechanical, stepwise progression — 'clock-time' (Bluedorn and Denhardt, 1988; Levine, 1997). But multi-agent systems experience time in a dissimilar and non-uniform — and so non-linear — way. Temporal non-linearity encompasses concepts, or temporal experiences, such as 'novelty', 'regularity' and 'movability' (as listed by Butler, 1995: 390) — though such non-linearities extend beyond the personal experience of individuals. If we consider systems as networks of interactions and inter-relationships in multi-agent systems, we can understand phenomena such as self-organized criticality; co-evolution; and concurrence as examples of temporally non-linear phenomena.

In the case of self-organized criticality (Bak, 1997; Jensen, 1998), a critical point is reached at which change crashes, cascades or ripples inexorably across the system until the pent-up energy for change has been dispersed. Examples include avalanches, the spread of fads, cascading power failures, and revolutions. These system effects represent discontinuities in temporal behaviour, potentially shifting the system into a new set of behaviours or circumstances.

Co-evolution (Kauffman, 1995) also drives temporal change. Change in one system alters the environment of interacting or proximate systems; those must adjust their own configurations, behaviours or strategies, or their temporal behaviour, resulting in constant restlessness across the system-of-systems.

Lastly, the concurrence of change also can affect system. Temporal cycles may coincide, resulting in system disruption or demanding extra effort to maintain stability. Generally, change in deeper, slower layers, will affect upper, faster layers: a sudden shift in a deep layer may result in system shear (Brand, 1994).

In our case, the increasing instability of OLDSIS, culminating in withdrawal of support by its vendor, created a criticality and the impetus for cascading change. The introduction of STARS and STRIPES triggered co-evolution by forcing change on interfaces and dataflows within ASU's web-based course sign-on system and student information systems. In preparation for system change, ASU shifted timetable production from an annual to semi-annual basis. But doing so shifted timetable production workload to coincide with peak workloads in schools, placing extra stress on staff to balance competing demands. This is an example of concurrence — a non-linearity in one place in a system forcing consequential behavioural change elsewhere.

Synchronization: The third temporal characteristic is synchronization, which extends well beyond simple social interaction. In systems that work well, temporal cycles are both independent and interdependent. The closer their respective temporal behaviour, the more likely interacting system elements are to synchronize their behaviour, whether the systems are natural or artificial (Strogatz, 2003). Some natural cycles, such as the circadian rhythm, may diverge wildly in the prolonged absence of reinforcing cues. Synchronization can be forced, but at a cost, especially where the natural temporal behaviours are substantially different — as is evident in forced logistical systems (eg Khouja, 2003).

Organizational and biological systems use entrainment mechanisms, supraprocesses or events that reset subordinate or associate processes, holding them in synchrony for a period to ensure goals are achieved or stability ensured (Ancona and Chong, 1996). A university timetable is one such entrainment mechanism. It orders and reinforces organizational processes, and provides a basis for interaction and synchronization of the activities of students and staff. As such the timetable operates as a commons — the realization of compromises mutually co-evolved over many years between academics and administrators. A shift in such a socially critical structure may presage massive disruptions within the organization.

Emergent Temporalities

The heterogeneous agents comprising socio-technical systems exhibit temporal behaviour. Aspects of that behaviour will be regulated by an inherent, self-centered dynamic, but may alter in response to environmental or self-generated change. In particular, agents will tend to synchronize their temporal behaviour with others with whom they interact and share some temporal similarities. At a system level, we expect these behaviours to generate emergent temporalities as individuals collaborate.

For example, workloads may be dictated by influences external to the workplace yet intrinsic to it. Implementing STARS may seem a comparatively simple task, but if coinciding with other system demands, such as the start of semester, it may generate changes cascading across the system, altering internal workload patterns, and disrupting associated patterns, such as the working day of staff, system maintenance schedules, and lecture schedules. An emergent temporality may be a continuing, even a growing, lag between the work at hand and available resources, tipped by a new software implementation, while the system shifts into a new pattern of behaviour.

Such characteristics suggest that understanding temporal structures as linear sequences is insufficient; such sequences fail to capture the underlying dynamics and the deeper temporal behaviour inherent in systems. Similarly, the focus on 'interaction in the small' (Dix, et al., 1998) traditional within CSCW can lead to a failure to appreciate the richness and persistence of system behaviour resulting from temporal dynamics. And it may lead analysts and managers to assume eternity — that the system of tomorrow, next week, next year, will be that of today — at the risk of misunderstanding large system shifts due to criticality or shear.

Having identified the manifestations of time in systems, we introduce a conceptual tool that helps contextualize those behaviours within the circumstances of particular systems. For example, we identified an example of concurrence within our case, but what effect does that have on the delivery of a suitable version of STARS? Understanding how different temporal behaviours interact and fit together within the system can help resolve such issues.

Temporal trajectories: Temporal behaviour may build on and repeat itself, with that repetition contributing to wider temporal patterns with the system. For example, a lecture delivers information to students — that means of delivery may become embedded through its contribution to deeper social and organizational processes reinforced through practice and social artifacts. Or, lacking sufficient support and reinforcing behaviours — perhaps due to the level and pace of work, teacher knowledge, or the organizational culture — attempts to deliver information in that form may dissipate.

Temporal behaviour thus may be constrained by deeper institutional processes and work habits that support and reinforce existing programmes. For example, in our case, Central Timetabling considered standardizing university teaching weeks for courses. However this was abandoned due to factors external to the university, such as the timing of the Education School's teacher placement courses which are negotiated each year with other universities offering similar courses — not all universities can have their students placed in the same schools at the same time. Alternatively, an unpredicted, 'deep' event, such as the September 11 attacks, or an IT crash with critical data loss, may result in a massive system shift, cascading in unanticipated ways. September 11, for example, resulted in changes to American policy, the invasion of Afghanistan and Iraq, and ongoing changes to behaviour of organizations and individuals concerning communication, security, and risk.

Thinking about time as a system phenomenon allows us to consider the *temporal trajectory* of particular occurrences. Using notions of *instance, pattern, meso-layer* and *temporal layer*, we can talk about a system's temporal behaviour. Triangulating temporal trajectories helps understanding of the emergent temporal behaviour within the system. The use of arenas, the interaction of various 'social worlds' around issues of interest (borrowing generously from Strauss, 1993:226), allows us to encompass a wide range of temporalities, from the slow and taken-for-granted to the fast, eye-catching change of the moment.

An event, termed an *instance*, possesses simple characteristics of timing and duration. For example, a lecture is held at a particular time of day for a certain period. The instantiation of the activity possesses both timing, as compared to the clock and relative to other activities and agents in the system, and duration.

Repeated instances may generate a temporal *pattern*, which comprises rhythm, frequency and duration, and a higher level of complexity; e. g. a lecture is held each Monday for the duration of the semester, at 10am, for 50 minutes, in a particular space. We notice that staff and students attend and at the peripheries of the lecture students socialize or move directly on to another, common lecture.

Combinations of patterns across the whole or part of a system comprise a *meso-layer*, comprising increased complexity again. Here we find interacting patterns: lecture time is determined by other patterns (lecturer, student availability) and the physical environment (suitable teaching space), accounting for the complexity of the time-tabling process. Socialization depends on student group composition, environmental conditions, student schedules and the university's own rhythm — assignments and exams can alter social activity. We may find that asynchrony or differing temporal patterns form semi-permeable barriers to interaction (Axelrod and Cohen, 1999) .

The interlinking of inter-related temporal processes form *temporal layers*. At this point we can begin to conceive of the temporal behaviour of the system as an emergent outcome of temporal processes and structures of compositional agents and sub-structures. What here we refer to as layers possess system-wide attributes and are based on the periodicity of change; their contents need not be linked through interaction, but are of a temporal nature. Our understanding of layering improves as we merge our understanding of a number of temporal trajectories, and we can arrange the system conceptually in terms of the relative pace of change. To illustrate: fast layers, such as the interchange of information during a lecture, depend on slower layers, such as the families of subjects and degrees offered by the university; those in turn depend on yet slower layers, such as the teaching pedagogy of the university. A middle layer may be the university timetable, which mediates teaching practice and social interaction.

Temporal layers may be described through separate temporal trajectories, but only make sense in a system context: for example, for a course of study to 'fit' we need a relevant body of knowledge and organized interaction between students and lecturers. Understanding the whole as an emergent outcome of inter-related temporal meso-layers, patterns and instances helps us to understand why, for example, bureaucracies inherently are slow despite efforts at reform: their behaviour is an emergent outcome of the temporalities of their interacting components.

Working from instances, through patterns, meso-structures and layers, we can build narratives that offer insights into the system's temporal nature — in particular, to help identify emergent temporal behaviours. For example, understanding repetition as a temporal pattern helps us to look for synchronizing patterns that may support the repetition. Or if non-linearities or significant stresses are evident, we can look for a dominant entraining activity.

Triangulated temporal trajectories provide a structured means of understanding how the manifestation of time in systems — differential rates of change, non-linearities including concurrence and co-evolution, and synchronization — is apparent within the system of interest. Furthermore it provides a means of binding together fast-moving 'interaction in the small' with deep, slow behaviours that shape and constrain those faster elements. Thus by drawing our eye beyond events encountered linearly as an observer passing through the system — for example, Barley's (1990) experience and Dourish and Button's (1998) 'moment-by-moment' sequential organization — to patterns, the interaction of patterns, and finally to a temporal representation of the system, we can overcome our natural inclination to ignore those effects that lie beyond our cognitive range. Such effects range from the slow cultural and economic shapers of work to the transitory passage of data through technological systems (Zaheer, et al., 1999).

Revisiting the Case

We now revisit the case to expose, and structure, emergent temporalities. We investigate three distinct arenas, or areas of interaction, in the case to draw out the outcomes more clearly. The first arena focuses on the organizational context of the timetabling system: how the timetable is used by and shapes organizational work. The second, the scheduling arena, concerns the assumptions and system dynamics built into the software itself. This, as we'll see, proves to be a point of tension between client and developer: the client expects the software to reflect the organizational context while the developer is more interested in attainment of a workable, and saleable, product. Those tensions are played out in the project environment, which comprises the third and final arena we consider.

The organizational arena: Within the Australian university environment the academic year commences in February and primarily consists of two semesters running from February to June (semester one) and July to November (semester two). Some courses are also offered in a Summer Semester (December/January). Normally the Central Timetabling section is required to produce by each November a full-year timetable for the following academic year. However, ASU management approved a request to allow the Project Team to focus on producing only the first semester 2004 timetable; semi-annual timetabling has now been in place for two years.

Central Timetabling undertake the following tasks to produce a class timetable: collect data from departments and schools; perform data entry; validate the data; run the optimization; perform an initial adjustment of the automated timetable; publish a draft timetable for academic comment; incorporate feedback and adjust the timetable; and publish the official timetable prior to the start of semester.

To accomplish these tasks, Central Timetabling starts the process between five and six months prior to the start of semester. So as departments and schools enroll students for semester one in February, they also provide details of their projected timetabling needs for July. Running parallel but offset by four months is the process of producing the examination timetable, a second task assigned to STARS. The rhythm of the university year means there are two immovable deadlines by which a new class timetabling system must be tested and in place: September, for semester one of the following year; and March, for semester two.

The delivery dates for critical modules of STARS were missed on four occasions: either revisions were needed to overcome the interoperability, consistency or functionality issues which emerged in testing, or else the rising cadence of work as deadlines approached defeated the developers. On each occasion the decision was made to reduce the project scope and downgrade to STRIPES to produce the following semester's timetable simply on the basis of space optimization, whilst retaining preset days and times from prior years. (Kim and Kaplan (2005) cover the reasons why ASU could implement STRIPES but not STARS, including the limited optimization of STRIPES, which matched current practice at ASU; the temporal assumptions that remain embedded in STARS; and the changeable nature of STARS versus the mature stability of STRIPES.)

After the initial attempt to implement STARS in September 2003, a Stellar consultant, Myers, arrived in January 2004 with a revised version of STARS to retrain the Project Team. They encountered a number of critical bugs during training, so Stellar's lead programmer, "working more hours than human beings should", produced and shipped nightly builds of the software. But after Myers left, ASU found more critical bugs, including the inability to optimize; problems representing course delivery patterns; and date problems, thought to have been fixed in STRIPES. Time pressures, the lack of a working version of STARS, and Stellar's inability to provide a definitive delivery date, led ASU in late March to downgrade again from STARS to STRIPES for the semester two 2004 timetable, and again in September 2004 and January 2005. STARS, if delivered by March 2005, could not be used until the semester one 2006 timetable was due.

While ASU was able to tinker with timetable production, shifting from the annual to a semi-annual production of timetables, it could not alter the deeply embedded cycle of semesters. High school student matriculation and State tertiary admission board processing reinforce that cycle. As such, it is an inherent organizational rhythm — it can only be altered on the margins, as with the Education School mentioned earlier. The university timetable itself does not simply order staff, students and space; its production entrains the entire university. Despite that, STARS's delivery has proven slippery and immune from such coercion.

The scheduling arena: ASU is the first institution outside North America to implement Stellar's products and numerous temporal constraints were encountered, reflecting organizational and temporal assumptions inappropriate to the Australian environment. For example, Australia uses a day/month/year system, and not the American month/day/year representation embedded in earlier versions of STRIPES and re-encountered in STARS. Such assumptions are in principle easily solvable if the code was internationalized appropriately during development. That was not the case in STRIPES, and that lack of internationalization was carried through into STARS. For a system that deals ostensibly with when things occur that's a substantial problem: the system has to recognize that within a given year the 4th of June (04/06) is not before the 9th of February (09/02) and so not an error condition. Both the developers and ASU's project team would stumble over such misunderstandings constantly and unexpectedly. Although data packages exist that can handle these issues invisibly, Stellar did not use them; later attempts to 'hack around' these problems simply exacerbated them.

But the time-related problems encountered were not limited to dates. The project team experienced considerable difficulties translating Stellar's delivery models and traits to the Australian scheduling environment. For example, a course at ASU might consist of a two-hour lecture and two one-hour laboratories. These three classes are largely independent, and each can be scheduled independently of the other two — provided they occur at a time that the lecturer, students and space are free. In contrast, the delivery models inscribed within STRIPES and STARS would regard the same course as comprising two sections: a two-hour lecture section; and a one-hour laboratory section having two in-week repeats. Where a section has a repeated meeting within the week, for example Tuesday and Thursday, it is scheduled for the same time in the same room, with the same staff member; students are expected to attend all repeats. The difference is most pronounced for large courses at ASU that offer many classes — 'section clusters' — to meet the enrolment demand. Myers noted these differences, referring to the way that ASU timetables as being a "data issue that needs resolution":

"Section records are not properly clustered. Currently there is not one section record that has more than one days met. Very few sections have a repeating meeting pattern."

Myers' Notes

Scheduling issues thus rest on differences between Stellar's assumptions and the realities at ASU, in terms of date representation as well as temporal patterning. Given the diversity of scheduling arrangements in North America, Stellar could expect to find similar issues with temporal patterning in its home market.

The project arena: The timetabling project had processes that required working around temporal constraints. Notably, Stellar's interaction with ASU was affected by the time difference between North America and Australia. Not only was Stellar operating some 17 hours behind eastern Australia, but the time shift meant that of every week there was only four days overlap. The folklore of software development holds that these temporal offsets can be exploited to speed up development (eg Wright, 2005), but that was not the case here:

"You lose almost a day every time we talk to each other, you know, that makes it hard. So time goes by very, very slowly."

Director of Sales & Marketing, Stellar, interview, 8 September 2004

It also led to other 'temporalogically' correct statements such as the following

"On Monday we're going to have to make a decision...because we're at a pretty desperate point...Monday is Sunday and even then we're going to need to retest."

Project Manager, ASU, project meeting, 26 March 2004

Project development improved during Myers' January 2004 visit and the visit by the lead developer in September 2004. Physical and temporal proximity improved communication and helped synchronize behaviour, not least because Myers became aware of the timing constraints on the ASU project team.

"The trip that I made out there was just absolutely how can I say it, essential and productive towards being able to create a product that is going to totally suit your needs. Does that make sense? In other words I feel that it was a very productive and effective, we were able to collect a lot of information that has caused us to go in and make a tremendous amount of additions and changes to the program."

Myers, teleconference with Project Manager, 7 May 2004

Where possible, the synchronizing of behaviour helped to build social bonds as well. Stellar's lead developer shared office space and work purpose — ASU's implementation of STARS — with ASU's Project Manager during his visit. As both were smokers, they also began to synchronize their social behaviour.

It's clear that time differences have not helped the project's delivery. Bursts of progress are most apparent when Stellar sends a trainer or developer to work with the ASU team, deepening understanding, readjusting the product, and synchronizing activity — but lacking repetition, such effects are transitory.

Emergent Temporal Behaviour in the Case

Timetables entrain not merely that which they are scheduling, but in a university, they entrain the organization through their very production. The dominant temporal feature is the timetable itself; it acts as a commons, and can be highly sensitive to change. Failure to realize — both in terms of understanding and actuality — the place of the timetable within the client's organizational environment would be a contributing factor to the difficulties encountered within the project.

But first let us consider the project through temporal trajectories. While the case allows several points of entry, we start from the instance of a lecture and the resulting trajectory in each of the arenas. Table 1 sets out the temporal trajectories for the respective arenas (read down the columns); Table 2 explores the consequences of the emergent temporalities identified via Table 1.

	(a) Scheduling Arena	(b) Organizational Arena	(c) Project Arena
Instance	The delivery of a lecture to a class in a particular space.	Provide a resource (space, staff member, technology).	Allow a resource to be entered (one occurrence, Aust. format).
Pattern	Lectures delivered once a week, at the same time, but occurrence and place may vary (eg lab in week 4, early semester start)	Allocation of space; allocation of staff to teach courses in faculties; student lists per course; preparation of course materials.	STARS needs reconfiguring from the set US template to allow progressive flexibility through the semester. Exceptions difficult.
Meso-layer	Semester-based delivery of 14 weeks, mid-semester break, study week and exams. Some programs start earlier.	Timetabling and space schedules coordinate with course offerings, degree programs, tutor requirements. Shift from annual to semi-annual planning.	Efforts to realign STARS constrained time difference between teams, other clients. Delivery times must align with semester dates.
Layering	Timetable development; individual subject; degree; timetable structure; academic year; policy; institutional environment	Individual lectures; individual subject; timetabling; degree; timetable structure; policy; organizational & academic culture	Code; project team developer interaction; ASU/Stellar management interaction; delivery dates; contract; scheduling assumptions; business models

Table 1. Temporal trajectories within (a) scheduling, (b) organisational and (c) project arenas

Reviewing Table 1, we see that each arena has a different interpretation of a lecture. The first problem arises at the pattern level: Stellar has major problems translating ASU's scheduling pattern; its scheduling assumptions are embedded deep within the software, and hard to change. Another issue emerges at the meso-layer: Stellar is unable to match ASU's organizational rhythm. That rhythm reflects the timetabling cycle itself and entrains staff and student behaviour and the deployment of resources. It also reflects the deeper pattern of the academic year. Shifting to semi-annual production of the timetable was meant to enable the anticipated imminent delivery of STARS and make ASU more responsive to the market, but strained organizational resources elsewhere.

At the layering level, we find that the project arena changes more quickly than either the organizational arena or the slower scheduling arena. Layering allows us to identify the 'limiting resource' (Simon, 1996), the key constraint of the system. In Brand's schema (1994), the slow layers constrain the fast; here, scope for change is set by two factors: the scheduling layer, dictated by the timetabling cycle; and the scheduling assumptions embedded deeply within STARS.

Stellar's inability to grasp the Australian scheduling system, as evidenced by their failure to match the university's organizational cadence which is reflected in the delivery dates, is due to a set of assumptions concerning the organization of time that is deeply embedded in the software.

> "Some of the others might not have understood how embedded that was into the system and how many different places that had to be changed and modified and the kind of routines that we really needed to create to make sure that it was working right in the database and in display."
>
> Lead Developer, Stellar, interview, 1 September 2004

Myers, for example, considered the difference between Stellar's working assumptions and ASU's scheduling system as a 'data issue' — a matter of getting the data right, rather than of user practice or temporal behaviour.

Attempts to come to grips with the problem are not helped by time differences, and different temporal perspectives, between client and developer. ASU, working to a steady beat, see the project as slow and plagued by delay; Stellar, working between several customers and trying to meet deadlines, cannot match ASU's pace:

> We have five simultaneous STARS implementations going on right now and all have demanded attention at different times and I can see when I step back our attention going wooo [arcing back-and-forward hand motion] zooming from one client to another like that and ASU is one of those who have probably seen us give a lot of attention and then swing somewhere else."
>
> Director of Sales & Marketing, Stellar, interview, 8 September 2004

ASU believed that Stellar could adapt to their practices and that little or no customization would be needed, only to find out that some assumptions were deeply embedded into the Stellar products. Each organization came into the project with a constraint deeply embedded on a 'slow layer', and the assumption that the other's reciprocal constraints would be on a 'fast layer' (see Table 2). But because the family of constraints at issue exists on 'slow layers', it has become difficult for Stellar and ASU to work together and the project has ended up in a kind of limbo; a further example of an emergent temporality.

The temporal behaviour of the overall system emerges from the interactions of the temporal characteristics of the system and its constituents — the developers, their clients, the technology and the environment. Because of problems in deep layers, attempts to entrain development through artifacts such as milestones, contracts and deliverables, run into difficulties. The critical entrainment mechanism is the timetable production schedule itself. The time differences between client and developer contribute to the problem, but are insufficient cause of the continued delay to STARS. Instead, the limiting resource is Stellar's inability to account for the nature of lecture schedules over the semester at ASU within its system, and to do so in time to match the timetable production schedule.

Emergent Temporalities	Consequences		
	ASU	Stellar	User Domain
Time assumptions in STRIPES (unanticipated, a barrier to adoption) deeply embedded	Unable to meet public commitments to new system. Ongoing, and increasing, political and resource burden.	Increases resource commitments. Continuously underestimates or misdiagnoses problem; unable to meet contractual or subsequent verbal commitments	Continued use of old timetabling process, using STRIPES, but collecting data as for STARS. Users acclimated to what were to be transitory arrangements
Time differences across the Pacific	Acts as an interaction barrier, affecting communication and responsiveness between ASU and Stellar		
ASU needs to entrain Stellar to meet delivery dates	ASU wanted a rapid delivery, had assumed changes were quick, cosmetic and few. Use of legal threats.	Stellar commits to unachievable timetable; massive expectation mismatch.	Schools carry burden of semi-annual collection of data for Stars. Academics assume the status quo is optimized & meets their needs.
ASU's own time constraints are deeply embedded in wider socio-economic system.	ASU unable to shift its own schedule. When changes prove to be big and many, ASU can't evolve its own constraints,.	Stellar assumed no issues, a quick evolution, and a good fit between its product and ASU's system	ASU instituted semi-annual timetabling to match Stellar's promised delivery and improve optimization

Table 2: Emergent Temporalities in ASU, Stellar and in the User Domain

Implications

We believe that any deep consideration of the behavioral characteristics and drivers of collaborative systems must necessarily include a broad view of time. That means appreciating how time affects systems, and that system-level temporal behaviour emerges from the distinctive temporal behaviors of constituent elements.

Our case allows us to consider the effect of time and collaboration within a socio-technical system that is itself used to shape time and collaboration. Not only does the notion and impact of time differ in each of the arenas, its interaction through the collaboration of the system's participants yields unanticipated outcomes and shapes the overall system. Two temporal patterns dominate the system: the timetable as an entrainment mechanism both in its ordering and in its production; and the nature of ASU's scheduling paradigms, in particular how it differs from the system embedded in Stellar's software. A third temporal characteristic exacerbated efforts to resolve difficulties generated by these two patterns: the time difference between ASU and Stellar, which militated against synchronization of effort and deepening understanding. The resulting interplay of these deep temporal characteristics has left the project in limbo, while retaining a perception of progress through frenetic activity and tight deadlines. This emergent characteristic of time has not been addressed as far as we are aware.

A more 'traditional' approach to our case might have focused on the interaction of the client and developer teams, noting the effect of geographical time differences (eg Massey, et al., 2003) and possibly attributing the lack of delivery on fragmentary, opaque interaction, independent of deep temporal drivers. Such simplification of time has its uses: understanding the sequence of actions contributes to an understanding of 'interaction in the small' and allows tasks to be automated and routines formalized. But it risks underestimating the depth of complexity — the wickedness — of the work environment, and the possibility of temporal behaviour emerging from the inherent presence of time in systems.

From our analysis, we can draw some tentative guidance so as to help shape temporally sensitive design of collaborative systems. First, analysts and designers need to be aware of *patterns of temporal interaction*, and the contribution those patterns make to the overall temporal profile of the system. The timetable production cycle, for example, entrains other organizational processes.

Second, temporal behavior, like other behaviors, is often negotiated at the *interface of social spheres and policy arenas*. Temporal behaviors do not necessarily translate directly between arenas. Scheduling, for example, comprises deeply entrenched expectations, perceptions and behaviors; it changes slowly and so acts as a brake, or if understood, as a base for fast changing behaviors. Despite the strong entrainment mechanism of the timetable production cycle, it was not able to drive STARS to delivery, as deep scheduling problems had not been resolved.

Last, *encapsulation* is a common technique in software engineering; socio-technical systems and sub-systems are often 'black-boxed'. Both forms of encapsulation contain assumptions concerning the temporal behavior of their contents. Those assumptions may shape system behaviour, especially when system elements are tightly coupled, yet remain opaque to analysts, designers, developers and users; critical errors based on flawed assumptions may be perceived as a 'data problem'. Thus Stellar's assumptions concerning the scheduling profile of a university, deeply embedded within its software and based upon its past US-based experience, contributes to its current inability to deliver STARS.

Social and socio-technical systems always will be 'intransparent' in good part to external observers (Luhmann, 1995;1997). However, harnessing time as a framework may help mitigate that intransparency. For example, watching for patterns of activities and their interactions may reveal insights concerning system drivers, and contributors to system behaviour. Treating time simply as homogenous, uniform and step-wise contributes to intransparency. If failing to account properly for temporal phenomena can reduce the utility and functionality of a system, then better understanding of temporal behaviour holds the promise of providing systems developers with a variety of new conceptual tools, including: (1) levers for control through mechanisms for entrainment, or simply identifying points of tension and coincidence; (2) removal of controls, for example through the inverse of the previous point; and (3) by recognizing when parts of systems functionality are on the 'wrong' temporal layers (the system will allow them to evolve too quickly, or not quickly enough), the system can be rearchitected.

Conclusion

Time is a deep driver of system behaviour, contributing to the wickedness of the socio-technical design problem. Time manifests in many ways — differential rates of change, non-linearities though co-evolution, criticality, and concurrence, and entrainment and synchronization — and generates emergent behaviours at the system level. In our case, failure to understand these factors contributed to the repeated failure to deliver the STARS timetabling system. Rather than seeking to build quick fixes within ASU's temporal cycle, Stellar would have been better served by stepping outside of those immovable deadlines and working on resolving those issues deeply embedded within its own product. Deep, slow temporal layers must be resolved on their own terms — slowly. Rushing simply meant that the deep, systemic assumptions built into STARS could not be identified, challenged and properly re-engineered.

The use of time as a lens has helped us to understand such drivers, and the consequential temporal behaviour within the system. Without regard for time, analysts risk missing some of the rich behaviour that it generates within the system. Accordingly, we suggest that tools such as temporal trajectories offer useful scaffolding for extricating temporal behaviours. In particular, the trajectories allow a more holistic view of time, encompassing slow behaviours often disregarded in our focus on the workplace and on the present. We also suggest that designers watch for patterns of temporal interaction, particularly at the interface of social spheres and policy arenas, and that care be taken to consider the temporal assumption often embedded within sociotechnical systems.

References

Adam, B. (1990): *Time and Social Theory*. Temple University Press, Philadelphia.

Alexander, C. (1979): *A Timeless Way of Building*. Oxford University Press, Oxford.

Alexander, C. (2002): *The Nature of Order: Book One: The Phenomenon of Life*. The Center for Environmental Structure, Berkeley.

Ancona, D. and Chong, C.-L. (1996): 'Entrainment: Pace, cycle, and rhythm in organizational behaviour', *Research in Organizational Behavior*, vol. 18, pp. 251-284.

Axelrod, R. and Cohen, M. D. (1999): *Harnessing Complexity: organizational implications of a scientific frontier*. The Free Press, New York.

Bak, P. (1997): *How Nature Works*. Oxford University Press, Oxford.

Bannon, L. J. (1995): 'The Politics of Design: Representing Work', *CACM*, vol. 38, no. 9, pp. 66-69.

Barley, S. R. (1990): 'Images of Imaging: Notes on Doing Longitudinal Field Work', *Organization Science*, vol. 1, no. 3, August 1990, pp. 220-247.

Beer, S. (1974): *Designing Freedom*. John Wiley & Sons, London.

Bluedorn, A. C. and Denhardt, R. B. (1988): 'Time and Organizations', *Journal of Management*, vol. 14, no. 2, pp. 299-320.

Brand, S. (1994): *How Buildings Learn*. Penguin Books, New York.

Brown, S. L. and Eisenhardt, K. M. (1997): 'The art of continuous change: Linking complexity theory and time-paced evolution in restlessly shifting organizations', *Administrative Science Quarterly*, vol. 42, no. 1, March 1997, pp. 1-34.

Butler, R. (1995): 'Time in organizations: Its Experience, Explanations and Effects', *Organization Studies*, vol. 16, no. 6, pp. 925-950.

Dix, A., Ramduny, D. and Wilkinson, J. (1998): 'Interaction in the large', *Interacting with Computers*, vol. 11, pp. 9-32.

Dourish, P. (1995): 'Developing a Reflective Model of Collaborative Systems', *ACM Transactions on Computer-Human Interaction*, vol. 2, no. 1, March 1995, pp. 40-63.

Dourish, P. and Button, G. (1998): 'On "Technomethodology": Foundational Relationships Between Ethnomethodology and System Design', *Human-Computer Interaction*, vol. 13, pp. 395-432.

Fehr, E. (2002): 'The economics of impatience', *Nature*, vol. 415, 17 January 2002, pp. 269-272.

Gell, A. (1992): *The Anthropology of Time: Cultural Constructions of Temporal Maps and Images*. Berg, Oxford.

Gersick, C. J. G. (1988): 'Time and Transition in Work Teams - toward a New Model of Group Development', *Academy of Management Journal*, vol. 31, no. 1, March 1988, pp. 9-41.

Gersick, C. J. G. (1994): 'Pacing Strategic Change - the Case of a New Venture', *Academy of Management Journal*, vol. 37, no. 1, February 1994, pp. 9-45.

Huy, Q. N. and Mintzberg, H. (2003): 'The rhythm of change', *MIT Sloan Management Review*, vol. 44, no. 4, pp. 79(6).

142

Jensen, H. J. (1998): *Self-Organized Criticality: Emergent Complex Behaviour in Physical and Chemical Systems*. Cambridge University Press, Cambridge.

Kaplan, S. and Seebeck, L. (2001): 'CSCW as a Complex Adaptive System', in W. Prinz, M. Jarke, Y. Rogers, K. Schmidt and V. Wulf (eds): *ECSCW'01*, Kluwer, Dordrecht, 2001, pp. 359-378.

Kauffman, S. (1995): *At Home in the Universe*. Oxford University Press, New York.

Khouja, M. (2003): 'Synchronization in supply chains: implications for design and management', *Journal of the Operational Research Society*, vol. 54, pp. 984-994.

Kim, R. M. and Kaplan, S. M. (2005): 'Co-Evolution in Information Systems Engagement: exploration, ambiguity and the emergence of order', in P. J. Ågerfalk, L. Bannon and B. Fitzgerald (eds): *3rd Int.Conf. on Action in Language, Organisations and Information Systems*, pp. 166-180.

Lee, H. and Liebenau, J. (2000): 'Time in Organizational Studies: Towards a New Research Direction', *Organization Studies*, vol. 20, no. 6, pp. 1035-1058.

Levine, R. (1997): *A Geography of Time*. Basic Books

Luhmann, N. (1995): *Social Systems*. Stanford University Press, Stanford, California.

Luhmann, N. (1997): 'The Control of Intransparency', *System Research and Behavioural Science*, vol. 14, pp. 359-371.

Massey, A. P., Montoya-Weiss, M. M. and Hung, Y. T. (2003): 'Because time matters: Temporal coordination in global virtual project teams', *Journal of Management Information Systems*, vol. 19, no. 4, Spring 2003, pp. 129-155.

McCarthy, J. (2000): 'The paradox of understanding work for design', *International Journal of Human-Computer Studies*, vol. 53, pp. 197-219.

Murphy, R. (2001): 'Nature's Temporalities and the Manufacture of Vulnerability: A study of sudden disaster with implications for creeping ones', *Time & Society*, vol. 10, no. 2/3, pp. 329-348.

Nowotny, H. (1994): *Time: The Modern and Postmodern Experience*. The Polity Press, Cambridge.

Orlikowski, W. J. and Yates, J. (2002): 'It's About Time: Temporal Structuring in Organizations', *Organization Science*, vol. 13, no. 6, November-December 2002, pp. 684-700.

Reddy, M. and Dourish, P. (2002): 'A Finger on the Pulse: Temporal Rhythms and Information Seeking in Medical Work', *Proceedings of the 2002 ACM conference on Computer supported cooperative work*, ACM Press, New York, NY, pp. 344-353.

Seebeck, L. and Kaplan, S. (2004): 'Understanding Time in System Design', in N. Callaos, J. Bemley, H. Tsuji, S. Nomura and J. Choo (eds): *8th World Conference on Systemics, Cybernetics and Informatics*, International Institute of Informatics and Systemics, Orlando, Vol. X, pp. 299-304.

Simon, H. A. (1996): *The Sciences of the Artificial*. The MIT Press, Cambridge.

Sorokin, P. A. and Merton, R. K. (1937): 'Social Time: A Methodological and Functional Analysis', *The American Journal of Sociology*, vol. 42, no. 5, pp. 615-629.

Strauss, A. (1993): *Continual Permutations of Action*. Aldine de Gruyter, New York.

Strogatz, S. H. (2003): *Sync*. Theia, New York.

Suchman, L. (1995): 'Making Work Visible', *Communications of the ACM*, vol. 38, no. 9, September 1995, pp. 56-64.

Wright, R. L. (2005): 'Successful IT Outsourcing: Dividing Labor for Success', *SoftwareMag.com*, (http://www.softwaremag.com/L.cfm?Doc=2005-04/2005-04outsourcing — 24 May 2005).

Zaheer, S., Albert, S. and Zaheer, A. (1999): 'Time Scales and Organizational Theory', *The Academy of Management Review*, vol. 24, no. 4, October 1999, pp. 725-741.

Zerubavel, E. (1981): *Hidden Rhythms: Schedules and Calendars in Social Life*. University of California Press, Berkeley.

H. Gellersen et al. (eds.), ECSCW 2005: Proceedings of the Ninth European Conference on Computer-Supported Cooperative Work, 18-22 September 2005, Paris, France, 143–162.

Managing Currents of Work: Multi-tasking Among Multiple Collaborations

Victor M. González, and Gloria Mark

Department of Informatics, University of California, Irvine: U.S.A.

{vmgyg, gmark}@ics.uci.edu

Abstract. This research reports on a study of the interplay between multi-tasking and collaborative work. We conducted an ethnographic study in two different companies where we observed the experiences and practices of thirty-six information workers. We observed that people continually switch between different collaborative contexts throughout their day. We refer to activities that are thematically connected as working spheres. We discovered that to multi-task and cope with the resulting fragmentation of their work, individuals constantly renew overviews of their working spheres, they strategize how to manage transitions between contexts and they maintain flexible foci among their different working spheres. We argue that system design to support collaborative work should include the notion that people are involved in multiple collaborations with contexts that change continually. System design must take into account these continual changes: people switch between local and global perspectives of their working spheres, have varying states of awareness of their different working spheres, and are continually managing transitions between contexts due to interruptions.

Introduction

Collaboration among information workers has long received attention in CSCW. However, a new perspective is now beginning to focus on information work: people's involvement in a multitude of projects and initiatives (Belloti et al. 2004; Czerwinski et al. 2004; Fussell et al. 2004; Mark et al. 2005). In fields as diverse as finance, software development, consulting, and academia, we are finding that it is commonplace that information workers are involved in multiple collaborations that occur in parallel. This demands that individuals enact specific efforts to coordinate, manage and track those collaborations and the activities associated with them.

Viewing a person's work in terms of multiple collaborations has particular relevance for the field of CSCW. Most CSCW studies of office work have focused on sole collaborations, in both distributed or collocated environments, too numerous to list here (e.g. Ackerman et al. 1997; Mark et al. 1999; Rogers 1994; Rouncefield et al. 1994) Other studies though, that recognize that people are involved in multiple and simultaneous projects, have not consolidated findings in order to identify strategies that individuals use to cope with the demands of multiple collaborations and activities (Buscher et al. 1999). Therefore, following this perspective that people must manage multiple activities, we propose to examine collaboration not as an isolated experience in a particular context but rather as an ongoing stream of activities where people move in and out of different collaborative contexts based on circumstances.

Focusing on multiple collaborations leads us to ask how information workers can manage their different collaborations over the course of a day. We are interested in examining how people manage transitions among activities and how they maintain continuity when their activities are fragmented.

In this paper we present the results of an analysis of the multi-tasking practices of thirty-six information workers as they were observed *in situ*. Based on this analysis, we argue that individuals adopt particular strategies that enable them to manage their work while multi-tasking. These strategies include a constant renewal of overviews of their various collaborations, managing transitions as these collaborative contexts change and maintaining a flexible window of focus across activities.

Related Work

Previous studies have recognized that information workers are typically involved in multiple activities and collaborations (Hudson et al. 2002; Perlow 1999; Sproull 1984). It has been argued that the need to multi-task seems to be increasing as companies increasingly more experience a flattening of organizational hierarchies, adopt team-oriented forms of organization, constantly change organizational structures, relax the formalization of job roles, and demand employees to focus on multiple and varied initiatives (DiMaggio 2001). The nature of work today for many information workers resembles what used to be exclusive to top-level managers, i.e. characterized by fast-paced and varied activities, frequent fragmentation of actions and constant interpersonal interactions (Mintzberg 1973).

Many studies have highlighted that information workers often experience interruptions during the execution of their activities (O'Conaill and Frohlich 1995;

Rouncefield et al. 1994). Due to the accessibility of other co-workers, people often find themselves engaged in informal interactions thematically unrelated with the activity they were working on before an interruption. It is recognized that collaborative work demands these kinds of interactions as they serve both social and work oriented functions, and fundamentally, they serve as flexible mechanisms to cope with changing circumstances and problem-solving (Kraut et al. 1993; Whittaker et al. 1994).

How information workers cope with the management of multiple activities and interruptions is still not well understood. It is often said that multi-tasking involves the management of a set of diverse aspects such as time, contacts, documents or even physical space (Belloti et al. 2003; Blandford and Green 2001; Boardman and Sasse 2004). However, it is not clear how, in practice, individuals can juggle priorities and what strategies they use to achieve this.

Collaborations and Working Spheres

Distinguishing between the collaborative relationships that individuals establish and the practical activities involved in those collaborations is a starting point for understanding multi-tasking. For example, in order to design a software component a developer can establish a collaboration with a business analyst who is particularly knowledgeable about the subject. In this collaboration, they will divide their labor for the specification, design, implementation and testing of the component. The practical activity of developing a particular software component creates a collaboration among those two individuals. Thus, as individuals define the demands of their practical activities, they also define collaborations with relevant individuals.

We refer to these practical activities that individuals pursue as *working spheres*. Thus, a working sphere is a unit of work that serves to describe work efforts that people pursue in practice in order to meet their responsibilities. A working sphere can refer to short-term tasks, such as fixing a software component, routine work such as daily maintenance of equipment, events such as a provider's exhibition, or long-term projects such as implementing a new infrastructure for a client. More precisely, we define a working sphere as a unit of work that, from the perspective of the individual, has a unique time frame, involves a particular collaborative structure, and is oriented towards a specific purpose (González and Mark 2004). As a unit of work, a working sphere thematically connects sets of actions enacted by an individual such as phone calls, working on documents, e-mail messages, interactions, and so on[1].

---

1 Compared with other types of conceptualizations, a working sphere is closer to the notion of *activity* as defined by Activity Theory, in the sense of connecting sets of actions toward particular objects (Leont'ev, 1978). However the notion of *working sphere* lacks an emphasis on high-level motives as the notion of

Collaborations clearly are often based on more than one working sphere. In some cases, individuals maintain a collaboration across time as they become involved in sequential working spheres (e.g. working on different software components which are part of a sustained long-term project). In other cases, collaborations demand simultaneous involvement in working spheres that have different purposes, time frames or collaborative structures. For example, the developer and analyst in the previous example can be simultaneously involved in two different working spheres: the development of a software component to be shipped by the end of the month and the evaluation of a new financial product to be completed by the end of the week.

Considering both the collaborations and the working spheres that individuals are involved in suggests that multi-tasking involves not only managing and keeping track of working spheres, but also managing the collaborations related to working spheres.

Research Setting and Methodology

The analysis presented here is based on an empirical investigation aimed to understand the strategies that information workers use to manage multiple activities. As opposed to taking a managerial perspective on work as in, e.g. (Sproull 1984), for our research we are especially interested in analyzing the practices of different kinds of information workers, with different roles in the organization and different levels of involvement in projects. Our investigation was conducted in two different companies. ITS is a company that acts as an outsourcer providing information technology and administrative services for major financial bond management companies. The size and volume of operations of their current client, CORI, demands that ITS serve them exclusively, currently having no other clients. Within ITS we observed informants working in two different teams. The JEB team focuses on supporting the financial systems used by the brokers in CORI. The AUG team focuses on the administrative operations managed in behalf of CORI, supporting the systems used to transfer money to financial institutions and the consolidation of accounts. The other study was conducted at Venture, a company specializing in providing specialized consulting services to small and medium-size medical practices. Hundreds of medical practices around the U.S are currently using a proprietary software solution provided by Venture, which covers their billing, financial and administrative needs. At Venture we observed people from many different teams.

Thirty-six informants participated in our study. Fourteen informants were observed in the JEB team, ten in the AUG team and twelve in Venture. The set of

---

activity does (e.g. becoming a project leader) and focuses instead on practical short-term purposes (e.g. enrolling and attending the training sessions on leadership).

informants covered personnel in varied positions and job roles including eleven managers, three project leaders, nine financial-business analysts, eight software developers, three support engineers, and two sales executives. In total, the study comprised more than 920 hours of systematic observation with an average of about 26 hours per informant.

Each informant was systematically observed, using a shadowing technique similar to the one used by Mintzberg (1973), during a minimum of three working days, and then was extensively interviewed. For the observation, a researcher sat with the informant at her cubicle and followed her to formal and informal meetings or other activities outside the cubicle whenever it was possible. The researcher used a time watch and notepad to record details of any actions performed by the individual and the activities towards which those actions were directed. Details such as the topic and fragments of conversations, people participating, and documents and applications involved, were carefully recorded with as much precision as possible. At the end of each day, or during breaks (e.g. lunch), informants were asked for clarifications about some of the actions observed. Data collected from each informant include transcripts of interviews, reports of observation, field notes, pictures and other documents.

The data were analyzed through a comparative analysis using grounded theory (Strauss and Corbin 1998). Through coding our data, we contrasted the behavior, experiences and strategies for multi-tasking among our informants, and produced a set of conceptual categories that consolidated our understanding about processes explaining multi-tasking. Data were also analyzed to identify the time duration and frequency of the working spheres that individuals engaged in.

The identification of working spheres was based on combining different sources of information. First, the informants themselves knew that we aimed to identify the different things they were working on each day. That influenced some individuals to naturally verbalize about some of their working spheres as they performed their work, without explicitly requesting them to do so. Sometimes at the beginning of the day they mentioned what they were planning to do; other times during the day they pointed out the purpose of the things they were doing. A second source resulted from the comments made by informants while interacting with co-workers. They referred to the things they were doing at the moment, e.g.: *"As soon as I'm done with the ATRACK stuff I will move over the R6 spec"* or *"I cannot take it right now, I am attending the Jim's production issue"*. These comments were noted. A third source of data came from informal short interviews conducted with the informants at the end of each day, which served to clarify events and interactions. This part was emphasized on the study with the AUG team at ITS and at Venture, where we used a paper format that informants completed each day by listing the things they worked on. Finally, a fourth source of information came from the post-observation interviews in which we inquired about the working spheres observed.

Characteristics of Multi-tasking: A Scenario

To illustrate how our informants multi-task, we present a scenario that describes the dynamics of their involvement in multiple collaborations and working spheres during a morning. The following scenario, taken directly as it was observed, illustrates the experiences of David, a manager at ITS:

At 8:40 a.m., while preparing documents for a 9:00 a.m. meeting about SIGMA, David notices a new email from Steven, a business analyst from CORI, the ITS client. David expected a message from Steven in regards to R6, a major software release scheduled for the next quarter, but this e-mail is about another issue: Steven is having problems getting reports from the Blotter-system that David supervises. This issue becomes an additional unexpected working sphere that David will have to attend to this day. He calls Steven to find out more about the problem. After talking to him, he phones Phil, a developer in his team to explain the problem and explore some solutions. While talking to Phil, David is interrupted by the sudden presence of his boss Marti and Andrew who come with a question about the official holidays for the office in Munich, Germany. David was involved with Munich's operations earlier, but this working sphere is now peripheral for him as they only seek his opinion. At 9:03, David politely stops the conversation and leaves for his SIGMA meeting. He passes by Phil's cubicle and calls him as he is also involved in this initiative and is attending the meeting. Forty-five minutes later at 9:48 a.m., he is back and ready to continue his investigation on the Blotter-system but after looking briefly at Steven's message, Phil and Gian show up in his office with questions about a different project. At 11:00 a.m., he is alone again, returns to the email from Steven, and phones Shin, a database administrator. During the previous conversation, Phil pointed to Shin as the right person to help solve the problem. While talking to Shin, he says: "I will call you later", as he notices the presence at his office door of people from the TGS team and he turns to attend to them. At 11:31 a.m., he runs over to his boss's office to discuss about the GAPS initiative, another working sphere that is central to him, as he has responsibility for it. At 11:38 a.m., he is back in his office, checks his voice mail message, and listens to a message from Shin. It seems that the source of the problem was identified and Shin is asking David to contact Mike, another UNIX administrator, who Shin believes can fix the problem. He decides to go with Phil and together they go to talk with Mike.

This description of one of David's mornings serves to illustrate how his work is characterized by the constant switching between expected and unexpected working spheres. As other studies of office work have described (e.g. Suchman and Wynn 1984), we noticed that the situated nature of David's work led him to adjust his plans to cope with changing circumstances. Thus, David handled a stream of working spheres that included previously defined ongoing efforts (e.g. the SIGMA initiative), but also unexpected requests to solve problems (e.g. the Blotter-system) or to provide consultation for colleagues (e.g. questions about the Munich office). This constant switching among expected and unexpected working spheres led David's work to be quite fragmented.

A graphical representation of all David's activities on that day illustrates the degree of fragmentation and the constant transitioning back and forth among different working spheres. In figure 1, we distinguish between *normal* working spheres that are attended to in a non-expedited fashion and *urgent* working spheres, attended to promptly. We found that some problems faced by people at ITS were very urgent compared to others, e.g. the Blotter-issue, because they jeopardized CORI's operation with the risk of potential major financial losses. David, due to problems with some servers, had to engage in three urgent working spheres later that day. We also distinguish between *central* working spheres where the individual is more involved in the collaboration and responsible for the outcomes versus *peripheral* working spheres in which one's involvement in the collaboration is limited. For instance, a working sphere such as SIGMA represents for David a central area of concern as he is leading efforts within his team. In contrast, David's involvement in the Munich working sphere is peripheral as he is asked to help due to his expertise. His involvement was limited as shown by the brief conversation he had with Mike and Andrew.

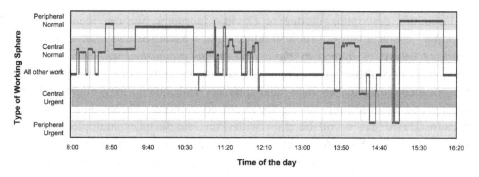

Figure 1. Map of David's activities in working spheres throughout the day.

We found that David experienced rapid switching among working spheres at certain points of the day. In total, he engaged in 14 different working spheres, nine that were central for him, and five with peripheral involvement. Of those working spheres, three were urgent. His involvement with workings spheres is characterized by brief segments of continuous engagement in each sphere (averaging 6 min. 32 sec., s.d. 10 min. 2 sec.). What is interesting is the fact that those working sphere-segments are composed of chains of actions (e.g. telephone calls, interactions) also of very brief duration (averaging 1 min. 29 sec., s.d. 1 min. 25 sec., excluding meetings and lunch). Figure 2 shows a detail of how these chains of actions comprise a segment of a working sphere. This gives a detailed view of how work is fragmented.

150

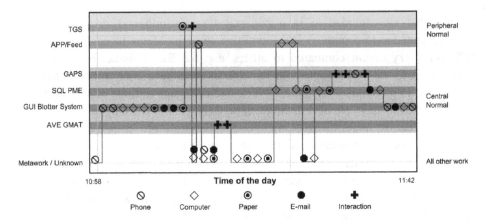

Figure 2. Detail of actions and working spheres (from 10:58 to 11:42 A.M.)

From this description of one of David's mornings, we can identify three important characteristics of multi-tasking. First, we can see that *multi-tasking of working spheres is framed by the collaborations established with others.* Some collaborations with the same people can involve more than one working sphere. In this scenario, when an individual interacts with others, they might end up talking and multi-tasking among those shared working spheres. For example, because David has a collaboration with Phil that includes multiple working spheres (e.g. the SIGMA initiative, the Bottler-issue and other projects), we observed that while interacting they often jumped from one working sphere to another to discuss different issues. These kinds of collaborations with multiple working spheres impose challenges as people must be prepared to multi-task among them on demand. Consequently, people must manage their work from multiple perspectives: not just in terms of individual and independent working spheres, but also in terms of managing the *entire* collaboration that frames a set of working spheres.

Second, we can see that *multi-tasking often is characterized by spontaneity in the way that working spheres originate and are assigned to people.* As we described before, David multi-tasked among working spheres that were expected, as they were in his agenda, and working spheres that arose unexpectedly. Thus, the way that a working sphere is enacted in practice is determined by the circumstances while executing it, but also by the spontaneous way in which working spheres are originated and assigned to one. As the scenario shows, the Blotter-system's issue arose unexpectedly and David had to adjust his plans for that day and to devote attention to solving the problem fast. More importantly, the working sphere was given to David in an informal way and not through any of the formal mechanisms established by ITS to assign work (e.g. a project request form). Hence, we can say that the spontaneous way that characterizes how people get involved in some working spheres shapes the way multi-tasking is done in practice. People must constantly adjust priorities and re-define their agendas by including new working spheres "on the fly".

Finally, the scenario serves to highlight that people *multi-task among collaborations and working spheres that have different levels of maturation.* Working spheres and collaborations are gradually defined as people become aware of the demands of their assignments. Often it is not possible to know all the details of a working sphere initially, such as the level of involvement required, its time frame, outcomes expected, and its collaborative structure. The Blotter-system's working sphere development depicts, in a very time-compressed way, the gradual definition that other collaborations exhibit over longer periods. As we can see in the scenario, the subset of individuals involved in the resolution of the problem with the Blotter-system was gradually defined as David interacted with more people to clarify the problem, defining *how* and with *who* it could be solved. Consequently multi-tasking and managing working spheres with different levels of maturation can be challenging as people have to plan and manage work for spheres with well established times frames, resources, and collaborative structures, but also for other spheres for which just partial information exists.

Continual Switching of Working Spheres

We found that David's involvement with a large number of working spheres and their degree of fragmentation is common among the other informants.

Type of working sphere*	Central		Peripheral		
Condition	Normal	Urgent**	Normal	Urgent**	All
Avg. #. W.S. per day	**8.72**	**0.92**	**3.02**	**1.03**	**12.22**
	5.06	0.70	2.35	0.78	5.30
Avg. Time/W.S. per segment	**0:11:57**	**0:08:36**	**0:05:24**	**0:04:41**	**0:10:29**
	0:04:00	0:06:14	0:03:38	0:04:52	0:02:51
Avg. Total Time/W.S. per day	**0:45:08**	**0:21:28**	**0:08:03**	**0:08:11**	**0:33:58**
	0:20:44	0:16:08	0:05:46	0:06:34	0:12:04

Table I. Average number of working spheres (W.S.) and segment durations. Means are in boldface and standard deviations are in normal font. *Results correspond to 35 informants as one was an outlier. ** The data correspond to 27 informants who handled urgent spheres during observation.

As table I shows, the information workers that we studied engaged in an average of about 12 working spheres per day. Among those, about nine of them were central working spheres for the individuals while the rest demanded just peripheral involvement. The continuous engagement with each working sphere before switching was very short, as the average working sphere segment lasted about 10.5 minutes.

The brief involvement in multiple working spheres and their fragmentation is a clear challenge that our informants face everyday. All our informants recognize that they must engage in an explicit effort to keep focused on what they do and, in case of fragmentation, they have to be able to recover and maintain the continuity of the working sphere. There is a struggle to keep focused, as well described by one of our informants, Adam, a financial analyst at ITS, who commented about the characteristics of this effort and compared it as navigating through a river:

> "Sometimes you just get going into something and they [call] you and you have to drop everything and go and do something else for a while. But I generally just have a pretty good idea of what is needed to be done, what my major tasks are. And just knowing that, I mean, it is like, it's almost like you are weaving through, it is like, you know, a river, and you are just kind of like: "Oh these things just keep getting in your way", and you are just like: "get out of my way" and then you finally get through some of the other tasks and then you kind of get back, get back along the stream, your tasks, that's a weird analogy [laughs], but there are always currents that kind of take you, tend to take you in another direction, and you just have to know if you should be following that."

The analyst's river analogy reflects that information workers have to make an explicit effort to keep "*along the stream*" of their working spheres in spite of "*currents*" that can divert their attention. Moreover, the analogy also reflects that individuals need to maintain a level of awareness about all their major working spheres in order to be able to assess whether they should switch or remain focused on the current working sphere at any particular moment. In the next section we address how in practice our informants enact those efforts to consolidate knowledge about what their "major tasks" are, how they maintain awareness of working spheres other than the one in which they are currently engaged in, and how they efficiently switch among their working spheres as necessary.

Fundamental Processes Involved in Multi-tasking

We argue that the multi-tasking behaviors observed with our informants can be better understood over time, encompassing past, present and future engagements in working spheres. Over time, working spheres evolve, transform and multiply as individuals identify collaborations and enact purposeful activities with other members of their teams. The course is experienced by individuals, but also shaped by them, as they are actively involved in starting, redirecting and abandoning work efforts. Based on our analysis, we discovered that individuals use three fundamental processes to manage multi-tasking as work moves along its temporal course. These processes involve a *constant renewal of overviews* of the working spheres in which one is engaged, the adequate maintenance of a *flexible window of focus* over working spheres demanding attention, and the *management of transitions* leading to switching among working spheres. These three processes are enacted and combined as individuals move throughout their days, and influence, and are influenced by, the collaborations established with others. We draw from our data to illustrate these processes in the following sections.

Continual Renewal of Overviews

We argue that to effectively multi-task, people must gain an *overview* of the working spheres in which they are currently engaged. An overview contains the knowledge about the scope and purposes of a set of working spheres, their temporal constraints, degree of development, and the next actions to conduct in each one. With such an overview, information workers can maintain a state of preparedness; they can make better judgments with respect to their priorities and can move in and out of working spheres as circumstances change or opportunities arise. People might start the first hours of the day by gaining an overview through verification using artifacts, consulting with co-workers, or monitoring communication channels with pending messages. However, given the changing nature of their work, our informants, along their day, continually renew overviews of their working spheres in order to make sure that the current working sphere is the one that must be attended to at that particular moment. A description of how this process occurs can be seen in the experience of Louis, a project leader at ITS:

It is 9:02 a.m., Louis is arriving at the office, and he is checking some reminders from his computer calendar about some meetings he has today. He then opens his e-mail inbox to check for messages. "Nothing new, nothing new", he mumbles as he scrolls down the list with a 3-line summary of each message. Suddenly he stops at one of them "Oops! This one". He looks at the message content briefly. "OK, let's see, what else?" he says as he continues checking the list of messages. Finishing that, he turns over a small paper notebook on the left side of his desk. "My notebook with the day-to-day stuff" he says, as he starts making annotations on it and turning over previous pages, "moving some items", he says. As he annotates on his notebook a list of items to complete today, he turns over a whiteboard hanging on one of the walls. On the whiteboard, he also has a list of things: "Those are like my bigger projects and the things I have to do". At 9:12 a.m., he turns to his computer, takes the phone and starts dealing with one of the items listed in his notebook. During the next two hours, he works on different items, leaves the cubicle a couple of times, and makes a few phone calls. At 11:14 a.m. he comes back from a meeting with George, his boss, and while taking his notebook and looking at it he says: "OK I took care of one thing, but for this one George has other plans. Let's hold that one". He leaves the cubicle again to talk to other people and defines details for another project. Louis continues his day attending to some meetings, preparing a report for people in Munich, and covering other items listed in his notebook. At the end of the day and just before leaving, he takes a look at his notebook, checks his annotations, and then turns over the whiteboard and makes some changes. He mumbles: "Things are cooking".

As we can see in the scenario, people gain an overview of their working spheres through a process that consolidates information from many different sources. In Louis' case, this process includes consulting information in his notebook, checking his whiteboard, and going through summaries of his e-mail messages. We found that other informants use agendas, daily planners, or other artifacts either in paper or in digital form for the same purpose.

Furthermore, the scenario highlights that to manage their multi-tasking, individuals represent information about their working spheres with different levels of aggregation using both digital and physical artifacts. Overviews can provide *local* or *global* perspectives of the working spheres depending on the level of aggregation. A local perspective refers to the day-to-day things that people must do. Louis used a notebook to maintain a list of particular actions to be done in the following days (e.g. making phone calls, preparing reports, asking someone a question, etc.). In parallel, people also maintain a *global* perspective of their working spheres and as one informant indicated, this provides them with: "*the big picture of things that I am suppose to be working on*". In Louis' case, this global perspective was maintained in his whiteboard. Although Louis primarily uses two physical artifacts to manage his working spheres (notebook and whiteboard), he complements them with digital tools such as his electronic calendar. In contrast, we found other informants relying more on digital information systems as their jobs revolve around them. Such is the case of developers or analysts who commonly use systems to keep track of their software items to be developed or tested in a particular release. Reports from those systems help keep people informed on what they are supposed to do each day.

The role of collaborations that individuals establish with others is central to understanding the mechanisms that generate overviews. To some extent, as we have discussed, gaining an overview is based on a person's effort to individually articulate their own work (i.e. defining what should be done, with what resources, the timeline, etc.). However, it is also clear that any individual overview originates first as a product of articulating the work collectively (Strauss 1985). Consequently, when individuals gain an overview, identifying the working spheres and setting priorities, they do so by aligning their overview to the overall goals that the collective effort aims to achieve. We observed that this alignment of overviews of their working spheres gets done in practice through formal and informal interactions with collaborating partners (cf Strauss 1985).

Through formal meetings, individuals can acquire information on the status of others' working spheres which helps consolidate their own overview. Meetings with the specific purpose of keeping people "*on the same page*" were very common at ITS and Venture as they allowed people to establish a common ground, refresh their collaborations, define dependencies, articulate their work, and discuss and validate their priorities with others. To some extent, those meetings also helped people anticipate the multi-tasking that they would be likely to experience through their collaborations. For example, an analyst mentioned that knowing what components the developers were involved in enabled her to plan in advance the testing of those components. This freed her from other time-consuming tasks on those days so she could be more responsive to the developers.

In contrast with formal team-based initiatives, we also found that overviews can be formed by individuals in a more informal way. We noticed that with certain regularity some of our informants "visit" people in their own team and in other teams to chat informally and get updated about their work and changes on it. This practice is explained by Albert, a senior developer at ITS:

> "I try to talk with the systems guys, Joe's group. Keep up with what they are doing. And I try to talk with the UNIX guys, keep up with what they are doing... if I spent an hour going around talking to people, that's really productive for me in getting my work done, because I found out what's going on and I can anticipate change and be very much more productive that way."

Thus, a typical day of our informants is characterized by a continual renewal of overviews of their entire set of working spheres. People update their overviews continually, through communication channels such as face-to-face interactions, email or voice mail, or by updating their reports in systems. Overviews are not only updated but also validated through interactions with other people, either formally or informally.

Maintaining a Flexible Window of Focus

A flexible window of focus refers to the ability of individuals to be immersed and attending to a particular working sphere, but at the same time, to be flexible and able to focus on things around them that can affect their other working spheres. As other authors have noticed (cf Heath and Luff 1991), we observed that our informants, while conducting their work, *monitor* the actions of their co-workers, checking their progress and status, as this helps them to adjust their own actions. However, we also observed that while monitoring, individuals focus their attention flexibly to filter and seek information relevant for their working spheres.

We found that the window of focus expands to cover both their *active* and *potential* working spheres. On one hand, based on their overviews, the individuals have a number of active working spheres that can draw their attention. Consequently, while conducting work in one of them, their focus is also partially oriented towards other working spheres. We noticed that people, as part of the process of creating their overviews, can develop a set of expectations in regards to the particular events or conditions that they should monitor that relate to those spheres (e.g. a person with whom they must talk, a device that has to be available, a paper format that has to be received, etc). Those events act as triggers that guide the multi-tasking among their active working spheres. On the other hand, we observed that because working spheres can arise unexpectedly, individuals attend to events that can have a direct impact on their areas of responsibilities and potentially, can become working spheres for them (e.g. problems on systems they supervise or requests from clients). By keeping a flexible window of focus over their areas of responsibility, they are able to cope with the unexpected way in which some of their working spheres originate and are assigned. Thus, as individuals conduct their work, both active and potential working spheres are focused on and distractions are filtered that have no relationship to their work.

The following scenario shows how the process of maintaining a flexible window of focus is experienced by John, a developer at ITS.

Today John is working against the clock. It is 11:18 a.m. and he is busy writing the documentation of the software code for the Upload process. He has been working on this working sphere for the last two weeks but, as he has been involved in other urgent working spheres, he is delayed. Yesterday he attempted to negotiate an extension of the deadline with his boss Leo, but he was not successful. The report of the Upload process has to be on Leo's desk at 9:00 a.m. tomorrow morning. As he works, he wears his headphones and plays some music, "Music helps me to focus", he mentions. After some time working he turns the volume down as he notices that Leo, who sits in an adjacent cubicle, is on the phone with the client. He stops working and listens to the conversation. However, as it seems that Leo's conversation is not really relevant for him, he continues preparing the report. At 11:55 a.m., Chris shows up and asks if John has plans for lunch. "I will order something, I have to get done with this report", says John and continues working. One hour later, while still working on the report, he listens to a conversation in James' cubicle as he talks to Eric about one of the software systems that John is supporting. He stops typing, takes out his earphones, and walks over to James' cubicle: "No James, you need a patch for that software". After discussing the patch that James has to install in the system, he returns to his cubicle and continues his work on the report.

In the scenario we can see how John listened and attended to matters that were related to his working spheres. He had to balance his focus over his current working sphere (i.e. the Upload process) with conversations happening around him. Similarly, John reacted to things that had no relation to his active working spheres, but that did have a direct impact on their areas of responsibility. For instance, while listening to James talking about a system that John was responsible for, John decided to focus on that conversation and clarified to James that he had to install a software patch for the system. This issue was unexpected and was not part of John's overview, yet it became a working sphere that he attended to that day, as it concerned his responsibility.

Maintaining a flexible window of focus requires that individuals be connected to the collective environment. As we observed in John's scenario, although he wore headphones and played music he kept listening to things around him and remained aware of the larger environment outside of his office. Beyond the events that occur nearby, other channels help individuals be connected to more distant events (e.g. e-mails, instant messaging, the phone or voice messages). We observed that the actual determination of the channels that individuals leave open depend on the communication requirements of both their active and potential working spheres. Based on the overviews of their active working spheres, our informants can expect that some communication channels convey information about particular spheres and therefore this affects their decision to leave them open. For example, some informants at Venture, while waiting to get calls from clients about approval of contracts, kept their cell phones on and handy as clients were likely to call their cell phone numbers. Also, based on their responsibilities, individuals rely on particular communication channels through which potential working spheres can emerge. For example, many of our informants play some role supporting users, and they had to always attend to phone calls from customers as those can be related to problems in the systems they support. We also noticed that given certain conditions, such as an approaching deadline, people can opt for closing most channels and even leave the office for a day or two and work from home. When co-workers were aware that the individual was working on a deadline, they helped her by limiting their interactions with her.

Thus, we observed that as individuals switch working spheres, they maintain a flexible window of focus over external events. The choice of whether to attend to an event is based on both its relevance for one's current working sphere, and one's overall responsibilities.

Management of Transitions

The management of transitions refers to the strategies used by information workers to facilitate their reorientation and engagement to a working sphere when moving from one working sphere to another. We observed that our informants experience different types of transitions that vary according to the way those working spheres intersect in time. Intersections can often result on challenges to resume working spheres later on and managing those transitions is important.

We found that our informants experienced *natural transitions* when an action is concluded (e.g. a phone conversation or the composition of an e-mail message) and no further action is required in that particular working sphere at that moment (e.g. the individual has to wait for a response from another person). In those cases, we noticed that in general, individuals try to reach a point of closure for their working sphere: making sure that nothing else has to be done, annotating details on documents, or putting away folders or documents associated with it. We observed that many times after a natural transition, individuals switched to another working sphere without interacting with any artifact or person to give them an overview. Other times, they renewed their overviews, by checking their e-mail for new or pending messages, went through their lists (e.g. to-do lists, agendas, etc) or even sought updates from co-workers. Once the overview was gained the individual moved to the next working sphere.

Many times our informants experienced *forced transitions* as a result of interruptions of one's current working sphere. In those situations people have to leave the current working sphere and turn to something else. We observed that a common mechanism to manage this transition is based on extending work in the current working sphere until a natural breaking point is reached. In this case, individuals, when interrupted by others, request them to wait so they could conclude the current action (e.g. finishing composing an e-mail message or typing a line of software code) and then give them their full attention. This strategy aims to minimize the level of disruption in the current working sphere by guaranteeing that it is left at a natural breaking point so that it can be easily resumed. Many of our informants pointed out that reaching natural breaking points was necessary in order to avoid losing track of the flow of ideas so as to be fully attentive to the interrupting working sphere.

We identified two main ways our informants managed abrupt transitions with respect to the immediate involvement in the interrupting working sphere. In many cases individuals accepted interrupting work and became fully involved in it until the request was done. This kind of involvement is typical when urgent working spheres serve as the basis for interruptions. These urgent spheres can have strong implications, for example, when requests refer to problems with financial transactions or legal operations. In contrast, in many cases, individuals opted for another strategy: they responded quickly to an interruption, took the necessary information and details about the request, and then followed it up later when they could easily turn away from other working spheres. This partial involvement helped them to be responsive and organize their work in a better way, but at the same time, allowed them to continue with the interrupted working sphere after a brief period, as is explained by Ronald a manager at ITS:

"...somebody called me and asked me a question I need to do research for and get back to them. I'll note it here [Outlook Tasks] so that I make sure that I don't forget. So when I get periods during the day when, 'OK I don't have any meetings', 'developers are all busy', this and that, I'll look here and see what I need to address."

We found that during interactions with another, our informants experienced *sequential* transitions among many working spheres as they discussed issues related to each one. We noticed this happening during conversations prior to the start of a formal meeting and in other kinds of informal interactions. Individuals took advantage of interruptions by people with whom they shared different working spheres by purposely engaging in sequential transitions. After talking about the interrupting working spheres, people tried to discuss other pending working spheres before the interaction finished. The following scenario illustrates that situation:

While working on an analysis, Jennifer is interrupted by the phone ringing: "Hello?... Hi Pam!". Pam, a trainer in Texas, is calling to give details about the training program at GTE, a new medical practice, as Jennifer called her earlier this week. However, Jennifer already has the information: "Don't worry Pam. I actually ended up figuring out that one," says Jennifer. They talk about that but then Jennifer turns to another working sphere, "What about East Bay Orthopedics? Are they signing the contract?". After discussing about East Bay, she ends the phone call and resumes work on her analysis.

We identified that in the case of abrupt transitions, individuals opted for different strategies to resume work. In some situations, the resumption is straightforward as people remember enough cues to facilitate the recovery. In other cases, we observed that if people have enough time before switching, they use post-it notes to annotate details that are useful for resuming the working sphere later on. Other informants annotated the actions performed for the working sphere as these were conducted. This indicates that people were preparing for interruptions; when they happened they could figure out where the work was stopped and could easily resume work in it. Finally, we also observed that many of our informants tried to recreate the last actions they did before the interruption. They went through each of the open applications in their computers or looked at the different documents on their desk trying to regain their train of thought.

Discussion

Understanding how information workers multi-task is fundamental for CSCW. Collaborations in practice are experienced as the intertwining of multiple working spheres, where people, along the course of the day, move in and out of different collaborative contexts based on circumstances. Furthermore, collaborations arise, evolve, and are defined in a situated manner as people delineate their work moment by moment and identify the subset of individuals that can contribute to achieve the purposes of their working spheres (Suchman 1987). Consequently, understanding the basic processes and strategies used in multi-tasking contributes toward understanding collaborative work itself.

The three fundamental processes that we identified highlight some optimal ways by which multi-tasking is achieved, as an informant described, to "*don't let anything fall through the cracks*". It should be clear that although each process is relevant for all our informants, we observed that the specific use of one or another strategy is based on personal preferences, job's characteristics, or the availability of resources. For example, to represent their overviews, some informants were more inclined towards annotating their working spheres in "to-do" lists, whereas others just used their email inboxes to list pending messages related to working spheres. Similarly, some types of job roles (e.g. project leaders) demanded more interdependence and required more interaction with others, whereas other work tended to be more solo. In some other cases individuals had access to particular tools such as instant messaging that facilitated awareness of the presence of co-workers beyond what can be understood by just listening to events in the hallway or other cubicles. Based on our findings, we discuss some of the challenges to support the different processes we discussed that are involved in multi-tasking.

Maintaining an overview of the working spheres in which one is engaged is based on the constant integration of information from many sources including digital and physical artifacts. People consolidate such information and use it to develop global and local perspectives of their working spheres. Local perspectives, containing those day-to-day actions to be done for their working spheres, were often represented in artifacts that are mobile (e.g. notepads), that afford flexible schemes to annotate information, that provide a space to draw on and discuss ideas with others, and that were often left open and visible on desks to serve as easy reminders of pending actions. On the other hand, global perspectives contained more high-level descriptions of working spheres and were always visible and represented in either whiteboards or printouts hanging on walls, or easily reachable on desks. We argue that technological support should be oriented towards helping individuals maintain both local and global perspectives of their working spheres, providing the ability to represent information in portable devices that can be located on their desks or hung on walls, and be connected and synchronized with other tools such as email, electronic calendars, or other systems. Similarly, those technologies can serve to link and share information about the progress that individuals have in their personal working spheres to the systems used by the organization to manage and coordinate team projects or manage customer requests.

Another challenge is for individuals to maintain a flexible window of focus over their different working spheres. There are clear limits on the degree to which individuals can monitor events around them. Consequently, technology can play a very important role in providing individuals with an expanded focus to be aware of events that might affect both current and pending working spheres. For this purpose, awareness information mechanisms should be designed to be configurable to reflect not only the status of collaborations, but also the status of particular working spheres in those collaborations (e.g. if a phone call was made, a document was signed or resources are available).

Finally, adequate tools do not exist to support transitioning between different working spheres. We argue that, due to the interactive nature of work, technologies should not only be oriented to reduce transitions due to interruptions, for instance by identifying when is appropriate to interrupt (Adamczyk and Bailey 2004), but, more importantly, oriented to make transitions beneficial for individuals. We argue that transitions due to interruptions can be optimized if individuals can remember and discuss those pending issues that they have with the persons interrupting them. We noticed that, lacking automated support for quickly retrieving information about shared working spheres and pending issues, our informants just opted to check their paper "to-do" lists, agendas, or mailboxes to verify if there are other pending issues. However, our informants commented that many times it was after the person was gone that they remembered those other things they needed to discuss with the interrupters. Technology should provide mechanisms to generate summaries of pending issues in working spheres so that interactions are optimized.

Conclusions

In this paper we have presented a view of collaborations that is different from that usually described in CSCW studies. We view that people are involved in multiple working spheres involving different sets of people and they continually change working spheres and collaborative contexts throughout the day. Work is thus very fragmented. We identified that our informants manage their multi-tasking by renewing their overviews, by maintaining a flexible focus on information relevant to current and future working spheres, and by managing transitions among their working spheres. We discussed how those processes can be supported by technology, and emphasized the importance of integrating information used to organize personal work with organizational information at the collective level. Our findings reflect and build upon previous CSCW studies, but also provide new perspectives to understand multitasking with multiple collaborations. We plan to conduct further analysis of our data to refine and improve our understanding.

Acknowledgments

We would like to thank all our informants at ITS and Venture. This research was supported by the National Science Foundation under grant no. 0093496, by the Center for Research on Information Technology and Organizations, and with grants from CONACYT and UCMEXUS.

References

Ackerman, M., D. Hindus, S. D. Mainwating and B. Starr (1997): 'Hanging on the wire: A field study on an audio-only media space', *ACM Transactions on Computer Human Interaction*, vol. 4, no.1, 1997, pp. 39-66.

Adamczyk, P. D. and B. P. Bailey (2004): 'If not now, when?: The effects of interruption at different moments within task execution' in: *Proceedings of CHI 2004*, ACM press, Vienna, Austria, pp. 271-278.

Belloti, V., B. Dalal, N. Good, P. Flynn, D. Bobrow and N. Ducheneaut (2004): 'What a To-Do: Studies of Task Management Towards the Design of a Personal Task List Manager' in: *Proceedings of CHI 2004*, ACM Press, Vienna, Austria, pp. 735-742.

Belloti, V., N. Ducheneaut, M. Howard and I. Smith (2003): 'Taking email to task: the design and evaluation of a task management centered email tool.' in: *ACM Conference on Human Factors in Computing Systems (CHI 2003)*, ACM, Fort Lauderdale; FL., pp. 345-352.

Blandford, A. E. and T. R. G. Green (2001): 'Group and individual time management tools: what you get is not what you need', *Personal and Ubiquitous Computing*, vol. 5, no.4, December 2001, pp. 213-230.

Boardman, R. and A. M. Sasse (2004): '"Stuff goes into the computer and doesn't come out" A cross-tool study of personal information management' in: *Proceedings of CHI 2004*, ACM press, Vienna, Austria, pp. 583-590.

Buscher, M., P. Mogensen, D. Shapiro and I. Wagner (1999): 'The Manufaktur: supporting work practice in (landscape) architecture' in: *Proceedings of the Sixth European conference on Computer supported cooperative work*, Kluwer Academic Publishers, Copenhagen, Denmark, pp. 21-40.

Czerwinski, M., E. Horvitz and S. Wilhite (2004): 'A Diary Study of Task Switching and Interruptions' in: *Proceedings of CHI 2004*, ACM Press, Vienna, Austria, pp. 175-182.

DiMaggio, P. (2001). The Futures of Business Organization and Paradoxes of Change. *The Twenty-First-Century Firm: Changing economic organization in international perspective*. P. DiMaggio. Oxford, Princeton University Press: 210-244.

Fussell, S. R., S. Kiesler, L. D. Setlock, P. Scupelli and S. Weisband (2004): 'Effects of Instant Messaging on the Management of Multiple Project Trajectories' in: *Proceedings of CHI 2004*, ACM Press, Vienna, Austria, pp. 191-198.

González, V. and G. Mark (2004): '"Constant, Constant, Multi-tasking Craziness": Managing Multiple Working Spheres' in: *Proceedings of CHI 2004*, ACM Press, Vienna, Austria, pp. 113-120.

Heath, C. and P. Luff (1991): 'Collaborative activity and technological design: Task coordination in London Underground control rooms' in: *Proceedings of ECSCW 91*, Kluwer Academic Publishers, Dordrecht, The Netherlands, pp. 65-80.

Hudson, J. M., J. Christensen, W. A. Kellogg and T. Erickson (2002): '"I'd Be Overwhelmed, But It's Just One More Thing to Do:" Availability and Interruption in Research Management.' in: *Proceedings of CHI 2002*, Minneapolis, Minnesota, pp. 97-104.

Kraut, R. E., R. Fish, R. Root and B. Chalfonte (1993). Informal communication in organizations: form, function, and technology. *Groupware and Computer-Supported Co-operative Work*. R. Baecker, Morgan Kaufmann, 1993: 287-314.

Leont'ev, A. (1978): Activity, Consciousness, and Personality. Englewood Cliffs, N.J., Prentice-Hall.

Mark, G., V. González and J. Harris (2005): 'No Task Left Behind? Examining the Nature of Fragmented Work' in: *Proceedings of ACM CHI 2005*, ACM press, Portland, OR, pp. 321-330.

Mark, G., J. Grudin and S. Poltrock (1999): 'Meeting at the desktop: An empirical study of virtually collocated team' in: *Proceedings of ECSCW'99*, ACM press, Copenhagen, pp. 159-178.

Mintzberg, H. (1973): *The Nature of Managerial Work*. Englewood Cliffs N.J., Prentice Hall.

O'Conaill, B. and D. Frohlich (1995): 'Timespace in the Workplace: Dealing with Interruptions' in: *Proceedings of CHI 95*, ACM, Denver, Colorado, pp. 262-263.

Perlow, L. A. (1999): 'The Time Famine: Toward a Sociology of Work Time', *Administrative Science Quarterly*, vol. 44, 1999, pp. 57-81.

Rogers, Y. (1994): 'Exploring Obstacle: Integrating CSCW in evolving organizations' in: *Proceedings of CSCW 94*, ACM Press, Chapel Hill, N.C., USA, pp. 67-77.

Rouncefield, M., J. A. Hughes, T. Rodden and S. Viller (1994): 'Working with "Constant Interruption": CSCW and the Small Office' in: *Proceedings of CSCW 94*, ACM, Chapel Hill, N.C., pp. 275-286.

Sproull, L. S. (1984): 'The Nature of Managerial Attention', *Advances in Information Processing in Organizations*, vol. 1, 1984, pp. 9-27.

Strauss, A. (1985): 'Work and the division of labor', *The Sociological Quarterly*, vol. 26, no.1, 1985, pp. 1-19.

Strauss, A. and J. Corbin (1998): *Basics of Qualitative Research: Techniques and procedures for developing grounded theory*, Sage.

Suchman, L. (1987): *Plans and Situated Actions: The problem of human machine communication*. Cambridge, Cambridge University Press.

Suchman, L. and E. Wynn (1984): 'Procedures and Problems in the Office', *Office: Technology and People*, vol. 2, pp. 133-154.

Whittaker, S., D. Frohlich and O. Daly-Jones (1994): 'Informal workplace communication: What is it like and how might we support it?' in: *Proceedings of CHI 94*, ACM, Boston, Massachusetts, pp. 131-137.

H. Gellersen et al. (eds.), ECSCW 2005: Proceedings of the Ninth European
Conference on Computer-Supported Cooperative Work, 18-22 September 2005, Paris,
France, 163–183.

The Duality of Articulation Work in Large Heterogeneous Settings – a Study in Health Care

Louise Færgemann, Teresa Schilder-Knudsen and Peter H. Carstensen
IT-University of Copenhagen, Denmark
faergemann@itu.dk, teresa@itu.dk, carstensen@itu.dk

Abstract. Based on an empirical study of articulation work in a health care setting this paper discusses core characteristics of articulation work in large settings. We argue that articulation work in large-scale settings is characterized by a dual nature, especially by a duality between articulation handled internally in a local work arrangement and articulation activities undertaken across boundaries of local work arrangements appears. We suggest that our understanding of articulation activities is related to a distinction between local and global work arrangements. We illustrate how cooperating actors involved in any given trajectory (e.g., a patient trajectory) have to articulate their activities in accordance with both a local and a global dimension. The distinction between local and global is important when aiming at understanding articulation work in large-scale heterogenous settings. The differences and their consequences are discussed. The paper conclude in some reflections on the challenges implied by the local/global variations, both for the analysis of large heterogeneous work settings and for design of IT support.

Introduction

A general trend in modern work settings seems to be that the work becomes more and more complex. Complex in the sense that it is characterized by complex problem solving and decision making activities, rule interpretation, cooperative work processes, etc. The demands for flexibility, faster production time, complex products, etc. are exploding.

The increasing complexity of the work activities, the situations to be dealt with, and the structures to be handled, often require involvement of many actors in the work processes. Since individuals have limited capabilities and capacities, the work arrangement required to conduct the work becomes cooperative. Cooperative work arrangements emerge in response to different requirements and may serve different generic functions such as augmentation of capacity, differentiation and combination of specialties and techniques, mutual critical assessment, and combination of perspectives (Schmidt, 1994).

When several actors having different competencies, perspectives, strategies, etc. are involved in a cooperative work arrangement, they become mutually interdependent in their work, i.e., "cooperative work occurs when multiple actors are required to do the work and therefore are mutually dependent in their work and must coordinate and integrate their individual activities to get the work done" (Schmidt, 1991). Mutual interdependence means not only sharing resources, but also that the involved actors mutually rely on the quality, feedback, etc. produced by the other actors, i.e., no matter how the division of labor is organized, the actors involved will be interdependent and need to interact with each other. In order to get the work done, they have to coordinate, schedule, integrate, etc. their individual activities. The actors have to articulate their work along the salient dimensions of who, what, where, when, how, etc. (Strauss, 1985).

When relatively few actors are involved, or the complexity of the work or its articulation is low, the actors may achieve the required articulation by means of modes of interaction and conventions from everyday social life such as talking, gesturing, monitoring the situation, etc. (Schmidt, 1994). Several studies indicate that actors in these situations are extremely good at handling the complexity of coordinating by means of ad-hoc modes of interaction (Harper et al., 1989, Heath et al., 1993). Problems will, however, often emerge in highly complex work when, for example, the cooperative work setting includes many geographically distributed actors; a large number of intertwined activities, actors, or resources; different areas of competence with different conceptualizations and goals; or when the work is carried out over a long time span.

The understanding and IT support of articulation work has been a recurring issue within CSCW research since Schmidt and Bannon (1992) suggested to make it a central theme. Articulation of the work in small scale settings and fairly delimited organizational settings such as control rooms (e.g., Heath and Luff, 1992; Harper and Hughes, 1993; Berndtsson and Normark, 1999) has drawn a lot of attention within CSCW. However, the nature of articulation work in large-scale settings such as health care has been less examined. Our general understanding of the basic characteristics of work carried out in large-scale settings is still insufficient and fragmented — and so is our understanding of the special characteristics of the articulation work undertaken in such settings. Based upon an empirical study this article provides insights into articulation work activities involving a large heterogeneous collection of actors who are geographically distributed — in our case the health care professionals involved in the period of pregnancy. Due to their geographical distribution the actors have to articulate their individual activities in order to take care of the patient and handle the surrounding patient trajectories.

An improved conceptual understanding of the nature of the articulation work and the underlying conditions are important when designing IT systems aiming at an effective, flexible, and adequate support of the collaboration undertaken. One of the main challenges for computer support in the health care area is to facilitate what is often described as 'shared care' among health care professionals. The aim of shared care is to ensure coherence and continuity over the patient trajectory, even though treatment involves several different and geographically dispersed actors. Our understanding of 'shared care' follows a definition commonly used in medical communities, namely a definition put forward by Pritchard and Hughs:

"Shared care applies when the responsibility for the health care of the patients is shared between individuals or teams who are part of separate organizations, or where substantial organizational boundaries exist." (Pritchard and Hughs, 1995).

Shared care is understood as an integrated and interdisciplinary collaboration related to a patient trajectory or patient care program where a common responsibility for treatment of the patient is shared between interdisciplinary teams that cooperate across units. Articulating the activities is a core aspect of the collaboration across units. Hence, an examination of the articulation work is an obvious starting point for a better understanding of shared care. Focus in our study has therefore been core characteristics of articulation work, not shared care as such.

As indicated in the introduction many researchers have pointed out that support of articulation work is essential for supporting complex cooperative work activities (e.g., Schmidt and Bannon, 1992), and as far back as in 1985 Strauss investigated medical work and the trajectories of work in order to establish a conceptual understanding of articulation work (Strauss et al., 1985).

Today there is furthermore a growing interest for health care studies within CSCW and a growing recognition of the problems with collaboration and coordination in health care. More specifically there is an increasing interest in electronic medical records within a CSCW perspective. Ellingsen and Monteiro (2003) examined which role knowledge representation — such as paper or electronically based records — play in the clinical work within one unit. Berg (1999) has investigated the implementation of electronically based records on a intensive care unit and presents a new understanding of information technology as embedded in work practice. Reddy et al. (2001) have examined the use of a shared information system within an intensive care unit and documented the need for many specialized representations in order to cope with the coordination demands. They have later also investigated the importance of rhythms in medical work (Reddy and Dourish, 2002). Bossen (2002) has also studied work and articulation work in hospital wards in order to inform discussions of the concepts of common information spaces, and Bardram and Hansen (2004) refer to a related study in their discussions of social awareness in a mobile hospital setting.

The CSCW related studies within health care mentioned above have primarily been focusing on the usage of artefacts and IT-systems, and most of them have primarily been concerned with the clinical work within one single unit (e.g., Berg, 1999; Reddy et al., 2001; Bossen, 2002; Bardram and Hansen, 2004). These influential and interesting studies contribute to highlighting central issues regarding computer support in health care, but they are not concerned with a deeper understanding of large-scale aspects of articulation work, and they do not explicitly address issues of heterogenous settings. The studies focused on implementation and use of already developed electronic medical records and investigations of the role of information technology in the medical work and clinical practices.

The study presented here has a different focus, namely the dual nature of articulation work conducted in distributed heterogeneous settings. Our study addresses large heterogeneous settings and investigates the articulation work handled, both within units and across unit boundaries.

In the following section, we briefly introduce our research approach. We then characterize the field study and the work setting investigated in our case: the period of pregnancy. Following this, we characterize the essential aspects of articulation work in patient trajectories. The paper concludes in a discussion on the nature of articulation work in distributed heterogeneous settings, and a few brief reflections on implications for CSCW design in such settings.

Research Approach

To obtain a coherent understanding of complex work settings and the work conducted, field studies can be an essential means (Yin, 1989; Orlikowski, 1993). As Schmidt points out the empirical study is essential for getting a coherent understanding of the nature of cooperative work and how it is unfolding:

"The primary role of workplace studies in CSCW is thus to dismantle the common-sense conceptions of cooperative work, take them apart, unpack and disclose the hidden practices of articulation work, and thus give us access analytically and conceptually to the intricate ways and means of the production of social order in cooperative activities." (Schmidt, 2000, p. 145).

This article is based upon an empirical study, heavily inspired by an ethnographic approach although the amount of time and resources for the project did not make it possible to conduct a full-scale ethnographic field study. The ethnographic inspiration is reflected in a lot of studies within CSCW, for example the studies of London Underground (Heath and Luff, 1992), Instrument Design (Carstensen and Sørensen, 1996), Air Traffic Control (Harper and Hughes, 1993,

Berndtsson and Normark, 1999), Medical care units (e.g., Reddy et al., 2001), and the early studies by Suchman (e.g., Suchman, 1983).

Many researchers have argued for the great potentials of an ethnographic approach within CSCW, and argued, for example, that "the ethnographic approach, with its emphasis on 'natives' point-of-view,' holism, and natural settings, provide a unique perspective to bring to bear on understanding users' work activities" (Blomberg et al., 1991, p. 123).

Our empirical work was primarily conducted at the Obstetrical Unit at the National Hospital of Denmark (Rigshospitalet). Focus was on interviewing and observing different people involved in the period of pregnancy to cover as many perspectives as possible. We started out by interviewing several pregnant women to get their key-perspective of the whole period of their pregnancy. Following this, we investigated the work and articulation activities of the professionals involved in patient care work. We interviewed midwives, maternity doctors and other specialists involved, as well as secretaries and nurses at the Maternity Ward. Furthermore, we studied how the professionals collaborated and communicated across organizational boundaries and units. Both actors in the Maternity Ward and in other units, such as the Cardiology Unit (involved in the care of pregnant women with heart diseases) and the Ultrasound Unit, were studied. Beside the health care professionals at the hospital, the general practitioners play a central role during the pregnancy period. Hence, our study includes this group too. Along with the interviews, we carried out observations at the Maternity Ward to see how the health care professionals conduct their work. In total, our empirical material includes 16 semi-structured interviews and 5 full day observations.

The field study was conducted over approximately four months and, as mentioned, was primarily based on observation, artifact analyses, and qualitative interviews (Patton, 2002). For all observations, interviews, meeting participation, etc. a summary was produced, and these summaries were then abstracted into general themes. These themes were identified from a first rough analysis. The abstraction of the data into themes was conducted as a collaborative brainstorm-oriented process. Although we did not start with a strict set of hypotheses, we did bring an articulated perspective. We explicitly addressed aspects like the organization of work, a 'typical' work day, the actors' use of artifacts, involved roles and competencies, and the internal and external articulation of activities, This resulted in a first very descriptive characterization of the work. From the first overall analyses, our data were reanalyzed with a more focused perspective. The research approach we applied can be characterized as qualitative research heavily inspired by theories and conceptualizations within CSCW. Conceptualizations suggested by Schmidt et al. of the work arrangement and the related field of work and the analytical distinction between work and articulation work (Schmidt and Simone, 1996, Carstensen, 1996) has played a central role. The understanding of articulation activities in this framework is heavily inspired by the conceptual work by Strauss (1985) and Gerson & Star (1986) on articulation work.

Studies like the one presented here make only limited claims regarding the generality of the findings. We have in our study focused on the richness of detail and relevance of the problems studied rather than general validity. This must be investigated through further studies.

Case: The Period of Pregnancy

Before we provide more detailed descriptions of the work investigated, let us briefly introduce the case, i.e., the period of pregnancy, and the organizational setting in which the patient care work is conducted.

During the period of gestation, the pregnant woman alternately consults her general practitioner and a midwife at a clinic for regular examinations, starting out with a consultation at the general practitioner. Furthermore, the pregnant woman is offered a nuchal fold scan and an ultrasound scan, which both take place at the Ultrasound Unit. Our studies illustrated that these examinations play a central role for the pregnant women because they here get to see their unborn child. When the pregnant woman goes into labour, she contacts the Maternity Ward, where midwives, nurses and maternity doctors are responsible for the delivery and post-delivery care.

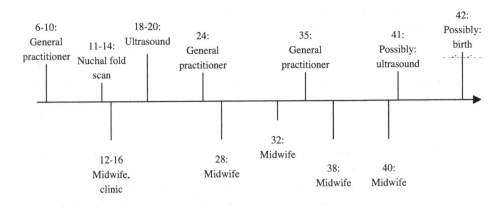

Figure 1: A time line for the period of pregnancy. The numbers indicate weeks.

The health care sector in Denmark is divided into a primary and a secondary sector. Every citizen is attached to a general practitioner, who takes care of patients' general medical condition. When specialist treatment is needed, when operations has to be carried out, etc., the general practitioner refers the patient to the secondary sector, the hospital. The primary and the secondary sector communicate and collaborate around the patients as they carry out different tasks and thus have different professional responsibilities for the patient. The general practitioner has his own clinic and works more or less on his own. This is in contrast to the work carried out at the hospital. Health care professionals at the hospital constantly collaborate with a lot of professional colleagues, both with colleagues having the same formal background and function and with other specialist groups. Hospitals are characterised by a high degree of specialization and are thus organizationally divided into many different units and employ many different types of health care professionals. In connection with pregnancy the Obstetrical Unit is the primary actor within the secondary health care sector. The Obstetrical Unit at Rigshospitalet employ 170 health care professionals and is divided into different units such as the Maternity Ambulatory, the Maternity Home, Maternity Ward, and a clinic with rooms for women giving birth. The Maternity Home takes care of uncomplicated births while the Maternity Ward takes care of the more complicated. The Obstetrical Unit primarily collaborate with the Ultrasound Unit, the Paediatrician Unit and the Anaesthesia and Operation Unit which all employ differently specialized health care professionals.

Midwives at the Maternity Ambulatory take care of the pregnant women during pregnancy, and they examine the condition of the unborn child such as weight and height. Midwives at the Maternity Ward and the Maternity Home are responsible for the care related to the delivery. The maternity doctors take care of all kinds of patients hospitalized with diseases within the obstetrical area, not only women in labour. The Maternity Home and the Maternity Ward are open 24-hours. The health care professionals thus work in shifts, an 8 hour day shift, an 8 hour evening shift and a night shift. During the day, approximately seven midwives and two obstetricians are on duty at the Maternity Ward. The midwives call the doctors (or physician or surgeons) when needed, for example when a birth is not in progress or when a caesarean operation might be needed. Every duty begins with a briefing among midwives and a conference among the doctors.

Health care professionals engaged at the Obstetrical Unit use a large number of documents and other artefacts to coordinate their work and keep updated information about the patients. Some artefacts such as notes, the obstetrical record, and notice boards in the briefing and conference room as well as phones are primarily used for internal coordination within Obstetrical Unit and between different units within the hospital. Other artefacts such as the record accompanying the pregnant woman (in Danish: 'vandrejournalen') are used for facilitating coordination between primary and secondary health care sector, i.e., between the general practitioner and the midwives at the clinic.

Articulation of Patient Trajectories

This chapter illustrates how the patient care activities are coordinated and exemplifies the communication among the different actors involved in the patient care. The intention is not to give a detailed and coherent picture of the work and its articulation, but rather to provide examples and illustrations of the different types of articulation undertaken, and to exemplify coordination activities conducted locally and across boundaries, and to show how this coordination involves issues of global articulation.

At the Maternity Ward where our studies primarily took place life is hectic. Following one midwife during her day duty revealed insights into the articulation work needed to take care of the pregnant women and women in labour.

Briefing

Every duty begins with a short briefing between midwives from the previous shift and midwives who have just arrived. The briefing takes place in the meeting room, which is the only common meeting place for the midwives. At daytime duties midwives arrive just before 7:00. The actors from the night shift report to the day duty about new incomers and the status of the hospitalized women: Are they in labour, how is the birth proceeding, etc.? They go through patients on the basis of their records. The records play an important role during duty. The records contian crucial information about the hospitalized (and not yet hospitalized) women. During duty the midwives update the records when the changes occur when they obtain essential information about the patients. The briefing lasts 10-15 minutes. Briefings are frequently interrupted by the phone or sudden events which call for the attention of the midwives, but each midwife seems to get the information she needs despite the interruptions and disturbances.

The chief midwife from the previous shift is also responsible for briefing the doctors coming in for the next duty. This briefing takes place at the doctors' conferences involving only doctors and the chief midwife and is held every morning at 8:00. After the midwife's briefing, doctors from the previous shift brief the incoming shift about hospitalized patients, and opinions about further treatment of each patients are shared. At the end of the conference, the medical superintendent makes a superior division of labour between the doctors depending upon their expertises and skills, and presents the planned activities (e.g., caesarean operations) to be carried out during the duty. Already planned activities make out an important structuring mechanism for the health care professionals. It helps structuring the duty and to make as much as possible 'predictable'. At the briefing the medical superintendent might, for example, inform his colleagues that three planned caesarean operations have to be carried out, although the norm allows for only one planned operation during a shift. As the Obstetrical Unit take care of many caesarean operations, a cross-disciplinary team has been established to take care of planned operations. Between 5 and 8 operations are carried out on every Wednesday. Like the midwives' briefing the doctors' conference is characterized by interruptions and disturbances (primarily from the phone), but we observed less private talk at the doctors' conference, and the door is kept closed during the meeting.

Both at the briefing and at the conference the actors try to plan and coordinate the activities for the duty. By taking into consideration the events that occurred during the previous shift they try to predict which activities and actions to expect. During the previous shift the situation of some of the hospitalized patients may have changed and these changes may call for specific actions. Based on the briefings, informal conversations during these, and information derived from records, the health care professionals get an overview of the state of affairs at the Maternity Ward at the beginning of each new duty. When a proper overview has been obtained, the chief midwife and the medical superintendent are responsible for making an overall division of labour for each group. This overall division of labour between midwives is explicated and made available by means of a notice board in the meeting room. The notice board reflects which midwife is responsible for which pregnant woman or woman in labour, and it reflects the state of the patient. The midwives aim at updating the notice board frequently so that it reflects the current situation. Midwives' briefing session and doctors' conferences illustrate articulation work and coordination activities conducted locally, that is, within the Maternity Ward or the Obstetrical Unit.

An Epidural Blockade

During our observations of the midwives' briefing session the phone was ringing and answered by a midwife. She agreed to take over a woman in labour from a colleague at the Maternity Home. The woman in labour suffered from severe pain and the midwife judged an epidural blockade was necessary. The woman in labour therefore had to be moved from the Maternity Home to the Maternity Ward. Formally, the midwives have to ask for a doctor's advice before ordering an epidural blockade. Due to lack of time and resources this procedure is not always followed. The midwife at the Maternity Ward prepared the woman in labour for the blockade as soon as she arrived and called an anesthesiologist, who is always responsible for giving the blockade. Unfortunately the anesthesiologist was occupied with another patient, as he was treating a badly injured patient hospitalised in emergency when the midwife called him. The anesthesiologist and his colleagues at the department of anaesthesia had to give priority to this patient and the midwife and the woman in labour at the Maternity Ward had to wait 30 minutes for his assistance.

The example illustrates how the health care professionals coordinate internally but also across units (across work arrangement boundaries) involving issues of what we describe as 'global articulation' as well. Further, it exemplifies the interdependence between the different health care professionals. The midwife depends on the competencies of the anesthesiologist, and her working rhythms thereby become dependent of the rhythms of other units (see Reddy & Dourish, 2002 for an interesting discussion of this issue). The priorities of the midwife might be in conflict with the priorities of anesthesiologist. The example also indicates that it often is not possible for the health care professionals to plan, coordinate, and prioritize their individual activities within one single unit in isolation, since many events and activities are part of a larger whole and have to be coordinated accordingly.

As soon as the epidural blockade was done the midwife was supposed to fill out the patient's record. This is the procedure for all actions the health care professional take. But in the specific situation the midwife didn't have time because she was called to assist at a caesarean operation. When she showed up in the operation room, another midwife, an operation nurse, an operation-assisting nurse, two obstetricians, a pediatrist, and an anesthesiologist were already gathered. Before the operation the two midwives agreed on the division of tasks related to the operation.

A Caesarean Operation

A caesarean operation is an example of interdisciplinary teamwork. Health care professionals from different units and with different skills and competencies have to work together to manage the task. This indicates the occurrence of coordinative activities across boundaries involving issues of global articulation work.

After the caesarean operation the midwife went to the meeting room and filled out the record for the epidural blockade and the record for the operation. When carrying out a caesarean operation different records and documents have to be filled out, such as a birth registration, a record of the newborn baby, and a 'standard sectio' document. A 'standard sectio' is a standardized schema to be filled out when a planned caesarean operation is carried out. This standard document has been pre-produced to facilitate the documentation process, which is a very time consuming activity for the actors.

Caesarean operations take up a lot of resources. The formation and establishment of the sectio team helped the different units and departments in planning and allocating their resources. More than one planned caesarean operation per weekday violates the norm and is therefore not very popular with the other departments that have to assist the Obstetrical Unit. As mentioned earlier, it sometimes happens that the medical superintendent requires more than one operation. This decision can then force other departments and units to allocate spare resources unexpectedly.

The Centre for Pregnant Women with Heart Diseases

Another formalized initiative is the establishment of the Centre for Pregnant Women with Heart Diseases. This is a virtual center based on an interdisciplinary teamwork of obstetricians, cardiologists, anesthesiologists, nurses, and midwives with special training in heart diseases. This team at first carries out a screening of the woman to judge whether a pregnancy is to be recommended at all. If possible, they produce on a plan for the pregnancy before it occurs, including the different medical perspectives. Depending on her situation, the woman might need a heart operation before her pregnancy, and during pregnancy her medicine must be adjusted and other factors reconsidered.

The center is an example of the need for formalization when conducting interdisciplinary teamwork across boundaries effectively. The initiative illustrates how health care professionals in this case meet to integrate different medical perspectives on the same patients. In this situation the actors not only try to analyse and act upon the current situation. They also aim at establishing a prospective plan for the patient.

Back at the midwives' meeting room a secretary entered the room and informed the participants that a general practitioner had called to tell that he had just admitted a pregnant woman to the Maternity Ward because of irregularities he had identified during his examination. The secretary placed a post-it note on the table with the name of the pregnant. When doctors at the hospital take over a patient from the general practitioner, they make an effort of informing the general practitioner about the situation of the patient. The process of admitting and informing between the general practitioner and the specialists thus illustrate an example of cross-boundary communication and coordination.

Much cross-boundary coordination takes place between professionals that do not know each other and do not have frequent contact. At the same time it is worth noticing that the process of information exchange between the general practitioner and specialists is not formalized. The level and quality of the information tend to be 'accidental', and essential information might get lost since the information-handling process depends upon the individual actor.

The woman admitted by the general practitioner came in and one of the midwives examined her in a delivery room. A scanning of the carriage of the child's head was needed and the midwife decided to call one of the obstetricians. He turned out to be occupied elsewhere and suggested the midwife to carry out the scanning herself, as he estimated that she was qualified to do so. She did not agree with this, but since she was left alone with the patient she had no choice. In situations where more complicated scannings are required the women are sent to the Ultrasound Clinic.

This example indicates that a strict division of labour is difficult during the hectic life at the Maternity Ward. New situations and professional challenges arise continuously and must be handled on an ad hoc basis. The roles (doctors, nurses, and midwives) are important as the title indicates an area of competencies. However, a flexible interpretation of the role and the matching competencies and qualification is needed during the practical work with the patients.

As our field study indicates patient trajectories are characterized by a high degree of temporal complexity. Patient trajectories are unpredictable and cannot be planned, since complications can suddenly arise. The uncertainty makes it difficult for the health care professionals — i.e., the cooperative work arrangement — to plan and coordinate the necessary activities at hand. Hence diagnosing, treatment, and care are correspondingly becoming increasingly complex. To meet the increased demands, the actors become more and more specialized. The different groups of specialists and units are characterized by high degree of heterogeneity. The collaborating actors have different educations, titles, competencies and qualifications, and often very different goals and perspectives. A consequence of this professional specialization is the geographical distribution of actors across specialized units. At the same time the increasing challenges arising from more complex patient trajectories will inevitable demand more interdisciplinary teamwork in the future. The collaboration, as well as its articulation, are challenged by the distribution and heterogeneity of the work force. Coherence in patient trajectory ('shared care') can only be achieved if actors collaborate and articulate their individual activities within and across units.

From our study we can outline a first rough categorization of the articulation activities. Articualtion activities are related to (1) The process of orientation, (2) Access to an overview of the state of affairs of the field of work, and (3) The process of integrating different perspectives on relevant situations.

The process of orientation concerns all activities related to getting access to relevant updated information about the patient. Orientation takes place in a formalized way at briefings and conferences and through patient records and notes. It does, however, also take place in an ad hoc manner during the duty when — for example — two midwives discuss the situation of a patient when they meet in the corridor. Mutual orientation is essential for the patient care work.

Access to an overview of the state of affairs of the field of work helps the actor to consider the patient in a general view. This is important, as examinations done by one unit or shift influence what has to be done by other units and so forth. A general view of the patient has great importance in the attempt to facilitate coherence in the patient trajectories.

The health care professionals also need to integrate different perspectives on the patient in order to establish a general professional view. As for the process coping with orientation and getting the overall picture, the integration of perspectives depends heavily on articulation activities, both within a unit and across work arrangement boundaries. The study also indicates that shifts between local and global articulation work happens constantly and continuously and that actors engage in both local and global coordination at the same time. It has, furthermore, clearly illustrated the constant change between ad hoc and formalized articulation activities.

Discussion

Our studies have illustrated that articulation work within large scale settings is characterized by a dual nature, both regarding formalized vs. ad hoc based coordination, and regarding local vs. cross-boundary (global) articulation activities.

The duality of formalized vs. ad hoc coordination is well-described. Suchman (1987) pointed at the gap between planned formal processes and the ad hoc based nature of the situated actions. Many others have discussed the dimension of ad hoc articulation to formalized articulation work (e.g,. Carstensen, 1996, Kraut and Streeter, 1995, Schmidt, 1994), and within CSCW a number of studies of the consequences of working in large settings exists (e.g., Grinter et al., 1999).

What we suggest here is a more explicit conceptualization of the local-global duality. An improved conceptualization of the duality can contribute to a better and more fine-grained understanding of cooperative work and its articulation. When unpacking the duality between articulation conducted within a unit (such as the Maternity Ward) and articulation conducted across units in the primary and the secondary sector, we can extrapolate a distinction between local and global work arrangements and the corresponding local and global articulation work.

The distinction between local and global appeared to be highly relevant for the work settings we have investigated, and it has to be addressed explicitly in large-scale heterogeneous settings. However, the question is: What does it mean, and what are the implications and consequences with respect to analysis of work settings and development of IT support? First of all we must investigate the concept of local and global and investigate when the distinction is relevant. Furthermore, we should seek to establish useful boundaries between the local and the global settings, and investigate to what extent these boundaries are static, respectively dynamic.

As fields of work, the patient trajectories are characterized by a high degree of temporal complexity. Complications may suddenly arise. The lack of predictability makes it difficult for the cooperative work arrangements to plan and coordinate the involved activities. As mentioned when presenting our empirical findings, unexpected examinations and activities (e.g., a caesarean operation) are often needed. Furthermore, the patient trajectory itself is geographically dispersed and many units are involved. The fact that health care become more and more specialized increases the dispersion further. The result are more complex patient trajectories involving many different units and specialties. Each specialty in the care and treatment has different competencies and responsibilities towards the patient. As an example, the general practitioner and the midwives are responsible for different examinations of the women at different points in time during her pregnancy. To put it differently they are both acting in each their *local field of work*. For the midwives at the Maternity Ward, the local field of work is the care of women in labour, and the examinations done at the general practitioners' clinic make out his local field of work. The midwife is part of one *local cooperative work arrangement* — the Maternity Ward. And similarly the general practitioner is part of another local cooperative work arrangement — his clinic. When aiming at understanding the local field of work it is necessary to talk about a corresponding *global field of work*. The global field of work is constituted by all of the patient trajectoriesto be undertaken at different places by different health care professionals.

The global field of work should be understood as the total web of patient trajectories which health care professionals are involved in at the time. Together the web of patient trajectories constitutes a global field of work with a concomitant *global cooperative work arrangement*. The global cooperative work arrangements are all the health care professionals — despite units — involved in any given patient trajectory. The subset of the web of patient trajectories being parts of a number of patient trajectories constitutes the local field of work of a local cooperative work arrangement at a given point in time. For example, the subset of of the patient trajectories related to the birth giving for non-complicated births constitutes the local field of work for the Maternity Home.

Actors involved in patient trajectories handle a web of distinct activities, such as a nuchal fold scan, ultrasound scan, examinations of heart beat rhythm, or examination of the weight and height of the unborn children. Together, all these individual activities — which are carried out geographically dispersed by different health care professionals — constitute the total amount of examinations and controls, ie., the activities required to handle the global field of work. This illustrates the distinction between local and global: We consider it local articulation work when actors within one unit collaborate and articulate their activities to carry a single type of examination such as the ultrasound scan. And it becomes global articulation work when focus on this single ultrasound scan is coordinated as just one out of many types of examinations during pregnancy.

There are two central dimensions of complexity of articulation work related to the global field of work, i.e., the total web of patient trajectories in which health care professionals are involved. That is (a) an organizational and spatial dimension implies the different analytical types of articulation work that are carried out internally or across units or sectors. We define these different types of articulation activities as internal, semi-internal, semi-external, or external (discussed below). And (b) a temporal dimension along which different articulation activities takes place. Activities taking place at different points in time can be associated. Activities are associated when an actor, while conducting an activity here and now, has to take into consideration which other activities have been carried out before, or how the activity will influence activities to be carried out later on. We can thus think of this as *associated articulation activities*. This type of association appear in the processes of getting access to relevant information, getting an overview of the state of affairs and integrating different perspectives. Examples of this could be an actor taking the notes written by another actor in the record into consideration before deciding on the sequence of a set of actions. Associated articulation activities can occur both locally (e.g., a midwife at the Maternity Ward applying notes written by another midwife) or globally (e.g., when information provided by the general practitioner is used for planning).

Let us, for a while, take a look at our empirical observations. Where do the distinction between local and global articulation work express itself? In our case, we identified different types of articulation work in which the actors were involved. As indicated above, our studies suggested four analytical types of articulation work: (1) internal, (2) semi-internal, (3) semi-external and (4) external. By internal articulation work we think of activities where the health care professionals within a single unit — e.g. the Maternity Ward or the Ultrasound Unit — coordinate their activities, etc.; for example, when the midwives coordinated and planned their work at briefings.

The semi-internal type of articulation work is similar to the internal. It occurs when collaborating actors in two closely coupled units (e.g., the Maternity Ward and the Maternity Home) coordinate their work and activities. An illustration is when the midwife at the Maternity Home contacted the Maternity Ward about the pregnant woman with a lot of pain related to her labour. We term it semi-internal because midwives at the Obstetrical Unit have duties on both the Maternity Ward and the Maternity Home. Analytically, we would often think of them as belonging to the same local work arrangement, but it is distinct from internal because the Ward and the Home are geographically separated as two distinct units, each having its own 'clients' and formalized coordinative activities such as briefing meetings and planning the duty.

We use the term semi-external articulation work when two separate organizational units (like the Obstetrical Unit and the Cardiological Unit or the Ultrasound Unit) collaborate and articulate their work. An example of this is when different specialized doctors, physicians, and midwives meet to coordinate and plan their care work with respect to a pregnant woman with a heart disease, as it is the case with the Center for Pregnant with Heart Diseases. Although the articulation activities are conducted within one organization we would usually analyze it as global articulation conducted across boundaries of work arrangements.

The fourth type of articulation work is external. This term is used when the health care professionals coordinate across sectors, e.g., when the general practitioner admitted a pregnant woman directly to the Maternity Ward and called the midwives to brief them about the situation. In a more indirect manner, it also takes place through the registration of the examination results in the record associated to the pregnant woman, or when the general practitioner admits one of his patients for examinations at the clinic. In these situations all coordination is handled trough mediated interaction facilitated by artifacts, not through direct face-to-face interaction. When the articulation work is external we consider it global.

It should be mentioned that these four types of articulation work cannot be regarded orthogonal categories, and it is not essential whether we name the different types of articulation work internal or semi-internal, or semi-external or external articulation work. What is essential is that there are different types of articulation work, and that each type has its own characteristics. We will elaborate this point further in the following.

Having sketched the important dimensions of organizational (and spatial) distance and temporal distance, let us elaborate the discussion of the complexity of local and global articulation work a bit further. The local collaboration and concomitant articulation activities are often characterized by a high degree of ad hoc coordination. Actors within a single unit —a local cooperative work arrangement — often have direct access to each others medical knowledge and capacity. When working together within a local cooperative work arrangement, it is easy for the health care professionals to monitor which colleagues are available at a given time. Our study showed that face-to-face interaction plays an important role for the collaboration, and that local articulation work often is based on immediate access and visibility. Within a local cooperative work arrangement, it is also fairly easy to gain an overview of the state of the field of work.

Handling the global articulation work across boundaries is much more complex. Actors do not in the same way have direct accesses to each others' knowledge and capacity. Often, they will not even know to whom to direct questions, comments, or suggested re-planning or re-scheduling, and they usually have no overview of who is available from the other units at the time. There is no immediate access to the state of affairs in other settings, and applying the traditional social skills of face-to-face coordination is not an option. The geographical distribution also complicates the possibility for gaining an overview of the state of the field of work. Lack of overview has severe consequences for handling the shared care. The collaboration and articulation work across unit boundaries is therefore much more demanding and is more dependent on a high degree of formalization in the interaction and coordination undertaken. Global collaboration, and thus global articulation, means great challenges to the actors' articulation activities.

Our studies cannot provide clear insights into the relation between organizational (and temporal) distance and demands for formalization of the articulation activities, but a relevant hypothesis seems to be that the longer organizational or temporal distance the stronger demand for formalization of the articulation activities. The local/global duality of the collaborative activities makes it difficult for the individual actors to know whom to brief, how much and which information to provide to others, and when to do it. The uncertainty is aggravated further by the fact that much of the articulation is handled via associated global articulation activities. Furthermore, the global field of work (the web of patient trajectories) is dynamic and highly unpredictable. This causes huge challenges for the planning processes. Formalized coordination processes are therefore called for, but at the same time a high degree of flexibility is required in order to cope with all the exceptions. Not only is the field of work dynamic. The articulation work activities are themselves dynamic due to the continuously shifts between local and global articulation, and the shifts between synchronous articulation interaction and asynchronous associated articulation activities. The uncertainty and the dynamics of the articulation activities were clearly illustrated in the example where a midwife and an anesthesiologist had to re-schedule how an epidural blockade was to be given and by whom.

The global dimension is very important and has to be taken into consideration, but the distinction between local and global dimension of articulation work is analytical. The dimensions mutually constitute each other and cannot be addressed in isolation. For example, the local articulation work conducted by two midwives in a unit is part of a whole (a global field of work and a global cooperative work arrangement), and the midwives must often take global aspects into consideration when articulating their activities, even when their work can be considered local. From the point of view of the actors we can state that, in order to be able to coordinate and plan their activities properly, the actors needs a sufficiently detailed picture of the state of affairs in the global field of work. The case is often such that the actors are well informed about status in the local field of work, whereas it is hard or impossible to quickly glance the state of the global field of work (of which the local field of work is a part). This poses both challenges and possibilities when it comes to IT support of global articulation work activities.

Above we have presented a very preliminary conceptualization of some of the central aspects of coordination and planning activities conducted in a global setting. A more detailed, coherent and elaborate conceptual framework for understanding the situation is called for. We need concepts for analyzing the global work arrangement and for characterizing the required global articulation work. It is out of the scope of this paper to present a detailed discussion of this, but we will submit a few open questions and problems.

For practical work analysis — conducted in order to establish a proper basis for discussing and designing support systems — a number of new challenges naturally occour. First of all, when analyzing a local work arrangement in a large-scale setting, the global dimension must be explicitly addressed. Conceptualizations of how the local unit is associated to the larger global setting and which aspects of the external relations that need detailed investigation are required. For now, it is not clear how to identify which global factors play a role for the local field of work and the corresponding local cooperative work and what the role may be.

When considering specific design of IT support, issues on how to support the different types of articulation work — it being local or global — become essential. We should consider how to support the process of information collection, getting an overview, and integration of perspectives across the spatial and temporal dimensions in the global work arrangement. Our study partly indicated that the longer the organizational or spatial distance is, the more formal structures for articulation activities should be considered. This could indicate that IT support of cross-boundary articulation activities should formalize the processes, but an IT-based system could also be a means of making ad hoc planning and coordination across bouadaries possible, for example by making the global field of work more easily observable. To support actors in undertaking the required global articulation activities the actors must be provided with an understanding of the global associations. This raises questions as to how to make the associations evident for the actors when they undertake their work, planning, and coordination. For the specific case of shared care of patients, the question will be how to provide an overview of the global articulation work with respect to the patient trajectory, for example how to 'visualize' the global aspects related to the activities actors conduct in order to undertake their (local) obligations. Issues related to this also concern the publishing of relevant information from one actor to others in the global work arrangement, but outside of the local work arrangement. Our study has pointed at a number of occasions where actors have a wish for providing information to other actors without knowing whether the information is required or who will be the user.

Conclusion

Based on an empirical study of a heterogenous large-scale health care setting we have shown that articulation work is characterized by a dual nature of local vs. global collaboration and articulation work activities. We have also exemplified the dimension of formalized vs. ad hoc articulation. We have documented how cooperating actors involved in handling the care and treatment required for patient trajectories have to articulate their activities in accordance with both a local and a global work arrangements (and the concomitant local and global field of work). We have furthermore discussed how the articulation work can be regarded as internal, semi-internal, semi-external, or external. In the discussions we have described how the local and global settings and activities are heavily intertwined, and we have illustrated that both local and global aspects must be taken into consideration during the articulation of the work. Over the last 20 years CSCW has been confronted with severe problems related to how to support what we would call local articulation work. What we argue here is that in order to support collaboration in large-scale heterogenous settings, we need a much richer conceptual understanding of the global aspects of the articulation work. This opens a variety of new questions and challenges for CSCW research and design.

Acknowledgements

This research could not have been conducted without the participation of the actors we have interviewed and observed. A warm and special thanks our contacts at the Obstetrical Clinic at the Rigshospitalet in Denmark for their openness and engagement in this project. Kjeld Schmidt and the anonymous reviewers provided many useful comments to previous versions of this paper. All errors remain our responsibility. The work has partly been funded by the HIT-project funded by the Danish National Research Councils.

References

Bardram, J. E. and Hansen, T. (2004): 'The AWARE Architecture: Supporting Context-Mediated Social Awareness in Mobile Cooperation', in C. A. Halverson and L. Terveen (eds.): *Proceedings of ACM Conference on Computer Supported Cooperative Work*, ACM, Chicago, 2004, pp. 192-201.

Berg, M. (1999): 'Accumulating and Coordinating: Occasions for Information Technologies in Medical Work', *Computer Supported Cooperative Work*, vol. 8, 1999, pp. 373-401.

Berndtsson, J. and Normark, M. (1999): 'The Coordinative Functions of Flight Strips: Air Traffic Control Work Revisited', In S. Hayne: *GROUP'99 - International ACM SIGGROUP Conference on Supporting Group Work*, ACM, Phoenix, Arizona, 1999, pp. 101-111.

Blomberg, J., Giacomi, J., Mosher, A. and Swenton-Wall, P. (1991): 'Ethnographic Field Methods and Their Relation to Design', In Schuler and Namioka (eds.): *Participatory Design: Principles and Practices*, LEA, pp. 123-154.

Bossen, C. (2002): 'The Parameters of Common Information Spaces: the Heterogeneity of Cooperative Work at a Hospital Ward', In C. M. Neuwirth and T. A. Rodden (eds.): *Proceedings of ACM Conference on Computer Supported Cooperative Work*, ACM, New Orleans, 2002, pp. 176-185.

Carstensen, P. H. (1996): *Computer Supported Coordination*, Risø National Laboratory.

182

Carstensen, P. H. and Sørensen, C. (1996): From the social to the systematic. Mechanisms supporting coordination in design, Computer Supported Cooperative Work. *Computer Supported Cooperative Work*, vol. 5, no. 4, 1996, pp. 387-413.

Ellingsen, G. and Monteiro, E. (2003): 'Mechanisms for producing a working knowledge: Enacting, orchestrating and organizing', *Information and organization*, vol. 13, pp. 203-229.

Gerson, E. M. and Star, S. L. (1986): 'Analyzing Due Process in the Workplace', *TOIS*, vol. 4, no. 3, 1986, pp. 257-270.

Grinter, R. E., Hersleb, J. D. and Perry, D. E. (1999): 'The Geography of Coordination: Dealing with Distance in R&D Work', In S Hayne (ed.): *GROUP'99 - International ACM SIGGROUP Conference on Supporting Group Work* ACM, Phoenix, Arizona, pp. 306-315.

Harper, R. H. R. and Hughes, J. A. (1993): 'What a f-ing system! Send 'em all to the same place and then expect us to stop 'em hitting. Managing technology work in air traffic control', In G. Button (ed.): *Technology in Working Order. Studies of work, interaction, and technology*, Routledge, London and New York, pp. 127-144.

Harper, R. R., Hughes, J. A. and Shapiro, D. Z. (1989): *The Functionality of Flight Strips in ATC Work*. The report for the Civil Aviation Authority, Lancaster Sociotechnics Group, Department of Sociology, Lancaster University.

Heath, C., Jirotka, M., Luff, P. and Hindmarsh, J. (1993): 'Unpacking Collaboration: The Interactional Organisation of Trading in a City Dealing Room', In G. DeMichelis, C. Simone and K. Schmidt (eds.): *ECSCW '93. Proceedings of the Third European Conference on Computer-Supported Cooperative Work*, 13-17 September 1993, Milan, Italy, Kluwer Academic Publishers, Dordrecht, 1993, pp. 155-170.

Heath, C. and Luff, P. (1992): 'Collaboration and Control. Crisis Management and Multimedia Technology in London Underground Control Rooms', *Computer Supported Cooperative Work*, vol. 1, no. 1-2, 1992, pp. 69-94.

Kraut, R. E. and Streeter, L. A. (1995): 'Coordination in Software Development', *Communications of the ACM*, vol. 38, no. 3, 1995, pp. 69-81.

Orlikowski, W. J. (1993): 'CASE Tools as Organizational Change: Investigating Incremental and Radical Changes in Systems Development', *MIS Quaterly*, September 1993, pp. 309-340.

Patton, M. Q. (2002): *Qualitative Research & Evaluation Methods (3 Edition)*, Sage Publications, Thousand Oaks, London, New Dehli.

Pritchard, P. and Hughs, J. (1995): *Shared Care. The Future Imperative*, Royal Society of Medicine Press, London, UK.

Reddy, M. and Dourish, P. (2002): 'A finger on the pulse: temporal rhythms and information seeking in medical work', In C.M. Neuwirth and T.A. Rodden (eds.): *Proceedings of ACM Conference on Computer Supported Cooperative Work*, ACM, New Orleans, 2002, pp. 344-353.

Reddy, M., Dourish, P. and Pratt, W. (2001): 'Coordinating Heterogenous Work: Information and Representation in Medical Care', In W. Prinz, M. Jarke, Y. Rogers, K. Schmidt, and V. Wulf (eds.): *ECSCW'01: European Conference on Computer Supported Cooperative Work* (Eds,.) Kluwer Academic Publishers, Bonn, Germany, 2001, pp. 239-258.

Schmidt, K. (1991): 'Computer Support for Cooperative Work in Advanced Manufacturing', *International Journal of Human Factors in Manufacturing*, vol. 1, no. 4, 1991, pp. 303-320.

Schmidt, K. (1994): *Modes and Mechanisms of Interaction in Cooperative Work*, Risø National Laboratory.

Schmidt, K. (2000): 'The Critical Role of Workplace Studies in CSC, In P. Luff and C. Heath, (eds.): *Workplace Studies*, University Press, Cambridge, England, pp. 141-149.

Schmidt, K. and Bannon, L. (1992): 'Taking CSCW Seriously: Supporting Articulation Work', *Computer Supported Cooperative Work,*, vol. 1, no. 1-2, 1992, pp. 7-40.

Schmidt, K. and Simone, C. (1996): 'Coordination Mechanisms: Towards a Conceptual Foundation of CSCW Systems Design', *Computer Supported Cooperative Work*, vol. 5, no. 2-3, 1996, pp. 155-200.

Strauss, A. (1985): 'Work and the Division of Labor', *The Sociological Quarterly*, vol. 26, no. 1, pp. 1-19.

Strauss, A., Fagerhaugh, S., Suczek, B. and Wiener, C. (1985): *Social Organization of Medical Work*, University of Chicago Press, Chicago and London.

Suchman, L. A. (1983): 'Office Procedures as Practical Action: Models of Work and System Design', *TOIS*, vol. 1, no. 4, 1983, pp. 320-328.

Suchman, L. A. (1987): *Plans and situated actions. The problem of human-machine communication,* Cambridge University Press, Cambridge.

Yin, R. K. (1989): *Case Study Research: Design and Methods*, Sage Publications, Beverly Hills.

H. Gellersen et al. (eds.), ECSCW 2005: Proceedings of the Ninth European Conference on Computer-Supported Cooperative Work, 18-22 September 2005, Paris, France, 185–204.
© 2005 *Springer. Printed in the Netherlands.*

Maintaining Constraints in Collaborative Graphic Systems: The CoGSE Approach

Kai Lin, David Chen, Chengzheng Sun and Geoff Dromey

School of Information and Communication Technology, Griffith University, Brisbane, QLD 4111, Australia

Kai.Lin@student.griffith.edu.au, {D.Chen, C.Sun, G.Dromey}@griffith.edu.au

Abstract. A constraint specifies a relation or condition that must be maintained in a system. It is common for a single user graphic system to specify some constraints and provide methods to satisfy these constraints automatically. Constraints are even more useful in collaborative systems, which can confine and coordinate concurrent operations, but satisfying constraints in the presence of concurrency in collaborative systems is difficult. In this article, we discuss the issues and techniques in maintaining constraints in collaborative systems. In particular, we also proposed a novel strategy that is able to maintain both constraints and system consistency in the face of concurrent operations. The strategy is independent of the execution orders of concurrent operations and able to retain the effects of all operations in resolving constraint violation. The proposed strategy has been implemented in a Collaborative Genetic Software Engineering system, called CoGSE, for maintaining the tree structure constraint. Specific issues related to CoGSE are also discussed in detail.

Introduction

Existing graphic systems fall into two groups, General Graphic system (GG), such as XFig, Illustrator, etc., and Special Application system (SA), such as AutoCAD, Rational Rose, etc. The former provides users with vast graphic manipulation functions and its application is broad. The latter offers sophisticated functions for specific applications, which is specially designed to maintain constraints and relations among objects in specific graphic systems. SA is advanced in satisfying constraints automatically. For instance, Rational Rose always ensures that no cycle appears in a graph representing Class hierarchy, even though it cannot be used as a general graphic tool.

Maintaining constraints automatically is even more advantageous in collaborative systems than in single user environments, which can confine and coordinate concurrent operations. It is extremely effective to deal with complicated tasks in collaboration scenarios. For example, when people work collaboratively to design a project using Java Class notation, many conflicts may arise if a system only relies on individuals to maintain Java single inheritance constraint. A task, which demands people to work collaboratively, is often complex and may contain many requirements and constraints. Thus, it is very practical and powerful for collaborative systems to maintain constraints automatically on behalf of users.

On the other hand, satisfying constraints in the presence of concurrency in collaborative systems is difficult. Concurrent operations may result in some constraints becoming difficult to satisfy even though they may be maintained easily in single user environments. For example, a horizontal-line constraint, which requires that the y values of the both endpoints of any horizontal-line should be equal, is difficult to maintain when two users concurrently change both endpoints of a horizontal-line to different vertical positions. In addition, interferences among constraints may be very intricate and difficult to coordinate in collaborative systems.

Collaborative graphic systems satisfying constraints automatically are rare, even though much work has been done on collaborative graphic systems (Sun and Chen, 2002, Ignat and Norrie, 2004). In these systems, graphic objects are independent of each other and no constraint is maintained. These collaborative graphic systems provide flexible functions for users to represent arbitrary graphic notations, but they lack constraint maintenance functions. Hence, they are not applicable to complex collaborative graphic applications, such as collaborative CAD and CASE.

To meet the requirement of high responsiveness in the Internet environment, replicated architecture is widely adopted in collaborative systems. Shared documents are replicated at the local storage of each collaborating site, so that operations can be performed at local sites immediately and then propagated to remote sites (Sun *et al*, 1998, Begole *et al*, 2001). However, maintaining consistency among replicas is more complex than sharing a single copy of centralized data, especially in collaborative systems with constraints.

The objective of this paper is to analyze constraint maintenance in collaborative environments and devise strategies to achieve both constraint satisfaction and system consistency in collaborative graphic systems adopting replicated architecture.

The rest of this article is organized as follows. The next section introduces constraint maintenance. We discuss problems of constraint maintenance in collaborative systems and propose a novel strategy that is able to maintain both constraints and system consistency in the face of concurrent operations. The strategy is independent of the execution orders of concurrent operations and able to retain the effects of all operations in resolving constraint violation. In the third section, we describe the application of the proposed strategy in Collaborative Genetic Software Engineering (CoGSE) system. Comparison with related work is introduced in the fourth section and the major contributions and future work of our research are summarized in the last Section.

Constraint Maintenance

A constraint specifies a relation or condition that must be maintained in a system (Sannella *et al*, 1993, Borning *et al*, 1986). For example, resistors must obey Ohm's law. A graphic application, such as Rational Rose that represents UML concept, may specify many requirements and constraints. From the view of graphic editing systems, these requirements and constraints confine the relations or states of graphic objects.

Constraints and Constraint Satisfaction Functions

There are two kinds of constraints: static constraint, which describes a relation or condition that must be maintained at all times, and temporal constraint, which is relevant to time and event and can be described as trigger events and their responses (Borning *et al*, 1986). For example, a horizontal-line constraint is a static constraint, which requires that the *y* values of the both endpoints of any horizontal-line should always be equal. The description, "when object *A* moves, object *B* should be highlighted", defines a temporal constraint, which only highlights *B* when *A* moves and imposes no restriction on *B* when *A* is still.

Users' operations may violate constraints. For example, there is a constraint which defines that the color of an object, *A*, representing a traffic light, can only be red, green or yellow. The execution of any operation that intends to change *A* to other colors will violate the constraint. An operation, *O*, is a constraint violation operation, if its execution causes a violation of the condition or relation specified by a constraint. On the other hand, user operations may generate the events specified by a temporal constraint and trigger some responses.

A system may contain several constraints. For any constraint C_i, there is a set of Constraint Satisfaction Function (CSF), $FS_i=\{F_1, F_2,..., F_n\}$, for making that relation or condition hold. Given an operation O that violates C_i, the execution of a selected $F_i \in FS_i$ will satisfy the constraint. For example, a horizontal-line constraint, which restricts *left-endpoint.y=right-endpoint.y* of any horizontal-line, has two CSFs to satisfy it. They are (1) *left-endpoint.y←right-endpoint.y*, and (2) *right-endpoint.y←left-endpoint.y*. Function (1) means that if *right-endpoint.y* changes, *left-endpoint.y* should be modified to the same value, and function (2) changes *right-endpoint.y* according to *left-endpoint.y* when *left-endpoint* changes its vertical position.

In graphic systems with constraints, operations may be blocked by constraint satisfaction functions. For instance, an operation that intends to color an object, representing a traffic light, to blue will be blocked. In collaborative systems, if an operation is blocked at the site where it is generated, it will not be propagated to remote sites.

On the other hand, the execution of a user operation in a graphic system may trigger some constraint satisfaction actions. For example, after a user moves *left-endpoint* of a horizontal-line, a constraint satisfaction function will be triggered to change the position of the *right-endpoint* of the line.

A Constraint Satisfaction Problem in Collaborative Systems

It is obvious that constraints are difficult to satisfy in collaborative systems regardless that they may be maintained easily in single user environments. A critical issue is that concurrent operations may result in constraint violations, which is illustrated in the following two scenarios:

Scenario 1. A horizontal-line constraint, C_1, which restricts *left-endpoint.y* =*right-endpoint.y* of any horizontal-line, has two CSFs to satisfy it. They are (1) *left-endpoint.y*←*right-endpoint.y*, and (2) *right-endpoint.y*←*left-endpoint.y*. Two users concurrently move both endpoints of a horizontal-line to different vertical positions.

In scenario 1, the horizontal-line constraint is difficult to maintain if both users' operations retain their display effects.

Scenario 2. Constraint C_2 confines that objects *A* and *B* should not overlap with each other and there is a CSF of C_2, which blocks any operation violating C_2. On the initial document state, *A* is at position P_a and *B* is at P_b. Two users concurrently move *A* and *B* to the same position P_c from different sites.

In scenario 2, the constraint violation is generated by concurrent operations. Even though both operations can satisfy constraint C_2 at their local sites, their executions at remote sites violate this constraint.

There is a contradiction between satisfying constraints and retaining operations' display effects in both above scenarios. The display effects of all operations cannot be retained while maintaining the constraints. The problem is caused by concurrent operations competing to satisfy the same constraint in different ways. To characterize these operations, we define competing operations group.

Definition 1. A Competing Operations Group of constraint *C*, denoted by COG_C, is a set of users' operations, $\{O_1, O_2, ..., O_n\}$, such that:

(1) For any $O_i \in COG_C$, there is $O_j \in COG_C$. O_i and O_j are concurrent,

(2) The executions of all the operations in COG_C will result in a constraint violation of C, which cannot be restored if all these operations retain their display effects,

(3) For any $O_j \in COG_C$, the executions of all the operations in $COG_C - O_j$ will not generate the condition described in (2).

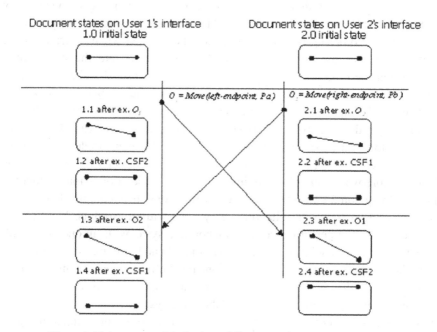

Figure 1. Maintenance of the horizontal-line constraint generates divergence

If $COG_C \neq \{ \}$, to maintain constraint C, one operation in COG_C will lose its effect when all the operations in COG_C have been executed. If different operations lose their effects at different sites, divergence occurs, as shown in figure 1, which represents scenario 1. The document states observable from each user's interface are illustrated by rectangular boxes with rounded corners, with labels 1.0 to 1.4 for user 1 and 2.0 to 2.4 for user 2. Two concurrent operations are generated in the scenario: $O_1 = Move(left\text{-}endpoint, P_a)$ by user 1, and $O_2 = Move(right\text{-}endpoint, P_b)$ by user 2. At the site of user 1, left-endpoint is first moved to position P_a, resulting in the document state shown in the rectangular box 1.1. Next, constraint satisfaction function (2) of the horizontal-line constraint will be invoked to satisfy the constraint. When O_2 arrives and is executed at user 1's site, it will invoke the execution of constraint satisfaction function (1) of the horizontal-line constraint. A similar process occurs at the site of user 2. After the executions of both users' operations at each site, O_1 loses its effect at the site of user 1 and O_2 has not any effect at user 2's site. Therefore, the final results at the two sites are not identical, even though the constraint is maintained at each site.

In figure 1, operations are executed in different orders at two sites, which generate divergence. If operations can be executed in the same order at each site, both constraint satisfaction and system consistency can be achieved. Serialization undo/redo strategy ensures that operations are executed in the same order at each site according to their total ordering relation. Thus, this strategy can be adopted in collaborative systems with constraints. In scenario 2, two users concurrently execute O_1 and O_2, which move A and B to the same position P_c respectively. Suppose O_1 total ordering precedes O_2, O_2 will be blocked when it arrives at the site of user 1, because its execution at the site will violate the overlapping constraint. On the other hand, before O_1 is executed at user 2's site, O_2 will be undone. The execution of O_1 at the site of user 2 will cause O_2 to be blocked as well. Thus, both constraint and system consistency are maintained. Nevertheless, applying undo/redo strategy to satisfy constraints has many demerits. First of all, some operations may be blocked/aborted. In the above example, O_2 will be blocked at each site. Therefore, it cannot restore its effect even when O_1 is undone. Moreover, undoing/redoing a user operation may involve undoing/redoing some constraint satisfaction functions. It is complicated or may be impossible to achieve in collaborative systems with constraints. Finally, this strategy degrades the performances of collaborative systems. If an operation with a smaller timestamp is delayed, we may have to undo and redo many operations to execute the operation. Interactive applications need efficient performance to meet the demands of real-time direct manipulation. Therefore, it is undesirable to adopt this strategy to maintain constraints in collaborative systems.

It is common that concurrent operations form competing operations group in collaborative graphic applications. For instance, concurrent user operations generate cyclic Class hierarchy in a collaborative CASE system and different users concurrently connect the outputs of different circuits to the same input of a circuit in a collaborative CAD application, etc. Being able to solve this problem is crucial in the development of complex collaborative graphic systems. The challenge is that the solution should be able to maintain both constraints and system consistency. Moreover, it should be independent of the execution orders of concurrent operations.

Constraint Maintenance in Collaborative Systems

If concurrent operations form a competing operations group of constraint C, to maintain the constraint, one operation in the COG_C will have to be removed. Thus, if each site chooses the same operation in the COG_C to remove, both constraint and consistency can be maintained.

There are two methods that can be applied to remove an operation from a COG_C: blocking/aborting and masking. The blocking/aborting strategy eliminates operations' effects. Thus, if an operation is blocked/aborted, it cannot play any role afterwards. Furthermore, in collaborative graphic systems, operations may be blocked at remote sites. This can cause confusion since the operations are not blocked immediately after generation. The alternative to blocking/aborting is masking. The masking concept is original from Multi-Version-Single-Display (MVSD) strategy in CoWord (Sun *et al*, 2004, Xia *et al*, 2004). When an object is updated by conflicting operations, multiple versions of the target object are maintained internally, but only one version is displayed at the user interface (Sun and Chen, 2002, Sun *et al*, 2004). MVSD adopts priority strategy to ensure consistency of the single displayed version at all collaborating sites. In distributed systems, an operation's timestamp can be used to represent its priority. After executing a group of conflict operations in any order, the single displayed version is the effect of the operation with the highest priority amongst all the operations in the group. Other operations are masked and their display effects are overwritten. However, even though an operation is masked, it still has a chance to recover its display effect in the future, such as when the operation with the highest priority is undone. Therefore, masking strategy retains all operations' effects. In the case of constraint violation caused by concurrency, it is usually better to preserve all users' work, rather than to destroy any user's work. Thus, we advocate using masking strategy to ensure the satisfaction of a constraint. For instance, in scenario 2, two users concurrently execute O_1 and O_2, which move objects A and B to P_c respectively. If O_2 is masked to satisfy the overlapping constraint, when O_1 is undone, O_2 may recover its display effect.

The problem of masking dealt with in constraint maintenance is more complicated than the one presented in CoWord (Sun *et al*, 2004). In CoWord, if two conflict operations are executed in the ascending order of their priorities, the operation with a lower priority will be masked automatically. Otherwise, the operation with a lower priority will be transformed to satisfy system consistency. In both cases, the operation with a lower priority is masked. However, to satisfy a constraint, concurrent operations may be masked explicitly even though they are executed in the correct sequence at each site. Concurrent operations, which cause a constraint violation, may target different objects. Hence, they cannot mask each other automatically. For example, in scenario 2, no *Move* operation can be masked automatically by the execution of the other *Move* operation. Moreover, it is difficult to apply Operational Transformation (OT) under this condition. How to mask operations to satisfy a constraint is application dependent. In the next session, we will discuss how to mask operations explicitly in a concrete collaborative graphic system.

Based on the above discussion, we can satisfy constraints by adopting a masking strategy. In scenario 1, when O_2 is ready for execution at user 1's site, a competing operations group of C_1, $COG_{C1}=\{O_1, O_2\}$, is formed. If each site masks the operation that has the biggest timestamp value in any COG_{C1} and O_1 total ordering precedes O_2, O_2 is masked at the site of user 1 and has not any effect, as shown in figure 2. On the other hand, when O_1 is ready for execution at the site of user 2, we will obtain the same competing operations group of C_1, $COG_{C1}=\{O_1, O_2\}$. Because the timestamp value of O_2 is bigger than the timestamp value of O_1, O_2 will be masked. In the above example, the execution of O_1 at the site of user 2 will mask O_2 automatically.

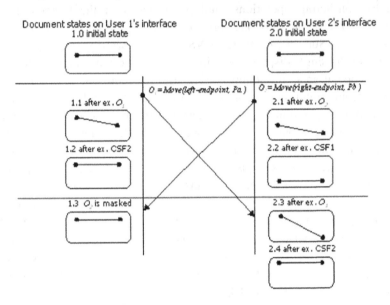

Figure 2. Maintaining the horizontal-line constraint and system consistency

At each site, O may generate many competing operations groups. We use a notation of $COGS_C{}^O=\{COG_1, COG_2, ..., COG_n\}$ to represent a set of COG_C of constraint C generated by applying operation O to the current document state of a site.

Definition 2. A Competing Operations Group Set of constraint C generated by operation O: $COGS_C{}^O=\{COG_1, COG_2,..., COG_n\}$ is a set of competing operations groups, such that for any $COG_i \in COGS_C{}^O$, $1\leq i\leq n$:

(1) COG_i is a competing operations group of C,
(2) $O \in COG_i$,
(3) For any $O_j \in COG_i$, either $O_j=O$ or O_j is an executed user operation at the site and has display effect (i.e. O_j is not masked) on the current document state.

Concurrent operations may be executed in any order at each site. Therefore, an operation O may generate different competing operations group sets at different sites. Under this condition, the above masking approach may generate divergence. For example, there is a constraint C restricting that no cycle should occur in a directed-graph. Suppose the initial document contains two nodes A and B. Three users concurrently generate operations: O_1 adds a directed edge from node A to B and both O_2 and O_3 add directed edges from node B to A, as shown in figure 3-1.

Suppose our strategy is to mask the operation with the lowest priority in each COG_C to satisfy the constraint. We use the notation $O.priority$ to represent the priority of operation O. In this example, $O_2.priority>O_1.priority>O_3.priority$.

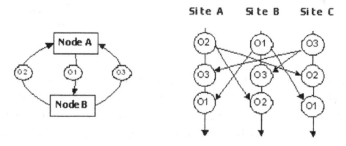

Figure 3-1. Maintenance of a non-cycle constraint

At site A, the execution order of the three operations is: O_2, O_3, O_1.

(1) O_2 is a local operation at site A, which can be executed with the constraint satisfaction on the initial document state, as shown in figure 3-2.

(2) When O_3 is ready for execution, $COGS_C^{O3}=\{ \}$, therefore, it can be executed, as shown in figure 3-3.

(3) When O_1 arrives, its execution on the current document state will form two cycles. Thus, $COGS_C^{O1}=\{\{O_1, O_2\}, \{O_1, O_3\}\}$. Because of $O_2.priority>O_1.priority$, O_1 should be masked. $O_1.priority>O_3.priority$, then O_3 should be masked. Thus, only O_2 may have display effect. However, if O_1 is masked, the executions of O_2 and O_3 can ensure the constraint satisfaction. Therefore, only O_1 will be masked under this condition, as shown in figure 3-4.

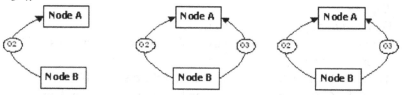

Figure 3-2. Execute O_2 Figure 3-3. Execute O_3 Figure 3-4. Mask O_1

At site B, the execution order of the three operations is: O_1, O_3, O_2.

(1) O_1 is a local operation at site B, which can be executed with the constraint satisfaction on the initial document state, as shown in figure 3-5.

(2) When O_3 is ready for execution, $COGS_C^{O3}=\{\{O_1, O_3\}\}$, because of $O_1.priority>O_3.priority$, O_3 is masked, as shown in figure 3-6.

(3) When O_2 is ready for execution, $COGS_C^{O2}=\{\{O_1, O_2\}\}$, because of $O_2.priority>O_1.priority$, O_1 is masked and O_2 is executed, as shown in figure 3-7.

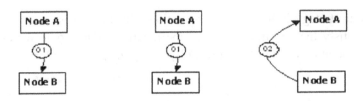

Figure 3-5. Execute O_1 Figure 3-6. Mask O_3 Figure 3-7. Mask O_1 and Execute O_2

After the three operations are executed at both sites, convergence is not maintained. The problem is that at site B, after O_1 is masked, O_3 should restore its display effect. As we mentioned previously, a masked operation may get a chance to restore its display effect when its concurrent operations are undone or masked. In the above example, when O_1 is masked, O_3 and O_2 will not generate competing operations group of C. Therefore, both of them can have display effects with the constraint satisfaction.

In collaborative systems with constraints, each time an operation O_i is masked to satisfy constraint C, all the masked operations that have lower priorities than O_i should be checked. If their executions on the new document state can satisfy constraint C, they will be unmasked. On the other hand, unmasking an operation O_j may cause other operations that have lower priorities than O_j be masked.

We can formally define the effects of the above approach. Suppose there is a constraint C and a set of operations, $OS=\{O_1, O_2,..., O_n\}$, which represent all the operations that should be executed at a site. Applying the above strategy, after executing all the operations in OS (concurrent operations can be executed in any order), we will obtain the same result $R=\{O_1', O_2',..., O_m'\}$. R is a set of operations, such that:

(1) $R \subseteq OS$,
(2) For any $O_k \in R$, O_k has display effect,
(3) For any $O_k \in R$, the executions of O_k and other operations in R cannot generate any COG_C,
(4) For any O_j, while $O_j \in OS$ and $O_j \notin R$, if the display effect of O_j is masked to satisfy C, the executions of O_j and other operations in R must generate COG_C and at least in one of these COG_C, O_j is the operation that has the lowest priority.

The following two procedures implement the above strategy that maintains both consistency and constraints in collaborative systems.

```
Procedure ConstraintMaintenance(O)
  {
   mGroup=GetMaskGroup(O)
   if O∈mGroup, then mask(O) and return
   else if mGroup≠{ } then for each Oi∈mGroup, mask(Oi)
   execute(O)
   if mGroup≠{ }, then {
```

```
1) Find Os that is the operation in mGroup with the
   highest priority.
2) In priority descending order, for any masked
   operation, Oj, if Oj.priority<Os.priority, do {
       mGroup=GetMaskGroup(Oj)
       if mGroup={ }, then unmask(Oj)
       else if Oj∉mGroup, then {
           for each Om∈mGroup, mask(Om)
           unmask(Oj)
       }
   }
}
```

When an operation O that may violate constraint C is ready for execution at a site, procedure *ConstraintMaintenance* will be invoked. It calls procedure *GetMaskGroup* to obtain a group of operations to be masked to satisfy constraint C. If the group contains any operation: (1) If O is in the group, O will be masked, otherwise (2) O can be executed after all the operations in the group are masked. After an operation, O_i, is masked, all the masked operations, which have lower priorities than O_i, will be checked in the descending order of their priorities. If their executions on the new document state can satisfy constraint C, they will be unmasked.

The implementation of procedure *GetMaskGroup* is shown as follows:

```
Procedure GetMaskGroup(O)
{
   noEffectGroup={ }
   COGSo=C.getCOGS(O)
   if COGSo≠{ }, then
       for any COG in COGSo, add the operation with the
       lowest priority in the COG to noEffectGroup
   return noEffectGroup
}
```

The input of the above procedure, O, is the operation which may generate competing operations group of C at a site and the output, *noEffectGroup*, contains a group of operations to be masked to satisfy C. Function *C.getCOGS( )* obtains $COGS_C^O$ (represented as *COGSo* in the procedure). If $COGS_C^O \neq \{ \}$, operations that have the lowest priorities in each $COG_C \in COGS_C^O$ are grouped into *noEffectGroup*. The implementation of function *C.getCOGS( )* is constraint dependent.

The above masking strategy can maintain both constraints and consistency in collaborative systems, which is independent of the execution orders of concurrent operations and able to retain the effects of all operations in resolving constraint violation. It can be adopted in many collaborative applications, including CAD, CASE, spreadsheets, graphical interface toolkits, simulation systems, etc. For instance, it may be used by:

- A graphical interface toolkit application to maintain consistency between application data and the graphic object used to display this data, when operations concurrently modify the application data and its display representation,
- An object-oriented CASE system to avoid concurrent user operations forming cyclic Class hierarchy,
- A simulation system representing current and voltage relationship of a complex circuit to confine that concurrent operations always satisfy Ohm's law,
- A graphic editing system to coordinate the concurrent operations that update graphic objects, such as coordinating the operations that concurrently change the *left, right* and *width* of a rectangle.

To illustrate the applicability of this approach, we will discuss the application of the proposed strategy in Collaborative Genetic Software Engineering (CoGSE) system in the next section.

Constraint Maintenance in Collaborative Genetic Software Engineering System (CoGSE)

Collaborative Genetic Software Engineering (CoGSE) system is a collaborative CASE (computer-aided software engineering) system based on Genetic Software Engineering (GSE). In this paper, it is used as a concrete system to demonstrate constraint maintenance in collaborative environments.

Introduction to Collaborative Genetic Software Engineering System

GSE is a methodology for software development. It uses states to characterize systems behavior and exploits the notion of state differently by making explicit use of the component-state relationship and by limiting component-component composition to a tree-form rather than a directed-graph form (Dromey, 2001, 2003). This yields an economical notation, called behavior-tree, for expressing both requirements and designs.

Using behavior-tree notation we can translate each individual functional requirement, use case, constraint or system behavior, expressed informally in natural language, into its corresponding formal graphic behavior-tree representation. Behavior trees capture/express behaviors in terms of state transitions and component interactions (Dromey, 2001). For example, expressing the behavior or requirement that "when the door is opened the light should go on" we can use a notation shown in figure 4:

197

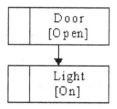

Figure 4. Door-Light requirement

Real-time Collaborative Genetic Software Engineering (CoGSE) system allows a group of users to view and edit the same behavior-tree representation at the same time from different sites. CoGSE is an Internet-based collaborative CASE system that adopts replicated architecture and is implemented in the programming language Java. The interface of CoGSE is shown in figure 5. CoGSE provides several benefits, such as easy interaction between clients and designers, sharing document easily and collaboratively integrating requirements into a design, etc.

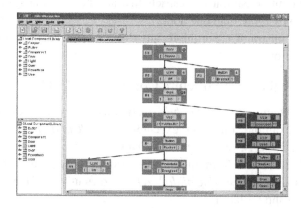

Figure 5. The Collaborative Genetic Software Engineering (CoGSE) system interface

Special Objects, Operations and Constraints in CoGSE

We use the notion of a node to describe a component in behavior-tree representation. A node can be expressed as a rectangle in graphic systems. A node, *N*, has many attributes, among which *parent* attribute denotes the parent node of *N* and *childrenList* contains all the children nodes of it. In CoGSE, each arrowed line, named edge, from a parent node to a child node represents the parent-child relation graphically. The state of an edge is dependent on the two nodes it links. In CoGSE, when a node moves or changes its size, its relevant edges will be redrawn automatically.

An *add-child* operation, *O=addChild(X, Y)*, generates parent-child relation between nodes *X* and *Y*. The execution of *O* in CoGSE has three effects:

(1) Set *Y.parent=X*,

(2) Add Y to X's *childrenList*, and

(3) Create an edge from X to Y to represent the parent-child relation graphically.

Each *add-child* operation has a mask signal bit. If $O=addChild(X, Y)$ is a newly arrived operation, the effect of masking O is to set mask signal bit of it. On the other hand, if O is an executed operation that has display effect, masking O means:

(1) Set mask bit of O,

(2) Delete Y from X's *childrenList*,

(3) Set $Y.parent=null$, and

(4) Delete the edge between X and Y from the graphic system.

In GSE, the behavior-tree notation is deliberately restricted to a tree like structure rather than being allowed to grow into a directed-graph (Dromey, 2001). Hence, there are two constraints, which represent the tree structure constraint, must be maintained in CoGSE:

(1) Single parent constraint C_P restricts that any node in the system cannot be pointed to by more than one node.

(2) No-cycle constraint C_N prohibits any cycle from occurring in behavior-tree representation.

Maintenance of the Tree Structure Constraint in CoGSE

The concurrent executions of *add-child* operations may violate the tree structure constraint. For example, one user executes $O_1=addChild(A, D)$ and the other executes $O_2=addChild(B, D)$ concurrently. Thus, C_P is violated, because node D is pointed to by both A and B. In another scenario, two users concurrently execute $O_1=addChild(A, B)$ and $O_2=addChild(B, A)$. The executions of the two operations will form a cycle and violate C_N.

For any *add-child* operation $O=addChild(X, Y)$ which is ready for execution at a site where the current document state is DSc, we can get $COGS_{Cp}^{O}$ of constraint C_P:

(1) If $Y.parent=null$ on DSc, $COGS_{Cp}^{O}=\{\ \}$,

(2) If $Y.parent=Z$ on DSc, there must be an operation $O_i=addChild(Z, Y)$ which has been executed and has display effect. Therefore, $COGS_{Cp}^{O}=\{\{O, O_i\}\}$.

On the other hand, we can obtain $COGS_{Cn}^{O}$ of constraint C_N by finding all the directed paths from node Y to X on the current document state of the site. If there are n different directed paths from Y to X, after the execution of O, n cycles will be formed. Therefore, there are n competing operations groups of C_N in $COGS_{Cn}^{O}$. Each COG_{Cn} contains O and a set of operations that form a directed path from node Y to X.

In CoGSE, the maintenances of C_P and C_N may interfere with each other. For example, if three users concurrently generate operations, $O_1=addChild(A, B)$, $O_2=addChild (C, B)$ and $O_3=addChild(B, C)$, the executions of these operations will violate both C_P and C_N. Because the executions of O_1 and O_2 make B be pointed to by two nodes and O_2, O_3 form a cycle. If constraint satisfaction strategy of C_P is to mask O_2 and C_N is to mask O_3, then only O_1 will have display effect. However, if O_2 is masked to satisfy C_P, there is not any cycle anymore. Therefore, O_3 should not be masked.

The strategy to coordinate constraint maintenances of C_P and C_N is straightforward. We use a notation $COGS_{Tree}{}^O = COGS_{Cp}{}^O + COGS_{Cn}{}^O$ to represent all the competing operations groups of the tree structure constraint generated by applying O to the current document state of a site. If O is the operation which has the lowest priority in a $COG \in COGS_{Tree}{}^O$, it will be masked. As a result, other operations in each $COG \in COGS_{Tree}{}^O$ can be executed with the tree structure constraint satisfaction and will not be masked. On the other hand, if O is not the operation that has the lowest priority in any $COG \in COGS_{Tree}{}^O$, an operation in each $COG \in COGS_{Tree}{}^O$ will be masked to satisfy the tree structure constraint.

The following example is used to demonstrate the above approach. In figure 6, suppose the initial document contains three nodes A, B and C. Three operations, $O_1=addChild(A, C)$, $O_2=addChild(B, C)$ and $O_3=addChild (C, B)$, are generated concurrently and $O_1.priority>O_2.priority>O_3.priority$.

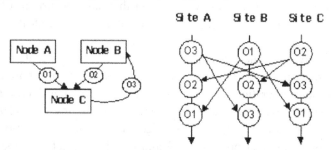

Figure 6. An example of maintaining the tree structure constraint in CoGSE

At one site, the execution order of the three operations is: O_1, O_2, O_3.

(1) The execution of O_1 on the initial document state ensures the satisfactions of both C_P and C_N, so that it can be executed directly.
(2) When O_2 arrives, it will be masked, because the executions of O_1 and O_2 violate C_P and $O_1.priority>O_2.priority$.
(3) Even though the executions of O_3 and O_2 will cause the violation of C_N. As O_2 is masked, O_3 can be executed with the satisfactions of both C_P and C_N.

Therefore, after the executions of the three operations, both O_1 and O_3 have display effects, but O_2 is masked.

At another site, the execution order of the three operations is: O_2, O_3, O_1.

(1) The execution of O_2 on the initial document state can ensure the satisfaction of the tree structure constraint, so that it can be executed directly.
(2) When O_3 arrives, it will be masked, because the executions of O_2 and O_3 violate C_N and $O_2.priority>O_3.priority$.

(3) When O_1 is ready for execution, O_2 will be masked, because the executions of O_1 and O_2 cause the violation of C_P and $O_1.priority > O_2.priority$.

(4) After O_2 is masked and O_1 is executed, O_3 will be checked. Because the executions of O_1 and O_3 do not violate the tree structure constraint, O_3 is unmasked.

Thus, after the executions of the three operations, both sites obtain the same results. The proposed masking strategy maintains both the tree structure constraint and system consistency, which is independent of the execution orders of concurrent operations.

Conflict Management in CoGSE

Different from constraints that may restrict the relations and states of many objects, a conflict is always isolated to an independent graphic object. In collaborative graphic systems, two concurrent operations, which update the same attribute of an object, conflict with each other. In this paper, we adopt the definition of conflict as below:

Conflict relation "$\otimes$": Two *update* operations U_a and U_b conflict with each other, expressed as $U_a \otimes U_b$, if and only if: (1) they are concurrent, (2) they are targeting at the same object, and (3) they are updating the same attribute (Sun and Chen, 2002).

In collaborative graphic systems with constraints, the execution of a user operation, O, may trigger some constraint satisfaction functions whose executions will generate other operations. Hence, we can use a notation $E(O)=\{O_1, O_2,..., O_n\}$ to represent the execution of a user operation O. For any $O_i \in E(O)$, either O_i is O or it is an operation generated by a triggered constraint satisfaction function. The executions of two user operations O_a and O_b will conflict with each other, if $E(O_a)=\{O_{a1}, O_{a2},..., O_{an}\}$, $E(O_b)=\{O_{b1}, O_{b2},..., O_{bm}\}$, there are $O_{ai} \in E(O_a)$, $O_{bj} \in E(O_b)$, and $O_{ai} \otimes O_{bj}$.

Two *add-child* operations may conflict with each other if they add edges pointed to the same node, but this kind of conflict will be solved as a result of constraint maintenance. On the other hand, *update* operations, which manipulate the graphic attributes of the graphic objects in CoGSE, may conflict with each other. For instance, two concurrent *update* operations move a node to different positions. Conflict management may interfere with constraint maintenance, even though an *add-child* operation cannot interfere with any *update* operation. For example, if conflict resolution adopts serialization undo/redo strategy, many *add-child* operations may be undone and redone to manage a conflict.

In CoGSE, Multi-Vision-Single-Display strategy (MVSD) is adopted as conflict resolution (Sun *et al*, 2004). MVSD has two distinct merits:

(1) It retains all operations' effects when conflicts occur.

(2) Different from serialization undo/redo strategy, which may impact many operations executed at a site, MVSD adopts operational transformation strategy and influences no operation except the ones involved in conflicts.

In CoGSE, constraint maintenance strategy only masks *add-child* operations, while MVSD only impacts *update* operations. Both strategies are independent of the execution orders of concurrent operations. Thus, constraint satisfaction and conflict resolution strategies will not interfere with each other.

Related Work

There is a large body of research related to constraint maintenance in graphic systems. Much work contributed to constraint maintenance in single user graphic environments (Borning *et al*, 1986, Myers, 1991, Wilde *et al*, 1990). The prevailing strategies in these systems, which implement constraint satisfaction methods intelligently to enforce system constraints, are adopted in our research. However, maintenance of constraints in concurrent environments has many new features, which cannot be handled by single user strategies.

CAB (Li *et al*, 2001), SAMS (Skaf-Molli *et al*, 2003), and CoDesign (Wang *et al*, 2002) are related to constraint control in collaborative environments. CAB presents an active rule based approach to modeling user-defined semantic relationships in collaborative applications and explores a demonstrational approach for end-user customization of collaboration tools to support the definition of those relationships. Constraints in CAB include those for coordination between distributed users such as awareness, access, and concurrency control, which are beyond the scopes of graphic objects. However, just as its author stated that many complications in maintaining constraints in collaborative environments, such as how to handle constraint violations and coordinate interferences among constraints, are not investigated in CAB.

The intention of SAMS is to achieve semantic consistency by integrating semantic constraints to the operational transformation approach. SAMS uses the language developed in xlinkit to describe static constraints. It also discusses the questions as to where the constraints are imposed and checked and what measures should be taken in case constraints are violated. However, SAMS is based on XML resources. Its application in other environments has yet to be investigated. Moreover, it does not ensure constraint satisfaction. When a constraint is violated, it just informs users to compensate it by undoing operations or modifying objects' states.

CoDesign intends to achieve semantic preservation in real-time collaborative graphic systems and devises semantic expression to express constraints. The proposed semantic expression describes constraints as attribute and value pairs. Thus, it is only suitable for representing constraints that restrict the states of objects. It cannot represent temporal constraints and the constraints confining relations among objects. Moreover, CoDesign also uses loose constraint satisfaction strategy that allows constraints be violated. Neither SAMS nor CoDesign investigates the relationship of constraints and no measure is taken to ensure constraint satisfaction in both systems.

By comparing with the above approaches, CoGSE adopts a novel strategy that is able to maintain both the tree structure constraint and system consistency in the face of concurrent operations. The strategy is independent of the execution orders of concurrent operations and able to retain the effects of all operations in resolving the tree structure constraint violation. Moreover, the interferences among constraints are handled in CoGSE.

Conclusion and Future Work

Constraints are very useful in CAD, CASE, and other applications. However, maintaining constraints in real-time collaborative systems is a challenging task. The difficulties are caused by concurrent operations that violate constraint(s). Being able to solve this problem is crucial in the development of complex graphic applications, such as collaborative CAD and CASE.

In this paper, we proposed a generic masking strategy to solve this problem. This solution ensures constraint satisfaction while retaining operations' effects. Our solution does not require operations to be undone/redone to achieve convergence, as undoing and redoing operations may not be possible in most systems due to the complexity of constraint satisfaction functions. We applied our solution to Collaborative Genetic Software Engineering (CoGSE) system to maintain the tree structure constraints. For these constraints, we investigated the problem of constraint interference and proposed a coordination strategy to resolve such interference.

The proposed strategy can be applied to many applications, including CAD, CASE, spreadsheets, graphical interface toolkits, simulation systems, etc. For instance, if we treat the nodes in CoGSE as Java classes in a collaborative CASE system, the proposed tree structure constraint maintenance strategy can be adopted directly to maintain Java single inheritance constraint and prevent cyclic Java Class hierarchy.

We are currently investigating conflict resolution in collaborative systems with constrains. In such systems, conflict resolutions are tightly coupled with constraint maintenances. Resolving a conflict may repair a constraint violation automatically and vice versa. This investigation may result in a more efficient method for constraint satisfaction.

Another issue we are investigating is a generic solution to coordinate interrelated constraints to achieve system consistency and constraint satisfaction. Two significant difficulties of coordinating interrelated constraints in collaborative graphic systems are:

(1) How to detect the interferences among constraint satisfaction actions? The executions of constraint satisfaction functions may interfere with each other and the interferences may propagate. Thus, the interferences among constraints may be very difficult to detect.

(2) How to coordinate constraint satisfaction actions? If some constraints interfere with each other, some strategies should be devised to determine whether all of them can be satisfied. If not, other strategies should be applied to choose operations to mask. Moreover, masking operations in multi-constraint collaborative systems may cause other interferences, which should also be coordinated.

The relationship of constraints can be very complex. If a collaborative system allows users to define constraints dynamically, there must be some strategies to coordinate the contradictory constraints, constraints' conflicts and interferences. All the above issues are currently being investigated and will be reported in subsequent publications.

References

Begole James et al. (2001): 'Resource sharing for replicated synchronous groupware', *IEEE/ACM Transactions on Networking*, vol. 9, no. 6, Dec. 2001, pp. 833-843.

Bharat, K. and Hudson, S. E. (1995): 'Supporting distributed, concurrent, one-way constraints in user interface applications', *In Proceedings of the ACM Symposium on User Interface Software and Technology, ACM*, New York, pp. 121-132.

Borning, A. and Duisberg, R. (1986): 'Constraint-based tools for building user interfaces', *ACM Transactions on Graphics*, vol.5, no.4, Oct. 1986, pp. 345-374.

Chen, D. and Sun, C. (2001): 'Undoing any operation in collaborative graphics editing systems', *In Proc. of the ACM 2001 International Conference on Supporting Group Work*, Sept. 2001, pp. 197-206.

Dourish, P. (1995): 'Developing a reflective model of collaborative systems', *ACM Transactions on Computer-Human Interaction*, 2(1), Mar. 1995.

Dourish, P. (1996): 'Consistency guarantees: Exploiting application semantics for consistency management in a collaborative tookit', *In Proceedings of the ACM Conference on Computer Supported Cooperative Work, ACM*, New York, pp. 268-277.

Dromey, R.G. (2001): 'Genetic Software Engineering – simplifying design using requirements integration', *IEEE Working Conference on Complex and Dynamic Systems Architecture*, Dec. 2001.

Dromey, R.G. (2003): 'Using behavior trees to design large systems by requirements integration', *(Invited Paper) Dagstuhl-Seminar 03371, Scenarios: Models, Transformations and Tools, International Conference and Research Seminar for Computer Science*, Sept. 2003.

Edwards, W.K. (1997): 'Flexible conflict detection and management in collaborative applications', *In Proceedings of the ACM Symposium on User Interface Software and Technology, ACM*, New York, pp. 139-148.

Ignat, C.-L, Norrie, M.C.(2004): 'Grouping in collaborative graphical editors', *ACM Conference on Computer-Supported Cooperative Work*, Chicago, USA, Nov. 6-10, 2004, pp. 447-456.

Lafore, Robert (2003): *Data Structures and Algorithms in Java, Second Edition*, Sams Publishing, 2003.

Li, D. and Patrao, J. (2001): 'Demonstrational customization of a shared whiteboard to support user-defined semantic relationships among objects', *ACM GROUP'01*, Sept. 30-Oct. 3, 2001, Boulder, Colorado, USA, pp. 97-106.

Lin, K., Chen, D. et al. (2004): 'Tree structure maintenance in collaborative genetic software engineering system', *Proceedings of the Sixth International Workshop on Collaborative Editing Systems, ACM,* Chicago, USA, Nov. 6-10, 2004.

MacLean, A., Carter, K., Lovstrand, L. and Moran, T. (1990): 'User-tailorable systems: Pressing the issues with buttons', *In Proceedings of ACM CHI'90 Conference*, 1990.

Monfroy, E. and Castro, C. (2003): 'Basic components for constraint solver cooperations', *Proceedings of SAC,* 2003.

Myers, B. A. (1991): 'Graphical techniques in a spreadsheet for specifying user interfaces', *In Proceedings of ACM CHI'91 Conference on Human Factors in Computing Systems,* User Interface Management Systems, 1991, pp. 243-249.

Sannella, M. et al. (1993): 'Multi-way versus one-way constraints in user interfaces: experience with the DeltaBlue algorithm', *SOFTWARE—PRACTICE AND EXPERIENCE,* vol. 23(5), pp. 529-566.

Skaf-Molli Hala, Molli Pascal and Ostér Gerald. (2003): 'Semantic consistency for collaborative systems', *the Fifth International Workshop on Collaborative Editing Systems Hosted by the 8th European Conference of Computer-supported Cooperative Work,* Helsinki, Sept. 15, 2003.

Sun, C., et al. (1998): 'Achieving convergence, causality-preservation, and intention-preservation in real-time cooperative editing systems', *ACM Transactions on Computer-human Interaction,* 5(1), Mar. 1998, pp. 63-108.

Sun, C. and Chen, D. (2002): 'Consistency maintenance in real-time collaborative graphics editing systems', *ACM Transactions on Computer-Human Interaction,* vol. 9, no.1, Mar. 2002, pp. 1-41.

Sun, C. (2002): 'Undo as concurrent inverse in group editors', *ACM Transactions on Computer-human Interaction,* vol. 9, no. 4, Dec. 2002, pp. 309-361.

Sun, D. et al. (2004): 'Operational transformation for collaborative word processing', *ACM Conference on CSCW,* Chicago, USA, Nov. 6-10, 2004.

Valiente Gabriel (2002): *Algorithms on Trees and Graphs,* Springer Verlag, Nov. 1, 2002.

Wang, X.Y, Bu J.J and Chen, C. (2002): 'Semantic preservation in real-time collaborative graphics designing systems', *The Fourth International Workshop on Collaborative,* New Orleans, USA, 2002.

Wilde, N. and Lewis, C. (1990): 'Spreadsheet-based interactive graphics: from prototype to tool', *In Proceedings of ACM CHI'90 Conference on Human Factors in Computing Systems,* Application Areas, 1990. pp. 153-159.

Xia, Q. et al. (2004): 'Leveraging single-user applications for multi-user collaboration: the CoWord approach', *ACM Conference on CSCW,* Chicago, USA, Nov. 6-10, 2004, pp. 162-171.

H. Gellersen et al. (eds.), ECSCW 2005: Proceedings of the Ninth European
Conference on Computer-Supported Cooperative Work, 18-22 September 2005, Paris,
France, 205–224.

Empirical Investigation into the Effect of Orientation on Text Readability in Tabletop Displays

Daniel Wigdor and Ravin Balakrishnan

Department of Computer Science, University of Toronto, Canada

dwigdor/ravin @dgp.toronto.edu

Abstract. Tabletop collaborative groupware is a newly re-emerging field in CSCW. The use of a tabletop display presents a unique challenge to interface designers: how to optimally orient displayed objects for viewing and manipulation by users situated at various locations around the table. A great deal of CSCW research has been conducted under the implicit assumption that textual elements should be oriented directly toward the reader, despite research that demonstrates that a simple, straight-on orientation is not necessarily ideal in all circumstances. Absent from this ongoing research dialogue, however, has been an empirical examination of user performance of reading text on tabletop displays at non-zero orientations. In this paper, we present two studies which examine the effect of text orientation on common tasks: the reading of a small piece of text, and the serial search for a label. We found that, though statistically significant, the effects of orientation on the performance of these tasks were less dramatic than might have previously been assumed. From this, we hope to help guide collaborative groupware designers as to when orientation should be "corrected".

Introduction

In recent years, a great deal of research has been conducted into the design and implementation of tabletop interactive systems; for example, the works of Ringel et al. (2004); Rogers et al. (2004); Shen et al. (2003); Shen et al (2004); Streitz et al.

(1999); Streitz, et al. (2002); and Wu and Balakrishnan (2003). Especially exciting about this domain is that a tabletop application can be targeted to simultaneous use by multiple users seated around the table. This organization, however, creates a problem unique to the domain: how should on-display objects be oriented?

Research has been conducted into how participants in non-computer based, table-centered collaborative tasks make use of orientation (Tang 1991; Kruger et al. 2003). These investigations have shown that users prefer a straight-on orientation for reading text, and orient objects towards themselves, others, or in-line with shared artifacts to ease reading in different circumstances. They have discovered, however, that in a collaborative setting, a straight-on orientation toward the reader is not *always* desired or exercised. In fact, orientation is employed as a tool to aide in interaction with other users. Despite this, it seems that designers of collaborative research systems have, in general, opted to attempt to orient text towards the reader, as seen in Bruijn et al. (2001), Rekimoto et al. (1999), Shen et al. (2003), Shen et al. (2004), and Streitz et al. (1999). Thus, there is a tension between a desire to allow for the use of orientation as an aid to collaboration, and the designers' assumption that users need to have textual elements oriented towards them.

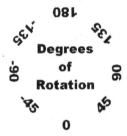

Figure 1. Degrees of rotation as referred to throughout this paper. In all cases, angles are measured relative to the edge of the table at which the participant was seated.

Absent from this previous work is a thorough investigation into the parameters for determining *when* a solution to the text orientation problem should be applied in the context of tabletop groupware. Although users seem to prefer a "normal" orientation of text (Kruger et al. 2003), and studies in the psychology literature in non-tabletop situations with constrained user head and body movement by Tinker (1972) and Koriat and Norman (1984, 1985) indicate that readability is compromised when text is oriented, is it possible that there are circumstances where it might be appropriate to ignore this preference in favour of a less preferred orientation that may aide collaboration in other ways? Is orientation so critical for text readability that design elements must be sacrificed in order for it to be addressed? Without empirical data quantifying the extents to which readability is compromised in less-preferred orientations on tabletops, it is difficult to make informed choices when confronted with these tradeoffs. Our present work provides such empirical data via two experiments that examine the effect of text orientation on the performance of tasks common to tabletop collaborative groupware. Based on the results, we hope to provide insights for system designers as to when the issue of text orientation takes precedence, and when it can be safely ignored. Although very infrequently done in the field of human-computer interaction, replication and extension of experimental work is an important aspect of research. Our work also contributes in this regard by re-examining and extending the studies of readability of text orientation by Tinker (1972) and Koriat and Norman (1985) to tasks relevant to the new domain of tabletop displays, and where users' head and body movements are unconstrained.

Throughout this paper we will be referring to various textual rotations. To help orient the reader, we will refer always to anticlockwise rotations of text. Figure 1 demonstrates the various orientations used in our experiments.

Related Work

Of relevance to the present work are two areas of research: first, an examination of how the issue of reading orientation has been addressed by researchers of tabletop collaborative groupware will provide context for the present research. Second, research in the field of cognitive psychology concerned with reading, especially of text at non-horizontal orientations, is reviewed.

Orientation in Collaborative Groupware Research

An examination of the role of artifact orientation in collaborative settings has been presented by Tang (1991) and Kruger et al. (2003). The lessons they present are clear: orientation has a role to play in collaboration, and any simple, one-sized-fits-all algorithmic solution to the issue of orientation of screen artifacts will deprive participants of some of the richness of interaction afforded in paper-based tasks. What they also provide is a clear demonstration of the intuitive notion that users regard text presented in a "normal" orientation as more readable. They both agree that, similarly to what was reported by Fitzmaurice et al. (1999), users do not always orient artifacts in the same right-angled orientation found in most modern GUI. For example, orientation for readability is often used as a mark of ownership, and re-orientation towards a collaborator is a strategy for passing-over or signifying a desire to share.

From this research, we make two important observations: 1. right-way orientation of artifacts is an important theme in tabletop collaboration, and 2. that users regard the orientation of task objects as important cues for ownership and collaborative behaviour.

Despite the tradeoffs inherent in the above observations, systems continue to be designed that attempt to "solve" the issue of text orientation. For example, by taking advantage of advanced display technologies, in both Agrawala et al. (1997) and Matsushita et al. (2004), users view a common scene orientation, but textual object labels are oriented toward each participant. Additionally, many systems attempt to dynamically and automatically re-orient objects; Kruger et al. (2003) present a thorough review of these algorithmic approaches, to which we refer the reader for more information. The reasoning behind these approaches seems sound: if text is easier to read at a particular orientation, an ideal approach would always present that orientation to any user attempting to read the content. It is their implicit contention that right-way up reading is so important that the group-dynamic affordances described in previous research should be sacrificed. But, how real is the tension between readability and system flexibility?

In an attempt to answer this, we now examine the research in text orientation that has been conducted in the field of cognitive psychology.

Human Ability to Read Text at Various Orientations

Research into the effect of graphical considerations on reading performance began with Huey (1898). Although the issue of orientation was not discussed, the effect of vertical vs horizontal alignment of words was examined, as well as the effect of partially occluding portions of characters. The issue of orientation and its effect on reading was first explored in detail by Tinker (1972). He conducted two experiments: in the first, subjects performed the Chapman Cook Speed of Reading Test at various orientations (Chapman 1923). The Chapman-Cook test involves the presentation of a paragraph, where a single word "spoils the meaning" of the text. The subject is required to identify this word, either by crossing it out, or speaking it aloud. The speed of reading is measured by how quickly this is accomplished. In this experiment, Tinker (1972) found that the reading of text rotated at 45° in either direction was, on average, 52% slower than reading normally oriented text, and text rotated at 90° in either direction was 205% slower on average. In the second experiment, participants performed the Luckiesh-Moss Visibility Meter to determine the physical visibility of rotated text (Luckiesh 1944). Tinker (1972) discovered that the speed of reading was affected much more dramatically by orientation than was visibility, and thus concluded that visibility was not the only factor that contributed to the decreased speed of reading at non-standard orientations.

Koriat and Norman (1984) used a text-reading task to evaluate the relative merits of two theories of how mental rotation is performed. Although this was informative to the present study, it was their later work (1985) which examined the issue of readability of rotated text in more detail. Specifically, they examined the effect of rotating text on the identification of strings as words or non-words. They found that performance of their task in the range of -60° to 60° degrees from the horizontal was not significantly variable, but that a performance cliff was reached once rotation exceeded 60° in either direction. Once this cliff was reached, word/non-word identification speed decreased by more than 120% (Koriat and Norman 1985).

The work of both groups seems to confirm the intuitive notion that reading orientation should be a key concern to designers of tabletop systems. However: their work is not directly applicable to tabletop collaborative groupware research. First, rather than allow participants free and natural movement during the experiments, the position and orientation of their heads was constrained. Second, in both sets of experiments, readability was determined by how quickly non-conforming strings were identified. In the Tinker (1972) study, this was done at the semantic level, as participants were required to find the word in paragraphs that spoiled their meaning. In the Koriat and Norman (1985) experiment, this was done at the syntactic level, as the study consisted of the presentation to the participant a series of strings of characters, which subjects were required to identify as either words or non-words. Though this experimental design enabled them to answer their research questions, we note that the identification of non-conforming or gibberish strings is not directly applicable to real user interface scenarios. In most applications, textual artifacts consist of either common words or domain terms that might be expected by the user. This assumption might aide in the reading of text at varying orientations, and so should be considered when evaluating user performance of reading at varying orientations.

In our studies, we attempted to provide a more "natural" environment where user head movements are not constrained, and measured the performance of reading non-gibberish text at various orientations. It was our hypothesis that, given this environment, the effect of orientation on task-performance would be less dramatic. If this were the case, we believe that the tension between orientation as a tool for collaboration and the apparent need to use the "right" orientation for text readability can be relaxed, and systems could begin to be designed that heed the observations of Tang (1991) and Kruger et al. (2003).

Experiment 1

Goals: Although we were certain that orientation would have a statistically significant effect on text reading performance (based on the results in the literature), we wished to measure the strength of the effect at each orientation. We also wanted to conduct an experiment that would measure performance in an actual collaborative tabletop environment as compared to the artificially constrained environments used by Tinker (1972) and Koriat and Norman (1985). To this end, we present the text to the user on a tabletop, and allow participants free movement of their body and head, to allow for any tendency toward personal re-orientation. We also wished to examine how the type of information presented might affect performance. We presented three types of stimuli: a single word, a short phrase, and a 6-digit number. In order to ensure that participants could easily comprehend the words and phrases, single word stimuli were only simple, 5-6 letter words, while the phrases presented were coherent and meaningful.

It was our hypothesis that the effect of orientation on reading of a single word would be less dramatic than what Koriat and Norman (1985) observed. Because our set consisted of only common words, participants would be able to trust their immediate identification of a rotated word, rather than graphically examine each character, as was required in the Koriat and Norman (1985) experiment. Further, we believed that the performance in reading longer phrases would be better than what Tinker (1972) reported. Because our phrase set consisted only of short, logical phrases, participants would be able to rely on the context of the surrounding text to aide in identification of harder to read words. Lastly, we believed that the reading of numbers would be most affected by orientation, since no particular grouping of the numbers could be assumed. Thus, we expected that our results in this situation would be similar to that previously reported.

Apparatus: Text was presented to the user using a ceiling-mounted digital projector, and was projected onto a DIAMONDTOUCH tabletop, introduced by Dietz and Leigh (2001), at which the participant was seated. Although the DIAMONDTOUCH is intended for touch-input, we used it only as a display screen since object manipulation was not required in our experiment. While we could have just as easily projected the image onto any tabletop surface, we chose the DiamondTouch since it is one of the common platforms for tabletop research and has a diffuse surface that results in high-quality imagery. The text was presented in a sans-serif font, and rotated in software to be presented to the participant. There was no apparent degradation in the quality of the rendering at the various orientations.

Text entry was facilitated by a standard QWERTY keyboard placed directly in front of the participant, who was seated at a chair placed directly in front of and centered on the longer side of the table. The system was driven by a windows-based Intel Pentium 3.0GHz system, equipped with an NVIDIA GeForce FX Go5700. Figure 2 illustrates the experimental environment.

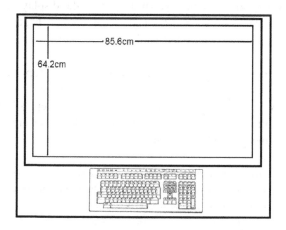

Figure 2. Top-down diagrammatic view of the experimental apparatus.

Participants: Fifteen participants, recruited from the university community, volunteered for the experiment. 12 were male, 3 were female. 13 spoke English natively, while the remaining 2 reported to be excellent readers. All self reported as excellent typists. Participants received no compensation for their participation.

Procedure: Users were repeatedly presented with a string which they were asked to read, memorize, and type-in to the system. We wished to measure how long they would spend reading the text before they were sufficiently confident that they would remember it long enough to type-in to the system.

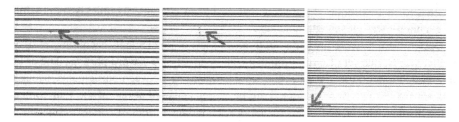

Figure 3. (a) Orienting crosshair primes the participant as to the location of text. (b) After 0.65 seconds, the crosshair disappears and is replaced by the rotated text. (c) As the subject begins to type, the text disappears from the screen. The black arrow is for illustration only and was not present in the actual experiment.

The strings consisted of 5-6 letter words, 6-digit numbers, and 6-7 word phrases. The words and numbers were randomly selected and generated, while the phrases were selected from the corpus developed by MacKenzie and Soukoreff (2003). The location of each string on the screen was primed with the display of a red cross for 0.65 seconds before the appearance of the text. When the user began to type, the text would disappear from the screen, but would return whenever "escape" was pressed. Figure 3 illustrates the procedure:

Timing began when the string was first displayed, and stopped when the user began to enter input. In order to prevent participants from "racing through the experiment", they were required to enter perfect input, and were told to correct their entry if it was incorrect when they pressed "enter". Trials where such correction occurred were not included in our timing analysis. Participants were given initial instructions as follows:

> The experiment will require you to read some text on screen. Each time text is presented, you should memorize it (as quickly as you can), and then start to type it into the computer. When you begin to type, the text will disappear from the screen.
>
> At any time, you can view the text again by pressing "escape".
>
> You will be required to enter the text absolutely correctly. If you make a mistake, the system will tell you, and ask you to correct your entry. Press enter to begin the experiment.

Before each priming/string was presented, they were given the following on-screen instruction:

> You will now be presented with a red cross, which will shortly be replaced with text. Read the text, keeping in mind that you will need to remember the text it long enough to type it into the computer after it disappears. When you are ready, type the text in to the computer. If you make a mistake the system will alert you. Press "space" to begin.

To ensure that participants understood what was required, they were allowed a practice dataset consisting of several short phrases. They were instructed to enter as many as was required to become familiar with the apparatus. Participants were directed to rest as required between strings, but to continue as quickly as possible once a phrase was presented on-screen.

Design: Strings were presented in three datasets of 96 elements each: one set of 5-6 letter words, one set of 6 digit numbers, and one set of 6-7 word phrases. The order of presentation of the datasets was counterbalanced between-participants using a latin-square. Strings were presented on the screen centered at one of the four corners of the display, and in one of 8 orientations, including straight-up, and each position around the compass at 45 degree increments. Within each dataset the position and orientation of a string was randomized, but controlled such that each position and orientation at that position was presented an equal number of times. The content of each dataset was fixed, such that all participants entered the same strings in the same order. In summary, the design was as follows:

3 datasets (single word, number, short phrase) X
4 on-screen positions (each corner of the tabletop) X
8 orientations (starting at 0°, in 45° increments) X
3 strings at each position/orientation X
15 participants
= 4320 strings entered in total.

All orientations were measured relative to the side of the table at which the participant was seated. Because head and chair positions were not constrained beyond the need to reach the keyboard to enter text, the exact orientation of the presented strings relative to the participants' eyes was not measured. Assuming a comfortable typing distance, as was generally observed, the angle of the 0-degree oriented-text relative to the centre of the participant's nose was approximately 12° for the upper-quadrant cases, and 17° for the lower-quadrant cases, well within the range of orientations shown to have little effect on reading speed in the works discussed previously.

Alternative experimental designs: Two alternative experimental designs were considered, but rejected in favour of the design we have presented. We will briefly present each of the designs and explain why we rejected them:

Stroop: The Stroop test is one of the most famous in cognitive psychology. As first demonstrated by Stroop (1935), it was found that participants were slower to identify the color of a string if the text was an interfering color name than if it was not the name of a color. It is believed that the participants were reading the text more quickly than they were identifying the color, and that the string was interfering with the identification of the color.

Our first experimental design consisted of a modified Stroop test, where the strings would be presented in various orientations. We believed that the Stroop effect would continue to assert itself, and so demonstrate that the participant was able to quickly read the text. We rejected this design for two reasons: first, we wished to measure performance of reading of various types of strings. Second, we realized that, even if the effect continued to assert itself, that we would be demonstrating only that reading speed was above the color-identification threshold. While informative, this would fail to measure with sufficient fidelity the effect of orientation on reading performance.

Read aloud: A read aloud design would have consisted of the presentation of text at various orientations, the user reading the string aloud, and the measurement of the total time required to read the text. This design would have mimicked the design presented by Huey (1898). We chose not to employ this design for two reasons: first, limitations in speech recognition technology would limit our reporting accuracy.

Second, differences between silent and spoken reading speed would limit the efficacy of the experiment in demonstrating reading performance at varying orientation.

Results: We discarded from the timing data all trials where the participant entered erroneous data which was then subsequently corrected. Orientation did not have a significant effect on error rate ($F_{7,26} = 1.40$, p = .1990). The type of stimuli did have an effect on errors ($F_{2,26} = 34.04$, p < .0001), with mean error rates of 15%, 8%, and 4% for single word, short phrase, and number treatment respectively.

As expected, orientation had a statistically significant effect on speed of reading: single word ($F_{7,10} = 28.0$, $p < .0001$), short phrase ($F_{7,10} = 64.28$, $p < .0001$), and numbers ($F_{7,10} = 7.76$, $p < .0001$). Pairwise means comparisons of entry time of all types of text indicated that orientations of -45°, 0°, and 45° were not significantly different from one another, but were significantly different than the rest. In the single

-135° and 135° were not significantly different from one another, but were significantly different from those at -90° and 90°. In the number condition, time to entry of stimuli presented at all orientations beyond -45° and 45° were not significantly different from one another. The location of presentation of the stimuli among the 4 on-screen position did not significantly affect performance time ($F_{3,26} = 1.95$, p = .12).

	Single Word			Short Phrase			6-Digit Number		
	μ (secs)	σ	% off 0°	μ (secs)	σ	% off 0°	μ (secs)	σ	% off 0°
-135°	1.19	0.67	64.70	3.82	1.52	107.13	2.85	1.06	17.48
-90°	0.92	0.40	26.60	2.66	1.07	44.25	2.85	1.63	17.19
-45°	0.78	0.60	7.98	2.07	1.02	12.62	2.36	1.17	-2.71
0°	0.72	0.22	-	1.84	0.86	-	2.43	1.57	-
45°	0.77	0.22	5.93	1.97	0.70	7.19	2.39	1.19	-1.65
90°	0.91	0.37	25.78	3.09	1.30	67.71	2.78	1.21	14.56
135°	1.35	1.00	86.42	3.90	1.97	112.82	3.01	1.24	24.26
180°	1.11	0.57	53.67	3.69	1.89	100.27	3.03	1.16	24.87

Table I. Summary of mean (μ) and variance (σ), of reading times, and percentage deviation from mean reading time for un-rotated text of the same type for each orientation, and each of the three conditions. Excludes trials where erroneous data was entered and subsequently corrected.

As we hypothesized, the effect of orientation on reading speed was far less dramatic than had been previously reported. Contrary to our hypothesis, however, the effect of rotation on 6-digit numbers was the least dramatic of the three conditions. Table I summarizes the mean rates for each orientation and condition.

Figures 4-6 are boxplots for time required to read the stimuli under each condition, broken down by screen-quadrant. Our results correspond with those of Koriat and Norman (1985) in that, for the word and phrase conditions, the worst mean performance for reading stimuli in the upper quadrants of the screen was 135° in the upper-left quadrant, and -135° in the upper-right quadrant. Since the participant was positioned at roughly the centre of the table, these orientations represent text written bottom-to-top, and away from the participant.

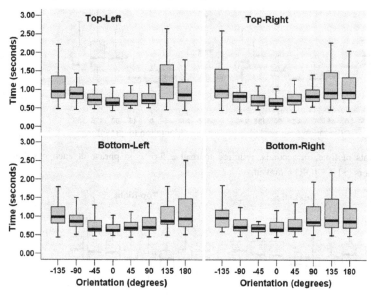

Figure 4. Boxplots of time, in seconds, required to read a single word at each position and orientation. Outliers (>1.5 * IQR) removed.

216

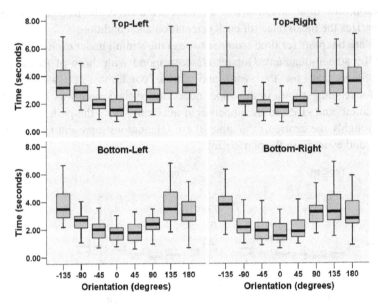

Figure 5. Boxplots of time, in seconds, required to read a 5-6 word phrase at each position and orientation. Outliers (>1.5 * IQR) removed.

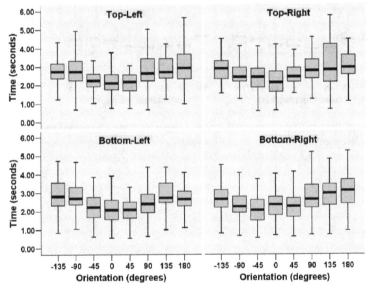

Figure 6. Boxplots of time, in seconds, required to read a 6-digit number at each position and orientation. Outliers (>1.5 * IQR) removed.

Experiment 2

Goals: A common task in many applications is the serial search: examining many on-screen elements in search of a desired target. Given the results of the previous experiment, we wished to examine the effect of orientation of target and distracters on efficiency in conducting a serial search. We hypothesized that although the amount of rotation of the target and distracters would have a significant effect on performance, the degree of this effect would be less than previous experimental results might suggest. We also hypothesized that a field with more greatly rotated targets and distracters might provide more visual cues, and thus aide in learning. We believed that, over time, this learning would mean that search times for the all-orientations condition would be reduced more than those of the no-orientations condition.

Apparatus: The apparatus used was identical to that in Experiment 1.

Participants: Nine participants recruited from the university community volunteered for the experiment. 7 were male, 2 were female. 6 spoke English natively, while the remaining 3 reported to be excellent readers. Participants received no compensation for their participation.

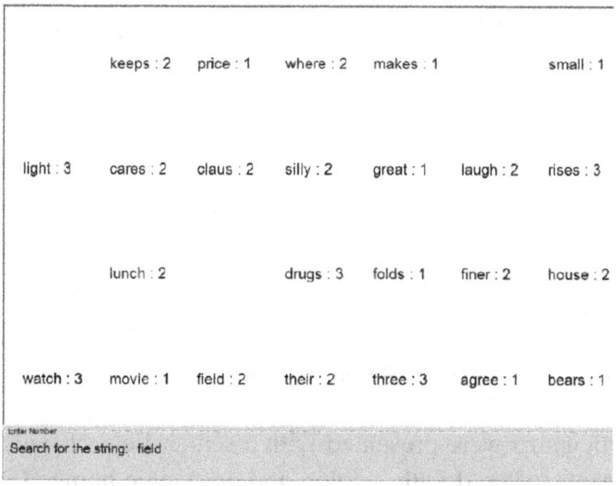

Figure 7. Serial search task with all targets oriented at 0°.

218

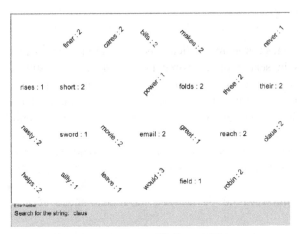

Figure 8. Serial search task with targets oriented at -45°, 0°, and 45°.

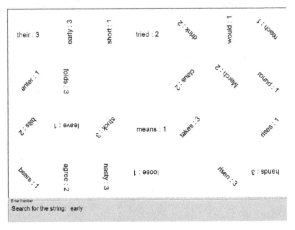

Figure 9. Serial search task with targets at all 8 orientations.

Procedure: Participants were presented with a search field of randomly positioned 5-6 letter words, each suffixed with a colon and an Arabic numeral between 1 and 3 (eg: "silly : 2"). For each trial, the position, rotation, and text of each of the words remained the same, but the suffixing numeral was randomly changed. For each trial, participants were told to search the field for a given word (different for each trial), and indicate when they had found it by entering its suffixing numeral using the keyboard.

Three datasets were used, which varied only in the degree of orientation of the constituent strings. In the first dataset, each of the strings was presented "right side up". In the second, strings were drawn at randomly assigned rotations of -45°, 0°, and

45°. In the third, strings were randomly assigned rotations of all 8 multiples of 45°. Figures 7-9 demonstrate the three treatments.

Initial instructions were given to the participant as follows:

> This experiment is broken into three parts. For each part, you will, 72 times, be presented with a field of strings, each ending with a ":" followed by a number. Each of the 72 times the field will be the same, except that the numbers at the ends of the strings may change. Each time, you will be asked to find a particular string, and indicate to the computer which number it ends with. If you give an incorrect reply, the system will ask you to try again.

> Please relax between presentations, but once you have started a trial, find the string and give the input as quickly as you can.

> You will be given the opportunity to rest between each presentation. Please do not take long breaks while you are completing a block. You may rest as long as you like between blocks.

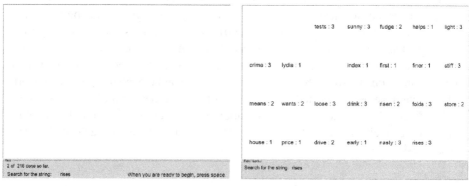

Figure 10. Left: Screen displaying search target to the participant. Right: the search field presented once the subject presses the "space" key, and timing starts for the search.

The string to find was presented first, and participants then pressed a keyboard button to display the field. Timing began when the field was displayed – Figure 10 demonstrates this sequence:

Timing began when the string was first displayed, and stopped when the subject entered a numeral. Participants were required to enter perfect input, and were told to correct their entry if it was incorrect. Trials with erroneous entries that were subsequently corrected were not included in the analysis.

To ensure that participants understood what was required, they were allowed a practice dataset consisting of several typical searches. They were instructed to conduct as many as was required to become familiar with the apparatus.

Design: Searches were conducted for each of the three datasets. For each dataset, an identical field of 24 5-6 letter words was repeatedly presented. Participants were asked to search for each string in the field on three different occasions within each dataset, resulting in 3x24 = 72 searches per dataset.

220

The order of presentation of the datasets was counter-balanced between participants using a Latin-squares design. The assignment of words to treatment, the order of searches, and the makeup (position and orientation) of the field was randomized between participants. In summary, the design was as follows:

3 datasets (no rotation, small rotation, complete rotation) X

24 strings per dataset (position and orientation randomized) X

3 searches per string (search order randomized) X

9 participants

= 1944 searches conducted in total.

Results: As before, trials with erroneous input were discarded from the analysis. There was no significant effect for treatment on error rate ($F_{2,215} = 0.28$, p = .75), indicating that orientation did not mislead the subjects. As expected, the orientation of the target and distracter words had a statistically significant effect on the search time for the target ($F_{2,215} = 9.80$, p < .0001), though pairwise means comparisons revealed that the search time for the zero and some rotation treatments were not significantly different from one another. As we hypothesized, the difference in performance time between the all-rotations treatment and the others was less dramatic than might have been expected: the mean performance times for the search tasks were 3.3, 3.4, and 3.9 seconds for the no-rotation, small rotation, and complete rotation tasks respectively. Figure 11 is the boxplot for search time for each of the three search tasks.

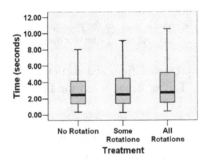

Figure 11. Boxplot of time required for the serial search under each of the three target / distracter orientation conditions: 0: all oriented towards the user, 1: all oriented at -45°, 0°, or 45°, 2: all oriented at one of the 8-compass positions. Outliers (>1.5 * IQR) removed.

Learning of the field did take place: search number had a significant effect on the time required to conduct it ($F_{71,215} = 1.57$, p < .005). Contrary to our hypothesis, however, there was no interaction effect between search number and dataset ($F_{142,215}$

= 7.19, p = .84), indicating that the degree of orientation did not affect the learning of the field.

Discussion

The results of our first experiment confirmed our primary hypothesis: that although significant, the effects of orientation on reading speed are not as large as previous work might have suggested. Where Tinker's (1972) test found a performance penalty of over 200% for reading of a paragraph once text is oriented at 90°, we found penalties of only 26%, 54%, and 17% for short words, phrases, and numbers respectively. Although our results do not refute the notion of a performance cliff at 60° as was found by Koriat and Norman (1985), what is clear is that if such a cliff exists, the depth of the plunge is not nearly as dramatic as they reported.

We attribute the differences in our results to two key experimental differences: the experimental condition, and the experimental task. Unlike the previous work, our participants were free to move their bodies and orient their heads to aide in rotated reading as they would be able to do in real use of tabletop groupware applications. Furthermore, our task required the reading and understanding of words and phrases that were consistently and reliably "real", so participants could trust their first-glance understanding of the text, rather than second-guess and scrutinize as was required in the Tinker (1972) and Koriat and Norman (1985) experiments.

We were surprised by the finding that 6-digit numbers suffered less from rotation-speed effect than did words and phrases. In our post-experimental interviews, several subjects reported that, when reading numbers, they would begin to type almost right away, and rely on their visual memory of the stimulus as they continued to enter the remaining digits, rather than carefully scanning each digit. We were unable to find references to this behaviour in previous work, which suggests an area of future research.

In the second experiment, our primary hypothesis that orientation would have a significant but minor effect on serial-search, was confirmed. We found that the average search time to find a target word among 23 distracting words suffered only a (statistically insignificant) 3% increase between the zero and some-rotation conditions, and only an 18% increase between zero and all-rotations conditions.

The effect of orientation on task performance is even less significant in the serial search task than it is on the reading task. If we consider the results of single-word reading from the first experiment, and weight the difference in speed of reading from the zero-rotation condition by the proportion of strings in the search field that were at that orientation, we find that a speed difference of 5% in the -45° to 45° condition

$(1/3 \times 0\% \ (0°) + 1/3 \times 7.98\% \ (-45°) + 1/3 \times 5.93\% \ (45°) = 4.6\%)$, and a speed difference of 34% $(1/8 \times 64.7\% \ (-135°) + 1/8 \times 26.6\% \ (-90°) + \ldots 1/8 \times 53.7\% \ (180°)$ = 33.89%) in the all-rotations condition, would be expected, versus 3% and 18% determined empirically. Thus, serial search of a field of short words is affected less than is the reading of an individual word rotated by the same amount. This finding might be of significance to those conducting general research in the serial-search task.

Although the hypothesized learning did take place as participants continued to make 72 searches within the same field, there was no difference in the learning effect due to text orientation. This was contrary to our secondary hypothesis, which was that when strings were presented in varying orientations, learning of the locations of those strings would be enhanced over a field of uniform rotation. With only three repetitive searches of the same item within a given field and all done within a short timeframe, our experiment was able to only evaluate immediate learning and not long-term recall. It is possible that varying orientations may aide in longer term recall of items, and is worthy of further research.

Conclusions

In collaborative tabletop groupware systems there is a tension between orienting textual data towards the user to facilitate readability, and orientation of interface objects to facilitate interaction, cognition, and communication as observed by Tang (1991) and Kruger et al. (2003). Our experimental results agree with those seen previously that orientation has an effect on speed of reading, and that if maximum reading speed is desired and the position of the intended reader is known, text should be oriented directly towards that user. What we have seen in our study, however, is that if circumstances require it, presenting text at non-optimal orientation does not as severely impair reading performance as previous studies had suggested.

Because the studies by Tang (1991) and Kruger et al. (2003) related primarily to task artifacts in a real-world setting, they offer little guidance as to how system artifacts, such as menus, alerts, and dialogs, should be presented. Our experimental results clearly demonstrate that the effect of orientation on reading labels, numeric and textual data, and performing serial searches, is less dramatic than might have been previously assumed. This indicates that tabletop interface designers could err towards supporting dynamic orientation of artifacts in favour of orienting for readability when they are forced to make a tradeoff between the two choices. Further to this, when presenting shared textual system artifacts, orientation alone does not necessitate that multiple copies or rotating labels be used to allow use by all users, thus saving screen space.

Another way of thinking about this issue is that designers should not attempt to create interfaces that orient text for maximal readability at all costs, or spend all their efforts on such designs, since the impact of slightly rotated text is not as significant as they might naively assume.

Aside from the practical design implications, our work also contributes new data to the empirical literature on readability of oriented text. In contrast to previous work by Tinker (1972) and Koriat and Norman (1984, 1985) that studied the impact of orientation on readability in the task of identifying non-conforming or gibberish strings within other strings, our work provides empirical data for four different tasks: searching for a word in a field of words and reading of non-gibberish words, phrases, and numbers at various orientations. Finally, while the previous research artificially constrained participant's head and body movements, our experiments were carried out in a more natural unconstrained setting, thus providing more ecologically valid data that can be reliably interpreted by designers and experimentalists alike.

Acknowledgments

The authors would like to thank Jonathan Deber, John Hancock, members of the DGP Lab, Mitsubishi Electric Research Labs, experimental participants, and the ECSCW reviewers.

References

Agrawala, M., Beers, A., McDowall, I., Frohlich, B., Bolas, M. and Hanrahan, P. (1997): 'The two-user Responsive Workbench: support for collaboration through individual views of a shared space', *Proc. of the 24th annual conf. on Computer graphics and interactive techniques*, ACM Press/Addison-Wesley Publishing Co. 1997, pp: 327-332.

Bruijn, O. and Spence, R. (2001): 'Serendipity within a Ubiquitous Computing Environment: A Case for Opportunistic Browsing', *Proc. of the 3rd int. conf. on Ubiquitous Computing*, pp: 362-370.

Chapman, J. (1923): *Chapman-Cook speed of reading test*. Ames, IA, Iowa State University Press.

Dietz, P. and Leigh, D. (2001): 'DiamondTouch: a multi-user touch technology', *Proc. of the 14th annual ACM symposium on User interface software and technology Orlando, Florida*, ACM Press, pp: 219-226.

Fitzmaurice, G., Balakrishnan, R., Kurtenbach, G. and Buxton, B. (1999): 'An exploration into supporting artwork orientation in the user interface', *ACM CHI 1999 Conf. on Human Factors in Computing Systems*, New York, NY, ACM, pp: 167-174.

Huey, E. (1898): 'Preliminary Experiments in the Physiology and Psychology of Reading'. *The American Journal of Psychology*, vol. 9,, pp: 575-586.

Koriat, A. and Norman, J. (1984): 'What is rotated in mental rotation?', *Journal of Experimental Psychology: Learning, Memory, and Cognition*, vol. 10, pp: 421-434.

Koriat, A. and Norman, J. (1985): 'Reading Rotated Words', *Journal of Experimental Psychology; Human Perception and Performance*, vol. 11, number 4, pp: 490-508.

Kruger, R., Carpendale, S., Scott, S. and Greenberg, S. (2003): 'How people use orientation on tables: comprehension, coordination and communication', *Proc. of the 2003 int. ACM SIGGROUP conf. on Supporting group work*. Sanibel Island, Florida, USA, ACM Press, pp: 369-378.

Luckiesh, M. (1944): *Light, vision and seeing: a simplified presentation of their relationships and their importance in human efficiency and welfare*. New York, New York, D. Van Nostrand.

MacKenzie, S. and Soukoreff, W. (2003): 'Phrase sets for evaluating text entry techniques', *Extended Abstracts of the ACM CHI Conf. on Human Factors in Computing Systems*, pp: 754-755.

Matsushita, M., Iida, M., Ohguro, T., Shirai, Y., Kakehi, Y. and Naemura, T. (2004): 'Lumisight table: a face-to-face collaboration support system that optimizes direction of projected information to each stakeholder', *CSCW'04*, ACM Press, pp: 274-283.

Ringel, M., Ryall, M., Shen, C., Forlines, C. and Vernier, F. (2004): 'Release, relocate, reorient, resize: fluid techniques for document sharing on multi-user interactive tables', *Extended abstracts, 2004 conf. on Human factors and computing systems*, Vienna, Austria, ACM Press, pp: 1441-1444.

Rogers, Y., Hazlewood, W., Blevis, E. and Lim, Y. (2004): 'Finger talk: collaborative decision-making using talk and fingertip interaction around a tabletop display', *Extended abstracts of the 2004 conf. on Human factors and computing systems*, Vienna, Austria ACM Press, pp: 1271-1274.

Rekimoto, J. and Saitoh, M. (1999): 'Augmented surfaces: A spatially continuous work space for hybrid computing environments', *Proc. of the SIGCHI conf. on Human factors in computing systems*, ACM Press, pp: 378-385.

Shen, C., Lesh, N. and Vernier, F. (2003): 'Personal digital historian: story sharing around the table', *Interactions*, vol. 10, number 2, pp: 15-22.

Shen, C., Vernier, F., Forlines, C. and Ringel, M. (2004): 'DiamondSpin: an extensible toolkit for around-the-table interaction', *Proc. of the SIGCHI conf. on Human factors in computing systems*, pp: 167-174.

Streitz, N., Prante, T., Muller-Tomfelde, C., Tandler, P. and Magerkurth, C. (2002): 'Roomware©: the second generation CHI '02 extended abstracts on Human factors in computing systems', Minneapolis, Minnesota, USA ACM Press, pp: 506-507.

Streitz, N., Geuler, J., Holmer, T., Konomi, S., Miller-Tomfelde, C., Reischl, W., Rexroth, P., Seitz, P. and Steinmetz, R. (1999): 'i-LAND: an interactive landscape for creativity and innovation', *Proc. of the SIGCHI conf. on Human factors in computing systems*, Pittsburgh, Penn., ACM Press, pp: 120-127

Stroop, J. (1935): 'Studies of interference in serial verbal reactions', *Journal of Experimental Psychology: General*, vol. 18, pp: 643-662.

Tang, J. (1991): 'Findings from observational studies of collaborative work', *Int. Journal of Man-Machine Studies*, vol. 34, no. 2, pp: 143-160.

Tinker, M. (1972): 'Effect of angular alignment upon readability of print', *Journal of Educational Psychology*, vol. 47, pp: 358-363.

Wu, M. and R. Balakrishnan (2003): 'Multi-finger and whole hand gestural interaction techniques for multi-user tabletop displays', *Proc. of the 16th annual ACM symposium on User interface software and technology*, Vancouver, Canada ACM Press, pp: 193-202.

H. Gellersen et al. (eds.), ECSCW 2005: Proceedings of the Ninth European
Conference on Computer-Supported Cooperative Work, 18-22 September 2005, Paris,
France, 225–245.

An Evaluation of Techniques for Reducing Spatial Interference in Single Display Groupware

Theophanis Tsandilas and Ravin Balakrishnan
Department of Computer Science, University of Toronto, Canada
{fanis, ravin}@dgp.toronto.edu

Abstract. When several users interact with Single Display Groupware (SDG) (Stewart et al., 1999) applications over a shared display, the potential exists for one user's actions to spatially interfere with another's (Tse et al., 2004; Zanella and Greenberg, 2001). We empirically evaluate four techniques for mitigating spatial interference in SDG: shared display with object ownership, spatially split display, shared display with uniform transparency between users' data, and shared display with gradient transparency from one edge of the display to the other. Apart from time and error performance measures, we also consider the impact of each technique on user's voluntary partitioning of the available display space. Results show that the best approach in terms of performance is to share the entire display with appropriate use of transparency techniques for minimizing interference, and allow users to decide for themselves how they wish to partition the space, rather than pre-partitioning it for them. Results also show that complete sharing may result in misuse of screen space and demonstrate the potential of gradient transparency as a technique that effectively balances costs and benefits of both sharing and partitioning.

Introduction

Single Display Groupware (SDG) (Bederson et al., 1999; Stewart et al., 1999) enable multiple physically co-located people to interact concurrently using a single shared display, but with each user having their own input devices. In an SDG environment using indirect input technologies such as mice, physical contact or interference between users are typically minimal and thus the body cues and social protocols used to mediate shared-space interaction in the physical world

(Pinelle et al., 2003) are less likely to be sufficient to prevent possible interference in the virtual realm. For example, one user could, perhaps inadvertently, activate a window that obstructs another user's work area on a shared display.

Tse et al. (2004) examined the problem of spatial interference in SDG to determine whether users tend to naturally separate their workspaces and avoid any interference without the need for verbal negotiation or the use of special interaction techniques. They conducted a user study in which pairs of users completed a series of collaborative tracing and drawing exercises. The experiment showed that interference was rare as collaborators naturally organized their interaction with the shared display to minimize spatial overlap. This result indicates that the role of techniques that resolve interference in shared displays is less important, and designers should rather focus on how to exploit and promote the implicit partitioning naturally made by users.

The above result was based on a specific type of application where tasks could be split into partial subtasks that could be completed within a small space. Therefore, users did not have any reason to interfere. Morris et al. (2004) report, however, that observations of groups of people interacting with SDG have shown that conflicts between users' actions often arise, which may be either accidental or intentional. For instance, interference may be unavoidable when a task involves handling large objects such as whole windows and users interact close to each other. As Hutchings and Stasko (2004) observe, everyday interaction involves coordination of multiple windows and space management is an important issue even in single-user displays. Besides, we believe that the interesting question is not whether collaborators in SDG would naturally try to avoid interference when its cost is high, but whether the performance of collaborators could improve by applying interaction techniques that reduce the cost of interference.

In addition, there may be situations in which multiple people interact with the same display to perform tasks that do not involve collaboration. For instance, such situations may arise in front of public displays. As users may be strangers, social protocols may not be strong and interaction techniques may be needed to prevent users from dominating the space of the display. Moreover, the physical location of a user in front of a display may not be explicit or determined in advance. Vogel and Balakrishnan (2004) suggest that interaction styles may change as the user transitions from distant to close interaction with a shared public display. During this process, the new user will possibly have to interfere with the workspace of existing users and even negotiate or compete for screen space.

Thus, although interference in SDG may not *always* occur, there are enough scenarios in which they do pose a problem. As such, it is important to design SDG systems with appropriate techniques for minimizing interference, with a sound understanding of the relative strengths and weaknesses of the techniques. Researchers have developed interface components that reduce interference, e.g., (Gutwin et al., 2003; Shoemaker and Inkpen, 2002; Yerazunis and Carbone,

2001; Zanella and Greenberg, 2001) – discussed in the next section, and evaluated them with reference to the standard completely shared display baseline in terms of task performance. However, there has not been a systematic evaluation of how multiple different techniques for reducing spatial interference in SDG perform relative to one another, and perhaps more importantly how they influence the natural partitioning of display space. Our present work is an attempt to provide some empirical data in this regard.

Related Work

An overview of problems arising when multiple people use a single display was presented by Bederson et al. (1999) and Stewart et al. (1999). Their work focused on collaboration in front of a single display and mainly investigated navigation conflicts that arise when users try to navigate in different areas of the shared data space. They suggested the following solutions to address navigation conflicts: (1) use a social protocol to negotiate and manage conflicts; (2) use a locking mechanism that prevents a user from navigating when another user is working; (3) use dynamic views to provide temporarily decoupled views; (4) split the display into one area per user; and (5) disallow any navigation. Shoemaker and Inkpen (2002), on the other hand, suggested that different users should be provided a different channel of output so that privacy is preserved and interaction conflicts are resolved. This, however, requires users to wear special CrystalEyes glasses. A similar approach was adopted by Yerazunis and Carbone (2001). Morris et al. (2004) proposed a set of coordination policies to resolve conflicts. Their work focused on conflicts caused by global user actions or by the access and manipulation of objects rather than conflicts arising from spatial interference.

The problem of spatial interference in SDG was examined by Zanella and Greenberg (2001), who proposed the use of transparent widgets. They conducted an experimental study in which pairs of users played a type of game. The first user in each pair tried to complete a simple drawing task. The second user tried to disturb the task of the first user by popping up and clicking either an opaque or a transparent menu. As expected, the transparent menus reduced interference and improved the performance of the interfered player. A limitation of the above experiment is that it simulated a worst-case scenario where interference occurred constantly rather than the more realistic situation where interference is more intermittent. Further, interference was not caused by any real need of users for more space and, as a result, the experiment did not examine the trade-off between screen space and interference. Also, the experiment did not examine how transparency could promote space separation. Our present work investigates this implication of using transparency.

The use of transparency as a means of reducing interference between overlapping workspaces has also been investigated in personal displays. Harrison et al. (1995a, 1995b) suggested the use of semi-transparent interface objects to support both focused and divided attention. Gutwin et al. (2003), on the other hand, explored the notion of *dynamic transparency* which adjusts the level of transparency with respect the position of the user's cursor. According to Tse et al. (2004), dynamic transparency could be used to impose separation between the workspace of two users working on the same display. However, this argument was not further elaborated on or experimentally evaluated. Our present work investigates the value of object-centric dynamic transparency.

Techniques for Reducing Spatial Interference

Building upon previous work (Gutwin et al., 2003; Harrison et al., 1995a; Harrison et al., 1995b; Hutchings and Stasko, 2004; Tse et al., 2004; Zanella and Greenberg, 2001), we identify three main techniques for managing screen space such that interference between the workspace of two or more concurrent users is minimized:

Shared screen. Users are allowed to utilize the entire screen, but can only interact with objects that are owned by them or globally shared. The advantage of this technique is that it allows users to move freely around the display and define by themselves the boundaries of their workspace. Its efficiency, however, highly depends on social protocols. It does not prevent situations where "greedy" users extend their workspace into large areas of the screen, thus intruding into the workspace of other users and disturbing them.

Split screen. Splitting the screen into one area per user ensures that interference between the workspaces of two users cannot occur. Splitting can be initiated either by the SDG system according to a splitting protocol or by its actual users. For instance, the Dynamo system (Izadi et al., 2003) allows users to interactively define private regions on a shared display. Splitting eliminates interaction conflicts, but it restricts users into the space that is allocated to them. Traditional techniques of space navigation such as panning and zooming can relax the problem of limited space.

Layers. Each user is provided with a different layer of interaction as shown in Figure 1. Each layer may be visible to multiple users, but its contents can only be manipulated by its owner. In a collaborative environment a layer could belong to more than a single user. Interference between layers can be reduced by controlling the transparency of the top layer. We extend the uniform transparency used by Zanella and Greenberg (2001), by proposing several unique ways in which transparency can be applied, as discussed in the following sections.

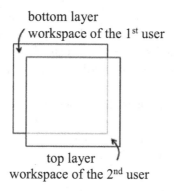

Figure 1. Splitting interaction into layers

Uniform Transparency on Overlapping Areas

Interference between layers can be reduced by simply applying transparency on the areas of the top layer which overlap with areas of the bottom layer. As demonstrated in Figure 2, the appearance of objects is not affected as long as there is no overlap between them. The main advantage of this technique is that users are allowed to use the whole space of the display while the use of transparency is limited to overlapping areas. This can be considered as object-centric dynamic transparency. The disadvantage of the technique is that since there is no defined separation between the working areas of any two users, greedy users can utilize more of the display and dominate over others who seek to avoid interference.

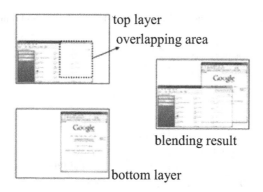

Figure 2. Applying transparency (alpha = 50%) to the areas of the top layer that overlap with areas of the bottom layer.

Varying Levels of Transparency

Another option is to divide the display into two or more partitions using varying levels of transparency. Each user has "transparency dominance" in one portion of the display, within which their content is displayed with maximum opacity while other users' content is displayed more transparently underneath. Consequently, users are encouraged to restrict their working space to the area which provides most visibility to their data. However, users can still use the other portions of the display to place objects that are temporarily inactive or out of the current focus of their ongoing task.

Figure 3 shows two techniques that divide a workspace using transparency. The first technique applies two levels of transparency to different halves of the top layer (Figure 3a). As a result, the transition between the two workspaces is discontinuous. The second technique (Figure 3b) adjusts the transparency level using a continuous function, which is shown in Figure 4. As a result, transparency smoothly decreases as users' interaction moves away from their area of dominance.

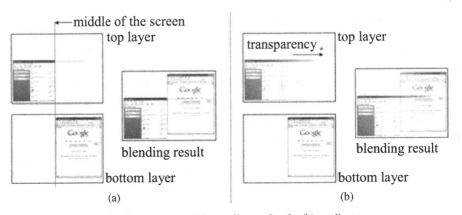

Figure 3. Varying levels of transparency: (a) two discrete levels, (b) gradient transparency.

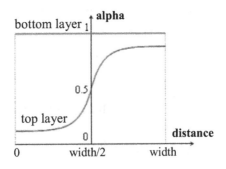

Figure 4. Function controlling the transparency of layers.

The above techniques have been designed so that no user has advantage over the other user. However, transparency levels could be adjusted in favour of a particular user. This might be useful when the task of this user requires additional space or has a high priority. Conversely, high transparency levels could be used to penalize aggressive users.

Taxonomy of Techniques

Figure 5 presents a taxonomy of techniques used to manage interference when multiple users work on the same display. The techniques are examined with respect to two main factors: (1) level of interference, and (2) level of sharing. There is trade-off between these two factors. Separation may result in less freedom in how to manage space and eventually decrease user performance. On the other hand, sharing results in more overlapping between users' workspace which may translate into more interference and reduced user performance. Completely sharing and completely partitioning a display are the two extreme cases. The goal of transparency-based techniques is to reduce the gap between these extremes and improve user performance.

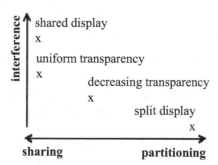

Figure 5. Taxonomy of techniques

Experiment

Goals

We conducted a controlled experiment to evaluate the role of different display partitioning and transparency techniques in reducing interference between the workspace of two users sharing a single display. More specifically, we examined four different techniques: (1) shared display (SHARED), (2) split display (SPLIT), (3) display with uniform transparency on overlapping content (TRANS), and (4) display with decreasing gradient transparency from one vertical edge to the other (GRAD). Following Zanella and Greenberg (2001), we hypothesized that transparency would reduce interference and, as a result, would improve task performance. Similarly to the above work and to other approaches that have studied the effects of transparency (Gutwin et al., 2003; Harrison et al., 1995b), we used task-completion time as the main measure of user performance.

The experiment isolated situations in which the trade-off between space freedom and interference becomes a significant factor in user performance. Such situations can emerge even in cases where users collaborate. As opposed to the experiment in Zanella and Greenberg (2001) where interference was reinforced by the rules of a competitive game, our experiment was designed so that interference naturally emerges as a result of the nearness between the users' working spaces as well as the space limitations posed by the display. In addition, our experiment examined transparency to a finer level of granularity and investigated how the different techniques promote space separation.

Apparatus

Two-mouse interaction was implemented using the MID package (Hourcade and Bederson, 1999). Since MID supports only older versions of the Windows operating system (Windows 98/ME), we used MID's capability of sending mouse events through a TCP/IP socket connection. As a result, our experimental system required two different machines being connected through a TCP/IP connection. The main components of the experimental software ran on a 2GHz P4 PC with Windows XP. This machine had a Dell UtraSharp 18-inch Flat Panel LCD Monitor, which was used to display the workspace of both users. The mouse of this machine was used by the user sitting at the left side of the monitor. The second mouse was provided by a Dell laptop running Windows XP and was used by the user sitting at the right side of the monitor. The laptop ran software responsible for sending events from the second mouse device to the main application. The software was built on Java 2 SDK, version 1.4.2. We employed Jazz's (Bederson et al., 2000) multilayer architecture to separate the surface of interaction between multiple users and developed cameras that affected the transparency of visual objects. The selection of the particular platform was also directed by future plans to develop zooming-based interaction techniques to reduce interference in SDG.

The experiment was run on a low screen resolution 800x600, as high-screen resolutions resulted in slight delays in the case of the two transparency techniques. The reason for such delays is that current versions of Java 2D did not support hardware acceleration in the presence of multiple transparency levels. Future versions of Java will possibly address this problem. We note that the low resolution used by the experimental system did not add any bias against any of the four techniques as object sizes were selected with respect to this resolution. In addition, the experimental task did not involve tiny font sizes or pictures so the low resolution did not affect the legibility of objects.

Task

The experimental task consisted of a series of drag-and-drop subtasks. More specifically, each user owned two windows. The movement of a window was constrained by the size of the display (800x600 pixels). The model of activation and movement of a window was identical to the model used by popular operating systems such as Microsoft Windows. As shown in Figure 6, each window contained 10 characters randomly positioned within the main area of the window. Characters could be either upper-case letters ('A'-'J') or lower-case letters ('a'-'j'). The user's task was to match the characters between the two windows. Matching was performed by dragging a lower-case character from one window and releasing it on top of the corresponding upper-case character on the other window. The task was completed after the user matched all the 10 letters in alphabetical order.

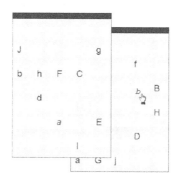

Figure 6. Experimental task. User drags lowercase characters in alphabetical order from one window and drops it on the matching uppercase character in the other window. In this example, after finishing with 'a/A' the user drags 'b' to match it with 'B'.

The size of windows was 270x390 pixels. This size was selected so that although completing the task in half of the display's space (400x600) was feasible, completing the task using the whole display was significantly faster. The above task is representative of common computer tasks that require a relatively large space in order to be completed, such as copy-and-paste and drag-and-drop actions between different windows. In contrast to Zanella and Greenberg (2001) where the experimental task simulated a worst-case scenario, where users were continually interrupted with interfering pop-up objects, our task simulates the more realistic situation where two users try to accomplish their tasks as fast as possible within a limited screen space deciding on their own whether they should interfere or not.

Figure 7 shows screenshots of the experimental setup when both users try to complete the task, using the four different display techniques. The borders and content of the windows owned by the user sitting at the left side of the monitor (Red Player) were coloured red, and the borders and content of the windows owned by the other user (Blue Player) were coloured blue. In the case of the shared display, when users clicked on top of a window that they owned, this window was brought into focus possibly covering the view of the other user. Deadlocks were avoided by allowing windows to be activated even if hidden by windows of a different colour. As shown in the figure, the split display was enhanced with a scrolling mechanism, which allowed users to use a total space equivalent to the entire display (800x600 pixels). Scrolling could be quickly performed by dragging the mouse left or right while pressing the right mouse button.

234

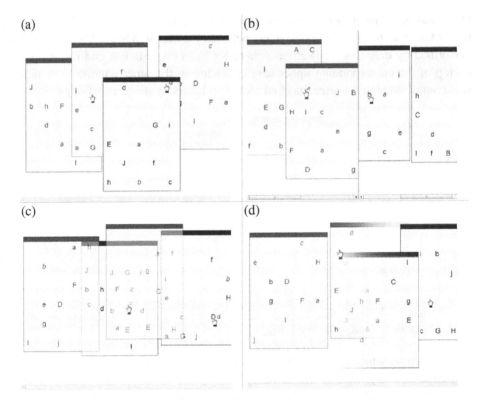

Figure 7. Evaluated techniques. (a) Shared display (SHARED), (b) split display with scrolling (SPLIT), (c) uniform transparency layered display (TRANS), (d) display with decreasing gradient transparency from one vertical edge to the other (GRAD).

Participants

16 undergraduate students, 13 male and 3 female, 18-23 years old, participated in the experiment. All the participants attended a first year undergraduate course in Computers Science. They were randomly grouped into 8 pairs. In total, there were 5 male-to-male pairs and 3 male-to-female pairs.

Design

A full factorial design with repeated measures was used. Each pair of participants completed 18 similar tasks for all the four evaluated techniques. For each task, a different arrangement of the letters in a window was set. Also for each task, windows were differently positioned around the left side (left user) or right side (right user) of the screen. The order in which the 18 tasks were performed was randomized for each technique and for each pair of participants. The order in which the pairs were exposed to the techniques was balanced using a Latin square. More specifically, each technique appeared exactly twice as first, second, third and fourth in the sequence. In summary, the experiment was designed as follows:

8 pairs of participants (16 participants) ×
4 techniques ×
18 tasks per technique

= 576 tasks in total

For each technique, in addition to the 18 main tasks, participants had to complete 3 practice tasks.

Measures

We examined two dependent variables measuring user performance: (1) task-completion time, and (2) number of errors. For task completion time, we define *MaxTime* as the time taken by the user who was the slowest for the applicable task, and *MinTime* as the time taken by the faster user for the same task. We define *Errors* as the sum – across both users – of the number of user attempts to drag and drop an incorrect letter and unsuccessful user attempts to drop a correct letter to the appropriate position.

In addition to time and errors, we measured the maximum screen space (*Width*) in pixels occupied by a user when completing a particular task. For a particular user, *Width* was measured as the distance from the side of the screen which was closer to physical location of the user. The maximum value that *Width* could have was 800 pixels and was measured only until the fastest user ("winner") completed his or her task, i.e., it was measured only for the time that both users were active.

Procedure

The experiment was performed in a single session lasting 70-80 minutes. Participants were asked to complete their tasks as fast as possible without being concerned about whether they disturbed the workspace of the other user. The purpose of this instruction was to guide user behaviour and discourage users from adopting non-optimal strategies. Participants were neither encouraged nor discouraged from interfering. They were rather left to decide on their own about which space-management strategy would best facilitate their task. This behaviour may seem artificial, since social protocols would possibly discourage users from disturbing each other even if such a selfish behaviour helped them to complete their task faster. However, if we know that a particular interaction technique improves the performance of both users when they act selfishly, then we can also conclude that the same technique will improve user performance in other situations.

Participants were asked to rest after each task. After a user's task was finished, his or her windows were locked, and the user had to wait for the task of the other user to be completed. Both participants in a pair had to agree in order to continue to the next task. At the end of the experiment, participants completed a questionnaire asking them to report how competitively or cooperatively they behaved during the experiment, to rank the four techniques, and give free-form comments.

Results

Measurements for 4 out of the 576 tasks were missing. ANOVA tests were performed after replacing missing values by the mean scores (time or number of errors) performed by the same participant for the same technique. We also examined outliers independently for each type of user (left-sided and right sided) and each technique. A value was considered as an outlier if it appeared three standard deviations away from the corresponding mean value. Rather than completely ignored, outliers were replaced by the worst (maximum) non-outlier score performed by any of the two users for the given technique. They accounted for 2.1% of the time measurements and 3.7% of the error measurements.

As the distributions of the time measurements were skewed, significance tests were performed on the inverse of the time measurements *1/Time*, which represent *task-completion frequencies*. This approach ensured the reliability of the significance tests since the resulting distributions were very close to normal. Clearly, a fast performance corresponds to a high task-completion frequency. Deviations from normality observed for the error distributions could not be corrected with simple transformations. However, additional statistics (mean, median, range) discernable in the boxplot of Figure 9 support the results of the significance tests.

Task Completion Time

Figure 8 shows the mean times performed by the "winners" and "losers" of the tasks for all the four techniques. There was a significant main effect for techniques on *1/MinTime* ($F_{3,21}=19.625$, $p<.001$). Their effect on *1/MaxTime* was also significant ($F_{1.619,11.336} = 13.38$, $p=.002$) [1].

As shown in Figure 8, TRANS was the fastest technique, followed by GRADS, while SPLIT was the slowest one. Post-hoc pairwise comparisons showed that mean differences were significant for the pairs (SHARED, TRANS), (SPLIT, TRANS), (SPLIT, GRAD), and (TRANS, GRAD). No significant difference was found between SHARED and SPLIT and between SHARED and GRAD. Table I summarizes these results. The differences are clearer in the case

---

[1]   Wherever degrees of freedom are reported as decimal numbers, the Greenhouse-Geisser's correction has been used to correct violations of the sphericity assumption.

of the *1/MinTime* measure, as *MinTime* measures the time in which both users were active and interference was more intense. In addition, *MaxTime* was more vulnerable to outliers and noise. We can notice, though, that both measures follow similar trends, which shows that all the techniques helped or hindered the task of both "winners" and "losers" in the same way.

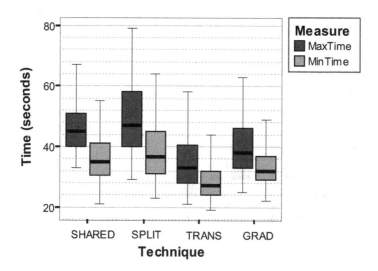

Figure 8. Boxplot illustrating MinTime and MaxTime scores for each of the four techniques.

Table I. Pairwise comparisons for 1/MaxTime and 1/MinTime (task-completion frequencies)

Techn (1)	Techn (2)	Sig. [a] (*1/MaxTime*)	Sig. [a] (*1/MinTime*)
SHARED	SPLIT	1.000	1.000
SHARED	TRANS	.069	.021 *
SHARED	GRAD	1.000	.299
SPLIT	TRANS	.004 *	< .001 *
SPLIT	GRAD	< .001 *	.024 *
TRANS	GRAD	.206	.036 *

a. Computed using Bonferroni's adjustment.
* The mean difference is significant at the .05 level.

We should note that the overall mean times were similar for Red and Blue Player (38.9 vs. 38.1 seconds, respectively). As a result, we did not observe any significant main effect of the type of the player on *1/Time* ($F_{1,14}$ = *.002, p=.969*). Besides, we did not observe any significant interaction effect between the type of player and the tested techniques ($F_{3,42}$ = *.670, p=.575*).

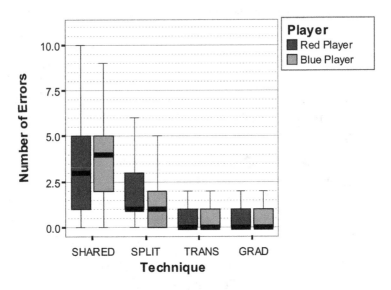

Figure 9. Boxplot illustrating the number of errors for each of the four techniques.

Table II. Pairwise comparisons for Errors

Technique (1)	Technique (2)	Sig. [a](*Errors*)
SHARED	SPLIT	.002 *
SHARED	TRANS	< .001 *
SHARED	GRAD	< .001 *
SPLIT	TRANS	< .001 *
SPLIT	GRAD	.002 *
TRANS	GRAD	1.000

a. Computed using Bonferroni's adjustment.
* The mean difference is significant at the .05 level.

Errors

Figure 9 illustrates the mean number of errors made by users when using each technique. There was a significant main effect for technique on the number of errors ($F_{3,21}$=*98.480, p<.0001*). Table II presents the results of pairwise comparisons between the techniques. All pairs except (TRANS, GRAD) showed significant differences between the techniques. In summary, the SHARED technique was the worst in terms of number of errors made by users, while the SPLIT technique was the second worst. The mean number of errors for the two transparency techniques was similar.

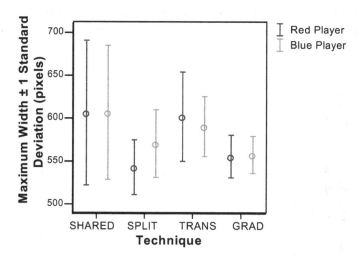

Figure 10. Maximum screen widths occupied by users for each of the four techniques.

Table III. Pairwise comparisons for Width

Technique (1)	Technique (2)	Sig. [a] (*Width*) Red Player	Sig. [a] (*Width*) Blue Player
SHARED	SPLIT	.027 *	.003 *
SHARED	TRANS	1.000	.431
SHARED	GRAD	.257	.002 *
SPLIT	TRANS	.004 *	.021 *
SPLIT	GRAD	.728	.196
TRANS	GRAD	.046 *	<.001 *

a. Computed using Bonferroni's adjustment.
* The mean difference is significant at the .05 level.

Use of Screen Space

Figure 10 illustrates the variance of *Width* among the techniques. Users typically utilized a space larger than the half of the screen (400 pixels) as this strategy fa-

240

cilitated their tasks. The greatest screen-space consumption was made when the two sharing techniques were used (SHARED & TRANS). This means that users did not try to limit interaction to a small area close to their side as such a strategy did not seem to be effective in terms of speed. On the other hand, the two splitting techniques (SPLIT & GRAD) provided less freedom to the users. As a result, user interaction was limited in a smaller area of the screen. The ANOVA test showed a significant main effect of the technique variable on *Width* ($F_{1.543,10.804} = 10.734$, $p=.004$ for Red Player, and $F_{3,21} = 27.523$, $p<.0001$ for Blue Player). In addition,

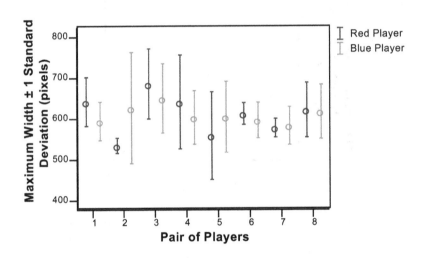

Figure 11. Maximum screen widths occupied by each participant (SHARED technique)

pairwise comparisons showed significant differences for the following pairs of techniques: (SHARED, SPLIT), (TRANS, SPLIT) and (TRANS, GRAD) for both Red Player and Blue Player, and (SHARED, GRAD) for Blue Player. These results are demonstrated in Table III.

An interesting result is the great variance of maximum widths in the case of the SHARED technique. This could be attributed to users employing different strategies of screen space usage depending on the attitude of the "opponent" user, as indicated in Figure 11. Interestingly, users of the same pair synchronized their strategies as corresponding mean values and variances appear to be similar. This implies that users did not allow their "opponents" to dominate the space as such an approach would result in a slower performance. Exception to this phenomenon was the strategies adopted by the users of the second pair: Red Player was very conservative with screen usage, while Blue Player was rather aggressive.

Observations and Subjective User Feedback

We observed a variety of different behaviour demonstrated by participants. Although participants were instructed to act selfishly, it seems that social protocols were not totally disregarded. Most participants exhibited friendly, sharing, behaviour while a few were highly competitive. Surprisingly, a participant commented that she got annoyed by the "lack of consideration" of the other user.

The difference in participants' attitudes was also demonstrated by their answers to the questionnaire. Four participants declared that they strongly agree or agree with the statement "I always tried not to disturb the other player", while six participants strongly disagreed or disagreed with the statement. Six participants were neutral. Likewise, seven participants said that they strongly agree or agree with the statement "I interfered with the other player as long as this facilitated my task". Three participants disagreed, while six were neutral. Participants were also asked to rank the four techniques that they used. Although the great majority (11 of 16) ranked the SHARED technique as the worst, no clear preference for the other techniques could be inferred.

Discussion and Future Directions

Space-Usage Strategies

Our results indicate that when space was not restricted, users did not necessarily divide the large shared space into completely separate individual ones, but rather worked in partially separate areas with significant overlap (Figure 10 & 11). This result contrasts with the observations by Tse et al. (2004) and indicates that the type of task can significantly impact space usage and interference strategies. We acknowledge, however, that as the experimental procedure directed users to adopt optimal strategies in terms of performance, social protocols may have not had the effect that they would have in real situations. An interesting question that future work needs to explore is whether and to what extend users would naturally adapt their space-usage strategies to the interaction technique used to handle interference. Would users decide to overlap their workspaces given that such an approach would improve their combined utility? If not, how could designers of SDG encourage users to revise traditional social protocols and adopt strategies that would optimize their tasks?

Sharing versus Partitioning

According to our results, performance was worst in terms of the time measure, when the system split the screen into two separate areas (SPLIT condition).

Scrolling added an additional cost which delayed the completion of the tasks. However, the SHARED condition resulted in high error rates, which together with participants' subjective answers indicate that the latter's performance was actually the worst one. On the other hand, providing interaction layers with uniform transparency on overlapping content was particularly beneficial, as indicated by the fastest performance times and lowest errors in our TRANS condition. The new gradient transparency technique we developed was not as effective as uniform transparency in terms of task performance time, but had similarly low error rates. Although this result advocates against the explicit partitioning of the screen when transparency is used, separation may be beneficial in several cases. The GRAD condition resulted in a more economical use of space, and thus, it could be used to discourage aggressive users from dominating the display. Explicit partitioning, however, assumes the system's knowledge about the position of users. The answer to the dilemma between sharing and partitioning a display may also depend on how much collaboration between users a task involves. We have

(a)　　　　　　　　　(b)

Figure 12. Transparency lens affecting: (a) a circular area around the cursor; (b) the active object.

worked on implementations that employ more than two layers of interaction. This allows the coexistence of both shared surfaces, which are more suitable for collaborative tasks, and gradually fading surfaces, which are more suitable for independent tasks. In future work, we plan to assess the usefulness of these implementations.

Limitations of Transparency

Results show that transparency-based techniques reduced interference and improved user performance. Nevertheless, we should be careful about how to generalize this result. In our experiment, the distribution of targets was relatively sparse and windows had simple backgrounds. The effectiveness of transparency has shown to reduce when background complexity becomes high (Gutwin et al., 2003). Several techniques could relax this limitation. Figure 12 demonstrates implementations of magic lenses (Bier et al., 1993) which locally reduce the transparency level of a region surrounding the cursor of a user (Figure 12 (a)) or the transparency level of a whole object (Figure 12 (b)). *Dynamic transparency* (Gutwin et al., 2003), *context-aware free-space transparency* (Ishak and Feiner, 2004), and *multiblending* (Baudisch and Gutwin, 2004) are additional techniques that could be used to effectively handle the trade-off between legibility of content and interference in SDG applications.

An additional limitation of our experiment is that colour was used to differentiate between objects of the two players (red and blue). The value of transparency could plausibly decrease if no colour separation was used as there would be an additional overhead for recognizing which objects belonged to whom. However, in real usage, users will probably be quite aware of the objects that they are currently working on, and usage context will further aid in object identification. Also, simple techniques can be used to reduce this problem, for example by subtly and uniquely highlighting each user's objects. Detailed investigation of this issue is worthy of future research.

Conclusions

We have presented a controlled study investigating the impact of four space sharing techniques in SDG. Our study focused on situations where interference between users naturally emerges as a result of space limitations imposed by the display. Our results have clearly shown the value of using transparency "when needed" for facilitating overlapping use of space in an effective manner. Taken as a whole, our results suggest that the best strategy for space management in SDG is to allow users to share the entire display with appropriate use of transparency techniques for minimizing interference, and decide for themselves how they wish to partition the space, rather than pre-partitioning it for them. On the other hand, gradient transparency results in more economical usage of space and therefore could be possibly used to effectively balance between user performance and space misuse. Future work needs to test the implications of our results in realistic collaborative environments and explore legibility issues concerning the use of transparency. We are also planning to test the application of the proposed techniques in displays shared by more than two users and explore techniques for reducing interference in SDG that do not use transparency, for example, techniques based on zooming.

Acknowledgments

Special thanks to Matthew Boulos for his help in recruiting participants and John Hancock for setting up the experimental hardware. We also thank all the people who participated in our user studies, Anastasios Kementsietsidis and members of the DGP Lab for their valuable feedback.

References

Baudisch, P., and Gutwin, C. (2004). 'Multiblending: displaying overlapping windows simultaneously without the drawbacks of alpha blending', *ACM CHI Conference on Human Factors in Computing Systems*, pp. 367-374, ACM Press.

Bederson, B. B., Meyer, J., and Good, L. (2000). 'Jazz: an Extensible Zoomable user interface graphics toolkit in Java', ACM *UIST Symposium on User Interface and Software Technology*, pp. 171-180, ACM Press.

Bederson, B. B., Stewart, J., and Druin, A. (1999). 'Single Display Groupware', Technical Report CS-TR-4086, University of Maryland, USA.

Bier, E. A., Stone, M. C., Pier, K., Buxton, W., and DeRose, T. D. (1993). 'Toolglass and Magic Lenses: The See-Through Interface', *ACM SIGGRAPH Conference on Computer Graphics and Interactive Techniques*, pp. 73-80, ACM Press.

Gutwin, C., Dyck, J., and Fedak, C. (2003). 'The Effects of Dynamic Transparency on Targeting Performance', *Conference on Graphics Interface*, pp. 101-110.

Harrison, B. L., Ishii, H., Vicente, K. J., and Buxton, W. A. S. (1995a). 'Transparent Layered User Interfaces: An Evaluation of a Display Design Space to Enhance Focused and Divided Attention', *ACM CHI Conference on Human Factors in Computing Systems*, pp. 317-324, ACM Press.

Harrison, B. L., Kurtenbach, G., and Vicente, K. J. (1995b). 'An experimental evaluation of transparent user interface tools and information content', *ACM UIST Symposium on User Interface and Software Technology*, pp. 81-90, ACM Press.

Hourcade, J. P., and Bederson, B. B. (1999). 'Architecture and Implementation of a Java Package for Multiple Input Devices (MID)', Tech Report CS-TR-4018, University of Maryland, USA.

Hutchings, D. R., and Stasko, J. (2004). 'Revisiting display space management: Understanding current practice to inform next-generation design', *Conference on Graphics Interface*, pp. 127-134.

Ishak, E. W., and Feiner, S. K. (2004). 'Interacting with hidden content using content-aware free-space transparency', *ACM UIST Symposium on User Interface and Software Technology*, pp. 189-192, ACM Press.

Izadi, S., Brignull, H., Rodden, T., Rogers, Y., and Underwood, M. (2003). 'Dynamo: a public interactive surface supporting the cooperative sharing and exchange of media', *ACM UIST Symposium on User Interface and Software Technology*, pp. 159-168, ACM Press.

Morris, M. R., Ryall, K., Shen, C., Forlines, C., and Vernier, F. (2004). 'Beyond "social protocols": multi-user coordination policies for co-located groupware', *ACM CSCW Conference on Computer Supported Cooperative Work*, pp. 262-265, ACM Press.

Pinelle, D., Gutwin, C., and Greenberg, S. (2003). 'Task analysis for groupware usability evaluation: Modeling shared-workspace tasks with the mechanics of collaboration', *ACM Transactions on Computer-Human Interaction*, vol. 10, no. 4, pp. 281-311.

Shoemaker, G., and Inkpen, K. (2002). 'Single display privacyware: augmenting public displays with private information', *ACM CHI Conference on Human Factors in Computing Systems*, pp. 522-529, ACM Press.

Stewart, J., Bederson, B. B., and Druin, A. (1999). 'Single display groupware: a model for co-present collaboration', *ACM CHI Conference on Human Factors in Computing Systems*, pp. 286-293, ACM Press.

Tse, E., Histon, J., Scott, S. D., and Greenberg, S. (2004). 'Avoiding interference: how people use spatial separation and partitioning in SDG workspaces', *ACM CSCW Conference on Computer Supported Cooperative Work*, pp. 252-261, ACM Press.

Vogel, D., and Balakrishnan, R. (2004). 'Interactive public ambient displays: transitioning from implicit to explicit, public to personal, interaction with multiple users', *ACM UIST Symposium on User Interface Software and Technology*, pp. 137-146, ACM Press.

Yerazunis, W. S., and Carbone, M. S. (2001). 'Privacy-Enhanced Displays by Time-Masking Images', *OzCHI Australian Conference on Computer-Human Interaction*.

Zanella, A., and Greenberg, S. (2001). 'Reducing Interference in Single Display Groupware through Transparency', *ECSCW European Conference on Computer Supported Cooperative Work*, pp. 339-358, Kluwer Academic Publishers.

H. Gellersen et al. (eds.), ECSCW 2005: Proceedings of the Ninth European
Conference on Computer-Supported Cooperative Work, 18-22 September 2005, Paris,
France, 247–264.

Cellular Phone as a Collaboration Tool that Empowers and Changes the Way of Mobile Work: Focus on Three Fields of Work

Eriko Tamaru, Kimitake Hasuike, and Mikio Tozaki

Human Interface Design Development, Fuji Xerox Co., Ltd., Japan

{eriko.tamaru, kimitake.hasuike, mikio.tozaki}@fujixerox.co.jp

Abstract. The development and spread of cellular phones have been remarkable in recent years, and these phones are becoming an integral part of the social infrastructure. Owing to mobile technology, especially cellular phone technology, the way of working that entails being unconstrained by time and space has flourished. Over a period of five years, we have investigated various fields of work that involve mobile workers such as sales representatives and repair technicians. Cellular phones were observed to have had a significant influence on task organization and the structure of communication in these fields of work. This paper describes how mobile workers have incorporated this new technology into their work creatively and constructively. Furthermore, it describes how cellular phones have changed the relationship between and enhanced the communication network among coworkers and customers. As a result, we demonstrate how cellular phones are evolving into a type of collaborative tool that supports collaborative work between mobile workers, instead of a communication tool that merely connects two individuals. In other words, based on ethnographical observation, we show that cellular phones are a fundamental element of CSCW technology for mobile workers.

Introduction

The way of working has become increasingly multifaceted in the past few years, enabling workers to choose from a wider range of employment. People can now choose to work in a manner that is unconstrained by time and location and suits their lifestyle or work style preferences (Froggatt, 2001). In addition to such change, the progress and rapid spread of mobile technology, especially cellular phone technology, is remarkable. In this study, we focus on the mobile work style and the use of cellular phones in the workplace. Further, we investigate the different ways in which cellular phone technology can aid and abet mobile workers.

In former times, people's lifestyles and forms of work changed drastically with the proliferation of the telephone (Fischer, 1992). In the same manner, the cellular phone has also affected the work style and social communication network among people. Cellular phones were initially introduced as a commodity for business people, but it rapidly spread among the youth in many countries (Rheingold, 2002). Various investigations have reported that the communication pattern of the youth and the manner in which they structure their time are changing with the use of cellular phone technology (Ling and Yttri, 2002; Weilenmann, 2003).

Most studies on cellular phones focus on their social, recreational, and familial use. On the other hand, very few studies focus on the use of cellular phones in the workplace. Currently, in the world of business, the number of people whose nature of work involves being mobile is fast increasing. From the viewpoint that it is more efficient to work at a more productive location rather than a fixed office, a person's workplace shifted to the location that would result in higher productivity. Cellular phone technology is one of the most powerful technologies that support such mobile workers.

For the past five years, we have investigated many workers in several workplaces. In most studies on workplaces, researchers have focussed on the interaction between the work and the technology employed (Engestrom and Middleton, 1998; Heath and Luff, 2000; Luff, et al., 2000; Goodwin and Ueno, 2000). In this paper, we focus on mobile technology, with particular emphasis on cellular phone technology. Cellular phones have undergone remarkable changes in these five years, and they have greatly influenced the working styles of mobile workers. People have grown accustomed to cellular phones and are now able to organize their work more efficiently. In this paper, we report on how the cellular phone has changed the working style and communication pattern of mobile workers over the past five years, citing examples from case studies on their ethnography.

Evolution of Cellular Phone Technology in Japan

This section outlines the trends and areas of changes of mobile media, focusing on cellular phones in Japan (Okada and Matsuda, 2000; Ito, et al., 2005).

Introduction Period

In Japan, the full-fledged cellular-phone service business began in 1987. Initially, however, a cellular phone terminal could only be rented and communication charges were high, thereby placing this technology beyond the reach of the common people and limiting its scope to business purposes. Early cellular phone usage was very different from the current trend of individual usage. For example, one cellular phone was shared among team members, and if a member were required to work outside office premises, s/he would be given the phone. Alternatively, at a construction site, only the site representative carried a cellular phone and made or received calls on behalf of the entire team. Thus, since a cellular phone was expensive, it was used more on an organizational level rather than an individual one. Current cellular phone usage has changed drastically from when it was an exclusive product. The fact that it was expensive lent a special significance to its usage. Business people mainly desired cellular phones because, rather than their functions, 'owning a cellular phone' became a status symbol, representing an 'up-and-coming business person'. Therefore, they sometimes deliberately flaunted their phones by using them in public spaces (e.g. carrying on loud conversations on their phones while commuting in trains). Plant (Plant, 2000) described such usage as 'The Flashy Peacock: proud and extroverted, using mobile primarily for show'.

Spread of Cellular Phones to Common Users

In the mid-1990s, cellular phone technology progressed rapidly, resulting in intense competition among carriers in the growing market. By this time, cellular phones had also gradually spread to common users because of the following reasons: reduction in size and weight of a mobile terminal, shift from rental to compulsory purchase of a terminal, reduction in communication charges, etc. Moreover, a simple and cheap cellular phone called PHS (personal handy-phone system) also accelerated the spread of cellular phones among the youth. During this time, the mail function was also introduced, and the cellular phone began to exhibit signs of shifting from a telephone to a colourful communication medium.

Development of Information Terminals for Cellular Phones

The evolution from a telephone to an information terminal began with the release of NTT DoCoMo's 'i-mode'® in 1999. Many PHS users shifted to a different cellular phone. This initiated the rapid spread of cellular phones. Currently, in addition to being an information terminal with mail and Internet functionalities, the cellular phone has been developed to serve as a multimedia terminal, providing photographs, music, games, etc. According to statistics provided by the Ministry of Public Management, as of 2004 (white paper, 2004), the number of cellular phones had exceeded 80 million, and no less than 89.5% of these phones had an Internet terminal. Thus, it can be considered that many people use cellular phones for their mail and Internet functionalities. Following this trend, cellular phone usage has changed greatly from the notion of 'The Flashy Peacock' in the 1980s.

We will now demonstrate the practical application of a cellular phone in business, including the changes that have taken place in the past five years.

Ethnography of a Mobile Worker: Three Fields of Mobile Work

In the past five years, we have investigated various workplaces. In this paper, we focus on mobile workers and cite examples from the following three case studies on their ethnography. The outline of the three fields of work and the investigation methods are described below.

Mobile Sales

In 1999, we investigated the sales operation section in a certain office equipment manufacturing company. The sales representatives of this section mainly sell office equipment such as copiers and printers. In order to enhance the abilities of the sales representatives, the work style was strategically reformed—they were provided with mobile technology in the form of notebook PCs, cellular phones and secure ID cards. These mobile tools enabled them to work at anytime and from anywhere (Figure 1). The number of visiting customers was therefore expected to increase significantly. The concerned section was located in central Tokyo, and their sales territory extended from the central area to the suburbs. Most sales representatives commuted either by train, on foot, or by motorbike, but those responsible for the suburbs mainly commuted by car. Although sales representatives are essentially mobile workers, they visited their office and met their colleagues in person in the morning, visited customers in the day and returned to the office in the evening. However, with the introduction of mobile technology, they were able to connect to an intra-network from any customer site or distributed office. The purpose of mobile work was to reduce various lead times and improve sales efficiency.

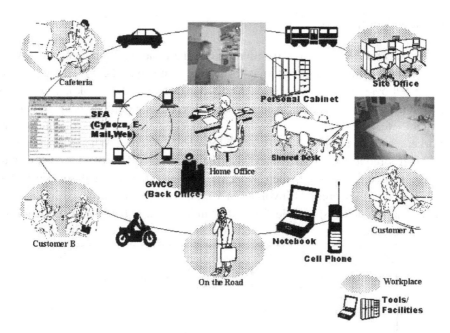

Figure 1. Mobile work environment of the target sales section

This investigation was conducted for about two weeks in 1999 by using the 'self-photo study' technique (Tamaru, et al., 2002; Hasuike, et al., 2003). In this study, each sales representative was provided with a disposable camera and was requested to photograph their workspace, tools, documents and coworkers during a typical work day (Figure 2). Interviews were conducted at a later date on the basis of the photographs, where the workers were questioned about the nature of their work, the use and applicability of the documents and technologies, etc. The subjects comprised three sales teams and nine sales representatives.

Figure 2. Various workplaces for mobile sales (photographs taken by sales representatives)

Service Technicians

For the second field of work, we investigated the repair and maintenance section of a certain office equipment manufacturing company. The investigation was conducted over five years from 1999 to 2004 (Ueno and Kawatoko, 2003). This section is responsible for the maintenance and repair of equipment such as copiers, printers, etc. and the network systems connecting these pieces of equipment. Workers from this field are also essentially mobile workers. When they receive a customer's request for repair, they visit the residence/office of that customer to fix the machine. Although their work mainly entails individual service at the customer site, they are also involved in various other team activities because all team members are responsible for maintaining the area that has a profusion of customers and machines. One team comprises five to ten service technicians.

Self-Dispatch System							
Call List			**Visiting List**				
NO	Client	Technician in Charge	NO	CE	Client	Completion Time (Estimate)	
103856	AAA Electric	Suzuki	01	Suzuki	EEE Industry	14:00	
204986	BBB Corporation	Tanaka	02	Suzuki	FFF Electric	15:30	
294857	CCC Department	Suzuki	03	Tanaka	GGG Electric	14:30	
491837	DDD Electric	Satoh	04	Satoh	HHH Corporation	15:01	
•	•	•	05	Satoh	III Store	16:00	
•	•	•	•	•	•	•	
•	•	•	•	•	•	•	
•	•	•	•	•	•	•	

Figure 3. Self-dispatch system (display example of notebook version)

A unique cellular phone Web application has been introduced for the workers of this section. They carry a cellular phone that serves as a Web terminal in order to use a mobile application called 'self-dispatch system' (Tamaru and Ueno, 2005). They voluntarily coordinate their schedule for visiting customers using this mobile application. The self-dispatch system visualizes the calling lists (which indicate the status of the repair jobs) and the technicians' visiting lists (which indicate the statuses of the team members) (Figure 3). Using this system, team members can infer the location and status of their colleagues.

The primary mode of transport in central Tokyo is a motorbike. Service technicians carry small replacement parts, manuals and a notebook PC on their motorbikes. In the suburbs, they commute by car.

We conducted a shadowing investigation to understand the activities at the client site. This investigation was carried out for one month each in 1999, 2002 and 2004, and in each of those years, we observed several service technicians. In addition to shadowing, we conducted interviews in order to gain a greater understanding of their activities. We interviewed several tens of people over the five years, such as service technicians, a technical specialist, the developer of the self-dispatch system, etc.

Office Design Company Sales

The sales section of an office design and furniture supplier company was investigated in 2004. The section under consideration mainly deals with office design rather than furniture supply. The sales representatives handle a wide range of activities—office layout design, construction and relocation.

The role of the sales representatives is to investigate the needs and problems of a customer, provide consulting services, propose new ways of working and recommend designs for advanced workplaces that tackle all the problems faced by a customer (Duffy and Powell, 1997; Zelinsky, 1998). These representatives deal with several issues, such as working styles, office layouts, document management, information infrastructure, etc. On receiving an order, they coordinate with the members of various workplaces, such as information infrastructure vendors, office furniture companies, designers, office equipment companies, construction contractors and building management companies. Sales representatives serve as project managers who facilitate the smooth completion of a project.

The team size of the concerned section is quite small, including only three sales representatives. Their service territories mainly lie within Tokyo and they commute primarily by train or on foot. Similar to the mobile sales investigation, we conducted a self-photo study in this investigation. In this case, we requested the representatives to photograph their work activities for one week—not only mobile work but also activities conducted in the office (Figure 4). Individual interviews were held subsequently. We then conducted a meeting with the sales representatives to discuss the data recorded by each member. During this meeting, the team members realized the differences between their own roles and those of their colleagues and further discussed these differences.

Meeting at a home office

Connect with a customer via mobile mail while commuting in a train

Meeting at a construction site

Telephone at a representative's desk

Figure 4. Work activities of the office design company's sales representatives (photographs taken by sales representatives)

Three Points of Interest

Since the time of the investigation and the fields of work of the above-mentioned case studies are different, we cannot draw a simple comparison among them. However, we proceed by discussing the relationship between mobile work, mobile technology and mobile workers. Furthermore, we discuss how these relationships have changed in these five years by citing characteristic examples from the three case studies. We now describe the viewpoints emerging from the above discussions.

(1) How people changed the way they organized work by cellular phones or how people accepted cellular phone technology and successfully applied it to their work

The introduction of cellular phones has evidently exerted a great influence on the way of working. However, working styles have not necessarily changed with the emergence of cutting-edge technology. People are constantly seeking creative ways of selecting the appropriate technology and applying that technology to their work activities. In this paper, we have focused on the creative ways in which mobile workers have suitably applied cellular phone technology to their work.

(2) How people reorganize the relationships with their coworkers using cellular phones

A mobile worker does not usually function only at an individual level. As a member of an organization, s/he has to maintain relations with colleagues; however, the strength of these relations may vary. In this paper, we discuss how mobile workers connect with their colleagues in a distributed work environment and how they reorganize their communication patterns using cellular phones.

(3) How workers connect with their customers using cellular phones and how this has effected a change in customer relations

Mobile technology has significantly influenced not only relations with colleagues but also customer relations. The relationship between a worker and a customer is essentially the same as that between the organizations to which they belong. We discuss the influence of mobile technology on the relationship between a worker and a customer and how their organizational relationship has changed with the introduction of cellular phones as a personal communication tool.

Reorganizing the Way of Working by Means of Mobile Technology

In this section, we discuss the manner in which mobile workers reorganized their working styles using cellular phones by citing examples of mobile sales representatives and service technicians.

Task Delegation by Sales Representatives

By changing to a mobile work style, sales representatives were able to work from anywhere outside their home offices. They could work not only from fixed workplaces such as at a site office or a car but also temporary workplaces such as the road and in small spaces at a customer site. However, it is difficult to accomplish a time-consuming task from a temporary workplace. When sales representatives work outside their home offices, the back office plays an important role in coordinating their actions. Sales representatives are accustomed to organizing their tasks by means of task delegation utilizing back office functions and mobile tools (Figure 5).

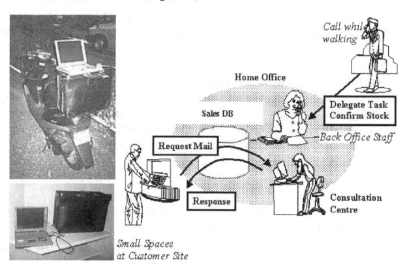

Figure 5. Work organization by task delegation

Delegation to office staff by means of a cellular phone

Upon receiving an order from a customer, a sales representative creates a shipping order after returning to her/his home office. If the stock is verified before returning, s/he can complete the shipping order smoothly. When requesting for an order outside the home office, s/he delegates a check task to a back office staff member via cellular phone. By doing this, s/he can work efficiently from the home office. Of course, at present, it is possible to check the stock via current cellular phone technology; however, the sales department did not employ such technology in 1999. Although restricted by technology, sales representatives developed creative methods for checking stock. By means of cellular phones and appropriate task allocation between the back office staff and themselves, they could carry out a pseudo inventory check anytime and from anywhere. This approach equalled the current technology of carrying out an inventory check using only a cellular phone.

Delegation to a consultation centre via electronic mail

When calling on customers, sales representatives are often asked various questions. However, certain questions cannot be answered immediately. After the visit, the sales representatives forward the questions to a consultation centre (which provides the necessary information to the sales representatives) via electronic mail by setting up their notebook PC in a small space at the customer site. In most cases, the centre replies to the sales representatives by the time they reach their home offices, and the sales representatives can then immediately forward the required information to the customer by e-mail. If the sales representatives were required to search for this information by themselves, the information would reach the customer on the following day at the earliest. In the case described above, the turnaround time is reduced by 'delegation'. Through the combination of back office assistance and mobile tools, sales representatives can dedicate themselves to more pressing tasks. Here, a cellular phone functions as a data communication terminal to access to the intranet.

In these two cases, sales representatives organized their tasks using not only mobile technology but also other resources, such as human resources. This is a key factor in successfully applying the new technology to their work (Brown and Duguid, 2000).

Parts Supply by Service Technicians

The method of supplying replacement parts has changed due to the occasional application of cellular phone technology. Here, we describe how service technicians reorganized their work entailing parts supply by using cellular phone technology.

Bottom-up approach among team members

As stated by J. Orr (1992; 1996), service technicians usually troubleshoot according to the problem at hand rather than completely relying on a manual. They structure an effective repair method depending on the status of the territory they cover and the status of the problem. However, procuring replacement parts often hinders the efficient execution of the repair method. If unable to obtain replacement parts when visiting a customer, they only perform emergency measures and revisit the customer upon obtaining the necessary part to carry on complete repairs.

Since numerous models and types of machines exist, it is difficult to carry along all types of replacement parts. Service technicians attempt to guess which parts will be required before the visit by evaluating the self-dispatch system or directly contacting the customer to enquire about the status of the problem. However, their ability to make an accurate guess is limited due to inadequate information. Therefore, efficient supply of parts to the client site is essential.

A basic method of ensuring parts supply is to contact a parts warehouse. They supply the required parts via a motorcycle delivery service. However, service technicians work at distributed sites. Thus, when the client site is at a distance from the parts warehouse, the supply may get delayed. This entire process is sometimes time-consuming. To avoid a delay in service, the technicians utilize the self-dispatch system that allows them to track the statuses of their team members to determine who is nearest to them at that time. They then call the nearest colleague to enquire whether s/he has the required parts. If available, they coordinate the method of transferring the parts. Apart from the parts supply system established by an organization, service technicians have created their own new method of parts supply.

Since team members can track each other's statuses on the self-dispatch system, it is important that a technician strategically follow her/his coworker's network without making reckless calls depending on only her/his personal network. In addition, the essential function of cellular phones, which is to connect individuals, promotes the coordination by effectively linking distributed colleagues. These two points support the organization of the bottom-up collaborative approach for parts supply.

Centre Approach for parts supply

Recently, a new cellular phone application for parts supply was introduced. The parts management system is centralized and uses a parts database. With this system, a service technician calls the central warehouse, which searches the database and locates the nearest warehouse that has the required parts. The parts are then delivered to the client site. By utilizing the GPS function of a cellular phone, this new application maps the parts delivery process with respect to the service technicians on a particular network. Once the parts are dispatched from the warehouse, the service technician receives a mail on her/his cellular phone providing tracking information such as the current location of the required part and the time it will be delivered. Since this new tool enables an accurate prediction of the delivery time, service technicians have developed a sense of security and are now capable of planning their work more efficiently.

It is speculated whether this new method of parts supply is quicker and more efficient than conventional methods. Irrespective, this method has certainly imparted a sense of security to service technicians. The ability to predict the delivery time of the parts has significantly facilitated the ease in planning work. In the former bottom-up approach, since it was difficult for technicians to carry many parts with them, their colleagues, too, did not usually have the parts they required. They would therefore frequent warehouses of nearby back offices to obtain the required parts. The probability that a technician can acquire replacement parts from her/his colleagues is, in fact, rather low. However, such methods were only resorted to because of the anxious feeling of 'procuring the parts as soon as possible', even if it would be faster to directly return to the back office in a calm and rational fashion. On the other hand, the purpose of the new tool is to not only reduce the waiting time for parts but also facilitate efficient time management at the client site. The use of GPS enabled an accurate prediction of the delivery time and thus enabled technicians to devise effective repair plans. Therefore, it can be said that GPS played a large role in organizing the way of working and in reassuring a technician.

Communication with a Colleague

A cellular phone is essentially a communication tool that connects people. Similar to mobile workers, people who work at diverse locations can contact their coworkers via cellular phones at any time. In this section, we describe how the relationship among colleagues and their patterns of communication have changed over the past five years.

Informal Collaboration Work by a Self-Dispatch System

At a basic level, service technicians work as a team. They can constantly track their team members by using a self-dispatch system and are conscious of the existence of their colleagues as they work. On one occasion, a technician (A) consulted the self-dispatch system and called his colleague (B) who was working in a company (C). A had previously visited C and had fixed a machine there. Although he might have resolved the problem, he remained somewhat anxious. However, upon referring to the self-dispatch system on the current occasion, he learnt that the same machine (at C) was giving trouble again and that B was working on it. A became increasingly anxious and telephoned B to enquire whether the same problem was encountered. Thereafter, it was revealed that it was not the same problem.

Thus, service technicians are conducting collaborative work informally using the self-dispatch system on a cellular phone. This mapping of a colleague's location and status facilitates collaborative work. Moreover, the communication function of a cellular phone aids technicians in establishing a direct link to their colleagues.

Communication by Mobile Mail

Initially, mobile mail was not adopted in the workplace, but this has changed over time. Although mobile mail was available since 1999, it was seldom used in business. As the use of mobile mail gradually increased among common users, many service technicians began using this function for personal purposes. Moreover, their organizations recommended the use of mobile mail as it proved cost effective. In such a scenario, some technicians began using the mail function for various purposes, e.g. connecting with a colleague, posing a question, connecting from a back office, etc. The exchange of mail messages had explicit purposes such as arranging for certain parts to be collected or even organizing lunch meetings. In this manner, service technicians who are familiar with mobile mail and use it in their personal life pioneered the use of this function in their team communication.

Collaboration using the 'multiple addressing mail' function

In 2004, the use of mobile mail became widespread and the number of people fully acquainted with the use of a cellular phone increased. In such a situation, its practical functions transcended individual use and permeated the realm of business. The 'multiple addressing mail' function can be cited as an example. Similar to mailing lists on the Internet, this function enables a mail to be transmitted simultaneously to all registered members. Upon discovering its convenience in personal use, the head of a certain team was keen on using this function in his work. He therefore introduced it to his team members and promoted its use.

At the time of observation, the team had been using this function for two months. However, it was obvious that this function had transformed the conventional communication pattern (individual network) among team members. While the tool remained unchanged, it could now link all team members. Earlier, questions could only be exchanged between two individuals; however, the multiple addressing mail function enables all team members to share messages and learn about problems simultaneously. When one technician is unable to resolve a confounding issue, another who has a solution can transmit it to the colleague. This also allows other technicians to learn about the types of problems encountered in their field and thus increase their knowledge. In this manner, an individual query is shared among all team members via the multiple addressing mail function.

Furthermore, they occasionally send messages like 'Today, I (A) will spend all day with a specialist (B) at the client office (C) because of a severe problem. I'm sorry for the inconvenience.' Until now, such information was only available to them indirectly via the self-dispatch system; however, by sending such messages, they receive this information directly. Such information increases awareness of team members, and it is interpreted as 'We should support A because he is unable to visit other customers.' This usage of mobile mail clearly differs from the conventional method. A similar situation was observed in the usage of the self-dispatch system. However, it should be noted that the multiple addressing message function is not a specialized tool like the self-dispatch system but a basic function of mobile mail.

The salient features of the multiple addressing mail function are as follows:

- Transmitting messages to all members enables the sharing of problems, statuses of team members and, of course, troubleshooting information. The conventional mobile mail is shared only by people who exchange messages. Note that these two functions have different capabilities.
- Team members began to exchange messages that do not require individual replies, such as context and awareness information.

As mentioned above, mobile mail, which was initially only a communication tool linking people (colleagues), has now become a collaboration tool realizing a shared context within a team and enabling informal collaboration work among service technicians.

Chat Meeting by Mobile Mail

The next example of communication among colleagues involves three project members managing the construction of a new office. The three members usually planned to meet in the morning. On one occasion, one of the members sent a message by mobile mail saying, 'I will be late for the appointment.' However, the other two members had already reached the office. The delayed member was expected to reach the office an hour later by train. As soon as they received notification of the delay, the three members began exchanging mails such as 'How did yesterday's proposal go?' and 'Please reply with the details at the earliest.' This form of communication was similar to a chat but via mobile mail. By chatting via mobile mail, the members had covered all the points on the agenda for the meeting that morning.

Two of the three members of the concerned project were mobile workers working in different time zones. Thus, coordinating a meeting was difficult. Usually, two of the members arrived at office early while the third was delayed. Since the member who usually arrived late commuted by train for an hour in the morning, s/he effectively utilized this time by communicating with the other two members via mobile mail. This frequent exchange of mails could be considered as a chat meeting. In this case, an advanced function such as multiple addressing mail was not used, but the ordinary mobile mail function was used for chatting in a short span of time. Thus, mobile mail facilitated a pseudo-remote meeting. Hence, this form of communication, which was conventionally used to connect individuals, has again been demonstrated as a collaboration tool used to efficiently conduct a remote meeting.

Worker–Customer Relations

In the preceding section, we described how mobile technology effected a change in the communication network among colleagues. In this section, we describe how mobile technology has affected the relationship between a mobile worker and a customer. When sales representatives are scheduled to visit a customer, they first call the customer to enquire whether it is suitable for them to visit the customer's office. In this regard, the cellular phone was a very effective tool in maintaining customer relations. However, the relationship between a sales representative and a customer is essentially the same as that between the organizations to which they belong. Therefore, as noted above, when a customer requires certain services, s/he calls the office of a sales representative and not the sales representative directly. In a similar manner, a sales representative does not divulge her/his personal cellular phone number to the customer. The customer's query is received via the back office. However, with the complete proliferation of mobile technology, a new trend is emerging with regard to worker–customer relations, as demonstrated by the following example.

Customer Directly Contacts the Sales Representative

A sales representative of the office design company checks her mobile mail while commuting to work by train. In this case, she has just taken charge of a new project of relocating a certain office. She is very busy and is continuously travelling from one location to another. For this reason, her customers and colleagues complain that she is often inaccessible. She has therefore provided the project members with not only her cellular phone number but also her cellular phone mail address. They can now be assured of contacting her via mobile mail, even when she is visiting other customers or commuting. The client of the new project had several concerns and frequently communicated with the sales representative via mobile mail. On one occasion, her phone signalled the arrival of a new mail after midnight; however, since it was very late, she did not check it at that instant. When checking her mail on the train the next morning, she noticed that the mail she received the night before was from her client and promptly replied. Such an occurrence is fairly common. Occasionally, the exchange of mails would lead to a chat meeting, similar to the above-described communication with a colleague.

'I am worried about the security of our entrance. Is there any solution?'

'Did you manage yesterday's problem? Please reply as soon as possible.'

'I received the solution from the building maintenance company a little while back. I will send the formal report by FAX.'

Such exchanges of messages were frequent. Exchanging messages for a short span of time is similar to conducting a meeting. Thus, since mobile workers are constantly on the move, e.g. at customer sites, it is difficult to contact them.

Therefore, many people find it easier to contact mobile sales representatives via mobile mail rather than phone calls. This led to sales representatives gradually providing customers with their cellular phone mail address.

Thus, the relationship between a customer and a sales representative was transformed into that between two individuals rather than two organizations. In this manner, mobile technology has shifted the relationship between a sales representative and a customer from an organizational level to an individual one. As mentioned above, mobile technology has especially effected changes in the style of communication—'from a communication tool for individuals to a collaboration tool for a team', 'from an organizational relationship to an individual one'.

Implications

Effective Utilization of Existing Social Infrastructure

From the viewpoint of adapting to the new tool, the process of introducing cellular phone application tools that use the GPS function is of great interest. The number of advanced trials carried out for physical distribution systems, which are used to track and map the current status and location of replacement parts, has been increasing over the past few years. For example, some systems use the IC tag technology for tracing. However, such systems require newly built infrastructure, which requires immense investment. However, systems using GPS have the following characteristics.

(1) Cellular phones have already spread in the market and many of them are GPS enabled.

(2) This system does not directly trace replacement parts. Instead, it tracks people carrying a GPS-enabled cellular phone. It is based on the idea that 'the replacement parts are carried by people'.

On the basis of these two characteristics, it is important to introduce such systems without changing the infrastructure. Cellular phones are already becoming the basic infrastructure of the social communication network system. Therefore, by effectively utilizing the existing infrastructure of mobile networks and terminals, the swift construction of a cost-effective system became possible.

With regard to task delegation of mobile sales representatives and the bottom-up approach for parts supply by service technicians, each worker effectively applied cellular phone technology to her/his work environment. The example depicting the use of cellular phone by a central warehouse for supplying replacement parts demonstrates how an organization can effectively structure a new task by successfully integrating existing organizational work and social infrastructure. It is thus important for individuals as well as organizations to adapt to cellular phone in order to structure their work effectively.

Lightweight Collaboration Tool

Earlier, the cellular phone was used as a communication tool connecting individuals with individuals. However, the latest trend is that cellular phones play the role of a 'collaboration tool' and not a 'communication tool' (Churchill and Wakeford, 2002). As demonstrated by the example of service technicians, cellular phones are used to share a gamut of information and contexts required for teamwork, which is very different from a tool that links only individuals. Cellular phones support communication, information sharing and context sharing among team members. This is in complete agreement with the aim of CSCW technology.

This also applies to the use of cellular phones for chat meetings. Cellular phones need not offer a remote meeting function for this type of usage. Large-scale CSCW technology that connects remote locations through multimedia applications via broadband is not suitable for mobile workers. Rather, a cellular phone that simply connects an individual with an individual and transforms itself into an ad-hoc remote conference system is preferred. A mobile worker can use this lightweight meeting system anytime and from anywhere, which is more convenient than a complete remote conference system.

Thus, by the creative usage of a worker, a cellular phone now plays the role of a collaboration tool rather than a communication tool.

Importance of Long-term Interaction between Cellular Phone Technology and Usage

As observed in the case of parts supply, the new technology has changed a service technician's way of work. This technology has gradually permeated the entire working world and led to the creation of a new way of work. As mentioned above, service technicians can identify the location of a certain part using a self-dispatch system. This gives rise to the need for a system that visualizes the current location of a part. The new GPS parts system satisfies this need. In addition, this system is advantageous in terms of the ease in planning work and provides a sense of security. This system and the way of work have evolved mutually.

Such interaction is also visible in communication among service technicians. Although initially hesitant towards the use of mobile mail, service technicians soon recognized the potential of this feature. Its advantages became apparent with the introduction of new functions such as multiple addressing mail. Thereafter, mobile mail was accepted by service technicians. Thus, it is important to examine the manner in which technology and its usage mutually influence each other and evolve by adaptation.

Summary and Conclusion

Sales representatives and repair technicians are essentially mobile workers. They constantly visit customers and work at customer sites. Their workplace is not a fixed office; rather, they work at various locations such as customer sites, coffee shops, trains or cars. However, they never work in isolation but as part of a team, always maintaining contact with coworkers, superiors, project members and customers.

Technological support is an essential component for the mobile worker whose nature of work entails being on the move. Although CSCW technology had evolved to support people working in different workplaces, conventional full-featured CSCW technology that integrated broadband networks and multimedia technology did not necessarily suit a mobile worker's working style. Instead, recently developed cellular phone technology enables mobile workers to organize their work more efficiently. By effectively utilizing human resources, including coworkers and support staff, mobile workers have successfully adapted cellular phone technology to their work.

Furthermore, although cellular phones do not directly support remote meetings, mobile workers often conduct these meetings using mobile mail as a chatting tool. Such usage was promoted by the mobile mail characteristics of 'being contactable at any place and being lightweight'. These features enabled mobile workers to restructure their work efficiently. This suggests that the conventional full-fledged CSCW technology would not be able to sustain a mobile worker's working style. A cellular phone is a simple communication tool; it can thus promote the reorganization of work by effectively utilizing social and human resources.

Moreover, the proliferation of cellular phones has effected a change in not only the working style and communication pattern but also the relationship between mobile workers and customers. Essentially, the relationship between a customer and a sales representative is inter-organizational. However, sales representatives contact customers directly using a cellular phone, which is a tool to connect individuals. This has led to communication using mobile mail. This concept of 'calling sales representatives directly' is very different from 'calling sales representatives via a company'. A cellular phone is owned by an individual. Thus, customers and sales representatives can connect with each other anytime and from anywhere. Although mobile workers have now established certain boundaries between their work and private lives, such changes will affect the relationship between a company and a worker.

In this paper, we describe the manner in which cellular phones can be used in the workplace based on ethnographic data from three fields of work and discuss how cellular phones have affected the communication pattern and working style of mobile workers. In future, we will discuss the design of cellular phones for business use and will also consider the interaction between technology evolution and the changes necessary for long-term usage.

Acknowledgements

We would like to thank Dr. Naoki Ueno and Dr. Yasuko Kawatoko, co-researchers on the service technicians research team. They gave us valuable discussions and suggestions. Furthermore, we would like to thank all the participants of this study—the mobile sales representatives for taking excellent photographs and the service technicians for their patient cooperation in our five-year investigation. Their contribution to this research is greatly appreciated.

References

Bellotti, V. and Bly, S. (1996): 'Walking away from the desktop computer distributed collaboration and mobility in a product design team', *Proceedings of CSCW'96*, ACM Press, 1996, pp.209218.

Brown, J. S. and Duguid, P. (2000): *The Social Life of Information*, Harvard Business School Press.

Churchill, E. F., Snowdon, D. N. and Munro, A. J. (eds.) (2001): *Collaborative Virtual Environments: Digital Places and Spaces for Interaction - Computer Supported Cooperative Work*, Springer-Verlag.

Churchill, E. F. and Wakeford, N. (2002): 'Framing mobile collaborations and mobile technologies', in Brown, B., Green, N. and Harper, R. (eds.): *Wireless World – Social and Interactional Aspects of the Mobile Age*, Springer-Verlag, London, 2002.

Fischer, C. S (1992): *America Calling: A Social History of the Telephone to 1940*, Univ of California Pr.

Froggatt, C. C.(2001): *Work Naked: Eight Essential Principles for Peak Performance in the Virtual Workplace* (The Jossey-Bass Business & Management Series), Jossey-Bass Inc Pub.

David N. Snowdon, D. N., Elizabeth F. Churchill, E. F. and Frecon, E. (eds.) (2004): *Inhabited Information Spaces: Living With Your Data - Computer Supported Cooperative Work*, Springer-Verlag.

Duffy, F. and Powell, K. (1997): *The New Office*, Conran Octpus

Engestrom, Y. and Middleton, D. (1998): Cognition and Communication at Work, Cambridge University Press.

Goodwin, C. and Ueno, N.(2000): *Mind, Culture, and Activity*, Volume7, Number1&2, 2000, Lawrence Erlbaum Associates, Publishers, London.

Hauike, K., Tamaru, E. and Tozaki, M. (2003): 'Methods for exploring workplace activities and user contexts employing intermediate objects - self-photos, personal view records, and skit performance', *Proceedings of HCI International 2003*.

Heath, C. and Luff, P. (eds.) (2000): *Technology in Action - Learning in Doing: Social, Cognitive and Computational Perspectives*, Cambridge University Press.

Ito, M., Okabe, D, and Matsuda, M. (eds.) (2005): *Personal, Portable, Pedestrian: Mobile Phones in Japanese Life*, MIT Press.

266

Lave, J. and Wenger, E. (1991): *Situated Learning: Legitimate Peripheral Participation -Learning in Doing: Social, Cognitive and Computational Perspectives*, Cambridge University Press.

Lesser, E. L., Fontaine, M. A. and Slusher, J. A. (2000): *Knowledge and Communities - Resources for the Knowledge-Based Economy*, Butterworth-Heinemann.

Ling, R. and Yttri, B. (2002): 'Hyper-coordination via mobile phones in Norway', in Katz, J. E. and Aakhus, M. (eds.): *Perpetual Contact – Mobile Communication, Private Talk, Public Performance*, Cambridge University Press, pp.139-169.

Luff, P. and Heath, C.(1998): 'Mobility in Collaboration', *Proceedings of CSCW'98*, ACM Press, 1998, pp.305-314.

Luff, P., Hindmarsh, J. and Heath, C. (eds.)(2000): *Workplace Studies Recovering Work Practice and Information System Design*, Cambridge University Press.

Nelson, L., Bly, S. and Sokoler, T. (2001): 'Quiet Calls: Talking Silently on Mobile Phones', *Proceedings of CHI'2001, ACM Press*, 2001, pp.174-181.

Okada, T. and Matsuda, M. (eds.) (2000): *Keitai-gaku Nyumon (Understanding Mobile Media)*, Yuhikaku, Toko (in Japanese)

Orr, J. (1996): *Talking About Machines: An Ethnography of a Modern Job Collection on Technology and Work*, Cornell University Press.

Orr, J. and Crowfoot, N. C. (1992): 'Design by Anecdote - The use of ethnography to guide the application of technology to practice', *Proceedings of PDC'92*.

Plant, S. (2000): 'On the mobile: The effects of mobile telephones on social and individual life', *http://www.motorola.com/mot/doc/0/234_MotDoc.pdf*

Rheingold, H. (2002): *Smart Mobs: The Next Social Revolution*, Cambridge, Mass: Perseus.

Tamaru, E., Hasuike, K. and Tozaki, M. (2002): 'A Field Study Methodology Using Self-Photography of Workplace Activities', *Proceedings of Design Research Society 2002 International Conference.*

Tamaru, E. and Ueno, N. (2005): 'Design of Keitai Technology and its use among service engineers', in Ito, M., Okabe, D, and Matsuda, M. (eds.): *Personal, Portable, Pedestrian: Mobile Phones in Japanese Life*, MIT Press 2005, pp.237-256.

Ueno, N. and Kawatoko, Y. (2003): 'Technologies Making Space Visible', *Environment and Planning*, A35, pp.1529-1545.

Weilenmann, A. and Institute, V. (2003): '"I can't talk now, I'm in a fitting room": Formulating availability and location in mobile phone conversations', *Environment and Planning*, A35(9), pp.1589-1605.

Wenger, E., Richard A. McDermott, R. A. and Snyder, W. (2002): *Cultivating Communities of Practice: A Guide to Managing Knowledge*, Harvard Business School Pr.

White Paper (2004): *Information and Communications in Japan: Building a Ubiquitous Network Society That Spreads Throughout the World*, Ministry of Public Management, Home Affairs, Posts and Telecommunications, Japan.

Zelinsky, M. (1998): *New Workplaces for New Workstyles*, The McGraw-Hill Company, Inc.

H. Gellersen et al. (eds.), ECSCW 2005: Proceedings of the Ninth European
Conference on Computer-Supported Cooperative Work, 18-22 September 2005, Paris,
France, 267–286.

Representations Can be Good Enough

Jacki O'Neill, Stefania Castellani, Antonietta Grasso, Frederic
Roulland, and Peter Tolmie
Xerox Research Centre Europe, Grenoble, France

{name.surname}@xrce.xerox.com

Abstract. When working remotely with physical objects obvious problems of reference
arise because of the lack of a mutually shared object. Systems aiming to support such
work tend to be based on understandings of face-to-face interaction and frequently use
video. However, video introduces new interactional problems. This paper describes a field
study of remote interaction around objects that is telephone-centred, namely in a call
centre for troubleshooting office devices. We describe how breakdowns in mutual
orientation stem from three main problematics: 1) The inadequate fidelity of operators'
support resources; 2) The lack of mutual access to indicative resources; 3) operators'
lack of direct access to customers' actions and orientation. From this analysis, we have
developed a design proposal for supporting such work. Rather than using video, we
propose that utilising a linked problem representation would address these problems. To
this end we describe our proposal for a bidirectional remote visualisation of the
troubleshooting problem.

Introduction

A recurrent area of research interest in CSCW relates to how remotely situated
people can work together when this work involves physical objects in the local
environment of one or more of the participants (Fussell *et al.*, 2000; Gutwin &
Penner, 2002; Kraut *et al.*, 1996; Kuzuoka *et al.*, 1994; 2000). Such work
produces a number of interesting issues, centering on how to make the object at
the local site available in someway to remote sites such that remote and local
participants can work with it. When remote interactions take place around such
objects obvious problems arise from the fact that the object is not mutually shared.
What are trivial matters of reference in face-to-face situations, such as mutual

orientation, establishing mutual understanding of referents, pointing, gesturing, knowing what people are doing or have done become problematic when participants are remote.

A number of different systems have been developed in an attempt to make local artefacts available remotely such that local and remote workers can work collaboratively on them. The prime approach to this problem so far has been to take face-to-face interaction around physical objects as the basis for systems design. Such systems aim to recreate aspects of face-to-face interaction around remote objects and tend to use video as the medium for bringing local objects to the remote site (e.g. GestureMan (Kuzuoka at al, 2000) and the work of Fussell *et al.* (e.g. 2004)). However, a common problem with video is that not only does it fail to recreate the richness of face-to-face interaction it also introduces new interactional problems for its users, something made evident in the early work on media spaces (Heath & Luff, 1991 & 1992).

Our research has taken an alternative approach to design in these circumstances. Rather than treating face-to-face interaction as a starting point, we began by examining a situation in which remote interaction around objects already occurs. Our field of interest was telephone support for copier-repair where local users (customers) have a problem and remote technical support experts (operators) attempt to talk the customers through troubleshooting that problem. This study follows in a tradition of studying the telephone-mediated work of call centres, both in general (see for e.g. Whalen, 1995; Bowers & Martin, 2000) and, more specifically call centres for large office devices (e.g. Whalen & Vinkhuyzen, 2001; Whalen et al, 2002). We present here the findings from a field study of this domain, with an emphasis on the methods the interactants use to establish co-orientation to and co-ordination of action around a non-mutually-shared object. Studying object work as it is carried out in a call centre enables us to examine the minimal support required to make such interactions effective. Thus avoiding many of the difficulties relating to how one might extract from the manifold richness of face-to-face interactions just which features are necessary for remote work. This is not to say that studying face-to-face interactions cannot give insights into how such interactions might be supported remotely, rather that the call centre provides an ideal opportunity to examine existing remote object-focused work from which new ideas for technology support might be derived. We now turn to, firstly, the existing work on supporting remote collaboration and, secondly, Whalen's work on remote support in a document machine call centre.

There are a number of systems designed to support remote collaboration around locally situated objects using video and audio in an attempt to create mutual co-presence with the object. One such system is GestureMan (Kuzuoka, 2000), a mobile robot with wireless video communication and a laser pointer, designed to support gesture between remote participants. It was tested in a series of naturalistic experiments described by Luff (2003) which uncovered new interactional problems arising from its use. Participants lacked reciprocal views, making acting on objects in the local and remote environment difficult because they could not design their conduct to be sensible and recognisable to other people. Mediation of action through the robot makes the coordination of such action difficult and orienting to objects also required work by both parties. Participants talked directly *about* the orientation itself, to overcome such problems. Luff concluded that conduct and ecology are reflexively related and by creating new environments, with technology supporting remote participants, the relation between action and the relevant ecology may be fractured, causing interactional problems.

Kraut, Fussell, Siegel and others carried out a series of experiments to understand the key visual information required in collaborative physical tasks (their tasks being bicycle repair and robot building) and thus the requirements of technologies to support such tasks (e.g. Kraut, Fussell & Siegal, 2003; Fussell, Setlock & Parker, 2003; Fussell *et al.*, 2004). They described how visual information is used to time instructions and for pointing and other deictic expressions. They implemented a number of different video arrangements (see for example, Fussell, Setlock & Kraut, 2003). However, they too found that video introduced new interactional problems, including dislocation of gesture and lack of reciprocal views. They concluded that the task view was the most important and that gesture needed to be embedded in the task environment. To this end a new system, DOVE (Drawing Over Video Environment), was developed to enable gesture around the task object (Ou *et al*, 2003). DOVE enables participants to share a workspace via video, with representational gestures and pointing done by over-laying pen-based gestures on the video stream. Testing (Fussell *et al.*, 2004) showed that the system was primarily used for pointing (75% of drawings).

To summarise then, a number of systems have been developed to support remote work around physical objects which attempt to recreate the salient features of face-to-face interaction. However, in the creation of new environments for interaction many of these systems fragment the relationship between action and its relevant environment, introducing new interactional problems which can make even seemingly simple activities problematic (Luff, 2003).

In this paper we examine the features of object-focused work in an *already established* remote environment, that of a machine troubleshooting call centre. Whalen and Vinkhuyzen (2001) studied call centres in the same domain, describing how the expert system, implemented in the call centre to enable the operators (Customer Service and Support Representatives, CSSRs) to diagnose machine problems and direct calls to the relevant hardware or software support services, embodied misconceptions about knowledge and expertise. Primarily that the expertise could reside within the system, utilised by non-expert CSSRs and that the CSSR-customer interaction was a unproblematic one, requiring merely that the CSSR enters, exactly, the customers problem report and repeats verbatim questions from the system. However, in practice this ignores how the CSSRs working knowledge of the technology and sensitivity to the user's circumstances, by necessity, shape the way they handle the problem. Thus Whalen and Vinkhuyzen outlined the common-sense practices used by operators to circumvent the system and do practical troubleshooting with the remote party. In effect, because of the non-expert status of the CSSRs this troubleshooting tended to revolve around arriving at a point where a service call could legitimately be made. The CSSRs made judgments and interpretations of the customers input, but with little machine knowledge they had to primarily use their interactional understandings, orienting to the call as a service encounter. This is in contrast to the work of operators with machine knowledge examined in both Whalen and Vinkhuyzen study and our study, who can utilise these understandings along with their interactional understandings to diagnose and fix machine problems. In the Whalen and Vinkhuyzen call centre the expert operator was the exception, whereas in ours they were the rule. In the call centre described in this paper, the operators are trained and the expertise is seen to reside with them, with support from a knowledge base rather than residing within the (expert) system. Indeed, even their titles could be seen to reflect this, that is Technical Support as opposed to Customer Service and Support Representatives. Some features of the work however can be seen in common and where such similarities occur they will be highlighted. However, although both papers examine work in similar organisations, the organisational process of the call centres differs (the non-experts and expert system in one versus the trained staff and knowledge base in the other) as does the analytical perspective. Whereas Whalen and Vinkhuyzen describe in detail the 'expert system; CSSR; customer' interaction we are primarily examining the 'technical support; customer; machine' interaction.

For such interaction the critical requirement is the ability to mutually attend to the machine and engage with it, not necessarily to be actually co-present or to recreate co-presence with that object. One issue that this work brings to light, and which will be explored in the discussion, is the relationship between the work to be supported and the optimal nature of the support. We suggest that a representation of the troubleshooting problem, from herein called the 'problem representation' can be good enough to support such interaction. A proposal for how such a problem representation might be designed is given later on in this paper. Although it has yet to be implemented, the proposal is firmly grounded in this research into remote work with physical objects. The work of remote experts giving help to customers attempting to fix problems with their office devices will be described in the next section, followed by the proposed problem representation which will then be discussed in the light of the previous work described.

Fieldwork Observations

The field work consisted of a three week ethnographic study of a European Call Centre for a copier and office device company. The study involved observing the operators at work. Data was collected through field notes, video and audio recordings[1]. The call centre in question provides telephone support across Europe for customers with problems with their office devices (copiers, printers, MFDs, etc.). Operators lead the customer through a process of troubleshooting the problematic device. This work involves a number of activities:

- Operators first elicit an initial problem description from the customers. This initial problem description is often partial and the full description of the problem, as it appears to the customer, may be provided during the course of the interaction. For instance multiple symptoms will not necessarily be described all at once.

- Next operators and customers collaboratively work up the initial description into a fuller description from which they can begin to arrive at possible solutions. Often the operators require additional information about the machine, which they get via the customer. This may involve getting the customer to carry out tests on the machine. This collaborative production of the problem description was also noted in Whalen and Vinkhuyzen where with non-expert CSSRs it caused problems of diagnosis which they observed did not occur where the CSSR had the expertise to probe the customer further for a more precise description.

- Then the operators and customers work collaboratively to troubleshoot the machine, with operators giving the customers instructions to carry out and customers reporting back on the results of their actions.

In this paper we will show how operators and customers work together to create and maintain a mutual orientation to the device through talk. It is this shared orientation that enables the remote troubleshooting to take place. Operators have a number of methods for dealing with their lack of direct access to the machine in question and these will be examined, along with how and where breakdowns in this mutual orientation may occur and how such breakdowns are repaired.

Establishing Shared Referents

Operators and customers engage in interactional work to establish shared referents in the absence of mutual access to the device. We elaborate here on how the shared understandings that Whelan and Vinkhuyzen noted with their expert users are arrived at. An important aspect of this is how operators and customers question one another's descriptions to ensure they are referring to the same thing.

---

[1] For legal reasons only the operator side of telephone conversations could be recorded on audio. Customer utterances were recorded in the field notes.

For example, in Extract 1, the customer reports a problem with a particular part of the machine, 'the paper feed'. The operator questions the customer, re-describing the referent according to its use ('where you put the originals in').

Extract 1[2]

1.   C - I've got a problem with the paper feed
2.   O: Um hum (.) You are talking sorry you are talking where you put the originals in aren't you

Operators also perform checks to ensure that the customer knows what part they are referring to. Thus one method of establishing shared referents is to reformulate descriptions according to different features of that referent, such as function, colour, shape, relative position, and so on.

Operators frequently use such descriptors to make their instructions understandable, adapting their utterances for the customer. Since many customers have relatively little technical knowledge about office printing devices, operators often use vernacular-type descriptions, occasionally with textual indicators (e.g. 'Can you just open the exit cover for me, the one that says CopierCo[3] on it'), to indicate parts rather than relying on technical terminology alone.

The manufacture of the machine with different coloured parts aids this location of referents. Operators know their machines well, describing machine parts from memory in such a way as to make it easy for the customer to locate them. In their work as operators they have evolved a comprehensive grammar of reference, reformulation and redirection. This stands in contrast to the 'helpers' seen in many of the previous studies outlined above who had little expertise in such remote help giving. Where the customer is able to locate the parts easily and follow the operator's instructions it is not necessary for the operator to be able to see what the customer is doing or where the customer is looking. The customer's verbal responses, combined with the operator's knowledge of the machine, are often enough for the operator to be able to indicate and clarify referents and give sequential instructions.

Directing Customers Through Sequences of Actions

As we have already indicated, operators must give instructions to customers regarding parts of the machine and/or sequences of actions to be carried out on those parts, even though they themselves do not have direct access to the machine. They therefore make use of the methods described above for accurately and adequately giving instructions to customers. Although operators frequently devised instructions 'off-the-top-of-their-heads', at times they utilised additional

---

[2] Where customer turns were not recorded in the field notes they are omitted.

[3] CopierCo is a fictitious name for purposes of anonymity.

resources to situate their instructions in relation to the machine. These resources are comprised of:

- *The knowledge base*: operators have access to a searchable knowledge base of solutions on their PCs, containing images of the various instructions. Operators use this as a visual aid from which instructions can be devised. For instance, one operator was observed pointing at an image on the knowledge base while instructing a customer through a set of actions, using colour and positioning descriptors to identify the parts:

Extract 2

1. O: ok and where you have door a you have like um a set of four grey rollers
2. <as she says this she points to them in the picture on her screen>[4]
3. on er a metal bar just above that there's a piece of black plastic and [...]

- *Menu maps*: operators use menu maps to lead the customer through their on-screen options. We shall examine the adequacy of menu maps below.
- *Miming*: operators are frequently seen miming actions whilst simultaneously describing them to the customer. Whalen and Vinkhuyzens expert CSSR was also seen to gesture while talking. Miming is used in the absence of the device to establish the sequence of actions that the customer must undertake. As with the pointing above, operators frequently used gestures despite this resource being unavailable to the customer.
- *Going to the machine*: most machine models are available in the call centre. Operators often leave their desks and physically go to these devices 'to see what the customer is seeing', enabling them to describe parts and action sequences more precisely.

The above resources enable the operators, in the absence of direct access to the problematic device, to visualise the machine and the sequence of actions to be carried out upon it. Although these resources, along with an operator's knowledge of the machine, are often adequate for troubleshooting, there are two problems that can arise with their use. Firstly, these are *generic* resources *representing* the problem device, not the problem device *itself* and thus their fidelity is not always adequate for troubleshooting. Secondly, the indicative information involved is not available to the customer, making it a lost resource and requiring the operator to translate it into verbal instructions.

These issues can feed into situations where the troubleshooting process encounters trouble or even breaks down completely. Such trouble arises for the operator in establishing what it is that is going on at the customer end and for the customer in attempting to put the operator's instructions into practice.

---

[4] Text in < > brackets indicates an action.

Establishing the State of the Machine and Related Artefacts

As suggested above, at times it is not enough for the purposes of troubleshooting to know a machine in general, rather the specific state of *this machine here* or its related artefacts, such as copies, becomes important. At various points in the interaction, operators need to establish what the state of the machine or related artefacts is. Their understanding is of necessity mediated by the customer.

Operators may check the state of the machine to enable them to give relevant and appropriate instructions. For example, they may ask if all the doors are closed. Operators also ask customers to tell them what some part or other of the machine looks like because knowing what a machine in general looks like is not the same as knowing what the machine looks like in just this instance. Yet it is often features of this particular machine *here and now* which are pertinent for troubleshooting. To uncover the relevant features here and now (or, as Garfinkel would put it, the *haecceities* of the problem (Garfinkel & Weider, 1992)), operators get the customers to examine their machine or to elaborate on prior descriptions.

Extract 3

1   O: Um and can you tell me when you look in is the tray still lying flat or is it
2   er a bit off does it look as though it's skewed by any chance?
3   O: It does look? Ok I just wonder if we can sort that out now

In Extract 3 the operator asks for information on the tray, proposing possible alternative scenarios, 'lying flat' or 'skewed' (1-2), to help the customer understand what they are looking for. These alternatives relate to the possible causes of the problem and thus are relevant for the troubleshooting process. The customer confirms that it seems to be skewed and the operator begins the process of rectifying the problem (3). By asking the customer about the state of the tray the operator is exploring ways of narrowing down the problem space (either by eliminating or finding a cause of trouble if the tray is flat or skewed, respectively).

Another method used is 'drilling down', where the operator asks a series of successive questions to get all the necessary detail and ensure a common understanding. For example, refining an understanding of an image quality problem by questioning the customer on the state of the copy, e.g. 'Is it all creased up?', 'Is the whole page creased up or half the page?', and so on. Both of these methods can help operators to refine the problem space, propose causes and suggest solutions. However the lack of direct access can result in incorrect instructions, for example asking the customer to 'open up the top cover' when it is already open or directing the customer to 'a blue plastic guide' when it is in fact green. Customers, of course, are able to and do correct such mistakes.

Where Mutual Orientation Breaks Down

Where customers cannot identify the part or other referent which the operator is describing, the operator must attempt to disambiguate the referent. This has to happen with little knowledge of the customer's actual orientation and the state of the machine. Two examples of this are presented below, the first in which the customer cannot locate a part, and the second in which the customer cannot find an entry on a menu map.

Disambiguating confusion: locating parts

Difficulties can arise in locating and identifying physical parts of the machine and the only methods available to the parties to resolve these involve further talk. This might include repeating instructions, reformulating descriptors and terms, or elaborating descriptions (e.g. by describing relative position or functional features (where the paper comes in/goes out, and so on)). Several examples were seen where understanding relative directions, in particular, right and left caused considerable trouble for the customer and took much effort to resolve. Extract 4 shows the work to resolve the location of some doors.

Extract 4

```
1    O: ok it's probably saying open the upper left hand side door? Probably one of right
2    there's two doors there that you open there's the first door that opens downwards and
3    then there's a door in front of that which is the hot area of the machine so you don't
4    touch that area and you just need to check that to see if there's any paper sticking
5    out that you can actually remove just to see if if you know you can remove it there
6    O: yeah course no problem take your time
7    <C goes away> (long wait) <C returns>
8    O: hello
9    C – can only find the big door and the little side door.
10   O: Yeah yeah yeah you know the when you slide the finisher away from the machine
11   you can open the upper left hand side door that opens downwards? Then just in front
12   of that there's another door and that's where the hot area of the machine is so don't
13   you don't touch the roller or anything just jus you're just looking for any paper that
14   you're able to actually
15   C – can't see any paper and there's only one door
16   O: No the the with the first bit you've got an upper left-hand side door and a lower
17   left-hand side door now the upper left-hand side door has two doors that you can open
18   the lower one (doesn't)
19   C – I'll go and check.
20   O: OK no problem
21   <C goes away> (long wait) <C returns>
22   C – I managed to retrieve the paper
```

In lines 1-5 the operator gives a detailed description of what the customer should do, including describing the doors to open according to their relative locations and opening mechanisms. The customer goes to do this, but returns unable to locate the right doors (9). The operator reconfigures her description twice (10-14 and 16-18) the second time because of the customers contradiction 'there's only one door' (15). This time the customer succeeds in locating the door and retrieving the paper (22).

We can see that the work in this case arose because the customer could not find what the operator was referring to. This was problematic to resolve because the customer only had limited understanding of what exactly the operator needed her to orient to. The only methods available to the operator and customer to resolve these issues and disambiguate the instructions are those available through further talk. Where instructions do not seem to be working, operators reiterate and reconfigure their descriptions, often repeatedly, both checking that the customer is doing the right thing, and reformulating them to make them more understandable. However, if operators had a better understanding of exactly what customers were orienting to, such reformulation would be far more straightforward. Additionally if customers had easy access to what the operator was referencing instruction would be more straightforward. The operator also does not know exactly what it is that the customer is doing at any one point, so cannot help the customer by correcting his errors as he makes them.

Disambiguating confusion: menu maps

Extract 5 is a further example where the customer cannot locate what the operator is directing him to, this time with regard to on-machine menus.

Extract 5

```
1    O: Ok can I get you to go into the front panel and select menus
2    O: Ok then scroll until you see printer set up menu
3    C – printer set up menu
4    O: Ok then scroll until you see energy star/power saver
5    C – energy star
6    (silence)
7    O: you're not seeing it no
8    <C reads list of menu options >
9    O: ok so I'm just quickly going through the menu map that I have here myself ok
10   <O looks at the menu map on screen> <C reads list of menu options again quietly>
11   O: ok can I just bear put you on hold for one second just want to check something
12   with a colleague of mine
13   <O talks to colleague who tells him that if it's not there it is turned off. Returns to desk>
14   O: hello karl?
15   O: Yeah sorry about that delay there ok yeah if that's not appear if that option's not
16   appearing on your front panel then it it would mean that that option has already
17   been selected it has been switched off already so that it's basically it won't say
18   after an hour or something go into this standby mode () it's
19   C – it does go into standby
20   O: does sorry
21   O: ok see  if if it is going into that that option should be
22   O: ok
23   O: ok because that's what I've been advised if it's not showing up on on that menu
24   page then it has been disabled in the machine. […]
```

Initially the customer is following the operator's instructions without problem (1-3), with the customer repeating back what the operator has directed him to (3). Then the operator asks the customer to scroll to the energy star (4) which the customer repeats as before (5). Trouble is signalled by a silence (6) which prompts the operator to propose an explanation for the silence 'you're not seeing it no' (7). The customer reads through the list of menu options (8), thereby making them available to the operator[5]. The operator checks his on-screen menu map. Operators often use menu maps as a way of visualising what a customer is seeing and thus enabling them to direct the customer through a series of actions. Menu maps are a stand-in for the fact that the device on which they are working is not mutually shared. However, as menu maps are an idealised instance of the menu, they *do not show what the customer can actually see*. In most cases, of course, this may be good enough. Whilst the exact labelling of menu options may not always be the same as on a customer's machine, for the most part operators can easily get round this by saying 'can you see something like...' or offering several different variations on likely names[6]. However in this case, the fact that the menu map is not the same as the customer's actual menu is more tricky to deal with.

While the operator is checking his menu map the customer re-reads the options from his own more quietly (10). Having checked the menu map and finding the energy star on it as expected, the operator excuses himself (11-12) and goes to check with a colleague (13), who explains that if it is not there then it has already been switched off. The operator explains this to the customer (15-18) but the customer disputes it (19 and between turns 20 & 21, 21 & 22 and 22 & 23[7]). The operator responds by reiterating that it has been disabled (21 & 23-24), then moves on[8]. Thus this difference between the idealised version of the menu map and the customer's actual menu required additional work to 'resolve'[9], with the operator first trying his own resources then having to take time out of the call to consult with a colleague.

We can see, then, that such trouble arises where what the customer can see appears to differ from the operator's description or where the customer just cannot see, for whatever reason, what it is the operator is describing. There is a difference

---

[5] One of the features of the phone is that just what is and is not shared is readily available to both parties, as demonstrated here.

[6] Although this is a noted problem in the non-English language groups if the operators are using English menu-maps as their translations can be quite different from the formulised menu-map translations.

[7] Customers wording between these turns not available.

[8] Interestingly this non-acceptance of the customers assertion that the machine does go into standby resembles somewhat Martin & Rouncefield's (2003) finding that only where the bank actually has a letter sent by the customer are they accountable for it, if they only have records they are only accountable to them and if they have no records of the object it does not exist. Here of course it is the behavior of the object rather than the object itself that is being held up to question, but it seems that where the customers report of the behavior of the object differs from some expected behavior, as confirmed by a colleague, it is the customers account that can be disregarded.

[9] Indeed, we can only say it was resolved in that the operator moved on to other troubleshooting activities, rather than that consensus was reached between the customer and the operator.

278

between locating physical parts and locating menu items which stems from a level of certainty. That is, the operator can be fairly certain that a part of the machine, doors, handles, etc., will be there for a particular model of the machine. In that case if the customer cannot locate it, it makes sense to reformulate and reiterate the directions until the customer *can*. In such situations it is assumed that the source of the trouble lies in the direction of the customer. However, with menus it is a rather different situation. Menus can be reconfigured in a way that changes them but which is not necessarily obvious to the user or presumptively certain to an operator. For instance, in the above example one possibility is that the energy saving feature had been switched off. Hence the energy star was no longer present on the menu, although this was disputed by the customer. Hardware can of course be reconfigured, but the presence or absence of a finisher, for example, is relatively easy to determine. Changing the settings on menus, by contrast, can effect what does or does not appear. Thus an operator can be less certain of the source of trouble when such issues arise .

Instruction in practice

Giving and following instructions is a collaborative activity designed for and by the co-participants. Instructions are designed to be timely and appropriate. Operators attempt to fit the instructions with customer activities and their situation (e.g. step-by-step if at the machine, in bigger chunks if having to move between the machine and the phone) and use appropriate language. As in Extract 5 (1-5) operators often time their instructions according to the activities of the customer. However, as described above operators only have limited access to what the customer is doing and orienting to. Access is limited to what is provided through customer feedback, though operators do, of course, work using assumptions of what is happening on the basis of their understandings of how such troubleshooting episodes usually proceed. However, as shown in Extract 6, this presumption is not always equal to overcoming the absence of personal access.

Extract 6

1   O: That's where the paper would normally um feed through ok so er it's just in there
2   that you're feeding the paper that you're putting the page in?
3   O: Is it?
4   O: Hello?
5   C – yes

In this sequence, which arose during a call where the customer was having problems following the operator's instructions, the operator asked the customer a question (1-2) then, on receiving no reply, twice prompted the customer for an answer (3-4). This occurred because the operator did not know what was going on at the customer site. Indeed, the operator remarked at the time that 'sometimes you wonder what they are doing'. Also later in the call the operator repeatedly asked the customer questions along the lines of 'Does that make sense?' 'Is that working?'. This is because when they get no feedback from the customer they have to try to work out what is going on. The production of such utterances in the absence of feedback is a systematic feature of talk (Sacks, 1992). The absence of a response to a question is highly accountable and typically leads to truncated repetitions such as the one visible in Extract 6 (line 3) (Atkinson & Drew, 1979; Heritage, 1984; Schegloff, 1972)[10] . The difficulty with this call was compounded by the fact that the customer had to put down the phone in order to follow the operator's advice.

Currently, then, both the customer and the operator must work together to disambiguate referents and instructions and to establish a mutual orientation to the object. Although this often works well, it can create difficulties where parts cannot be identified or instructions followed. Where this happens the mutual orientation to the object is lost.

To summarise, troubleshooting the machine is a collaborative activity and is based on a mutual orientation to the device. However, the lack of mutual access to the problem device can result in breakdowns in this mutual orientation which stem from a number of problematics:

1) The operator's resources to visualise the problem device are *generic* resources representing some type of device in general rather than the haecceities of this particular problem. Consequently, their fidelity is not always adequate for troubleshooting.

2) The lack of mutual access to indicative resources means that the operator's gestures are not available to the customer. Instead they require translation through talk. Similarly, customers can only indicate the source of their misunderstanding through talk.

3) The customer's orientation and actions are not directly available to the operator. In that case the operator must rely on a customer's feedback to situate and disambiguate instructions.

In the next section we will outline a design proposal to address these problematics.

Bidirectional Visualisation of the Troubleshooting Problem

To address the problematics outlined above (generic rather than indexical resources, lack of mutual access to indicative resources, lack of direct access to customers orientation and actions) we examined ways in which the features of the actual troubled device itself might be made available to both parties. Primary here is finding ways to enable them to mutually orient to it, share indicative

---

10   The conditional relevance of utterances in these kinds of situations is more generally discussed by Schegloff (1968).

information such as gesture, and enable customer actions to become available to the operator. One such way is to provide the interacting parties with a *representation of the troubleshooting problem itself.* Such a representation would provide a resource for both coming to an understanding of the problem and mutual orientation and interaction. To this end, support could come from providing a shared object (i.e. the problem representation) to which customers and operators could mutually orient and refer which would reflect the actions of the customer. One of the crucial aspects of the telephone is that it gives a clear understanding for both parties of what does and does not fall within the shared space. Therefore, any solution that will be supporting this interaction should do the same, rather than creating the additional problems which arise where the boundaries and extent of the shared space as against the local space are not clear. To achieve this we propose to use a distinct representation of the machine and its troubles rather than focusing on video to connect the local and remote parties. Using this kind of representation offers a number of potential advantages. These include a ready recognisability of what is shared or purely local and low overheads in equipment.

Making Use of Representations

The design proposal outlined here is based around the creation of a bi-directional, shared visualisation of the troubleshooting problem (BDV). This problem representation will consist of a linked 3-D model of the device and a number of means of interacting with this model. The BDV will be presented on the device itself at the local site (on the kinds of medium sized screens increasingly available with modern devices) and on the technical support operator's terminal at the remote site. The representation is *linked* to the device itself, such that actions on the device are shown on the representation, e.g. if a user opens a door, that door will appear open on the representation. This is enabled through the many sensors that already reside on such devices. In addition both the customer and operator are able to indicate parts on the machine, and the operator is able to demonstrate visually actions which should be performed (for example, lifting a handle and sliding a toner cartridge out of the machine). The customer will access technical support through audio-visual communication channels located on the machine itself. The audio channel will enable the customer to converse with the operator. The visual channel will show the BDV. Thus the machine becomes the infrastructural mediator between users and technical support.

The BDV enables *both parties* to have a real time understanding of the actions which are being or should be performed on the machine. These provide a resource for overcoming the troubleshooting problems we have described. The machine will enhance an operator's understanding of the problem and thus aid the discovery of a solution. It will then mediate between the operator and the customer enabling them to mutually arrive at a solution despite not having mutual access to the problem source, i.e. the machine. The solution we envisage will allow:

- The creation of a dynamic virtual visual representation of the troubleshooting problem including a visual representation of the machine and interaction controls.

- Customers and remote operators to access a personalised view of the representation, which they can manipulate in a coordinated way where interactions on one side are captured, transmitted and appropriately made visible to the other side.

- Customers and operators to identify in their representation a component of the machine by indicating it.

- Operators to define on their view of the representation actions to be performed by users on selected components of the machine. This will be achieved through visual images, animations and descriptions of solutions being dragged and dropped from other resources, for instance the knowledge base. These actions will be transmitted to the customer via their representation.

- Customers to interact with the representation by manipulating the machine itself. That is sensed actions that the customer carries out on the machine will be shown on the representations. These actions will be transmitted to the operator via their representation.

- The local device menus to be made available to the remote operator so that they can direct the user through the correct navigation path. This is particularly pitched at problems and solutions which involve the user navigating the menu (as was shown, for example, in Extract 5).

A number of benefits could arise from using the BDV. We propose that these would both give advantages over the current situation and provide support for the troubleshooting interaction that is *good enough* at minimum interactional and equipment overheads. Benefits include the fact that many aspects of the state of the machine, such as doors open, trays pulled out, etc. would be evident to the operators without having to ask the customers. In addition changes to the state of the machine would enable the operators to get an understanding of the customer's actions, that is as the customer opened doors, removed machine parts and so on this would be represented on the operators BDV enabling them to 'see' what the customer was doing. Operators would be able to indicate parts and actions to the customer and customers would be able to indicate parts to the operators. Situating the instructions in the stream of activity would be aided by the representation as the operator would be able to 'see' what the customer had done more or less as it happened and thus give the next instruction. Reciprocal viewpoints are supported and operators and customers should be able to co-ordinate and co-orient around the representation of the object. Although just as with any other tool or artefact to be used during the service interaction, the BDV would have to be weaved into the interaction with the customer (Whalen, Whalen & Henderson, 2002). This is of course is already the case with the operators existing tools and indeed the machine itself (as we could see with the work to situate instructions within the stream of activity on the device). To this end the design of the BDV will need to take into account its use in interaction, and how exactly the features described will be implemented will need to be specified during the design process. In addition, like other such tools it is likely to introduce its own specific interactional difficulties which will only come to light upon implementation. However, with careful and iterative design we feel that the BDV could offer a useful alternative, in appropriate domains, to previously specified solutions and facilitate current interaction. The solution also contains non-representational aspects for menu-based instructions, where the operator can view the same interface as the customer.

The BDV is not designed to be an expert or other such system, rather it is a *communication tool* to be used by technical support and the customer alongside the audio interaction in troubleshooting the device. Although the representation is an idealised version of the object rather than the object itself, because it is tied to the actual machine, it is closer to the object than those representations already used (menu maps, machines, etc.). Although at first it may seem to be a relatively basic and simple representation, this seemingly shallow representation is actually able to capture salient indexical information so that the haecceities, the 'just thisness' of the problem (Garfinkel and Weider, 1992) can be explored and revealed. Here the focus is solely upon making available the orders of detail relevant to getting the troubleshooting job done instead of leaving the interactants still in need of uncovering saliency from a relatively undifferentiated video stream.

Discussion

The field work exposed three areas of work that operators and customers do to make remote troubleshooting work. These are:

1) *Establishing shared referents and mutual orientation* to the device through talk. For example, operators question customers, reformulate descriptions, use appropriate non-technical language, and so on.

2) *Establishing the state of the machine.* Customers mediate between the machine and technical support. Operators use checks, drilling down, offering proposals, etc. to narrow down the problem space. Customers report back on actions they have performed and resultant machine status.

3) *Situating instructions.* Operators are knowledgeable about the machines and have additional resources for visualising the device, thus supporting their

interaction with the user despite not having direct access to the device or the user's orientation or actions upon it.

Breakdowns in mutual orientation stem from three main problematics:

1) The inadequate fidelity of operators' generic support resources.

2) The lack of mutual access to indicative resources.

3) The operators' lack of direct access to customers' actions and orientation.

The BDV aims to address these problems by providing a shared object around which both parties can mutually orient. This shared object, being a representation of the device, is linked to the device itself thereby simultaneously increasing fidelity to the specific problem device and enabling the operator to view many of the customer's actions as they are undertaken. In addition indicative resources are provided to both parties.

The related work we described earlier, in particular that by Fussell et al, has tended to examine the visual information available in face-to-face interaction in a decompositional way. For example Fussell, Kraut & Siegal (2000) describe how different types of the visual information (from gaze to participants bodies and actions) can be used in conversational grounding. This leads them to video as a mechanism for recreating this shared visual space. Rather than focusing on visual information in a decompositional way, examining the detailed practices of those engaged in remote object-focused work shows how talk, referring, etc. is embedded in the circumstances of getting the work done. By focusing on the practical work of troubleshooting we have begun to get an understanding of where troubles occur in this work. We have seen that although customers and operators are often able to establish a mutual orientation to the device in question, asymmetries of access can also all too easily result in their mutual orientation breaking down. Where it does break down the parties have to rely on further talk to re-establish it and this can involve considerably more interactional work. This focus on the work to establish a mutual orientation to the non-mutually shared device led, in this case, to the idea that a problem representation could be good enough to support the troubleshooting interaction.

Another difference between our own study and the others that we have discussed is that we have studied the work of expert givers of help: people who are trained and work in the context of providing remote help on a day to day basis. Other approaches have resorted to using 'subjects' with no particular experience in help giving, relying instead upon the articulation of provided instructions. Our experts were seen to have developed skills in remote help giving, from hiding or accounting for the use of the system during interaction to miming the actions as they describe them to the customer. For example, in the bicycle repair task described in Kraut, Fussell & Siegal (2003), one issue was that helpers did not know when to intervene, yet here we can see that intervening as such (deciding when help should be provided) is not generally a problem. There are some difficulties with situating instructions but the operators have developed a grammar for appropriate instruction and reformulation.

The problem representation described here has a number of features which lead us to propose that it will be 'good enough' to accomplish this required order of enhancement. These features include: the ways in which parties could mutually orient their activities around the representation; an appropriate level of indicative resources; the fact that the state of the machine is available to both local and remote parties; and the linkage of the resource across sites allows for a high degree of fidelity to the troubleshooting problem itself. In addition, our solution is not about removing expertise from the hands of technical support, rather it is a communication tool designed to enable them to apply their knowledge more easily. That is, by providing some access to the remote object. Whalen and Vinkhuyzen comment on how CSSRs are disadvantaged by their lack of access to the remote object i.e. the machine and it's artefacts such as print outs, but that they have the rich resource of natural language to help them get an understanding of the machine problem but not the expertise to use it. In contrast Technical Support do have the expertise, however there are still aspects of the Technical Support-Customer interaction that can prove troublesome because of non-mutually shared access to the device. The BDV is an attempt to address this.

There are also a number of reasons which suggest that problem representations are more suitable than video for supporting *this* work. In particular these relate to the ways in which shared representations of this order should avoid the problems of fractured ecologies that video based systems introduce, since a common understanding of reciprocal views should be easy to achieve. In addition, the system outlined here is a more economical arrangement for the task at hand. Customers want to spend minimum effort troubleshooting their machines, so it needs to be made as simple and effective as possible. It is a solution that has the minimum overhead for all the parties concerned and is based on existing device features: sensors, medium-sized screens and high quality GUI (found on newer devices). Our solution does not require the user to wear or have any special equipment. In this situation low-cost video is certainly not likely to be good enough for many of the actual problems, whereas a good problem representation can have the advantage of clarity by not relying upon camera angles and orientations. Furthermore, it seems likely that if static cameras were used the number of cameras required would be prohibitive whilst the use of a mobile camera would negate many of the proposed benefits, requiring the operator to direct the customer to move the camera to the appropriate areas of the machine. Thus considering the limitations of other support and considering the actual requirements of the task, a problem representation tied to the actual object is likely to be 'good enough' for many of the kinds of troubleshooting that involve the participation of experts at remote sites.

Further research is still required, most particularly with regard to implementing and testing such a representation, but we hope that this paper has begun to contribute to an understanding of where other kinds of representation might be best suited to supporting interactions around remote objects. There are specific aspects of office devices that lend themselves to these kinds of representations well : newer models already have larger interfaces on them and they already have many sensors, allowing a degree of fidelity between the object and the representation that might be harder to accomplish in some domains. There are however other domains where similar levels of fidelity are available, another massive domain is vehicle repair. Vehicles are increasingly fitted with wireless technology and multiple sensors. The basic requirements of domains where such representations might be appropriate domains where mechanical manipulation of parts is required, there is the ability to repair on site and sensing infrastructure is viable. The size of many kinds of devices also makes low cost video solutions less appropriate than they would be for, say, a desktop task. It therefore seems sensible to suggest that design should be for the particular work-at-hand. That is, different work is likely to be more or less suited to different orders of representation.

Beyond all this, questions can also be posed regarding what can and should be represented and what adequate fidelity of a representation to an object might amount to in practice. For example, in the case outlined here will the proposed solution be adequate for specific aspects of the task such as instructing a customer through on-screen menus or for understanding and transferring information on the image quality of copies? These are issues that are subject to further investigation in the course of implementing the system described here.

So, to sum up, in this paper we have described the troubleshooting practices of remote experts and customers in order to delineate our reasons for proposing a different approach to designing support for such work. Other approaches have proposed video-based systems to recreate features of the face-to-face situation. Our research, by contrast, has suggested that, for many situations, a representation of the troubleshooting problem, tied to the source of the problem itself, would be 'good enough'.

References

Atkinson, J M, and Drew, P (1979) *Order in Court: the Organization of Verbal Interaction in Judicial Settings*, London: Macmillan

Bowers, J., and Martin, D. (2000). Machinery In The New Factories: Talk and Technology in a Bank's Call Centre. *Proceedings of CSCW 2000*, © 2000 ACM.

Fussell, S R, Kraut, R E, and Siegel, J (2000) 'Coordination of communication: effects of shared visual context on collaborative work', *Proceedings of the CSCW 2000 Conference on Computer Supported Cooperative Work*, 21-30, New York: ACM

Fussell, S., Setlock, L. & Kraut, R. (2003) Effects of head-mounted and scene-oriented video systems on remote collaboration on physical tasks. *CHI 2003*. 513-520

Fussell, S., Setlock, L. & Parker, E. (2003) Where do helpers look? Gaze targets during collaborative physical tasks. *CHI 2003 New Horizons*. 768-769

Fussell, S., Setlock, l., Yang, J., Ou, J., Mauer, E. & Kramer, A. (2004) Gestures over video streams to support remote collaboration on physical tasks. *HCI. 19*. 273-309

Garfinkel, H and Wieder, D L (1992) 'Two incommensurable, asymmetrically alternate, technologies of social analysis', in G Watson and R M Seiler (eds) *Talk in context: contributions to ethnomethodology*, New York: Sage, 175-206

Gutwin, C and Penner, R (2002) 'Improving interpretation of remote gestures with telepointer traces', *Proceedings of the CSCW 2002 Conference on Computer Supported Cooperative Work*, 49-57, New York: ACM

Heath, C & Luff, P (1991) Disembodied conduct: communication through video in a multimedia office environment. *Proc. Of CHI'91*. ACM Press. 99-103

Heath, C. & Luff, P. (1992) Media Spaces and communicative Asymmetries: Preliminary observations of Video-mediated Interaction. *HCI* 7(3). 315-346

Heritage, J (1984) *Garfinkel and Ethnomethodology*, Cambridge: Polity Press

Kraut, R E, Miller, M D, and Siegel, J (1996) 'Collaboration in performance of physical tasks: Effects on outcomes and communication', *Proceedings of the CSCW 1996 Conference on Computer Supported Cooperative Work*, 57-66, New York: ACM

Kraut, R., Fussell, S. & Siegal, J. (2003) Visual Information as a Conversational Resource in Collaborative Physical Tasks. *HCI Special Issue : Talking about things*. 18 (1&2). 13-49

Kuzuoka, H, Kosuge, T and Tanaka, K (1994) 'GestureCam: A video communication system for sympathetic remote collaboration, *Proceedings of the CSCW 1994 Conference on Computer Supported Cooperative Work*, 35-43, New York: ACM

Kuzuoka, H, Oyama, S, Yamazaki, K, Suzuki, K and Mitsuishi, M (2000) 'GestureMan: A mobile robot that embodies a remote instructor's actions', *Proceedings of the CSCW 2000 Conference on Computer Supported Cooperative Work*, 155-162, New York: ACM

Luff, P, et al (2003) Fractured Ecologies: Creating Environments for Collaboration. *HCI Special Issue : Talking about things*. 18 (1&2) 51-84

Martin, D. & Rouncefield, M. (2003) Making the Organization Come Alive: Talking Through and About the Technology in Remote Banking. *HCI Special Issue : Talking about things*. 18 (1&2). 111-148

Ou, J., Fussell, S., Chen, X., Setlock, L., & Yang, J. (2003) Gestural communication over video stream : supporting multimodal interaction for remote collaborative physical tasks. *ICMI'03*. ACM. 242-249

Sacks, H (1992) *Lectures on Conversation, Volumes I and II*, Edited by G Jefferson, Malden, MA: Blackwell

Schegloff, E A (1968) 'Sequencing in conversational opening', *American Anthropologist*, 70, 1075-95

Schegloff, E A (1972) 'Notes on conversational practice: formulating place', in Sudnow, D (ed), *Studies in Social Interaction*, New York: Free Press

Whalen, Jack (1995) 'Expert systems versus systems for experts: computer-aided dispatch as a support system in real-world environments'. In Thomas, P., (ed) *The Social and Interactional Dimensions of Human-Computer Interfaces*. Cambridge University Press. 161-83

Whalen, J.; Vinkhuyzen, E. (2001) Expert systems in (inter)action: diagnosing document machine problems over the telephone. In Luff, P., Hindmarsh, J., & Heath, C., (eds) *Workplace studies: recovering work practice and information system design*. Cambridge University Press. 92-140.

Whalen, J.; Whalen, M.; Henderson, K. (2002) Improvisational choreography in teleservice work. *British Journal of Sociology*. June; 53 (2). 239-258.

H. Gellersen et al. (eds.), ECSCW 2005: Proceedings of the Ninth European Conference on Computer-Supported Cooperative Work, 18-22 September 2005, Paris, France, 287–306.

Using Empirical Data to Reason about Internet Research Ethics

James M. Hudson and Amy Bruckman

Georgia Institute of Technology, USA

{jhudson,asb}@cc.gatech.edu

Abstract. Internet technology holds significant potential to respond to business, educational, and social needs, but this same technology poses fundamentally new challenges for research ethics. To reason about ethical questions, researchers and ethics review boards typically rely on dichotomies like "public" versus "private," "published" vs. "unpublished," and "anonymous" vs. "identified." However, online, these categories are blurred, and the underlying concepts require reinterpretation. How then are we to reason about ethical dilemmas about research on the Internet? To date, most work in this area has been grounded in a combination of theoretical analysis and experience gained by people in the course of conducting Internet research. In these studies, ethical insight was a welcome byproduct of research aimed primarily at exploring other ends. However, little work has used experimental methods for the primary purpose of contributing to our reasoning about the ethics of research online. In this paper, we discuss the role of *empirical data* in helping us answer questions about Internet research ethics. As an example, we review results of one study in which we gauged participant expectations of privacy in public chatrooms (Hudson & Bruckman, 2004b). Using an experimental approach, we demonstrate how participants' expectations of privacy conflict with the reality of these public chatrooms. Although these empirical data cannot provide concrete answers, we show how they influence our reasoning about the ethical issues of obtaining informed consent.

The Necessity of Empirical Work on Ethics

Starting in the early 1990's, the Internet grew from a tool used by a small population of specialists to a popular medium. Behavior of Internet users and accompanying changes in culture are of great interest to scholars from a wide variety of disciplines—computer science, management, education, sociology, anthropology, and more. In CSCW, we seek to understand the social and psychological influences of different media and different interface decisions so that we can better understand how to design environments that support and appropriately influence specific types of interaction (e.g., Bos *et al.*, 2004; Connell *et al.*, 2001; DiMicco *et al.*, 2004; e.g., Nardi *et al.*, 2004; Woodruff & Aoki, 2003). Thoughtful research on this new medium can help us both understand its present and shape its future. However, we must conduct such research ethically, or we risk both harming individuals and disturbing the very phenomena we seek to understand.

Research on the Internet raises a host of novel ethical challenges (e.g., Bassett & O'Riordan, 2002; Boehlefeld, 1996; Bruckman, 2002; Ess, 2002; Eysenbach & Till, 2001; Frankel & Siang, 1999; S. Herring, 1996a; King, 1996; Schrum, 1997; Walther, 2002; Waskul & Douglass, 1996). Traditionally, research ethics relies on distinctions such as "public" versus "private" spaces, "identified" vs. "anonymous" individuals, and "published" vs. "unpublished" information. However, online, these categories become blurred (Bruckman, 2002; Eysenbach & Till, 2001). Consequently, it can be difficult to translate our intuitions to the new domain of Internet research. The varied ethical codes stemming from different academic and professional backgrounds of researchers in CSCW and Internet research more generally further complicate matters. Despite significant efforts from the American Psychological Association (Kraut *et al.*, 2004), the American Association for the Advancement of Science (Frankel & Siang, 1999), and the Association of Internet Research (Ess, 2002), many questions regarding the ethical conduct of online research remain.

For example, a significant amount of CSCW research has focused on synchronous text-based, computer-mediated communication or "chat" (e.g., Bradner *et al.*, 1999; Churchill *et al.*, 2000; Farnham *et al.*, 2000; Halverson *et al.*, 2003; Handel & Herbsleb, 2002; Nardi *et al.*, 2000; O'Neill & Martin, 2003; M. Smith *et al.*, 2002). However, a host of particularly thorny ethical questions remain. Is it ethical to enter a chatroom and record the conversation for research purposes? Under what circumstances? Is it necessary to obtain consent from participants? If so, what kind of consent? Is it sufficient to announce the researcher's presence and offer users a way to opt out of participation? Is it feasible to announce the researcher's presence but only record data if participants type a command to opt in? Is the process of obtaining consent more disruptive than the actual study? How should data collected from chatrooms be protected? Is it necessary to change pseudonyms of participants in written accounts? Is it acceptable to retain chatroom logs for long periods of time, or should they be coded for target behaviors and then destroyed to protect the privacy of participants? These are just a few of the difficult ethical questions this new medium raises.

In this section, we describe two traditional approaches to answering these questions about research ethics: theoretical inquiry and case studies of research experience. Then, we use an important concept in research ethics—reasonable expectations of privacy—to show how these traditional approaches leave questions unanswered. We suggest that empirical data is needed to support our reasoning about research ethics.

The examples that we draw on in this paper focus primarily on the legal and ethical standards of research in the United States. In doing so, we do not suggest that this is the only legitimate perspective available. As the European Data Privacy Directive (1995; 2002) illustrates, reasonable expectations of privacy—and the resulting research ethics applied—will vary between cultural settings. Through this paper, we seek to illustrate how empirical research can illuminate new ethical considerations. Further empirical research is needed to understand how these issues vary from culture to culture. We explicitly consider international perspectives toward the end of this paper.

Traditional Approaches to Research Ethics

Due to the complexity of issues in research ethics, we often rely on theoretical inquiry to simplify or highlight different questions. Philosophy, for example, can help us to see specific cases as examples of categories of problems (e.g., Ess, 1996; Thomas, 1996a). Likewise, it can help us make sense of the assumptions underlying different practical approaches to research ethics. Beyond pure philosophic thought, we often use hypothetical case studies (e.g., Keller & Lee, 2003; King, 1996). These case studies help highlight specific troublesome areas in research ethics.

Practical experience in conducting research also informs our understanding of research ethics. It's not uncommon for researchers to run into ethical issues in the course of conducting other research, especially in the social sciences. Case studies of practice, grounded in experience, offer concrete examples about how researchers design and conduct experiments as well as how subjects respond to these experiments. These case studies complement theoretical inquiry by illustrating ways that reality differs from or is more complex than theoretical predictions. For example, Kipling Williams's studies of cyberostracism have highlighted issues of identifying distress while conducting an online experiment (Williams *et al.*, 2000). Brenda Danet's (2001a, 2001b) work has raised questions of ownership in online performance art. Sheana Bull and Mary McFarlane's (2000) work on risky sexual behaviors resulting from online encounters has dealt with issues of data collection and retention. Our own work has run into challenges of obtaining consent in online environments (Hudson & Bruckman, 2002).

Periodically studies come along that raise ethical issues which resonate with broader research communities. For example, Stanley Milgram's (1974) studies on obedience sparked numerous debates on how subjects withdraw consent. Laud Humphreys's (1970) studies of the "tearoom trade" lead to discussion of when public information should be considered private. Marty Rimm's (1995) studies of pornography on the Internet raised debate about both the misrepresentation of information in research reports and about how this information can be further (mis)represented in media reports about academic research and in social policy decisions (Thomas, 1996b).

Although case studies of research practice can shed light onto complicated ethical issues, they are not designed for that purpose. Instead, they encounter these issues while pursuing other research questions. Below, we use an important concept in research ethics—reasonable expectations of privacy—to illustrate how targeted empirical studies can play a complementary role to both theoretical inquiry and case studies of practice in informing our ethical reasoning.

Reasonable Expectations of Privacy

Questions of privacy—and, therefore, questions about the necessity of consent—often deal explicitly with the concept of "reasonable expectations." For example, in the United States, the Belmont Report[1] (Department of Health, 1979) sets up a "reasonable volunteer" as the standard by which to judge a consent process. The U.S. regulations on research state:

> Private information includes information about behavior that occurs in a context in which an individual can *reasonably expect* that no observation or recording is taking place, and information which has been provided for specific purposes by an individual and which the individual can *reasonably expect* will not be made public. (45 CFR 46, Section 102(f), emphasis added)

In conducting research on the Internet, both the American Psychological Association (Kraut et al., 2004) and the Association of Internet Researchers (Ess, 2002) caution that we must carefully consider reasonable expectations of privacy in determining the necessity of consent.

Not only is this concept embedded in our codes of research ethics, reasonable expectations are also fundamental to many privacy laws. For example, Charles Katz was convicted on illegal gambling charges based primarily on evidence from a tapped public phone. In the U.S. Supreme Court decision ("Katz v. United States, 389 U.S. 347", 1967), the court argued:

> The Fourth Amendment protects people, not places. What a person knowingly exposes to the public, even in his own home or office, is not a subject of Fourth Amendment protection. But what he seeks to preserve as private, even in an area accessible to the public, may be constitutionally protected.

In his concurring opinion, Justice John Harlan further elaborated:

> My understanding of the rule that has emerged from prior decisions is that there is a twofold requirement, first that a person have exhibited an actual (subjective) expectation of privacy and, second, that the expectation be one that society is prepared to recognize as "reasonable."

With this decision, the concept of *reasonable expectations of privacy* became embedded in U.S. law.

---

[1] In the United States, federal regulations governing the conduct of research are based largely on the findings of the Belmont Report. Like the Nuremberg Code (1949), the Belmont Report was written in the wake of a number of questionable research experiments in the U.S.

European Union Data Privacy Directives ("Directive 95/46/EC of the European Pariament", 1995, "Directive 2002/58/EC of the European Parliament", 2002) illustrates how varied historical experiences may cause expectations of privacy to differ from one culture to another (Habermas, 1962). Given that the Nazis used information collected from government databases to identify Jews during World War II, it's not surprising that the European Union takes a more stringent view of *reasonable* expectations of privacy than the United States. To further complicate matters, however, individual nations of the European Union implement this legislation differently.

In studying online environments, complicated issues of conflicting expectations of privacy arise. Online, national borders are permeable; it is simply impractical to design a study of naturally occurring groups in an online environment that does not risk including subjects from different nations and different cultures. When this happens, we cannot assume that the reasonable expectations of researchers are the reasonable expectations of research subjects.

This emphasis on subjects' *reasonable expectations*, however, begs the question: When and where do individuals expect privacy? When is this expectation *reasonable*? Theoretical inquiry and experiential case studies have provided us with some insight into these questions, but they remain largely unanswered.

Theoretical inquiry into reasonable expectations leads us to contradictory conclusions about whether or not consent is necessary before studying online environments. Some online environments are clearly intended to be public spaces. These environments do not restrict membership, have significant readership that does not participate (Nonnecke & Preece, 2000), and archive contributions in an accessible way. Based on these defining characteristics, it can be argued that individuals in these forums have no *reasonable* expectations of privacy and that consent issues are the same as they are for any public space (Kraut et al., 2004).

When conversations are not publicly archived, however, theoretical inquiry leads to divergent conclusions. For some researchers, unrestricted membership is the key to determining whether or not a space is public, and therefore whether or not it is accessible to researchers without consent (S. Herring, 1996a). Others, however, argue that the ephemerality of some online discussions creates a reasonable expectation that the conversation will not be recorded, even though it is clearly publicly accessible (Bruckman, 2002). Since these ethical stances are based on differing assumptions, theoretical inquiry is not likely to lead to a resolution. From a theoretical inquiry perspective, "reasonable expectations" remain problematic.

Case studies of research practice have also raised a number of questions about reasonable expectations. For example, Elizabeth Reid's (1996) study of one particular text-based online environment highlights an often neglected factor in understanding reasonable expectations of privacy. Namely, the disinhibiting effects of online communication (Dery, 1993; Joinson, 1998, 2003; Kiesler *et al.*, 1984; Spears *et al.*, 2001; Wallace, 1999) can reduce awareness that privacy might be at stake. As Reid (1996, p. 172) notes:

> In particular I began to doubt the wisdom of taking enthusiasm for my project to indicate both knowledge and acceptance of the risks that participation in it might entail. ... In online environments where consequences to the actual lives of participants can be hidden behind the illusion of a virtual/actual dichotomy, this tendency toward uninhibited behavior can make the social researcher's job seemingly easier and thereby place an added burden of responsibility on his or her shoulders.

Even though the spaces she studied were public, Reid argued the disinhibiting effects of online environments might lead to *reasonable* expectations of privacy. Likewise, Yatzchak Binik, Kenneth Mah, and Sara Kiesler (1999) describe a number of cases with negative consequences where individuals engaged in public conversations as if they were private. In their study of an online environment for gay and lesbian individuals, Elizabeth Bassett and Kate O'Riordan's (2002) further complicate matters by highlighting contradictions between management's view of the website as a public space to promote awareness of gay and lesbian issues and users who interacted on the various forums as if they were private spaces. As these studies illustrate, the tendency toward disinhibition in online environments raises questions about whether or not expectations from traditional public spaces reasonably apply in new online environments.

A Need for Empirical Work

Traditional approaches to ethical questions have involved either philosophic inquiry or case studies of issues that arose in the conduct of other research. Rarely do we see research aimed at gathering empirical data to support ethical reasoning. Though these traditional approaches to research ethics have significantly informed our thinking as a community, more is still needed. For example, although a significant amount of work using these traditional approaches has looked into notions of *reasonable expectations of privacy*, questions remain.

Gathering empirical data on these questions can help us reach some answers. Doing so, however, is not easy; it often requires a willingness to stand on potentially shaky ethical grounds. Where the benefits of doing the research outweigh the harm[2], though, we should be willing to conduct these studies. We must point out, however, that knowing what people do does not tell us what people should do. Knowing about how subjects feel, however, can provide us with evidence to inform our ethical reasoning.

In the next section, we describe one case study that illustrates how empirical data can shed light onto ethical dilemmas, specifically onto questions of

---

[2] The Belmont Report, like the Nuremberg Code (1949), takes an explicitly teleological perspective (Mill, 1998). Here, we follow this approach. In our discussion below, we include further analysis of this viewpoint, along with a discussion of deontological ethics (Kant, 1981) as an alternative perspective.

reasonable expectations of privacy. In doing so, we explicitly deal with the ethical challenges that arose in conducting this type of research.

Gathering Empirical Data: A Case Study

A number of research studies have illustrated how various psychological properties induced by online environments cause individuals to act as if public spaces were private (Bassett & O'Riordan, 2002; Binik et al., 1999; Hudson & Bruckman, 2004a; Joinson, 2003; Kiesler et al., 1984; Matheson & Zanna, 1988; Postmes & Spears, 1998; Reid, 1996; Wallace, 1999; Walther, 1996). In analyzing the ethical issues in any chatroom study, one key piece of information to understand is this: Do users of public chatrooms act as if studying them violates their privacy? How much do users object to being studied in a *public* online environment when they are aware of the study? Notions of privacy are based on implicit and constantly evolving social contracts (Habermas, 1962). These social contracts are often based on our experiences in the physical world (e.g., how far the sound of a voice will carry), which offer little guidance online. Therefore, we need to understand how participants in online environments interpret these social contracts so that we may consider appropriate strategies for ethically conducting research.

In this section, we describe one study that we conducted to help answer these questions (Hudson & Bruckman, 2004b). Through looking in detail at this study, we demonstrate that experimental research aimed at gathering empirical data plays a complementary role in answering some of these difficult ethical dilemmas. Although this type of research cannot tell us appropriate ethical positions, it can inform our reasoning by providing concrete data about how potential subjects might respond to various situations.

Method

To begin to understand whether participants react to online studies in public spaces as potential invasions of privacy, we experimentally studied how individuals in online chatrooms reacted to a variety of consent conditions. We designed a study where we entered a number of online chatrooms, informed the participants that we were recording them to study language use, and recorded how individuals responded. Specifically, we examined participants in chatrooms on ICQ Chat[3]. Since ICQ Chat uses IRC servers, we were able to conduct this study without worrying about proprietary software (such as MSN Chat). Also, ICQ Chat's web-based interface offered a population that is generally less technologically aware than standard IRC populations. Because of this web-based interface, we have reason to believe that individuals using ICQ Chat are somewhat more representative of the general population of Internet users than those on most other IRC servers. Note that our experimental setup addresses one

---

3   http://www.icq.com/ircqnet/

294

Condition	Message Broadcast
No Message	None
Recording Message	We are researchers recording this chatroom for a study on language use in online environments. For questions or comments, email study@mail.chatstudy.cc.gatech.edu. Thank you!
Opt Out Message	We are researchers recording this chatroom for a study on language use in online environments. If you don't want to be recorded, please whisper "Chat_Study opt out" to us. For questions or comments, email study@mail.chatstudy.cc.gatech.edu. Thank you!
Opt In Message	We are researchers and would like to record this conversation for a study on language use in online environments. If we may record you, please whisper "Chat_Study volunteer" to us. For questions or comments, email study@mail.chatstudy.cc.gatech.edu. Thank you!

Note The "study on language use" was chosen as a specific innocuous study

Table I. Announce Messages

particular kind of chatroom environment. In our discussion, we explore the available evidence for generalization of these results.

First, we downloaded a list of the available chatrooms each evening at 9:50 PM[4]. On any given day, the mean size (i.e., number of participants) of available chatrooms on most IRC networks tends to be positively skewed: there are a large number of small chatrooms, but fewer large ones. In order to ensure that we adequately covered the range of potential chatroom sizes, we arbitrarily divided the available chatrooms into four buckets: very small (2 – 4 participants), small (5 – 10 participants), medium (10 – 29 participants), and large (30 or more participants). This means we sampled a much larger percentage of the available large chatrooms than of the available smaller chatrooms.

Using these buckets, we randomly chose 16 chatrooms from each. Each set of 16 chatrooms were further (randomly) subdivided into groups of four. Each group of four was assigned to one of our recording conditions. In each condition, we varied the message we said to the chatroom. In the *No Message* condition, we simply entered using the nickname "Chat_Study" and said nothing. In the *Recording Message* condition, we entered as "Chat_Study" but announced that we were recording the chatroom for a study. The *Opt In Message* and *Opt Out Message* conditions were similar, but allowed individuals to choose to opt in or opt out of the study by typing a response. The exact messages used are listed in Table I.

Once chatrooms were randomly assigned to conditions, we entered the chatrooms (in a random order) and conducted the study. Upon joining a room, we waited one minute before posting our message. Then, we waited another five minutes before leaving the chatroom. If we had not been kicked out of the chatroom by this time, we posted the following message before exiting:

---

[4] Note that all times are Eastern Standard Time. The study lasted for two weeks.

This research is actually not about language use. Rather, it is designed to study how individuals in chatrooms react to researchers studying them. Further information is available at http://www.cc.gatech.edu/elc/chatstudy. Thanks!

By entering chatrooms two at a time and staggering our conditions, we were able to test 64 chatrooms within a one-hour period (10:00 PM – 11:00 PM).

For each chatroom, we noted the number of participants at the time we entered, whether or not a moderator was present, whether or not conversation occurred, and whether or not we were kicked out of the room. If a chatroom did not have a moderator or we did not observe conversation, it was removed from the study prior to data analysis. Running this study each evening from March 1 until March 14, 2003, we sampled 525 chatrooms. Of these, we retained the 137 chatrooms with moderators and active conversation for our data analysis.

Ethical Issues in Conducting this Study

Before delving into the results, there were a number of ethical issues that arose in the design and conduct of this study. In essence, this is a deceptive study conducted on 2260 subjects[5] without their consent. In conducting this research, we decided to work under the most restrictive of ethical stances—the human subjects model[6]. As such, we sought permission from Georgia Tech's Institutional Review Board[7] (IRB) for conducting this research. Our IRB had three primary concerns in reviewing this research: the use of deception, the lack of consent, and the potential for harm.

Responding to concerns over the potential for harm is quite difficult in a study designed to partially evaluate the potential for harm in studies like it. However, most reported case studies of significant harm as a result of this type of research have involved conversations about sensitive topics (Bassett & O'Riordan, 2002; Reid, 1996). Therefore, we agreed to review the names and (official) topics of all potential chatrooms before entering them to ensure that sensitive discussions seemed unlikely. While we never formally defined what we meant by "sensitive topics," we used emotional support groups such as "breast cancer survivors" as the prototypical discussions to avoid. In conducting the study, we encountered no such chatrooms. To further minimize harm, we limited the scope of our study to only comments directly pertaining to us. Specifically, after reading through the transcripts once, we removed all comments that were not directed to or about us. All data analysis was performed on these cleaned transcripts.

In addition to removing comments that did not pertain to us, we also replaced any usernames with randomly generated identifiers and removed all other

---

5 This represents the number of unique usernames involved in our study. There is not necessarily a one-to-one mapping between individuals and usernames.

6 For a discussion of other models for conducting Internet research, see Bassett and O'Riordan (2002).

7 In the United States, all research involving human subjects and conducted at or with a federally funded institution (e.g., universities) must be reviewed by an Institutional Review Board (IRB). With the authority to veto any proposed human subjects research, the IRB has a broad mandate to ensure that the research design adequately protects human subjects.

identifying information. As Bruckman (2002) points out, anonymity and pseudonymity in online environments raise difficult ethical challenges. Subjects using pseudonyms in online environments, for example, does not mean that the data is anonymous. In many cases, log file data from online conversations include information such as IP addresses, which has been labeled as identifying information in both the United States (45 CFR 160.514.b.2.i.O) and the European Union (Directive 2002/58/EC Section 28). Even with IP addresses removed, however, pseudonyms often function as individual identities in many online environments. It's not uncommon to find individuals who use the same pseudonym across a number of communities, making it easier to link a pseudonym with a physical person. Even when it is not possible to trace these pseudonyms to an individual's physical identity, however, users still can feel deeply invested in online identities. When a pseudonym is revealed in a research study, that user may still perceive harm.

In conducting this study, we did not take questions of harm lightly. This is certainly the most provocative study that either of us has conducted. After all, we hypothesized that subjects would find this type of research upsetting. As the results below show, subjects did feel annoyed and expressed high levels of hostility. Sometimes, however, when the scientific questions are important enough and the potential for harm can be minimized, doing research that aggravates subjects may be acceptable. Based on the steps we took to minimize the potential for harm, we believe that the scientific value of these research questions outweighed the annoyance that subjects expressed.

In social psychological traditions, there is a long history of using deception-based research when topics of concern are otherwise inaccessible (Korn, 1997). Although there are a number of approaches to dealing with consent issues in deception research, generally subjects in laboratory studies consent to participate in a research study, but are deceived about the exact nature of the research (Aronson et al., 1998). However, in field studies, some topics can only be studied when subjects are wholly unaware of the research. Given that people are notoriously poor at being self-reflective about privacy topics (e.g., Ackerman et al., 1999), we felt we could not simply ask potential participants about how they might respond to this type of research. Therefore, it was necessary to conduct this study using deception, without seeking consent to participate in the study. This was a decision that we did not take lightly.

When deception is justified, subjects should be debriefed to the extent possible about the true nature of the research. To do so, we pointed subjects to a webpage with information about our study before we left the chatroom. When doing field research without consent, however, decisions about debriefing require special sensitivity as they may cause further and unwarranted disruption (Aronson et al., 1998). We decided—with the help of our IRB—that we would not debrief chatrooms where we had been kicked out. This decision involved balancing subjects' right to be debriefed with their right to be left alone. Since we believed that kicking us out of the chatroom would indicate a strong desire to be left alone, we gave this right greater weight. We felt that the additional disruption would cause more harm than the benefit that debriefing provided.

Based on the U.S. federal regulations governing research, informed consent may be waived only when four conditions are met:

(1) the research involves no more than minimal risk to the subjects;

(2) the waiver or alteration will not adversely affect the rights and welfare of the subjects;

(3) the research could not practicably be carried out without the waiver or alteration; and

(4) whenever appropriate, the subjects will be provided with additional pertinent information after participation. (45 CFR 46.116.d)

After much discussion, our IRB felt that we met all four of these conditions and qualified for a waiver of informed consent. More discussion on waivers of consent is provided in the full report of our study (Hudson & Bruckman, 2004b).

Chatroom Consent Study Results

To analyze which factors contributed to whether or not we were kicked out of the chatrooms, we conducted a hierarchical logistic regression analysis. Our dependent variable was whether or not we were kicked out of the chatroom. Results from this analysis indicate that both size ($Wald_{(1)} = 5.407$, $p = 0.020$) and the number of moderators ($Wald_{(1)} = 7.491$, $p = 0.006$) significantly predicted when we were kicked out of chatrooms. Briefly, the likelihood of being kicked out of a chatroom decreased as the number of people present increased. We were twice as likely to be kicked out of a room with 5 people than a room with 18 people, holding other factors constant; for every thirteen additional people in a chatroom, the chances of being kicked out were cut in half. Conversely, increased numbers of moderators lead to increased chances of being kicked out.

In addition, our experimental conditions were significant predictors ($\chi^2_{(3, 137)} = 15.554$, $p = 0.001$) over and above all other variables. The No Message condition was significantly different from the other three conditions ($Wald_{(1)} = 12.286$, $p < 0.001$), but there were no other differences found between conditions. In other words, it did not matter what we said; any indication of recording the chatroom significantly increased our likelihood of being kicked out. In fact, holding other variables constant, we were nearly four times more likely to be kicked out when we said something.

Based on the results from the Opt In and Opt Out conditions, there is little reason to believe that these are viable ways of conducting research. In the Opt Out condition, we were kicked out of the chatrooms 72% of the time. With Opt In, it was 62% of the time. (There is no significant difference between these two conditions.) Of the 443 individuals who could have responded in the Opt Out condition, only two individuals opted out. A few others, however, did express what might be called a desire to opt out (e.g., "hey chat[8] fuk off", "yeah up urs chatstudy!!"). Of the 766 individuals in the Opt In condition, only four chose to do so. Even in this condition, some individuals expressed strong disagreement with the possibility of being recorded (e.g., "please leave Chat_Study u do not have permission ... now all we need is for Chat_Study to fuck Off."). For the most part, however, the negative comments we received in these two conditions were less frequent and less vehement than those we received in the Recording condition (e.g., "<deleted> kicks Chat_Study's ass so hard.... Chat_Study will be shitting out of it forhead for a week!", "Hey Chat_Study dont you ever talk to me like that again you fucking flaccid, nasty, skank ugly, idiotic no brained, small dicked, stinking nasty pimp daddy wannabe, go wave that limp nasty scab encrusted dick somewhere else bitch!"). During the course of running this study and the pilot testing, only one individual asked for more information about the study.

Discussion

Based on this study, we can say that participants in public chatrooms acted as if their privacy had been violated when they were made aware of the fact that we were studying them. Although there were a number of limitations to this study[9], the reactions of participants was consistent with what we would expect if the chatrooms were private spaces. If we accept that this indicates an expectation of privacy in public chatrooms, we must ask a number of questions. Is this expectation of privacy in a public environment reasonable? If so, what are the implications for conducting research on chatrooms ethically? Reasonable or not, what are the implications of expectations of privacy for designers of CSCW environments? In the next sections, we consider these questions.

Ethical Research Given Expectations of Privacy

If we accept that the data gathered in this study indicates that participants in public online chatrooms have an expectation of privacy, we must ask whether or not this expectation is reasonable. On one hand, we can argue that public chatrooms are (usually) unambiguously public. Given that fact, we have no ethical obligation to consider participants' expectations of privacy. Following this reasoning, we may study subjects in a public online chatroom as we would in any other public environment.

On the other hand, the nature of this new media and its (not-completely-defined) implicit social contracts surrounding privacy (i.e., Habermas, 1962) suggests that these expectations of privacy may, in fact, be quite reasonable. As in this study (Hudson & Bruckman, 2004b), research has shown over and over again that people in public, online environments often act as if these environments were private (Bassett & O'Riordan, 2002; Greist et al., 1973; Hudson &

---

8   We used "Chat_Study" as our username.

9   These limitations are discussed in detail in Hudson and Bruckman (2004b).

Bruckman, 2002, 2004a; Nardi et al., 2004; Sproull & Kiesler, 1991; Weisband & Kiesler, 1996). In other words, there is a mismatch between people's (often unspoken) expectations of privacy in computer-mediated environments and the reality of privacy. Research on disinhibition in online environments suggests that aspects of the online environment (e.g., the feelings of anonymity online or the ephemerality of text in chat or the (in)visibility of audience in blogs) may lead to this mismatch in expectations of privacy (Hudson & Bruckman, 2004a; Joinson, 2003; Kiesler et al., 1984; Matheson & Zanna, 1988). Thus, empirical data suggests that the expectation exists, and the medium may encourage it. Following this reasoning, it seems appropriate to accept people's feelings as valid, i.e. reasonable.

Assuming that expectations of privacy in public chatrooms are reasonable, we must ask questions about how to ethically conduct research on these chatrooms. Do we have a moral imperative to seek and obtain informed consent? What if the process of obtaining consent is potentially disruptive and harmful? This leads us to a central ethical question: If subjects are not aware that a researcher is recording the conversation in a chatroom, is there harm in violating their privacy? A teleological perspective such as utilitarianism holds that no harm has been done (Mill, 1998). A subject unaware of research cannot feel disrupted or harmed. Therefore, the benefits of the situation (to scientific understanding) outweigh the potential for harm. It is important to note that this line of ethical reasoning hinges on the (arguably tenuous) assumption that subjects will never become aware of the research. If subjects become aware of the research, a teleological perspective holds that we must now weigh the amount of harm against the potential benefits.

A more deontological perspective holds that there are certain rights that are fundamental (Kant, 1981). As the Belmont Report states:

> Respect for persons requires that subjects, to the degree that they are capable, be given
> the opportunity to choose what shall or shall not happen to them. ... An agreement to
> participate in research constitutes a valid consent only if voluntarily given. (Part C.1)

A violation of these rights, whether or not the subject is aware of the violation, constitutes harm. Therefore, violating a subject's right to consent to participate in a study is harm even if the subject is unaware of the violation.

Tied in with this question, we must ask about the ethics of harming potential subjects through the consent process. Our data indicates that chatroom participants kicked us out roughly two-thirds of the time when we attempted to obtain informed consent. Which is the greater harm – annoying two-thirds of potential subjects or not obtaining consent? This is a difficult question where reasonable people can disagree.

Although deontological reasoning may reasonably lead us to the conclusion that conducting this type of research is unethical, a teleological stance holds that this type of research is perfectly valid as long as the potential for benefits outweighs the (anticipated) potential for harm. Individual researchers, in partnership with ethics review boards, must decide for themselves whether or not it is ethically right to do so.

When doing this type of research, we believe that research in pre-existing chatrooms[10] can be conducted most productively when subjects are unaware of the study. There are three ways under the United States regulations governing academic research that we can go about doing research without the consent of potential subjects: (a) determine that the research is not human subjects research, (b) determine that the research is exempt from IRB oversight, or (c) convince an IRB to issue a formal waiver of consent. The first two of these approaches are problematic. Assuming that a researcher has decided it is ethically appropriate to conduct a given study without obtaining subjects' consent, we conclude that obtaining a waiver of consent from an IRB is the most appropriate way to conduct chatroom research under U.S. regulatory law. We discuss these conclusions in detail in (Hudson & Bruckman, 2004b).

Designing CSCW Systems for Expectations of Privacy

These findings have implications for CSCW beyond ethical issues in conducting research. Over and over again, research findings indicate that computer-mediated communication technologies lead users to expect a certain degree of privacy, even when they consciously know better (Joinson, 2003; Wallace, 1999). Individuals filling out surveys on a computer reveal much more personal information than they do on paper-based forms (Greist et al., 1973; Weisband & Kiesler, 1996). Power hierarchies in face-to-face and audio environments (France et al., 2001) seem to disappear in online discussions (Sproull & Kiesler, 1991). Shy students who would never say anything in a classroom have no problems interacting with the same teachers and classmates in chat environments (Bruce et al., 1993; Hudson & Bruckman, 2002, 2004a). Normally polite people get into vicious flame wars when they go online (Dery, 1993). Novice bloggers remain unconcerned about privacy (Nardi et al., 2004), despite the growing number of reported problems with unintended audiences reading blogs (e.g., Hart, 2005)

In short, there is often a mismatch between user expectations of privacy and the reality of privacy in Internet-based tools. As designers of communication tools, we have a special obligation to be aware of this. In designing new environments, we need to explicitly consider how design decisions may influence the expectations of privacy in users. Where appropriate, we should strive to make these privacy expectations match reality.

---

[10] For a discussion of emic versus etic styles of research, see Hudson and Bruckman (2004b). In Hudson and Bruckman (2002), we discuss an alternative approach involving creating new chat servers and inviting participation in this specifically-designated research environment.

Beyond the U.S. Perspective

Although the proceeding discussion took a U.S.-centric view on privacy, this is far from the only legitimate perspective. Notions of privacy develop in and through specific historical situations within specific cultural norms (Habermas, 1962). For example, Genevieve Bell (Bell, 2004, p. 92) illustrates just how different norms about privacy can be through her experiences conducting research in a number of Asian countries:

> In China, a male tea-server in a restaurant asked me whether I was menstruating—because it impacted the tea selection. Try to imagine the same question in a Starbucks in Cincinnati! In other places I have spent time, men consume pornography in public cybercafes because to do so at home would violate their homes and insult their families (and wives).

Privacy is a complex notion arising from various implicit social contracts between individuals based on specific historical perspectives. Attitudes vary about types of information that should be kept private and about whom the information should be kept private from (e.g., government, corporations, researchers, or other individuals and institutions).

Unfortunately, this seems to lead us to an impossible dilemma. With the breakdown of national and cultural barriers that is the hallmark of online interaction, any study runs a significant risk of including populations from many cultural backgrounds. Both formal (e.g., S. C. Herring, 1996b; M. A. Smith & Kollock, 1999) and anecdotal evidence (e.g., Cherny, 1999; Horn, 1998; Rheingold, 1993), however, suggests that online communities—like co-located communities—tend to develop their own unique norms over time. Through studying and understanding these norms, we can make more informed ethical decisions.

Conclusions

Traditionally, theoretical inquiry and case studies of research practice have constituted the majority of thinking in research ethics. Although both of these approaches are useful and provide valuable insight, they cannot completely capture all possible legitimate perspectives that our subjects might have (Habermas, 1990, 1993). When it is reasonable, ethical, and useful to do so, we need to consider using experimental techniques to gather empirical data that can help us to better understand our subjects' perspectives.

In this paper, we have examined how this approach helped to strengthen our understanding of reasonable expectations of privacy. Those wrestling with questions of privacy have often struggled with the vagueness of *reasonable expectations* (Bruckman, 2002; S. Herring, 1996a; Kraut et al., 2004; Reid, 1996). In our empirical work on the subject (Hudson & Bruckman, 2004b), we temporarily set aside questions of *reasonable* expectations in order to explore more thoroughly chatroom participants' *expectations*. With an empirical understanding of general expectations of privacy in one setting, we were able to have a more nuanced debate about what is reasonable. Of course, many questions remain, but an empirical understanding of expectations does inform the debate.

Other debates in research ethics—for example, the nature of *harm*—also need empirical data. In our own experiences[11], research ethics boards, such as IRBs, constantly struggle with predicting both the magnitude and probability of potential harm when evaluating research studies. Theoretical approaches can reasonably identify areas of potential harm, and case studies of research practice can describe actual harm, but these boards rarely have empirical data to inform their decisions.

As new media allow us to study increasing numbers of subjects in increasing varieties of cultural settings, it is becoming more and more important that we have solid empirical data contributing to our understanding of research ethics. This type of research can complement philosophical analyses and case studies, and can give us greater insight into balancing the need to protect human subjects with the need to further academic inquiry into the world around us. Gathering empirical data about issues in research ethics can help us (1) to identify particularly problematic areas and (2) to alleviate concerns of researchers and ethics review boards in innocuous areas. A greater emphasis on this type of research will help us relieve the tension between protecting our human subjects and conducting scientifically necessary research.

Acknowledgements

Special thanks to those who gave us feedback when conducting and analyzing these results, especially Susan Herring, Brenda Danet, and Charles Ess. We're especially grateful to the anonymous reviewers who took the time to provide us copious feedback. Thanks to the members of the Electronic Learning Communities (ELC) research group for their support.

References

Ackerman, M. S., Cranor, L. F., & Reagle, J. (1999). Privacy in E-Commerce: Examining User Scenarios and Privacy Preferences. In *Proceedings of the 1999 ACM Conference on Electronic Commerce* (pp. 1-8). Denver, CO: ACM Press.

Aronson, E., Wilson, T. D., & Brewer, M. B. (1998). Experimentation in Social Psychology. In D. T. Gilbert, S. T. Fiske & G. Lindzey (Eds.), *The Handbook of Social Psychology* (Fourth ed., Vol. 1, pp. 99 - 142). New York, NY: Oxford University Press.

Bassett, E. H., & O'Riordan, K. (2002). Ethics of Internet Research: Contesting the Human Subjects Research Model. *Ethics and Information Technology, 4*(3), 233 - 247.

Bell, G. (2004). Intimate Computing? *IEEE Internet Computing, 8*(6), 91 - 93.

Binik, Y. M., Mah, K., & Kiesler, S. (1999). Ethical Issues in Conducting Sex Research on the Internet. *The Journal of Sex Research, 36*(1), 82 - 90.

---

[11]   Hudson served on Georgia Tech's Institutional Review Board from late 2001 until mid-2005.

303

Boehlefeld, S. P. (1996). Doing the Right Thing: Ethical Cyberspace Research. *The Information Society, 12*(2), 141 - 152.

Bos, N., Shami, N. S., Olson, J. S., Cheshin, A., & Nan, N. (2004). In-group/Out-group Effects in Distributed Teams: An Experimental Simulation. In *Proccedings of the 2004 Conference on Computer-Supported Cooperative Work (CSCW)* (pp. 429 - 436). Chicago, IL: ACM Press.

Bradner, E., Kellogg, W., & Erickson, T. (1999). The Adoption and Use of Babble: A Field Study of Chat in the Workplace. In *Proceedings of the 1999 European Conference on Computer Supported Cooperative Work (ECSCW)* (pp. 139 - 158). Copenhagen, Denmark: Kluwer Academic Publishers.

Bruce, B. C., Peyton, J. K., & Batson, T. (Eds.). (1993). *Network-Based Classrooms: Promises and Realities*. New York, NY: Cambridge University Press.

Bruckman, A. (2002). Studying the Amateur Artist: A Perspective on Disguising Data Collected in Human Subjects Research on the Internet. *Ethics and Information Technology, 4*(3), 217 - 231.

Bull, S., & McFarlane, M. (2000). Soliciting Sex on the Internet: What Are the Risks for Sexually Transmitted Diseases and HIV? *Sexually Transmitted Diseases, 27*(9), 545 - 550.

Cherny, L. (1999). *Conversation and Community: Chat in a Virtual World*. Stanford: CSLI Publications.

Churchill, E., Trevor, J., Bly, S., & Nelson, L. (2000). StickyChats: Remote Conversations over Digital Documents. In *Proceedings of the 2000 Conference on Computer Supported Cooperative Work (CSCW)* (Vol. Video Program, pp. 350). Philadelphia, PA: ACM Press.

Connell, J. B., Mendelsohn, G. A., Robins, R. W., & Canny, J. (2001). Effects of Communication Medium on Interpersonal Perceptions: Don't Hang Up the Telephone Yet! In *Proceedings of the 2001 International ACM SIGGROUP Conference on Supporting Group Work (GROUP)* (pp. 117 - 124). Boulder, CO: ACM Press.

Danet, B. (2001a). *Cyberpl@y: Communicating Online*. New York, NY: Berg Publishers.

Danet, B. (2001b). *Studies of Cyberpl@y: Ethical and Methodological Aspects*: Case study prepared for the Ethics Working Group, Association of Internet Researchers (http://atar.mscc.huji.ac.il/~msdanet/papers/ethics2.pdf).

Department of Health, Education, and Welfare. (1979). *The Belmont Report: Ethical Principles and Guidelines for the Protection of Human Subjects of Research*. Washington, D.C.: OPRR Reports.

Dery, M. (Ed.). (1993). *Flame Wars: The Discourse of Cyberculture*. Durham, NC: Duke University Press.

DiMicco, J. M., Pandolfo, A., & Bender, W. (2004). Influencing Group Participation with a Shared Display. In *Proceeding of the 2004 Conference on Computer-Supported Cooperative Work (CSCW)* (pp. 614 - 627). Chicago, IL: ACM Press.

Directive 95/46/EC of the European Pariament. (1995). *Official Journal of the European Communities*.

Directive 2002/58/EC of the European Parliament. (2002). *Official Journal of the European Communities*.

Ess, C. (2002). *Ethical Decision-Making and Internet Research: Recommendations from the AoIR Ethics Working Committee*: Association of Internet Researchers (AoIR).

Ess, C. (Ed.). (1996). *Philosophical Perspectives on Computer-Mediated Communication*. Albany: State University of New York Press.

Eysenbach, G., & Till, J. E. (2001, 10 November). Ethical Issues in Qualitative Research on Internet Communities. *BMJ, 323*, 1103-1105.

Farnham, S., Chesley, H. R., McGhee, D. E., Kawal, R., & Landau, J. (2000). Structured Online Interactions: Improving the Decision-Making of Small Discussion Groups. In *Proceedings of the 2000 Conference on Computer Supported Cooperative Work (CSCW)* (pp. 299 - 308). Philadelphia, PA: ACM Press.

France, E. F., Anderson, A. H., & Gardner, M. (2001). The Impact of Status and Audio Conferencing Technology on Business Meetings. *International Journal of Human-Computer Studies, 54*(6), 857-876.

Frankel, M. S., & Siang, S. (1999). *Ethical and Legal Aspects of Human Subjects Research on the Internet*: American Association for the Advancement of Science (AAAS).

Greist, J. H., Klein, M. H., & VanCura, L. J. (1973). A Computer Interview by Psychiatric Patient Target Symptoms. *Archives of General Psychiatry, 29*, 247-253.

Habermas, J. (1962). *The Structural Transformation of the Public Sphere: An Inquiry into a Category of Bourgeois Society* (T. Burger & F. Lawrence, Trans.). Cambridge, MA: MIT Press.

Habermas, J. (1990). *Moral Consciousness and Communicative Action* (C. Lenhardt & S. W. Nicholsen, Trans.). Cambridge, MA: MIT Press.

Habermas, J. (1993). *Justification and Application: Remarks on Discourse Ethics* (C. P. Cronin, Trans.). Cambridge, MA: MIT Press.

Halverson, C. A., Erickson, T., & Sussman, J. (2003). What Counts as Success? Punctuated Patterns of Use in a Persistent Chat Environment. In *Proceedings of the 2003 International ACM SIGGROUP Conference on Group Work (GROUP)* (pp. 180 - 189). Sanibel Island, FL: ACM Press.

Handel, M., & Herbsleb, J. D. (2002). What is Chat Doing in the Workplace? In *Proceedings of the 2002 Conference on Computer Supported Cooperative Work (CSCW)* (pp. 1 - 10). New Orleans, LA: ACM Press.

Hart, K. (2005, May 6). Your Blog or Your Job? *The Washington Examiner*, http://www.dcexaminer.com/articles/2005/05/05/opinion/op-ed/64oped06hart.txt.

Herring, S. (1996a). Linguistic and Critical Analysis of Computer-Mediated Communication: Some Ethical and Scholarly Considerations. *The Information Society, 12*(2), 153 - 168.

Herring, S. C. (Ed.). (1996b). *Computer-Mediated Communication: Linguistic, Social and Cross-Cultural Perspectives*. Philadelphia, PA: John Benjamins Publishing Co.

Horn, S. (1998). *Cyberville: Clicks, Culture, and the Creation of an Online Town*. New York: Time Warner.

Hudson, J. M., & Bruckman, A. (2002). IRC Français: The Creation of an Internet-based SLA Community. *Computer Assisted Language Learning, 15*(2), 109-134.

Hudson, J. M., & Bruckman, A. (2004a). The Bystander Effect: A Lens for Understanding Patterns of Participation. *Journal of the Learning Sciences, 13*(2), 169-199.

Hudson, J. M., & Bruckman, A. (2004b). "Go Away": Participant Objections to Being Studied and the Ethics of Chatroom Research. *The Information Society, 20*(2), 127 - 139.

Humphreys, L. (1970). *Tearoom Trade: Impersonal Sex in Public Places*. Hawthorne, NY: Aldine de Gruyter.

Joinson, A. N. (1998). Causes and Implications of Disinhibited Behavior on the Internet. In J. Gackenbach (Ed.), *Psychology and the Internet: Intrapersonal, Interpersonal, and Transpersonal Implications* (pp. 43-60). San Diego: Academic Press.

Joinson, A. N. (2003). *Understanding the Psychology of Internet Behavior: Virtual Worlds, Real Lives*. New York, NY: Palgrave Macmillan.

Kant, I. (1981). *Grounding for the Metaphysics of Morals* (J. W. Ellington, Trans.). Indianapolis, IN: Hackett Publishing Co.

Katz v. United States, 389 U.S. 347 (U.S. Supreme Court 1967).

Keller, H. E., & Lee, S. (2003). Ethical Issues Surrounding Human Participants Research Using the Internet. *Ethics and Behavior, 13*(3), 211 - 219.

Kiesler, S., Siegel, J., & McGuire, T. W. (1984). Social Psychological Aspects of Computer-Mediated Communication. *American Psychologist, 39*(10), 1123-1134.

King, S. A. (1996). Researching Internet Communities: Proposed Ethical Guidelines for Reporting of Results. *The Information Society, 12*(2), 119 - 127.

Korn, J. H. (1997). *Illusions of Reality: A History of Deception in Social Psychology.* Albany: State University of New York Press.

Kraut, R., Olson, J., Banaji, M., Bruckman, A., Cohen, J., & Couper, M. (2004). Psychological Research Online: Report of Board of Scientific Affairs' Advisory Group on the Conduct of Research on the Internet. *American Psychologist, 59*(2), 105 - 117.

Matheson, K., & Zanna, M. P. (1988). The Impact of Computer-Mediated Communication on Self-Awareness. *Computers in Human Behavior, 4*(3), 221-233.

Milgram, S. (1974). *Obedience to Authority: An Experimental View.* New York, NY: Harper Perennial.

Mill, J. S. (1998). Utilitarianism. In R. Crisp (Ed.), *J.S. Mill: Utilitarianism* (pp. 47 - 110). New York, NY: Oxford University Press.

Nardi, B. A., Schiano, D. J., & Gumbrecht, M. (2004). Blogging as Social Activity, or, Would You Let 900 Million People Read Your Diary? In *Proccedings of Computer-Supported Cooperative Work (CSCW) 2004* (pp. 222 - 231). Chicago, IL: ACM Press.

Nardi, B. A., Whittaker, S., & Bradner, E. (2000). Interaction and Outeraction: Instant Messaging in Action. In *Computer Supported Cooperative Work (CSCW) 2000* (pp. 79-88). Philadelphia, PA: ACM Press.

Nonnecke, B., & Preece, J. (2000). Lurker Demographics: Counting the Silent. In *Preedeedings of the 2000 Conference on Human Factors in Computing Systems (CHI)* (pp. 73-80). The Hague, The Netherlands: ACM Press.

The Nuremberg Code. (1949). *Trials of War Criminals Before the Nuremberg Military Tribunals Under Control Council Law, 2*(10), 181-182.

O'Neill, J., & Martin, D. (2003). Text Chat in Action. In *Proceedings of the 2003 International ACM SIGGROUP Conference on Group Work (GROUP)* (pp. 40 - 49). Sanibel Island, FL: ACM Press.

Postmes, T., & Spears, R. (1998). Deindividuation and Antinormative Behavior: A Meta-Analysis. *Psychological Bulletin, 123*(3), 238-259.

Reid, E. (1996). Informed Consent in the Study of On-Line Communities: A Reflection on the Effects of Computer-Mediated Social Research. *The Information Society, 12*(2), 169 - 174.

Rheingold, H. (1993). *The Virtual Community: Homesteading on the Electronic Frontier.* New York: HarperCollins.

Rimm, M. (1995). Marketing Pornography on the Information Superhighway: A Survey of 917,410 Images, Descriptions, Short Stories, and Animations Downloaded 8.5 Million Times by Consumers in Over 2000 Cities in Forty Countries, Provinces, and Territories. *Georgetown Law Journal, 83*(6), 1849 - 1934.

Schrum, L. (1997). Ethical Research in the Information Age: Beginning the Dialog. *Computers in Human Behavior, 13*(2), 117-125.

Smith, M., Cadiz, J., & Burkhalter, B. (2002). Conversation Trees and Threaded Chats. In *Proceedings of the 2002 Conference on Computer Supported Cooperative Work (CSCW)* (pp. 97 - 105). New Orleans, LA: ACM Press.

Smith, M. A., & Kollock, P. (Eds.). (1999). *Communities in Cyberspace.* New York, NY: Routledge.

Spears, R., Lea, M., & Postmes, T. (2001). Social Psychological Theories of Computer-Mediated Communication: Social Pain or Social Gain? In W. P. Robinson & H. Giles (Eds.), *The New Handbook of Language and Social Psychology (Second Edition)* (pp. 601-624). New York, NY: John Wiley and Sons.

Sproull, L., & Kiesler, S. (1991). *Connections: New Ways of Working in the Networked Organization.* Cambridge: MIT Press.

Thomas, J. (1996a). Introduction: A Debate about the Ethics of Fair Practices for Collecting Social Science Data in Cyberspace. *The Information Society, 12*(2), 107 - 117.

Thomas, J. (1996b). When Cyberresearch Goes Awry: The Ethics of the Rimm "Cyberporn" Study. *The Information Society, 12*(2), 189 - 198.

Wallace, P. (1999). *The Psychology of the Internet.* New York, NY: Cambridge University Press.

Walther, J. B. (1996). Computer-Mediated Communication: Impersonal, Interpersonal, and Hyperpersonal Interaction. *Communication Research, 23*(1), 3-44.

Walther, J. B. (2002). Research Ethics in Internet-Enabled Research: Human Subjects Issues and Methodological Myopia. *Ethics and Information Technology, 4*(3), 205 - 216.

Waskul, D., & Douglass, M. (1996). Considering the Electronic Participant: Some Polemical Observations on the Ethics of On-Line Research. *The Information Society, 12*(2), 129 - 139.

Weisband, S., & Kiesler, S. (1996). Self Disclosure on Computer Forms: Meta-Analysis and Implications. In *Proceedings of Human Factors in Computing Systems (CHI) 1996* (pp. 3-10). Vancouver, Canada: ACM Press.

Williams, K. D., Cheung, C. K. T., & Choi, W. (2000). Cyberostracism: Effects of Being Ignored Over the Internet. *Journal of Personality and Social Psychology, 79*(5), 748 - 762.

Woodruff, A., & Aoki, P. M. (2003). How Push-To-Talk Makes Talk Less Pushy. In *Proccedings of the 2003 International ACM SIGGROUP Conference on Supporting Group Work (GROUP)* (pp. 170 - 179). Sanibel Island, FL: ACM Press.

H. Gellersen et al. (eds.), ECSCW 2005: Proceedings of the Ninth European
Conference on Computer-Supported Cooperative Work, 18-22 September 2005, Paris,
France, 307–324.

Community-based Learning: Design Patterns and Frameworks

John M. Carroll and Umer Farooq

Center for Human-Computer Interaction and School of Information Sciences and
Technology

The Pennsylvania State University, University Park, PA 16802 USA

jcarroll@ist.psu.edu, ufarooq@ist.psu.edu

Abstract. Information technology adoption and literacy are typically not first-order goals
for community-based volunteer organizations. Nonetheless, information technology is
vital to such groups for member recruiting and management, communication and visibility
to the community, as well as primary group activities. However, volunteer organizations
are often not able to make effective use of Internet-based technologies and content. They
lack resources of all sorts (money, skills, telecommunications infrastructure) as well as
organizational structures, protocols, and continuity to effectively cope with the rate of
change in Internet technology. We describe a *design pattern*, a standard solution schema
for a recurring problem, that proposes a self-sustained process in which volunteer
organizations identify and analyze their technology needs, and then learn about
information technology through active engagement in solving their own problems. The
pattern, called Community-based Learning, is grounded in our fieldwork experience in
several community computing projects. We discuss patterns and pattern frameworks as a
research approach to community computing.

Introduction

Personal computing and the World-Wide Web (WWW) have made information
technology (IT) far more accessible and versatile. More people interact
collaboratively with IT than ever before, and for many the key tool and
environment is their Web browser. However, most users of the WWW are

consumers and relatively passive observers, rather than producers and active participants. The WWW is a highly effective delivery channel for government and commercial information and medium for form-filling transactions, but it does not as effectively afford opportunities for creative and active end-user participation, such as designing Web sites and publishing of Web content.

Yet there has never been a time when it is more critical for everyone to relate to and to participate in IT actively and creatively. Many recreational, learning, and work activities require at least some IT skill, and this is becoming more pervasive. People who do not have these skills or who cannot acquire these skills may become marginalized in the society of the future.

The point of departure for our project is the observation that community-based volunteer organizations, like church groups, service organizations, arts and cultural groups, clubs and recreational groups, are paradoxically both more important and less well-supported than in the past. They are more important because they are bastions against the decline of community described by Bellah, Madsen, Sullivan, Swindler and Tipton (1986) and by Putnam (2000) among others, and because this sector of organizational activity is growing rapidly. In the state of Pennsylvania, for example, there are now 700,000 non-profit organizations, compared to only 12,500 in 1940. Moreover, non-profit organizations, which are largely community-based and rely heavily on volunteer labor, now account for about 10% of total employment in the state (Grobman, 2002).

(Nota Bene that many of our literature sources and analyses are deliberately restricted to American society, and more specifically to the states of Pennsylvania and Virginia. This is reflects the locations of our primary study sites. As far as we can tell from visits and discussions with European colleagues, the larger situation characteristics are not dramatically different in at least some other western societies. We simply do not know how our sources, observations, and analyses might generalize to other, especially non-western, societies.)

But community volunteer organizations are less well supported with respect to IT than in the past. No longer can an organization function with a typewriter and a telephone. Maintaining PCs, networks, and software, perhaps even servers, and obtaining or otherwise organizing training and other personnel support is an order of magnitude more expensive, financially and with respect to organizational structures.

Our premise is that the learning of key technology skills and the motivation for applying those skills are increased when people are empowered to become creators rather than consumers of technology. This premise derives from diverse research in psychology showing that *perceived control* is critical to effective engagement, learning and human development, and to the achievement of autonomous and sustained performance (Carroll, 1998; Deci and Ryan, 1985; Knowles, 1973; Ryan and Deci, 2000; Vygotsky, 1978).

This paper, in part, describes a "pattern", that is, a solution-schema, called "Community-based Learning". We draw upon discussions of design patterns in other disciplines such as architecture (Alexander, Ishikawa, Silverstein, Jacobson, Fiksdahl-King, and Angel, 1977) and software (Gamma, Helm, Johnson, and Vlissides, 1994). Patterns generally include a problem, a description of the problem's context, an analysis of relevant forces, that is, resources and trends that enable or constrain possible solutions to the problem, a statement of our solution to the problem, a discussion of how the resulting context, that is, how the problem context might be changed by adoption of our solution, and examples of the solution, pointers to instantiations of the pattern in our on-going work.

Patterns provide a common language to be shared among domain experts for codifying and developing design knowledge. For example, among Alexander's patterns is the Street Café pattern. The problem this pattern addresses is the need to enhance feelings of openness and access to people and activity in city spaces. The context is tightly packed, tall buildings and narrow streets, with many people anonymously hurrying along. The forces are construction and operation costs, the hassles of getting municipal approvals to open a café onto the sidewalk, the personal approach-avoidances of making eye contact and meeting others in public, and so forth. And so on. Documenting and analyzing the pattern provides a resource to designers and other design stakeholders for sharing and improving solutions.

In the balance of the paper, we first characterize the problem that our pattern, Community-based Learning, addresses, namely, that community volunteer organizations often cannot make effective use of Internet technologies and content. They have little control over their own IT and seldom participate actively in IT related activities. They need to use the Internet for member recruiting and management, communication and visibility to the community, as well as primary group activities. But they often lack relevant resources, including skills and equipment.

We then examine aspects of contemporary societal context bearing on this problem. IT is increasingly pervasive, and important to community organizations, but they and their members relate to it and participate in it in limited and fairly passive ways. Such passive interactions do lead to enhanced technology literacy and skills, but they also keep people from playing a more active and creative role in using technology (e.g., by becoming publishers of web content).

Thereafter, we present our solution to the problem. We advocate an active and collective process of problematizing technology, in which organizations recognize and analyze their technology practices and needs, and then learn about IT through contining engagement in solving their own problems. In the balance of the paper, we analyze how the original problematic context might be changed and improved by adoption of this solution, including aspects that go beyond the original problem statement. We exemplify how this solution pattern was implemented in real community settings.

More broadly, our concern, and the larger contribution of this paper, is to illustrate a research approach to codifying design knowledge in community computing through patterns and pattern frameworks. In community computing, where most technical interaction is deeply participatory and all about empowering people where they live, it is critical to be able to share design solutions. This is highly consistent with the developing methodological vision of pattern languages in CSCW and community computing (Erickson, 2000; Schuler, 2002).

Problem: Lack of Control over IT

Not so many years ago, it was a radical proposition to assert that community organizations could maintain information and manage activities through the Internet. Through the 1980s, community groups used the Internet to facilitate information dissemination, discussion, and joint activity pertaining to municipal government, public schools, civic groups, local events, community issues and concerns, and regional economic development and social services. Some of these projects have become touchstones of Internet activism—jobs, housing, and veterans' issues in the Berkeley Community Memory (Farrington and Pine, 1997), community health in the Cleveland Free Net (Beamish, 1995), problems of the homeless in the Santa Monica Public Electronic Network (Rogers, Collins-Jarvis and Schmitz, 1994), and public education and Native American culture in the Big Sky Telegraph (Uncapher, 1999).

In their decade, these projects were the leading edge of community networking. But in fact they were implemented on relatively simple networking software platforms—the file transfer protocol (ftp). People were inspired to be able to use this new medium to exchange civic information and perspectives with fellow citizens. But of course the broader context was that most civic and community-based organizations, and indeed most commercial and governmental organizations as well, were still operating in a world of typewriters and telephones.

Today, baseline expectations throughout western society about communication are different. One expects to be able to identify and access an organization's url (universal resource locator). One expects to be able to send or receive an email announcing a meeting. The pervasive adoption of email and the WWW present opportunities and challenges to community-based volunteer organizations. The opportunities are obvious. Organizations can get their message out for "free". Web communication may result in more time-efficient management of work, and so on.

The challenges are less obvious. The Web is easy and accessible to all, if accessibility means browsing. But when a community organization wants to post and serve current information about activities and new programs, it faces a host of issues — Who will design and create the Web site, the various pages, and the content in the pages? Who will maintain the site and contents, run the Web server, and update software? It is likely that no one in the organization has these skills. If so, it is unlikely that anyone wants to invest much time and effort into acquiring these skills.

The problem we are addressing is that community-based volunteer organizations experience a lack of control over their own IT. What makes the problem worse is that these organizations can have so little in-house expertise that they are not even able to recognize the extent to which they lack control, or to diagnose how they might begin to remedy the situation. An example from our own fieldwork was an environmental group who felt they were participating in IT activities over which they had control, because they had hired a commercial vendor to produce their web site. Indeed, when they wished to change the Web site design, they discovered that this outsourcing had deprived them of control. The vendor had all the knowledge, all the content, and all the code (Farooq, Merkel, Nash, Rosson, Carroll, and Xiao, 2005). Hence, part of the problematic lack of control over IT is not realizing that this problem exists in the first place.

Context: American Society and the Internet

A key context for the challenges that community-based organizations face with respect to control of their own IT is the rapid and pervasive growth of computing and the Internet during the past two decades. The WWW began as a way for elite military and academic groups to exchange information but has evolved rapidly into a powerful information source for ordinary citizens.

Our empirical work takes place in North America, chiefly in Pennsylvania and Virginia in the United States. Sixty three percent of American adults now use the Internet. Since 2000, the distribution of Internet users across gender, income, and race is surprisingly regular. Use of the Internet has become normal in daily life. On a typical day in 2004, 70 million adult Americans logged on to the Internet (about 35%), up from about 50 million in 2000. Fifty-eight million used email; 35 million got news; 24 million did job-related research; 24 million looked for political information. Ninety-four million Americans have used the Internet to find or to share health-related information; 97 million Americans have used government Web sites. Sixty-five percent of American Internet users believe that the Internet has helped their relationships with friends; 56% believe it has helped their relationships with their own family members. Sixty million American homes now have broadband Internet access, compared with 6 million in 2000. (All data are from Rainie and Horrigan, 2005).

These facts and trends contrasts interestingly with trends relating to the ability and interests of Americans in preparing for more active roles with respect to IT.

For example, undergraduate enrollments in computer science fell about 25% between 2000 and 2003 (Computer Research Association, 2003).

Moreover, as the Web has evolved, browsing, searching, and carrying out purchases has become easier and more accessible, while creating dynamic, interactive Web content has become increasingly more difficult, requiring server-based mechanisms (e.g., servers that support web-based discussion forums), embedded components written in other programming languages (e.g., Java applets, ActiveX controls, Flash, or JavaScript), or plug-ins that augment the user's browser and allow it to receive data in closed, proprietary formats. These advances create richer experiences for the passive information consumer on the Web, but they add technical obstacles for users interested in constructing novel, interactive functionality to their own creations.

Forces

Two of the key forces shaping the solution to the problem in this pattern are the lack of resources among volunteer community-based groups and the important role such groups play in social capital formation.

Lack of Resources

Community volunteer organizations generally lack financial resources, telecommunications infrastructure (high bandwidth connectivity), equipment, skills, and access to training. They lack almost every relevant resource to support an IT strategy. In our studies, we have found that it is typical for community organizations to have no budget line item for technology. In one case, a community organization we worked with only had Internet access via the home connections of its members; the organization as such had no connectivity other than its own phone line. Lack of resources is a force—it affects how community volunteer organizations will address the problem of having less control of their IT.

Lack of relevant resources is exacerbated by the fact that IT is generally *not* a core concern of these organizations. Not surprisingly, a local historical society is chiefly concerned with preservation of sites and artifacts, informal education programs, and interactions with school and community groups. Even though an outside consultant might conclude that IT is a key to addressing their primary concerns in an efficient and effective manner, they do not necessarily see it that way.

Social capital

Social capital is the generalized trust, social interaction, and mutual reciprocity throughout a group, a community, or a society (Coleman, 1990). Because community volunteer organizations depend upon intrinsic motivation and personal commitment, rather than material rewards, social capital formation and preservation is especially critical to their survival and growth (King, 2004). And the social capital produced through participation in these organizations is critical to the whole society (Putnam, 2000).

Indeed, many studies of contemporary American society have concluded that traditional mechanisms of social capital formation in American communities are in decline (e.g., Bellah, Madsen, Sullivan, Swindler, and Tipton, 1986; Putnam, 2000). For example, between the 1960s and the 1990s, participation rates in a variety of civic activities declined: Red Cross volunteering declined by 60 percent; participation in parent-teacher organizations declined by nearly half, membership in the League of Women Voters and in the Jaycees both declined by 40 percent; the number of people reporting that they attended a public meeting on town or school affairs in the past year has declined by more than a third; volunteering of Boy Scout troop leaders declined by a quarter; voter turnout in national elections declined by nearly a quarter; churchgoing and church-related activities declined by a sixth; the proportion of Americans who socialize with neighbors more than once a year declined by nearly a sixth.

In this societal context, the formation and preservation of social capital through participation in community groups has become of greater importance to the larger society.

Solution: Community-based Learning

An important alternative to formal pedagogy is learning *informally*. Informal learning refers to learning that occurs outside of classrooms, schools, and other formal instructional environments and activities, and it includes incidental, self-directed, and lifelong learning. People with existing and active commitments to their communities may find it more meaningful to learn about Web programming, for example, by helping to create a Web application for a community service organization, than by attending an intensive programming class. What we know about adult learners suggests that this would indeed be the case (e.g., Knowles, 1973).

In fact, informal learning represents an important part of the common culture of the Internet and its democratic and community roots (Rheingold, 1993). Informal learning of Web technologies often involves "learning by doing", for example, learning in the course of downloading and exploring new software, posting on newsgroups, getting product technical support, or copying and editing

314

useful or appealing Web pages. Such activities are often situated in "authentic" tasks, providing solutions to real, concrete problems that the learner faces either as an individual or as part of a group or community.

One solution to the problem of lack of control over IT is a self-sustained process of informal learning, in which organizations identify and analyze their technology needs, and then learn about IT through continuing engagement in solving their own problems. We describe this solution as comprising three facets: *reflection, analysis,* and *enactment* (see Figure 1). Reflection is a self-assessment on part of the community organization of its relationship to its own IT. It is more effective to come to the realization that there is a lack of control on one's own, than to be told there is a problem by another. Technology self-assessments and discussions of critical incidents within the organization are good approaches for this reflection. In the example, we discussed above, when the environmental group wanted to change their Web site and found that this would be a long and difficult process, they realized that they were not in control to the extent they wanted to be and needed to be.

Organizational competition with peer groups may also prompt reflection, such as multiple environmental organizations in a proximate community competing for project or operations funding from one government source.

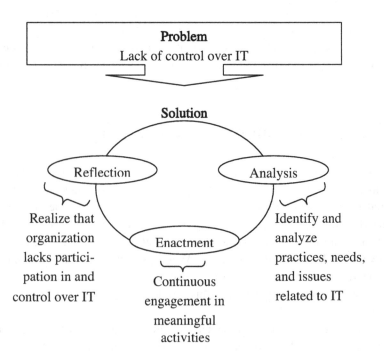

Figure 1. Solution schema for Community-based Learning.

The second facet is identification and analysis of organizational practices, needs, and issues related to IT. Community-based volunteer organizations are unique in that their work activities may be loosely coupled and minimally coordinated (Carroll, 2001) they depend primarily on volunteerism, they face a lack of financial and temporal resources, and so forth, which makes them unique. Technology needs and issues must be identified and analyzed in context of these unique structural features of community-based volunteer organizations. While technology provides many opportunities for these organizations to achieve their civic-oriented goals, community-based volunteer organizations still face formidable challenges in sustaining the use of technology (Merkel, Farooq, Xiao, Clitherow, Carroll, and Rosson, 2005). Part of the reason is that the adoption and use of technology is not aligned with their unique structure. Hence, these organizations must identify and analyze their organizational practices to see how IT can become a part of their organizational day-to-day activities. One way to achieve this is to develop technology plans by assessing the current status of work practices and technology-related activities in the organization (e.g., Techsoup, 2005).

The third facet of our pattern solution is enactment. The solution must be assimilated into everyday practices of the organization. In other words, learning about IT is an on-going facet of everyday activity, in the sense that Dewey (1916) described traditional models for situated learning as integrated into community activities, and in the sense that Lave and Wenger (1991) describe learning as the process of becoming a full participant in a socio-cultural practice. Enactment makes the solution sustainable (e.g., Merkel, Farooq, Xiao, Clitherow, Carroll, and Rosson, 2005).

The three facets are not stages. They are three aspects of the solution that can be discussed independently. Reflection, analysis, and enactment are all key to achieving more control over IT because they are interdependent. A community organization could be engaged in meaningful activities but may not realize that they are not in control of IT, or vice versa. The integration of these facets leveraged through the social mechanisms of the community allows community organizations to inspire and assist one another in learning about, utilizing, and developing skills for advanced IT tools and resources.

Resulting Context

It is difficult to project all the effects of any socio-technical innovation. Several likely consequences of Community-based Learning are the following:

(1) This pattern would help in achieving sustainable learning related to IT. IT is critical for community-based volunteer organizations to achieve their goals for many reasons: it increases their outreach to the larger geographical community, workload may be lightened by email and web-

based communication, and it may provide more convenience for interested stakeholders through features like online donations. However, with the fast-paced change in IT, these organizations have to continuously learn. Our pattern assigns sustainability a key role in the solution by emphasizing the need for *continuous* engagement in meaningful activities *over time.*

(2) This pattern would enhance organizational preservation of technical expertise. For community-based volunteer organizations, technical experts just like other volunteers are temporally volatile. They come, do an IT-related project(s), and go. Since these organizations cannot afford a continual supply of technical experts round the clock, it is natural for these organizations to consider preservation of technical *expertise* rather than *experts.* Our pattern solution, in effect, allows community organizations to develop IT-related knowledge management within the organization. Since community organizations would breed their own technical expertise, and would continuously learn and develop their IT skills over time, a culture of eliciting and packaging organizational memory emerges.

(3) This pattern would help to recast organizational practices related to IT. In our pattern solution, community-based volunteer organizations are cognizant of the fact that sustainable use of technology is key to their long-term success. Decision makers in such organizations make decisions by following a reflexive and proactive process of thinking about how particular technology-related decisions will affect the organizational goals and use of that technology in the near and far future. Part of this process involves perceiving how technology learning will be managed in their organization over time (e.g., Who will update the site when you are on vacation? Who will maintain the site if you, your technology person, or a volunteer leaves the organization?) and how will a long-term technology plan be incorporated as organizational practice (e.g., What will happen to the site when the grant runs out? Who is going to add content to these more dynamic features of the site?).

These consequences are some of the major ones that result from following our pattern solution. They all converge toward greater control over IT for community-based volunteer organizations. We now discuss our pattern solution with two examples in the next section that also illustrate some of the resulting context.

Examples

The Community-based Learning pattern can be illustrated in many community-oriented participatory action research (PAR) projects. Spring Creek Watershed Community (SCWC, http://www.springcreekwatershed.org) is a sustainable development, volunteer organization committed to regional environmental and economic planning, specifically, planning by watershed area rather that by individual municipalities. The organization works to explain this vision to the larger community, and to show how watersheds have an impact on quality of life and the local economy. We have been working with this organization during the past 18 months (Merkel, Xiao, Farooq, Ganoe, Lee, Carroll, and Rosson, 2004).

A major technology issue that SCWC faced was to redesign their web site. Before our involvement with the organization, SCWC hired a commercial vendor to develop and maintain their web site. SCWC was dissatisfied with the web site because it did not reflect their mission, overall goals, or the fact that they were a local organization concerned with environmental and economic planning. For example, whereas the goal of SCWC was local economic planning, influencing decision makers, and encouraging quality of life through watersheds, the web site depicted them as a generic tree-hugger group. Moreover, the vendor resisted any major restructuring of the web site and often times used his/her sole control over the community organization's technology to avoid changes. Critical incidents such as this forced SCWC to realize the problem. By delegating their web site design and maintenance to a commercial vendor, SCWC lacked control of IT because they were not active participants in web site related activities.

To address this problem, key stakeholders in SCWC first analyzed the situation. This was achieved by holding a kickoff meeting in which many volunteers from SCWC's social network were involved. The result of this meeting was that SCWC would itself redesign their web site so that they retain control over its management. The volunteers who attended this first meeting formed, by default, an informal technology committee that would deliberate over subsequent meetings to see SCWC's vision through.

During the web site redesign process, committee members had different perspectives on "design" that created tension between technical requirements and the need to organize information on the web site effectively. One of the more technical volunteers wanted to follow a rapid prototype approach by proposing several new designs for the web site, whereas another volunteer who had been working previously with SCWC suggested that content design should be done first. The latter proposal meant that layout design would be done afterwards—this would allow SCWC to focus on the organizational message they want to convey through their web site. Key stakeholders in SCWC agreed to the latter idea by being active participants in this negotiation process, trying to tease out the pros and cons of the different proposals put forward. This resulted in the creation of an expert-novice zone of proximal development that concretely led to achieving common ground and understanding through hierarchical modes of learning (Farooq, Merkel, Nash, Rosson, Carroll, and Xiao, 2005).

One way that key stakeholders from SCWC became active participants in the social context of the web site redesign process was through the use of scenarios as conceptual tools (Farooq, Merkel, Nash, Rosson, Carroll, and Xiao, 2005). Key stakeholders used scenarios to convey their input into the design process. Active engagement through scenarios had a direct effect in eliciting design, communicating design rationale, and resolving design conflicts. It also had an indirect effect by resulting in increased learning on part of the key stakeholders as they were now transitioning from legitimate peripheral participants to more core actors in the redesign process (Lave and Wenger, 1991).

The solutions adopted by SCWC had both short- and long-term implications. In the short-term, the current stakeholders in SCWC's web site have become more technology literate. For example, one of the key stakeholders before did not even know what HTML denoted, and now, after having engaged meaningfully in technology-related activities, is heavily involved in technical discussion forums and basic HTML coding. In the long-term, this solution will result in more autonomy over time, where learning is being captured and transformed into organizational expertise. Some evidence of this is currently being seen. For example, SCWC has incorporated technology-related knowledge management practices within the organization and has thus reduced the dependence on outside technical experts. SCWC now keeps a documented record of all their web site management activities, so that newer volunteers can come in and learn about how web site maintenance and update is done.

Another example of our Community-based Learning pattern comes from a project involving middle and high school science teachers in Giles and Montgomery counties (Virginia, USA) and researchers from Virginia Tech and the Pennsylvania State University (Carroll, Rosson, Dunlap, and Isenhour, 2003). This 5-year participatory action research project sought to facilitate resource and knowledge sharing among communities of teachers. This community included about 60 teachers, many of whom were intrinsically interested in sharing resources and knowledge with colleagues, and all of whom understood that they are under a sort of mandate to more effectively leverage one another. A special challenge for teachers is that they work all day in isolation from their professional colleagues. Moreover, the information technology in their classrooms is oriented to uses within the classroom, and not to supporting teacher collaboration.

A major focus of the project was helping teachers to articulate their frustrations with this situation and their interests and ambitions in collaborating more effectively within their community. This involved teacher-initiated identification of opportunities to share and exchange resources within their own teaching practices, and to recognize and analyze the ways in which IT did and did not support such practices.

A second focus of this project was the initial development and successive refinement of a web-accessible collaborative environment called Teacher Bridge (http://teacherbridge.org) to better support sharing and reusing a range of pedagogical artifacts, including lists of URLs, evolving lesson plans, and interactive activities. We tried to help the teachers to collectively establish new collaborative practices using the Teacher Bridge infrastructure.

For accessibility and familiarity, Teacher Bridge looks and behaves like a typical web site, with all content rendered as HTML and images. A key difference is that users can directly edit Web page content in the browser: Each page has an "Edit" link which supports editing and new page creation using a shorthand notation that requires no external authoring tools or knowledge of HTML. This design is intended to facilitate the kind of easy transition from browsing to authoring, and from authoring to collaborative authoring, that is supported in Swiki and similar wiki-based systems (Guzdial, Rick, and Kerimbaev, 2000).

Each page also has a "Full Editor" link that launches an interactive Java-based client. The Java client supports interactive authoring functionality that is not possible or practical using HTML-based forms. In our current implementation, this includes tools for drawing, creating data tables and charts, uploading files, and creating interactive maps. These data objects can have either static (text- or image-based) or interactive web representations and can be embedded in web pages created in the system.

The interactive client also supports synchronous collaboration. A user list displays the set of users currently logged into the system, and chat facilities provide a simple communication mechanism. All authoring tools also support synchronous interaction, so that users working together on the same object will see each other's changes as they are made. Our belief is that the integration of simple authoring tools, awareness features, and collaboration tools will encourage the kind of content reuse and skill sharing that was perhaps more common in the early days of the Web.

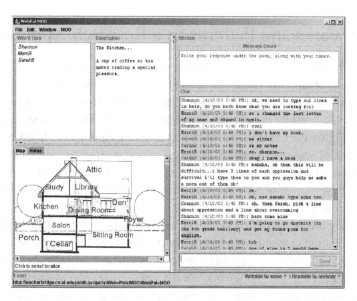

Figure 2. WebPals activity in Teacher Bridge.

An example teacher-designed project is WebPals (Figure 2), a reading and discussion activity for middle school students. The activity was originally created using a text-based multi-user domain (MUD). We developed a collection of Bridge objects for a graphical MUD, a set of "rooms" each with a user list, navigation map, message board, chat area for each, room description, and an optional object to swap with the map using a tab. The objects could be configured and copied easily to create new MUDs or, since each object has a web rendering and corresponding URL, each object could be accessed in a web browser. Adoption of this activity spread rapidly to other teachers; it seemed critical that the technology was demonstrated by peers, and could be quickly appropriated and repurposed.

Teacher Bridge was initially used by a handful of teachers and administrators. However, as part of a process involving the design of a new school website, the school administration decided to host a workshop to introduce Teacher Bridge to the entire staff. The workshop sessions, run by the teachers and administrators, walked groups of teachers through the process of setting up their own sites. In most cases, these were sites for individual teachers' classroom management, but in some cases, they were sites for groups of teachers, teams, or departments. As a result, many Teacher Bridge components were shared and reused among teachers (e.g., authentication privileges of web sites). The diversity of skills among the teachers actually helped strengthen the social network by distributing the burden of training. Using Teacher Bridge, no one teacher had to know everything, and no one teacher had to train everyone else.

Frameworks and Patterns as a Research Approach

Community-based Learning is a design pattern that is a specific solution to the recurring problem of lack of control over IT in community volunteer organizations. We believe that patterns, and related abstractions, offer a research approach that usefully couples codification and application of design knowledge. This is a highly desirable property in practical design domains like CSCW where many kinds of scientific knowledge necessarily converge and interact (see Carroll and Rosson, 2003, for general discussion). In the balance of this discussion, we describe how our approach recruits the notion of *frameworks* from software design to codify knowledge for design.

A framework is a reusable design of all or part of a system that is the skeleton of an application customizable by a software developer (Gamma, Helm, Johnson, and Vlissides, 1994). Frameworks are expressed in a programming language— they are code. A single framework usually contains several to many patterns, and in this sense patterns are narrower than frameworks (Johnson, 1997). Patterns are embodied in and illustrated through their roles in frameworks. Patterns are more abstract, and can be viewed as micro-architectural elements of frameworks. A well-known example in software engineering is the role of the observer, composite, and strategy patterns in the model-view-controller framework (Gamma, Helm, Johnson, and Vlissides, 1994).

In the CSCW domain of community computing, frameworks are the various types of community networks, community portals, and community organization Web sites. For example, Spring Creek Web site (section 7) instantiates a design framework: It consists of a shallow information hierarchy navigated by a permanently-displayed dynamic menu that foregrounds a statement of the organization's mission, a rationale, and a newsletter archive. The primary graphical content is a set of images depicting typical landmarks throughout the Spring Creek Watershed. This Web site is literally code, but more specifically it is a code base over which the Spring Creek organization now exerts substantial control. It exemplifies an application skeleton that could be immediately repurposed with a few cut-and-paste operations.

As described earlier, the *Community-based Learning* design pattern is an architectural element of this framework. The framework embodies and illustrates the pattern, but it also shows how the knowledge codified in the pattern interacts in design implementation with other patterns. For example, another recurring problem for community organizations is that of *preparing and disseminating newsletters* (Merkel, Xiao, Farooq, Ganoe, Lee, Carroll, and Rosson, 2004). This pattern is also evident in the Web site framework; the current newsletter and the newsletter archive are one click away from the homepage display of the organization's mission and strategic goals. This pattern (which we have not yet analyzed in the same detail as *Community-based Learning*) highlights the need to organize members to contribute content and editorial assistance, and to streamline the formatting of newsletter content into email, Web pages, and other formats (e.g., *pdf* file). It suggests, for example, solution approaches like Wiki-based interface through which organizational stakeholders can add newsletter content without worrying about the details of formatting tags, and possibly press a button to generate the newsletter as a *pdf* file styled according to a pre-defined template.

Another community-oriented design pattern could address the problem of *managing different volunteers* who have a variety of technical skills and vested interests. Within the web site framework, this pattern implies the problem of who does what on the web site while keeping organizational goals in mind. In our fieldwork, we have observed that community organizations want to micro-manage volunteers in relation to specific Web site tasks. In our work with Spring Creek, it was noted that they did not want all volunteers to be able to update the entire web site because it may be detrimental to the organization (volunteers' interest may not match organizational mission, volunteers may involuntarily delete vital content, etc). One possible solution that was discussed was to grant access rights to specific volunteers so they could change web site content only for the sections they had privileges to.

The *preparing newsletters* and *managing different volunteers* are two related patterns to *community-based learning*. We discussed these patterns in context of the *Web site* framework.

Linking patterns explicitly to pattern frameworks is a critical step in developing patterns as a medium for effectively codifying design knowledge. For example, Schuler's (2002) impressive pattern language collection has had limited utility and impact. This collection is organized as a searchable list. It does not link patterns to frameworks, either in the sense of providing concrete exemplification (i.e., code) or in the sense of illustrating how multiple patterns can work together. Thus, it does not provide enough support for bridging from knowledge to design.

First, using the notion of frameworks in community computing gives us an analytic lens to *concretely* study recurring problems in this domain. Patterns themselves are abstract constructs that have little meaning and implication without context. Frameworks add this context by tangibly illustrating the use of patterns. Community-based learning, for example, would be demonstrably weak as a pattern if it were not applied to the Web site framework.

Second, frameworks enable researchers and practitioners to apply multiple patterns *interdependently*. Without frameworks, patterns would exist in isolation with loosely conjectured relations amongst themselves. Frameworks strengthen these loose relations by evoking synergies and tradeoffs between multiple patterns. In the Web site framework example, granting access rights to different volunteers in the *managing different volunteers* pattern may conflict with learning through engagement in the *Community-based Learning* pattern. This is because the former means more time needs to be expended to manage different volunteers, which leaves less time to actively engage in meaningful activities, therefore implying decreased learning.

In community computing, organizations such as community-based volunteer organizations are needy for practical solutions they encounter everyday because of the multivalent challenges they face. In addition to practical solutions, the need for developing abstractions is clear in community computing if we want to inculcate a culture of developing coherent and reusable scientific knowledge in this inter-disciplinary domain. Community-based learning, as a design pattern, and our integrated approach, comprising frameworks and patterns, set a research trajectory to develop such practical *and* abstract models in community computing.

Acknowledgment

We thank our colleagues in the Civic Nexus and Teacher Bridge projects: Daniel Dunlap, Craig Ganoe, Philip Isenhour, Roderick Lee, Cecelia Merkel, Janet Montgomery, Dennis Neale, Michael Race, Mary Beth Rosson, Wendy Schafer, and Lu Xiao. We are grateful to the US National Science Foundation (grant numbers 0106552, 0342547, 0353101, 0429274) for supporting this research.

References

Alexander, C., Ishikawa, S., Silverstein, M., Jacobson, M., Fiksdahl-King, I., and Angel, S. (1977): *A Pattern Language: Towns, Buildings, Construction*, Oxford University Press, NY, USA.

Beamish, A. (1995): *Communities On-Line: Community-Based Computer Networks*, Masters Thesis, Department of Urban Studies and Planning, MIT.

Bellah, R., Madsen, R., Sullivan, W., Swindler, A. and Tipton, S. (1986): *Habits of the heart: Individualism and commitment in American life*, University of California Press, CA, USA.

Carroll, J. M. (1998): *Minimalism beyond the Nurnberg Funnel*, The MIT Press, Cambridge, MA, USA.

Carroll, J. M. (2001): 'Community computing as human-computer interaction', *Behaviour and Information Technology*, vol. 20, no. 5, pp. 307-314.

Carroll, J. M., Chin, G., Rosson, M. B. and Neale, D. C. (2000): 'The development of cooperation: Five years of participatory design in the virtual school', *Proceedings of ACM Symposium on Designing Interactive Systems: DIS'2000* (Brooklyn, New York, August 17-19 2000), ACM, New York, pp. 239-251.

Carroll, J. M. and Rosson, M. B. (2003): 'Design rationale as theory', in J.M. Carroll (ed.): *HCI models, theories and frameworks: Toward a multidisciplinary science*, Morgan-Kaufmann, San Francisco, CA, USA, 2003, pp. 431-461.

Carroll, J. M., Rosson, M. B. Dunlap, D. R. and Isenhour, P. L. (2003): 'Frameworks for Sharing Knowledge: Toward a Professional Language for Teaching Practices', *Proceedings of the 36th Hawaii International Conference on System Sciences: HICSS-36* (Kona, Hawaii, January 6-9 2003), IEEE Computer Society, Washington DC, USA.

Coleman, J. S. (1990): *The foundations of social theory*, Harvard University Press, Cambridge, MA, USA.

Computer Research Association. (2003): 'Taulbee Survey', accessed at http://www.cra.org/ on March 1, 2005.

Deci, E. L., and Ryan, R. M. (1985): *Intrinsic motivation and self-determination in human behavior.* Plenum, New York.

Dewey, J. (1916): *Democracy in Education*, Macmillan, New York.

Dunlap, D. R., Neale, D. C. and Carroll, J. M. (2000): 'Teacher collaboration in a networked community', *Educational Technology and Society,* vol. 3, no. 3, pp. 442-454.

Erickson, T. (2000): 'Lingua francas for design: Sacred places and pattern languages', *Proceedings of ACM Symposium on Designing Interactive Systems: DIS'2000* (Brooklyn, New York, August 17-19 2000), ACM, New York, pp. 357-368.

Farooq, U., Merkel, C., Nash, H., Rosson, M. B., Carroll, J. M. and Xiao, M. (2005): 'Participatory design as apprenticeship: Sustainable watershed management as a community computing application', *Proceedings of the 38th Hawaii International Conference on System Sciences: HICSS-38* (January 3-6, 2005, Big Island, Hawaii), IEEE Computer Society, Washington DC, USA.

Farrington. C. and Pine, E. (1997): 'Community memory: A case study in community communication', in P. Agre and D. Schuler (eds.), *Reinventing technology, rediscovering community: Critical explorations of computing as a social practice*, Albex, Greenwich, CT, USA, 1997, pp. 219-228.

Gamma, E., Helm, R., Johnson, R., and Vlissides, J. (1994): *Design Patterns: elements of reusable object-oriented software*, Addison-Wesley, Reading, MA, USA.

Grobman, G. M. (2002): *Pennsylvania Nonprofit Handbook: Everything You Need to Know to Start and Run Your NonProfit Organization*, White Hat Communications.

Guzdial, M., Rick, J., and Kerimbaev, B. (2000):' Recognizing and Supporting Roles in CSCW', *Proceedings of the Conference on Computer Supported Cooperative Work* (Philadelphia, Pennsylvania, December 2-6 2000), ACM Press, NY, pp. 261-268.

Johnson, R. E. (1997): 'Frameworks = (Components and Patterns)', *Communications of the ACM*, vol. 40, no. 10, pp. 39-42.

King, N. K. (2004): 'Social Capital and Nonprofit Leaders', *Nonprofit Management & Leadership*, vol. 14, no. 4, pp. 471-486.

Knowles, M. S. (1973): *The adult learner: A neglected species*, Gulf Publishing Company, American Society for Training and Development, Houston, TX, USA.

Lave, J., and Wenger, E. (1991): *Situated learning: Legitimate peripheral participation*, Cambridge University Press, New York.

Merkel, C. B., Xiao, L., Farooq, U., Ganoe, C. H., Lee, R., Carroll, J. M. and Rosson, M. B. (2004): 'Participatory design in community computing contexts: tales from the field', *Proceedings of the 8th Conference on Participatory Design: Artful Integration: Interweaving Media, Materials and Practices* (Toronto, Ontario, Canada, July 27-31 2004), ACM Press, New York, pp. 1-10.

Merkel, C. B., Clitherow, M., Farooq, U., Xiao, L., Ganoe, G. H., Carroll, J. M. and Rosson, M. B. (2005): 'Sustaining computer use and learning in community computing contexts: Making technology part of "who they are and what they do"', *The Journal of Community Informatics* [Online], vol. 1, no. 2, 134-150.
URL: http://ci-journal.net/viewarticle.php?id=53&layout=html.

Putnam, R. (2000): *Bowling Alone: The Collapse and Revival of American Community*, Simon & Schuster: New York.

Rainie, L. and Horrigan, J. (January, 25, 2005): 'A decade of adoption: How the Internet has woven itself into American life', *Trends 2005*, Pew Research Center, accessed at http://pewresearch.org/ on March 1, 2005.

Rheingold, H. (1993): *The Virtual Community: Homesteading on the Electronic Frontier*, Addison-Wesley, Reading, MA, USA.

Rogers, E. M., Collins-Jarvis, L. and Schmitz, J. (1994): 'The PEN Project in Santa Monica: Interactive communication, equality, and political action', *Journal of the American Society for Information Science*, vol. 45, no. 6, pp. 401-410.

Ryan, R. M., and Deci, E. L. (2000): 'Self-determination theory and the facilitation of intrinsic motivation, social development, and well-being', *American Psychologist*, vol. 55, pp. 68-78.

Schuler, D. (2002): 'A pattern language for living communication', *Proceedings of the 6th Conference on Participatory Design* (Malmo, Sweden, June 23-25 2002), CPSR, Palo Alto, CA, USA, pp. 434-436.

Techsoup. (2005): 'Technology Planning', accessed at http://www.techsoup.com/howto/articles.cfm?topicid=11&topic=Technology%20Planning on March 2, 2005.

Uncapher, W. (1999): 'Electronic homesteading on the rural frontier: Big Sky Telegraph and its community', in M. Smith and P. Kollock (eds.), *Communities in Cyberspace*, Routledge, 1999, pp. 264-289.

Vygotsky, L. S. (1978): *Mind and society: The development of higher mental processes*, Harvard University Press, Cambridge, MA, USA.

Wellman, B. (1982): 'Studying personal communities', in P. Marsden and N. Lin (eds.), *Social Networks and Social Structure*, Sage, Beverly Hills, CA, USA, 1982, pp. 61-80.

H. Gellersen et al. (eds.), ECSCW 2005: Proceedings of the Ninth European
Conference on Computer-Supported Cooperative Work, 18-22 September 2005, Paris,
France, 325–345

Expertise Sharing in a Heterogeneous Organizational Environment

Tim Reichling and Michael Veith

Institute for Information Systems and New Media, University of Siegen, Germany
{Reichling; Veith}@fb5.uni-siegen.de

Abstract. The term knowledge management (KM) has lost most of its magic during the
past few years: While knowledge has been identified as an important resource and key
factor for productivity gains and innovation in organizations, there seems to be no
generally applicable (and easy) way to utilize this resource. In this paper we present
results of a field study that was conducted within a major European industrial association.
The study focused on knowledge intense processes among the association and its
member companies which were supposed to be improved by KM strategies and systems.
The organizational setting appears to be unique in different ways: A grown and highly
decentralized organizational structure, goods that exclusively consist of human and social
capital and a distinct mutual unawareness of competencies and responsibilities within the
organization define our field of application.

Introduction

Cohen and Prusak (2001) predict that there is a high potential for companies to
increase productivity and speed of innovation cycles by enabling the actors to
build *social* and *human capital*. These terms refer to human resources like
abilities, social networks as well as explicit and implicit knowledge of employees
in organizations. One basic assumption is that the utilization of these resources
would be the next step in empowerment of companies in the technical and
engineering sector by enhancing knowledge intensive processes after "dimensions
of productivity" had reached their limits. This is where KM strategies and KM
systems are expected to lead to success.

The research field of KM is widely spread: It includes different domains
concerned with seeking, visualizing or structuring sources of knowledge. We

roughly differ between explicit and implicit / tacit knowledge where explicit knowledge can be easily externalized in documents or certain binary forms and implicit and tacit knowledge (expertise) cannot (Hinds and Pfeffer, 2003). Instead implicit knowledge (including experiences or practices) is closely bound to human actors. Hence IT supporting KM in terms of implicit knowledge includes groupware tools like recommender systems or yellow pages systems (YP) that focus on utilizing social and human capital rather than content[1]. Examples of those systems are *Who Knows* (Streeter and Lochbaum, 1988) or *Yenta* (Foner, 1997), *Expert Finder* (Vivacque and Lieberman, 2000) or *Expertise Recommender* (McDonald, 2000 and 2001). All these systems create and store user profiles by interpreting certain artefacts like emails, Java source code or documents. Furthermore these systems focus on expertise rather than content which purely repository-based systems are not capable of (cf. Ackerman, 1998; Ackerman and McDonald, 1996; Pipek and Wulf, 2003).

As mentioned above, there are several problems in applying these technologies in practice, i.e. in a native organizational environment, in which a large amount of actors is expected to use a common system. Actors often have different skills, goals or cultural backgrounds which can lead to the failure of IT systems (Grudin, 1988; Grudin and Palen, 1995). Even the successful application of new technologies can have unexpected individual or organizational outcomes that are contrary to the initial goals as Orlikowski (1996) or Wulf and Pipek (1999) describe. As we still know little about the practice in those knowledge intensive processes, we claim that sufficient pre-studies within the application field are highly important for successful applications of KM strategies. In this paper we present the results of a field study that is part of a three year lasting project aiming on the application of KM strategies in a major European national industry association (NIA[2]).

Setting

The association NIA has almost 3000 member companies from technical branches in the broadest sense. Thus NIA is divided horizontally into 37 sections, each dedicated to companies of a certain sector[3] (like "agricultural technology", "lifts and escalators" or "pumps and systems") and vertically into general departments (like "business administration", "law" or "taxes"). Additionally, there are several spin offs and other subordinate units like forums, projects and regional offices. Member companies pay for their membership according to their size. These

---

[1]   In literature the term 'knowledge management' is ambiguously used. Whether or not 'information management' should be covered by the term of KM is not a matter of this paper.

[2]   "NIA" is not the real name.

[3]   In the following we will use the term "sector" in the sense of branch of industry, whereas "section" will refer to GIAs sectoral departments.

payments are the only source of income for NIA. Members in turn are welcome to request NIA's services, when they need them. NIA defines its core competencies as:

- *Networking* (Introducing member companies to each other for business transactions)
- *Technical* or *professional support*
- *Representation:* (lobbying at governmental (or other important) institutions – this kind of service is offered by NIA exclusively)

In the main department of NIA about 450 employees are working in one of the organizations' sections or departments. The project setting includes one of NIA's sector organizations, the agricultural department and one of its member companies (AGRAR[4]) representing a "typical" member company. AGRAR has about 280 employees. Its core competencies are municipal equipment and seeding technology.

The main goals of the KM project, in which our study took place, were (a little abstractly) defined as "improving the quality of services that NIA offers to its members". In a way the project can be seen as a reaction to an observed trend that members start to doubt about the meaning of their membership, which was a given in past decades. Nowadays managers are expected to justify expenses by giving some well defined 'Return On Investment' (ROI). This certainly is hard to calculate for the membership in an organization 'dealing' with *support, network* and *representation.* So one of the projects goals is to better define and present its services to the members and to make NIA and its members 'move closer to each other'. This shall be done by improving the mutual awareness of each other: The awareness of NIA's services on the members' side and the awareness of the members' needs on NIA's side.

An illustrative example should sharpen the projects vision. In short: When developing a new agricultural tractor, one member company fell into trouble as this machine – when the design phase was long ago – appeared not to be conform to certain regulations concerning its physical dimensions. This was very painful since the error could have been avoided by turning to the NIA who was in possession of this spatial information. In turn NIA was not aware of the company's intention of developing this kind of agricultural machine, and thus was unable to inform the company. KM strategies are now expected to connect both – NIA and its members – more efficiently to each other and may avoid situations like the one described.

---

4   "AGRAR" is not the real name

Methods

The methodological approach we made to the field follows the theoretical framework of *Integrated Organization and Technology Development* (OTD). Wulf & Rohde (1995) describe OTD as an evolutionary concept which tries to put technological, organizational, and human factors into consideration of observations in working environments. Not only does the introduction and establishment of novel technology influence particular work processes; even organizational structures and human habits are affected. Keeping that in mind, human and organizational needs have to be taken into account when new software solutions (as in the underlying field) shall support working processes. Practically we realized the OTD guidelines by employing the ethno methodological concept of "Studies of Work" to set personal and interpersonal stresses into focus (cf. Flick, 2002: 39ff, Bergmann, 2003: 129ff and Harper et al., 2000). Beside the observation of the setting – including workplace observations, investigations of the technical infrastructure and workshops on specific topics - our research included 16 semi-structured interviews (that were conducted within three cycles) with employees and managers of NIA. The majority of the interviewees were employees of the agricultural section; the others worked in several vertical units such as the staff-, IT- or standardization departments. The two managers headed the agricultural section and the IT department, respectively.

For each interview cycle we drew up a particular guideline. This allowed us to modify the guidelines evolutionarily as we assimilated those to our experience we gained in the interviews we had already done. These guidelines included questions concerned with issues like "everyday life on the job", "working history within NIA", "communication and cooperation among others" and "knowledge management and expertise sharing".

Our technique to work with an interview guideline which stimulated narrative responses offered the test persons to answer in a relatively open, free and talkative manner. By doing so, we were given the opportunity to reflect the interviews regarding an organizational and cultural environment, which is not described by certain personal attitudes. Much rather, we recognize our findings in an interpersonal, organizational context (cf. Randall and Bentley, 1994). Therefore, we tried to stir the interviews as little as possible. In order to guarantee solid and valid results we used a tape recorder to avoid note taking during the interviews, which would have influenced the fluency of the conversations negatively.

In order to manage the resulting empirical materials appropriately and not too time-intensively we decided to split the analysis into five specific steps (cf. Schmidt, 2003):

1. Orientated towards our written material, we built up certain 'ex-post' categories for the analysis. On the one hand, this categorization

followed the three important OTD supporting pillars (technology, organization, and human factors), but on the other hand - strongly geared towards the interviews - subcategories emerged.

2. We put together the analytical categories to a kind of coding guideline, which helped us to cluster the data in terms of meaningful units. Each unit built its own focus on a specific problem.

3. We coded the material in order to depersonalize and generalize the data.

4. We built up nodes of correlating units which provided a quantitative overview of the material. This also gave us a clue which questions and problems might be most prominent and urgent, and had to be reconsidered in any case in later steps of the project.

5. Finally, we thought about possible hypotheses which had been derived from the previous steps of analysis. On the basis of those we wrote the next guideline for the following interview cycle.

We employed the five steps mentioned above for each cycle. This shows some equivalence with the concept of action research (cf. Mills, 2003). By doing so, we believe to have realized two important needs: (1) participation of the persons and (2) consideration of the processes. Following OTD, both are considerable quantities as personal habits and organizational processes are affected by possible novel software solutions.

Empirical Findings and Results

After analyzing the interviews certain topics appeared to be central in terms of KM. These topics can roughly be assigned to the domains of organizational structure, work processes and knowledge management. As a result of the open styled interviews these topics were not identical with those of our guideline. Particularly those topics that were not addressed within our guideline but emerged during the sessions can be seen as highly relevant. For instance, participants independently addressed the complex organizational structure, organizational transparency, and coherence within NIA. These topics were not part of the initial guideline but emerged during the interview sessions. In the following sections we will have a closer look at the results in these domains.

Complex Organizational Structure

When asked to describe their starting time at NIA, several interviewees stated that they were overwhelmed by its organizational complexity: The association was judged to be very complex even by its own employees. As interviewees stated independently – but in accordance to each other – it took them about two years to learn "how NIA works" and to gain an appropriate view over the organizational structure. In this domain experienced employees have an advantage over novices. As some of the interviewees claimed, this complexity is a result of NIA being a grown organization (see above), that was created by the fusion of several independent associations. Two of the interviewees described their image of NIA in a very illustrative way:

> "If you are here for a while, you see: The structure of NIA is gigantic, you certainly need two years to look through it. There are really different companies. And those are for themselves. There is the incorporated society. Then there is the incorporation of science where Mr. W. is working. Then there is the publishing house, the assurance and so on…"

> "We have managers for every unit. And they're doing things on their own."

In the latter quote another problem becomes obvious that is caught up below: The 'organizational coherence', which some participants are missing.

Organizational Transparency

The organizational structure that was felt to be very complex may have led to a loss of transparency that some of the interviewees felt as well. It was stated that it was sometimes difficult to find persons within the organization that were competent or responsible for certain issues. This was seen as very painful particularly in situations where requests of member companies were to be answered urgently (see also: *Social Networking*). So it was stated during the interviews that it was very useful to have a more transparent organization, and thus, to be able to find accountable and / or competent persons quickly. Participants described their expectations this way:

> "If we had a rough idea of what everyone is doing [within NIA] – which of course is unmanageable for 450 people – then for us this would be a giant step forward"

> "The goal is to create transparency. Responsibilities must be clearly defined and assigned unambiguously."

The interviewees were aware of the fact that NIA's 'complex structure' does not make it easy for member companies' employees to get in contact with the right person in NIA, in case they do not know this person in advance. From their experience, they knew that member companies' employees in general see NIA as one large entity without recognizing its substructures. Thus, when they request NIA for a service, they expect to be redirected to the 'right' person there, no matter to whom they call or mail to. When looking at problems of 'complexity' and 'transparency', it is not surprising that sometimes this redirection does not work properly. Situations occurred – as interviewees reported – in which requests of member companies were handed over from one colleague to the next several times as no one knew – or could find out – who was responsible for that request.

When discussing these identified problems during the interview sessions, the idea emerged to set up some kind of call centre within NIA that people can access to be directed to the right person quickly and liable. This idea was seen critically by some of the interviewees. First, for the employees at NIA – who in general are experts in very special domains – it is very important to be directly requested. They fear that members could be directed to a "wrong" person at NIA and then receive wrong information, which would be more painful than to be redirected several times – but finally access the right person. Second, – as one person stated – there was already a switchboard which was working with a good "score rate", i.e. it reliably connects to the right expert.

Handling Members' Requests

In the interviews we were told that there were no guidelines or standardizations for handling requests or sending newsletters to member companies. Although most of the interviewees would find this useful, they pointed to severe problems occurring when applying such general guidelines. These problems are a result of NIA being an entity of self-determined sections (see below). As participants stated self-critically, members sometimes were treated 'careless' in one of the following ways:

- Information is arbitrarily sent to members without a request or indication of interest.
- Response times for handling (given) requests are too long – or requestors are left unaware about the time it takes to handle their requests.
- The catalogue of services is not well defined, so members sometimes do not know which service they can access.

Another problem that was reported by the interviewees is an "inappropriate understanding of responsibility" that some employees turned out to have (in some isolated cases). Examples were given in the interviews about persons at NIA who had not realized at all that in the end the member companies pay their wages with their membership subscriptions. So it should be perfectly natural for NIA's personal to handle the customers' requests with the highest priority, which sometimes is not the case. One interviewee found that:

"...some have an attitude that they should take care of."

What she was talking about was an insufficient motivation to carefully handle members' requests, particularly in cases when these requests had to be directed to another of NIA's employees or even to another section.

Some participants on the other hand uttered that it was difficult to avoid delays when handling requests because this would often collide with other urgent tasks. So in cases of conflicting tasks, employees naturally priorize those tasks that are given to them by their boss in order to avoid troubles. One participant stated it this way:

"When I'm told to work off that position paper by my boss, it would be pretty stupid to work first on those ten requests."

An 'exemplary' way to handle users' requests when colliding with other tasks was described by one participant. Whenever she was unable to directly answer a request – which simply cannot be prevented – she first let the requestor know how long it would take her to answer that request. This way she gave herself the time to solve or delegate that request without leaving the customer "in the dark". Finally, when the request was ready to be answered she (or some colleague) called the customer. Such a pattern of behaviour does not seem to be always followed. However, the idea of applying some kind of standardization or guideline for handling requests is hard to apply as we see below. Furthermore, we are given some interesting examples for peoples behaviour when faced with 'guidelines' (below within 'knowledge sharing').

Organizational Coherence

In one of the citations above another problem is addressed that must be seen apart from the insufficient motivation that some employees show – which certainly is a common problem many organizations have to deal with. We can outline this problem as an insufficient *organizational coherence* that itself is likely to be another result of the "wild-grown" organization. Some of the participants feel that there were no uniform goals and directions by which NIA as a whole would be defined and can be identified. Instead in a subtle way several sections have an own political attitude according to the sector they serve for. For example the attitude NIA as a whole stands for is to 'avoid subsidizations by the state at all'. This attitude is not very useful with regard to the agricultural sector as it is one of the major receivers of subsidies. So according to the assessment of another participant the sections still are...

"...highly self-determined and this certainly has many advantages, but sometimes effects of friction occur."

Another participant said it this way:

"Each section, each department, each corporation within NIA is a story of its own."

A third participant added some interesting reasoning for NIA having a 'lack of coherence': She assumes that after the break down of the USSR in the early 90s "major questions concerning strategies and visions" came up, since one of NIA's previous predominant tasks was to keep alive connections with the eastern economy. She felt that there was no vision for NIA as a whole. In her words:

"[...] so there is missing [...] a major vision, and this must be given from the top. From there it can be broken down to each single section for orientation and it must be repeated and communicated continuously till the message arrives and is understood everywhere in the organization."

Although the majority of interviewees stated that colleagues of different sections "of course" would cooperate well, some of them conceded that there was a subtle competition between those sections that serve for similar or related branches. This subtle rivalry is likely to additionally increase the loss of transparency and the willingness to cooperate. Even it makes it more difficult to set up common guidelines for interaction with members.

Work Processes

The work of NIAs' employees (especially those of the agricultural sector) is dominated by providing services to members (*technical support, representation*), preparing for certain events (exhibitions, standards committee meetings) and projects which are peripherally done. As exhibitions mean a lot of work in advance and members' requests cannot be anticipated, the workload of the colleagues varies highly according to these events.

As the application of novel technologies often enforces changes within work processes (see above) it is necessary to justify these changes. Many of the participants also emphasize this phenomenon. Changes of established processes would only be accepted and persistently applied if the executives behave competently and are "sent from above" supporting an overall strategy. Support on one hand eases the introduction, whereas competence and good reasons enable acceptance and lasting impact on work processes.

Operating on projects is seen as highly innovative within NIA. Therefore, working in project teams appears to be a challenge for employees. Additionally, there is no standardized and integrated organizational concept for the initiation of projects. Our empirical findings clearly show that several attempts to standardize project work have been conducted, but have always been declined and prevented by particular decision-makers – seemingly for reasons of keeping power and influence. "This hampers innovation" is one participant's observation. The organization hinders itself in further development and assimilation to market conditions.

The same applies to other innovation proposals which employees suggest to improve the organizational growth. Technology is just one example, also non-technical "ideas of innovative working very often just peter out". One interviewee reported a very characteristic and typical example about her attempt to establish a 'virtual notice board' for handling sticky customers' requests. This tool should help employees to get in contact with particular experts – "this idea just seeped away into some filing cabinet". One possible reason for this phenomenon is the absence of a specific central office for innovations, which exclusively would be concerned with working on innovations and changing processes. As a result, innovative ideas would not simply get lost anymore. The idea of the notice board was discussed in detail during the interviews and is described below within the section of 'knowledge management'.

The experts' work in a specific section of the association is composed of dynamical constituents as well as 'regular' and recurring tasks. The dynamic components of work mainly consist of handling costumers' inquiries. As the amount of these questions can hardly be anticipated in advance, it is very arduous to organize them in time tables. Most utterances in the interviews clearly show that handling with inquiries is mostly reduced to "finding the right expert". In the first instance employees try to find internal experts. In particular cases, with regard to specific topics, even contacts to member firms or ministries are utilized to answer certain questions (see below). Furthermore, a few queries demand further inquiries or are delegated to other work units within the association. A common way to organize queries – as was uttered in the interviews – was to sort these open questions according to their "importance" for NIA. This importance is defined by two major criteria. Firstly, the actual size of a member company is of significance, as the membership subscription is based on size. As participants stated this ranking is further influenced by the engagement of a member company and its employees for 'NIAs' interests', e.g. external experts who work in the association voluntarily.

Other 'dynamic' components are exhibitions and trade fairs. These are dated in advance for certain times in a year – mainly in spring and autumn. During these periods the working day is primarily determined by preparations for these events, whereas other tasks are handled with less attention.

Recurring tasks are tasks of routine. For instance the work in the section of standardization, i.e. ISO and DIN, appears to be routine. Here "bureaucratic processes" mainly determine work and working load. The impact and importance of this work is enormous. In the "guiding committee", for instance, experts work out goals and future topics in the area of standardization. However, it is very hard to justify this effort for member companies, as this work is kept in the background and is done continuously, i.e. not on a member company's demand.

Moreover, the training period for new employees seems to be problematic. Most of our interviewees found it difficult to familiarize themselves with the new subject they had to work on. "I felt to be thrown in at the deep end" is a typical utterance we could gather. Additionally, some reported that their new position was vacant for some considerable amount of time, namely in the dimension of several months. Thus, a great deal of work "waited impatiently for the newcomers" as nobody else was responsible or had the time to handle the work coming up.

Social Networking

As we have already seen in the previous paragraph, in NIA building and maintaining social networks is a task of central importance: It is essential to have good contacts to persons in influential positions like ministries or standard comities but to member companies, as well. The interviewees reported situations in which a good relation led to success when drafts of laws or standards were to be adjusted to better fit certain members' interests or when some delicate information was needed. Building up one's social network was reported to take years. As social networks cannot be simply transferred to another person, it is very painful for NIA when colleagues leave the organization – either when they retire or are wooed away. This is another issue concerned with knowledge transfer that is described below. Actually for many of NIAs' employees *social networking* indeed is a major part of their job.

Yet, there is some kind of catalogue in written form, which lists contacts for specific topics. In response to the question whether this booklet eases the search for experts within NIA[5] appropriately, some interviewees uttered that very often it was pure chance to find an expert with support of the booklet. One participant was missing the opportunity to seek for experts by 'outlining his/her skills', as there is no such feature in the booklet. "The catalogue is too arbitrary" as each expert is allowed to "write whatever s/he likes to be in the booklet". However, as we see below ('Knowledge Management') there is evidence for 'expertise finding' to be very important in particular situations.

Knowledge Transfer

In this section issues concerned with knowledge transfer are being discussed. The term 'knowledge transfer' might have multiple meanings: It can be used in the sense of 'saving as much information, experience, practice or even reputation as possible' when employees leave the organization. It can otherwise be used to describe a 'common' documentation of the everyday work for the case of sudden fall out by illness to make it easier for colleagues to temporarily take over ones work. A third way to define knowledge transfer might be a 'desired awareness of the colleagues' activities' to have a broader view over the ongoing activities within the organization.

As we saw in the sections above when employees leave the organization, not only the work power of that person (that can be replaced by any person with similar skills) gets lost. Moreover the entire person's organizational knowledge, practices, experiences and social network get lost. These properties cannot simply be replaced by employing another person. Asked for possible solutions to that problem the staff departments' member suggested that it was a good practice to merge young and old employees within their departments to have a better information exchange among each other. Furthermore, a long term staff planning should be applied that includes some 'training period' (see above). In this phase – as far as possible – employees, who are going to leave the organization, should introduce their successors to the job, share their knowledge and link them to their social networks. Finally continuous know-how transfer among colleagues should be elicitated in some way (i.e. periodical meetings).

Beyond dealing with leaving personnel, knowledge transfer has been identified to be useful in general during the interviews: As mentioned above it should be

---

5   These experts may work in certain horizontal sections (the agricultural section, for example, as in our project) or in vertical sections (the IT or standardization department, among others).

possible for employees to stand in for a colleague who suddenly is unavailable. On the other hand this kind of personnel planning is said to be highly expensive as it recommends occupying two people to do one job over several weeks. Probably the monetary effects of covering one job by two people are easier to calculate than effects of knowledge transfer that does not take place. In 'real life' the colleagues in the office of the leaving person try to "train the new arrival", as those became familiar with the work of the leaving expert over the time.

Additionally when discussing issues of knowledge transfer within the interviews it appeared to be very hard to find suitable ways to realize it. The idea of periodical meetings was not new to one of the interviewees: He told about the "Friday-meeting" that took place once a week some time ago, but was declined after a while. A short extract taken out of the interview may outline why this kind of knowledge transfer has failed in the end, even though the interviewee felt that some kind of meeting in general was still important.

"[...] well, that Friday-meeting in my opinion is [stops] *very* [stops] improvable [felt slightly uncomfortable]"

"Shall we turn off the recorder [joking]?"

"Oh no, just keep it running. [pause] Well, I mean what I say. The point is, and this may sound a bit old-fashioned, but it's just the way it was that we had that Friday-meeting where everyone was given a few minutes to report what it [his actual work] was about. And then we have an agenda as some kind of checklist, that surely is reasonable and correct, but my impression is that people are scared to address certain topics. Maybe there is some kind of inner threshold: 'well, what I'm doing surely is not important, compared to what others are doing and then it's better to say nothing'. This is what I believe. Or they're looking around while someone else is reporting [...] and then one seriously reflects about, whether or not to report the next time. Well, I think there certainly is a need for further improvements in communication."

Later within the same interview, these meetings were addressed again[6]. It turned out that the section leader took part to give a short introduction followed by the other colleagues who then had the opportunity to shortly report about the past week. Another interesting detail came up:

"[...] and I had the impression: If you had nothing to say this was quite suspicious. And then – and this again is my personal view – this turned around completely: If you said something everyone was looking at you thinking 'oh no, not again wasting time, or whatever"

In the end this institutionalized meeting got cancelled as it was judged to be a waste of time. From this case we see that sometimes it is not easy to set up a quasi institutionalized kind of knowledge transfer since seemingly little 'frictions' obviously have led to the failure of the Friday-meetings. Some factors are likely to be a source of problems: Maybe it was not a good idea to have the section leader take part. This may have led to situations in which employees felt uncomfortable. The meetings mode may have an influence, as well. A formal set

---

6   At this point the earlier "Monday-meetings" were addressed. They were cancelled and later on replaced by the "Friday-meetings" which were discussed above.

up might turn out to be too formal (making participants feel uncomfortable) while an informal one can be too informal (leading members to a 'chat' instead of a serious discussion).

Information Management

When discussing about ways and strategies to inform and keep the employees of member companies up to date, it is certainly not surprising, that during the past few years email has become the medium of choice for sending out information. One of our interviewees was responsible for the 'newsletter' of the agricultural section. This is sent out to the members via email every second week. Its claim is to aggregate the most important actual information in a way that "if [members] read this, they do know everything that is important" as he told us. The newsletter was primarily directed towards the management. For developers and designers (technical) 'working groups' were a better way to receive important information. Besides the newsletter there is no other medium that is sent out periodically. The major part of information is sent out on demand.

To manage the large amount of addresses a proprietary system is used by all of NIAs employees. "AIM" (address information system) is a central database containing every known address of all the member companies (and its employees) and NIAs personnel as well. As the IT manager stated during the interviews, no "ordinary" CRM system was capable to fulfil the very special requirements defined by NIA. Here the main requirement was to have multiple entries for one person as one person (in the context of the work for/with NIA) was likely to have more than one well defined role. For instance – as the IT manager told us – members of NIA's technical staff often are also members of the standardization committee and the national institute of standardization, and even cover positions in European associations. Additionally, they were employees of NIA. This should be reflected by an address information system. AIM was implemented by a service provider and is redesigned and extended in an ongoing process.

The work with AIM, as a central database, is obligatory for NIAs employees. Sometimes, it is not without problems, as this is likely in case a common system is to be used by all the members of a large organization (see above). The employees' requirements of different departments are sometimes too high or simply too different to be realized within one application. For instance, as one participant stated, she would like AIM to be capable for seeking persons within the organization carrying certain competencies or responsibilities. But she assumed, that this would "break all dimensions" to have keywords stored which described the tasks of each of the employees. And the danger was too high, that certain keywords still were missing (this person later uttered an idea to overcome this problem, which is discussed below). Another participant stated that sometimes he was in doubt about the correctness of the database. He suggested, for the sake of reliability, the system should be checked periodically to verify whether the addresses are still correct.

Knowledge Management

The final part of the interviews was reserved for 'brainstorming and discussing KM solutions'. Since we were in the beginning of the KM project, we had only a very coarse vision of which KM strategy we should apply within NIA. So, almost any kind of KM solution or strategy was thinkable. In later interview sessions we focussed on KM solutions with respect to problems which had already been identified. The main 'problem' within NIA and thus – as we assume – the main opportunity for KM to be successfully applied was the 'transparency problem' that is described above. In short: Several of the interviewees uttered in some way that in NIA it was unclear who is responsible and who has skills or competencies within specific topic areas. As one participant expressed it:

"The plain information 'who's responsible for what?' is simply missing"

There was one basic idea of KM that was phrased by several interviewees in different ways: The most illustrative definition was given by one of them as "Google for NIA". This person had a vision of a YP system that supports finding people in NIA (rather than contents) based on personal attributes, such as *activities, interests, experiences,* or *responsibilities.* One of the participants explained his vision in the following way:

"It would be heaven, just to enter a keyword and then to get back exactly those ten experts [that I am seeking for]."

Another person gave a concrete example how the "Google for NIA" would improve his work:

"Just one example: I'm organizing our overall members meeting, that takes place from 1st to 2nd October in Weimar. So it would certainly be helpful to know, 'who has already been there?', 'who has organized meetings there?', 'which were the experiences?' and so on. And I would surely benefit from that."

An interesting remark was thrown in by another interviewee when discussing the 'Google idea':

"… that it becomes transparent, who's responsible for what, would be surely helpful. And this might be some kind of compliment for certain people; they can see themselves in a leading position within the organization (…). This can even be motivating."

In the latter quotation, another issue is addressed, namely the interviewee is giving a subtle reasoning for employees to take part in that system: People might feel some kind of 'glory' when being assigned as an expert for a certain topic area. Such a feeling may improve their motivation to keep their profiles up to date and to share their knowledge with others. As we see below the willingness to share knowledge must not be seen as naturally given in NIA.

A sticky question with regard to YP systems in general is how to create and update the user profiles (cf. Ehrlich, 2003; Pipek et al., 2003). Since most of the interviewees typically worked under time pressure and high work load, it seems to be unlikely that they would update their profiles periodically. On the other hand it became clear that a YP system would not be used in case the stored user profiles appeared to be outdated or simply erroneous. In the words of one participant:

> "It would surely be interesting, but it has to work properly. That would be a great thing if a system like that would exist and work properly."

Moreover, as another participant stated, employees feel "stressed by pointless questions" if they were erroneously recommended as an 'expert' for a certain topic area. This has already happened in the past when using the contact catalogue as described above.

An alternative suggestion that was made by one of the interviewees was a 'virtual notice board'. In her assessment NIA was too complex and too manifold to be effectively covered by a YP system. So her idea was to simply turn from a 'pull' to a 'push' concept: By having such a virtual notice board the system was no longer required to seek for people– which she judged to be erroneous – but the users themselves could react to requests of which they thought they were qualified for. We believe no one could explain this idea as illustrative as she did:

> "[…] it's like at the airport. Think about the luggage, that's exactly what I mean! 'This is my suitcase!' I can recognize mine out of a set of 50 black suitcases! […]. Which system is able to assign the suitcases to the people?"

By the way: Afterwards she told us that she had already written down this idea and "officially" suggested it as an innovative approach several times, but was never given any feedback. Even though the 'virtual notice board' approach has obvious advantages over the Google idea, it is expected to lead to problems when urgent requests were to be handled. As one participant stated, it was impossible for him to wait for "someone who is willing to accept a request". Maybe a combination of both approaches – push and pull concepts – would be suitable for NIA.

Another requirement was expressed by two of the interviewees working in the agricultural section: KM should make it possible to provide frequently requested information to members via the internet. Such a system should reduce the efforts of answering the same (or similar) requests again and again. It would additionally enable members – as they often desire – to independently seek for information instead of "bothering" NIA employees for simple information. Members should be given an efficient way to seek for information while NIA's employees were responsible for that content. Technical aspects of presenting the content on the website should be left to "specialists" who particularly care for that. The idea was certainly not, to get rid of taking care of the member companies. "We still are the ones to take care" but only in those cases where interactive advice is necessary – and wanted. As we think, this concept is very similar to Ackerman's answer garden (Ackerman, 1998) which then might become a part of a large-scale KM strategy.

The same concept might be applicable internally: One participant described his way to manage requests by means of his personal archive of contacts. He had built up this archive continuously over the time by adding contacts and skills every time a new expert has proved to be 'useful'. His archive now allows seeking for certain skills and appropriate experts.

Expertise Sharing

When discussing KM strategies during the interview sessions, we primarily focussed on the management of human resources rather then content. The concepts of a YP system ("Google for NIA") or a 'virtual notice board' certainly require the employees to actively take part, i.e. *share their knowledge/ expertise* – which they must be willing to and ready for. At this point the statements of different interviewees diverged. Several of our interviewees found it perfectly natural to share their knowledge with others and expected others to do so, as well. Others however expressed good reasons for themselves – and others – not to do so. Additionally some participants stated that the 'potential of knowledge sharing' was highly overestimated.

As one participant assumed, KM was primarily required by the younger employees having little experience. Those could profit the most by 'sharing' knowledge. In contrast older personnel will tend to reject the idea of KM as it would endanger their status by 'making their unique knowledge accessible for others'. So he suggested that it could be a good idea to create incentives for sharing knowledge in the sense of monetary rewards. According to his assessment...

> "[...] everything inside my head is mine. And I must keep it to myself, just like the winning lottery numbers, to increase or to keep up my market value."

Besides this obvious reason not to share their knowledge, other impeding factors of organizational or cultural nature were brought up by the same participant. As he stated, it was a typical behaviour of some of his colleagues to "strut in borrowed plumes". They would solve certain problems with the help of colleagues within NIA, and thereafter, declare it to be their own work. So colleagues with lower qualification appear as 'experts' who will be requested in the future instead of the real expert. This phenomenon leads to a loss of liability. Furthermore, as a result, it reduces the colleagues' willingness to share their knowledge. Finally, with respect to this behaviour, there would only be one way to make colleagues share their knowledge and this would be by paying them money. Asked whether standardizations or guidelines (mandating colleagues to share knowledge as part of their work) were capable to increase the colleagues' willingness to share knowledge, he spontaneously responded that "guidelines are to be avoided" which is redundant to comment.

It is still unclear to us whether there is a majority of people working in NIA thinking this way. If so, KM certainly cannot help. Some other arguments this interviewee stated surely are worth thinking about: As he explained there were several distinct kinds of knowledge[7]: Those that any person was able to utilize and those that only specialists could effectively use. For instance, a chemist would not be in danger of loosing his status as a specialist, if "all his formulas" became visible for others. Only specialists were able to understand them. This is different when knowledge was easily applicable by others. So owners of non-specialized knowledge would be much more careful than those of specialized knowledge.

Another question gained importance when discussing KM strategies: Is there really much potential for sharing knowledge? One of the interviewees was doubtful about that. In his opinion different sections (for instance) were so distinct that there was no 'common ground' to share knowledge. This seems to be true at least for sections that primarily stand for *representation* – as these sections mostly work with highly specialized content – rather then *support* or *networking*, which more often have to link several specialized expertise (see above).

However, as we saw in the sections above there still seems to be a sufficient potential for 'knowledge sharing' and thus cooperation with each other. This leads to another question that was discussed with the interviewees: If we assume that some YP system in the sense of 'Google for NIA' would really be working, then colleagues are expected to spend time helping each other. Taking the workers' heavy workload into account, cooperation among colleagues could be fostered by creating a balance sheet to bill internal services. Some of the interviewees argued that such a balance sheet would make it easier to legitimate the amount of time spent to help or cooperate with colleagues which otherwise might have been labelled as "lost time".

Conclusions

In this section we will discuss technical and organizational implications derived from the empirical findings. Certainly it is not possible to overcome each of the identified problems by some technical solution and / or a 'simple' organizational adjustment. According to the OTD approach introducing IT should be accompanied with (and cause) certain organizational changes. Additionally – according to Orlikowski (1996) – emerging organizational changes and outcomes should be expected. However, we believe that both, well chosen KM technology and appropriate organizational changes may play an important role in creating transparency, in improving services and in balancing the employees' workload. In the following, requirements are derived from the empirical findings and promising KM concepts are discussed in more detail.

The very special situation in NIA is defined by a complex organizational structure accompanied by a lacking transparency of the competencies and

---

[7]   The term 'knowledge' here is meant to include ‚information' as well.

responsibilities. Additionally we must assume to face subtle refusal of 'expertise sharing' as a result of the actors' heavy workload and a (subjective) necessity to keep up their 'market value'. The lack of coherent visions for the whole association (organizational coherence) makes it difficult to implement changes of technical and organizational nature within the organization. With regard to YP systems, we cannot expect the employees to keep their expertise profiles up to date (cf. Ehrlich, 2003; Pipek et al., 2003). In certain cases 'pull' concepts (e.g. virtual notice board) seem to be more promising than 'push' concepts (e.g. YP).

However, based on the statements of several participants we believe that there is a high potential for the 'Google idea' including some 'virtual notice board' functionality to be successfully applied. Even though the answer garden approach should be seen with some reservation in complex organizational settings – as Pipek and Wulf (2003) argue – it can be fruitful within a simple and well defined environment. Such a context could be given when providing frequently requested information to member companies. As NIA's employees are dealing with a large number of different software systems, it is highly risky to bother them by introducing yet another complex system on mandate which has to be learned first. Hence, 'Google for NIA' should appear as an 'offer' for the employees that they are welcome to use. Additionally the Google-metaphor refers to the ease of use that is required. An implementation of the Google-idea should be as easy to use as the original system. Furthermore the way of introducing the system should be well thought-out by the management to allow for an active participation of as many actors as possible.

In realizing the "Google for NIA" approach, we plan to draw on the *Expert Finding Framework* (Becks et al., 2004). The system supports finding co-learners and experts within an e-learning platform. However, it needs to be extended for organizational contexts where structured data describing the users' interests, skills or abilities is missing. E-learning platforms generally keep structured data such as a user's educational background and qualifications, a classification of content, a history of interaction (click stream), or test results. This information is typically kept up to date within the platform and thus provides accurate user profiles for algorithms to find appropriate actors. In contrast this kind of information cannot be assumed to exist within a 'typical' organizational setting. So we focus on developing an algorithmic framework which makes use of other users' artefacts that reflect users' actual interests, abilities and working context. This might be text files, emails, newsgroups entries, slides, or bookmarks. The tool should include a 'virtual notice board' functionality. However, introducing the tool within the organization is a matter of the next steps to be accomplished within the KM project.

In summary, in this paper the results of a case study are presented that was conducted within a unique organizational environment. Social and human capital – knowledge, experience, practice, social networks and the like – is the matter to be offered, utilized, 'sold' and exchanged. These actions take place within the association as well as between the association and its member companies. Our results and findings both confirm and extend or even disagree with assumptions that were made in the literature:

- As McDonald (2000 and 2001) states, when applying KM in terms of expertise sharing in an organizational context, it is necessary to have a detailed impression of the internal situation concerned with organizational culture, IT and coherence. This finding is fully confirmed by our results.
- Both push (i.e. YP systems) as well as pull concepts (i.e. virtual notice board) for expertise finding/sharing can complement one another and be alternatively used to create transparency in a complex and highly dynamic organizational field.
- The concept of Answer Garden is likely to be helpful in a certain, well defined context that we have described above. Nevertheless this concept is not likely to be successful as a large scale KM solution, as bilateral discussion is often the only way to handle sticky problems.

Acknowledgments

Our very special thanks go to all employees of NIA which have been involved in the KM project. We thank Andrea Bernards and Edith Faust who supported us finishing this paper. We are indebted to Volker Wulf who generously provided advice in writing up this paper.

References

Ackerman, M. S. and McDonald, D. W. (1996): 'Answer Garden 2: Merging Orgaizational Memory with Collaborative Help', in *International Conference on CSCW'96*, ACM Press, New York, pp. 97-105.

Ackerman, M.S. (1998): 'Augmenting Organizational Memory: A Field Study of Answer Garden', *ACM Transactions on Information Systems (TOIS)*, vol. 16, no. 3, 1998, pp. 203 – 224.

Becks, A., Reichling, T., Wulf, V. (2004): 'Expertise Finding: Approaches to Foster Social Capital', in M. Huysman and V. Wulf (eds.): *Social Capital and Information Technology*, MIT Press, Cambridge, 2004, pp. 333-354.

Bergmann, J. R. (2003): 'Ethnomethodologie', in U. Flick, E. von Kardorff, and I. Steinke (eds.): *Qualitative Forschung: Ein Handbuch*, Rowohlt Taschenbuch Verlag, Hamburg, pp. 118-135.

Cohen, D. and Prusak, L. (2001): *In Good Company: How Social Capital makes Organizations Work*, Harvard Business School Press, Boston.

Ehrlich, K. (2003): 'Locating Expertise: Design Issues for an Expertise Locator System', in M. Ackerman, V. Pipek, and V. Wulf (eds.): *Sharing Expertise - Beyond Knowledge Management*, MIT Press, Cambridge, 2003, pp. 137-158.

Flick, U. (2002): *Qualitative Sozialforschung : Eine Einführung*, Rowohlt Taschenbuch Verlag, Hamburg.

Foner, L. N. (1997): 'Yenta: a multi-agent, referral-based matchmaking system', in *Proceedings of the first international conference on Autonomous agents*. USA, ACM Press, New York, pp. 301-307.

Grudin, J. (1988): 'Why CSCW Applications fail: Problems in the design and evaluation of organizational interfaces', in *Proceedings CSCW '88*, Portland 26.-29. September 1988, pp.85-93.

Grudin, J. and Palen, L. (1995): 'Why groupware succeeds: Discretion or mandate?', in *Proceedings of the European Conference in Computer Supported Cooperative Work*, Kluwer Academic Publishers, 1995, pp. 263-278.

Harper, R., Randall, D., Rouncefield, M.: (2000): *Organizational change and Retail Finance: An Ethnographic Approach*, Routledge, London.

Hinds, P. J. and Pfeffer, J. (2003): 'Why Organizations Don't "Know What They Know"', in M. Ackerman, V. Pipek, and V. Wulf (eds.): *Sharing Expertise - Beyond Knowledge Management*, MIT Press, Cambridge, 2003, pp. 3-26.

McDonald, D. W. (2000): *Supporting Nuance in Groupware Design: Moving from Naturalistic Expertise Location to Expertise Recommendation*, PhD-thesis, University of California, Irvine.

McDonald, D. W. (2001): 'Evaluating Expertise Recommendation', in *Proceedings of the 2001 International ACM Conference on Supporting Group Work*, 2001, ACM Press, New York, pp. 214-223.

Mills, G. E. (2003): *Action research: a guide for the teacher researcher*, Upper SaddleRiver, Pearson Education, Inc, NJ.

Orlikowski, W. J. (1996): 'Evolving with Notes: Organizational change around groupware technology', in C. Ciborra (ed.): *Groupware & Teamwork*, J. Wiley, Chichester et al., pp. 23 – 60

Pipek, V. and Wulf, V. (1999): 'A Groupware's Life', in *Proceedings of the Sixth European Conference on Computer Supported Cooperative Work, ECSCW'99*. Netherlands, 1999, Kluwer Academic Publishers, pp. 199-218.

Pipek, V. and Wulf, V. (2003): 'Pruning the Answer Garden: Knowledge Sharing in Maintenance Engineering', in *Proceedings of the Eighth European Conference on Computer Supported Cooperative Work (ECSCW 2003)*, Helsinki, Finland, 14-18 September, Kluwer Academic Publishers, pp. 1-20.

Pipek, V., Hinrichs, J., Wulf, V. (2003): 'Sharing Expertise: Challenges for Technical Support', in M. Ackerman, V. Pipek, and V. Wulf (eds.): *Sharing Expertise - Beyond Knowledge Management*, MIT Press, Cambridge, 2003, pp. 111-136.

Randall, D. and Bentley, R. (1994): Tutorial on *'Ethnography and collaborative systems development II: practical application in a commercial context'*, CSCW '94, Chapel Hill, North Carolina, Sept, 1994.

Schmidt, C. (2003): 'Analyse von Leitfadeninterviews', in U. Flick, E. von Kardorff, and I. Steinke (eds.): *Qualitative Forschung: Ein Handbuch*, 2003, Rowohlt Taschenbuch Verlag, Hamburg, pp. 447-456.

Streeter, L. A. and Lochbaum, K. E. (1988): 'Who Knows: A System Based on Automatic Representation of Semantic Structure', in RIAO '88, Cambridge, MA, pp. 380 - 388.

Vivacque, A. and Lieberman, H. (2000): 'Agents to assist in finding help', in *Proceedings in the Conference on Human Computer Interaction (CHI 2000)*, ACM Press, New York, pp. 65-72.

Wulf, V. and Rohde, M. (1995): 'Towards an integrated organization and technology development', in *Proceedings of the conference on Designing interactive systems: processes, practices, methods, & techniques*, 1995, ACM Press, New York, pp. 55-64.

H. Gellersen et al. (eds.), ECSCW 2005: Proceedings of the Ninth European
Conference on Computer-Supported Cooperative Work, 18-22 September 2005, Paris,
France, 347–366.
© 2005 Springer. Printed in the Netherlands.

Local Expertise at an Emergency Call Centre

Maria Normark

School of Computer Science and Communication, Royal Institute of Technology
(KTH), Stockholm, Sweden

marian@nada.kth.se

Dave Randall

Department of Sociology, Manchester Metropolitan University, Manchester, UK

d.randall@mmu.ac.uk

Abstract. Some important research has been undertaken in recent years on knowledge
management within the CSCW community, drawing attention to the inherently social
properties of knowledge and how it is shared. Much of this work has demonstrated the
complex and sophisticated needs of so-called knowledge workers, and the requirement
for better understandings of knowledge sharing processes. The example we present in
this paper is that of knowledge work in emergency calls at SOS Alarm in Sweden, currently of interest because of a planned new system that will allow for centre-to-centre
case coordination and not only within the centre. What makes such a case interesting is
that workers in this context face an unlimited variety of incidents that require interpretation, decision and coordination, many of which require the deployment of local knowledge
and, as importantly, have to be dealt with in a timely fashion. In this paper we focus on
how a number of people work to combine their knowledge and expertise in a time effective way.

Introduction: Knowledge Management and Sharing Expertise

The argument we present in this paper concerns approaches to 'knowledge
management' or 'shared expertise' and it's relevance to safety and time- critical
domains. The case we examine below is taken from a wider project (Helgeson et

al, 2000, Normark, 2002a, Normark 2002b, Pettersson et al, 2002) dealing with Swedish emergency call centres. It deals with the way in which current arrangements rely on a local organization of knowledge and how this might be affected by the development of a new system that will support case coordination between the 20 existing centres instead of the current local case handling.

In principle, the development of new information and communication technology allows for the sharing and management of information virtually anywhere at anytime. Along with these technological affordances, however, has come the recognition that new technology must be accompanied by appropriate approaches to the problem of what is variously termed information, expertise or knowledge. Terms such as 'knowledge' and 'expertise' are not, and arguably cannot be, precisely defined for they range over some quite heterogeneous acts. Nevertheless, something of an opposition has developed, one in which 'expertise sharing' has developed as an alternative to 'knowledge management' (KM). That is, KM might be seen as an approach which stresses knowledge as data or information, and thus sees the attendant problems as being to do with structure and codification. The alternative has been a 'social' perspective. We would suggest there are two closely related elements in this alternative. Firstly, the emphasis on the 'social' has produced attention to the active ways in which knowledge is acquired, maintained, shared and 'passed on' and secondly, this has been accompanied by new methodological recommendations.

A specific contribution of CSCW to this field, then, has been firstly to emphasise the 'social' quality of expertise and thus how some of the more 'information theoretic' assumptions of knowledge management- broadly, the assumption that problems of knowledge are principally to do with encapsulating its structures and finding efficient ways to transmit it- do not adequately encompass the contextual character of its use. Researchers in the CSCW community, then, have taken a distinctive view of knowledge as being in part non-propositional; as residing in 'practices', and hence as being 'tacit' or 'local'. Critical reflections on both Organizational Memory and Knowledge Management have led to a re-thinking of these issues (see for instance Randall et al, 1996; Ackermann and Halvorsen, 1998; Ackermann et al, 2003; Groth and Bowers, 2001). Recently this critical stance has led to analysis and treatment of themes such as the organizational conditions which affect knowledge or expertise sharing in the local setting. This might involve attention to the conditions which limit it; to the technologies which might support sharing, and attention to the knowledge areas that might be shared. Ackermann et al stress that examinations of knowledge problems (and solutions) in and for the organization should be conceptualized as examinations of 'expertise sharing' in order to provide for the kinds of nuance and complexity that characterise real acts of expertise sharing and thus are likely to inform genuinely usable technologies under this rubric. Various broadly ethnographic contributions to this book show how, in a range of contexts, the activities of organizational members orient towards accessing the expertise of others in some complex and subtle ways. We find this approach very promising for CSCW. It is a route along which we might continue the process of moving beyond some sometimes narrowly defined interactional and technical problems of technologically mediated communication towards a more fruitful engagement with technology and the organization.

One approach, and it is the one we adopt, to dealing with this has been to characterise certain kinds of knowledge or expertise sharing as 'local'. This refers to the way in which some forms of knowledge have a relevance only in local circumstances and often remain invisible to the 'global' organizational view. It is therefore a subset of the more general category, 'expertise sharing'. Thus and for instance, what Randall et al (1996) have termed the 'Mavis' phenomenon, which refers to the way in which knowledge in an organization is socially distributed, turns out to be a significant aspect of organizational effectiveness (and not necessarily in ways predicted by organizational charts). Similarly, Harper et al (2000), have emphasised how knowledge of procedures, others' expertise, and of customer requirements are all locally deployed. One significant aspect of this is the idea of 'knowing who knows' (Groth, 2004).

Methodologically, these themes pan out into a search for adequate knowledge elicitation techniques that allow us to determine what knowledge is held and by whom, who else might need to acquire and use it, and how it is to be made available. In other words, getting beyond narrow conceptualizations of what the expertise in question might be requires an attention to the details of its use. The recognition that not all of the knowledge in question is explicit and propositional (and thus not straightforwardly codifiable) led to substantial use of concepts like 'tacit' knowledge, drawing on the work of Polyani (1967). The problem of uncovering this kind of knowledge has led to methodological reflections which have in turn stimulated a more 'ethnographically informed' approach. This has been evident more than anywhere else in the CSCW arena, where the problems of maintaining knowledge bases in contexts where personnel change; where knowledge is geographically and organizationally distributed, and where it might be difficult to ascertain what the relevant knowledge in question might be have informed a more sophisticated view.

A number of issues are related to the view of knowledge as socially distributed. They include, for instance, understanding of what knowledge might be; how knowledge is shared; what organizational and social obstacles might exist; the importance of 'local experts' and 'knowing who' (Randall et al, 1996), networks, trust and bias discounting (Strauss, 1993), and what appropriate technology for sharing expertise might look like. Fitzpatrick gives us a good example of the sophistication and nuance provided by such an approach (Fitzpatrick, 2003). She shows us, for instance, that while some knowledge sharing activities are explicit, putting the content to work most effectively was, in her example, critically dependent on knowing relevant context information. Having a good network of contacts was also critical to getting the work done. (ibid: 81-82) She goes on to distinguish between (generally codifiable) information 'in the large' and information 'in the small'. The latter case is where, *'much of the sharing is .... only triggered in the context of interpersonal relationships and only makes sense when interconnected and put to work with preexisting knowledge.'* (p82). It further involves 'finding-out' practices such as, *'finding out information in the large, finding out information in the small, finding out what people do now, and finding out what people are like.'* (p83). Information 'in the small', we would suggest, is more or less what we refer to in our use of the term, 'local knowledge'. We want to draw on this work in order to make comparisons with local knowledge work in another context. We do so not only because attention to aspects of 'information in the small' remains rare but also because Fitzpatrick describes her case precisely in terms of features such as being driven by 'ad hoc, unpredictable, event-driven demands' and the fact that the work is therefore to some extent time-critical. She further refers to information gathering as involving various strategies, two of which are 'just-in-time' and 'just-in-case' (p87). Such an approach we believe to be invaluable because it acts as a reminder that information gathering and sharing work is *occasioned.*

There is a need for more case studies with which to understand the varied ways in which local knowledge work might be complex, and understanding why this might be so. Significantly, in the organizational context we describe, the problem of expertise sharing is highlighted by the fact of a 'working' division of labour (Anderson et al, 1989). Here, expertise is shared among operators affected by local and time-critical problems, and engaged in achieving common goals, but undertaking different tasks in different places. We will argue that the means by which outcomes are successfully managed is a product of the relevant management of local knowledges by various parties.

Emergency Call Centre Work

Studies of 'centres of coordination' (Suchman, 1993) such as those of Hughes, et al (1991) and Heath and Luff (1991) identified features of control rooms pointing to the elegance of coordination solutions such that information could be obtained and acted upon 'at a glance' in and through the use of some quite mundane artefacts. Other research has similarly identified how artefacts in control rooms may be used to furnish solutions, prompt mutual awareness, and act as a locus for coordinated activity (see Goodwin and Goodwin, 1993, Watts et al, 1996). Similarly, work on emergency services emphasises the role of call-taking (Whalen, 1995), the cooperative nature of dispatch (see Martin and Bowers, 1999), 'talking to the room' (Artman and Waern, 1999) and the importance of redundancy and visibility (Tjora, 2004). In turn, Pettersson et al attempt to draw generic features of this work from the above studies and from their own observations of SOS Alarm (Pettersson et al , 2002). Other work shows how the successful emergency operator coordination not only consists of case decisions but also the reasoning that leads to the decisions (Normark, 2002).

As we have suggested, emergency services work suggests an interesting test case for knowledge management or expertise sharing issues. This is precisely because emergency service work, like other similar contexts (see e.g. Berndtsson and Normark, 1999) is time- and safety- critical. Proposed solutions for new organizational forms, then, must maintain these fundamental purposes. They must be more or less error-free, timely and comprehensive. A relevant assumption is that 'local' knowledges of a varied and sometimes subtle nature constitute one of the ways in which this work is currently achieved. If these knowledges are likely to be attenuated under the move to more global arrangements, then there is a *prima facie* case for analysis of their possible significance, especially as current solutions to time- and safety criticality are 'at a glance'. That feature, we suggest, makes some forms of expertise sharing in electronic form particularly problematic.

If our assumption above is correct, then it would suggest that some real attention needs to be paid to the nature, extent and frequency of local knowledge in use. The tricky problem for knowledge management in this context is that a range of different knowledges need to be encapsulated in such a way that accurate results can be delivered quickly and reliably to those who need to use it, precisely because the system is both time- and safety- critical. This leads us below to examine the character of practices, solutions, adjustments and knowledge in local settings. Not for the first time, ethnographic approaches to the study of expertise or knowledge management/sharing might reveal features of the expertise/ knowledge in question that might otherwise be overlooked. As Pettersson et al (ibid) point out, operators here work in the context of a range of ambiguities. Their training, knowledge and experience are critical. We consider our emergency call centre case relevant for understanding what the limits of viewing knowledge as generically *shared* might be. In other words, two conditions restrict the degree to which knowledge or expertise 'in the large' constitutes a solution to a knowledge management problem. Firstly, the particular set of work conditions in this instance are *highly* constrained by time considerations. Secondly, the planned organisational changes (which have to do with the reduction in cost entailed in providing for a range of centralized functions in distributed, and hitherto local, environments) involves increasing geographical remoteness from the location of incidents. If, as we state, a central feature of emergency services work as done today is that it relies on a set of local knowledges which are socially distributed both within and between different operational centres within a region, then it seems likely that globalised functions will be predicated on some sharing of expertise across more remote centres. What is particularly interesting for our purposes is the comparison between Fitzpatrick's (ibid) context and what we find at SOS Alarm. One difference is that creating 'a good network of contacts' is not currently so relevant, but might become necessary under the new arrangements. A similarity is that knowledge 'in the small' is most certainly triggered by events in exactly the way she describes.

Emergency Case Handling

SOS Alarm is the company (state-owned) responsible for managing telephone calls made to the emergency telephone number (112 in Sweden). SOS operators receive, categorize, document, dispatch and monitor the incoming cases. At larger SOS centres, a case is almost always coordinated between two operators, a call-taker and a dispatcher. The centres are equipped with computerized maps, maps made of paper, folders and a Computer Aided Dispatch system with a local database called CoordCom. SOS Alarm is (at the time of writing) developing a new computer system aimed at supporting the handling of different kinds of calls across the centres. In effect, this means standardising the technology use across all the 20 centres and at far as possible standardising work practices. Currently, collaboration between call-taker and dispatcher is entirely local. The new system, however, will allow for the emergency calls to be handled by any centre, e.g. the least busy one, though dispatch will remain within the local centre. In these circumstances, the distribution of knowledge now and in the future would seem to be a critical issue.

Our study was initiated by the SOS Alarm as a part of their development project and lasted about one year, involving not only observations in the Malmö centre but also visits to several of the other 20 centres in Sweden and other similar services (the police call centre in Malmö and bridge control at the Øresund Bridge). The purpose was to study collaboration and technology use in the current setting and suggest ideas for the future centre-to-centre setting. We participated in a reference group that met several times in order to discuss and prepare materials for the procurement process. The new system, which currently is under development, is large (estimated project cost ~10 000 000 Euro) and will not only cover national emergency service, but also commercial services such as the reception of automatic elevator alarms. We had an ethnographic approach in our studies with focus on collaboration in between operators and did about 15 observations of 1-2 days at a time. During the observations we did a few video recordings but mostly took notes because of the sensitive medical information that is exchanged in emergency dispatch service. Every video recording had to be stored and transcribed in the centres based on our secrecy agreement; otherwise we had full access to the centres. The child birth case presented in this paper is one such recorded case. This case is also analysed based on SOS Alarm's own audio tapes that we got access to.

We can trace the logic of information-handling at SOS Alarm from the moment a call is received at an SOS centre. For the call-taker, the first issue to be dealt with is whether the call is an appropriate emergency case to deal with at all (bearing in mind the large number of hoax calls made, and other forms of time wasting), followed immediately by a decision concerning the priority to be attached to the call (based on how serious the case is, and how immediate the response needs to be. Priority is allocated on a 1-4 scale.). Following on from this, decisions have to be made concerning the relevance of incoming and outgoing information, and in particular who needs to hear it and possibly act on it. This work is done while documenting and recording information and decisions in the CoordCom system. Operators often have medical knowledge, unsurprising given that many call receivers and dispatchers are ex-nurses and ambulance drivers. Other information that is recorded in the system will include the "where" and "who"; the address of the incident and who the ambulance should pick up.

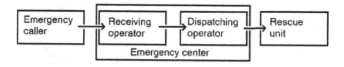

Figure 1. A general overview of the communication in an emergency case

As soon as some basic information is uploaded in the CoordCom database, the ambulance dispatcher can start dispatching (if it is a priority 1 case) while the receiving operator can continue to collect more information about driving directions, development of the accident, etc from the caller. S/he chooses among the resources that are suggested by CoordCom, based on proximity to the ambulance station and a set of other conditions. After calling the ambulance verbally on the radio, the operator sends out a mobitex message, a text message that gets printed out in the ambulance, containing the case information that was entered into CoordCom. The mobitex system is also used to send automatic status reports from the paramedics to the dispatcher. The dispatching operator then follows the progress of the ambulance or rescue vehicle through these status reports. S/he may also help coordinate information between different vehicles.

Local knowledge in use: The Childbirth Case

The case we describe is dealt with at the Malmö centre. [1]The Malmö centre covers the whole south part of Sweden (Skåne).

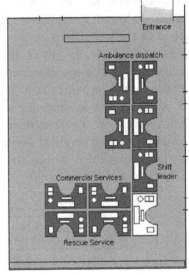

Figure 2. The Skåne region and the position of the tables at Malmö SOS center

Much of what we have described above of the database handling done by operators could be described as information-sharing 'in the large' insofar as it involves the use of standardized methods and technologies to allocate known resources to deal with identified events. We wish to show using one extensive case how information and expertises 'in the small'- knowledges that we will refer to as 'local' knowledge- are shared as well.[2] Knowledges and expertises of this kind are, however, characterized by two factors. Firstly, expertise in this context is geographically distributed across a number of different actors in the case and, secondly, the relevant use of knowledge and expertise is occasioned by, and arrived at through, the need for collaborative work to resolve problems. Again, one of the powerful factors driving this collaborative work is that the actors in the case do not know at the outset what the relevant forms of useful knowledge and expertise might be, nor do they know who might be in possession of them.

We have selected a quite mundane and everyday (although potentially life-threatening) case of a woman about to give birth to her baby to illustrate our themes. A crucial character of the work of receiving and handling emergency

---

1   In Malmö the GPS system in the ambulances is fully implemented, i.e. operators can follow the movements of the ambulances on the map computer.

2   There is always a trade-off between detail and coverage in empirical reporting. We opt for detail here, but readers should be aware that we saw many such cases.

cases, as stated, is that it needs to be done *fast* and with trustworthy technology. Local knowledge is therefore decisive in many situations in order for the operators to be able to grasp incoming information and to know what to do with it. In the analysis of the Childbirth case, we identify what situations engender the use of local knowledge, and thus what kind of information would be lacking if the operators were to be sitting in different rooms and not working with their own geographical area. An overview of the verbal exchanges between the participants in this case looks like this (the direction of the arrows show who contacted whom):

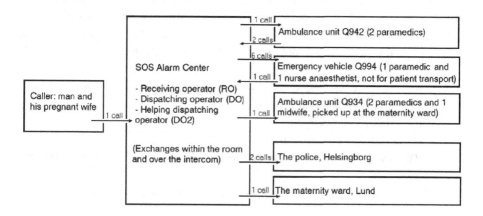

Figure 3. An overall picture of the parties and the number of conversations between them

15 calls in total are recorded during the course of this case. Talk in the room is not included. Text messages exchanged with ambulance units (so-called mobitex messages), including status reports that ambulance units send in as soon as they are dispatched, at the site, on their way to the hospital, and so on, are also not included. (This was because of limitations on our ability to record everything simultaneously and the existence of certain confidentiality issues.) As the overview shows, there are several different people involved in this case, and we count 14.

Call from Help Seeker to RO (Receiving Operator)

The ethnographer was sitting next to the dispatcher who would turn out to be responsible for the ambulance area in question (we were also able, later, to review the system recordings of the case.) The operator firstly receives a co-listening request from the receiving operator. A man, apparently the husband of the pregnant woman, initiates the call. The dispatcher receives the listening-in request after the need for an ambulance was established, and the tapes reveal that first interchange[3]:

> *4 Husband (HS): Yeah, hi, can you send an ambulance?*
>
> *5 Receiving operator (RO): What has happened?*
>
> *6 HS: She's very pregnant you see the waters have broken, you see and she's bleeding everywhere*

The wife of the caller is, it turns out, one week overdue in her pregnancy and her waters have broken. Her cries can be heard in the background and the receiving operator tries to calm down the situation by telling the husband that this is a natural occurrence when the baby is about to be born. The husband at this point asks the operator to talk to his wife directly. The operator tries to soothe the woman while the woman attempts to explain what is happening:

> *30 RO: Are there large blood lumps coming?... yes, I'm sending for an ambulance at once...so ... it is on its way to you now ...*
>
> *31 Wife (AB): [crying loudly]*
>
> *32 RO: ...so, so, try to calm down now*
>
> *33: Dispatching Operator (DO): I'm with you [only heard by the RO through the listen-in function]*
>
> *34: RO: OK...you know the baby is supposed to come out now [said to AB]*

When the caller indicates that his wife is bleeding heavily, the operator immediately reacts. She requests co-listening by the ambulance dispatcher (DO) through the CoordCom system. When the dispatcher answered the co-listening request, she says, "I'm with you", as is customary, and indicating attentiveness. Otherwise the dispatcher only listens. While the conversation is going on, both the receiving operator and the dispatcher have the case file on their screens. We should note here that the RO can see the DO who is sitting about 5 meters away and they can maintain eye contact.

Talking with Emergency Unit Q994

When the emergency call is finished, the receiving operator enters information into CoordCom and while doing that the two operators discuss matters through the still open co-listening connection. They agree that it is a priority 1 (serious) case and that they should send both an ambulance (Q942) and an emergency unit (Q994-which contains an anaesthetic nurse) as is customary with priority 1 cases at this centre. At this point, the dispatcher selects the units that will get this assignment. She contacts them through radio and sends mobitex messages to them, providing both an event code and also the information, "large lumps of

---

[3] These conversations were translated from Swedish

blood coming out". Since Helsingborg has the closest emergency hospital/maternity ward, it is put as the destination for the dispatch. Again, this simple action relies on a close knowledge of the local geography. Bearing in mind that relatively small towns are involved in this case, the dispatcher needs to quickly identify the nearest hospital. She does so in this instance without recourse to any map-based information, because in effect she knows the local hospitals by heart, which of them are the emergency hospitals, and their relevant codes.

Having been contacted and informed as to the nature of the problem via radio and mobitex, the 'anaesthetic' nurse, who is a member of the emergency ambulance team, decides that a midwife should be sent to meet them on their way to the hospital. The ambulance then calls the dispatcher. The following is an excerpt of a radio call from the emergency unit Q994:

> *64 Q994: Can you fix us a midwife from HBG, over [HBG= short for Helsingborg]*
> *65 Dispatching Operator: I can do that if you'd like, sh…*
> *66 Q994: Yup, my nurse anaesthetist .. kind of thinks so.*
> *67 DO: The nurse anaesthetist thinks that I should get a midwife?*
> *68 Q994: Yes, please*
> *69 DO: I'll solve it, will you go and get her?*
> *70 Q994: Nah, we don't really want to go to Helsingborg and get her, really…*
> *71 DO: No, it's Helsingborg, yes, all right, sorry, we'll solve it*

The pregnant woman lives in a small town, Landskrona. Helsingborg is about 200 km north of Landskrona and it is possible that the patient is in need of immediate emergency care. In order to get the midwife from Helsingborg to Landskrona, the dispatcher needs a fast vehicle, but at this point has no ambulance available. The operator misunderstands the paramedic, assuming that he is already close to the hospital. The paramedic uses the short hand expression HBG, he works in that area and perhaps it is a more obvious expression for him than for the operator, who is located in another city in the area. By using the map computer, the operator is able to see where the ambulances in the area are approximately. She judges that there are not enough available ambulances in the area if another ambulance is dispatched. The rule is that no one should have to wait more than 15 minutes for an ambulance so an area cannot be emptied of emergency units. The operator then decides to ask the police in order to get a unit that can transport the midwife from the maternity ward in Helsingborg to the ambulance containing the pregnant woman. The dispatching operator then gets help from another operator, DO2, who contacts the police (obtaining the number from the CoordCom system) while the DO contacts the maternity ward in Helsingborg. She calls the police in Helsingborg:

> *96 DO2: Hi, you don't have a…um…patrol available? Possibly?*
> *97Police (Po): Possibly? Well, yes,maybe…*

98 DO2: Well you see, we might need a midwife from Helsingborg to Landskrona quick as hell ... maybe!
99 Po: A midwife from Helsingborg?
100 DO2: Yes
101 Po: Towards..um..Landskrona
102 DO2: Landskrona...but it's not...it's not a done deal yet...
103 Po: It isn't...uhu
104 DO2: So we'll get back to you within a minute or two
105 Po: I can put someone on the road for now then

At this stage, it is not yet certain that a midwife is needed, since the ambulance and emergency car have not yet arrived at the woman's house. The receiving police officer promises to have a car ready by the hospital.

2nd Call from the Ambulance Q942

While the dispatcher is talking to the police, the ambulance arrives at the scene and discovers that the pregnant woman has been seeing a doctor in Lund, which is a town south of Landskrona. The ambulance personnel therefore decide to take her to Lund:

119 Q942: This midwife, you know
120 DO: Yes
121 Q942: She should be brought from Lund instead, because she is going to Lund, this one [the patient/mother]
122 DO: Okey dokey, but otherwise we have a police patrol at...um...the maternity ward in Helsingborg just waiting to bring one ...

Here we see new and relevant knowledge, which we will term biographical knowledge, being introduced from the ambulance driver. This emergent information has a clear impact on the subsequent decision to re-allocate the midwife role elsewhere. Given the fact that the ambulance is now on its way to the hospital in Lund, the driver contacts the dispatcher with a suggestion. It now makes sense if a midwife is brought from Lund to aid the patient, because the ambulance is heading in that direction and it will take less time for the midwife to meet up with it, the DO2 then calls the maternity ward in Lund instead:

138 DO2: We need to have a midwife that goes to Landskrona in a hurry and helps an ambulance that's on its way down
139 MW: Uhu, you do
140 DO2: Yes
141 MW: Well, then I'll send it...are you picking her up...?
142 DO2: Yes, an ambulance will come and pick her up

Here, DO2 contacts a new ambulance (Q934) in the Lund area in order to pick up the midwife at the hospital and meet the ambulance coming from Landskrona with the woman. DO2 calls the maternity ward in Lund and has it confirmed that a midwife is available, and an ambulance from the Lund area is sent to pick her up. Subsequently, we hear the following segment of conversation:

Call from the Q934 Ambulance (with the midwife)

159 Q934: They're at the motorway, then?

160 DO: Yes, they're at the motorway, you'll have to meet up with them there

167 Q934: Yes, but you don't know whether this is her first child or not? [the midwife wants to know]

168 DO: No, I don't know ... but we do have both an emergency unit and an ambulance unit there right now and so they will be going down ... Q942 and 994. Did you get the strip, or not? [the strip= the mobitex message that is printed in the ambulance with the main case information]

169 Q934: Yes we've got it

170 DO: Yeah, great

171 Q934: Hey, can we do it like this, that when you see that they have loaded...[the patient in the ambulance]

172 DO: Yes

173 Q934: ...can't you give us a ring so that we can hook up with them [that is, connect the two of them by radio]

By now, the midwife has been picked up by a 3rd unit (Q934). She asks the DO, through the paramedics, if this is the woman's first child, but no answer is forthcoming from the dispatcher. The DO then gives driving instructions to the paramedics, and then connects the two ambulances' radios so that they could talk to each other. While doing that, she also listens to the conversation. The DO then cancels the police unit and contacted the maternity ward at the hospital in Lund instead of Helsingborg in order to get a midwife (MW) that can be sent to the incoming ambulance. The plans work out and the units subsequently meet on the motorway and proceed to the hospital.

Various aspects of the case can be seen as germane to the problem of understanding and codifying knowledge or expertise here. Firstly, the knowledge deployed in this case is of various kinds, including specific knowledge concerning not only the geography of the area and the availability of resources but also biographical knowledge which becomes relevant as the case evolves. Secondly, the knowledge in question is not held by any single actor but is socially distributed. In this case, the emergence of relevant and timely knowledge is a feature of actors including the husband of the pregnant woman, the pregnant woman herself, the operator, the ambulance driver and the paramedic, the police, the nurse anaesthetist in the ambulance and the midwife who is eventually summoned. Thirdly, and as we shall argue below, what is particularly critical here is the way that what constitutes relevant knowledge cannot be identified at the outset but is emergent.

Combining Local Knowledge

We have deliberately limited our own investigation into relevant knowledge and expertise to a single case, precisely because even then we find that knowledge still takes a variety of forms and remains stubbornly resistant to codification. The importance of wall maps and computerised maps has been discussed elsewhere (Martin and Bowers, 1997; Pettersson et al, 2002), and here our observations lead us to distinguish between the factual information operators might deploy, and which is available in these maps, and *relevant* knowledge which is not. As suggested above, we think that our notion of relevant local knowledge here is akin to Fitzpatrick's 'knowledge in the small'. The various cases we discuss demonstrate the highly contingent nature of knowledge about location- so contingent that it is not easily provided in any hierarchical form. This knowledge, we stress, comes not only from professional experience, but also from the fact that the operators *live* in their area and know the community. Knowledge of matters such as the pattern of traffic jams, the shopping malls, the road works, the popular beaches, etc. comes from the fact that they have to some extent seen and experienced them directly.

Two relevant matters when dealing with the problem of expertise sharing in a time- and safety- critical environment seem especially salient. Firstly, various 'types' of local knowledge may be deployed at one time or another and secondly the relevance of these knowledges can be emergent.

Types of 'Local' Knowledge

In our SOS research, there are at least four different and very broad kinds of knowledge that are visible in local centre work but not currently accessible in any technology. These are:

Knowledge of the local geography and community. This includes local geographical features; weather patterns; the characteristics of buildings, as well as the different ways in which roads and landmarks might be described. It should be obvious that all local operators are, at least after some time, likely to know the names of geographical areas and the main streets to be found within them through accrued experience. But they also know something about local patterns and nicknames, etc, because they live in the community as well. This might be more important than it seems in that when callers introduce topics related to location,

361

they often do so in vague ways. Thus and for instance, we saw in a further instance an operator in Växjö centre receiving a 112 call meant for the Malmö centre (currently, phone calls may be received at another centre but they cannot deal with it directly and must re-route it to the appropriate centre). The caller in this case says that his friend has fainted and fallen down (hence a likely priority 1 case) "in a park here in Malmö". When the operator asks which park, the response is: "You know, the one in Malmö where they play petanque." Given that she is working in a different area, the operator has no idea where this might be and has to rely on the assumption that this kind of information will make sense to dispatchers and paramedics in Malmö. This kind of local knowledge is, of course, a very difficult type of information to disseminate simply because of its vagueness, but easy to resolve locally, hence:

Op1 (calling out in the room): Anna, you live in Södertälje, do you know if the Södergatan is close to the water?

Op2: Yes it is.

Operators, especially in urban areas, try to pinpoint the exact location by asking callers to give descriptions precisely, but failing this they rely on knowledge of where their colleagues live and may ask them. *Operators thus also act as local experts on their immediate living area.*

Knowledge of local context. The child birth case we describe above suggests knowledge of local context in two ways. It shows the relevance of biographical knowledge as it emerges, and knowledge about the distribution of medical expertise (where it is to be found, and how quickly). As we have demonstrated, important knowledge on which to base decisions about how to proceed comes from different sources including, in this case, the patient herself. There may be other kinds of knowledge of 'local context' that turn out to be relevant in other cases. They might include, knowledge of cultural differences between centres; of local dialects, and knowing the work 'style' of others (which in turn includes variations in tool use).

Knowledge of the 'rhythms of the city', temporal knowledge. That is, demonstrating awareness of what is going on currently in the area one works in, such as large festivals, road constructions, 'rush hour' patterns, etc It includes, for instance, knowledge in connection with time, or what we might call the 'rhythms of the city'. Thus and for instance, knowledge of traffic flows at rush hour, temporary circumstances such as traffic diversions or road works, and occurrences such as sporting events or other large meetings which might substantially affect traffic flow. Again, this kind of knowledge is often immediately available in virtue of operators' living arrangements.

The local variations we are able to identify are more or less taken for granted by operators, embedded as they are in the business of 'dealing with this case', and thus seldom remarked upon. It is, in consequence, difficult to pinpoint exactly what knowledges are displayed and who has them. We are certainly not confident that we have been able to describe all of the different knowledges that might prove relevant to a case, although we can state with confidence that the kinds of issue we mention here crop up more or less regularly.

Emergent Properties and Social Distribution of Knowledge

The second problem is that of the emergent properties of knowledge. The case we detail suggests that relevant knowledge is constructed at various different stages in the case, depending on how actors construe what is going on. 'Expertise combining' in this sense is a matter of actors contributing relevant knowledges at relevant times, in accordance with problems that arise and solutions that might be proposed. 'Knowledge' or 'expertise' in this context can refer to judgements concerning whether they need to introduce other actors to unfolding events. Thus and for instance, at the point of the initial call, the operator's problem is how to judge the severity of a case where the pregnant patient is 'bleeding everywhere ..' and to ensure that the necessary expertise will be present in a timely fashion by dispatching dispatch an emergency unit with a nurse/anaesthetist. The decision by that nurse upon arrival that a midwife will be required to accompany the patient to the nearest emergency hospital (some 200 km away) is an example of the same thing.

As the case unfolds, decisions need to be made about where that midwife is to be obtained from and how to get her to the ambulance. The first decision is to bring her from Helsingborg, where the maternity ward is located, in order to meet the emergency unit on the road. From here on, we see the emergence of a possible solution to the problem of the midwife, and subsequently a change of mind. Initially, the ambulance driver has to correct the operator's error in believing that the ambulance itself can pick up the midwife (the midwife is to come from Helsingborg, which is the destination of the emergency unit. Precisely the point is that the midwife should accompany the emergency unit to the destination). The operator establishes that there are insufficient units available and makes the decision to involve the Helsingborg police in the transportation of the midwife. All of this, it should be remembered, takes place before the ambulance and emergency unit arrive at the pregnant woman's home.

For this reason, the operator makes an arrangement with the police at Helsingborg (lines 102-105) whereby a car is made ready but not yet sent on its way. At this point, when the units arrive at the patient's home, new knowledge becomes available to the crew (lines 119-122). It seems that the patient has been seeing a doctor from another town (Lund) and thus the appropriate action is to take her to the hospital in this town. This means that the midwife should also be obtained from the same town so as to be able to meet the ambulance and emergency unit en route. An ambulance from the Lund area can now be made available to deliver the midwife to a meeting point (lines 138-142).

The ambulance carrying the midwife still has to rendezvous with the unit carrying the patient, and the next piece of data involves an exchange concerning where they are likely to meet up- it being the case that the operator is tracking both units (lines 159-174) At the same time, other requests for medical information are transmitted and the suggestion is made that it would be better if the two units are 'hooked up' for direct radio communication (170-174). Only at this point does the operator cancel the police unit from Helsingborg. Evident from our rehearsal of this case is the fact that relevant knowledge is not held by one person alone, nor can the relevant competence be presumed to be present in any individual's hands. Different actors at different times bring relevant knowledge and expertise to the table, combining them to find appropriate solutions.

Conclusions

As many studies have shown, 'elegant' or 'seamless' practices are easy to find in face-to-face work but not so easy to produce in distributed settings. When we factor knowledge and expertise into this, the degree of geographical separation- not just the fact of- makes a difference. We have tried to support and extend the argument of Fitzpatrick and others concerning the analysis of 'shared expertise' by establishing a limiting case. In our one extended case, certain background features define and limit the properties of expertise sharing in this environment. They are firstly that knowledge must be accessed relevantly, quickly and accurately. Of course, this is directly related to what kind of knowledge will turn out to be relevant. Secondly, that in some instances and regardless of the fact that cases are given different priorities at the outset, knowledge relevance is constructed by *ongoing* determinations of the urgency or seriousness of cases. Thirdly, that knowledge is socially distributed. It is not typically held by one expert and by one expert alone, nor can one assume equal levels and types of expertise across all parties to the encounter. This has particular ramifications when, as we see, some of the knowledge which becomes available is provided by mobile agents like ambulance drivers, or when particular medical expertise is required.

It is unlikely, in this context, that any near-future technology can encapsulate all knowledge in this domain, encode and structure it, and make it available to all operators. The case we deal with illustrates why. The relevance of knowledge depends on the emergent properties of situations; the socially distributed nature of expertise; and the need for it to be obtained in timely ways. It is thus not only the obtaining of knowledge that is of interest but the *organised properties* of knowledge seeking behaviour and how responses are adjusted (in accordance with how knowledge is offered) that are important. Compared to Fitzpatrick's (op cit) examples of acquiring knowledge in the small - how people in the office environment find out what people do know through browsing printers and noticing unexpected books at other people's desks - the SOS operators have to find out what people know during a time critical activity and thus in situ. This is what we label *expertise combining.* Expertise combining *within the SOS Emergency Centre is the organised work of several people, often in different locations and some of whom might be mobile, seeking and offering relevant knowledge in a suitable and convenient form that meets time- critical conditions.* The main reason for this, we argue, is that what constitutes relevant and useful knowledge is *emergent and cannot be easily identified or structured in advance of the particular case that arises.*

The obvious consequence of our deliberations is a 'categorical' problem. By this we mean that, even if we emphasise the problem of replicating local knowledges in one specific set of cases - relating to geographical location - there still appear to be many ways in which such cases might be categorised and embedded in systems. Appropriate categorisations may depend on the way in which any given case unfolds, and relevant knowledge has to be available in such a way that all actors have more or less immediate access to it. It should be apparent that at present the operator acts as a conduit for the dissemination of relevant knowledge and expertise, utilizing information from available technology such as map computers and some geographical and medical knowledge (and also on the basis of her knowledge of the limits of her own expertise). At the same time s/he is receiving, based on expertises and knowledge held by others, relevant information at timely moments. Appropriate technological support, then, must be embedded in a work regime where a working division of labour involves socially distributed knowledge of several different kinds.

Shared expertise systems currently available are not wholly suitable for such an environment insofar as time- and safety- criticality preclude them. 'Expertise finding' systems, while they may evolve organically to meet some needs, at present cannot deal with the 'timeliness' problems we raise. Creating and maintaining a knowledge base does not really deal with the problem of 'emergence'. The development of such expertise sharing systems in this context may ultimately prove useful, but only if they support a community of practice that adapts to the organisational needs for knowledge exchange (Pipek and Wulf, 2003).

The likely way forward is some combination of new resources. We see a role for the 'map based' kind of technology which already exists - a role in which various forms of local knowledge are embedded in the system. At the same time, the problems of emergence, the social distribution of knowledge and the various forms which local knowledge can take, mean that it alone is unlikely to serve. It needs to be accompanied by, we think, two organizational and cultural shifts: the development of a culture in which knowledge is built and embedded organically, and a move towards a more strategic role for some operators, whereby they can support the immediate work of call takers and dispatchers. In principle, local figures like shift leaders can be such experts in technological solutions. They could either provide knowledge directly or indirectly (on a 'knowing who knows' basis). The current case file does not contain all case related information and much of what could help in combining knowledge could be encouraged by a more elaborate case file where different kinds of information (map/comments/web pages etc) could be added. In a new and improved system it may be possible to provide more elaborate log, so that as much as possible of the operator's reasoning is visible in the case file. Another possible solution to the lack of local knowledge is to attach information, permanent or temporary, to addresses e.g. if a road is temporarily closed due to road work or if it is a festival going on (see also Halverson et al, 2004). These implications are dealt with in a current project where we have developed an emergency case handling and dispatch prototype that addresses several of these problems (see Normark, forthcoming).

References

Ackermann, M.S. and Halvorsen, C. (1998). *Considering an organization's memory*. Proceedings Conference on Computer Supported Cooperative Work, CSCW '98, Seattle, Washington, ACM Press

Ackermann, M., Pipek, V. and Wulf, V. (2003). *Sharing Expertise: Beyond Knowledge Management*, Cambridge, Mass. MIT Press

Anderson, R.J., Hughes, J.A. and Sharrock, W.W. (1989). *Working for Profit: The Social Organisation of Calculability in an Entrepreneurial Firm*, Avebury, Aldershot.

Artman, H., & Waern, Y. (1999). *Distributed Cognition in an Emergency Co-ordination Centre*, Cognition Technology & Work, Vol 1, pp. 237-246

Berndtsson, J. and M. Normark (1999). *The Coordinative Functions of Flight Strips: Air Traffic Control Revisited*. Proceedings of the Conference on Supporting Group Work, GROUP'99 Phoenix, Arizona, USA

Fitzpatrick, G. (2003). Emergent Expertise Sharing in a New Community, in M. Ackermann, V. Pipek and V. Wulf (eds.) *Sharing Expertise: Beyond Knowledge Management*, Cambridge, Mass., MIT Press: 81-106

Goodwin, C. and M. Goodwin (1993). Formulating planes: Seeing as a situated activity. In *Communication and cognition at work*. Y. Engeström and D. Middleton (Eds). Cambridge University Press.

Groth, K (2004) *Knowing who knows – an alternative approach to knowledge management*, PhD Thesis, ISBN 91-7283-889-2, Royal Institute of Technology, Stockholm

Groth, K. and J. Bowers (2001) *On finding things out: situating organisational knowledge*. Proceedings of the European Conference on Computer Supported Cooperative Work, ECSCW'01

Halverson, C., T. Erickson, et al. (2004). *Behind the Help Desk: Evolution of a Knowledge Management System in a Large Organization*. Proceedings of the Conference on Computer Supported Cooperative Work, CSCW'04, Chicago Illinois, USA.

Heath, C. and P. Luff. (1991). *Collaborative activity and technological design: Task coordination in London Underground control rooms*. Proceedings of the Second European Conference on Computer-Supported Cooperative Work, ECSCW '91

Helgeson, B., Lundberg, J., Normark, M., Pettersson, M., & Crabtree, A. (2000). *Redovisning av uppdrag i SOS Alarm AB:s Nova 2005 Teknik projekt* (541 00 010) . Ronneby, Sweden: Institutionen för arbetsvetenskap (IAR): BTH och SOS Alarm AB.

Martin, D., Bowers, J., & Wastell, D. (1997). *The interactional affordances of technology: an ethnography of human-computer interaction in an ambulance control centre.* Proceedings of the British Conference on Human Computer Interaction HCI'97. Cambridge: British Computing Society/Cambridge University Press.

Normark, M. (2002a). *Using technology for real-time coordination of work; A study of work and artifact use in the everyday activities of SOS Alarm.* Licentiate Thesis TRITA-NA-0122, ISBN 91-7283-239-8, Royal Institute of Technology, Stockholm.

Normark, M. (2002b). *Sense-making of an emergency call - possibilities and constraints of a computerized case file.* NordiCHI 02, Aarhus, Denmark, October 19-23.

Normark, M. (Forthcoming). *Transforming field observations into functions - on the use of ethnography in system design,* School of Computer Science and Communication, Royal Institute of Technology (KTH).

Pipek, V. and V. Wulf (2003). *Pruning the Answer Garden: Knowledge Sharing in Maintenance Engineering.* 8th European Conference on Computer Supported Cooperative Work, ECSCW'03 Helsinki Finland.

Randall, D. O'Brien J. Rouncefield M. and Hughes, J.A. (1996). *Organzational Memory and CSCW: Supporting the 'Mavis' Phenomenon.* Proceedings of the Sixth Australian Conference on HCI (OzCHI '96)

Strauss, A. (1993). *Continual Permutations of Action.* Aldine De Gruyter, New York

Tjora, A. (2004). *Maintaining Redundancy in the Coordination of Medical Emergencies.* Proceedings of the Conference on Computer Supported Cooperative Work CSCW'04, Chicago, IL, USA.

Watts, J. C., D. D. Woods, J. M. Corban and E. S. Pattersson (1996). *Voice Loops as Cooperative Aids in Space Shuttle Mission Control.* Proceedings of the Conference on Computer Supported Cooperative Work CSCW'96. ACM press: 48-56.

Whalen, J. (1995). Expert systems versus systems for experts: Computer-aided dispatch as a support system in real-world environments. In P. J. Thomas (Ed.), *The social and interactional dimensions of human-computer interfaces.* Cambridge University Press.

H. Gellersen et al. (eds.), ECSCW 2005: Proceedings of the Ninth European
Conference on Computer-Supported Cooperative Work, 18-22 September 2005, Paris,
France, 367–386.

Context Grabbing: Assigning Metadata in Large Document Collections

Joachim Hinrichs[1], Volkmar Pipek[2] and Volker Wulf[3]

[1]Institute for Information Management Bremen GmbH, Germany; [2]International
Institute for Socio-Informatics, Bonn, Germany and University of Oulu, Finland;
[3]University of Siegen and Fraunhofer FIT, Sankt Augustin, Germany
jhinrichs@ifib.de, volkmar.pipek@iisi.de, wulf@fb5.uni-siegen.de

Abstract Classification schemes are an important issue in the collective use of large
document collections. We have investigated the classification of technical documentations in two engineering domains: a steel mill and a sewerage plant company. In both
cases we found a coexistence of different classification schemes and problems resulting
from distributed local archives. In supporting human actors to maintain different classifications schemes while working on a common archive, we developed the concept of
context grabbing. It allows assigning context information efficiently in the form of metadata. Based on a document management system, a tool kit for context grabbing was
developed. Its evaluation in a sewerage service company allows us to comment on
important aspects of understanding the role of classifications in collaborative work.

Introduction

Knowledge management has become an important topic for the CSCW
community within the last couple of years (Davenport and Prusak 1998; Probst et
al. 1999, Ackerman et al. 2003). Since cooperative work is often based on
existing documents, document archives and their organisation are an important
research issue in the context of sharing knowledge. To maintain a shared
document archive proves to be a complex task. Large numbers of documents and
additional information need to be categorized, a task involving different actors
and stakeholders. This problem is of particularly relevant in the manufacturing

and engineering sector. Maintaining an appropriate structure in vast collections of technical documents is a challenge for practitioners as well as scientists (Carstensen and Wulf 1998, Trigg et al. 1999, Lutters and Ackerman 2002). Accessing specific documents can become a labour-intense and error-prone activity (Hinrichs 2000).

The transition from paper-based archives towards electronic document collections holds the opportunity to capture additional information about a document's context by enriching its representation with meta-data. Context in this sense can be understood as a document's set of present or past relationships in the world. Examples of a document's context dimensions are: objects (e.g., machines, plants) of the 'real world' the document refers to, other documents the document is related to (e.g. same project), human actors who created or accessed the document, or work processes in which the document was relevant (including administrative processes like accounting). A document's context consists typically of an immense variety of different dimensions. When making use of context in digital archives, a small selection of relevant dimensions is typically represented in specific attributes (metadata). Each attribute is defined by a set of values that represent the variation within this dimension of context (capturing one personal, physical, organisational, etc. aspect of a 'situation', see Klemke 2002). The representation of context–based meta-data can be used to constitute classification schemes that support human actors to structure large collections of entities (Simone and Sarini 2001).

The benefit of maintaining context data in digital archives has to be weighed against the effort necessary to capture and maintain the attributes' values for each of the many documents. To deal with this problem, we will propose the concept of 'Context Grabbing' which allows capturing attribute values efficiently. By maintaining a richer representation of context, context grabbing supports human actors to build their specific classification schemes on shared collections of documents.

Additionally, assigning context data is not a straightforward task, Documents and document collections become boundary objects (Star 1989) of different organisational communities, with different sets of 'relevant' dimensions of context that represent and establish the perspective of the respective community. 'Maintenance' of documents, metadata (context) and classifications becomes a matter of multilateral interest, with every actor or stakeholder expecting to find a manifestation of his/her perspective in the archive data available. Changing interests, perspectives and – thus – contexts require adaptable context representations, and 'tailoring' the metadata becomes a crucial task for maintaining document collections. The need for appropriate management support becomes even stronger if large amounts of 'new' documents have to be included in a collection.

In this contribution, we present our idea of providing 'context grabbing' techniques to support classification work in large document collections. These ideas have been informed by earlier research we discuss in the 'State of the Art' section, and by two case studies in industrial settings we we present and comment. After that, we describe one 'context grabbing' prototype we implemented and evaluated. In the concluding sections we discuss the ideas in a broader context of archive management.

State of the Art

In many domains cooperative work is based on collections of stored documents. Current file systems are insufficient for the administration of large amounts of documents. They restrict the users by limited indexing functionality and insufficient support to organize documents in an intuitive way (Dourish 2000). Another problem is the loss of context information when documents are passed on through different departments. Without additional documentation, information about the original context gets lost (Freeman and Gelernter 1996; Rekimoto 1999). Technical functions to record context and at a later point in time to restore previous compilations of the document stocks are missing (Lutters and Ackerman 2002). Even Document Management Systems (DMS) especially designed for the purpose of document administration often prove to be too rigid and are not sufficiently adapted to cooperative work processes (Timmermans 2000). In summary, the technical support for the classification of documents is too inflexible with regard to evolving schemes.

In order to analyse the use and evolution of classification systems, Bowker and Star (2000) gave the static notion of classification systems (as being a segmentation of the world with a set of consistent classificatory principles that operate on a disjunct and complete set of categories) a pragmatic turn. They suggested to accept anything that is "consistently called a classification system and treated as such" under this term. However, the use of the term with regard to the implications for the design of Information Technology (LaMarca et al. 1999) softened the sharp edges of the strict definition even more to allow the inclusion of all activities of classification that are relevant for work.

Various studies show that the order and classification of data are often linked to specific work conditions (Bowker and Star 2000) and that the compilation of the documents reflects the know-how of the actors handling the processes (Hertzum and Pejtersen 2000). While the file structures used are comprehensible and self-explanatory to individual users, the comprehensibility of the classification schemes gets lost at the collaborative level. Severe problems occur when classification schemes for cooperative processes are to be developed (Dourish 2000, Wulf 1997). Different terms and terminologies, but also different modes of operation and understanding complicate the process of coordination

(Bannon and Bødker 1997; Carstensen and Wulf 1998; Trigg et al. 1999). Classification schemes that are introduced in a centralised way and that cover the whole organisation are often too rigid and restrict the users in a disproportionate way (Hinrichs 2000; Pipek et al. 2002). The standards for building classification schemes (IEC 61346 – structuring principles, classification objects and codes) and for structuring technical documentation (IEC 61355 – classification for plants, systems and equipment) still have to be tested in practice. Categories arising by themselves during a more decentralized process often hold better opportunities (Bowker and Star 2000; Dourish 2000; Simone and Sarini 2001) to access relevant information.

With regard to classification schemes for storing and retrieving documents Simone and Sarini (2001) discuss case studies from the CSCW literature. With respect to the degree of centrality, they distinguish between endogenous and exogenous classification schemes. Endogenous classification schemes are defined by a high degree of overlap in common practice between the producers and the consumers of a classification scheme. Exogenous schemes are given in case a "relevant distance" in practice between producers and consumers of classification schemes exists. Simone and Sarini (2001, p. 28) assume that exogenous and endogenous classification schemes coexist and should be both supported by technical means.

When supporting different endogenous and exogenous schemes, capturing information about a document's various contexts seems to be crucial. The Placeless Documents approach offers an infrastructure for highly flexible document administration (Dourish 2000). Applications can be implemented which offer emerging classification schemes by allowing adding new attributes flexibly (LaMarca et al. 1999). While this is a very interesting approach in case new categories for classification come up, the more mundane question remains how to grab the values of these attributes efficiently.

In the Lifestream approach, document administration is supported by temporal information which is automatically recorded. Unlike traditional file structures that are organized in a hierarchical way, time bars represent the chronology of a work process and thus symbolize aspects of the temporal context (Freeman and Gelernter 1996, also in the Time-Machine Computing approach, Rekimoto 1999). Awareness services are often implemented as procedures that record a specific aspect of a documents context automatically (e.g. Fuchs 1998). The display of awareness information may be understood as (short-term) classification. However, automatic procedures are not always suitable to capture those dimensions of a document's context that are relevant for classification.

In more general considerations on 'organisational memories', Ackerman and Halverson (1999) explained that the documents in collaborative contexts themselves represent boundary objects - in the sense of Star (1989) - for the different actors (tasks, organisational entities) that use them, and active processes of decontextualisation (losing context) and recontextualisation (giving context) mark the crossing of these boundaries and counteract static notions of 'organisational memory'. If context is represented explicitly (as it is when using classification schemes in document collections), there is an immediate need for flexibility in representing the different contexts a document might pass through. As this process is highly dependent on unpredictable organisational changes that every company experiences, the problem to maintain changing context representations becomes a highly important task. The contribution of Ackerman and Halverson also demonstrates the importance of empirical work for understanding the pragmatics of archive maintenance, and for understanding the emergence of classification schemes. It also becomes clear, that there is a need for better technological support for these processes.

Case Studies

We have investigated the practice of document management in two different organisations running complex technical facilities. The first case study deals with the handling of drawings in maintenance engineering of a major German steel mill (Hinrichs 2000, Pipek et al. 2002, Pipek and Wulf 2003). The second case study investigates the document management practice of a company that runs the facilities for wastewater treatment of a major German city.

Running and maintaining complex technical facilities is highly cooperative work. It requires cooperation among different actors typically distributed across various organizational units. Running and maintaining complex technical facilities is highly constrained by the work carried out by other actors in the past. Here, technical drawings play a crucial role in representing states and history of technical facilities.

Organisations that run large-scale technical facilities have to handle vast amounts of drawings and other types of documentation. The two companies investigated employ rather different strategies with regard to the degree of centralization of the document archives. The focus of our analyses was on investigating the role of a document's context for storage and retrieval.

A Central Archive in a Steel Mill

We have investigated the maintenance engineering processes of a major German steel mill in the Ruhr area. The mill employs about 3,500 employees and is structured into rather independent plant operating units, such as the coke chambers or the blast furnace. Various central units provide services to these plants and manage the mill. The maintenance engineering process involves different central and decentral organizational units as well as external service providers. A central construction department inside the mill coordinates the planning, construction and documentation of the plants. Important parts of construction work have been outsourced to external engineering offices. In each of the different plants, a small group is responsible for the execution of the maintenance work, often supported by hired external construction companies.

Research Methods

The OrgTech project aimed at improving the maintenance engineering process by introducing groupware technologies over a period of three years (Hinrichs 2000; Pipek et al. 2002, Stevens and Wulf 2002). During the course of the project, the steel mill's central drawing archives turned out to be the crucial bottleneck of plant maintenance. Therefore, we investigated the practice of document storage and retrieval. The results are derived from a variety of different sources:

- Analysis of the work practice: 25 semi-structured interviews, workplace observations, further informal inquiries into special problem areas of work.
- Analysis of the documents, particularly the technical drawings and the descriptions of archiving facilities and processes.
- System evaluation: The existing archiving systems were examined (usability evaluation, with a focus on task adequacy).
- Project workshops: In a number of workshops organisational and technological interventions were discussed to improve the maintenance engineering process.

Empirical Findings

A central organizational unit, the archives group, is responsible for storing the documents that represent the technical state of the steel mill. The central drawing archive represents a history of 100 years. It contains more than 300,000 documents, such as technical drawings, technical descriptions, part lists, static information and calculations. A large part of these documents is filed in conventional paper form and saved on microfilm. In 1995, an electronic archiving system was introduced which contains more than 50,000 drawings, old documents scanned from microfilms or new ones stored in raster format. So far the central archive contains only few CAD files.

The classification scheme of the central archive is based on 'Basic Numbers' that break the mill down into plants and their components. However, this classification has been created for accounting purposes, and was not always meaningful for engineers. The 'Drawing Numbers', the other index, are used rather arbitrarily. The central archive gives sets of Drawing Numbers to internal and external engineers who assign them to drawings. They roughly classify drawings in the temporal order of their creation. These sets of numbers do not reflect the amount of drawings created within individual projects, a project may cover Drawing Numbers from different engineers and different number sets. It is the responsibility of the archives group to classify newly delivered drawings into the scheme of Basic Numbers, to add certain keywords to the documents and to enter the Drawing Numbers. The consistency of the paper-based archive has suffered from several changes in the classification schemes over the 100 years of the steel mill's history. Within the electronic archive about one quarter of the documents are not appropriately categorised according to the correct Basic Number or stored without keywords. Finally, the electronic archive system does not offer search functions beyond Drawing Numbers, Basic Numbers and keywords.

The central classification scheme and its implementation within the archive system are obviously problematic for maintenance engineering purposes. Information relevant for local work is not considered. To overcome these problems some engineers developed different types of local classification schemes that enabled them to deal with the problems of the central archive. One important context information is provided by project-specific 'Drawing Lists'. Whenever a project is finished, the internal or external engineers create a document that lists all the drawings that have been created or modified during the course of this project. After handing over the drawings to the central archive, the engineers of the internal construction department preserve the Drawing Lists in paper form in their offices. When searching for drawings they cannot find easily in the electronic archive, the engineers refer to the Drawing List to locate drawings from the same project.

While maintaining its own classification schemes, the internal construction department still uses the central archive to store the technical documents. In some plants, local classification schemes lead to the existence of local drawing archives. Annotated copies of drawings are stored by the actors who are responsible for the execution of the maintenance work in the local plants. These local archives can contain up to 500 drawings. Even 'physical' information, such as a drawing's position in a pile or the level of dust covering it, indicates when these drawings have last been used.

The existence of local archives has also implications for the quality of information provided by the central archive. The workers in the maintenance department of the different plants annotate their locally stored drawings when changes in the state of the plant happen without prior construction activities. For instance, plants can be modified without prior planning (and without the creation of any documentary drawing) when accidents happen. This 'sloppyness' also occurs when at the end of a budget year, work is carried out to use up still available funds. Since these annotations are only carried out in the local drawings, the local archives are often more accurate than the central ones.

Local Archives in a Sewerage Work Company

The second field of study was done in a company that runs the sewerage system of a major German city. The allocation of a fixed yearly budget to be invested into

into the extension and maintenance of the sewerage facilities is part of the contract between the city and the service provider. The company has about 400 employees. The technical services of the company are divided into operating and construction departments. There are two operating departments: one deals with the sewer system of about 1000 km length, the other runs two sewerage disposal plants and various pumping facilities. A construction department plans the extension and maintenance of the different facilities. It is divided into two groups: one deals with the sewers themselves, the other with over-ground facilities. External construction companies support both efforts.

Research Methods

The research with the sewerage service company directly focused on problems with handling the technical documentation. In a socio-technical approach, we accompanied the introduction of a document management system (DMS) by means of a socio-technical approach. The results presented in this paper have been collected from a variety of different sources between 2001 and 2003:

- Analysis of the work practice: >30 semi-structured interviews, workplace observations, and further inquiries into special problem areas.
- Analysis of the technical documents and the archiving processes.
- Analysis of the of the organisational appropriation of norms and standards for documentation and classification structures.
- Feedback workshops with the project's 'Steering Committee': Based on the results of the steps above, requirements for the selection of a DMS were specified and discussed with the steering committee of the project that involved stakeholders from all organisational units.
- Introductory workshops: Opportunities to improve the document handling with a DMS were discussed with engineers from all and with members of the steering committee.

Empirical Findings

In the beginning, the sewerage service company did not run a central archive for technical documentation. We found a broad variety of different locations all over the company, where technical documentations were stored. In our analysis, we focused on the construction process and the two operating departments.

The construction department initiated the process of technical documentation of a project, and planning and documentation efforts were intensified after a project's approval by the management. Usually a project was carried out by one engineer, larger projects by small groups of engineers, lead by a manager.

In a project, the engineers in the construction department kept electronic and paper-based folders in parallel. Most of the technical documents, especially CAD drawings, were created on the engineers' computers and stored on a file server. Each engineer had his own folder on a file server that he could structure according to his individual way of working and classifying. Those folders were only accessible for members of the same group in the construction department.

During the course of the project the engineers started to create a paper-based documentation, as well, resulting in up to 40 DIN A4 folders per project. When the responsibility of a project moved within the construction department or from the construction towards the operating department, only the paper-based version of the technical documentation was handed over. Often, the electronic version of most documents stayed only in the creator's folder on the file server. Electronic versions of drawings considered important were stored on a CD and attached to the physical folders. The operation department usually only got copies of the folders. Those were extended further as the work proceeded. The original documentation either stayed in the engineer's office, or was moved to the local archive of the construction department. 'Projects' are the main dimension for classifying technical documents. Within the project-related folders, the individual engineers were rather free to create the categories for structuring their documentation, and sometimes even individual schemes overlapped significantly.

An important basis for classification was provided by the standardised German 'scale of charges and fees for architects and engineers' (HOAI), which is also part of the professional education. The scale of fees distinguishes nine consecutive phases/activities in construction work (e.g. 'Planning', 'Detailing', etc.). This scheme was also applied for purposes of external subcontracting and internal controlling. So, in some cases the project folders got structured in this way. Other engineers created an internal folder structure based on the time of a document's creation or based on the document type (drawings, drafts, statistical calculations, protocols). One engineer kept specific folders that contained documents and notes that the engineer did not want to share with his colleagues later on in the process.

The engineers were offered some freedom to implement their project-specific classification schemes, although the relevant standards for documentation (DIN 6779 resp. IEC 61346) were well known in the organisation. The pattern of decentralization led to a couple of severe problems. Documents were redundantly kept in different locations, which left it unclear whether a document version represented still the actual state. The documentation in a local archive became incomplete in the course of time, since folders were taken away when needed and not returned. Archiving and working processes were also suffering from media discontinuities, since there was no direct linkage between the electronic documents and their paper versions. Lacking access to the appropriate documentation led to severe problems. Incomplete or inaccessible documentation e.g. lead to costly exploratory 'digging by hand' to avoid damaging power lines.

Supporting Classification Work

The two case studies indicate that a broad variety of context dimensions were selected by the different actors to create classification schemes for technical documentation. In both of the case studies, the historic context of a document's creation played a major role. In the case of the steel mill, the Drawing Lists were an important resource for finding those documents that were created in the same project. In case of the sewerage work company the historical context of creation was the main classification scheme for all technical documents. A second dimension in classification was provided by the structure of the facilities the drawings referred to. This was the main classification dimension in the steel mill. However, there were different versions of this scheme. The central archive was based on an economical interpretation that divided the plant up into cost centres while the plant operators' local archives were rather structured according to a technical interpretation of the plant's structure. In the sewerage service company, reference to the facilities was not used as a classification scheme, since the facilities did not have the complexity to make this necessary. Instead, the geographical position of the facility the drawing referred to was documented in each drawing as part of a descriptive set of information. Another dimension mapped historical aspects. The phase of a document's production in the engineering process was part of a documents' context in the case of the sewerage work company. An important dimension of classification with regard to local archives in the Steel Mill was the reference to the actor in charge. In both companies, local archives were kept in the actor's offices. When looking for certain documentation, one usually asked those engineers to provide help.

Interestingly, the different classification schemes do not always create fully distinct subdivision of the documents. For instance, geographical and technical interpretations of the structure of the plant do overlap in a considerable manner. A project-based classification overlaps greatly with one that is based on the 'engineer in charge'. Obviously there exist similarities between different context dimensions that could be exploited to maintain classification schemes efficiently.

Coexisting central and local classification schemes resulted from different tasks and work practices in the organisational subunits. The coexistence of different classification schemes led to the problem of a redundant storage of technical documents, which again led to inconsistent document bases. The transition from paper-based archives to electronic archives often results in the loss of a dominant (physical) order, but it also offers the opportunity to operate with several different classification schemes that can be extended with new attributes when needed. In decentralised architectures, synchronisation mechanisms can help maintaining a consistent database.

So far research on technical support for classification work has mainly focused on flexibility. Architectures should allow flexibly adding or modifying the represented dimensions of context (e.g. Trigg et al. 1999; Dourish 2000, Sarini and Simone 2001). However, it is not only a question of being able to define attributes flexibly. The more attributes of a document's context are modelled and the more dynamic they change, the more classification work results (cf. Trigg et al. 1999). To make this classification work more efficient, we have developed the concept of context grabbing.

Context Grabbing

Under the label of 'Context grabbing' we collect a set of techniques to support categorisation work in large document collections. The goal is to provide a time-efficient way to maintain context metadata of documents. These techniques can complement DMS, but also file sharing applications. They need to be customisable with regard to the existing local work practices.

We distinguish two possibilities to capture context information: automatically or computer supported. Since documents are created, manipulated and stored on computers many aspects of a document's context can be grabbed automatically. For instance the time of a document's creation or last modifications can be extracted automatically. Additionally, information about the set of other documents a document was ever stored with in a folder can be grabbed automatically (e.g., to produce the 'Drawing Lists' in the Steel Mill).

Capturing context automatically does not work if the relationships of a document (with actors, documents, tasks, etc.) are not represented in the computer. For instance, it is difficult to decide automatically which part of a plant a drawing refers to. This information has to be provided by those human actors who possess the relevant knowledge. Computer support should make their classification work more efficient.

Computer support in grabbing context information can be based on similarities either between the value sets of different documents or between value sets of different context attributes. Exploiting these similarities allows both, assigning attribute values in an automatic or computer-supported manner. For instance, in the sewerage work company we found that a project-based classification strongly resembles the one based on the 'engineer in charge'. So, in case the attribute 'engineer in charge' is newly created in a digital archive, its value can be assigned to individual documents by referring to the values of the attribute 'project number'. Since the value sets of different attributes show similarities but are typically not identical, fully automated, e.g. rule-based, approaches to the problem are not feasible. The human actor needs to stay in control.

We can distinguish two cases of context grabbing. In a first case, values of a newly created attribute have to be assigned or the values of an existing attribute have to be updated. In this case different values of the same attribute have to be assigned to many documents. Secondly, there are cases in which a newly created document has to be classified with respect to all relevant context attributes. These cases require different kinds of tool support.

In the first case one can exploit the similarity between the value sets of different attributes. The tools for assigning a value to a particular context attribute for a set of documents need mechanisms to specify the scope of validity of an assignment operation, maybe by exploiting the existing folder structure and the value sets of those attributes that are already defined. Since these specifications can become quite complex, users have to be supported in understanding them. In the second case, the user needs support to identify documents or sets of documents that already have been classified. These documents can then be taken as points of reference to copy the values of all of their context attributes. Here again the user should stay in control to check whether all the appropriate values get assigned.

The strategy to exploit similarities of classification dimensions for assigning meta-data not only requires appropriate editing functions. Since the similarities themselves are often hard to detect, additional support for detecting and visualising these similarities is also helpful. Relations between different documents that are represented by means of context attributes can be used by specific search tools to provide graphical representations. For instance, in case of the steel mill it would be very helpful for the engineers if all those documents could be displayed together that once had been stored in the same project folder.

A Tool Kit to Support Context Grabbing

We now describe our approach to support context grabbing to one of our fields of study. In the course of the project, the sewerage work company decided to introduce a document management system (DMS). Based on requirements developed in the initial phase of the project, windream[C1], a commercial DMS product, was chosen. Contrary to traditional DMS that run as separate document management applications, windream's document management functionality is integrated into the file management of the operating system. It adds functionality of a DMS such as version control, document life cycle management, differentiated access control, and a sophisticated search tool.

As an important prerequisite for our approach, windream supports the evolution of classification schemes by allowing to structure the meta-data as a basis for classification and to dynamically add new attributes to existing schemes. Beyond the typical features of operating systems, windream offers additional functions to grab values of a context attribute automatically (e.g. regarding data of a document's history). However, there is no appropriate support to assign values of context attributes manually to larger collections of documents. Administrators of windream can create 'index sheets', specific pop-up windows to enter values of a document's different attributes. Depending on the type of attribute, specific value sets and interface elements can be defined, as well. An example of such an 'index sheet' is presented in Figure 1.

---

[1] http://www.windream.com/

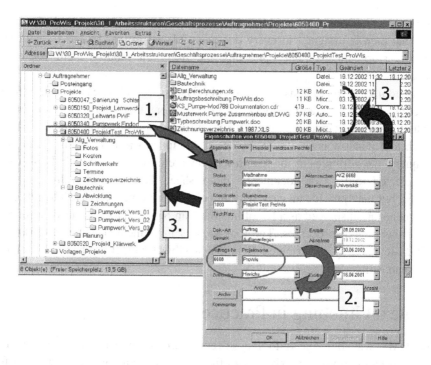

Figure 1. Context grabbing supported by the Windexer: (1) after selecting a folder, the index sheet appears, (2) values of specific attributes can be modified, and (3) assigned to selected documents

To make the manual assignment process in the sewerage work company more efficient, we implemented a tool kit based on the DMS. The tool kit consists of two applications, called Windexer and PreWindexer. The Windexer allows assigning a specific attribute value to a set of predefined documents. The PreWindexer supports the classification of newly created documents by assigning a whole set of predefined attribute values. The classification process via the Windexer operates on the basis of folders. When the Windexer is activated the folder's index sheet appears, (first step in Figure 1). The user can enter and modify attribute values (second step in Figure 1) that serve as the basis for assignment operations. For the assignment operation, the user can select which of the different attributes in the sheet should be assigned to what group of documents (by criteria like name of the creator, the date of creation, or the type of document; third step in Figure 1). Finally, a description of the operation in plain text is presented for user confirmation, and a list of altered documents is produced. For each assignment operation, the Windexer creates a unique identification number that is automatically assigned to all altered documents of the operation. This code number allows recreating the grabbing context by searching for the documents that have been "windexed" together.

The PreWindexer is a tool that helps assigning attribute values to newly created documents. The assignment of the attributes' values is again based on the index sheets assigned to the folder structure of the DMS, which provide the metadata that then is assigned to every document placed in that folder. Usually this happens automatically, but optionally the user can modify them for every operation.

The tool kit also contains a search tool (ContextSearch). It can be activated by selecting a folder or a document. After activating the search function in the context menu, a window to specify the inquiry pops up. The structure of the search tool window is similar to the one of the index sheet. To simplify entering the query, the attributes of the search window are initially filled with the value of the selected folder's or document's index sheet. These search values may be altered, but may provide an easy starting point for complex queries. The retrieved documents are displayed as a list of hits that can be saved and used as a reference for further search processes. The tool kit was implemented using Microsoft©'s DCOM-technology (Distributed Component Object Model) and the API of the windream software.

Context Grabbing in Practice

The DMS was introduced to the sewerage work company to overcome the problems caused by the coexistence of the various local archives. The tool kit for context grabbing played an important role in enabling the transition from the local archives towards a better integrated pattern of storage.

Introducing the DMS

The introduction of a DMS was the technological part of the management's agenda to improve the overall performance of the formerly state run company. On the organisational side, the construction department was split up and integrated into the two operating departments. The change in the formal organisation had an impact on the way the DMS was applied to centralise document management.

A pilot installation of windream was run for half a year on data from one completed project to experiment with the functionality, then a field trial was conducted with a small group of engineers. During that time the system was also presented to various actors from the two operating departments. During these presentations, requirements for the context specification using the index sheet were collected. Based on prototypical implementations of the index sheet, these requirements were discussed in the project's steering board. The integration of the local archives was prepared, and a centralised concept for document management was developed. A classification structure for the file repository was built. The folder structure resulting from prior archiving strategies built the basis that was complemented by the metadata of the index sheet that provided classifications according to work practice and technical standards for documentation (e.g. IEC

61346). The need for the suggested functions of Context grabbing became even more manifest with this experience. The training of about 60 actors during the introduction addressed DMS as well as toolkit functionality, and followed the new conventions on document management.

Classifying Documents

Our evaluation of the context grabbing tool kit covered about 50 workplaces that were observed for the period of about one year. Most of the experiences we were able to record came from field notes from informal communications during site visits and from the conversation in the steering committee. Additionally, 10 semi-structured interviews were conducted regarding the use of the DMS and our tools. The introduction of the DMS lead to far reaching changes in the handling of electronic documents: vast collections of individually structured documents suddenly got shared among different actors. To enable this transition the individual as well as the newly established organisation-wide classification schemes had to be entered into the system.

The generation of classification schemes in the DMS is restricted by its original functionality and its local configuration. Classification schemes relied on both, the folder structure (as the basis) and the index sheet of the DMS (as additional classification scheme). Each of the two departments worked in one folder. On the next structural level, three project phases were distinguished by corresponding folders: "planning", "detailing", and "operating" (based on HOAI), that again contained project folders with all documents belonging to that project. Folder movements followed the proceeding of a project. There was no general template about organising the project folders, but the engineers were asked to keep a flat structure. Project folders usually were created by project managers and then passed to the engineer carrying out the technical work.

While the structure of the individual project folder was still rather specific to the individuals in charge, the attributes represented in the index sheet allowed for additional classification schemes. Some of these attributes have an organization-wide meaning (e.g., the seven-digit project number also used in the ERP system). The value sets of other attributes are less well defined (e.g., the project name is an arbitrary character string chosen by the project manager). Interestingly, there is a considerable redundancy among certain attributes. The project number and the project name always characterise the same project, but both attributes were included in the index sheets since different actors are better able to interpret attribute values of the one or the other type. Some attributes of the index sheet represent super-/subclass relations. The reference number ("Aktenzeichen") was a superclass of name, location, coordinate and object name, 'object name' was the superclass of 'technical location', craft, project and order number. These super-/subclasses served as a flexible classificatory orientation for users.

The values of attributes are assigned and modified by various actors at different points in time. When launching a project the project manager uses the PreWindexer to configure the project folder. Values of the initially known attributes are suggested whenever a new document is stored in the folder. Typically also attributes such as project name and number, cost center, facility, engineer in charge, and status are assigned at that point. During planning, the engineer adds attribute values such as geographical coordinates, object name, and object location. When the project status shifts from "planning" to "detailing" additional attributes may have to be assigned or modified (e.g. time of completion, engineer in charge). The engineers in charge can also add comments in plain text (e.g. information about a customer). Depending on the internal folder structure and the time of assignment, for these activities the Windexer or the PreWindexer were used. When the construction work was finished, the project documentation was archived electronically. At the same time, copies of certain documents were created and passed to various actors (plant operators, external construction firms). In these copies, the classification provided by the folder structures is not present anymore. Thus, the folder-based classification schemes were fully duplicated by means of attributes of the index sheet.

The Windexer proved also helpful for the classification of documents of about 120 to 150 running and approximately 300 completed projects. After being transferred from the file server to the DMS, these documents had to be also classified. One problem in the course of the introduction was the workers' refusal to accept a delay of about 30 minutes until the context assignment was effective in the DMS. The delay was caused by a problem with the file locking mechanism of the office software used. The tools were only used to their full capacity when an immediate storage (and presentation) of context in the DMS was guaranteed.

Reconsidering Classification Work

When observing and supporting work that relates to classification schemes, it is important to understand the way how classifications are objectified, used and altered (Simone and Sarini 2001). Our studies as well as the evaluation of the context grabbing tool kit suggest that it is important to embrace deviations in the use of classification systems instead of fighting them with standardisation efforts.

Star's (1989) notion of boundary objects helps us to further argue in that direction. Documents are not simply 'work results', they also became the anchor of different perspectives on work goals and work processes. In the times of paper-based documentation, their location, attached markers and comments, and other 'physical' attributes often documented the state of work processes as well as the meaning of current work tasks. That way, work practices have made 'documents' meaningful beyond 'documentation'. They became boundary objects of different communities that collaborate in an organization to get work done. The 'context' every actor or group of actors subjectively associates with a document is a manifestation of the meaning the document has for their work, and it is as important as the documents' content[VW1].

Context has to be re-established every time the document is used, and 're-contextualisation' is an important activity in using organizational memories (Ackerman and Halverson 1999). Organisation-wide classification schemes are one way of maintaining (part of) a documents' context, but our experiences show the importance of local practices of context maintenance (e.g., copies, annotations), sometimes even their priority (e.g., higher accuracy of local archives in the steel mill). It is important to consider how we deal with these dynamics when designing the transition from physical to electronic archives.

The dangers for 'traditional' approaches that actors choose to maintain their contexts are manifold: Copying, arranging, annotating, modifying and sorting documents work differently with electronic archives. The seducing power to impose (finally!) a single classification scheme on all documents often tempts managers on all organizational levels. When classification schemes are centrally developed and imposed, power relations play an important, often dysfunctional role since they hinder the maturing of schemes (cf. Star and Bowker 2000). Before the implementation of the DMS, the engineers of the construction department of the sewerage work company were able to predefine the structure of the project documentation because they were the first to built up a local archive that was later copied. In a number of cases, their schemes influenced the way the succeeding actors in the operating departments went on in organizing a project's documentation. With a centralised approach this diffusion of schemes is not possible anymore. We see that on an individual as well as on a collaborative level the transition to electronic repositories holds challenges for context maintenance. But the danger does not always come from 'above': In a case study on the development of classification schemes in a German public administration, we saw that typists who had more experiences in classifying were able to impose their scheme for some time on their clients (cf. Wulf 1997).

To strengthen the argument, the effects and value of emerging classification schemes have to be the focus of additional practice-oriented research. From an action research perspective, we also need to better understand how to facilitate the negotiation processes that are necessary when local classification schemes merge.

Technological Support for Classification Work

Technologically, it is not enough to provide flexibility in classification schemes, e.g. by allowing the definition of new context attributes and value sets. The flexibility has to be complemented by appropriate tools to manage it even for large document collections. Automated approaches can only operate on the traces of context that are machine-readable (timestamps, etc.). To fully integrate appropriate context maintenance in document management systems, human actors have to be supported in modelling their context descriptions and maintain their individual perspectives, as it was the goal of our concept of context grabbing. This requirement can obviously lead to large numbers of non-disjunctive, even redundant context dimensions. Our experiences indicate that this is by no means a problem. When context visualisation is appropriately integrated into the user interface and supported by search tools, disadvantages due to a lack of transparency can be avoided. However, redundancy among attributes can have positive effects. The differences in the naming of redundant attributes can support local interpretation and sense making processes. Again, the challenge is not fighting congruency and redundancy, but dealing with it. Our concept successfully exploited congruencies between context dimensions for assigning context metadata to documents. Our case studies even indicate that the acceptance of a central electronic archive can be greatly increased when tools for managing local or individual context dimensions are provided.

We regard it as most important to further exploit those similarities, e.g. in asking how value sets of attributes produce subdivisions of document sets. Providing an editing tool that allows using these similarities in assigning context descriptions is just a first step. In our case studies, the congruency of attributes was easily recognisable for users familiar with the organisational aspects of the documents. But there may be similarities between attributes that are harder to detect. Here, automated support for detecting these congruencies is possible and would further improve the usefulness of the concepts presented here.

Classification Cultures

Simone and Sarini (2001) already focused on the importance of classification schemes for intra- and intergroup collaboration. One of the dimensions they described as important is the 'distance' between definition and use of classification schemes. They distinguish exogenous (external to common practice) and endogenous (derived from common practice) classification schemes to capture this distance. In the sewerage service company, the HOAI and documentation standards (IEC 61346) supported inter-group cooperation in classification work. Those were exogenous classification schemes, but very much 'in practice'. Similarly, the education of engineers in the steel mill provided a valuable background for classifications according to technological properties of the facilities. In our eyes, the dimension of 'distance between definition and use' in fact refers to a cultural distance between those defining a classification and those using it. The argument that frequent collaboration produces a shared culture of understanding which then again allows 'endogenous' classification schemes to occur just describes an effect of cultural dynamics at workplaces. A 'cultural' understanding of this 'distance' is not only a redefinition of terms, but it also suggests different research efforts to further deepen the understanding of the relation between collaborative work and classification schemes. In the light of this argumentation, a future analysis of the long-term effects of the context grabbing concept and tool kit is likely to suggest not only improvements for technological support, but also new theories on the emergence of classification schemes.

Conclusion

Especially when it comes to knowledge-intensive environments, classification work in order to allow a later retrieval of valuable information, is an important part of knowledge work. We were able to describe the experience from two field studies in industrial settings. Classification in practice happens on various individual and organisational levels, along different local and emerging classification schemes. Document Management Systems (DMS) aim to organize large document collections, but they usually treat documents as once and forever classified according to an acknowledged classification scheme. To allow a more flexible use of classification schemes in practice we suggested 'Context Grabbing' techniques to build and maintain classifications according to the context metadata of documents. A prototype for (semi-)automatically assigning context metadata attributes to large groups of documents has been evaluated in one of the fields. The results of the evaluation stressed the need to support the emergence of classifications, and to support the maintenance of large document collections also in order to maintain them as boundary objects of collaborating organisational communities.

As reliable and unambiguous as classification schemes have to be to be operable, there is no point in pretending a timeless validity in collaborative contexts. Praxis reinterprets and changes the schemes frequently. Classification schemes can be understood as coordination languages for search and retrieval of information. Approaches to support 'classification work' should take into account what makes language useful[VW2]: Enough stability to guarantee mutual understanding, and enough ambiguity to allow for emerging changes.

References

Ackerman, M.S., Halverson, C. (1999): Organizational Memory: Processes, Boundary Objects, and Trajectories. In: IEEE Hawaii International Conference of System Sciences (HICSS'99).

Ackerman, M.; Pipek. V.; Wulf. V. (2003) (eds): Beyond Knowledge Management: Sharing Expertise; MIT-Press, Cambridge.

Bannon, I.; Bødker, S. (1997): Constructing common information spaces; In: Hughes, J.; Rodden, T.; Prinz, W.; Schmidt, K. (eds): Proceedings of ECSCW 97, Kluwer, Dordrecht, pp. 81-96

Bowker, G. C.; Star, S.L. (2000): Sorting things out: Classification and its consequences, MIT Press, Cambridge, 2000

386

Carstensen, P.; Wulf, V. (1998): Common Information Spaces in Engineering Design: An Analysis of the Structure and Use of a Project File; In: Proceedings of Concurrent Engineering (CE 98), Tokio, 1998, pp. 127–135

Davenport, T.-H.; Prusak, L. (1998): *Working Knowledge: How Organizations Manage What They Know*. Harvard Business School Press, Boston, MA, USA

Dourish, P. (2000): Technical and social features of categorization schemes; In: Schmidt, K.; Simone, C.; Star, S.L.: Workshop Classification Schemes; CSCW 2000; Philadelphia, 2000; available at: http://www.isr.uci.edu/~jpd/publications.shtml

Freeman, E.; Gelernter, D. (1996): Livestreams: A storage model for personal data; ACM SIGMOD Bulletin, 1996

Fuchs, L. (1999): AREA: A Cross Application Notification Service for Groupware, in: S. Bødker, M. Kyng & K. Schmidt (eds): Proceedings of ECSCW '99, Kluwer, Dordrecht , pp. 61 - 80

Hertzum, M.; Pejtersen, A. (2000): The information-seeking practices of engineers: Searching for documents as well as for people; Information Proc. and Management 36; 2000, pp. 761-778

Hinrichs, J. (2000): Telecooperation in Engineering Offices - The problem of archiving; In: Dieng, R.; Giboin, A.; De Michelis, G.; Karsenty, L.: Designing Cooperative Systems; COOP 2000, IOS-Press, Sophia Antipolis (F), 2000, pp. 259-275

Klemke, R. (2002): Modelling Context in Information Brokering Processes; Dissertation with the Rhenanian-Westfalian Technical University of Aachen, http://sylvester.bth.rwth-aachen.de/dissertationen/2002/120/02_120.pdf, 2002

La Marca, A.; Edwards, W. K.; Dourish, P.; Lamping, J.; Smith, I.; Thornton, J. (1999): Taking the Work out of Workflow: Mechanisms for Document-Centred Collaboration, in: S. Bødker, M. Kyng & K. Schmidt (eds): Proc. of ECSCW 99, Kluwer, Dordrecht, pp. 1-20

Lutters, W.; Ackerman, M. (2002): Achieving Safety: A Field Study of Boundary Objects in Aircraft Technical Support; Proc. CSCW 2002, ACM, New Orleans, 2002, pp. 266 - 275

Pipek, V.; Hinrichs, J.; Wulf, V. (2002): Sharing Expertise: Challenges for Technical Support; In: Ackerman, M.; Pipek. V.; Wulf. V. (eds): Beyond Knowledge Management: Sharing Expertise; MIT-Press, Cambridge, 2003, pp. 111 - 136

Pipek, V., Wulf, V. (2003): Pruning the Answer Garden: Knowledge Sharing in Maintenance Engineering. in European Conference on CSCW, (Helsinki, Finland, 2003), Kluwer, 1-20.

Probst, G.; Raub, S.; Romhardt, K. (1999): Wissen Managen: wie Unternehmen ihre wertvollste Ressource optimal nutzen; 3. ed., Gabler, Wiesbaden, 1999

Rekimoto, J. (1999): Time-Machine Computing: A Time-centric Approach for the Information Environment, in Proceedings of UIST 99, ACM-Press, New York, 1999, pp. 45-54

Simone, C.; Sarini, M. (2001): Adaptability of Classification Schemes in Cooperation: What does it mean? In: Prinz, W.; Jarke, M.; Rogers, Y.; Schmidt, K.; Wulf, V. (eds): Proceedings of ECSCW 2001, Kluwer, Dordrecht, 2001, pp. 19-38

Star, S. L.: The Structure of Ill-Structured Solutions, in: Glasser, L.; Huhns, M. (eds): Distributed Artificial Intelligence – Volume II, Morgan Kaufmann, 1989, pp. 37-54

Timmermans, H. (2000): Was wird von Dokumenten-Management-Systemen zukünftig erwartet? In: EDM-Report, Nr. 1, Dressler Verlag, Heidelberg, 2000, pp. 64-71

Trigg, R. H.; Blomberg, J.; Suchman, L. (1999): Moving document collections online: The evolution of a shared repository. In: S. Bødker, M. Kyng & K. Schmidt (eds), Proceedings of ECSCW 99, Kluwer, Dordrecht, 1999, pp. 331-350

Wulf, V. (1997): Storing and retrieving documents in a shared workspace: experiences from the political administration; In: Proc. INTERACT 97; Chapman & Hall, UK, 1997, pp. 469-476

H. Gellersen et al. (eds.), ECSCW 2005: Proceedings of the Ninth European Conference on Computer-Supported Cooperative Work, 18-22 September 2005, Paris, France, 387–406.

Between Chaos and Routine: Boundary Negotiating Artifacts in Collaboration

Charlotte P. Lee

California Institute for Telecommunications and Information Technology, USA
University of California, Irvine, USA
cplee@uci.edu

Abstract. Empirical studies of material artifacts in practice continue to be a rich source of theoretical concepts for CSCW. This paper explores the foundational concept of boundary objects and presents the results of a year-long ethnographic study of collaborative work. This research questions the assumption that artifacts exist necessarily within a web of standardized processes and that disorderly processes should be treated as "special cases". I suggest that artifacts can serve to *establish and destabilize* protocols themselves and that artifacts can be used to push boundaries rather than merely sailing across them.

Introduction

Much CSCW research has been devoted to the role of inscription and material artifacts in cooperative work. Myriad ethnographic studies have documented the importance of inscriptions and material artifacts to the creation of shared understanding (Star and Griesemer 1989; Tang 1989; Bucciarelli 1994; Heath and Luff 1996; Pycock and Bowers 1996; Mambrey and Robinson 1997; Harper 1998; Perry and Sanderson 1998; Bechky 1999; Henderson 1999; Hertzum 1999; Brereton and McGarry 2000; Eckert 2001; Lutters and Ackerman 2002; Schmidt and Wagner 2002; Subrahmanian, Monarch et al. 2003). In particular, the relationship of material artifacts to coordinative practices has rightfully attracted a great deal of interest.

Empirical studies of material artifacts in practice continue to be a rich source of theoretical concepts for CSCW. Concepts such as boundary objects (Star 1987-

1989; Star and Griesemer 1989), coordination mechanisms (Schmidt and Simone 1996), prototypes (Subrahmanian, Monarch et al. 2003), ordering systems (Schmidt and Wagner 2005), and intermediary objects (Boujut and Blanco 2003) have been proposed as ways to theorize the role of material artifacts vis-à-vis coordinative practices, and by extension, to theorize collaborative work in general. These concepts overlap to form a patchwork quilt of frameworks that are moving us towards an increasingly sophisticated theoretical understanding of collaborative work.

The concept of boundary objects, in particular, has attracted a great deal of attention as a useful theoretical construct with which to understand the coordinative role of artifacts in practice. I will discuss how the concept of boundary objects came about and how the concept has been used as a catch-all for artifacts that fit uncomfortably within the definition. After an exploration of the foundational concept of boundary objects and presentation of the findings of a year-long ethnographic study of collaborative work, I question the assumption that artifacts necessarily exist within a web of standardized processes and that disorderly processes are to be treated as "special cases". I suggest that artifacts can serve to *establish and destabilize* protocols themselves and that artifacts can be used to push boundaries rather than merely sailing across them.

Boundary Objects

Boundary objects are a key innovation in the study of collaboration and information practices and systems. Many have suggested that the creation of boundary objects is key for collaboration between communities of practice (Star and Griesemer 1989; Wenger 1998; Bowker and Star 1999; Henderson 1999) and I agree. However, I believe there is some danger in relying too heavily on the concept when theorizing collaborative work.

Since Star and Griesemer (Star and Griesemer 1989) initiated the concept of *boundary objects*, it has been used in a wide variety of research areas including research on collaborative information systems, organization science, and information science (Krasner, Curtis et al. 1987; Mambrey and Robinson 1997; Albrechtsen and Jacob 1998; Van House, Butler et al. 1998; Bechky 1999; Henderson 1999; Garrety and Badham 2000; Pawlowski, Robey et al. 2000; Karsten, Lyytinen et al. 2001; Lutters and Ackerman 2002; Diggins and Tolmie 2003; Larsson 2003). Research employed the concept of boundary objects to show that a single object can be used for different purposes by different people (Larsson 2003), to theorize information systems as boundary objects between communities of practice (Pawlowski, Robey et al. 2000), and to explore activities surrounding boundary objects within information or work flow (Mambrey and Robinson 1997; Lutters and Ackerman 2002).

Boundary objects are described as objects that coordinate the perspectives of various communities of practice (Wenger 1998; Henderson 1999). The concept of boundary objects relies heavily on the concept of standardization and examples of boundary objects are typically things with a standardized structure such as forms, maps, and grades—or things with a naturally predetermined structure such as a bird. The question then arises as to how groups of people who lack standardized structures begin to collaborate.

When Star and Griesemer (Star and Griesemer 1989) first introduced the term *boundary objects*, they introduced boundary objects as one of two major factors that contributed to the successful cooperation between biologists and amateur naturalists. The other major factor, *methods standardization* was the less glamorous and less innovative of the two concepts and the title of the article reflects the favored status of the boundary objects concept; the title refers to boundary objects but not to methods standardization. Despite this, the concept of standardization is important to the boundary objects itself. Star and Griesemer discuss Joseph Grinnell, the museum's first director, and Annie Alexander, the museum's founder and amateur naturalist:

> Grinnell and Alexander were able to mobilize a network of collectors, cooperating scientists and administrators to ensure the integrity of the information they collected for archiving and research purposes. The precise set of standardized methods for labeling and collecting played a critical part in their success. These methods were both stringent and simple—they could be learned by amateurs who might have little understanding of taxonomic, ecological or evolution theory. They thus did not require an education in professional biology to understand or to execute. At the same time, they rendered the information collected by amateurs amenable to analysis by professionals. The professional biologists convinced the amateur collectors, for the most part, to adhere to these conventions—for example, to clearly specify the habitat and time of capture of a specimen in a standard format notebook (Star and Griesemer 1989).

The director and founder of the museum, two people in managerial positions, engineered methods standardization. While Star and Griesemer found methods standardization to be necessary, they did not find it to be sufficient for cooperation across diverse social worlds. Other means for cooperation, namely boundary objects, were found to be necessary. Boundary objects are created when groups from different worlds work together. Shared work creates objects which inhabit multiple worlds simultaneously. In *Sorting Things Out*, Bowker and Star (1999) describe the concept of boundary objects.

> Boundary objects are those objects that both inhabit several communities of practice and satisfy the informational requirements of each of them. Boundary objects are thus both plastic enough to adapt to local needs and constraints of the several parties employing them, yet robust enough to maintain a common identity across sites. They are weakly structured in common use and become strongly structured in individual-site use. These objects may be abstract or concrete. Star and Griesemer (1989) first noticed the phenomenon in studying a museum, where the specimens of dead birds had very different meaning to amateur bird watchers and professional biologists, but "the same" bird was used by each group. Such objects have different meaning in different social worlds but their structure is common enough to more than one world to make them recognizable, a means of translation. The creation and management of

boundary objects is a key process in developing and maintaining coherence across intersecting communities (Bowker and Star 1999).

Boundary objects arise over time from durable cooperation among communities of practice. Star lists four types of boundary objects (Star 1987-1989; Star and Griesemer 1989):

- *Repositories* which are 'piles of objects that are indexed in a standardized fashion such as libraries'.
- *Ideal Type* which does not accurately describe the details of any one locality or thing but is abstract and vague and therefore adaptable, such as a diagram or atlas.
- *Coincident Boundaries* which are common objects which have the same boundaries but different internal contents, such as the political boundary of the state of California.
- *Standardized Forms* which are standardized indices that serve as methods of common communication, such as forms.

While Star notes that this list is by no means exhaustive, it is interesting to note that two of the four types of boundary objects listed have standardization as a key component. Repositories are indexed in a *standardized fashion* and standardized forms are *standardized indexes.* Furthermore, it could be argued that political boundaries or atlases also relay on standardized forms of both measurement and representation. This is particularly interesting given that methods control and boundary objects were said to be two different strategies for cooperation across social worlds. Standardization is integral to the definition of boundary objects.

Standards and boundary objects are entwined concepts that both arise over time from durable cooperation among communities. The dependence of boundary objects on the concept of standardization is inherently problematic for theorizing incipient, non-routine, and novel collaborations. Theories are needed to explain how collaborators from different communites of practice, that lack pre-exisiting standards, use material artifacts to collaborate. The empirical research undertaken for this study follows a newly-formed, interdisciplinary design group. Lacking standardized processes and objects for collaboration, the collaborators created what I will call *boundary negotiating artifacts.* My point is not that there is a strict dichotomy between standardized and nonstandardized processes and work. Rather I am seeking to increase the profile of the role of material artifacts in the non-routine work commonly found in incipient interdisciplinary design. As I will discuss later, boundary negotiating artifacts and boundary objects are likely to be related and to vary in prevalence along a continuum from routine to non-routine work.

Building on the Concept of Boundary Objects

Since the introduction of boundary objects, ethnographic research has expanded on the theory. Studies have revealed the importance of providing contextual information about boundary objects in order for the objects to be useful. For example, understanding the context of a boundary object's inception, including its history and surrounding negotiations, is a necessary precursor for boundary objects to be intelligible to those in the receiving community of practice (Mambrey and Robinson 1997; Bechky; Henderson; Lutters and Ackerman 2002; Diggins and Tolmie 2003; Subrahmanian, Monarch et al.). Boundary objects may need to be augmented with additional contextual information in order to be effective in other words.

Research has also documented cases where boundary objects failed for various reasons (Henderson 1999). Bechky's (1999) ethnographic work of engineers, technicians and assemblers involved in the production of semiconductor equipment manufacturer found that boundary objects were not always enough to negotiate shared understanding:

> The occupational communities negotiated a shared understanding through the use of boundary objects, but they were not always enough. Boundary objects can fail to serve as a translation tool when they are not plastic or flexible enough to be used by all groups. Because these groups had different experiences with the objects and spoke different languages, misunderstanding resulted, particularly between engineers and assemblers. These misunderstandings were resolved through verbal translation into the language of drawings or by the offer of a tangible definition, which provided the context needed for shared understanding (Bechky 1999).

Bechky found that the assemblers found engineers' drawings to be too abstract and ambiguous. The drawings were clear to the designers who created them because they were familiar with the context in which they were created, but the assemblers need additional context in order to understand the drawing. While Bechky does not go so far as to suggest that these drawings are not boundary objects, one may conclude that they are not. By definition boundary objects are supposed to satisfy the informational requirements of different communities of practice.

In her ethnographic work on design engineers, Henderson (Henderson 1999) found that the boundary object concept required amendment in order to describe the way that designers actually use artifacts. Consequently, she coined the term *conscription devices* to mean a type of boundary object that enlists group participation, are receptacles of created knowledge, and that are adjusted through group interaction.

> The focus of conscription devices is the process, while the focus of boundary objects is product. During the design process conscription devices exert a powerful influence. Participants find it difficult to communicate about the design without them (2003).

Unfortunately, Henderson does not elaborate on the concept and ultimately posits conscription devices as a type of boundary object. I would argue that objects that are used and adjusted through simultaneous group interaction are not a new type of boundary object, rather, while similar and related, they are not actually boundary objects at all.

Examples of boundary objects such as birds, political borders, or repositories are described as passing from one community of practice to another with little or no explanation. Boundary objects are supposed to "satisfy the informational requirements of each community of practice." Yet some of the things we call boundary objects do not seem to actually satisfy the informational requirements of each community of practice because they required considerable additional explanation and discussion to be intelligible.

Other work has suggested more strongly that the boundary object concept requires amendment (Boujut and Blanco 2003; Subrahmanian, Monarch et al. 2003). Subrahmanian et al (2003) propose the broad concept of *prototypes* based on their observations of artifacts and activities that support systematic updating of boundary objects and their observations of organizational changes that rendered boundary objects unable to support activity. Prototypes are described as verbal, gestural, and virtual representations and models, protocols, process graphs, and physical artifacts that serve as partial or complete representations of the product or process that is being produced. Prototypes are described as boundary objects but also as representations that are necessary to support the understanding of boundary objects. The first case study found that even in a stable organizational environment, boundary objects may require a fair amount of updating in order to continue to satisfy the information needs of the collaborating parties. The second case study highlighted that boundary objects can be somewhat brittle. In the face of organizational instability, existing boundary objects failed and new prototypes and boundary objects needed to be created to support work. Subrahmanian et al (2003) raise important points: Boundary objects may fail due to changes in the organization context or structure; There is a broad class of representations and activities that dynamically change their representational status in the achievement and breakdown of shared understanding that are not boundary objects.

Another concept that amends boundary objects is that of Intermediary Objects (Boujut and Blanco 2003). Intermediary objects are intermediate states of a product. Intermediary objects are representations, but they are also the traces as well as the outputs of a collaborative transformational process. A sketch, for example, is a conjecture that is evaluated and confronted by collaborators who have other constraints.

> More precisely we think that co-operation can be considered as a process of "disambiguation" if it is properly framed. Negotiation and compromise setting are particular ways for creating specific shared knowledge. The concept of intermediary objects can provide a tool that allows the production of a conceptual frame that formalizes and represent this shared knowledge through objects and various representations (Boujut and Blanco 2003).

While Boujut and Blanco (2003) note, in passing, that intermediary objects act as boundary objects. I suggest they may be something quite different.

Rather than pushing the limits of the concept of boundary objects, it would be fruitful to consider that the concept of boundary objects may not be up to the conceptual heavy lifting that many of us have been trying to assign it. Others have noted this before, not only critiquing boundary objects but also common information spaces, workflow systems and coordination mechanisms as forming a picture that is "rather patchy and incoherent" and as collectively forming a defective foundation for CSCW (Schmidt and Wagner 2005). While I don't presume to singlehandedly lay that foundation. I may be able to identify weaknesses in the existing foundation.

Case Study: Museum Exhibition Designers

This research used ethnographic methods to understand how a team of designers used physical artifacts and social practices to collaborate. I wanted to find out what communities of practice were involved, what sorts of practices they used, and how they used artifacts.

The site for the fieldwork was a project to design a traveling exhibition about wild and domestic dogs. The project was sponsored by a large natural history museum, hereafter referred to as the Natural History Museum. An interdisciplinary team of designers, most of them located on-site, was charged with the responsibility to design the exhibition.

At any given time there was a core group that worked intensively on the project and a peripheral group of participants who made occasional contributions through participation in meetings and provision of information or artifacts. The core design team was comprised of educators/writers, exhibit designers (an industrial designer and graphic artist by training), a builder, and off-site scientific advisors/curators.

I used ethnographic methods such as participant-observation and interviewing and also used documentary analysis. Data was collected at the Natural History Museum for over a year between December 2001 and March 2003. I spent well over two hundred hours in the field with members of the exhibition design team and collected over a thousand pages of field notes, documents, and photographs. I have used pseudonyms for the names of people and places to protect the privacy of individuals who have participated in this research.

The Dogs Group as Intersection Between Communities of Practice

Design is often fraught with conflict. Rather than characterizing such contests as a battle of individual wills, it is helpful to explore the Dogs project group as an intersection between different communities of practice. In a very real way, the members of the Dogs Group brought sets of practices, values, and meanings with them to work. Some of these practices are embodied in staff member's know-how and expertise regarding exhibit-oriented reifications (e.g. how to build a kiosk, how to write at a certain grade level), but along with task-oriented practical skills, communities of practice teach members related practices, attitudes, and norms as well. Sometimes these practices, attitudes, and norms conflict directly with those of other members of the Dogs Group.

Interviews revealed that each team member had multiple self-identified affiliations to communities of practice such as departments, functional units within departments, previous occupations, education, training, other museum genres, and professional associations. They each cited these affiliations as motivation for specific actions (Lee 2004).

To a surprising extent, contests in the collaboration between communities of practice were invisible to participants. The curators worked on the project off and on over a period of two years and yet never became privy to the communities of practice at work within the museum. Certainly they understood that there were conflicts and that different people had different jobs, but even after the exhibition had been successfully opened they were unclear about the roles of each of the team members and to what extent they had been involved in the creation of the exhibition. They certainly never came to understand what functional units were involved in the creation of Dogs and that they mapped to different communities of practice.

The curators were never privy to the participation and affiliation of three key team members in a professional museum studies association that advocated a reduced role for exhibition curators. Knowledge of the philosophical differences engendered by this association, would likely have changed the way that things transpired amongst the team if not the ultimate outcome. While not always resolved to universal satisfaction, the conflicts and negotiations that occurred enabled the team to coordinate themselves and successfully collaborate to produce a complicated museum exhibition.

Boundary Negotiating Artifacts

This research found designers using artifacts and surrounding practices to iteratively coordinate perspectives and to bring disparate communities of practice into alignment, often temporarily, to solve specific design problems that are part of a larger design project. The discussion that follows will describe five types of boundary negotiating artifacts that do not fit the definition of boundary objects: 1) self-explanation, 2) inclusion, 3) compilation, 4) structuring, and 5) borrowing. Self-explanation *artifacts* were created by and for either a single individual or two to three members of the same community of practice working in tight collaboration. Four types of artifacts were created for crossing and negotiating boundaries between communities of practice: *inclusion, compilation, structuring,* and *borrowing.* Each artifact was created for specific purposes and was used differently by members of the Dogs Group.

1) Self-explanation artifacts (e.g. notes, tables, concept sketches) were the most difficult to study as they were rarely presented directly to others and were typically created while Dogs Group members worked in the privacy of their offices. The designers used self-explanation artifacts for learning, recording, organizing, remembering, and reflecting. While created and used privately, self-explanation artifacts were sometimes indirectly presented to others through the creation of inclusion artifacts or compilation artifacts.

Self-Explanation Artifact Example 1: Hannah's Table for Section 4

Hannah, an educator, was responsible for generating the label copy for a section of the exhibition about what people do to help dogs, section 4. While working on her own, Hannah created a table to organize elements of section 4. Hannah's table was an innovation because up to that point she, and also Emma, had relied primarily on the narratives, which were essentially scripts for the exhibition, and her meeting notes. Hannah used her table to organize the information that she was getting from various sources, to remind herself of the artifacts associated with each exhibit and the personal stories and a scientific issues to cover in the label copy. Eventually, Hannah used her self-explanation artifact to develop and refine her label copy, a structuring artifact. Self-explanation artifacts are surrounded by a web of practices such as recording, remembering, collecting, and organizing.

Self-Explanation Artifact Example 2: Martin's Journals

For over twenty years Martin has been keeping journals relating to his work as an exhibit designer. His journals included illustrated notes on science and technology topics and sketches of ideas for interactive electrical-mechanical museum exhibits. Martin also used his journal as a place to collect ideas and images. Sometimes he would visit a museum and would see a quote that he particularly liked and record it in his journal. When his work took him to foreign countries he made rough sketches of things he had seen and he pasted local postage stamps in his journal. When I asked him about the quotes and postage stamps, he said that they were things that he liked that were potential material for future exhibitions.

In his role as a designer at NHM many of Martin's exhibit concepts were brand new, but his ideas were also very much influenced by what he had seen and created in the past and had recorded in his journal. On one occasion, Martin used a concept from an old journal for a new exhibit idea. He then created a new sketch that was used as an inclusion artifact (discussed below). Martin used his journals to record pleasing, useful, and potentially useful information and images, to remind himself of personal stories and feelings, and to explore scientific issues and exhibit ideas. His journals were a tool for learning, remembering, and reflecting.

2) Inclusion artifacts were used to propose new concepts and forms. These artifacts were created from self-explanation artifacts and went through an informal screening process of group discussion whereby an idea embodying different concepts and forms (e.g. sketches or text) originating from one community of practice would be proposed to others. This screening process entailed communal gatekeeping whereby the group would use the inclusion artifact as a reference or symbol for the new idea.

Inclusion Artifact Example: Object Theater

Inclusion artifacts can be used to create alliances with sympathetic communities of practice to exert pressure on still other communities of practice. Martin tried to include an inclusion artifact on his own behalf, but also on behalf of the curators, when he designed an exhibit he called Object Theater. Object Theater was a theater that displayed artifacts depicting dogs from different cultures and eras and related those artifacts to dog myths and legends using audio or video recordings. The theater was important to Martin because he wished to emphasize that dogs are part of human culture—a theme that had been strongly encouraged by the curators. In fact, the curators had expressed disappointment that the exhibition did not have more content about dogs and culture.

The educators were initially very reluctant to include the theater for practical reasons—the exhibition was already well behind schedule and the object theater required a large amount of additional work including researching and choosing specific myths and legends, identifying, locating, and borrowing appropriate artifacts, writing and recording a script, or filming a storyteller, and editing the audio or video. Many of these tasks would need to be undertaken by the already over-burdened educators themselves. While the educators liked the concept and visual impact of the theater, they were wary of the amount of work it would entail. The educators actually discouraged Martin from presenting his drawing of the object theater, an inclusion artifact, to the curators because they feared that the curators would then insist upon its inclusion. Eventually, this is exactly what happened. During the next meeting the curators again complained about the lack of culture in the exhibition and Martin took advantage of the opportunity to engage in including practices, specifically presenting a sketch of the object theater.

When the curators saw Martin's drawing they recognized a chance to include more culture in the exhibition and they then persuaded the rest of the group to accept the theater as part of the exhibition. Martin belonged to a community of practice of traditional exhibition design whereby exhibit designers would translate curator's ideas into exhibits and Martin used the object theater to create an alliance with the curators who held views similar to his own.

Martin successfully used including practices to have his including artifact incorporated into the exhibition, but it is important to note that engaging in including practices does not necessarily entail the successful acceptance of an inclusion artifact. One can engage in including, yet fail to gain acceptance of one's inclusion artifact. Inclusion artifacts are embedded in a web of practices that can be considered including practices—presenting, accepting, rejecting, and reserving judgment.

3) Compilation artifacts (e.g. tables, technical sketches) were used to coordinate both media and the designers themselves. The designers used compilation artifacts to bring two or more communities of practice into alignment just long enough to develop a shared and mutually agreeable understanding of a problem and to pass crucial information from one community of practice to another. This process of alignment and sharing of information facilitated the creation of shared understanding about each exhibit and the exhibition as a whole. This process of alignment was continually necessary as knowledge was distributed across functional specialties (e.g. sculpture, taxidermy, education, etc.) and elements of each exhibit were constantly evolving. While inclusion and compilation artifacts often fully or partially incorporated self-explanation artifacts, structuring artifacts often fully or partially incorporated inclusion and compilation artifacts.

Compilation Artifact Example: Angela's Table for the Graphic Designers

One day I observed Angela (Exhibit Designer) and Emma (Educator) cooperating to turn Emma's images and artifacts table (a self-explanation artifact) into a compilation artifact that was to be given to the graphic designers. Angela explained to me that she was trying to help the graphic artists by putting together a new table. Emma's document, Dogs Images and Artifacts, listed the images and artifacts for each exhibit, but within each exhibit were several discrete labels. Emma's document did not relate each image and artifact to its corresponding label. The graphic artists didn't know which images went with which labels.

Angela, with help from Emma, created a compilation artifact by collecting information from various sources. The information necessary to create Angela's table came from Emma's table, label copy, folders, and from Emma herself. By going through the act of compiling, all this information was funneled into one table that was formatted specifically for the graphic designers; Angela created a bridge between Emma and the graphic designers. As they filled in the table, they innovated with terminology and with the information structure of the table. For example, they had to figure out how to represent single labels that contained multiple images, they also had to figure out how to indicate that the graphic designers may choose amongst several images, or if they had to include all the images listed. Additionally, they created shorthand for: the state of an image, how to code the component type, and how to indicate repeating items. While Angela's table came very close to being a boundary object, it was not a boundary object because Angela developed names for the fields on the fly and needed to decide how to communicate instructions to the graphic designers as she went along. Additionally, when it came time to give the tables to the graphic designers, Angela found it necessary to explain how to read the tables.

Compilation artifacts are involved in a web of compiling practices: remembering, gathering, organizing, discussing, anticipating needs, presenting, and explaining. Angela and Emma used the table to coordinate both media and themselves. The table provided a focus for finding and organizing media. Lacking a boundary object, Angela was able to use her tacit knowledge of graphic design to create a compilation artifact that augmented her brokering role. Ultimately Angela used her table to bring two communities of practice into alignment just long enough for the communities to pass crucial information from one to another.

4) Structuring artifacts (e.g. exhibition narrative, exhibition concept map) were plentiful throughout the design of the Dogs exhibition. The structuring artifacts created by different members of the Dogs team often competed with each other for primacy. The curators, the educators, and one of the exhibit designers each had a vision for the exhibition and their vision was made manifest in their structuring documents and their expectations for how their structuring documents would be used. Like compilation artifacts, structuring artifacts are used to coordinate media and understanding but, unlike compilation artifacts, structuring artifacts are also used to establish ordering principles, establish tenor in narrative forms, and to direct and coordinate the activity of others.

Structuring artifacts were often at the center of heated struggles between communities of practices and were sometimes used to push and negotiate boundaries themselves—quite different from boundary objects which move across boundaries from one community of practice to another with relative ease.

Structuring Artifact Example 1: The Curator's Narrative

The curators, Brad and Elaine, wrote a large text that I'll call the *curator's narrative*. The curator's narrative contained chapters for each of the topic sections that the NHM Dogs staff had agreed upon. Within each chapter, the curators had isolated sub-topics and written one to four paragraphs about each. Additionally, the curators included detailed suggestions for illustrations or photos, indicated what should be wall panels or kiosks, and suggested what exhibits might look like. The curators believed that their narrative provided the framework for which topics and sub-topics would be included in the exhibition and how they would be organized. One of the curators was stunned to discover that the museum staff seemed to be removing and changing whole concepts.

In fact, the educators were using the curator's narrative, but they were using it as a source of material, rather than as a framework, for the whole exhibition. Because of their affiliation with the visitor studies community, Emma and a few other members of the staff believed that it was their professional responsibility to remove, shorten, and simplify the text of the exhibition. The educators did not accept the curator's narrative as the primary structuring artifact for the exhibition—a fact that the curators fought throughout the duration of the project.

The curator's narrative was a structuring artifact. Like all structuring artifacts, the curator's narrative showed the structure of the final design product. As a structuring artifact, it was concerned mostly with the organization of concepts, however it also dealt with how those concepts would be expressed in text, graphics, and physical forms. The curators had introduced one structuring artifact, but Dogs Group members introduced structuring artifacts of their own. Sometimes structuring artifacts were compatible and sometimes they competed.

Structuring Artifact Example 2: Educator's Narratives and Label Copy

The curators produced a narrative, a structuring artifact, but the educators Hannah and Emma, created their own narrative for the exhibition which quickly supplanted the curator's narrative as the structuring artifact for the exhibition. The educator's narrative was derived from the curator's narrative and was intended to facilitate the organization of the exhibition as a whole. The educator's narrative, like the curator's, was divided into agreed-upon sections and corresponding topics. From there the educators began to impose their own structure on the narrative. Topics were moved, combined, and finally given exhibit titles and component and label numbers. The resulting educator's narrative also provided a concise summary of topics and any preliminary ideas for the physical design of exhibits. Early narratives dating from late 2001 covered the first three sections of the exhibition and were quite similar in structure to the curators' narrative. Changes from that point on were incremental with some topics being rethought, added, or eliminated based on discussions amongst the NHM Dogs staff and, to a lesser extent, also the curators. The narrative was redistributed every few months to keep people apprised of changes in the order of exhibits, additions of sub-topics, or the assignation of different numbers for existing exhibits. The narrative became the dominant structuring artifact.

From December of 2001 through early February 2002 Emma and Hannah gradually began to spend less time deciding and elaborating on what should be listed in the narrative and more time conveying and explaining listed items to Martin, Angela, Evan, and Brent. Hannah and Emma began to spend more time on several other exhibition-related activities. One of these activities was writing the label copy for the exhibition. The educator's narrative had distilled the curator's narrative to its simplest form, essentially an outline form that could be easily scanned and reorganized. The label copy then took the educator's narrative and constructed new text based on a combination of the curator's narrative, conversations with the curators and other dog experts, the educators own investigations, and encounters with artifacts created by other members of the Dogs Group such as Evan's Dog Component List and Martin's concept maps.

Gradually the label copy supplanted the educator's narrative as the dominant structuring artifact—the master artifact.

The educator's narrative, and later the label copy, was used to coordinate the activity of the entire Dogs Group. Like compilation artifacts, structuring artifacts are used to coordinate media and understanding, but unlike compilation artifacts, structuring artifacts are also used to establish ordering principles and tenor of narratives.

Structuring Artifact Example 3: Concept Maps and the Notion of Hierarchy

Martin's concept maps were bubble diagrams that showed the structure of sections of the exhibition. Early drafts of the concept maps were hand drawn and were created by Martin, Elaine, and Brad and were comprised of a large bubble with the main idea for the section and smaller bubbles containing sub-topics that were linked to the main idea with simple lines. Each sub-topic could be linked to a set of lesser sub-topics that were in bubbles that were smaller yet. Later versions of the concept maps were drafted by Martin on his computer and printed out for meetings. The maps also included section numbers from the educator's narrative and replaced the singular bubble shape with three or four different shapes to indicate hierarchic level.

Martin intended for the concept maps to fulfill two functions: re-organize sub-topics into related clusters within the exhibition sections, and establish a hierarchy of ideas so that more important topics could be visually emphasized in the exhibition. While Elaine, a curator, was familiar with the purpose of concept reorganization, unlike the educators, she was unaware of the role of the concept map as a tool for establishing a visual hierarchy. In contrast the educators, Hannah and Emma, believed that the concept map was purely for helping the exhibit designers with the three and two-dimensional design of the exhibition. It was no wonder then, that they expressed some frustration when Martin presented later versions of the concept map to the Dogs Group and Brad and Elaine began to rearrange concept bubbles. With their understanding of the role of the concept map, Emma and Hannah saw Brad and Elaine's second round revisions of the concept maps as an unfortunate side effect: changes on the concept map generated a lot of additional work. The act of the curators rearranging the concept map meant that the educator's narrative would also have to be rearranged and the label copy that had already been written would have to be revised.

Martin believed that his role as a designer went beyond the design of the two and three dimensional elements of the exhibition. He believed that his role should include designing the structure of the concepts within the exhibition. He also thought that the concept map was a way that he could directly engage the curators in the conceptual design of the exhibition. Martin's structuring artifact was produced partially to help his own community of practice, but he also used it indirectly to help that of the curators because he believed that the message of an exhibition should come from the curators.

Hannah and Emma sat patiently through a couple iterations of Martin's concept maps with the understanding that they were helping Martin to put concepts in a hierarchy of importance for the purpose of emphasizing concepts visually. But ultimately, the concept map was hardly used for that purpose. Most of the exhibition was comprised of kiosks and the size and shape of the kiosks were limited to two basic styles. The decision to use only two basic styles was a business decision to make fabrication easier and faster. The exhibit designers had control over placement of kiosks, wall panels, and islands within the space of each section; However, these decisions were largely determined by practical (e.g. safety and flow) and aesthetic concerns (e.g. making the view of the next section attractive from the point of view of the section in which one is standing). Ultimately the exhibit designers themselves actually had fairly little to work with in order to visually emphasize concepts deemed particularly important. Furthermore, the graphic designers never saw the concept map. Despite Martin's intentions, the concept map was hardly used to influence the visual prominence of the various exhibits. However, it was very much used to promote an alternative to the structuring artifact of the educator's narrative.

The concept map structuring artifact was also used to direct the activity of others and, less successfully, to create shared understanding. Structuring artifacts are used to coordinate media and understanding but, unlike compilation artifacts, structuring artifacts are also used to establish ordering principles, establish tenor of narratives, and to direct the activity of others. Structuring artifacts can be used to promote alternative ordering principles and alternative protocols that shake the status quo.

5) Borrowed artifacts are artifacts that are taken from its creator in one community of practice and used in unanticipated ways by those in another community of practice. Designers use borrowed artifacts to augment their understanding of design problems. The practice of borrowing occurs when communities of practice are in close proximity.

Example: Brent's Physical Design Collages

In January of 2002, the fabrications coordinator, Brent, spoke to the NHM Dogs staff to ask for more specifics about the exhibits that were to comprise the final exhibition. He was concerned that he did not have enough information to allocate human resources in the upcoming months. Brent needed to know what sorts of exhibits were going to be built and how many of each type. He was not getting the type of information he needed in order to begin building the exhibition. The rest of the Dogs Groups replied to his request with pleas for patience—they would get to it soon.

Consequently, Brent decided to create a self-explanation artifact from several artifacts: two versions of the educator's narrative, the exhibition floor plan, and the concept sketches. He incorporated these three different types of documents into a self-explanation artifact without the knowledge of the producers. Using scissors, he cut pieces from the documents he had gathered and pasted them to blank sheets of paper. Each fully assembled sheet represented one exhibit.

Brent created a self-explanation artifact in much the same way that Emma created her Images and Artifacts table. However, in this case we have a borrower from one community of practice borrowing artifacts from two other communities of practice: exhibit design and education. The concept of borrowed artifacts is focused on the procurement of an artifact and not its creation. Therefore borrowed artifacts are can be used as another type of boundary negotiating artifact, sometimes being physically transformed in the process. In our example, Brent takes objects that he finds useful and adopts them for his own purposes: creating a self-explanation artifact.

The importance of borrowed artifacts is that they imply a special kind of relationship between communities of practice. The communities of practice must be in close enough proximity that they are aware of the artifacts created by other communities of practice, and while not having dual membership, is in a trusted position whereby he or she has access to those artifacts and can appropriate them for his or her own community of practice to further the goals of the project. Furthermore the community of practice that produces the artifact bears no burden for making their product intelligible or useable for the borrower's community.

Discussion of Boundary Negotiating Artifacts

Each type of artifact is entangled in a mesh of practices. The Dogs Group was relatively unaccustomed to working together and was also unaccustomed to working on a project of this size and complexity so some practices were more evolved than others.

The practices surrounding self-explanation were fairly evolved because each team member had years of specialized experience with artifacts in their own field. Each team member had years of specialized training and experience that helped them create self-explanation artifacts for recording and analyzing ideas in ways that were understandable and helpful to themselves and to those from similar backgrounds.

The practices surrounding inclusion artifacts were fairly simple: involving creating and proposing on the part of the artifact's creator; and accepting, rejecting, or reserving judgment on the part of the receivers (the other communities of practice). Including, and the related practices of accepting and rejecting, took up a great deal of time during the meetings of the Dogs Group. These practices were stable and occasionally including practices would take place without the actual creation of an inclusion artifact.

Unlike with self-explanation and inclusion artifacts, the practices surrounding compilation artifacts and structuring artifacts were not well-developed and required the development of new practices. This resulted in confusion and conflict. The curators, educators, and the exhibit designer each produced their own structuring artifacts and they each had their own expectations for how their own artifacts and those of others would be used.

Boundary negotiating artifacts are used to: record, organize, explore and share ideas; introduce concepts and techniques; create alliances; create a venue for the exchange of information; augment brokering activities; and create shared understanding about specific design problems. The taxonomy of boundary negotiating artifacts and its sub-concepts of inclusion, self-explanation, compilation, structuring, and borrowed artifacts illustrates artifacts in the context of their use.

Implications for CSCW

Boundary negotiating artifacts may be considered to be an extension of previous work on coordinative artifacts such as ordering systems, intermediary objects, and prototypes. The concepts of structuring and compilation artifacts resonate with the concepts of ordering systems (Schmidt and Wagner 2005) and intermediary objects (Boujut and Blanco 2003)—and to a lesser extent to the concept of prototypes (Subrahmanian, Monarch et al. 2003).

Simultaneously, boundary negotiating artifacts are a first step towards a theory of boundary negotiating which is a model of collaboration that: 1) does not presuppose fairly high levels of coordination, 2) does not focus on coordinative aspects of artifacts at the expense of disruptive aspects, and 3) involves artifacts that are not "standardized inscribed artifacts (Schmidt and Wagner 2005)" such as those found in ordering systems. A great deal of boundary work has to do with the discovering, testing, and pushing of boundaries. By extension collaborative work can involve discovering, making, testing, developing, and arguing over practices and how to instantiate those practices into intermediary artifacts and end products.

Strauss (1988) noted that projects could be mapped according to two axes: from routine to non-routine and from simple to complex. On these axes projects fall along a continuum. Routine projects have project paths that have been traversed frequently, with clear and anticipatable steps, experienced workers, an established division of labor, stable resources, and strategies for managing expected contingencies. Non-routine projects would have projects paths that have been traversed infrequently, with unclear steps, inexperienced workers, an unclear division of labor, etc. Complex work includes that which has many workers and many types of and levels of workers, a complicated division of labor, variable worker's commitments, possibly more than one explicit project goal, and a complex organization context for the projects. A simple project would have few workers, few types and levels of workers, a simple division of labor, similar levels of commitments from workers, an explicit project goal and a simple organizational context. If we apply Strauss' definition, Star and Grisemer's prototypical boundary objects (1989) were part of a somewhat routine and fairly simple project because Grinell and Alexander were in the position of having stable resources, had the authority to dictate clear and anticipatable steps, had experienced workers, an established division of labor, an explicit project goal and a simple organizational context. Perhaps boundary objects are found primarily in fairly routine or fairly simple work projects. Boundary negotiating artifacts on the other hand might be more prevalent in projects that are fairly non-routine and fairly complex.

We might consider that not only do projects fall along the two dimensions Strauss described, but particular constellations of artifact types may also correspond with project location on those two axes. At each point in space, perhaps a whole taxonomy of artifacts including, but not limited to, boundary negotiating artifacts and boundary objects, may be prevalent.

The artifacts I saw in use mostly did not have a standardized format and were not devised in a collaborative process. Collaborative work can be highly contested and practices and artifacts are not always well understood. Alignments can be partial, shared understanding between groups can be spotty, and these breaks in alignment extend to understanding and use of representational and coordinative artifacts. Further research might explore more fully the relationship, or lack thereof, between boundary objects and boundary negotiating artifacts. The concept of boundary objects is important and is deserving of more research, but we must also push past the assumptions of standardization and stable boundaries between communities on which it lies. Perhaps boundary negotiating is part of a process by which methods are developed and become standardized (Remember *methods standardization* the less glamorous sibling of boundary objects?) Or perhaps, even more intriguingly, future work may find that boundary negotiating is an alternative form of collaborative work that is advantageous for certain types of circumstances (e.g. short term or highly innovative projects).

Conclusion

Since beginning this work, I was asked by someone in the CSCW community, "Isn't this just a story about people behaving badly?" The answer is no. This is a story of perfectly nice people with a common goal behaving rationally on a project that was highly complex and non-routine. Could the assumption of well-ordered and deliberate progression in the design process be clouding our vision? Might we be dismissing complex and non-routine collaborations as "people behaving badly" so that we can return to the safety of standardized artifacts and stable organizational contexts? Perhaps the artifacts and protocols found in these situations can be most easily codified into our computational systems, but for the purposes of creating a theoretical foundation for CSCW we should try to do more.

In his work on the articulation process and project work, Strauss (1989) noted that that articulation work is but a constituent element of the articulation process. Articulation work refers to the putting together of tasks and aligning lines of work in the service of work flow. The articulation process includes articulation work, but also includes *interactional processes* such as negotiating, persuading, education, manipulating, and coercing. Furthermore, he noted that these interactional processes occur at different levels of organizations and require continual alignment. Articulation work as Strauss conceived it in occurred within an organization and within a project group that was subject to manipulation and coercion. It's not a pretty picture of collaboration, perhaps, but indeed this is much closer to the picture formed by this research.

I have attempted to document a movement within CSCW that branches out from the concept of boundary objects and forms a new constellation of theoretical constructs that lie in the considerable space between chaos and routine. Conducting additional studies of how incipient collaborations create and use artifacts to negotiate and establish boundaries, and that explore the relationship between boundary negotiating artifacts and boundary objects may prove to be fruitful for developing increasingly sophisticated theories of collaborative work.

Acknowledgments

The author gratefully acknowledges Phil Agre and Paul Dourish for reading several drafts and Jennifer A. Rode for providing eleventh hour comments. Any oversights are strictly the responsibility of the author.

References

Albrechtsen, H. and E. K. Jacob (1998). "The Dynamics of Classification Systems as Boundary Objects for Cooperation in the Electronic Library." *Library Trends* **47**(2): 293-312.

Bechky, B. A. (1999). Crossing Occupational Boundaries: Communication and Learning On a Production Floor. *Industrial Engineering*. Palo Alto, Stanford University: 114.

Boujut, J.-F. and E. Blanco (2003). "Intermediary Objects as a Means to Foster Co-operation in Engineering Design." *CSCW Journal* **12**: 205-219.

Bowker, G. C. and S. L. Star (1999). *Sorting Things Out: Classification and Its Consequences*. Cambridge, MA, The MIT Press.

Brereton, M. and B. McGarry (2000). An Observational Study of How Objects Support Engineering Design Thinking and Communication: Implications for the Design of Tangible Media. *CHI 2000*.

Bucciarelli, L. (1994). *Designing Engineers*. Cambridge, MA, MIT Press.

Diggins, T. and P. Tolmie (2003). "The 'Adequate' Design of Ethnographic Outputs for Practice: Some Explorations of the Characteristics of Design Resources." *Personal and Ubiquitous Computing* **7**(July): 147-158.

Eckert, C. (2001). "The Communication Bottleneck in Knitwear Design: Analysis and Computing Solutions." *CSCW Journal* **10**(1): 29-74.

Garrety, K. and R. Badham (2000). "The Politics of Socio-technical Intervention: An Interactionist View." *Technology Analysis & Strategic Mangement* **12**(1): 103-118.

Harper, R. (1998). *Inside the IMF: An Ethnography of Documents, Technology and Organizational Action*, Academic Press.

Heath, C. and P. Luff (1996). Documents and Professional Practice: 'Bad' Organizational Reasons for 'Good' Clinical Records. *CSCW, Boston, MA*, ACM.

Henderson, K. (1999). *On Line and On Paper: Visual Representations, Visual Culture, and Computer Graphics in Design Engineering*. Cambridge, MA, MIT Press.

Hertzum, M. (1999). Six Roles of Documents in Professionals' Work. *ECSCW, Copenhagen, Denmark*.

Karsten, H., K. Lyytinen, et al. (2001). "Crossing Boundaries and Conscripting Participation: Representing and Integrating Knowledge in a Paper Machinery Project." *European Journal of Information Systems* 10(2): 89-98.

Krasner, H., B. Curtis, et al. (1987). Communication breakdowns and boundary spanning activities on large programming projects. *Empirical Studies of Programmers: Second Workshop*. G. M. Olson, S. Shepard and E. Soloway. Norwood, NJ, Ablex: 47-64.

Larsson, A. (2003). Making Sense of Collaboration. *GROUP '03, Sanibel Island, FL*, ACM.

Lee, C. (2004). The Role of Boundary Negotiating Artifacts in the Collaborative Design of a Museum Exhibition. Ph.D. Dissertation, Department of Information Studies. Los Angeles, University of California, Los Angeles: 299.

Lutters, W. G. and M. S. Ackerman (2002). Achieving Safety: A Field Study of Boundary Objects in Aircraft Technical Support. *CSCW 2002, New Orleans, Louisiana, USA*, ACM.

Mambrey, P. and M. Robinson (1997). Understanding the Role of Documents in a Hierarchical Flow of Work. *Group 97, Phoenix, AZ*, ACM.

Pawlowski, S. D., D. Robey, et al. (2000). Supporting Shared Information Systems: Boundary Objects, Communities, and Brokering. *21st International Conference on Information Systems, Atlanta, GA*, Association for Information Systems.

Perry, M. and D. Sanderson (1998). "Coordinating Joint Design Work: the Role of Communication and Artefacts." *Design Studies* 19(3): 273-288.

Pycock, J. and J. Bowers (1996). Getting Others to Get it Right: An Ethnography of Design Work in the Fashion Industry. *CSCW, Boston Massachusetts*.

Schmidt, K. and C. Simone (1996). "Coordination Mechanisms: Towards a Conceptual Foundation of CSCW Systems Design." *Computer Supported Cooperative Work: The Journal of Collaborative Computing* 5(2-3): 155-200.

Schmidt, K. and I. Wagner (2002). Coordinative Artifacts in Architectural Practice. *Cooperative Systems Design. A Challenge of the Mobility Age*. M. Blay-Fornarino et al. (eds.) Amsterdam, The Netherlands, IOS Press: 257-274.

Schmidt, K. and I. Wagner (2005). "Ordering Systems: Coordinative Practices and Artifacts in Architectural Design and Planning." *CSCW Journal* 13: 349-408.

Star, S. L. (1987-1989). The Structure of Ill-Structured Solutions: Boundary Objects and Heterogeneous Distributed Problem Solving. *Distributed Artificial Intelligence*. L. Gasser and M. N. Huhns. San Mateo, CA, Morgan Kaufmann. II: 37-54.

Star, S. L. and J. R. Griesemer (1989). "Institutional Ecology, 'Translations' and Boundary Objects: Amateurs and Professionals in Berkeley's Museum of Vertebrate Zoology, 1907-39." *Social Studies of Science* 19: 387-420.

Strauss, A. (1988). "The Articulation of Project Work: An Organizational Process." *The Sociological Quarterly* 29(2): 163-178.

Subrahmanian, E., I. Monarch, et al. (2003). "Boundary Objects and Prototypes at the Interfaces of Engineering Design." *CSCW Journal* 12: 185-203.

Tang, J. C. (1989). Toward an Understanding of the Use of Shared Workspaces by Design Teams. Department of Mechanical Engineering. Stanford, CA, Stanford University.

Van House, N. A., M. H. Butler, et al. (1998). Cooperative Knowledge Work and Practices of Trust: Sharing Environmental Planning Data Sets. *CSCW 98, Seattle, Washington*, ACM.

Wenger, E. (1998). *Communities of Practice*. New York, NY, Cambridge University Press.

H. Gellersen et al. (eds.), ECSCW 2005: Proceedings of the Ninth European
Conference on Computer-Supported Cooperative Work, 18-22 September 2005, Paris,
France, 407–426.

Coordination and Collaboration Environments for Production Lines: A User Acceptance Issue

François Laborie[1], Stéphane Chatty[2] and Claude Reyterou[1]
[1] EADS Corporate Research Center, France, [2] IntuiLab, France
francois.laborie@eads.net, chatty@intuilab.com, claude.reyterou@airbus.com

Abstract. The Airbus Visual Line (AVL) project, now deployed on the A380 assembly line, was propelled by the desire to foster collaboration and coordination among aeronautical Final Assembly Line teams while going beyond the simplistic – repressive concept of "andon boards" (Monden, 1993). We introduced an environment composed of large public displays and semi-public interfaces to support this collaborative process, so as to enhance team awareness and facilitate coordination among the multi-disciplinary actors. Acceptance of such a coordination system on the shop-floor is a difficult issue. The difficulty is mainly due to the increasing complexity of sub-systems to assemble, the increasing amount of teams involved, the ever-shortening time to market and the circumspection of all actors regarding a 'monitoring' system. This article proposes solutions to facilitate team acceptance in the design of highly distributed coordination environments. The acceptance challenge is developed along three major factors, information targeting, information clarity and privacy concerns. From the points it develops, this article aims at facilitating Computer Supported Collaborative Work (CSCW) environments development in complex coordination system such as industrial production lines, building and construction sites, large naval or aeronautical maintenance contexts.

Introduction

Industrial production lines are seldom considered in the CSCW literature about collaboration and coordination, but they are an extremely relevant field of study. A first reason is the exponential complexity of the products manufactured, which requires an ever-increasing range of expertise during the production phase. Large teams from different technical backgrounds are involved all over the manufacturing process. Another reason is the reduction of time to market, which forces formerly sequential activities to be performed synchronously by different teams. Furthermore, tasks are growingly interdependent, and one's activity can be influenced by the activity of other teams. Therefore, coordination on the production lines is subjected to several issues: distribution of the information space all over the shop floor and sometimes over several factories, huge size of this information space, heterogeneity of the actors' background and interests, and interdependencies within the information space.

Existing coordination systems, mainly developed throughout the 70's, have targeted the resolution of isolated problems (Monden, 1993). Those alarm systems have gained the negative image of a repressive system among the shop floor actors: one of activity monitoring and repression of faults. Evolution of current production practices towards complex distributed tasks and closer relations between operators and support team forces coordination systems to shift towards more comprehensive and less repressive collaboration and coordination processes. Therefore, acceptance of the distributed coordination environment among the different actors becomes a complex challenge when designing for the shop-floor.

Based on a concrete project now deployed in the largest factory in Europe, the Airbus A380 final assembly line, we claim that the acceptance of a distributed coordination environment is driven by three major criteria:

- **Information targeting** – how to define a consistent information transfer to very different teams and hierarchical levels in different locations?
- **Information legibility** – how to transmit highly detailed information, such as a plane assembly planning, to a large audience distributed in a huge area?
- **Information privacy** – how to convince end-users that a dynamic coordination system is not aimed at monitoring their activity?

This article reports on our experimental study of these criteria through the Airbus Visual Line (AVL) project. This project, which went through a research phase in 2002 and 2003, was aimed at enhancing coordination among distributed teams on the assembly lines. Its success led to its industrial deployment in 2004.

The next section looks at related works and existing frameworks for all three criteria. We then describe the aeronautical final assembly lines, set the scope of the study, and introduce the AVL environment. The three following sections develop each of the three criteria through their application within the AVL environment. The last section presents the results of the research project, based on field observation and questionnaires, to assess the level of acceptance reached through the application of the three criteria to the AVL project.

Related Work

Background: Shop Floor Coordination and the Andon 'Alarm' Systems

The use of public displays in the manufacturing process has generally focused on efficient notification of periodic production line failures to the support teams, thus facilitating coordination over simple sequential operations. The *andon* system (Monden, 1993) made famous by Toyota is simply a way to report the occurrence of a problem on the assembly line ('andon' is the Japanese for 'signal'). In case of a problem the operator pulls an alarm string and an electronic board is activated. Typically a yellow signal indicates a problem (missing part, defective assembly, etc) and a red signal indicates the problem is so severe the operator has to stop the line. The team manager or the support team then comes for assistance.

The andon system left a very negative image, because whenever an operator has to pull the andon string, the whole line is stopped and the faulty operator is pointed out by his co-workers. Human contact and solidarity are very important factors on aeronautical assembly lines. A repressive system, or an environment assimilated as a monitoring system by end users, would thus not be accepted on the shop-floor. Respect of information privacy is always a very delicate point for public systems (Jancke et al., 2001; Tollinger et al., 2004). User acceptance regarding privacy issues is certainly the most sensitive and delicate aspect to be considered during the coordination and collaboration environment design.

Targeting Large Distributed Groups with Public Information

Many studies have addressed the need to support collaboration and group-based activities using large interactive displays. Early projects, such as LiveBoard (Elrod et al., 1992), focused on supporting collaborative activities through large electronic whiteboards using novel interaction techniques. Those works have been extended in more recent projects by embedding several interconnected displays in the environment to support more complex collaboration activities. Examples as iLand (Streitz et al., 1999) and iRoom (Johanson et al., 2002) proposed complete interactive environments and investigated novel ways to share information and control between the multiple displays during meetings.

Another approach has been to use large displays to support communication and coordination of groups and teams. Several projects augmented notice boards and bulletin boards found in community areas, thus focussing on the communal spaces rather than the whiteboard in meeting rooms. For example, Plasma Poster (Churchill et al., 2003) and Community Wall (Grasso et al., 2003) were designed to enable people to post and annotate information onto a large public display available to a community of users.

Other applications have exploited the large displays to promote shared awareness by making the information of other's activities available to a community of users. The Notification Collage (Greenberg et al., 2001) and the Semi-Public Display (Huang et al., 2003) augment features associated with community notice boards with an aggregated overview of the activities of a community of users. Kimura (McIntyre et al., 2001) makes a user's current and past activities available to others. Those systems use large peripheral displays to provide background awareness of activities that users have performed.

The use of large interactive boards in communal spaces, or "public" spaces, also found application for "walk-up and use" collaborative activities. The Blueboard (Russel et al. 2002), and its modified version for NASA space mission scientists: the MERBoard (Tollinger et al., 2004), enables identified users to quickly display, manipulate and exchange personal information available on the network. The Dynamo (Brignull et al., 2004) further enhances this personalised information sharing capabilities by enabling several users to simultaneously "carve" their own collaborative space in the public interactive surface.

As observed by Xiao et al. (2001) and investigated by all those projects, the large public boards used in communal spaces can support a very broad spectrum of group activities. By using the persistence of information and playing on the ubiquitous aspect of the large-scale displays in the workplace those large displays can induce asynchronous collaboration among groups and enhance coordination. We based our investigations on those findings to design the AVL environment. However, researchers demonstrated that it can be very difficult to get the users to spontaneously use the collective display. Churchill et al. (2003-2) and Agamanolis (2003) found that users were initially reluctant to use the system and needed constant encouragements to interact with it. Jancke (2001), stresses that the quality and adequacy of information conveyed is critical for the environment relevance, and thus to arouse users' interest.

Visualisation of Highly Detailed Information

Andon systems and most coordination systems focus on the notification of single events. This avoids the trouble to transmit the complete information space to the end users and only convey single, uncorrelated alarms. However, Schmidt and Bannon (1992) demonstrated the need to recontextualise information in order to facilitate information appropriation, and this is confirmed by Xiao (2001). The problem faced with production lines is the size of the contextual information to be passed over. Several Human Computer Interface-related studies have covered the issue raised by large and detailed data visualisation. The Perspective Wall (Mackinlay et al., 1991) or the Fisheye (Noik, 1993) involve geometrical deformations of the information representation in order to better visualise details. Baudisch et al. studied focus plus context systems (2002) for cartography applications, potentially usable in a multi-user schema. Their system is composed of a high-resolution display providing focus, embedded in a larger, lower-resolution system displaying the context.

Context of the Study: the Airbus Assembly lines

Our study took place in the Airbus aeronautical final assembly lines in Toulouse (France). On an aeronautical final assembly line, the aircraft goes through several stages before completion (eight to fifteen stages for one plane program). To each stage corresponds a physical station in the huge assembly plant (see Figure 1). The process is not purely sequential: a few dozens of actors team and support each other for executing hundreds of required operations during the several days the plane stays at the assembly station. For each station there are three types of actors:

- the **operators** perform the assembly tasks. Upon day and night shift alternations they take over the tasks left pending by other teams. They may receive assistance from the support teams for specific issues;
- **support teams**, as for andon systems, perform timely interventions for specific actions (logistics, quality, technical issues) signalled by the operators, and assure the action follow-up. The support team's offices are usually located some distance from the station, up to 200 metres in some cases;
- the **station manager** is in charge of the overall station organization. He or she must have a synthetic view of the current station status as well as an insight of the prospective organization of the station.

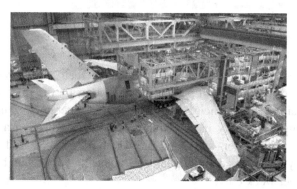

Figure 1: Airbus A380 assembly line station number 40.

The complexity of this inter-disciplinary relationship, each actor bringing its specific requirements, is the key of the final assembly line coordination. From those inter-dependencies, we have identified the following three main types of information a coordination system should convey:

- *Task specific information (operational view)*: details of the technical tasks to perform (documents, tooling…), specific task allocated resources and status.
- *Notification system (tactical view)*: similar to andon notifications, it deals with isolated events and alarms.
- *Planning management (strategic view)*: visualization of overall progress, actions follow-up and impacts forecast; it is the longest term view.

The Previous System

A paper-based coordination system is currently used on the lines. A0-sized pages display a very detailed planning of the tasks to be performed on the station. The planning is called a *balancing,* because it results from a process of evenly distributing the tasks across the available work time and technical competences. It is located nearby the station gathering area (see Figure 2). The balancing organises the station operators' activities much like a classical planning would: resources on the left and an associated time line of operations on the right.

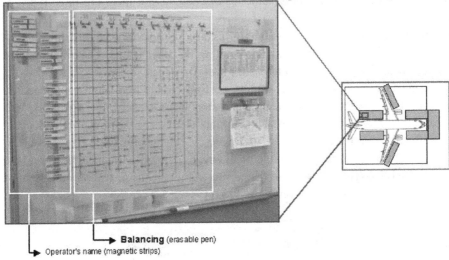

Balancing (erasable pen)
Operator's name (magnetic strips)

Figure 2: Paper-based coordination system and location on the station

Operators update the balancing by reporting their work progresses with an erasable pen, drawing lines of percentage of work achieved on top of a photocopy of the balancing. The balancing is mostly used by operators, to help teaming and daily planning, especially in case of night and day shifts on a same task. The coordination with other actors is mostly verbal and based on experience. Consequently, operators do not update the balancing very often: between once per day to once per week only.

With that system, a delicate issue for the collaboration is the link with support teams, not only for problem reporting (logistics, technical issue …) but as well for quality checks and validations. Usually, operators facing a problem or needing to validate an operation have to walk over to the support offices, write a report and verbally notify the appropriate support person - if found.

Designing the Airbus Visual Line (AVL)

By timely conveying the relevant information to a large audience, a coordination system could significantly reduce the time loss associated with the search of a person on the assembly station or distant support office for notification of some sort (Monden, 1993). It would also enhance the actors' awareness of each others' activities, giving way to "natural" management and coordination on the station (Xiao et al., 2001), empowering the shop floor with knowledge and a vision of their current activity. The AVL environment was designed based on those concepts, trying to create a common information space from the distributed, overlapping information places (Bertelsen & Bødker, 2001).

The Design Process

Given the complexity of our context, we adopted for the AVL project a strong participatory design strategy. Iterative and participatory design methodologies are not uniformly employed by the industry. Whereas they are used up to the industrial stage in information and telecommunication industries (Lindholm et al., 2003), for complex systems such as control or supervision environments they are mainly used by research centres (Mackay et al., 1998; Da Silva et al., 2000). To our knowledge, the application of a user centred methodology to one of the most sensitive sectors of the aeronautical industry was a premiere. The design process followed four phases:

The first phase of the AVL design has been the presentation of a scale one, low-cost, proof of concept of the envisioned AVL system to the end-users.

Then followed a user centred design phase to determine the AVL functionalities. Through participative design meetings, we illustrated design alternatives and saved a precious time over long, time-consuming debates. Concrete images of the future system interface started to take form in the users' mind. In parallel, semi-structured observation of current work practices helped to define the exact context on the assembly line.

The illustrator phase then saw three AVL systems designed, implemented with the help of a visual designer, and tested on three Airbus final assembly stations for a two-month duration. During this phase a very strong support was provided to the assembly line teams testing the AVL illustrators. AVL functionalities were completed throughout the illustrator phase based on regular meetings with the teams, whiteboard located near the public display for free comments, a continuous follow-up and semi-structured observations. This phase brought invaluable insight on the users' perception of the system and of the users work practices.

Finally, following the experiment, all participants were given a questionnaire to gather their feedback. A discussion of the questionnaire results and of some of the observations and interviews will be given in the Results section of this article.

System Overview

In exploring the current work practices on the stations, we realised that the needs for information visualisation were closely related to the actor's activity and location. Because of the station size, all information is highly distributed: from the operator's location anywhere on the plane, to the management information on the station's gathering area and even to the support offices dozens of meters from the station. As a result, the common information space we designed matches this distributed geography (see Figure 3) by providing relevant common information tailored to the physical place on the station.

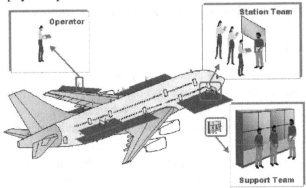

Figure 3: AVL interfaces overview

The AVL environment is based on three major interfaces, all giving access to views of the common coordination space:

- **private input devices**: the primary issue was to enable real time inputs of information on the common information space. A dedicated interface has been designed to enable mobile operators to access and update the coordination space from their location on the station. Using nomadic devices (pen-tablet computer), simple and intuitive interfaces have been designed for declaring the completion of tasks (see Figure 5);
- **large public displays**: what we call the public space is located in an open space, nearby the station and the support team offices. All actors have to pass in front of it to reach their working place. This 2 metres by 1.5 metre retro-projected screen displays a large view (minimum 1600 x 1200 pixels) of the whole station balancing status (see Figure 4). The accessibility of the board, located in a public space, and its size that can simultaneously accommodate several users are key characteristics of a coordination system. The station status displayed is legible from 10 meters to 1.5 meters with different granularity of details depending of the user's distance. Therefore, beyond its use as peripheral awareness display and 'at a glance' overview, the public display can provide highly detailed information on given tasks (task number, percentage of completion, current and past alarms for a given task ...);
- **semi-public displays**: Garbis (2000), in the context of control rooms, stressed the use of a large public display as a medium for reference and discussion among team members. Based on similar observations, a smaller shared display was designed to facilitate discussion among teams of operator directly

on the station. Because of their specific location and usage, we refer to Huang et al.'s (2003) definition: "because the information of these displays is intended to support members of a small, co-located group within a confined physical space, and not general passer-by, we call our system a Semi-Public Display." The semi-public displays are 40 inches screens located directly on the station displaying an interactive vision of the coordination space (see Figure 4). Interaction capabilities have been kept very low to privilege the ease of use. A user, through a mouse interface, can browse the planning, zoom and seek for detailed information on specific operations.

Figure 4: AVL illustrator: Large Public Display (left) and semi-public display (right)

Information Relevance for a Multi-disciplinary Public

Information is distributed on the shop floor. Each actor, by his or her actions, participates to the creation of the common information space. However, depending on their specific role, location and current action, all actors will not need the same view of the information space to perform their tasks. The challenge here is to define the specific information view required for each actor. We focused on the three specific views (or levels) of the common information space: **task specific information** (operational view), **notification information** (tactical view), and **planning management information** (strategic view). By analysing how all actors manipulate each of those three views we identified the distribution of the coordination information in the physical space. Based on this cartography, the contents and location of each coordination elements can be deduced.

Task specific information is typically directed towards operator teams. This information is the core of the coordination system. Observations and interviews showed that operators essentially used task specific information on the station itself. The closer to the operator's workplace, the more detailed the information must be. For instance, specific information, such as technical document for the task one operator was assigned, must be directly accessible on the spot, where the

416

operator is performing his action. It is, as well, directly on the station that the operator can the most easily notify progresses on the task or specify a task status.

On the other hand, on the station's meeting space, where operator teams gather, task-specific information is also used, but only as a reference for discussions. For instance, we observed a team manager and two operators assembled in that space to discuss the daily planning, and seeking the exact reference of a task to support that discussion. Similar situations occurred with station managers about the status of a particular task.

Task specific views can therefore be split in two different uses. The first is directly on the station, where a detailed view must be accessible and information regarding the properties of the task can be modified. The second is on the public and semi-public gathering areas, where references to the task are made, and only the task status is relevant. Therefore, we proposed mobile, personal channels of communication for the operators on the station (see Figure 5) and clear references to the tasks information in the public areas displays. Personal peripheral information channels avoid monopolising public displays for personal information retrieval, and permit nomadic, on the spot information access.

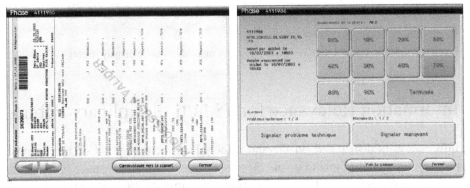

Figure 5: AVL operator interface, for consulting tasks (left) and reporting progress (right)

Notification information, on the other hand, is aimed at the support teams and is, by definition, unpredictable regarding its occurrence. Mc Crickard and Chewar (2003) define this type of interruption as "high interruption", as it should require a strong attention allocation from the user in case of an occurrence. Reactivity is equally expected to be high (a 10 minutes reactivity would be satisfactory), but detailed comprehension is generally not important: the support team only needs to identify the alarm bearer and contact him. We do not expect the support team to seek more details about the alarm on the screen because, as explained earlier, the coordination environment must not substitute to the rich human-human interactions that already exist. Given our notification goals (high interruption and efficient reactivity), McCrickard & Chewar recommend the use of an alarm system. The main challenge for us was to notify the support team in a non-intrusive way for the rest of the station. A non-intrusive parallel notification system, such as a personal beeper, has been envisioned. Still, after participatory design meetings with end-users and management, it was decided that the alarms should be visible by all actors, as for the andon boards systems, and that they should convey contextual information regarding the task and resources impacted. This would allow for a shared knowledge of the ongoing station issues among all support teams.

The AVL balancing interface, publicly visible, provides an implicit knowledge of all station actors' activities. This mutual knowledge gives birth to a "natural" coordination. We observed for instance support teams prioritising their reaction to alarms depending on the task's impacts on the balancing, or notifying another support team that one of their alarms was on. The public display alleviates much of the burden of a centralised coordination by facilitating the direct management of interdependencies.

The third information view, **planning management**, is based on the two previous information views combined with the time and resources allocation. It is essentially directed towards the station managers, even though all actors use this view as a public awareness system. We identified two main usages for the planning view. The main one is the "at a glance" usage, in order to grasp a global vision of the station status. Such a vision should be easily accessible by all actors; we chose to make it available in the public places through the large public displays. The second usage is for discussions and reference regarding the station organisation. This usage requires a more detailed vision of the planning view and usually involves several actors. The closer to the product, the more task-related the discussions become. This is the justification for the semi-public displays. The semi-public displays, located directly on the assembly station, facilitate more operational discussions than the large, public displays. They enable more detailed views and interactions with the task specific views, while keeping a contextual overview of the planning management.

Regarding the specific information the planning view should convey, Reddy et al. (2001), in the scope of a medical coordination system, stress the importance of retrospective and prospective representations of the same information for a coordination system. In our case, the global view of the balancing, displayed on the public screens (see Figures 4,6), offers a clear global vision of all tasks status, fulfilling the retrospective requirement. Additionally, the interface must convey three types of prospective view of the same balancing:

- *The moving timeline*: enhances the time/progress perception indicating the percentage of work achieved and objectives at that time.
- *Upcoming issues anticipation*: expected supply delays notified ahead of time by the logistics support team.
- *Visual impact of current alarms*: based on the balancing critical path, if an important task has an active alarm on, all of the impacted tasks are highlighted on the interface.

418

Once defined, the three views must be appropriately conveyed to the end users through the environment's interfaces. Problems arise there, particularly regarding the **legibility** of the large public displays. Indeed, several layers of detailed and complex information must be merged into a single view. The next section discusses the design challenges faced when displaying large, detailed information for heterogeneous groups.

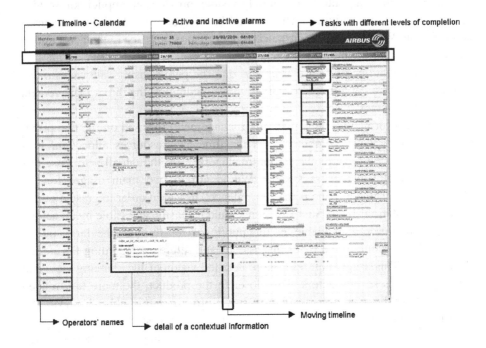

Figure 6: The AVL public interface layout

Targeting Large Groups with Detailed Information

Problems faced when designing distributed coordination interfaces are essentially due to two factors: the huge size of contextual information to display on the public interfaces, and the combination of several layers of information. This section details the solutions proposed for both issues.

Displaying Highly Detailed Information

The balancing, or station planning, is made of thousand of operations allocated to the station teams. Unlike classical planning the station balancing is almost never completed linearly. Some operations may remain pending at the early stages of the balancing while, for logistic priorities, some minor operations planned for the end of the balancing may be completed in an early phase. On top of that come foreseen supply issues on upcoming tasks and pending minor technical alarms. Therefore, to offer a synthetic view of the station, i.e. the contextual overview, the whole station status must be displayed on the public interfaces.

An AVL particularity was the collective use of the large data set to display. After experimenting different HCI solutions with end-users, we eventually proposed a design inspired from Noik's Fisheye view (1993) (see Figure 7). The fish-eye geometrical distortion is limited to the time axis, thus facilitating the horizontal correlation between the resource – operator's name – and a particular task-line. In its "normal" configuration, when no one is interacting with the public display, a fisheye-view of the full station balancing is displayed, centred on the present date and time. This configuration allows any passer-by to see the current station status as well as a detailed view of the same day tasks.

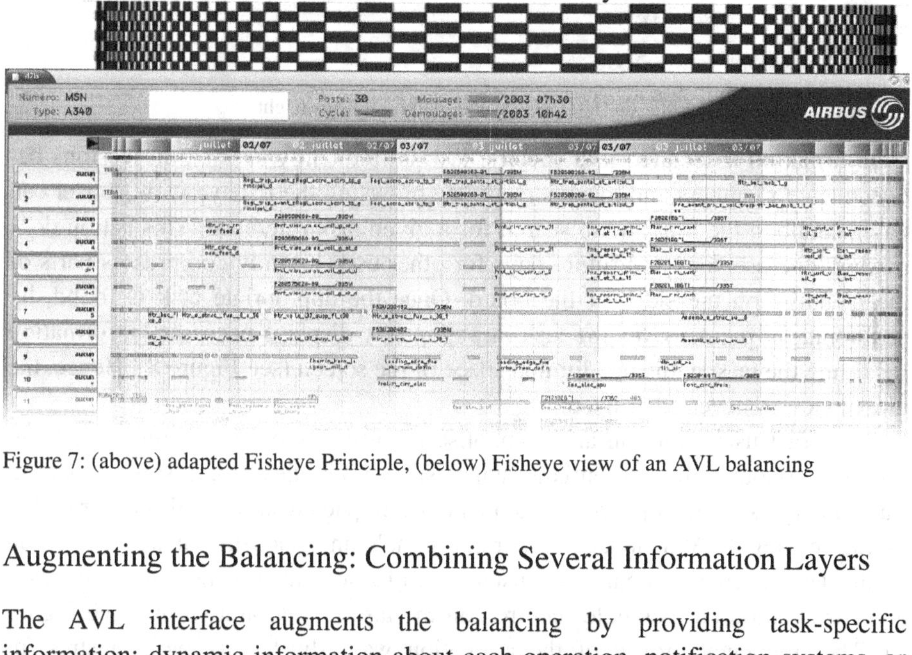

Figure 7: (above) adapted Fisheye Principle, (below) Fisheye view of an AVL balancing

Augmenting the Balancing: Combining Several Information Layers

The AVL interface augments the balancing by providing task-specific information: dynamic information about each operation, notification systems, or an omnipresent moving timeline to mark the present day and time. Thus, we have had to propose a visualisation metaphor that would conciliate a detailed view for the person/group interacting directly with the system, together with a general view for passers-by or more remote readers. Moreover, the large public display is intended to be simultaneously accessible by all station members, hence we had to prevent one user from monopolising the public space as was reported by Russell in the BlueBoard experiment (2002). This requirement implies that all relevant information displayed on the public board, i.e. the synthetic station view, should remain as much visible as possible to the audience no matter what specific interaction one user or a team is performing on the board.

We achieved this by limiting the interaction capabilities to non-obtrusive information retrieval, and always displaying the whole AVL planning on the large public boards. If a user asks for detailed information about a task, it should be conveyed in a manner that does not block other users from accessing the rest of the displayed information at a distance. We describe here two design choices, one for task-related information retrieval, and the other for alarm notification.

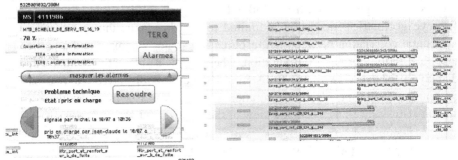

Figure 8: contextual information (left); active and inactive alarms (right)

Information associated to a specific task is frequently used in discussions between team members and management. By browsing the fisheye view, a user can navigate along the timeline to search for a given task reference. This action does not hide the previous and future days for other users, it only compresses parts of the planning on the sides of the board. Once the appropriate task is found, by positioning a pointer over the task, a popup box displays necessary information regarding the task status in a limited space of the screen (see Figure 8). Hence, the global view is never obstructed.

To attract user attention and symbolise the urgency of alarms on an ambient display without using potentially aggressive modalities (loud sounds, strong flashing lights) we proposed to augment the impacted tasks with colour-coded fading rectangles. Whenever an operator signals an issue, the impacted task, on all displays, changes colour – for instance red for technical, yellow for logistics – and fuzzy coloured rectangles centred on the task extend and shrink (see Figure 8). The frequency profile of the animation was adjusted to avoid a stressful feeling when looking at the interface. Then, when a support team member decides to handle the alarm, he/she selects it and signs in. The animation automatically stops, and the colour remains until the issue has been completely cleared.

Acceptance as a Major Challenge

Efficiency, effectiveness and … satisfaction

As discussed in the previous sections we argue that the visual coordination system enhances the effectivity – better coordination – and efficiency – increased reactivity – of the station work. How could such a system not meet user acceptance?

Given the system's dependence to user inputs for its relevance, a problem could emerge if end-users refused to participate and provide information. This would be a sure sign of reject and the system's failure.

We sought to play on several factors to facilitate end-user adhesion. Even though our study occurred in an industrial context, we could not guarantee the system's relevance if it had been perceived as a monitoring system, spying on users' performances. Such an issue can be compared to the public awareness system's privacy issues noted by Jancke et al. (2001). The risk of user rejection had been identified in the early phases of the AVL project. It has been confirmed during the project illustrator phase as several users came to us and raised the question of our exact motivations while we were presenting the system. The main concerns were regarding a fear of activity monitoring, moral harassing and loss of human contact between all station actors.

In order to facilitate end-user adhesion we have used two types of arguments:
- *reflective arguments* explaining the AVL concept,
- *affective strengths* of the interactive system.

Reflective Arguments

No potentially personal information is available through the system's interface. The only information displayed is directly related with the program, excluding competencies, immediate user presence, and all the privacy-related issues.

By setting-up a user-centred design process we sought to facilitate user appropriation of the system from the early phases of the project. Hence, by involving the end-user in a reflection on their own activity, many of them realized the system's benefits and decided to support the project.

The last of the factors has been a strong communication, demonstrating the system's benefits and discussing the potential user reticence. The illustrators were visible by all assembly line teams. The three AVL systems have implemented on three major Airbus final assembly lines stations, each receiving visits from other station operators and team members seeking explanations, offering comments ... little by little the idea settled down.

Affective Arguments

From its physical location on the station, the public display is clearly visible by all the station actors and potential passer-by (client, assembly line manager ...). Any operator can clearly see his/her name written on the board's line. All active or unresolved alarms denote of pending tasks for the concerned support team. All actors are therefore implicitly involved in the system. This argument is playing on the degree of percolation (Galam&Mauger, 2003) a physical notion used by sociologists, it shows that all actors are directly or indirectly aware of each others' activity, thus creating a web of awareness leaving no room for unwanted behaviour to develop, namely inefficiency.

In order to put forward each actor's role, not only are all displayed information associated with an actor's name, but the system's detail must be carefully chosen: small enough for each action to be visible in the system, but large enough to avoid irrelevant information overflow. Two concrete example to illustrate this idea:

- Task progress detail: operators can only increase task progress by steps of 10%, so that a small improvement in the task progress can be notified at the end of a shift for instance.
- Alarm handling: only two actions are possible for support teams: taking note of an active alarm – stops the flashing – and resolving the alarm – suppresses the highlighting –, therefore no change will be noticed until the problem is completely solved.

Through those incentives actors find a motivation to provide information to the environment, as their contribution to the project is made visible.

Another factor for user acceptation has been the visit of important managers to the station while the system was experimented. Even though this argument only prevails for the experimentation phase, it greatly contributed to the feeling of recognition of the shop-floor and facilitated the system appropriation by the teams.

Finally, in the industrial context, final interface aesthetic is not an insignificant argument for user acceptance. The system's interface has been seen as a projection of the user's own work, therefore nice finishing touches can imply the seriousness of the system proposed and of the user using it. The design of the operator's input interface (see Figure 4) gave a feeling of simplicity and intuitivity to the end-users, hence facilitating their acceptance.

Evaluation Results

The best proof of success of the AVL design is probably its industrial deployment on the A380 final assembly lines, thus validating the end-user acceptance and the AVL environment's adequacy with industrial needs.

However, all over the design process several observations and data collection methods have also been applied. We first describe the results of observations and interviews performed with the previous paper-based system. We then discuss the results of questionnaires filled after using the AVL illustrators.

Before: Structured Observation and Interviews.

Structured observations have been conduced before the first illustrators were set-up on the assembly lines to understand current work practices. Two days of observation of work practices have been complemented by nine targeted interviews of a chosen set of station actors. Observation and interviews were all concordant concerning the following statements:

Regarding collaboration between operators and support team, each operator used to walk to the support office two to five times per shift, with an average of 30% unsuccessful visits, i.e. when the support expert was absent. Missing parts were the most frequent problems reported. An average of 30% of visits were to remind the support of a pending alarm.

Regarding existing coordination system use (balancing): the system used to be updated by operators once every two days on average. As a direct comparison, AVL logs show that system's updates have been made two to four times per shifts, usually around breaks or in case of alarm.

After: Questionnaires Results

Questionnaires have been distributed after the experiment to all teams who participated to the three illustrators on the final assembly lines. In total, 41 out of the 45 questionnaires have been collected and analysed. A total of 40 multiple-choice questions were answered. The main objective was to assess user's perception of what was achieved by the new system. We analyse here the user's answers for each of the three criteria.

	Overall system adequacy
System adapted to activity:	94%
Improvement of the activity:	72%
Ease of use – Intuitivity:	50% less than 1 day
(how long to use the system)	100% less than 2 days

	Information consistency – Location specific interfaces
Improved *operational* activity – Nomadic view	95%
Improved station *management* – Public view	95%
Improved *notification* of alarms – Public view	85%

Table 1 Questionnaire results – System adequacy and Information relevance (overview)

Our first concern was to evaluate AVL's overall adequacy with the station activity, not only for the station managers but for all the multidisciplinary bodies of users (**information relevance**). As shown in Table 1, despite their specific activities, *all users* highly rated the adequacy of AVL with their activity, most noting an improvement of their daily work with AVL (72%). Users also acknowledged an improvement of their specific activities in relation with the three information views delivered by AVL (*operational, notification, management*).

As shown in Table 2 and validated by empirical observations of the system in use, users validated the adequacy of the system to transmit **clear detailed information** to large panel of users simultaneously performing different tasks.

424

However, 29% of the users would expect the system to display more details on particular items. The on-station semi-public displays partly answer this point, but we believe that there is still room for improvement in the design solution adopted.

Information Legibility – Targeting large groups with detailed information	
Improved **vision of the station status**	86%
Improved **legibility of the balancing** through the multiple views (*fisheye & compressed*)	97%
Sufficient **level of detail** in the public views	71%

Table 2. Questionnaire results - Information legibility (overview)

Importance of the last factor, **information privacy**, was more difficult to evaluate. We believe that the strong adhesion of all users is a significant indicator that no concerns regarding privacy issues were raised. Indeed, on top of all questionnaires, interviews and group meetings, a total of 66 written proposals have been posted by stations actors directly on dedicated boards nearby the large public display. Those contributions to improve the project's functionalities and specifications prove the strong appropriation of the project by all users and their will to contribute to its adequacy with their actual needs.

These results appear to validate the importance of all three criteria on the system acceptance, and are confirmed by the large adhesion of end-users, from operators to management, that led to the successful industrial implementation of AVL on Airbus A380 assembly lines. The coming years will now show whether, as expected, this success yields improvements in coordination and productivity on the final assembly lines.

Conclusions

We presented the design process and methodology of AVL, a coordination system for aeronautical assembly lines' teams using a set of large public displays, semi-public displays and private interfaces to support coordination and collaboration among the multi-disciplinary distributed actors. We particularly investigated the key features to facilitate user acceptance of such a coordination system. The system design was developed through three acceptance factors: information relevance, information accessibility and privacy concerns. The results of formal evaluations as well as the industrialisation of the project suggest that the design solutions associated to these three acceptance factors have been a success.

This article describes the transposition of CSCW concepts to the production lines context and demonstrate the relevance of this field for future CSCW work. Through the AVL public and semi-public displays concepts, it highlights how public interfaces can transmit relevant information to multiple simultaneous users and how those interfaces can conciliate different levels of legibility depending on the user distance. It finally illustrates how graphical design and user-centred design process can influence the ever increasing acceptance and motivation issues.

Acknowledgements

All visual designs were produced by Jean-Luc Vinot, as well as the Bleriot-tiny font. We are indebted to the many actors from Airbus involved in the project, from operators to the top management. And many thanks to Intuilab and EADS CRC teams for their dedication and support.

References

Agamanolis, S. (2003) *Designing displays for Human Connectedness.* In Public and Situated Displays. Social and Interactional Aspects of Shared Display Technologies. K. O'Hara, M. Perry, E. Churchill and Russell, D. (Eds), Kluwer, 2003, 309-334.

Baudisch, P., Good, N., Bellotti, V., Schraedley, P. (2002) *Keeping Things in Context: a Comparative Evaluation of Focus Plus Context Screens, Overviews, and Zooming.* In Proc. of CHI'2002, ACM Press, 259-266.

Bertelsen, O. W., Bødker, S. (2001)*Cooperation in Massively Distributed Information Spaces*, in Procs ECSCW 2001, Bonn, Germany, 16-20 Sept 2001, Kluwer Academics Publishers.

Brignull, H., Izadi, S., Fitzpatrick, G., Rogers, Y., Rodden, T. (2004) *The Introduction of a Shared Interactive Surface into a Communal Space.* In Proc. CSCW 2004. ACM Press. pp 49-58.

Churchill, E.F., Nelson, L. Denoue, L., Murphy, P., Helfman, J. (2003) *The Plasma Poster Network.* In *Public and Situated Displays. Social and Interactional Aspects of Shared Display Technologies.* K. O'Hara, M. Perry, E. Churchill and Russell, D. (Eds), 233-260.

Churchill, E.F., Nelson, L. Denoue, (2003-2*) Multimedia Fliers:Information Sharing With Digital Community Bulletin Boards..* In *Public and Situated Displays. Social and Interactional Aspects of Shared Display Technologies.* K. O'Hara, M. Perry, E. Churchill and Russell, D. (Eds), Kluwer. 2003, 233-260.

Elrod, S., Bruce, R., Gold, R., Goldberg, D., Halasz, F., Janssen, W., Lee, D., McCall, K., Pederson, E., Pier, K., Tang, J., Welch, B. (1992) *LiveBoard: a Large Interactive Display Supporting Group Meetings, Presentations and Remote Collaboration.* In Proc. of CHI'92, ACM Press. pp 599-607.

Galam, S., Mauger, A. (2003) *On reducing terrorism power: a hint from physics.* In Physica A, Volume 323, Elsevier Science B.V. Editors, 695-704.

Garbis, C. (2000) *Communication and Coordination Through Public and Private Representations in Control Rooms.* In Proceedings of CHI2000, ACM Press, 67-68

Greenberg, S., Rounding, M. (2001) *The Notification Collage.* In Proc. CHI 2001, ACM Press 514-521.

Grasso, A. (2003) *Supporting communities of practice with large screen displays.* In Public and Situated Displays. Social and Interactional Aspects of Shared Display Technologies. K. O'Hara, M. Perry, E. Churchill and Russell, D. (Eds), Kluwer, 2003, 261-282.Huang, E. M., Mynatt, E. D. (2003) *Semi-Public Displays for Small, Co-located Groups.* In Proc. Of ACM CHI2003, ACM Press, 49-56.

Jancke, G., Venolia, G., Grudin, J., Cadiz, J., Gupta, A. (2001) *Linking Public Spaces: Technical and Social Issues.* In Proc. of CHI 2001, ACM Press, 530-537.

Johanson, B., Fox, A. Winograd, T. (2002) *The Interactive Workspaces Project: Experiences with Ubiquitous Computing Rooms.* IEEE Pervasive Computing Magazine 1(2), April-June 2002.

Lindholm, C., Keinonen, T., Kiljander, H. (2003) *Mobile Usability. How Nokia changed the Face of the Mobile Phone.* McGraw-Hill, New-York.

Mackay, W., Fayard, A.L., Frobert, L., Medini, L. (1998) *Reinventing the Familiar: Exploring an Augmented Reality Design Space for Air Traffic Control.* In Proc. CHI'98, ACM Press.

MacIntyre, B., Mynatt, E.D., Voida, S., Hansen, K.M., Tullio J., and Corso, G.M. (2001). *Support for multitasking and background awareness using interactive peripheral displays.* In Proc. UIST 2001. Orlando, Florida: ACM Press, pp. 41-50.

Mackinlay, J. D., Robertson, G. G., Card, S. K. (1991) *The Perspective Wall: Detail and Context Smoothly Integrated.* In Proc. SIGCHI'91, ACM Press, 173-179.

McCrickard, S. D. and Chewar, C. M. (2003) *Attuning notification design to user goals and attention costs.* In Communication of The ACM Vol 3, March 2003, ACM Press, 67-72.

Monden, Y. (1993) *Toyota Production System: An Integrated Approach to Just-In-Time*, Second Edition, Industrial Engineering and Management Press.

Noik, E. G. (1993), *Exploring Large Hyperdocuments : Fisheye View of Nested Networks.* In Proc. ACM Conference on Hypertext and Hypermedia (HT'93), ACM Press 192-206.

Reddy, M.C., Dourish, P., Pratt, W. (2001) *Coordinating Heterogeneous Work: Information and representation in Medical Care.* In Proc. ECSCW'01, 239-258.

Russell, D., M., Drews, C., Sue, A. (2002) *Social Aspects of Using Large Public Interactive Displays for Collaboration.* In Proc Ubiquitous Computing conference (UbiComp 2002), Göteborg, Sweden, 229-236

Schmidt, K., Bannon, L. (1992) *Taking CSCW Seriously: Supporting Articulation Work.* In Computer-Supported Collaborative Work. An International Journal, vol. 1, no. 1-2, 7-40.

Da Silva, A.M., Calani Baranauskas, A.C. (2000) *The Andon System: Designing a CSCW Environment in a Lean Organization.* 6th International Workshop on Groupware (Criwg 2000), IEEE Computer Society Eds., 130-133.

Streitz, N., Geißler, J., Holmer, T., Konomi, S., Müller-Tomfelde, C., Reischl, W., Rexroth, P., Seitz, P., Steinmetz, R. (1999) *i-LAND: An interactive Landscape for Creativity and Innovation.* In. Proc. CHI'99, ACM Press 120-127.

Tollinger, I., McCurdy, M., Vera, A.H., Tollinger, P. (2004) *Collaborative Knowledge Management Supporting Mars Mission Scientists.* In Proc. CSCW'04, ACM Press pp 29-38.

Xiao, Y., Lasome, C., Moss, J., Mackenzie, C., F., Faraj, S. (2001) *Cognitive Properties of a Whiteboard: A Case Study in a Trauma Centre.* In Proc ECSCW 2001, Bonn, Germany, Kluwer Academics Publishers 259-278.

H. Gellersen, K. Schmidt, M. Beaudouin-Lafon, and W. Mackay (eds.). *Proceedings of the Ninth European Conference on Computer-Supported Cooperative Work, 18-22 September 2005, Paris, France*

Sharing the square: Collaborative Leisure in the City Streets

Barry Brown[1], Matthew Chalmers[1], Marek Bell[1], Malcolm Hall[1], Ian MacColl[2], Paul Rudman[1]

[1]Department of Computing Science, University of Glasgow, Glasgow, UK [2]School of IT and Enginnering, University of Queensland, Brisbane, Australia

Abstract. Sharing events with others is an important part of many enjoyable experiences. While most existing co-presence systems focus on work tasks, in this paper we describe a lightweight mobile system designed for sharing leisure. This system allows city visitors to share their experiences with others both far and near, through tablet computers that share photographs, voice and location. A collaborative filtering algorithm uses historical data of previous visits to recommend photos, web pages and places to visitors, bringing together online media with the city's streets. In an extensive user trial we explored how these resources were used to collaborate around physical places. The trial demonstrates the value of technological support for *sociability* - enjoyable shared social interaction. Lastly, the paper discusses support for collaborative photography, and the role history can play to integrate online media with physical places.

Introduction

Supporting co-presence, collaboration and shared experiences between distant individuals are long-standing goals of CSCW research (Gaver, 1992). The many limitations of current collaborative technologies, such as telephones and video conferencing, have prompted researchers to explore new ways of sharing space, objects and presence. Techniques such as moving cameras (Kuzuoka et al., 1994),

428

laser pointers (Keiichi et al., 1999), multiple screens (Gaver et al., 1993) and mobile robots (Paulos and Canny, 1997) have all been used to support shared interactions. However, despite some successes current systems require considerable set-up and configuration and are predominantly designed for use in stable office or work settings. In this paper, we present a more lightweight approach focusing specifically on *mobile* users and collaboration as part of *leisure*. Building on ethnographic studies of tourism (Brown and Chalmers, 2003), previous systems (Brown et al., 2003), and conceptual work on weaving media together (Chalmers, 2004), the *George Square* system uses a small, portable tablet PC to allow a mobile visitor to explore a city while sharing his or her location and activity with others. The tablet is connected via the Internet to other users running the same software on other tablet or desktop PCs. This supports collaboration around both the online and physical aspects of the place being visited. The scenario we explore in this paper is of a tourist visiting a city square, sharing that visit with a companion who is at home, however our system is generally applicable to sharing of places at a distance.

Four key collaborative resources are provided. First, users' locations are tracked using GPS and displayed on a map, with non-mobile users able to move an equivalent avatar by clicking on the map. This supports a shared sense of context in terms of location. Second, users can share photographs taken from an attached camera. Third, users' behaviour is recorded and compared to the history of others' past behaviour, producing a focused set of recommendations of places, web pages and photos displayed on the map. Lastly, the system uses voice-over-IP to support talk between participants.

In an extensive trial of the system we studied how the system could support a shared visit to a city square across the Internet. In particular, we describe how the system supported the enjoyable aspects of shared visiting, in particular *sociability* (Simmel, 1949), the experience and enjoyment of shared experiences with others. In use, the shared conversational resources of the system proved to be of primary importance in that photos and webpages provided visitors with topics to discuss during their shared visit. Along with collaborating around the viewing of photographs, participants also shared the taking of photographs—collaboratively creating and arranging photographs of the square. Lastly, the system's use of history, through the recommendation system, worked to bring together online aspects of the visited square with the physical site. Broadly, this paper underlines the potential of mobile CSCW systems when designed for leisure and sociability.

Previous Work

City visiting has been a popular area for research in mobile information systems, in particular (Cheverst et al., 2000) and other PDA–based systems (Abowd et al.,

1997; Fesenmaier et al., 2000). Indeed, as mobile phones and other portable devices become more advanced, tourism is one obvious application area. A number of phone operators have released city guides that can be accessed on one's phone (e.g. http://www.lonelyplanet.com/mobile/), however these and other commercial technologies have had limited success. Generally, these systems are based around a 'walk–up, pop–up' model in which information, such as text or pre–recorded speech, is pushed at a user based on his or her current location (Oppermann et al., 1999). There has been little explicit support for *collaboration* between visitors (with rare exceptions such as *Sotto Voce* (Grinter et al., 2002)).

Our earlier ethnographic studies of tourism underlined (Brown et al., 2003) the importance of collaboration as a key part of visiting, and of leisure more generally (Urry, 1990, p131). Indeed, tourists already put considerable effort into sharing their visit with distant others – such as through travelogues, or sending photos home from their holiday. In turn, online collaboration has recently developed into a popular form of leisure in its own right, in the form of online games. This suggests the value of experimenting with new forms of shared leisure experiences that bring these aspects together.

The Lighthouse system (Brown et al., 2003) supported collaborative museum visiting by connecting online interactions with traditional visit experiences. This system was designed for collaboration between online museum visitors and those visiting an actual museum. A group of visitors, each in a different location, used VR, 2D maps, the web and audio links to share a museum visit. The on–site visitor in the museum used a PDA with an ultrasonic tracking system to communicate with two online co-visitors using a virtual reality (VR) and web version of the museum that we had created. In a trial of this system, we highlighted how users could bring together digital and physical exhibits through their interactions. Visitors would share and interact around exhibits which were physically in the museum for some visitors, and were presented as web pages to others, forming what we called 'hybrid exhibits'. These were exhibits that linked places and electronic information about them, through visitors' collaboration.

Although this system demonstrated the feasibility of collaborative leisure experiences, the system itself had a number of limitations. The system was restricted with regard to mobility, since its use was fixed to one location, and not easily scalable beyond the Lighthouse, since web and VR versions of each new setting would have to be produced at some cost and effort. The differences between users were also artificial in that the design imposed a restrictive model of distinct PDA, web and VR users, rather than allowing users to choose their own configuration of devices and tools. Lastly, visitors were to a large extent passive consumers of the content of the museum, rather than having the opportunity to leave lasting comments or contributions themselves.

System Overview

To address these limitations, we have developed support for collaborative leisure further with the *George Square* system. This system breaks with our previous work in a number of ways. It is designed for use outdoors in the city streets, working anywhere a network connection is available. In this less constrained setting, content is much harder to produce, so its usage involves the sharing of existing digital resources that are available, such as maps and web pages, and content that users themselves produce, such as photographs.

Figure 1. Example usage of the system and screenshot showing a map that displays each user's location (1), thumbnail photos (2), recommended locations, web pages (3) and photos (4), and each user's recommendation list (5).

When using the system each tourist can visit the city much as they would in a normal city visit. On a handheld tablet PC, the visitor's location is tracked using a GPS unit and shown (e.g. 1 in Figure 1) on a map of the city. Maps are automatically downloaded over the Internet from a map server, allowing the system to be run anywhere with map data available. As an alternative to tracking location via GPS, visitors can select a 'manual position' mode, and then click on the map to specify their position. As a visitor moves around the square, he or she can take photographs of attractions using an attached camera. The pictures are geo-referenced and shown on all users' maps at the location where the picture was taken (2). These pictures are also shown in temporal order on a shared 'filmstrip' view at the top, alongside buttons to control the map's zoom level, briefly highlight a position on the map, change positioning mode and take a photo.

A key finding from our earlier studies of tourism was that tourists often need to combine information from guidebooks and maps. A design goal was therefore to experiment with visualisations that combine their functionality. George Square uses previous activity to filter information for visitors. Users' movements and activity are logged in a database, recording the attractions in the square each user encountered, web pages browsed and photographs taken. The last few minutes' log entries are used to find periods of time with similar context and activity data in the logs of all previous visitors. This is the first stage of the Recer collaborative filtering algorithm (Chalmers et al., 1998), which we use here to find attractions and web pages (3) accessed by previous visitors in similar contexts. Pictures taken by visitors in similar contexts are also recommended (4). These recommendations are displayed on each user's map, and in a legend below each map (5). In order to support sharing and discussion, other's recommendations are displayed 'ghosted' on the map. Map icons for web pages and photos can be clicked to view the related content in detail. Lastly, a voice–over–IP subsystem allows visitors to talk as they visit together.

The system supports a range of different scenarios. Our main scenario is shown in figure one – mixed groups of users either physically visiting a place or visiting online. Through the system visitors share their photos, voice, location and web pages. Physical and online visitors can be guided around a place, or an online visitor could 'piggyback' on the experiences of a physical visitor. However, a single visitor can also use the system, visiting a new place, taking photographs and browsing web pages using the system's recommendations. The system also supports users who are all distant from the area but interacting via the Internet. The latter scenario is important since our observational studies of city visitors emphasised that the visit itself is only one part of a visitor's experience; the 'pre-visit' and 'post-visit' have an important role for both planning and sharing. Our design therefore supports users in planning their visit in advance, and in reviewing their visit afterwards. The database log generated from earlier visiting is used to generate a web page: a travel weblog. One can browse the web pages generated from one's visit, look at a temporally–ordered list of all the pictures, web pages and places that one has visited, and explore a map based on the one used during the visit but summarising one's visit in a spatial presentation (this post-visit 'blog' will be discussed in more detail in a forthcoming paper.)

The use of past activity to build up content in the form of webpages and photographs gives the system considerable flexibility. It can be run in a new city with the minimum of reconfiguration—new content does not need to be produced in advance, since it will automatically accumulate from usage of the system. Together these features develop further the concept of collaborative leisure, in the form of a lightweight mobile system that can be run almost anywhere with a minimum of configuration, pre–authoring and setup.

Technical Overview

The implementation challenges for George Square were typical of collaborative mobile systems, in that we needed a dynamically changing set of devices working together as peers without continuous reliance on a central server and supporting users and devices joining or leaving at any time.

The hardware of our system consists of a lightweight tablet PC with attached compact flash GPS unit and a USB 'stalk' camera. Headphones and mic were plugged into the unit, and the built–in WiFi was used for communications. In our trials, to provide Internet access, a temporary wireless network was bridged to a publicly available WiFi 'hotspot'. This allowed users to browse and search the web, and to follow links to information provided by our system.

For our software we used the EQUIP distributed tuple space system (Greenhalgh, 2002), middleware which supports a peer-to-peer communication model between networks of sensors and output devices via stores (or 'spaces') of records (or 'tuples'). EQUIP is used to send data both between different machines and system components. Tuple space events support sharing data between components as well as network communication, allowing the flexible combination of components. By using a peer–to–peer architecture, each component can also be used without reliance on a central server. The event–based architecture allows devices and users to leave or join at any time, with dynamic and automatic reconfiguration. Events describing user activity and sensor readings (e.g. GPS) are recorded by logging components, and entered into a database. These logging components also continually run algorithms comparing recent activity with historical logs, to create anonymous recommendations. After each visit, we aggregate individuals' databases, so that their logs add to the shared source of recommendations for future users.

The Trial

We ran an extensive user trial of the George Square system in the streets of Glasgow. In evaluating the system we were sensitive to how it could support enjoyable interactions around new places, rather than an optimal, yet potentially sterile, experience. Our focus was thus on the lessons we could learn for designing for enjoyment, as much as evaluating how well our specific system performed.

Procedure

We ran a trial with 20 participants, in pairs of two, recruited as pairs of friends. We chose a mix of locals (10) and visitors (10) to the city, recruiting participants through the city's tourist information centre, language schools and our university. Ages ranged from 19 to 35, with 13 female and 7 male participants. Participants were paid for their time at the end of the visit. Each trial lasted between 35 and 60 minutes, with a post-trial debriefing of 10 minutes.

Each pair of users was taken to George Square, an open city square (125 meters by 90 meters) in the centre of Glasgow. This square is a focus for tourists in the city, has a number of statues, monuments and gardens in it, and is surrounded by several major civic buildings. One user was taken to an indoor venue on the corner of the square (the *indoor visitor*), and one visitor was taken out to the square itself (the *outdoor visitor*). The outdoor visitor was given the tablet computer as described previously, while the indoor visitor sat at a conventional laptop PC, equipped with a USB camera (Figure 1). While the indoor visitor did have limited visual access to the square, a frosted window and the seating arrangement meant that all but a corner of the square was obscured from view.

The scenario we used for this trial was of two friends sharing a visit to George Square, communicating via the system – one physically located in the square and the other remote. Participants were asked to freely explore the square, learning how to use the system and sharing their visit to the square. To specifically test all the aspects of our system, for the last ten minutes of the trial visitors were also given a short list of tasks to complete, such as sharing a photograph of the square, and finding out the height of the statue in the centre of the square.

Analysis

While we had designed our system for a specific application area, we were also charting a new social experience with many differences from existing city visiting. The popularity of online social experiences (such as games and chat) underlines the potential value of new computer mediated social experiences, although we were unsure if this would transfer to the outdoors. Our approach was therefore to explore what worked, and did not, rather than compare the experience strictly to conventional visits. A range of data from each trial was collected: video tapes of the outdoor visitor, video of the indoor visitor, audio recording of the participants' communication, and log data of the system and users' behaviour. For analysis we combined the shared audio channel and the video images into a single video stream. From the logs, we generated a 'replay' visualisation of the system as seen by the trial participants, and this was superimposed onto the video stream. We also analysed transcripts of the post–trial debriefings, and our general observations of the use of the system. Our aim was to inform future design, accordingly, we chose a technique known as *interactional analysis* (Heath and Luff, 2000), based on paying close attention to the details of how users interact with each other and with technology, usually through the analysis of video. We paid special attention to where the participants used the resources provided by the system, such as location awareness. Having a visualisation of the system's behaviour allowed us to better interpret users' reactions to system events. In particular, situations where participants were confused showed something of where the system could be improved to better support collaboration or understanding.

Results

In use, the system presented a novel and seemingly enjoyable experience for trial participants, with all participants exchanging photographs, and using their location and recommendations in their interactions around the square.

Division of Leisure

A key concept in the study of work situations has been the working division of labour that develops as individuals collaborate around tasks and activities (Anderson et al., 1989). In our trials, a complementary *division of leisure* developed. While exactly the same software was used for both indoor and outdoor participants, differences in the visitor's situation gave different capabilities to each user. The indoor visitor used a laptop with a larger screen, keyboard and mouse. He or she could type URLs and interact with multiple web pages more easily. However, this user was stationary. The outdoor user, through their presence in the square itself, could move around to different statues and attractions, taking photographs of statues and of other events out in the square. These differences in situation led to a clear division in what users did:

	Outdoor Users	Indoor Users	Total
Pictures Taken	214 (78%)	61 (22%)	275 (100%)
Web Pages Browsed	25 (20%)	98 (80%)	123 (100%)

Table 1. Number of actions by type of user (N=20)

The indoor user predominantly searched the web for information about particular statues, whereas the outdoor user would take pictures and relay information about the different statues and their plaques. As one of our outdoor participants put it: "if you can't type, you can't surf the web". These results were confirmed by our analysis of the videos. In these, participants form a division of activities by asking the other visitor to either take photographs or find out information, overcoming the limitations of their own situation. For example, one outdoor visitor takes a picture of a statue of William Gladstone and then asks the indoor visitor to look up information on the web:

```
Out:   (Takes photo) Oh There it goes
In:    Did you take it? (.) Ah yeah got it
Out:   Can you look up something about William Gladstone?
```

As with a division of labour, this division between visitors was not fixed or total, e.g. some web pages were browsed by the outdoor user. Indeed, the recommendation system would suggest pages to browse, placing icons on the map that were then clicked to open the page. In this way, the outdoor visitor viewed some relevant web pages without having to type in a URL or search terms. This system allowed the visitors to form a flexible division of leisure, with participants collaborating so to make the most of their different situations.

Sociability

Of all the resources provided by the system, the voice connection proved to be the most valuable for creating a sense of shared experience. Users continually talked about what they were doing, what they had done and what they were going to do. Yet conversation during the trial was not purely functional; it ranged widely covering different aspects of the square, such as the different buildings, people in the square, shared past events, and even the wildlife in the square such as the ever–present pigeons. As an historic square in the centre of Glasgow, George Square contains many statues of the 'great and the good' from British and Scottish history, e.g. Prince Albert and Robert Burns. Much of the talk of the visitors centred around trying to place these statues in history, and understanding a little of who was beyond the somewhat opaque information given on each statue's plaque:

```
Out:  On the statue to James Oswald it says given by a few good friends
In:   (Browsing a web page) Eh (.) I think he's a MP it says he was one of the
      first Glasgow MPs. He was elected in 1841 and the statue was erected in
      Charing Cross and then moved to George Square
Out:  No way
In:   So they obviously thought he was good enough
```

As could be expected with a tourist visit, the more factual 'high cultural' aspects of the square were combined with the more playful. Here the tourists move quickly from talking about statues in the square, to chatting about the pigeons in the square, taking photographs of the pigeons and joking around these pictures:

```
Out:  I'll take some more. I'll take one of a horse
In:   No I don't want to see that I've got one of those. Take one of a pigeon
Out:  Pigeon? What about will I take one of Barry
In:   With a pigeon
Out:  K wants to see a picture of you with a pigeon
In:   Feeding a pigeon
Out:  What? You can't feed the GPS system to a pigeon (laughs)
```

These sorts of conversations are notable for their playful and non-goal focused nature. Our earlier ethnographic work has emphasised that tourism is as much about shared enjoyable experiences as it is about the specific place being visited. Research in CSCW often ignores these experiences, and more broadly the importance of the enjoyment of companionship with others (Brown and Bell, 2004). The sociologist Simmel (1949) argued for the importance of the shared experience of enjoyable conversation—an experience he called 'sociability', where the purpose is not external to that experience but rather is that experience itself. As he put it, when we engage in the company of others (in its purest form) we engage for the company itself (Davis, 1997). For pleasurable and enjoyable city visiting, many of these aspects of life come to the fore, for example the enjoyment of shared experiences and conversation with family and friends, in a setting that supports these experiences and this conversation.

As can be seen in the extracts above, the George Square system had some success in supporting these sociable interactions. Shared photographs, recommendations and web pages acted as 'local resources' (Sacks, 1995, vII p96) for conversation, in that objects that were seen in common could be used as topics to talk about. For example, in the following extract the outdoor visitor has just sent a picture of the Cenotaph (pictured) to her co-visitor. This prompts a discussion about a previous shared experience:

```
In:   Reminds me of the other day when we went to the
      cemetery.
Out:  (laughs) Why?
In:   Eh I don't know. Because of the crosses and all
      that.
```

Alternatively, local resources could lead to photo requests:

```
Out:  There's a shopping centre nearby there I went to a Scottish party with
      Scottish dancing… It was really really nice and the people either they
      were drunk or they were crazy. I think it was half and half
In:   Can you take a picture?
Out:  From the shopping center, yes if you like (takes picture)
```

The different features of the system did thus not just support narrowly defined tasks, but were resources for sociability. The visitors could use what the system provided to talk and share their experiences. Rather than focus on specific clearly defined goals (such as making sure they saw a list of attractions) the visitors could enjoy each other's company, talking about and around the different aspects of the square and the city.

In particular, photographs acted as rich 'seen in common' objects that could be used as topical resources for conversation in this way. They gave users something to talk about, in a similar way to the events and attractions of traditional tourist visits. Shared photographs could be used to comment on and talk around objects in the square, either through direct talk about the features of an object (such as the height of a column or statue), or by referring to events or memories evoked by the photograph. In this way the relatively simple ability to send a photograph and talk as that photograph was taken helped to produce the sociability of the shared visit.

Collaborative Photography

There was a clear distinction between the use of photographs in our trial, and the "photo talk" discussed in previous studies (Frohlich et al., 2002). While digital cameras add the ability to share photos the instant after they are taken using the camera's LCD display, photography is predominately directed towards viewing and sharing much later on, in a different location. The acts of production and consumption are disconnected from each other in terms of time and location. In the George Square system, the ability to share the photographs taken brought these two acts together temporally, even though it involved people in two different locations. Rather than taking photographs to be kept for later, photographs would be taken for sharing in that instant, serving as a conversation topic at that point in time:

```
Out:  I'll take a picture of the stone lions for you
      they're very majestic
In:   Get him to take a photo of you and the lions. Get
      a photo of him [videoing you]
Out:  [Hang on]. Oh. Lion lion back up I can't really
      see. Ok come on. There you are can you see how
      bi(h)g they arr. (2s)
Out:  Have you got it?
In:   Noooh. Oh there it is (.) Very Elvis.
```

Here a photograph of the stone lions in the square is taken by one visitor and automatically sent to the other. After some joking talk about the size of the lions ("can you see how big they are"), the indoor visitor receives the picture and gives a humorous description of the lions: "Very Elvis". Both the taking of the photograph and its reception are tied together in time and integrated into the conversation. Indeed, photographs often had a sequential organisation, in that the meaning of a particular photograph would depend on previous photos and the discussion around them. For example, a photo would be taken as an elaboration of a point made around a previous photograph. While we had told participants that we would give them access to their photographs after their trial, the instant sharing of photos allowed photos to act more like exchanges in conversation than as a way of capturing memories for later.

Furthermore, the features for sharing of photos produced collaboration not only around receiving photographs but also around *taking* photos. Visitors talked about the photograph they were taking as they framed the photo and waited for it to be sent to the other visitor. This talk also included requests from the other visitor for particular photographs, asking each other to take photographs of particular attractions, sometimes rejecting the photos taken and asking for a different one. The choice of what to photograph thus developed over time as visitors talked about different statues in the square, photographing and re-photographing them as they talked.

Sending of photographs is very different to using a continuous video stream, in that taking a photograph is an explicit action. Participants would work around framing photos, taking photos, and waiting for comments or confirmation from the other visitor. The taking and sending of a photo became a shared event, and the photographs taken by our trial participants were chosen specifically to elaborate certain points being discussed, or as pictures of specific features of the square. An undifferentiated video stream would have far less of this deliberate identification. The shared persistence of photographs in the system allowed visitors to talk about a picture, rather than having to potentially hold a camera steady to talk about a particular object.

Walking with Maps

As one of the most familiar of tourist artefacts, most of us have used maps while visiting a new place. In our system, much of users' interaction and collaboration took place around a map overlaid with information, photographs and web pages—information they needed to bring together to use the system. The outdoor visitor also had to relate the map information to what he or she could see in the square, using that information to decided what to do.

Since the map in our system was shared between visitors, it served both *collaborative* and *informative* purposes (as do conventional maps (Brown and Laurier, 2005)). These two aspects were often combined and at times conflicted. The map displayed where the users were in the square, and the photographs they had taken. In addition, recommendations of web pages, places in the square and photographs taken by others were generated by running the previous history of visits to the square through a collaborative filtering algorithm (Figure 2). Each visitor also saw the co–visitor's recommendations ghosted on the map.

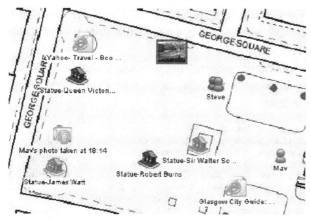

Figure 2. A screenshot of the map showing recommended places, photos and webpages. One's own recommendations shown in full colour while one's co-visitor's are shown 'ghosted'.

One example of an informative use of the map involved an early trial participant browsing the 'Wikipedia' pages about William Gladstone—pages that were then recommended to later trial participants who went to that statue. The recommended web pages were positioned on the map and acted as geographically specific web bookmarks taken from others' past behaviour. These recommendations proved particularly useful to the outdoor visitors, since they could view these recommended web pages by clicking on them, without having to navigate the web. In addition, due to the collaborative filtering algorithm, statues in the square visited frequently by users were recommended more often than others.

These informative uses of the map worked in combination with collaborative uses of the map. Web pages and recommended places on the map were used by visitors when they talked about different places in the square. The indoor user, for example, would ask the outdoor user to go to a particular attraction by using the name listed under the icon on the map. The recommendation algorithm, as well as being informative, took on a role in collaboration by labelling the square. Yet this conflicted with the recommendation's role as suggestions of where to go or what to read next. As an outdoor visitor got close to a recommended place, that label often disappeared because (for our collaborative filtering algorithm) there was no longer any need to suggest that place—because he or she was already there. Rather frustratingly for our users, this meant that the shared labels disappeared just at the point where (or when) they wanted to talk about them.

This tension between informative and collaborative uses caused further dilemmas in our design. Much of the literature on electronic maps argues that maps should be rotated as a user turns (Montello, 2003). This overcomes what are known as 'alignment effects', i.e. the problems that users have in reading a map to find what places are in their visual range. By automatically rotating the map around the visitor as he or she turns, the map always faces the 'right way' up. Unfortunately, as experience with the Lighthouse system showed, users frequently used relational terms to refer to objects on the map, e.g. "I'm right above you now". These terms, which would have an ambiguous meaning if the system rotated the map, causing problems for collaboration.

However, collaborative aspects of the map could work to improve its effectiveness. By talking around places on the map, visitors could help each other to find places and objects:

```
In:   Or see if you can get that --------------->
      picture of that human rights plaque that's just
      near you just now. There's a human rights
      plaque that's just near you I've circled it
      don't know if you [can see]
Out:  [Human rights] plaque. Well I can't but I'm
      walking (.) Oh wait a minute Hold on (laughs)
      hhh I've got a thing (.) no I can't. Put your
      icon where it is
In:   Like here
Out:  Alright well I don't know where that is but I'll walk towards you.
```

Here the participants are trying to find the 'human rights plaque' in the square; a particularly difficult attraction to find as the plaque is small and embedded into the ground. In just this short conversation, the visitors talk about each other's divergent viewpoints, refer in conversation to the different parts of the map, and of the square and finally decide where to go next using their location. Only by talking about the map, the square, so they find the plaque and start moving towards it.

Location and pointing

A specific issue of importance in the design of electronic maps is their ability to show users' location – a topic extensively discussed in the literature although predominantly from a technical direction (with the notable exception of (Benford et al., 2004)). In our trials location was important in the way it helped visitors understand each others' context. Location could be set either via a GPS unit, or via a self–reported location given by clicking on the map. With the exception of one trial, when the GPS unit had poor accuracy, the indoor visitors used manual positioning and the outdoor visitors used GPS positioning. The map proved to be a focal point of collaboration for both the indoor and the outdoor visitor. The indoor visitors made use of the outdoor visitors' location to access the local context of the outdoor visitor. For example, by referring to a statue that the indoor visitor could see was 'right next to you':

```
In: Take a picture of the Robert Burns statue.
    It's right next to you.
```

When an outdoor visitor talked about a particular statue, his or her location could be used to find what statue he or she was actually talking about. The outdoor visitor's *implicit* location could be used to find out what they were looking at when it was automatically updated from the GPS readings.

However, the indoor visitor had to move his or her position explicitly. This led to the indoor visitor's position having a different meaning to that of the outdoor user. Instead, the indoor position was used *explicitly* for deixis, that is to point to parts of the map. This need to move thus made position more a gestural resource than an implicit indicator of context. For example, in this extract the indoor visitor moves her icon around the map to point to the different squares on the map, asking if they are all statues:

Inside visitor moves her icon around the map as she refers to the different statues

```
In:   The circles in the corner?
Out:  Yeah that's all statues again
In:   There's lots of little squares like this one
      this one this one this one.
      That's all statues?
Out:  Yeah all of them.
```

The indoor visitor uses her position to refer to points on the map. While the system had specific telepointer support for gesturing on the map, users often simply moved their avatar around to gesture at different points on the map.

Design Implications

Although George Square was designed to support city visiting, the synchronous aspect of its collaboration are similar to a wide range of collaborative applications, from instant messaging to picture messaging. Therefore, we will attempt to draw implications more broadly for the design of CSCW systems, in particular for systems with an application to leisure. We make three main points: firstly we argue that CSCW systems should provide resources not only for completion of narrow goals, but also for sociable interactions between users. Second, we argue that collaboration around photos can be about not just photo sharing but also shared photo taking. Lastly we discuss how history can be used both to manage the information displayed to users and also as further support for collaboration.

Designing for Sociable Interaction

The first lesson we draw from our trials is that in designing CSCW systems we should provide resources not only for specific tasks and goals but more broadly for sociable interactions. The George Square system was not used only for specific tasks in the square, but more broadly for sociable interactions around the square. The key distinction here is between designing for goal centred activities or activities where we obtain pleasure in the experience itself.

Earlier studies of tourism have emphasised to us the value of these interactions as part of tourism. Sociable interaction, while not necessarily goal–oriented, is not without purpose. Rather it is part of the flow of an enjoyable experience; 'talk for the sake of talk' is the very stuff of sociability. Interactions of this kind are an often–neglected aspect of collaborative systems, since there is a traditional focus on supporting the task, rather than talk around that task. However in creating enjoyable collaborative environments, particularly those used for leisure, this sort of talk is important in how it can help to create shared experiences. We enjoy doing things with others not only because of the activity itself but also because we can naturally talk around that activity. Systems should support users' interactions around the tools they use, rather than simply the use of those tools.

Key to supporting such interactions in George Square were the 'local resources' that the system provided. These were topical resources in the environment, which the system shared and made available to others. In particular, our trial participants used shared photographs in this way, to tell stories inspired by photos and to express their opinions on different aspects of places. The photographs, while being taken and after being taken, acted as resources for conversation about their experiences and for more general chat. This underlines how systems can support sociable interaction through relatively simple mechanisms.

Photos are one important resource, but other collaborative features can be used to support sociable chat. For example, in an instant messaging client we have recently been experimenting with sharing screenshots and a history of system commands used. Although in some ways quite different to the sharing of photographs in George Square, sharing selected parts of ongoing and recent activity also provides local resources for talk.

Collaboration Around Photo Taking

While the popularity of camera phones shows the value of the sharing of photographs between mobile devices, camera phones currently support only the asynchronous sending of photographs (via MMS) or mobile video-conferencing (on 3G phones). While this is not without value, it lacks much of the important synchronous social interactions which take place around photography (Kindberg et al., 2005). The coupling of both taking and sharing photographs was a particularly powerful use of photographs in our trials. This suggests that mixed modes of interaction around photos on phones may provide more value to users. For example, phones or other mobile devices could support augmenting phone calls with the ability to take photographs and then talk around those photos. Photographs in this context are potentially more valuable for collaboration than a video stream, since the static shared display of a photograph supports talk around specifically aspects of that photograph. Taking a photo can also be an event in itself, differentiating one moment over others, whereas a video stream would show an undifferentiated flow.

We found other features also helped support this richer interaction, for example the georeferencing of pictures on a map and the persistent display of photographs on the map or in a timeline or 'filmstrip'. These allowed users to relate the current image to previous photographs and to the people, artefacts and buildings in the areas that the photographs were taken in, and hence to request particular photographs, to reject the photos taken and ask for a different one, and so forth. Timestamping of images is already common in digital cameras and phones. We suggest that designers can use map–based and time–based displays of photographs and other aspects of recent activity to share photographs on mobile phones, PDAs or even cameras. These features could support collaboration around both photo viewing, and photo taking.

Using the Past for Filtering and Collaboration

A last lesson we draw from George Square is how the past can be used as a filter to prevent information overload, and to connect online content with specific places. A key problem with maps, and visualisations more generally, is the need to keep the display clear from irrelevant details. This is particularly true in mobile contexts where devices may have a small or restricted display. Through collaborative filtering algorithms, systems can use statistically significant patterns in previous users' actions to automatically prioritise relevant information. Future applications could emphasise or prioritise objects used by users with similar histories to a particular user, with similar periods within their histories (as in George Square), or with particular significance to the current user, e.g. friends or relatives explicitly chosen by the current user. Of course, users might also use more explicit means to select relevant information, via queries for example, but 'implicit queries' (Rhodes, 2003) made by tracking ongoing activity can offer useful information in a lightweight way. One additional lesson we draw is that collaborative filtering of information is more than simply a means of recommendation—it is also a resource for ongoing collaboration. In our trial the displayed map items were used both as a source of information and in the collaboration between users.

Our recommender made use of historical data to weave together online information with urban locations. Photographs taken and web pages browsed by users, such as the Wikipedia page on William Gladstone used near his statue, were stored as an archive of information about particular locations. Without this gradual adaptation to users' behaviour, a large amount of context would have had to be manually entered in the locations that we judged to be appropriate for visitors. Instead, our system made use of patterns of co-occurrence of location and browsing, to place information in contextually relevant locations on the map (Chalmers 2004). This suggests a broad method for making use of people's behaviour to connect together information and locations, complementary to the pre–authored content.

Ongoing and Future Work

The George Square application takes many of the features of synchronous groupware systems such as instant messaging and conferencing software, and moves them to a mobile context. In our future work we are experimenting with both expanding the mobile features of our system, as well as integrating aspects of the system into desktop applications. The functionality from George Square is being integrated into instant messaging (IM) software, expanding the use of IM to more mobile contexts. In particular, we are exploring the use of photographs within instant messaging software and awareness of location. This is to support not only discussions around current photos, but the taking of new photos during interaction. In a very different context, we have also been experimenting with a version of George Square tailored for scientists collaborating with remote colleagues in monitoring urban pollution, where tablet PCs each have an attached carbon monoxide sensor and relate ongoing pollution readings to databases and simulations of urban pollution.

Currently, the George Square system is limited by hardware constraints and by reliance on one wireless network. The tablet PCs we used have a relatively limited battery life (under two hours) and while lightweight are still beyond a size desirable for carrying around longer than a few hours. We have ported the bulk of George Square to both smartphones and PDAs, and are piloting recommender and map systems that use ad hoc networks to spread information in a peer–to–peer way between PDAs. These different form factors enable longer–term and wide–ranging use of the system, in that users can choose to use the system over longer periods such as a whole day, and need not rely one local wireless network for communications or on one particular server for storage. In future trials, we plan to experiment with more asynchronous forms of collaboration for visitors, collecting photographs and comments over days of travelling in a wide area of the city.

Conclusion

This paper has presented a study of the George Square co-visiting system. The main goal of this system was to support geo–spatial collaboration around a place as well as the information about that place, with a particular focus on support for leisure. The system supports city visitors sharing their visit with those at a distance. A trial uncovered how, through the different resources the system provided, visitors could accomplish a shared visit. In particular we discussed how users achieved a division of leisure, used the local resources that the system provided, and collaborated around photography and maps.

Mobile technologies offer the possibility of access to large bodies of information on distant servers and stores, through information-seeking tools such as search engines and recommenders. More importantly, perhaps, they allow new forms of interaction with other people, both mobile and stationary. In George Square we have focused on these collaborative applications with a lightweight system that supports rich interactions between users. This paper shows how we can design systems to support interaction that weaves these apparently disparate places, times, and media into a coherent, manageable and even pleasurable whole.

Acknowledgements

The authors would like to thank Steve North and Chris Greenhalgh for their help in developing George Square, and Eric Laurier and Jon Hindmarsh for helpful comments on an earlier draft. The work documented in this paper is supported by the Equator EPSRC grant (GR/N15986/01).

References

Abowd, G. D., C. G. Atkeson, J. Hong, S. Long, et al. (1997): 'Cyberguide: A mobile context-aware tour guide', *ACM Wireless Networks*, Vol. 3, pp. 421-433.

Anderson, R. J., J. A. Hughes and W. Sharrock (1989): *Working for profit: The social organisation of calculation in an entrepreneurial firm*, Aldershot:Gower.

Benford, S., W. Seagar, M. Flintham, R. Anastasi, et al. (2004): 'The Error of our Ways: The experience of Self-Reported Position in a Location-Based Game', in Proceedings of *Ubicomp '04, Nottingham, September 2004*, Springer.

Brown, B. and M. Bell (2004): 'CSCW at play: there as a collaborative virtual environment', in *Proceedings of CSCW 2004, Chicago, IL*. New York, ACM Press, pp. 350-359.

Brown, B. and M. Chalmers (2003): 'Tourism and mobile technology', in K. Kuuttie*t al* (Eds.): *Proceedings of ECSCW 2003, Helsinki, Finland*. Dordrecht, Klewer Academic Press, pp. 335-355.

Brown, B. and E. Laurier (2005): 'Maps & journeying: an ethnomethodological approach', *Forthcoming in: Cartographica*.

Brown, B., I. MacColl, M. Chalmers, A. Galani, et al. (2003): 'Lessons from the lighthouse: Collaboration in a shared mixed reality system', in *Proceedings of CHI 2003, Ft. Lauderdale*. New York, ACM Press, pp. 577-585.

Chalmers, M. (2004): 'A Historical View of Context', *CSCW Journal*, Vol. 13, no. 3, pp. 223-247.

Chalmers, M., K. Rodden and D. Brodbeck (1998). The order of things: activity-centered information access. Proceedings of WWW 1998, pp. 359-367.

Cheverst, K., N. Davies, K. Mitchell, A. Friday, et al. (2000): 'Developing a Context-aware Electronic Tourist Guide: Some Issues and Experiences', in *Proceedings of CHI '2000*. The Hague, Netherlands, ACM Press, pp. 17-24.

Davis, M. S. (1997): 'Georg Simmel and Ervin Goffman: Legitimators of the sociological investigation of human experience', *Qualitative Sociology*, Vol. 20, no. 3, pp. 369-388.

Fesenmaier, D., S. Klein and D. Buhalis, Eds. (2000): *Information and communication technologies in tourism*, Springer.

Frohlich, D. M., A. Kuchinsky, P. C., D. A., et al. (2002): 'Requirements for photoware', in *Proceedings of CSCW '02*. New York, ACM Press.

Gaver, W. (1992): 'The Affordances of Media Spaces for Collaboration', in *Proceedings of Computer Supported Cooperative Work, CSCW'92. Toronto, Canada.*, ACM Press, pp. 17-24.

Gaver, W. W., A. Sellen, C. Heath and P. Luff (1993): 'One is not enough: multiple views in a media space', in *Proceedings of the SIGCHI conference on Human factors in computing systems*, ACM Press, pp. 335--341.

Greenhalgh, C. (2002): EQUIP: a Software Platform for Distributed Interactive Systems. *Equator Technical Report 02-002*. Nottingham, University of Nottingham.

Grinter, R. E., P. M. Aoki, M. H. Szymanski, J. D. Thornton, et al. (2002): 'Revisiting the visit: understanding how technology can shape the museum visit', in *Proceedings of CSCW 2002*, ACM Press, pp. 146-155.

Heath, C. and P. Luff (2000): *Technology in action*, Cambridge university press.

Keiichi, Y., Y. Akiko, K. Hideaki, O. Shinya, et al. (1999): *GestureLaser and GestureLaser Car: development of an embodied space to support remote instruction*, Kluwer Academic Publishers, Copenghagen, Denmark.

Kindberg, T., M. Spasojevic, R. Fleck and A. Sellen (2005): How and why people use camera phones. *HP Technical reports HPL-2004-216*. Bristol, UK, HP Labs.

Kuzuoka, H., T. Kosuge and M. Tanaka (1994): 'GestureCam: a video communication system for sympathetic remote collaboration', in *Proceedings of the 1994 ACM conference on Computer supported cooperative work*, ACM Press, pp. 35--43.

Montello, D. (2003): 'Navigation', in P. Shah and A. Miyake (Eds.): *Handbook of visuospatial cognition*. Cambridge, Cambridge University Press.

Oppermann, R., M. Specht and I. Jaceniak (1999): 'Hippie: a nomadic information system', in *Proceedings of HUC 1999*, Springer Verlag.

Paulos, E. and J. Canny (1997): 'Ubiquitous tele-embodiment: applications and implications', *Int. J. Hum.-Comput. Stud.*, Vol. 46, no. 6, pp. 861--877.

Rhodes, B. (2003): 'Using Physical Context for Just-in-Time Information Retrieval', *IEEE Transactions on computers*, Vol. 52, no. 8, pp. 1012-1014.

Sacks, H. (1995): *Lectures on conversation: vol 1 & 2*, Basil Blackwell, Oxford.

Simmel, G. (1949): 'The sociology of sociability', *The American Journal of Sociology*, Vol. 55, no. 3, pp. 254-261.

Urry, J. (1990): *The Tourist Gaze: Leisure and travel in contemporary societies*, Sage, New York.

H. Gellersen et al. (eds.), ECSCW 2005: Proceedings of the Ninth European Conference on Computer-Supported Cooperative Work, 18-22 September 2005, Paris, France, 449–468.

Informing Public Deliberation: Value Sensitive Design of Indicators for a Large-Scale Urban Simulation

Alan Borning*, Batya Friedman†, Janet Davis*, and Peyina Lin†
*Department of Computer Science & Engineering; †The Information School
University of Washington
Seattle, Washington, USA
{borning, batya, jlnd, pl3}@u.washington.edu

Abstract. We investigate informing public deliberation regarding major land use and transportation decisions with the results from a sophisticated computer simulation of urban development. Our specific focus is on indicators that portray key results from the simulations. Our design addresses a number of challenges, including responding to the values and interests of diverse stakeholders, making documentation ready-to-hand, and balancing the value of fairness with presenting a diverse set of advocacy positions. We use Value Sensitive Design as our theory and design methodology; our theoretical framework also draws on Habermas's theories of legitimation and communicative action. Our work contributes to CSCW as an example of designing a system for effective use in an environment with multiple stakeholders who have fundamental disagreements, and we conclude by drawing lessons for other environments with these characteristics.

Introduction

Public deliberation and debate over major issues, at local, regional, and national levels, plays a central role in democratic society. We investigate informing such deliberation with results from computer simulations, to help stakeholders understand the long-term consequences of different choices. Facilitating more informed decisions is one side of the coin, but another is supporting the legitimacy of the *process* by which the decisions are made. Our research is guided by the Value Sensitive Design theory and methodology (Friedman, 1997; Friedman, Howe, and Felten, 2002; Friedman, Kahn, and Borning, in press), an approach to the design of technology that accounts for human values in a principled and comprehensive manner throughout the design process. This exploration is grounded in investigations of UrbanSim (Waddell et al., 2003; Waddell and Ulfarsson, 2005), a system for simulating the development of urban areas. UrbanSim is designed to inform public deliberation and debate around major decisions regarding land use and transportation by projecting the long-term impacts of different alternatives. However, the techniques and lessons learned should be applicable to other uses of simulation to support public deliberation, and more generally to enhancing the legitimacy of applications of complex computer systems in the public sphere.

One important characteristic of this problem domain is that it centers on public deliberation and decision-making involving multiple stakeholders. Another is that there are often long-standing disagreements, both on particular projects or legislation, and on the overall approach to urban land use and transportation. These are often rooted in fundamental value conflicts among the stakeholders about issues such as the environment, economic growth, or equity. A third is that the decision-making process can be informed by using modeling and simulation to help reveal the long-term consequences of alternative choices, and that such models can also raise issues themselves, such as concerns regarding "black box" simulations or the input assumptions. From the beginning, our designs have been shaped by these characteristics—in particular the context of a dispute-filled environment, in contrast to more cooperative work environments. These characteristics are shared by other important domains, such as long-range budget forecasts, and environmental issues such as global warming, or biodiversity.

CSCW is concerned with understanding the needs of people who do cooperative work and designing systems to support them. Our work contributes to CSCW as an example of designing a system for effective use in an environment in which participants have fundamental disagreements. That conflict is inherent in cooperative work is well recognized, for even though the core of cooperative work is interdependence in work, this is "by no means necessarily harmonious" (Schmidt and Bannon, 1992, p. 8), and "successful cooperation depends on how conflict is handled" (Easterbrook, 1993, p. 3). Yet, the urban planning context requires a different view of conflict. Conflict between stakeholder groups is often what Pace (1990) calls "competitive conflict" among "entrenched" participants: "[t]his may occur where participants have opposing basic beliefs, values or principles which they believe must be mutually exclusive" (Easterbrook, 1993, p. 25). Competitive conflict may also be seen in groups' formative stages or within functional teams around power relationships.

Much of the work on group decision-making and deliberation seeks to structure interactions between participants. For example, Decision Support Systems focus on the provision of a decision model (Kraemer and King, 1986). Collaboration tool-based Group Support Systems are intended to support and structure group deliberation (Davison and Briggs, 2000), as are "argumentative" or "discursive" information systems such as Issue-Based Information Systems (Isenmann and Reuter, 1997). In contrast, here we seek to inform rather than to structure deliberation.

In this paper, we first provide an overview of UrbanSim and the role of indicators in presenting its results. We then describe our theoretical framework, including our methodological framework of Value Sensitive Design, and our conceptualization of legitimation and transparency, drawing on Habermas's theories of communicative action. The bulk of the paper presents the iterative design and formative evaluation of a component of UrbanSim: an Indicator Browser that integrates live Technical Documentation with a chooser for selecting indicators to use to summarize key results from UrbanSim simulations. We conclude with a discussion of directions for future work and implications for other domains that feature multiple stakeholders with strongly held, conflicting views.

UrbanSim Overview

In many regions in the United States, there is great concern about traffic congestion, resource consumption, pollution, loss of open space, lack of sustainability, and sprawl. Elected officials, planners, and citizens in urban areas grapple with these difficult issues as they develop and evaluate alternatives for such decisions as building a new rail line or freeway, establishing an urban growth boundary, or changing incentives or taxes. Nor are these problems confined to the U.S. In urban regions in Europe, for example, there are often significant disagreements regarding the balance between spending on auto-oriented facilities, public transit, and bicycles; transportation taxes (e.g., on petrol, or fees for taking autos into the city center); or how best to move toward sustainable development.

For example, a regional planning agency might be considering alternate approaches to adding transport capacity, such as a major upgrade to the rail system vs. a new ring motorway around the urban core. To help compare these alternatives and their long-term impacts, the agency might use UrbanSim to simulate the development of the region for the next 30 years under alternative plans, in particular the interactions between transportation and land use, along with their environmental impacts. In assessing the long-term effects of building the ring motorway, we need to consider not only what portion of the current transportation demand can be accommodated by the proposed motorway, but also its effects on land development in the long term around the urban fringe—the motorway might induce additional auto-oriented development in its vicinity, which would in turn add additional traffic, filling the motorway and perhaps creating yet more demand for road capacity. Predicting the future is of course a risky business. In this example, unknown factors that could significantly affect the long-term outcome include the price of oil, possible breakthroughs in technology, or unexpected major shifts in population. Yet we do have to make decisions now, with the information we have. As E.F. Schumaker (1973, p. 240) observed, "The future cannot be forecast, but it can be explored."

To date, UrbanSim has been applied experimentally in the U.S. in metropolitan regions around Eugene/Springfield, Oregon; Seattle, Washington; Honolulu, Hawaii; Salt Lake City, Utah; Houston, Texas; and Phoenix, Arizona; with other applications in process. Internationally, it is being applied experimentally in Paris, France; Tel Aviv, Israel, and elsewhere. It played a significant role in helping settle a lawsuit in Utah regarding a major freeway construction project out-out-court (Waddell and Borning, 2004); the first major use in a public planning process is scheduled to take place in the Puget Sound (Seattle) region beginning in summer 2005. The system is Open Source software, under the GNU Public License, and freely available for download from www.urbansim.org. The system continues to evolve, with the addition of improved and new models.

In urban planning, indicators (Gallopín, 1997; Hart, 1999) are often used to monitor changes in a region with respect to specific attributes of concern. In UrbanSim, simulation results can be presented using the same set of selected indicators for all the policy alternatives being considered, thus aiding the assessment and comparison of different scenarios. For example, suppose that we are interested in fostering compact, walkable, more densely populated neighborhoods within the urban area, and curbing low-density, auto-oriented development ("sprawl"). In the urban planning literature, population density is regarded as one of the key indicators of the character of development (e.g., dense urban, low-density suburban, rural, etc.). We can then monitor population density to understand current trends, and also use UrbanSim to assess and compare the impacts of different policies on population density 30 years in the future. In addition, modelers use UrbanSim indicators diagnostically, to learn about the system's internal operation, to help assess whether it is operating correctly, and to debug problems. In the work reported here, we are concerned with both evaluative and diagnostic uses.

Theoretical Framework: Value Sensitive Design

Our research in this area is guided by the Value Sensitive Design theory and methodology, a theoretically grounded approach to the design of technology that accounts for human values in a principled and comprehensive manner throughout the design process. Key features of the methodology are its interactional perspective, tripartite methodology, and emphasis on direct and indirect stakeholders.

Value Sensitive Design is an interactional theory: values are viewed neither as inscribed into technology nor as simply transmitted by social forces. Rather, people and social systems affect technological development, and technologies shape (but do not rigidly determine) individual behavior and social systems.

Value Sensitive Design employs a tripartite methodology, consisting of conceptual, empirical, and technical investigations. These investigations are applied iteratively and integratively, with results from new investigations building on and integrating earlier ones. *Conceptual investigations* comprise philosophically informed analyses of the central constructs and issues under investigation. For example, how does the philosophical literature conceptualize certain values and provide criteria for their assessment and implementation? How should we engage in trade-offs among competing values in the design, implementation, and use of information systems? *Empirical investigations* focus on the human response to the technical artifact, and on the larger social context in which the technology is situated. The entire range of quantitative and qualitative methods used in social science research may be applicable. *Technical investigations* focus on the design and performance of the technology itself. Technical investigations can involve either retrospective analyses of existing technologies or the design of new technical mechanisms and systems. The work reported here represents a snapshot of this iterative process: we present our conceptual, empirical, and technical investigations so far, but (as described in the Future Work section) intend to build on these in additional work.

A third key aspect of Value Sensitive Design is its focus on both direct and indirect stakeholders. The direct stakeholders here are the urban modelers and technical planners who use UrbanSim and manipulate its results. The indirect stakeholders are those who don't use the system directly, but who are affected by it. In the case of UrbanSim, the indirect stakeholders include all the residents of the region being modeled, as well as residents of nearby regions.

Early in our conceptual investigations in the present project, we made a sharp distinction between *explicitly supported values* (i.e., ones that we explicitly want to support in the simulation) and *stakeholder values* (i.e., ones that are important to some but not necessarily all of the stakeholders). Next, we committed to several key moral values to support explicitly: fairness and more specifically freedom from bias (Friedman and Nissenbaum, 1996), representativeness, accountability, and support for a democratic society. In turn, as part of supporting a democratic society, we decided that the system should not *a priori* favor or rule out any given set of stakeholder values, but instead should allow different stakeholders to articulate the values that are most important to them, and evaluate the alternatives in light of these values. Note that explicitly supported values are *not* the same as designer values—they are subjected to a principled analysis of arguments for their inclusion rather than simply being a matter of personal preference. We identified comprehensibility, and subsequently legitimation and transparency, as key instrumental values.

Legitimation: A Habermasian Perspective

UrbanSim's legitimacy is crucial for its effective use as part of the urban planning process. Stakeholders who do not see the use of UrbanSim as legitimate may never accept decisions that are informed by its use, and may disengage from discourse about urban planning, reducing the diversity of stakeholders present at the table and undermining democratic participation. If stakeholders who do not see UrbanSim as legitimate do choose to stay at the table, their constant questioning of simulation results may detract from discourse about what really matters in the outcome of adopting a course of action.

Our conceptualization of legitimation—its central role in the political process, and what allows a political process to be legitimate—draws primarily on the work of Jürgen Habermas (1979, 1984). The legitimation of an urban planning process depends on a huge number of factors. The modeling software forms only one small part, and even the best-designed system could be used in a process lacking in legitimacy. Since most of these factors are out of our control, in this work we concern ourselves with the *legitimation potential* of the modeling system, rather than the legitimation of the entire process in which it plays a part.

Communicative action plays a key role in legitimation potential. Habermas defines communicative action as speech in which all participants aim towards mutual understanding, without manipulative or strategic actions. In communicative action, each utterance implicitly raises four validity claims: to the comprehensibility of the utterance, to the truth of its propositional content, to the truthfulness of the expression of the speaker's intent, and to the rightness and appropriateness of the utterance with respect to existing norms and values. UrbanSim is just one voice in public discourse about urban planning. It does not dictate the truth; rather, it informs a process of coming to an understanding. As it is used in the course of deliberation, information from and about UrbanSim will raise the four validity claims of communicative action. To provide legitimation potential for the use of UrbanSim, we as designers should do our best to ensure these claims are well grounded. First, the information UrbanSim provides should be comprehensible to the range of stakeholders. Second, UrbanSim's models and results should be a reasonable representation of reality. Third, UrbanSim should be transparent with respect to its inner workings and design, so that stakeholders can see that the model and its results are truthfully represented in the deliberation. Fourth, UrbanSim is cast in the role of a source of relatively neutral, technical information in a highly political process. To rightly fulfill this role, and in the interest of fairness to all stakeholders, UrbanSim should provide information that is as unbiased as possible. The information provided should be appropriate and relevant to the policy context.

Those who have access to information such as that provided by UrbanSim have a power advantage in discourse. In the interest of permitting an equal agreement, as many stakeholders as possible should have access to UrbanSim. Many different presentations may be required so that results can be comprehended by stakeholders with differing expertise and accepted by stakeholders with differing norms and values. While the Technical Documentation is intended primarily for modelers and planners, our Indicator Perspectives mechanism, which lets different organizations present perspectives on how UrbanSim output should be used in making policy decisions, is intended for a wide range of interested stakeholders.

Though Habermas has been criticized (sometimes strongly), for our purposes there is much of value here. Indeed, we embrace critiques such as that of Nancy Fraser (1992), who argues that the ideal of the public sphere must be reconstructed to permit the participation of all. According to Fraser, even after everyone is formally licensed to participate in the public sphere, informal barriers such as that of differing communication styles remain. These barriers can be reduced through a multiplicity of publics that give members of subordinated groups safer venues in which to find their voice, so that they can better articulate and defend their interests in the larger public sphere. The Indicator Perspectives mechanism supports multiple publics in that it allows members of particular groups to formulate positions in discourse amongst themselves and then articulate those positions to the larger public.

Transparency and Comprehensibility

The term "transparency" appears in contexts of human-computer interaction, modeling, and public policy, all of which have relevance to UrbanSim. In both human-computer interaction (e.g., Herlocker et al., 2000) and modeling (e.g., Lee, 1973; Fleischmann and Wallace, 2005), "transparency" is used to designate the opposite of a "black box" system, which hides all information beyond its inputs and outputs. In the public policy literature, the term "transparency" is widely used to designate mechanisms for public disclosure of information. Finel and Lord (2000) capture the notion of transparency as a glass box in emphasizing the visibility of the internal characteristics of a government. For simulation models, transparency provides evidence of the system's "truthfulness": that the output reflects the true behavior of the models and is not strategically manipulated. However, a simple "glass box" notion of transparency is insufficient. It is important to make the purpose and assumptions of the system apparent so that stakeholders can assess when its assumptions do not hold or its purpose is incompatible with the goal of the deliberation. Furthermore, Value Sensitive Design leads us to consider transparency for both direct and indirect stakeholders, who will have differing expertise with respect to urban planning, simulation, computer systems, and the region in which UrbanSim is applied. Therefore, transparency is needed at a number of levels—in the reports read by elected officials and the public, in documentation about simulation outputs, in model specifications, and in the availability and comprehensibility of the simulation code itself.

The Design Problem: Challenges with Indicators

We turn now to the design problem that is the focus of the current paper: how can we create an interaction design around indicators for UrbanSim that will provide improved functionality, support stakeholder values, enhance the transparency of the system, and contribute to the system's legitimation? When we began our work, the code to produce indicator output from UrbanSim was intertwined with the simulation code itself, and adding a new indicator was not straightforward. No single list of the implemented indicators existed, and no single place contained the definitions of the indicators or other details that would be needed by modelers and planners working with UrbanSim. There was no easy mechanism for ensuring that indicator documentation was current, including documentation for how indicators were computed. And none of the above information was ready-to-hand (Friedman, Howe, and Felten, 2002; Winograd and Flores, 1986), that is, easy to access in the course of interacting with UrbanSim. With the design and development of the Indicator Browser, we set out to remedy this situation in a way that would help to support the process of legitimation through increased access to and transparency of the indicators. Specifically, we set out to address the following design challenges:

(1) *Fragmentation of indicator information*, in many different sources.
(2) *Lack of ready-to-hand indicator information.*
(3) *Diverse sources and competing definitions for indicators.*
(4) *Difficulty of comprehending indicator information.*
(5) *Difficulty of inspecting and understanding how indicators are computed.*
(6) *Sometimes outdated or inaccurate information.*
(7) *Difficulty of adding and modifying indicators (and corresponding documentation), due in part to the system architecture.*
(8) *Concerns regarding perception of bias in the indicator information,* including what information is provided about the indicators and how they are organized and presented to the user.
(9) *Potentially inadequate representation of stakeholder values,* including a cogent argument for why a given indicator is important and relevant for assessing a particular policy.

We hypothesized that the transparency of the system would be directly enhanced by addressing the first six design challenges. Moreover, we believed that stakeholder representation could be better supported with mechanisms to easily add new indicators. While at the start it was unclear how much progress we could make on any of the first seven design challenges, from our perspective there was little controversy that making progress on any of these would be beneficial.

The last two design goals—that of addressing perceptions of bias and of supporting specific stakeholder value representation—provided a greater challenge, in that they represented a tension between the competing goals of neutrality and value advocacy. In this case, what we sought to make transparent was the purpose of information: when information was of a more neutral flavor and when it clearly represented a specific stakeholder perspective.

The Design Process: The Indicator Browser

In this section we describe our iterative Value Sensitive Design process around the development and informal formative evaluation of the Indicator Browser. Our purpose is to convey how we thought through the value implications of our work and how those analyses impacted our design work. We highlight the integrative nature of our design work, moving among conceptual analyses of transparency, legitimation, representation, and freedom from bias, technical development of the actual Indicator Browser design and implementation, and empirical investigations in the form of informal (and eventually more formal) formative evaluations.

Prototype 1: Envisioning the Indicator Browser

The first problems we addressed concerned information fragmentation, the lack of ready-to-hand information, and balancing tensions between neutrality and value commitments. Our first prototype (Prototype 1) was sketched on a whiteboard (Figure 1) and shortly thereafter developed in MICROSOFT ACCESS (Figure 2). This version divided the screen into two parts: the top part showing the specific indicators a user had selected and the bottom part showing the available indicators to select from. In addition, it grouped the indicators into eight overarching categories and showed the number of indicators selected from each category. The idea was to make visibly salient to users which categories were well represented by any given indicator selection, and which categories less so. We also envisioned a system that would allow users to click on the name of an indicator to bring up ready-to-hand information about that indicator, as well as sample output, though these features were not implemented until Prototypes 2 and 3.

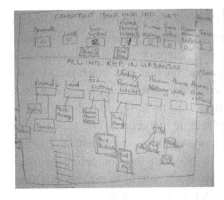 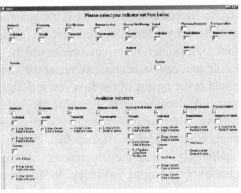

Figure 1. Whiteboard sketch of Prototype 1, showing "Construct Your Own Indicator Set" (top) and "All Indicators Represented in UrbanSim" (bottom), grouped by categories.

Figure 2. Screen shot of Prototype 1, showing the users' selected indicator set with the number of selected indicators per category (top) and the "Available Indicators" (bottom), grouped by categories.

Prototype 2: Refining the Indicator Browser and Developing the Technical Documentation

The initial sketch of the Indicator Browser realized in Prototype 1 led naturally to the need for two key developments: (a) a change of platform to a web-based implementation that could be readily connected to the working UrbanSim simulation and (b) ready-to-hand Technical Documentation for each of the individual indicators. The former development would allow for a close coupling of the Indicator Browser with the running models and position us to develop live documentation for the indicators; the latter development would increase transparency and comprehensibility of the indicators by providing easy access at the time of use to accurate, useful information about each indicator. With Prototype 2 we set out to design and implement these changes.

At this stage key disagreements arose within the design team regarding categorization schemes that might be perceived as biased and as a result undermine the system's legitimacy. Our discussions here were extensive, lasting many months, and nearly bogged down the development of the Indicator Browser. To help move past this log-jam, in Prototype 2 we implemented more than one categorization scheme and put the selection of the categorization scheme into the user's hands. Figure 3 shows one scheme; clicking on the tabs at the top provide a display of the indicators in alternative schemes.

As shown in Figures 3 and 4, Prototype 2 is implemented as a series of web pages. Figure 3 shows the main Indicator Browser page (similar to Prototype 1) with the list of all available indicators now on the left (categorized by Economics, Environment, and Social) and the indicators selected by the user on the right. In

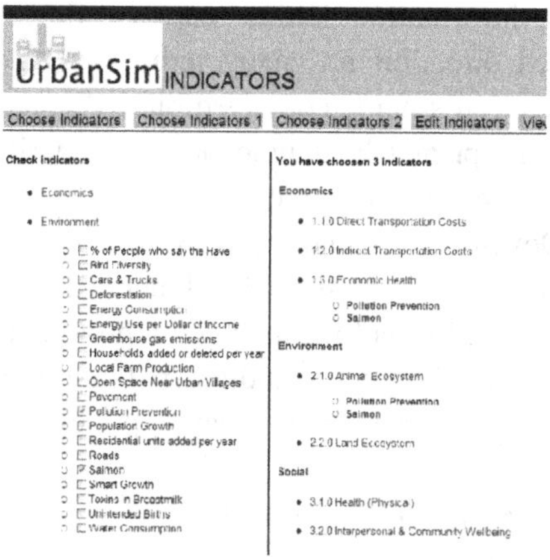

Figure 3. Screen shot of Prototype 2, showing all indicators (left) and user selected indicators (right), categorized as Economics, Environment, or Social. The "Choose Indicators" tabs at the top allow the user to choose among different categorization schemes for the indicators.

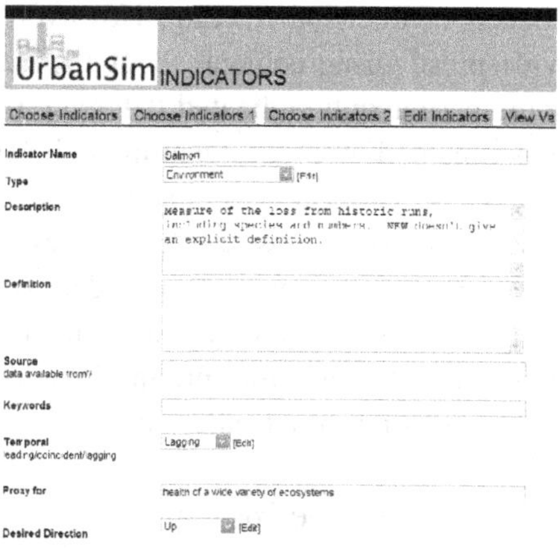

Figure 4. Screen shot of Prototype 2, showing the Technical Documentation about the "Salmon" indicator. Sections shown include indicator name, type, description, definition, source, keywords, temporal relationship, proxy for other indicators, and desired direction of change.

addition, Technical Documentation was created for each indicator. Figure 4 shows sample documentation for the "Salmon" indicator for the Pacific Northwest. Once reasonable Technical Documentation had been developed for the 40 implemented indicators, we began to engage in formative evaluation to refine the content, organization, and presentation of this information.

Informal Formative Evaluation and Iterative Design of Prototype 2

To test our design intuitions, we conducted a series of informal-formative-evaluation/redesign cycles of the Technical Documentation with nine participants, five with a modeling background and four with a policy background. Within each evaluation/redesign cycle, the participant was asked to think aloud while browsing the Technical Documentation in the presence of a facilitator, who made note of the participant's comments and suggestions. We also asked the participant questions about particular documentation elements. Following each evaluation session, changes were made in quick iteration so that each subsequent participant engaged with a slightly improved version of Prototype 2.

Taken as a whole, the formative evaluation guided our redesign to better achieve our design goals. Much of the strongest feedback we received was with respect to neutrality. Early versions of Prototype 2 included a section for the desired direction of the indicator, which we thought would be useful in the context of decision making. However, the information in this section reflected widespread disagreement about the desired direction for many indicators, and some participants indicated that even the section's name conveyed bias. We also experimented with designating indicators as primarily diagnostic or primarily evaluative. Several participants pointed out to us that some indicators we had designated as diagnostic (e.g., "Acres of Developable Land") would in fact be of policy interest to some stakeholders (in this case, real estate developers). Based on this feedback, we eliminated this distinction; instead we included a prominent comment in a new "Interpreting Results" section for the few indicators that report on simulation artifacts and thus are not at all appropriate for evaluating policies.

Prototype 3: The Indicator Browser with Live Technical Documentation and Indicator Perspectives

With the current version of the Indicator Browser (Prototype 3), we completed the work of connecting the web-based Indicator Browser to the live UrbanSim simulation, refined the Technical Documentation in response to the informal formative evaluation reported above, and developed a means for stakeholder groups to advocate for particular value perspectives set apart from the system's Technical Documentation. The decision to create a new separate area within the Indicator Browser for organizations to express their views emerged in response to the need to balance competing requirements for neutrality (the Technical Documentation) and value advocacy (the Indicator Perspectives). In this section, we describe each of these components and highlight how they contribute to our goals for transparency and comprehensibility.

Live Technical Documentation

With an eye toward providing useful, "ready-to-hand," comprehensible information about each indicator as well as minimizing perceptions of bias, we refined the Technical Documentation to include the following sections, as shown in Figure 5: (1) indicator name; (2) definition of the indicator; (3) advice for interpreting indicator results; (4) units of measurement and precision of the results; (5) related indicators; (6) a specification of how the indicator can be computed; (7) any known limitations of the indicator; (8) how the indicator relates to the simulation models; (8) the indicator's source and evolution, as well as examples of its use; (10) the SQL code that is used to compute the indicator from databases of simulation results; and (11) input and expected output for a test to verify that the SQL code computes the indicator results correctly.

This Technical Documentation is "live" in that the SQL code and tests are extracted directly from the code-base each time they are displayed. This guarantees that what the user reads in the Technical Documentation is current.

Figure 5. Screen shot of Prototype 3, showing the current Technical Documentation for a particular indicator, in this case "Acres of vacant developable land."

Figure 6. Screen shot of Prototype 3, showing the Indicator Perspective for Northwest Environment Watch.

Moreover, the Technical Documentation is easily updated and extended. And, in keeping with our design goal to create an underlying architecture that can incorporate new indicators readily (Freeman-Benson and Borning, 2003), Technical Documentation can be easily added to the system as new indicators are implemented. Thus we are able to support the extensibility of indicators in UrbanSim, not only technically, but from the user perspective as well.

Indicator Perspectives

As much as possible, the Technical Documentation is intentionally neutral, yet the planning process is rife with strong opinions and perspectives. How then might stakeholders use the indicators to represent and express their strongly held opinions? Here we have taken an approach—Indicator Perspectives—that allows stakeholders to tell a story and advocate particular values and criteria for evaluating outcomes. The Indicator Perspectives position organizations to present their own perspectives on which indicators are most important for evaluating policy alternatives, and how those indicators should be interpreted. We believe that these perspectives will be useful to stakeholders and decision makers because the organizations have well thought-out positions and can present them clearly and coherently. In contrast to the Technical Documentation, which is intended to cover all the indicators in a fairly neutral way, Indicator Perspectives can focus on a small set of indicators in a potentially opinionated way. Indicator Perspectives are intended to provoke thought and public deliberation, as well as to give groups a venue in which to state their positions.

We are currently in the early stages of developing Indicator Perspectives. We have partnered with three local organizations to construct perspectives for the initial prototype: a government agency (King County Budget Office, which publishes the King County Benchmark Reports), a business association (Washington Association of Realtors), and an environmental group (Northwest Environment Watch). In keeping with our explicitly supported value of representativeness, we choose initial partners who cover a wide range of views. Later, we plan to provide opportunities for involvement to all who are interested, actively soliciting partners as needed to help ensure coverage of the political and policy space. Figure 6 shows one prototype perspective, based on the Cascadia Scorecard, a monitoring program developed by Northwest Environment Watch.

Evaluating the Indicator Browser with Urban Planners

At this formative stage of our design process, we sought to systematically evaluate several key aspects of the Indicator Browser and its component pieces. While we hypothesized that we had solved key aspects of the information fragmentation problem (both in terms of consolidating information and making it ready-to-hand) and would positively impact task performance (e.g., comprehension and evaluation of indicators), we had not tested our redesign work. We also hypothesized that design features such as providing live SQL code, limitations of the indicators, and test case information would increase comprehensibility and transparency of the indicators. There were also unresolved design issues concerning the categorization of indicators, tools for on-demand testing of indicators, incorporating region-specific documentation, and maintaining the visibility of unused indicators. To answer these and related questions, we conducted a small user study focusing on the Technical Documentation with urban planners interested in UrbanSim, who constitute the primary audience for the Technical Documentation. (Since we were in the early stages of developing the Indicator Perspectives, we decided to evaluate this component with a broader range of stakeholders at a later date.)

Participants and Method

Eight current or prospective UrbanSim users (2 women; 6 men) participated. Participants were recruited at an UrbanSim user group meeting and had at least some urban planning experience (Range: 1 to 22 years; $M = 10.5$ years).

Each participant was engaged in a semi-structured interview for approximately one hour and fifteen minutes. The value-oriented interview questions and tasks drew in structure on prior research (Friedman, Kahn, and Hagman, 2004). The first group of questions explored the participants' current work practices, including their estimates of the time it would take to complete various tasks related to indicators and the number of sources they would need to consult. The participants were then asked to identify values and policies important to land use and transportation in their own regions, and to record these on cards. Following a demonstration of the Indicator Browser, participants were asked to perform short tasks using the Technical Documentation (e.g., defining an indicator in their own words, describing the relationship between two indicators, identifying three indicators to assess a particular concern). Participants were then asked about design tradeoffs with respect to ten current or future design decisions for the Technical Documentation. Each design trade-off was presented in terms of two alternate views with the rationale tied to transparency and comprehensibility supporting each view, e.g., for live SQL code:

> View 1: One person told me that including the SQL code in the documentation is helpful. Reading the code helps you to know what's really going on when the indicator is computed. Including the code in the documentation makes it easy to find. It's also easy to compare the code to the definition of the indicator and the specification of how it should be computed. Even if I don't read the code, it's reassuring to see it there and know that it's the actual code that is run to compute the indicator values. It's just more transparent that way.

> View 2: Another person told me that including the SQL code in the documentation is not very helpful. Other sections of the documentation, like the definition and the specification, provide all the information you will usually need about how the indicator is defined and how it's computed. The code is lengthy and hard to read compared to these other sections. If you need more information, you can always go find the source code somewhere else.)

Participants were asked to identify the view more like their own. Finally, participants were asked to identify indicators that would be informative for evaluating scenarios with respect to the values or policies they identified at the beginning of the interview. A subsequent telephone interview was conducted with seven of the eight participants to supplement incomplete work practice data.

All interviews were audio recorded for later transcription. A coding manual was developed to code evaluations and responses to content questions. Data were coded by two independent coders trained in the coding manual. Intercoder reliability was assessed through testing Cohen's kappa at the $\square = .05$ significance level; all tests were statistically significant, with $k = .74 - .94$ depending on question type. For the short tasks, time to complete each task was recorded, as well as whether the participant consulted the Technical Documentation. A domain expert assessed whether each task was completed correctly.

Results

For the task performance questions, participants required much less time to complete each of the four tasks using the Indicator Browser than with their traditional work practices (Table I). For 26 of the 27 tasks (96%) for which we have both estimates and data on task performance, the time it took the subject to complete the task using the Indicator Browser was less than the estimated time that they gave based on current work practice. The overall median estimated time was 20-60 minutes, while the actual median time to complete the tasks was only

| Task | Median Time to Complete Task | | Actual performance less than estimated current practice? | Wilcoxon p-value |
	Estimated Time in Current Practice	Actual Time using Indicator Browser		
1. Define Nonresidential Square Feet	10-20 min.	1.7 min.	6 out of 7 (86%)	.014*
2. Discuss relationship between Residential and Household Density	10-20 min.	2.8 min.	7 out of 7 (100%)	.009*
3. Find three indicators of economic growth	20-60 min.	2.4 min.	7 out of 7 (100%)	.009*
4. Explain what Jobs-Housing Balance says about commute times	20-60 min.	2.0 min.	6 out of 6 (100%)	.022*

Table I. Task Performance. An asterisk (*) denotes significant differences at the $p = .05$ level between estimated time to complete tasks in current practice and actual time using the Indicator Browser.

Feature	Description	p-value
Categorize Indicators	In the Indicator Browser opening screen, the indicators are grouped according to some categorization scheme (the specific scheme is not specified) rather than alphabetized.	.035*
Interpreting Results	In the Technical Documentation, the Interpreting Results section provides advice for understanding what the indicators signify and how to use them to answer different kinds of questions.	.008*
Limitations	In the Technical Documentation, the Limitations section provides information about pitfalls in using the indicator as well as when to avoid using the indicator altogether.	.008*
Live SQL Code	In the Technical Documentation, the live SQL code section provides access to the code used to compute the indicator; the "live" SQL code is extracted from the code-base at display time.	.008*
Test Cases	In the Technical Documentation, the Test Cases provide SQL code that is run to test the indicator.	.008*
Do Not Display All Categories	In the Indicator Browser opening screen, the categories are always displayed even if no indicators from a given category are selected.	.060
Do Not Distinguish Diag. & Eval. Indicators	In the Indicator Browser opening screen, indicators are designated as evaluative or diagnostic.	.164
Do Not Include Test-On-Demand	In the Technical Documentation, the Test-on-Demand section allows the user to run the indicator Test Cases from the web.	.125
Layered Documentation	In the Technical Documentation, include region-specific information along side of the UrbanSim software documentation.	.453
Specific Categorization Scheme	In the Indicator Browser opening screen, choose between two competing categorization schemes, one based on non-expert conceptions and one on the urban planning literature.	1.000
Comprehensive List of Indicators	In the Indicator Browser opening screen, provide a comprehensive list of indicators for stakeholder values about regional land use, transportation, and environmental impacts, including those that UrbanSim may not yet support.	1.000

Table II. Design Tradeoffs. An asterisk (*) denotes features that were preferred by a significant number of participants at the $p = .05$ level.

2.1 minutes, indicating a substantial improvement. Participants were also asked to estimate the number of sources they would need to consult in their current work practice to complete the tasks. For each of the four tasks, the median was two to three sources. By comparison, each participant who successfully completed the task in the study did so using only one source, the Indicator Browser. Of the 31 tasks performed by the 8 subjects, 25 were completed successfully (81%).

The design tradeoff questions, in which participants were asked to select one of two views, were analyzed using a binomial test. Table II provides a description of the specific design features and summarizes the quantitative results. As shown in Table II, nearly all participants preferred categorizing the indicators in the Indicator Browser opening screen ($p = .035$) as well as including sections for each indicator in the Technical Documentation on Interpreting Results ($p = .008$), Limitations ($p = .008$), Live SQL Code ($p = .004$), and Test Cases ($p = .008$).

Regarding linking values and policies with indicators, participants generated a total of 31 values and policies related to urban planning in their regions (Range: 3-4; M = 4), 18 of which were within UrbanSim's current scope of land use, real estate, employment, and demographic indicators (Range: 1-4; M = 2). Participants were later asked to identify indicators that they believed would inform discussion of those values and policies. Of the values that were within UrbanSim's current scope, 6 were not considered due to time constraints, and 2 were deemed by the participant to be unsuited to the use of indicators. For 9 of the 10 values and policies (90%) for which participants attempted to identify indicators, participants were able to find informative indicators.

Discussion

Taken together, the results on task performance and design trade-offs indicate that much is working here to support comprehensibility and transparency of indicators in UrbanSim. In particular, the results on current work practice and task performance with the Indicator Browser provide strong support that the current design—with cohesive ready-to-hand Technical Documentation—has made progress toward addressing the problem of information fragmentation. The significant positive assessments from the design trade-off questions confirm our decisions to include the Interpreting Results, Limitations, Live SQL, and Test Case sections to improve the policy relevance and transparency of the Technical Documentation. In addition, results provide some support that we were successful in providing indicators that are appropriate to values and polices that are important to the stakeholders in the participants' regions.

Other results point to directions for future design. For example, though all participants supported some form of categorization, there was no consensus on which scheme to use. These results suggest a need for further investigation of categorization schemes, as well as design of a ready-to-hand mechanism for choosing among multiple categorizations along the lines of our earlier implementation in Prototype 2. Also, further work is needed on how to handle regional information.

Lessons Learned and Future Directions

We believe the research reported here represents a successful application of Value Sensitive Design theory and methodology to the problem of informing public deliberation using sophisticated computer models. In this section we reflect on the lessons learned thus far and their broader implications.

First, the distinction between explicitly supported values and stakeholder values has held up well throughout our research. Because explicitly supported values are subject to a principled analysis of arguments for their inclusion, this distinction provides a strong response to the concern that the system simply reflects the personal values of the designers. We recommend making this same distinction in the conceptual analysis in other CSCW domains that feature multiple stakeholders with strongly held, divergent values.

Second, the identification of legitimation potential as an instrumental value has allowed us to draw on the rich theoretical work of Jürgen Habermas as well as that of some of his critics, and provided a useful way to reconceptualize the organization of some of our original explicitly supported instrumental values. Habermas's theory of communicative action in turn leads to a set of testable design goals (comprehensibility, accuracy, transparency, relevance, and freedom from bias). For UrbanSim, legitimation potential is in support of the moral value of fostering a democratic society, but an analogous move could be made in other CSCW domains in which the legitimacy of the use of a system may be in question.

Third, for complex systems such as UrbanSim, minimizing information fragmentation and providing ready-to-hand documentation can go some distance toward the goals of comprehensibility, transparency, and relevance. Specific techniques that we used, and that could be gainfully employed in other contexts, include live code and tests (integrated with the documentation), as well as integrated discussion of limitations and how to interpret results.

Finally, to address the tension between possible perceptions of bias on the one hand, and value advocacy and engaging citizens in the democratic process on the other, we provide both relatively neutral technical information and also a diverse spectrum of advocacy positions, distinct but interlinked. As discussed earlier, work on the Indicator Perspectives is in the early stages. However, we are optimistic that this work will unfold to provide additional lessons for balancing value advocacy with freedom from bias in other contested domains.

Planned work includes improving the comprehensibility of the information for the range of stakeholders, integrating the Indicator Perspectives more closely with the other components of the Indicator Browser, and providing better support for comparison and discussion of different perspectives. Finally, we intend to deploy and evaluate the Indicator Browser and Indicator Perspectives in a real decision-making context; our plan is to do so in the upcoming revision of VISION 2020, the regional growth and transportation plan in the Puget Sound (Seattle) area.

In conclusion, we have provided a snapshot of an ongoing research project on informing public deliberation with the results from sophisticated simulations. We believe that the lessons learned so far—in particular, regarding the use of Value Sensitive Design, the strong distinction between explicitly supported values and stakeholder values, the focus on legitimation, minimizing information fragmentation and providing ready-to-hand-documentation, and techniques for balancing value advocacy and neutrality—can be valuable in other CSCW domains involving multiple stakeholders with strongly held, divergent values.

Acknowledgments

Thanks to Peter Kahn and Paul Waddell for many useful discussions of the underlying ideas; to Ann Hendrickson, Bjorn Freeman-Benson, Jon Fuchs, Casey Huggins, Charles Naumer, and David Socha for help with the design and implementation of different versions of this system; to Stephanie Collett, Shireen Deboo, Nicole Gustine, and Jessica Miller for help with the formative evaluation; to Lance Bennett for discussion about Habermas; to Brian Gill for his assistance with statistics; and to our user study participants. This research has been supported in part by the U.S. National Science Foundation under Grant Nos. EIA-0121326 and IIS-0325035, and in part by gifts from IBM and Google.

References

Davison, R. M., and Briggs, R. O. (2000): 'GSS for Presentation Support', *CACM*, vol. 43, no. 9, pp. 91-97.

Easterbrook, S. M., Beck, E. E., Goodlet, J. S., Plowman, L., Sharples, M., & Wood, C. C. (1993). 'A Survey of Empirical Studies of Conflict', in S. M. Easterbrook (Ed.), *CSCW: Cooperation or Conflict,* Springer-Verlag, London, pp. 1-68.

Finel, B. I. and Lord, K. M. (2000): 'The Surprising Logic of Transparency', in B. I. Finel and K. M. Lord (eds.): *Power and Conflict in the Age of Transparency*, Palgrave, New York.

Fleischmann, K. R. and Wallace, W. A. (2005): 'A Covenant with Transparency: Opening the Black Box of Models', *CACM*, col. 48, no. 5, pp. 93-97.

Fraser, N. (1992): 'Rethinking the Public Sphere: A Contribution to the Critique of Actually Existing Democracy', in C. Calhoun (ed.): *Habermas and the Public Sphere,* MIT Press.

Freeman-Benson, B., and Borning, A. (2003): 'YP and Urban Simulation: Applying an Agile Programming Methodology in a Politically Tempestuous Domain', *Proceedings of the 2003 Agile Development Conference*, Salt Lake City, Utah, June 2003.

Friedman, B. (ed.) (1997): *Human Values and the Design of Computer Technology*, Cambridge University Press and CSLI: New York, NY and Stanford, CA.

Friedman B., Howe, D. C., Felten, E. W. (2002): 'Informed Consent in the Mozilla Browser: Implementing Value Sensitive Design', in *Proceedings of the 35th Hawaii International Conference on System Science.*

Friedman, B., Kahn, P. and Borning, A. (in press): 'Value Sensitive Design and Information Systems', to appear in P. Zhang & D. Galletta (eds.): *Human-Computer Interaction in Management Information Systems: Foundations*, M.E. Sharpe, New York.

Friedman, B., Kahn, P. H., Jr., and Hagman, Jr. (2004). 'The Watcher and The Watched: Social Judgments about Privacy in a Public Place', in *Online Proceedings of CHI Fringe 2004*. Vienna, Austria.

Friedman, B. and Nissenbaum, H. (1996): 'Bias in Computer Systems', *ACM Transactions on Information Systems*, vol. 14, no. 3, July 1996, pp. 330-347.

Gallopín, G. C. (1997). 'Indicators and Their Use: Information for Decision-making', in B. Moldan & S. Billharz (Eds.), *Sustainability Indicators: Report of the Project on Indicators of Sustainable Development* (pp. 13 - 27): John Wiley & Sons Ltd.

Habermas, J. (1979): *Communication and the Evolution of Society*, T. McCarthy (trans.), Beacon Press, Boston.

Habermas, J. (1984): *The Theory of Communicative Action*, Vol. 1, T. McCarthy (trans.), Beacon Press, Boston.

Hart, M. (1999). *Guide to Sustainable Community Indicators* (2nd Edition). North Andover, MA.

Herlocker, J. L., Konstan, J. A., and Riedl, J. (2000): 'Explaining Collaborative Filtering Recommendations', in *Proceedings of CSCW 2000*.

Isenmann, S. and Reuter, W. D. (1997): 'IBIS—a Convincing Concept...But a Lousy Instrument?', in *Proceedings of ACM Designing Interactive Systems*.

Kraemer, K. L. and King, J. L. (1986): 'Computer-Based Systems for Cooperative Work and Group Decisionmaking: Status of Use and Problems in Development', in *Proceedings of CSCW 1986*.

Lee, D. B. Jr. (1973): 'Requiem for Large-Scale Models', *Journal of the American Institute of Planners*, vol. 39, no. 3, May 1973, pp. 163-178.

Pace, R. C. (1990): 'Personalized and Depersonalized Conflict in Small Group Discussions: An Examination of Differentiation', *Small Group*, vol. 21, no. 1, pp. 79-96.

Schmidt, K. and Bannon, L. (1992): 'Taking CSCW Seriously: Supporting Articulation Work', *Computer Supported Cooperative Work: An International Journal*, vol. 1, no. 1 pp. 7-40.

Schumacher, E.F. (1973): *Small is Beautiful: Economics as if People Mattered*, Harper, New York.

Waddell, P., Borning, A., Noth, M., Freier, N., Becke, M., and Ulfarsson, G. (2003): 'Microsimulation of Urban Development and Location Choices: Design and Implementation of UrbanSim', *Networks and Spatial Economics*, vol. 3, no. 1, pp. 43-67.

Waddell, P., and Borning, A. (2004): 'A Case Study in Digital Government: Developing and Applying UrbanSim, a System for Simulating Urban Land Use, Transportation, and Environmental Impacts', *Social Science Computer Review*, vol. 22 no. 1, pp. 37-51.

Waddell, P., and Ulfarsson, G. (2005): 'Introduction to Urban Simulation: Design and Development of Operational Models', forthcoming in P. Stopher, K. Button, K. Haynes and D. Hensher (eds.): *Handbook in Transport, Volume 5: Transport Geography and Spatial Systems*, Pergamon Press.

Winograd, T. and Flores, F. (1986): *Understanding Computers and Cognition: A New Foundation for Design*, Norwood, New Jersey, Ablex.

H. Gellersen et al. (eds.), ECSCW 2005: Proceedings of the Ninth European
Conference on Computer-Supported Cooperative Work, 18-22 September 2005, Paris,
France, 469–488.

The Work to Make a Home Network Work

Rebecca E. Grinter, W. Keith Edwards

GVU Center, College of Computing, Georgia Institute of Technology, USA
{beki, keith}@cc.gatech.edu

Mark W. Newman, Nicolas Ducheneaut

Palo Alto Research Center, USA
{mnewman, nicolas}@parc.com

Abstract: Recently, households have begun to adopt networking technologies to interconnect devices within the home. Yet little is known about the consequences for households of setting up and living with these complex networks, nor the impact of such technologies on the routines of the home. In this paper, we report findings from an empirical study of households containing complex networks of computer and audio/visual technologies. Our study finds that home networks require significant household effort not just to coordinate their use, but also their set up and maintenance. We also show how the coordination around networking has to be worked into the routines of the home and the householders.

Introduction

In his CSCW 94 paper "The Work to Make A Network Work", John Bowers reported study findings from a government organisation that deployed and used a network of CSCW applications. At the time, one of the unusual features of the people studied was their degree of familiarity with CSCW. In the 15 years since

Bower's study, the general awareness and use of networked collaborative technologies has changed.

One change centres on the use of networked collaborative technologies at home. Today, householders use collaborative applications such as email, WWW, and IM, for recreational as well as for work purposes. However, as domestic computer usage has increased, the difficulty of sharing a single machine at home has lead to a new trend: the adoption of home networking technologies that allow the Internet to be shared among multiple machines. Beyond just the Internet, however, these home networking technologies offer the promise of delivering many more applications to our smart homes.

Yet, little is known empirically about the consequences for a household that has the type of complex network required to deliver such advanced services. This paper reports findings from a study that sought to address that question. Our study found that home networks represent a complex collaborative household endeavour in virtually all of their aspects including design and maintenance as well as use.

This paper begins by reviewing the literature on household collaboration and the role of computing in such collaboration. We then describe our methods and the participants in our study. Our findings are organised around three themes: the myriad of networks that exist in households, the household tensions that emerged because of the clash of individuality and collectivity in the networks, and the collective challenges that householders faced in administration and troubleshooting. The discussion focuses on the collaborative work required to make home networks work, how that coordination is further complicated by the tension between invisibility and comprehensibility, and why it creates an integration paradox in domestic technology.

From Domestic Computing to Domestic Networking

In the last few years, CSCW research has shifted from an exclusive focus on the office to examine collaboration in other settings such as the home. In this context, two lines of complementary research have emerged: studies that focus on domestic collaboration and studies examining the role of computing (which is closely coupled to the adoption of the Internet) in domestic settings. In this section, we review each in turn.

Domestic Collaboration: Routines and Technologies

One theme of home-based CSCW research has emphasised the need to study how people collaborate at home, often with the purpose of informing the design of domestic technologies. This focus of research takes as one of its motivations the belief that computer application development has evolved from a theoretical grounding in paid-labour work, and as a consequence has resulted in design practices that tend to emphasise efficiency and production (Hindus, 1999), which may not be appropriate for the home. Early results from studies in this tradition have highlighted the nature of routines in the home (see for example, Harper, 2003). Routines can be thought of as the interactions householders pursue in order to organise their domestic life (Crabtree & Rodden, 2004; Edwards & Grinter, 2001).

Studies of domestic routines have had two foci. The first of these is an explication of the routines themselves, often with an eye toward developing insights that could be applied to design. For example, studies of how families coordinate the arrival, processing and output of postal mail show that families need not always explicitly negotiate the division of work (who collects the post from the box or the floor, for example) because they can rely on the visibility of the letters and bills themselves, as well as a shared sense of where various postal items should end up (Crabtree & Rodden, 2004). Another study of routines examined the use of calendars in the home and found that shared orientation to the artefact was essential for family members' explicit negotiation around event scheduling (Crabtree & Rodden, 2004).

The second focus of studies of domestic routines has examined the role that technology plays in these routines. For example, Tolmie and others (2002) highlight how technologies such as alarm clocks play an integral role in complex coordination routines such as "leaving the house," without calling attention to the technologies themselves. They argue that this invisibility in use provides a different criterion than the more usual notions of perceptual invisibility often touted as a principle for designing new technologies.

In contrast with Tolmie and others, O'Brien and others' (1999) study of set-top box use showed both the positive and negative impacts that technologies had on household routines. Their study highlighted how use of the television was often intertwined with temporal routines (such as coordinating departure activities) and spatial routines (such as demarking current ownership and control of shared spaces) in the house. Simultaneously, they also discovered that sometimes these technologies overtly dictate the use of the physical areas in the home. For example, in their study of a family with an open plan living room, the use of the television and stereo in that room by any householder not only dictated the use of that entire space, but also limited the possibilities of other householders to access the services provided by those technologies.

These tensions between the use of technology and the use of the space in which it resides have been solved by homeowners in a number of ways. One solution to the difficulties of multiple demands on technology and space noted by O'Brien and others was the purchase of equipment to make the technology more mobile. Televisions on carts, or small enough to be carried to another section of the house, along with portable stereos allowed numerous families to workaround some of the contention of routines. Indeed, as we shall discuss in the next section, similar tensions around computer usage led a number of families in our study to adopt home networks that, in principle, allowed the resources of the network to be distributed across multiple devices, in multiple spaces.

Domestic Networks: From Internetworking to Networking

An important and related line of research has focused more exclusively on the role of the computer at home. As early as the mid-1980's, a few researchers were beginning to examine computing at home (Vitalari, Venkatesh & Gronhaug, 1986). These early studies reported that the primary use of a computer at home was as an extension of the computer in the office.

Today, studies show that families use their home computer for a variety of recreational activities, many of which are made possible by the presence of the Internet (Cummings & Kraut, 2002; Kraut et al., 1999). For example, Venkatesh and others (2003) groups these non-work activities into shopping, information gathering, learning, and communications. Another area of use for the computer is as a source of entertainment, including gaming (Ducheneaut & Moore, 2004) and also music playing on the machine itself (Brown, Sellen & Geelhoed, 2001; Voida et al., 2005).

For all of these reasons, it is not surprising that some studies of domestic computing comment on the difficulties those householders have in sharing the computer. For example, Frohlich and others (2001) described how families experienced resource contention when trying to share a single machine. They also highlighted how dedicated appliances were not always perceived as the best solution by householders, who often wanted the flexibility that access to a "general-purpose" computer provided.

For those households that choose to invest in multiple home computers, Internet access can become another potential source of contention. Although contention over the management of Internet access from multiple machines via a single landline has not often been reported in studies of home computing use (Rainie & Horrigan, (2005) being a notable exception), it is noticeable that broadband adopters typically have more than one machine in their household (Horrigan & Rainie, 2002).

Broadband adopters also share another important feature in common: their degree of familiarity with networking (Anderson et al., 2002; Horrigan & Rainie, 2002). Perhaps due to this familiarity, it is these families that have taken the next step towards distributing Internet access around the house—as well as potentially solving the problems of sharing computer peripherals such as printers and scanners—by purchasing intra-home networking equipment. Specifically, some households have begun to create and install rich home networks, comprising not just infrastructure technologies such as hubs, routers, gateways, and wireless access points, but also application-oriented devices such as media players and centralised storage.

Whether consciously or not, these networked households represent a step towards realising a commonly touted vision of the "smart home" (Harper, 2003). Visions of the smart home portray home life surrounded by computational devices that varyingly respond, predict, and monitor occupants' activities. Implicit in these notions of ubiquitous and smart home technologies is the assumption of an in-home network that allows the devices and services to communicate with each other as well as the occupants and the outside world.

One version of the smart home begins with a specially designed house that provides the network if not the appliances themselves. As Randall (2003) observed in his own unique study of householders temporarily living in such a smart home, the possibilities of the network were not always seamlessly realisable by the occupants. However, given the dominance of old housing stock, it seems unlikely that many people will experience their smart home as a new purchase (Edwards & Grinter, 2001). Rather, people will more likely attempt to make their homes "smarter" by adapting their existing physical infrastructure (Rodden & Benford, 2003).

This research represents a step towards an empirical understanding of what the consequences are for families who decide to set up and live with a complex network of these technologies. Rather than assuming that the network would produce a set of possibilities, we wanted to understand what options householders sought from their network, and how they collectively set about setting up and maintaining a home network that would provide them with the services of their choice.

Our findings are organised around three themes: the myriad of networks that exist in households, the household tensions that emerged because of the clash of individuality and collectivity in the networks, and the collective challenges that householders faced in administration and troubleshooting. The discussion focuses on the collaborative work to make the networks work, how that coordination is further complicated by the tension between invisibility and comprehensibility, and why it creates an integration paradox.

Study: Participants and Methods

In order to study the work to make the home network work, we conducted an empirical study of households with "advanced" technology set-ups. Our choice of such early adopters was motivated by a desire to understand the routines and tensions that result from such complex networks, which we believe will be representative of more and more homes in the near future. For the purposes of this study, the *advanced* qualifier restricted our participation pool to homes that possessed a minimum of two computers, connected both to each other and to the broader Internet.

Further, for the purposes of this study, we considered the *home network* to be not just the computing elements installed in the home, but also the Audio/Visual (A/V) devices installed there. As has been noted many times previously, data and media networks are converging, and are becoming interconnected. This was demonstrated in our sample group, as a number of the participating households had attempted to integrate their computer and A/V networks, for example, to stream MP3s to their stereo. Moreover, studies such as those by Petersen and others (2002) suggest that users already struggle with the complexities of A/V technologies; we wanted to see how the potentially more complex interplay of data and A/V would impact the routines in the home, and the use of the technologies.

Our participants consisted of 14 individuals in 7 homes. Each household was composed of dual-income two-adult family, and all families worked in professional occupations. All but one family lived in old housing stock (ranging from the 1930's to the 1960's), and all of the families lived in houses that did not contain any type of specialised wiring support for home computer networking, such as CAT6 Ethernet wiring throughout the house.

Unsurprisingly, in each household there was at least one person with considerable networking knowledge.[1] In all households network knowledge came from either advanced formal education (undergraduate degrees in computer science that covered networking) or many years of experience as a systems administrator or related profession. This—in and of itself—says much lot about the work required to make a home network work. By contrast, the other members of each household had a much broader range of experiences with networks. Although these other users shared much less in common, one striking feature was that they had all used networked technologies in corporate or educational settings themselves, which was another significant change since Bower's study. While some experienced network use in high-tech industries, others had learned about networks in other professions.

The study consisted of four activities. First, participants were asked to produce a "Home Inventory" of the technologies they had at home. The inventory consisted of three lists. The first asked householders to indicate whether they owned certain types of technology in categories including Home A/V, telecommunications, home automation, and in-home networking. The second asked participants to identify the locations of these technologies throughout their homes. The third list asked the occupants to list their mobile devices such as cellphones, MP3 players, and so forth.

These lists served two purposes. First, they allowed the research team to gain insight into the types of networks and devices that we might see during the later

---

[1] Although the general awareness of the possibilities created by networks has grown, studies like Kiesler and others' (2000) reminds us of the usability problems giving networking novices technologies originally designed for systems administrators.

phases of the study. Second, the information allowed us to determine participants' "Tech Home Rating," a system devised by the Consumer Electronics Association (CEA) that claims to help end-users assess the technological state of their home. Surprisingly given our selection criteria, most of our participants (6 of 7 households) scored 3 out of a total of 5, implying that their home was only moderately technological. The one exception was a household that achieved a rating of 4, closer to CEA's "technologically advanced" rating. Despite these middle ratings, the next phases of our study allowed us to assess just how much technology these households owned.

This next phase consisted of three activities that all took place in the context of a home visit; two researchers visited each household. The home visit began with a sketching exercise, where we asked each householder to draw three diagrams: their home computer network, their home audio-visual network, and their vision of what they would like in an integrated home network. We asked the householders not to interact with each other so that their diagrams would reflect their own perspectives about their home networks.

The second activity, which represented the main part of the home visit, consisted of a tour of the home by the householders. The purpose of the tour was to visit the locations of components in the network. At each site, we would stop and discuss what we were being shown, and talk about its purpose, problems that it generated, and also provided an opportunity for the householders to raise issues that they wanted us to know about their networks and its uses.

Finally, the home tour concluded with a short interview designed to review what we had just seen and ask questions about other aspects of the home network that may not have been visible or obvious during the tour itself. In total, most of the home visits took between 2 and 3 hours including the sketching, touring, and interview activities.

At Home with Networking

In this section, we present the findings from our study organised into three topics. First, and as we soon discovered, the apparently simple question of *what constitutes* a home network was much more complex in practice. Second, we learned that there is a tension that householders must balance concerning the individual nature of certain types of devices and the collaborative nature of certain media. Third, the setup, administration, and troubleshooting of home networks required a division of labour in the household; this division of labour was not always completely agreed upon.

What is a Home Network?

The term *network* often conjures up a vision of *a single, well-orchestrated* collection of connected devices. The cohesive singularity implied by term is often used to emphasize the possibilities that fully connected devices can bring to householders—for example, the ability to interact with all devices on the network from any point of contact. Yet, in our studies we found that households embodied a much richer notion of networking, which was at once more pluralistic and less cohesive.

Audio-visual (A/V) systems, which were typically the older of the two types of networks that people had in their homes, illustrated some of those properties. In all homes we found a "primary" A/V network, which typically resided in the living room and included all the most recent A/V component purchases.

Families described this network, and the space that it occupied, as the place that they "came together" to utilise the services that this A/V network provided. Although in the majority of our cases, we found that families generally agreed about how they used the various services this network provided, we were also surprised to learn about difficulties that three of the families were having with television, and how this in turn shaped their A/V networks.

Half a century after the arrival of television into many people's homes, almost half of the families we visited were still actively considering its role in their homes and trying to determine the boundaries of acceptable use. In once case, the householders had developed a shared policy about the acceptable amount of television use, in relation to other activities such as talking to each other, reading or hobby time. This family would routinely decide that they were watching too much television, at which point the television would be disconnected from the network and stored away. Somehow, as they explained, the television always found a way to return—for example, because someone wanted to watch a particular program. Significantly, their network had to accommodate the routine arrival and departure of the television set.

In another case, the householders disagreed about the place of television in their A/V network, with one member enjoying the television and the other believing that television had no place in the home. Their compromise illustrates another common phenomenon in homes: the presence of *multiple* A/V networks. In this case, the television was not a part of the primary A/V network, but was installed in a "secondary" A/V network, a place where this one member of the household could watch.

A number of families had such secondary A/V networks, which were present in a variety of locations, but never in the living area of the house. For example, a secondary network might appear in a master bedroom where family members watched television before sleeping, or in a home office where one family member worked but might still want to watch television or listen to music.

Another common feature of these secondary A/V networks was the age of the components that comprised them. Components typically migrated into secondary networks as householders upgraded their primary A/V network. Consequently, secondary networks had components of dramatically different ages, which as a collection presented significant integration challenges.

In comparison with A/V networks, it was much harder to identify how many computer networks existed in the homes we visited, because generally the structures of such networks are not visually apparent. A/V networks located in specific regions of the house, connected through tangible wires and in a relatively localized topology, were easier to "see" than the computer networks. Visually, much of the computing network often appears to be unified and cohesive, as all components are connected to each other, to the broadband modem, and out to the Internet.

Yet, through interviews and diagrams we came to learn that some households had much more complex data network than were visually discernable. For example, several households needed to create a distinction between their "personal" home network, and their "work" home network (on which corporate machines at home were connected). Whether it was for reasons of taxation (being able to take certain deductions on equipment used for business purposes), or ownership (software developed using corporate resources would belong to the corporation), or data protection (ensuring that personal machines did not accidentally connect to the corporate network), the home computer "network" was rarely as simple and unified as it first appeared.

One distinctive feature we found in some households was an *open wireless network*, providing free Internet access to anyone in the area. Unlike "accidental" open wireless networks, attributed to householders' ignorance about how to secure the network, our householders had deliberately chosen to allow anyone within range to connect to their network, and the Internet. The motivation for doing so was often described in terms of "neighbourliness": these homeowners wanted to offer not just friends and houseguests, but also their neighbours the ability to share their network resources. While householders recognised the potential for network abuse, the opportunity to be neighbourly, with those within wireless range, appeared to make some households feel appropriately part of their community.

Comparing computer and A/V networks also revealed a difference in the degree of personal ownership of devices in the household. Householders frequently referred to computers as belonging to someone, but rarely spoke about A/V devices—even those they used exclusively—as "mine." This difference in orientation towards devices—as belonging to people on a computer network, and as being situated in a space on the A/V network—also influenced how technology migrated in the household. Unlike A/V networks, when new computers arrived, old ones migrated to a new owner, which in turn could trigger location changes, such as physical desk swaps or network topological changes, that were a consequence of the change of ownership.

Beyond the complexity of the technologies themselves, Home A/V and computer networks illustrate the complex relationships between devices, householders, the services the network provides, and (perhaps competing) household visions of what constitutes acceptable use, all of which in turn is reflected in the devices present on the home network and how their users describe them. The answer, then to our question of what a home network is turned out to be a set of relationships and beliefs, layered over a set of interconnected and disconnected technologies, which was surprisingly complex in implementation and subject to ongoing change by the household.

Individuality and Collective Action

Our home visits suggested that home networks generally, and certain types of devices specifically, created a coordination challenge around online media such as photographs. This challenge arose because of a tension between the desires of householders to organise media collaboratively, versus the fact that this media was stored on individually owned devices. We first observed this tension in a household where all the householders had their own personal digital cameras and photograph repositories. This household experienced acute coordination difficulties in trying to manage their online photographs as a shared family collection—something that worked well with their traditional physical photo collection that lived in a box—because their images were stored on separate machines owned by the individual who had taken the picture. An aborted attempt to integrate these individual collections was made even more painful by the fact that each householder's private collection was organised differently, and the sorting scheme of each collection was not comprehensible to the householder trying to merge them together. Householders worried that they would some how "lose" the their collective experiences as they were scattered across machines and potentially subject to deletion or inaccessibility (such as if one individual took their machine off the network).

We found similar concerns in other homes. In most households media coordination problems extended beyond photographs to include other types of media, including collaboratively produced content such as music and letters. We also noticed that two devices seemed to especially exacerbate the tension between individuality and commonality: iPod and TiVo.

The iPod, Apple's portable music player, must be associated with a specific computer from which it gets its music. However, since most computers in the households we visited were individually owned, each iPod tended to gather one person's music only. This would not have been a problem if each iPod had been used exclusively by that person, but it was often used in conjunction with a secondary A/V network, either at home or in the car. Householders without iPods resented the difficulty in listening to their music in contrast to the convenience of the iPod owner.

TiVo is a brand of Personal Video Recorder (PVR), a specialised computer used in an A/V network that allows people to record television programs to a hard drive, replay them, and skip advertisements.[2] TiVo also collects data about the programs users record, in an attempt to produce a model of viewing habits that can be used to make recommendations about other programs a user might like to view. While all the homeowners were enthusiastic about TiVo's core features, a number of households experienced problems with TiVo's recommendation system.

This problem stemmed from the fact that multiple people used a single TiVo, TiVo has a single viewer model of recommendation—in other words, there is no way to separate usage data in such a way that different recommendations can be made for different people in the home. This tension manifested itself in a number of ways. In one household that had two TiVo's (one for each member of the household), each person "owned" one TiVo. Unfortunately, only one householder's TiVo was connected to the primary network, so it was that person's recording habits that tended to influence the programs that got watched on the primary network even when the other householder was present and wanted to watch TV. Another household, with a single TiVo, attempted to resolve this problem socially, with one member of the household being the only person "allowed" to operate the TiVo and influence how the TiVo generated the data that it would use to make recommendations. The most common model was that any divergent viewing habits among the owners were overloaded into one TiVo, and householders either competed to "turn" TiVo into their own, or accepted that its suggestions were going to be an eclectic hybrid of various householders interests, sometimes right, and mostly representing an alien middle-ground.

In all of these cases, tensions existed in both the computer and A/V networks, where individually owned devices, or services that assumed individual use, conflicted with householders' desires to collectively share and manipulate media.

Administration and Troubleshooting

One dominant theme in all the households we visited was the ongoing challenge of setting up and troubleshooting their networks. Again differences emerged between A/V and computer networks. Although the cables and remotes belonging to the primary and secondary A/V network presented problems, it seemed to be the home computer network that generated the worst difficulties. Of course, one can argue that these problems are the result of trying to migrate technologies such as TCP, IP, DNS and NAT, which were designed to be used by skilled systems

---

[2] In the USA, where this study took place, the brand TiVo has become synonymous with PVR. Even the few families who owned non-TiVo PVR's referred to their device as a TiVo.

administrators, into people's homes. Yet it seems likely that these technologies will persist in their dominance, and in turn the work to make the home network work will involve meeting the challenges presented by these technologies.

From a collaborative perspective, one feature of the set-up and troubleshooting work was the emergence of a complex and sometimes contested division of labour among the householders. Typically, the person with most networking knowledge was responsible for setting up and maintaining the network infrastructure. In the majority of households the person responsible for setting up and maintaining the computer network was also the same person who supported the A/V networks.

This particular division of labour was accepted in most households, especially given the typically significant difference in knowledge among householders about how computer networks work. The sketching exercise revealed this difference vividly, with one person usually producing detailed network diagrams while the others produced diagrams that contained only a small subset of the devices in the network. Unsurprisingly, the devices that were most commonly missing from sketches included infrastructure devices such as routers, firewalls, hardware VPNs, and—less commonly—the broadband modem. When such devices were sketched by the less knowledgeable householder they were often labelled something like "network doodads." And yet, of course, without knowledge of these devices, infrastructure maintenance is unsurprisingly difficult.

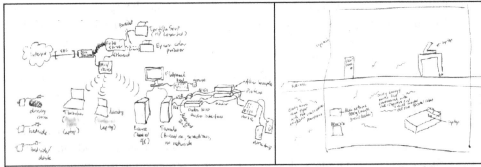

Figure 1. Two sketches of the same home network illustrating individual differences in perception of the structure of the home network. The sketch on the left is by the home "systems administrator," while on the right is by another home resident.

This difficulty manifested itself most clearly when these householders needed to troubleshoot the network and the "systems administrator" was not home. For example, one householder described a week in which he did not have Internet access, because the other person was out of town. Although his troubleshooting skills included rebooting not just his machine but also the DSL modem, they did not extend to considering the actual solution, which was to reboot a router. In other words, without the ability to understand the whole network, troubleshooting the network—let alone installing or modifying the network—becomes virtually impossible.

For some non-systems administrators in the household, troubleshooting the network got increasingly difficult as the home networks evolved. For example, in one household we found a person who did not typically administer the home network infrastructure, but regretted that fact. In particular, this person felt that they had the skills to take on some, if not all, of this responsibility, but because they had not been involved in the initial network setup or subsequent changes, now felt that they did not understand the network well enough to troubleshoot it.

Ultimately in our households, one householder typically recognised the need to take full responsibility for the network infrastructure; these householders unanimously resented the amount of time they spent adding, reconfiguring, and debugging the network. Almost all the systems administrators described instances where trying to provide new functionality in the network—like network printing for Windows machines, or debugging something that had gone wrong—took days of their "leisure" time.

The task of administration includes not just infrastructure support but also device support; often, the device support division of labour caused more tensions than the infrastructure support division of labour. In particular, where householders ascribed ownership to a device, there was confusion about whose responsibility it was when it went wrong. Even householders who did not desire or did not feel capable of troubleshooting their own machines would often administer the look and feel of their computers, as well as make decisions about the organisation of files and the installation of software onto their machines. This made that same machine much harder for the systems administrator to understand, and potentially troubleshoot. Many of our householders felt a sense of uneasiness when discussing the division of labour associated with the machines that made up the network.

Two other challenges for those responsible for the network came from the need to coordinate with outsiders, and the need to understand history. One episode illustrates both of these well. One household described how they kept losing their Internet access. One of their earliest attempts to solve this problem involved calling the local telephone company to see whether they had faulty equipment or a bad telephone line.

This first step in troubleshooting oriented us to the presence of numerous outside parties involved in the setup and maintenance of home networks. Satellite, cable and Internet providers needed to be engaged to provide the basic infrastructure of the A/V and computing networks. Then, other companies providing specific services, such as IP-based telephony or the TiVo PVR's recommendation subscription service were involved. When we asked householders to list how many companies they paid regular bills to in order to make their network work they often listed between 3-7 outside entities.

Unfortunately, having outside agencies involved in the provisioning of the network increased the likelihood of network related problems for these households. For example, people who came out to install various pieces of equipment tended to have installation scripts that drastically under-estimated the complexity of the networks into which they were adding functionality. Assuming that the television (rather than the receiver) produced the sound in the primary A/V network was a common mistake made by satellite installers; these installers would not leave until they had "correctly" set up the dish work with the television, consequently disabling the receiver.

The second step of troubleshooting for the family with Internet connectivity problems — once they had determined that the telephone line and DSL equipment was not at fault — was to begin to search for problems inside the house. They identified a list of potential problems sources and addressed these in turn. Ultimately, a decision to move a computer and its monitor to a different room caused them to realise that the true source of their problem was that their electrical circuitry was old enough that the quantity of equipment on a single circuit was degrading power to the DSL modem to the point that it was dropping the network connection.

These householders, like many others in this study, lived in housing stock that came from the first half of the 20th century; in many ways the design of these houses caused additional challenges for householders. Another home visit revealed how network complexity increased due to the fact that telephone jacks were not located near the site of the primary A/V network. However, devices in that network required a telephone line so that they could routinely make connections over a dial-up modem connection to receive information, such as television schedules and service upgrades. This led the family to add another network: a wireless connection that allowed their devices located in the living room to communicate outside the house using the telephone jack in the dining room.

Setup, administration, and troubleshooting the home networks revealed a complex division of labour among householders. Two somewhat overlapping divisions of labour seemed to exist in most households: these divisions of labour concerned separation of infrastructure and end-user device responsibilities. Adding to the difficulties for the householders were the relationships they had to manage with outside agencies required in the setup and ongoing maintenance of the network. A final complexity came from the lost knowledge about what previous outside agencies had done, and whether it was adequate (electricians/telephone engineers and the electrical/telephony infrastructure).

Discussion

In this section, we explore some of the broader themes that emerged from our examination of the routines surrounding home networking.

The Collaborative Work Required to Make the Network Work

Much like studies of single device usage in the home, our study has highlighted the importance of ownership, space usage, and routines around the applications that networks provide. With regards to the home network, there is a tension between ownership and the utility promised by the network. For example, the tendency of computers to be personally owned conflicts with desires around collaborative ownership and management of family photos.

Beyond such tensions, however, our study has highlighted how much collaborative work is required simply to make the network work—to let householders get to the stage where they can begin to incorporate the services offered by their network into their lives. Further, our study reveals that the work required to make the network work involves not just the householders themselves, but also parties outside the home, with whom the householders must interact and rely upon in order to realize their vision of useful home networking.

Troubleshooting revealed the many types of collaboration clearly. Householders turned not just to each other—according to their respective divisions of labour—but also to people outside the house when they needed help debugging their network. The sheer number of outsiders, and the potential that problems could involve coordination among them, was daunting to many householders, and something that would, as one person said "keep the network on the to-do list in one form or another for months."

Still more parties were often represented in the design of the home networks. Often these parties appeared in the "social network design" of the household. For example, neighbours and houseguests influenced some households to provide open networks. The corporations that householders work for, as well as potential hackers, influenced people to close off sections of their networks. Even the government could shape a home network by encouraging technical separations based on tax reasons.

Householders took all these outsiders' potential and actual needs and then combined them with their own internal desires for their network. While families' needs are often framed in utilitarian terms ("I want to connect to the Internet") our interviews with families revealed strong moral imperatives involved in home network design: our families' "values" drove the selection and configuration of services and devices on the network. Indeed, in aspiring to open and close networks from various outsiders, the same type of moral order was also being used.

The balance between individuality and collectivity played out in the maintenance of the home network and the devices on it as well. Even though one householder typically was responsible for the network infrastructure itself, many of the devices on that network were "owned" by a particular person in the home. Successfully troubleshooting the network often required breaching normal practices, for example, to change settings on a machine owned by another person in the home, so that it could function appropriately on the home network.

Finally, and most problematically in some ways, notions about the functionality desired in a home network often made coping with the network difficult, as new desires brought about evolution of the home technical infrastructure. This constant evolution of the network, while bringing new functionality, also changed the way that current work, created tension among the householders. This surprisingly (almost frighteningly) constant evolution of the household networks also fed into problems with invisibility and comprehensibility, which we discuss next.

Invisibility and Comprehensibility

Computing infrastructures are often described as invisible (for discussion see Chalmers, (2004)). Whether because networks are physically hidden, or because they have become so embedded into practice, these technologies seem to disappear (Star, 1999). Invisibility, and the need for comprehension, played out in very complex ways in the households we studied.

First, there were empirical challenges for the researchers. Diagrams helped to capture some of the complexity of home computer networks that was not apparent from their physical appearance. In particular, in the case of data networks, there is no outward sign of the logical structure or of the "reach" of these networks.

Second, there was an interesting tension between householders' desires for invisibility and comprehensibility in their home networks. All the households we visited made an effort to minimise the physical visibility of their networks. Cables were typically hidden behind and underneath furniture and often were referred to as the "rats nest". Other families replaced cables with wireless solutions, and then proceeded to hide the antennae in plants around the house. We found speakers, hubs, DSL modems and even computers hidden in cupboards, behind family pictures, inside desks and even under the couch. Families seemed to largely do this for aesthetic reasons: hiding those "little blinky lights" out of view, or "trying to be tidy".

Yet, this physical disappearance did little to help householders, particularly those less familiar with the networks, engage in the setup and maintenance of the network itself. In particular, not being able see devices or their relationship to others in the network reinforced householders' senses that their home network did not contain a variety of technically essential components. This disappearance prevents some from considering infrastructure technology (hubs, routers) as potential sources of problems when troubleshooting.

Of course, visibility alone does not guarantee comprehensibility. In this study, discussions around media usage illustrated how householders could see other devices and content on their networks, and still not make sense of it. Pictures, spread across multiple machines, could not be bought together in a family archive, because householders could not make sense of others' organisation schemata. TiVo added another dimension to content management. Homeowners could readily cope with the basic functionality of these systems, but the tension that arises through a device used in a shared setting that provides individually oriented recommendations caused homeowners to try to control recommendations through both technical and social means.

Ultimately, this study suggests that invisibility and comprehensibility are both desirable aspects of home networks. Currently, however, these goals are often conflated in the physical embodiment of the device itself. Once a device is out of sight, it is often out of mind. Tools that provide views of the network oriented around the services the network provides—rather than the devices that comprise it--might greatly aid householders in working together on family solutions to not just media sharing problems, but also the set-up and administration of the devices and infrastructure itself.

The Integration Paradox

The difficulties in administrating and troubleshooting the home network led to something we term the *integration paradox*. Integration—whether through single devices embodying a variety of functions, or pre-integrated collections of components—seemed very attractive to householders experiencing the challenges of administering diverse networks.

Yet, while integration seems like a potential solution, integrated devices have their own problems. This is well illustrated by the following quote

> Oh, yeah, if someone would sell me an integrated box, I would buy it. Really. In fact, *we'd buy two of them.*" [Emphasis added]

The paradox of integration turns on the simultaneous desire to have integrated components that reduce the work to make the network work, while achieving the same flexibility of functionality potentially provided by non-integrated components.

A similar type of paradox also played out in households around the remote. Most families showed us their large collection of remote controls, most of which arrived in the home as components were purchased. Several households also had a universal remote, purchased to reduce the number of remotes required to operate the system; the goal of such a purchase was to achieve integration of device control, if not of components.

Again, the paradox of integration arose in these cases. In practice, universal remotes worked for a few members of some households—typically those who told us that they understood the programming model of the remote itself. A surprisingly large number of householders, however, used the universal remote in conjunction with *at least one other remote.* Typically the universal remote would be used most often, and a secondary remote would be needed because it contained a few "key buttons". Again, the flexibility provided by the remotes in combination seemed to override any potential interface benefits that might be had by using one remote alone.

Conclusions

In this paper, we have sought to empirically begin the process of exploring the question of what it means for households to set up, live with, and support complex networking technologies. Moving beyond some of the usability issues with the technologies themselves—and there are many—networks raise many issues for households, most of which involve ongoing collaboration among householders to resolve. Networks not only make the collaborative production and consumption of media and services possible, but they take coordination to produce and consume themselves.

Of course, this study can only be a beginning point in a larger empirical and design research program. Our findings, while emerging from data about end-users experiences of networking in the wild come from a small portion of the population. In particular, our data was drawn from USA residents' homes, belonging to more-affluent-than-average middle-class families, and consequently represents one part of the population being targeted by corporations that have visions of networked homes and a myriad of services that will be delivered into those houses.

Yet, despite potential limitations of this study, it has already surfaced key problems with visions that networked homes. Most particularly, technical networks—as well as the technologies that they connect—enter into social networks that connect householders to each other, and to the outside world in a complex set of coordinated relationships. Future work exploring how other kinds of families, in other places and with other types of technical and social collaborative agendas, set up and live with networks of technologies has much to offer our understanding of precisely what it means to design devices for home networks.

Acknowledgements

We'd like to thank the people who participated in the study. Thanks to John Bowers for an inspirational title for this paper. We appreciate all the helpful comments and suggestions from the reviewers.

References

Anderson, B., C. Gale, A. P. Gower, E. F. France, M. L. R. Jones, H. V. Lacohee, A. McWilliam, K. Tracey, and M. Trimby. (2002): Digital Living—People-Centred Innovation and Strategy, BT Technology Journal, vol. 20, no. 2, pp. 1-20.

Brown, B., A. J. Sellen, and E. Geelhoed (2001): Music Sharing as a Computer Supported Collaborative Application. In Proceedings of the 7th European Conference on Computer-Supported Cooperative Work ECSCW '01, Bonn, Germany, Sept 16-20. Kluwer, pp. 179-198.

Chalmers, M. (2004): A Historical View of Context, Computer Supported Cooperative Work (CSCW), vol. 13, no. 3, pp. 223-247.

Crabtree, A. and T. Rodden. (2004): Domestic Routines and Design for the Home, Computer Supported Cooperative Work (CSCW), vol. 13, pp. 191-200.

Cummings, J. N. and R. Kraut. (2002): Domesticating Computers and the Internet, The Information Society, vol. 18, no. 3, pp. 221-232.

Ducheneaut, N. and R. J. Moore (2004): The Social Side of Gaming: A Study of Interaction Patterns in a Massively Multiplayer Online Game. In Proceedings of the ACM Conference on Computer Supported Cooperative Work (CSCW '04), Chicago, Illinois, Nov 6-10. ACM Press, pp. 360-369.

Edwards, W. K. and R. E. Grinter (2001): At Home With Ubiquitous Computing: Seven Challenges. In Proceedings of the UbiComp 01, Atlanta, GA, Sept 30-Oct 2. Springer-Verlag, pp. 256-272.

Frohlich, D. M., S. Dray, and A. Silverman. (2001): Breaking Up is Hard to Do: Family Perspectives on the Future of the Home PC, International Journal of Human-Computer Studies, vol. 54, no. 5, pp. 701-724.

Harper, R. (ed.) (2003): Inside the Smart Home. Springer, London, UK.

Hindus, D. (1999): The Importance of Homes in Technology Research. In Proceedings of the Second International Workshop on Cooperative Buildings (CoBuild'99), Pittsburgh, PA, October 1-2. Springer-Verlag, pp. 199-207.

Horrigan, J. B. and L. Rainie (2002): The Broadband Difference: How Online Americans' Behavior Changes with High-Speed Internet Connections at Home. Pew Internet Foundation, Washington D.C.

Kiesler, S., B. Zdaniuk, V. Lundmark, and R. Kraut. (2000): Troubles With the Internet: The Dynamics of Help at Home, Human Computer Interaction, vol. 15, no., pp. 323-351.

Kraut, R., T. Mukhopadhyay, J. Szczypula, S. Kiesler, and W. Scherlis. (1999): Information and Communication: Alternative Uses of the Internet in Households, Information Systems Research, vol. 10, no. 4, pp. 287-303.

O'Brien, J., T. Rodden, M. Rouncefield, and J. Hughes. (1999): At Home with the Technology: An Ethnographic Study of a Set-Top-Box Trial, ACM Transactions on Computer-Human Interaction, vol. 6, no. 3, pp. 282-308.

Petersen, M. G., K. H. Madsen, and A. Kjær. (2002): The Usability of Everyday Technology—Emerging and Fading Opportunities, ACM Transactions on Computer-Human Interaction, vol. 9, no. 2, pp. 74-105.

Rainie, L. and J. B. Horrigan (2005): A Decade of Adoption: How the Internet has Woven Itself into American Life, Report, Pew Internet Foundation, Washington, D.C.

Randall, D. (2003): Living Inside a Smart Home: A Case Study, in R. Harper (ed.) Inside the Smart Home, Springer-Verlag, London, UK, pp. 227-246.

Rodden, T. and S. Benford (2003): The Evolution of Buildings and the Implications for the Design of Ubiquitous Domestic Environments. In Proceedings of the ACM Conference on Human Factors in Computing (CHI '03), Fort Lauderdale, FL, Apr 5-10. ACM Press, pp. 9-16.

Star, S. L. (1999): The Ethnography of Infrastructure, American Behavioral Scientist, vol. 43, no. 3, pp. 377-391.

Tolmie, P., J. Pycock, T. Diggins, A. MacLean, and A. Karsenty (2002): Unremarkable Computing. In Proceedings of the ACM Conference on Human Factors in Computing Systems (CHI 02), Minneapolis, MN, Apr 20-25. ACM Press, pp. 399-406.

Venkatesh, A., E. Kruse, and E. C.-F. Shih. (2003): The Networked Home: An Analysis of Current Developments and Future Trends, Cognition, Technology and Work, vol. 5, no. 1, pp. 23-32.

Vitalari, N. P., A. Venkatesh, and K. Gronhaug. (1986): Computing in the Home: Shifts in the Time Allocation Patterns of Households, Communications of the ACM, vol. 28, no. 5, pp. 512-522.

Voida, A., R. E. Grinter, N. Ducheneaut, W. K. Edwards, and M. W. Newman (2005): Listening In: Practices Surrounding iTunes Music Sharing. In Proceedings of the ACM Conference on Human Factors in Computing (CHI '05), Portland, Oregon, Apr 2-7. ACM Press, pp. 191-200.

Index of Authors